DERIVATIVES, RISK MANAGEMENT & VALUE

Second Edition

DERIVATIVES, RISK MANAGEMENT & VALUE

Second Edition

Mondher Bellalah

CY Cergy Paris University, France & MIT Tunis, Tunisia

World Scientific

NEW JERSEY • LONDON • SINGAPORE • BEIJING • SHANGHAI • HONG KONG • TAIPEI • CHENNAI • TOKYO

Published by

World Scientific Publishing Europe Ltd.
57 Shelton Street, Covent Garden, London WC2H 9HE
Head office: 5 Toh Tuck Link, Singapore 596224
USA office: 27 Warren Street, Suite 401-402, Hackensack, NJ 07601

Library of Congress Cataloging-in-Publication Data
Names: Bellalah, Mondher author
Title: Derivatives, risk management & value / Mondher Bellalah,
CY Cergy Paris University, France & MIT Tunis, Tunisia.
Other titles: Derivatives, risk management and value
Description: Second edition. | New Jersey : World Scientific, [2026] |
Includes bibliographical references and index.
Identifiers: LCCN 2025042384 | ISBN 9781800618718 hardcover |
ISBN 9781800618725 ebook for institutions | ISBN 9781800618732 ebook for individuals
Subjects: LCSH: Derivative securities | Risk management
Classification: LCC HG6024.A3 B445 2026
LC record available at https://lccn.loc.gov/2025042384

British Library Cataloguing-in-Publication Data
A catalogue record for this book is available from the British Library.

For any available supplementary material, please visit
https://www.worldscientific.com/worldscibooks/10.1142/Q0551#t=suppl

Desk Editors: Aanand Jayaraman/Gabriel Rawlinson

Typeset by Stallion Press
Email: enquiries@stallionpress.com

Dedication

I dedicate this book to the President of the Tunisian Republic, His Excellency, Pr. Kais Saied, in recognition of his continuous and pivotal support for science and its applications in Tunisia. Over the past five years and more, the scientific achievements of Tunisian researchers in various fields have been of great importance. I do believe that the distinction of scientific research in Tunisia, in relation to other countries in the Euro-Mediterranean region, stems from the particular efforts of the Tunisian President and Government.

In the fields of finance and IT, the scientific community and I in Tunisia were fortunate to benefit from His Excellency's particular attention. Indeed, by organizing annual international conferences focused on finance, IT and artificial intelligence, fintech, cryptocurrencies, risk management, and derivatives, Tunisian institutions gained a remarkable international reputation. With these opportunities, PhD students, college professors, and professionals were able to communicate with professors and experts from leading American and European universities and institutions, including the opportunity to interact with Nobel laureates in economics and finance, such as H. Markowitz, J. Heckman, and E. Prescott.

Another important insight into Pr. Kais Saied's role is related to the establishment of national awards to strengthen the mechanics of scientific research at undergraduate and graduate levels. Such awards boost one's willingness to improve the Tunisian economy and its ability to meet the new challenges posed by the international context.

Mondher Bellalah

Preface

This book covers all areas of risk management in financial and non-financial institutions.

In the first part, we focus on various risks, including market risks, operational risks, and credit risks. Managing these risks is crucial in the banking industry. We also cover policies, procedures, and capital requirements as specified by international regulators (Basel II, III, and IV). Internal capital adequacy processes, or ICAAP, and stress testing are analyzed as implemented in the financial system.

In the second part, the book covers all types of financial markets: banking, insurance, stock exchanges, and commodity markets. The operating mechanisms are explained, as well as the role of these markets in the economy. Particular attention is given to market participants who engage in hedging, arbitrage, and speculation.

The following parts propose the use of different types of derivatives across all markets (organized and unorganized). These instruments can be used for risk management purposes.

Special attention is given to exotic derivatives and their valuation. Quantitative aspects are presented in all chapters. The book can be used by academic researchers and students as a reference and in courses at various levels. It can also serve as a reference for professionals in the banking industry and stock exchanges, particularly in the areas of hedging risks, pricing derivatives, and implementing simple and complex risk strategies.

Bonne lecture.

About the Author

Mondher Bellalah, after obtaining his PhD in finance in 1990 at France's leading university, Paris Dauphine, began his career both as a professor of finance — teaching at leading institutions such as HEC Paris, INSEAD, the University of Maine, Paris Dauphine University, Cergy-Pontoise University (now CY Cergy Paris University), ESSEC (Cergy-Pontoise, France), and the MIT Foundation — and as an international finance expert, banker, and consultant in portfolio management and in all areas of risk and corporate governance. He worked initially as a trader and market maker on the Paris Bourse (stock exchange) before being put in charge of BNP's financial engineering research team as Head of Derivatives and Structured Products and Risk Management.

Professor Bellalah has served as an advisor to numerous leading financial institutions, including BNP, Rothschild Bank, Euronext, Houlihan Lokey Howard & Zukin, Associes en Finance (where he was part of the team that built the CAC 40 Index in 1987), NatWest Bank, the Central Bank of Tunisia, Dubai Holding (Dubai Capital Group and Dubai Group), NBK, and UAB. He has also held several positions, including chief risk officer, managing director in alternative investments, head of capital markets, and head of trading. He is now acting as an independent non-executive director at Bank ABC, as well as chairman of the Board Risk Committee and a member of the Corporate Governance Committee. He is also a member of the Board Governance Committee and the Board Nomination Committee.

Professor Bellalah has enjoyed a distinguished academic career as a tenured professor of finance and researcher for about 37 years. During this time, he has authored more than 30 books and 200 articles in leading academic and professional journals, and he was awarded the prestigious Turgot Prize for the best French-language book on modern finance, risk management, and derivatives in 2005. A new edition of the book will be published in 2026. He was awarded a Doctor Honoris Causa in Paris.

Contents

Part I

Banking Risk Management

Chapter 1

Risk Management and Governance in Banks and Financial Institutions

Chapter Outline

The structure of the chapter is as follows:

1. Section 1.1 defines the risk mission statement, which covers the overall risk philosophy of a bank.
2. Section 1.2 introduces the general principles, which cover the overarching guidelines for risk management and outline the enterprise-wide risk management activities of the bank. It details the high-level organization, authorities, and processes relating to the risks faced by the bank as part of its normal business operations and their management.
3. Section 1.3 covers the risk strategy, which includes the overall approach for establishing, communicating, and monitoring all material risks of the bank through organizational roles and responsibilities, risk appetite statements, policies, risk limits, processes, controls, and systems in pursuit of its strategic and business objectives.
4. Section 1.4 is devoted to risk governance, which covers the roles, responsibilities, and reporting lines to ensure adequate segregation of duties in order to allow independence and avoid conflicts of interest in pursuit of the bank's business objectives and strategy.

Abbreviations: Table 1.1 lists the words that are standard in the financial industry.

Table 1.1. Standard words in the financial industry.

Word/Term/Abbreviation	Definition
ALCO	Asset and Liability Committee
AML	Anti-Money Laundering
Board/BoD	Board of Directors
BRC	Board Risk Committee
BTIC	Business and Technology Investment Committee
CEO	Chief Executive Officer
CFO	Chief Financial Officer
CB/CB	Central Bank
ERM	Enterprise Risk Management
EXCOB	Executive Management Committee of the Board
GMRC	General Management Risk Committee
GMCC	General Management Credit Committee
ICAAP	Internal Capital Adequacy Assessment Process
Management	The Executive Management
MIC	Management Investment Committee
ORM	Operational Risk Management
ORAP	Operational Risk Assessment Process
PSC	Premises Steering Committee
RA	Risk Appetite
RAS	Risk Appetite Statement
RMG	Risk Management Group
TORs	Terms of Reference

Introduction

This chapter provides guidance on the roles and responsibilities exercised within the risk function and the terms of reference of the management risk-related committees of a bank or financial institution. It provides a practical account of the way the risk management group and management committees operate. It defines the industry best practices followed by those of bank employees and contractors when performing their functions.

Most of the risk management in banks refers to the work of the Basel Committee on Banking Supervision (BCBS). The BCBS is a committee of banking supervisory authorities that was established by the central bank governors of the Group of Ten countries in 1974. The committee expanded its membership in 2009 and again in 2014.

All references to the work of BCBS are available at the following website: Wikipedia: https://en.wikipedia.org/wiki/Basel_Committee_on_Banking_Supervision (updated 2025).

A risk charter is effective from the date of approval by the board risk committee (BRC), and subsequently by the board of directors (BoD or "the board"), and remains valid until rescinded, amended, or superseded with the approval of the BRC and board. The aim of risk management is to manage upside risks (opportunities) and downside risks (threats) and to maximize returns on the associated risks while comprehensively identifying and assessing risk situations, without attempting to find all potential risks, in order to be able to manage them in an effective, well-informed manner. Importantly, this chapter is based on my professional experience in several financial institutions. For further reading, the reader can refer to Bellalah and Zouari (2015) and Bellalah *et al.* (2017).

1.1. Risk Mission Statement

Risk management is a necessary function required by regulators around the world. It exists in all charters of banks.

Risk management information is available on references in websites at the end of the chapter of the European Banking Authority: "Guidelines on internal policies, procedures and controls to ensure the implementation of Union and national restrictive measures".

A bank's risk management mission statement aims to:

- protect the bank's stakeholders and thereby contribute to shareholder value, providing the bank with a framework enabling proactive identification of those risks that may impact the ability of the business to achieve its objectives;
- promote a culture of risk awareness, continuous control improvement, and risk reduction to create a flexible, low-risk profile organization capable of rapid response to business opportunities and the emergence of new risks;
- balance the potential to offer value-added and revenue-increasing services with the risks arising from them to ensure an appropriate risk–return tradeoff is maintained (in line with the bank's approved risk appetite).

The bank's risk management mission statement also aims to:

- adhere to market-recognized industry practice in the identification, measurement/assessment, management, and reporting and control of risks, as certified by auditors, regulators, and other independent bodies;
- improve risk awareness and risk transparency in general, as well as identify, assess, control, and review key risks which impact the bank from both internal and external environments;
- provide comprehensive risk information through early warning indicators to business units, management, and the board on the status of risk within the bank;
- ensure that direct losses arising from inadequate processes, systems, people, and external events are identified and resolved promptly;
- derive commercial benefit by minimizing regulatory (and consequently economic) capital requirements by lowering its risk profile.

1.1.1. *Risk management framework*

Risk management is viewed as a continuous process operating at all levels and the various components of the risk management framework that link the bank and individual risk policies. For a comprehensive review of the risk management framework, the reader can refer to Bellalah and Simon (2000) and Bellalah and Abdel Rahman (2000).

Most of the risk management framework descriptions can be found on websites such as the European Banking Authority: "Guidelines on internal policies, procedures, and controls to ensure the implementation of Union and national restrictive measures" (updated 2025).

The risk management cycle within the bank is based on the identification of risks as the starting point in the risk management process, both at a business and the bank level. It is also based on the assessment of the bank's exposure to identified risks. The bank's risk management mission also refers to the development of action plans to mitigate losses where the probable loss exposure exceeds the bank's tolerance and to monitor risks in relation to the assessment of the bank's exposure.

1.1.2. *Risk culture and ownership*

"Culture" can be defined as the set of shared attitudes, values, goals, and practices that characterizes an organization.

An essential element of the success of the risk management framework is the recognition by all employees of the need to carry out their responsibilities effectively and to communicate when chapter violations and other problems are detected.

Clearly written, distributed, and readily available procedures are fundamental to the detection and communication of risk issues.

The key characteristics of the bank's risk culture are as follows:

- The bank succeeds if everyone takes ownership of risk as part of their responsibility.
- Everyone is expected to make risk decisions in the best interests of the bank.
- Risk ownership is an active, ongoing responsibility of the business.
- The risk management group provides and communicates a clear and unambiguous framework of policies, principles, and processes for risk ownership and review.
- All risk decisions have a clear, identifiable "audit trail".

The characteristics of the bank's risk culture require the bank's staff to be accountable for the risk within their areas of responsibility and decisions taken; therefore, a clear audit trail is essential. In holding people accountable, the bank differentiates between unforeseeable consequences and deliberate violations of policies/mandates.

The characteristics also require that the bank work to create a climate in which staff can talk openly about risk or problems at a sufficiently early stage, with the emphasis on solutions.

In addition, it is required that the bank openly discuss and learn lessons from mistakes or misjudgments.

The bank ensures that all employees receive risk training as appropriate and ongoing guidance in risk issues through risk management.

Finally, job descriptions for all staff throughout the bank should clearly outline roles and responsibilities, including risk management obligations.

1.1.3. *Risk and control assessment*

Risk and control assessment is an empirical element or component within the bank's risk management framework.

Sound internal risk control is essential for prudent operations of the bank and to promote stability of the financial system as a whole. Risk control entails the entire process of policies, procedures, and systems an institution needs to have in place to prudently manage all risks resulting from its financial transactions and to ensure those risks remain within the bank's risk appetite. The impulses for risk control are generated from a comparison of planned and actual risk situations and risk strategies.

For a comprehensive review of risk management frameworks, the reader can refer to Bellalah (2004a).

The purpose of risk evaluation is to assess the bank's risk profile, which involves comparing the level of risk found during the analysis process with risk tolerance established considering the context.

The bank's methodology for risk assessment should aim to identify, prioritize, and profile the complete portfolio of risks across business and functional areas within the bank.

The bank's risk is identified through the use of process mapping and/or questionnaires, control self-assessments, and key risk indicators (KRIs). This analysis assists in identifying key business activities and processes, functional dependencies, process stress points, process duplication, institutionalized processes that reduce the integrity of the control environment, the adequacy of controls for chapter processes, or the adequacy of controls relating to automated processes such as transfers of data between IT systems.

The chief risk officer is responsible for developing a methodology and framework for selecting, monitoring, capturing, validating, analyzing, and reporting on KRIs. The risk management department works with the business units and functional areas to select appropriate indicators that capture key risk trends at this level and develop generic bank-wide indicators that track risk trends on an enterprise basis.

The bank uses a range of quantitative tools and metrics for monitoring and managing risks. Some of these tools are common to a number of risk categories, while others are tailored to the particular features of specific risk categories. The following are the most important quantitative tools and metrics currently used and proposed by the bank to measure, manage, and report risk:

- credit ratings;
- stress testing, which requires stress simulations performed regularly to evaluate potential losses resulting from extreme market movements;
- control activities and segregation of duties;
- value at risk (VaR) for market risk, which is defined as an estimate of the potential loss of income over a given time period within a given confidence level due to changes in the market level of profits and foreign exchange rates and prices;
- earnings at risk (EaR) for interest rate risk;
- mismatch analysis for liquidity risk;
- limits for concentration risk;
- portfolio risk reporting.

For a more detailed analysis, the reader can refer to Bellalah (2004b) and the later chapters in this book.

1.1.4. *Effective internal control systems*

The scope and nature of effective internal control systems should be consistent with the bank's business model and level of activity.

An effective internal control system should ensure several tasks, as described in the following.

The bank should consider the nature and size of its operations, diversification of activities, transaction size and complexity, degree of risks associated with each area of the bank's activities, level of control exercised by the management on the daily operations, degree of centralization of work management, and extent of reliance on automated information systems.

The bank's organizational structure should be proportionate to the size and nature of its various banking activities. The assets of the bank should be protected against any losses resulting from misuse or mis-disposal thereof. Disposal of the assets must be in accordance with the resolutions and recommendations of the board.

The risks involved in the bank's business should be properly identified, assessed, and followed up. Hence, adequate information security is necessary, in accordance with the International Accounting Standards or any other regulatory criteria determined by the central bank. Through this, areas of potential conflict of interest are identified, minimized, and subject to thorough independent scrutiny.

The management team must be capable of managing and controlling the financial position's elements (capital adequacy, liquidity, profitability, asset quality, and associated risks) on a regular basis and at the right time.

The internal audit department must possess both independence and competence, and its scope, procedures, and periodicity of audit must meet the level of risk encountered in the different activities of the bank.

Reliable information systems are essential to provide adequate and comprehensive information to cover all material risk-related activities. The structure of the bank should be such that it provides for channels of communication to ensure information flows downward, upward, and laterally (across departments) among divisions. Good downward communication ensures all staff fully understand the bank's objectives, strategies, and expectations and adhere to policies and procedures in line with their responsibilities. Information flow upward is necessary for management to be aware of the risks being encountered at operational levels in achieving organizational goals and to take prompt corrective actions. Communication across departments is vital to ensure that information is shared and activities are coordinated toward achieving organizational goals.

1.2. General Principles

The chief risk officer is approved by the BRC and given final approval by the board of the bank after consultation with the General Management Risk Committee (GMRC) and the General Management Credit Committee (GMCC). The purpose is to outline the enterprise-wide risk management activities of the bank. It details the high-level organization, authorities, and processes relating to the risks faced by the bank as part of its normal business operations and their management.

1.2.1. *Guiding principles for risk management activities*

The following guiding principles apply to all risk management activities:

Approval: All business activities which commit the bank (legally or morally) to deliver risk-sensitive products and any business proposals require approval by authorized individuals or committees prior to commitment.

Independence: There should be a clear separation between commercial and risk management functions.

Transparency: Risk management structures, policies, and procedures should be transparent, based on consistent principles in written form and well-communicated.

Committee: Decisions regarding the approval of and changes to chapters, products, portfolios, and large or high-risk exposures are taken by an appropriate committee.

Approval authority: Authorities are delegated by the board through the chief executive officer (CEO) and reflect the delegate's (committee or individual) level of expertise and adequate segregation of duties.

Risk and return: The risk element is duly taken into consideration while deciding on the appropriateness of pricing exposures so as to ensure risk–return matching.

Business responsibility: Business units are responsible for the selection of clients and for managing all business activities with those clients within approved limits.

These guiding principles and the underlying elements of the risk charter are dictated by the bank's policies and central bank guidelines.

1.3. Risk Strategy

Risk appetite is an overall approach for establishing, communicating, and monitoring all material risks of the bank through organizational roles and responsibilities, risk appetite statements, policies, risk limits, processes, controls, and systems in pursuit of its strategic and business objectives.

A comprehensive risk appetite framework and resulting risk appetite statement (RAS) are the cornerstone of an effective risk appetite.

Risk appetite is one of the core factors in the process of measuring additional capital required to cover the various risks faced by the bank.

1.3.1. *Definition of risk capacity*

Risk capacity is defined as the maximum amount of risk the bank can assume while meeting minimum statutory capital and liquidity requirements (inclusive of capital and liquidity management actions).

Since the bank is managed within the risk appetite, and the risk appetite is intended not to exceed risk capacity, risk management and quantification processes are built around the risk appetite rather than risk capacity.

1.3.2. *Definition of risk appetite*

Risk appetite is the level and nature of risk that the bank is willing to take on in pursuit of its strategic business objectives, subject to constraints imposed by debt holders, regulators, and customers. It is expressed in terms of qualitative and quantitative limits. Risk appetite is formally articulated in the bank's RAS.

RAS translates the bank's strategy into measurable goals, optimizing risks embedded in business and also allocating available capital resources to ensure sustainable performance. Defining risk appetite is the responsibility of the chief risk officer and is approved by the BRC after recommendations from the GMRC and GMCC, as it is closely linked to defining the overall strategy of the bank. Risk appetite provides an anchor for strategy, risk, and finance and aligns these three functions.

1.3.3. *Components of a risk appetite framework*

The risk appetite framework aims to ensure that the risk taken is aligned with the business strategy. It is understood at appropriate levels of the bank and adequately priced and rewarded.

Table 1.2. Components of a risk appetite framework.

Governance structure	The governance sets out the roles and responsibilities of the functions of the bank in embedding its risk appetite.
Risk appetite statement (RAS)	The formally articulated RAS of the bank.
Risk appetite chapter	The policies and processes that embed the risk appetite across the bank.
Risk appetite adherence	The controls and thresholds put in place to ensure adherence to the risk appetite.

The framework consists of the following components, as summarized in Table 1.2.

Governance structure: The BRC is the ultimate owner of the bank's risk appetite and has overall responsibility for setting and approving it. This involves determining the nature and extent of the significant risks the bank is willing to take in achieving its strategic objectives.

The chief risk officer, along with the consultation of the GMRC, operates and makes decisions based on the set risk appetite limits. They receive regular reports on the actual compared to the limits and are also notified in case of any breaches of limits based on report frequency.

The management takes part in the reviews and discussions on risk appetite setting, debates on the limit structure with business units to support implementation, and also monitors the business profile against limits and tolerance levels.

Risk appetite statement: The bank should adopt the RAS as a formal articulation of the type, quality, and amount of risk that the bank is willing to accept in pursuit of strategic and business objectives. It is a tool for senior management to understand the critical linkages between strategy, business plans, and risk. RAS should address the needs of all stakeholders involved by acting as a governor of risk and a driver of current and future business activities. The central bank expects banks to submit their risk appetite statement and link it to their internal capital adequacy assessment process (ICAAP) and stress testing.

Risk appetite: To meet the stated objectives of the risk appetite framework, the bank should manage the material risk types. It should specify the amount of risk the bank is willing to seek or accept in pursuit of its long-term objectives. It indicates the parameters within which the bank would want to conduct its activities.

Risk appetite adherence: The inclusion of threshold structures within the risk appetite framework is integral to embedding a consistent risk appetite across the bank's businesses by cascading strategic targets into operational thresholds. Emphasis is placed on integrating a comprehensive framework of early alerts and portfolio profiling, on both baseline and stress views, with respect to the risk appetite boundaries. An effective risk appetite promotes active portfolio management by proactively assessing external and internal risks. To meet this objective, the bank leverages industry and macroeconomic trends and analysis. Doing so allows the bank to assess and mitigate these evolving risks as well as ensure that we are within the risk appetite boundaries.

1.4. Risk Governance

1.4.1. *The board of directors and the committees of the board*

Board of Directors: The board has the ultimate responsibility for the management of all risks assumed and faced by the bank, which it does through several board committees it has established to assist it in performing its duties. The BoD reviews and approves all risk policies and maintains oversight of all bank risks through reports received from the BRC, board credit committee (BCC), GMRC, and GMCC.

Board Credit Committee: The BCC is responsible for evaluating and granting counterparty credit facilities and approving the bank's investment activities within authorized limits.

Board Risk Committee: The risk appetite and its governance are set by the BRC. This committee is responsible for all aspects of enterprise risk management, including, but not restricted to, credit risk, market risk, operational risk, legal risk, regulatory risk, liquidity risk, and financial risks.

Management Committees: At the management level, the CEO is delegated by the board to create management committees, either permanently or *ad hoc*, to perform roles and responsibilities determined by him or her. The terms of reference, structure, and authorities of the management committees are to be endorsed by the board executive committee. The following management committees have been established by the CEO: the executive management committee, the GMRC, the GMCC, the business and technology investment committee (BTIC), the asset and liability committee (ALCO), the management investment committee (MIC), and the premises steering committee.

The terms of reference for these committees can be found in their respective committee charters.

1.4.2. *Risk management group*

Mission and objectives of risk group:

The risk management group is an independent risk organization that works closely with the business units to support their activities while safeguarding the bank's risk profile.

The primary objectives of the risk group are to:

- ensure adherence and compliance of individual transaction and portfolio performance to agreed terms and chapters;
- institute prudent risk control mechanisms across the bank;
- review commercial and retail credit transactions and highlights risks;
- ensure compliance with UAE and other applicable laws and regulations;.
- maintain the primary relationship with local regulators (when matters pertain to the risk-related circulars).

Responsibilities:

The risk group presides over all risk management activities of the bank and has the following as its primary focus:

- Work with commercial business units, finance, internal audit, and other stakeholders in the development of risk policies and procedures.
- Periodically review and function as custodians of all risk policies of the bank.
- Approve risk exposures within delegated authorities.
- Analyze and provide recommendations for appropriate risk limits.
- Monitor creditworthiness of clients and counterparties together with commercial business units.
- Together with commercial business units and the active involvement of the legal department, actively manage special and remedial assets.
- Recommend and maintain adequate levels of loss provisions for non-performing loans and other impaired assets of the bank, in compliance with the bank's policies and regulatory guidelines.
- Develop and maintain custody of risk management tools, methodologies such as stress testing, sensitivity analysis, and portfolio testing.
- Provide input into new product papers.
- Monitor local legal and regulatory compliance (when matters pertain to risk-related circulars).
- Monitor, control, and report on risk exposures.
- Develop risk management procedures and portfolio management tools.
- Proactively identify and manage any new or existing risks or risk processes not identified above.
- Take on general responsibilities regarding staffing and career development of risk, legal, compliance, and fraud management professionals.

Summary

Risk evaluation of the bank's risk profile involves comparing the level of risk found during the analysis process with risk tolerance established when the context was considered.

The methodology for risk assessment must identify and profile the portfolio of risks across business and functional areas.

The chief risk officer is responsible for developing a methodology for selecting, monitoring, capturing, validating, analyzing, and reporting on KRIs. Risk management works closely with business units to select appropriate indicators that capture key risk trends at this level.

The bank uses tools and metrics for managing risks. Some tools are common to a number of risk categories, while others are tailored to the particular features of specific risk categories.

The following are the most important quantitative tools and metrics currently used and proposed by a bank to measure, manage, and report risks: credit ratings, stress testing, control activities and segregation of duties, VaR for market risk, EaR for interest rate risk, limits for concentration risk, and portfolio risk reporting.

References

Bellalah M and Y Simon (2000). Options, Contrats à Terme et Gestion des Risques Financiers. *Economica.*

Bellalah M and K Abdel Rahman (2000). Gestion des Risques dans un Cadre International. *Economica.*

Bellalah M (2004a). *Gestion des Risques et Produits Dérivés Classiques et Exotiques.* Dunod, Prix Turgot.

Bellalah M (2004b). *Gestion des Portefeuilles.* Pearson Education.

Bellalah M and S Zouari (2015). Portfolio credit risk models and name concentration issues: Theory and simulations. *International Journal of Business.*

Bellalah M, O Masood and SM Ghauri (2017). Basel III implementation outcome in Islamic banks. *The Journal of Risk.*

Websites

European Banking Authority: Guidelines on internal policies, procedures and controls to ensure the implementation of Union and national restrictive measure (updated 2025).

Wikipedia: https://en.wikipedia.org/wiki/Basel_Committee_on_Banking_Supervision (updated 2025).

Chapter 2

Market Risk Management

Chapter Outline

This chapter is organized as follows:

1. Section 2.1 is devoted to risk governance.
2. Section 2.2 proposes general statements of the market risk function in the banking industry.
3. Section 2.3 defines market risk management strategy.
4. Section 2.4 is devoted to the market risk management framework.
5. Section 2.5 explains the use of internal market risk models.
6. Section 2.6 is reserved for interest rate or profit rate risk guidelines.
7. Section 2.7 explains foreign exchange risk guidelines.
8. Section 2.8 develops equity risk guidelines.
9. Section 2.9 is reserved for commodities and inventory risk.
10. Section 2.10 explains options risk.
11. Section 2.11 develops trading book guidelines.
12. Section 2.12 is reserved for the investment management guidelines.
13. Section 2.13 describes market risk identification and measurement.
14. Section 2.14 deals with market risk capital charges for financial contracts.

15. Section 2.15 explains market risk monitoring and reporting guidelines.
16. Section 2.16 introduces risk reporting in banks and financial institutions.

Introduction

The purpose of this chapter is to address the specific approaches for mitigating market risks arising from a bank's business and key activities. This chapter covers the responsibility of the board of directors, the risk committee, the executive investment committee, and the risk management department (RMD). All roles and responsibilities mentioned in this chapter should be performed by the relevant departments, taking into consideration the bank's delegation of authority (DoA). The RMD, or risk management function, in a bank or financial institution is responsible for identifying and managing the bank's overall market risk exposure. Most of risk management in banking is guided by the Bank for International Settlements.[1]

It is worth noting that this chapter is based on my professional experience in several financial institutions and standard regulatory texts from the Basel Committee on Banking Supervision (BCBS) and the Financial Stability Board. For an introduction to market risk management, the reader can refer to Bellalah and Abdel Rahman (2000) and Bellalah (2004a, 2004b).

2.1. Market Risk Management Identification: Processes and Governance

The bank should follow sound risk governance principles, laying emphasis on the articulation of clear roles, responsibilities, and reporting lines. It should adhere to sound governance principles laid down by the local central bank (or regulatory authority) for corporate governance and its governance structure for market risk. The following sections articulate the bank's governance framework for market risk management. The governance structure includes various stakeholders, such as the board of directors (BoD), the risk committee, the executive investment committee, the asset liability

[1](https://www.bis.org (updated 2025)) and the Financial Stability Board (https:// www.fsb.org › ... › Monitoring of Priority Areas (updated 2025)).

management committee, the chief risk officer (CRO), the chief investment officer (CIO), and the chief finance officer (CFO).

2.2. General Statements

The risk division must establish limits based on the market risk appetite of the bank to mitigate risks related to foreign exchange, profit rate, equity, and liquidity; limit excesses should be forwarded to the risk and chapter committee, or as deemed appropriate as per the delegation of authority matrix. Market risk must be monitored daily by the middle office to ensure that no limit breaches have occurred.

The bank must have an adequate system of internal controls over its market risk management process. A fundamental component of the internal control system involves regular independent reviews and evaluations of the effectiveness of the system and, where necessary, ensuring that appropriate revisions or enhancements to internal controls are made.

Stress testing should be performed to determine the effects of abnormal market movements and their impact on the value of the bank's portfolios. Contingency plans should be developed for certain scenarios. The bank should have an adequate contingency plan in place due to sudden adverse market movements. Also, an adequate segregation of duties between trading, deal processing (operations), and accounting functions should exist.

The CRO has the overall responsibility of oversight of the market risk function. The internal audit function is responsible for checking adherence to the market risk management chapter through *post facto* testing of controls. The bank can establish a risk analytics and testing unit to conduct daily middle office activities. Alternatively, it can implement effective systems for conducting such middle office activities. For a more detailed analysis, the reader can refer to Bellalah and Bouheni (2020), Bellalah and Butt (2019), and Bellalah *et al.* (2017, 2022).

2.3. Market Risk Management Strategy

The bank's strategic plan determines the extent of trading and investing activities that are considered to be core (or non-core) to its activities. The bank's risk appetite and investment strategies guide the chapter regarding the types of financial instruments that it is permitted to trade and invest in, as well as which department or function has overall responsibility for these activities. Risk can be mitigated by diversifying the bank's investment holdings across different sectors and asset classes.

The fundamental principles underlying the market risk process are outlined as follows:

- the risk committee, with the CRO's oversight of the market risk management process;
- adequate and clearly defined risk management policies and procedures consistent with the nature and complexities of the market risk exposures;
- clearly defined and documented roles and responsibilities of all parties (individuals and committees) involved in the market risk management process;
- full compliance with the regulatory standards and requirements;
- strong control (identification, measurement, and control procedures) over risks inherent in new products/services before they are introduced.

The fundamental principles underlying the market risk processes also include adequate segregation of duties between risk position takers and the market risk control function. They require adequate market risk measurement systems that capture all material sources of market risk. They include material hedging or risk management initiatives approved by the risk committee.

Market risk processes need adequate operating and risk limits to contain exposures within reasonable levels (in line with the bank's risk appetite). They also require periodic and adequate stress and scenario testing. The principles underlying the market risk process necessitate adequate and timely Management Information Systems (MIS) and reporting to the governing body, senior management, and, where appropriate, individual business line managers. They need periodic independent assessment of the market risk management process (policies, procedures, and measurement approaches) by internal and external auditors and other experts. They implement adequate capitalization in order to commensurate with the level of market risk.

2.4. Market Risk Management Framework

The framework consists of a bank-wide definition of market risk and lays down the principles of how market risk is to be identified, assessed, monitored, and controlled/mitigated. The bank uses the standardized approach for calculating the market risk capital charge. The standardized methodology uses a "building-block" approach in which specific risks and the general market risks arising from debt and equity positions are calculated separately. The framework is consistently implemented throughout the bank, and staff at all levels should understand their responsibilities with respect to market risk management. The framework is subject to periodic internal audit reviews.

2.5. Use of Internal Market Risk Models

The bank should use an internal model to calculate its market risk capital requirement or any standalone components of its market risk capital requirement, provided such models have been approved in writing by the regulator or market authority. In case the bank chooses to use internal models, then the bank should ensure that a robust stress testing framework is in place. For more details about models, the reader can refer to Bellalah and Zouari (2015) and Bellalah *et al.* (2015, 2016).

Regulators usually only grant approval for the use of an internal risk model if the use of the model to calculate the market risk capital requirement has been approved by another appropriate regulator. Regulator is satisfied having been provided by the bank with such opinions from independent experts as it may require, that the model adequately addresses the market risk requirements.

Regulators grant approval for the use of an internal risk model if the use of the methodology is integrated into the governance and control framework of the bank. Specifically, the governing body and senior management of the bank receive and review appropriate reports in respect of the entity. They should be satisfied that: the bank's risk management system is conceptually sound and is implemented with integrity; the bank has sufficient numbers of staff skilled in using sophisticated models not only in the trading area but also in the risk control, audit, and, if necessary, back-office areas; the bank's models have a proven track record of reasonable accuracy in measuring risk; and the bank regularly conducts stress tests.

In determining whether an internal value-at-risk (VaR) model meets the standard for regulatory approval, the bank focuses on qualitative and quantitative standards, the specification of market risk factors, and stress testing with a combination of internally developed models and the standardized methodology. The bank can also use internal models developed by its risk analytics unit, provided those models are tested by independent validators.

2.6. Interest Rate or Profit Rate Risks Guidelines

The bank accepts and manages interest rate or profit rate risk as an inherent part of its business. Interest rate or profit rate changes affect the bank's earnings by altering net profit income and the level of other profit-sensitive income and operating expenses. Additionally, interest rate or profit rate changes affect the underlying economic value of the bank's assets, liabilities, and off-balance sheet instruments.

Interest (rate or profit rate) risk management strategy for the bank is explained as follows.

The bank must clearly identify the interest (rate or profit rate) risk-sensitive products and activities it wishes to engage in. It should minimize the maturity mismatches between its assets and the balances from fund providers. An ALM system can be used to monitor maturity mismatches. The bank establishes a limit structure to monitor and control the interest rate or profit rate risk, which must be approved by the risk committee.

The bank may enter into Shari'a-compliant transactions in order to hedge exposures arising from day-to-day banking and investment activities. The interest rate or profit rate risk exposure can be managed by evaluating each new product/activity with respect to the risk introduced by it. The primary forms of interest rate or profit rate risk faced by the bank can be divided into three categories: repricing risk, yield curve risk, and basis risk.

All financings are priced on a floating rate basis, and the funding profit basis is matched with the financing pricing basis.

The RMD ensures that a system is in place for the timely identification and measurement of interest rate or profit rate risk, including that arising from new products or services.

The RMD ensures that interest rate or profit rate exposures are monitored on a periodic basis and set in accordance with the changes to the corresponding risk exposure. The following measures can be used for interest rate or profit rate risk measurement in the banking book repricing gap analysis.

Repricing gap analysis: It measures the arithmetic difference between the interest rate or profit rate-sensitive assets and liabilities. Based on the contractual maturities of financial instruments or assumptions regarding these instruments, gap analysis shows the cash flows, including those, on a cumulative basis, of a portfolio, sub-portfolio, or product by maturity segment (e.g., up to 3 months, 3–6 months, 6–12 months, 1–3 years, over 3 years, etc.). The gap report shows the exposure released during a particular time period and the outstanding exposure during a particular time period.

Earnings-at-Risk (EaR): It measures the loss of net profit income resulting from upward/downward interest rate or profit rate movements over a particular time horizon. It is computed as the sum of marginal gaps (calculated for each time bucket in the repricing gap analysis), each weighted by the product of the average time left until the end of the horizon period and the expected interest rate or profit rate movement for the gap period.

The bank only carries out a repricing gap analysis to monitor interest rate or profit rate risk. The approach is reviewed periodically by the bank to assess its suitability and to consider a possible inclusion of EaR analysis to monitor its interest rate or profit rate risk. Business managers must inform the treasury and investments division and the risk division whenever the bank approves fixed-rate financings above the acceptable threshold set in light of the credit section. The treasury will assess the potential for hedging the customer's and the company's exposure to interest rate or profit rate risk and take the appropriate action. Minimum capital requirement for interest rate or profit rate risk is expressed in terms of two separately calculated charges:

Specific risk, which is the interest rate or profit rate risk, stemming from each security position (short or long).

General market risk, which is the interest rate or profit rate risk within the portfolio, where long and short positions in different securities or instruments can be offset. The risk division sets the interest rate or profit rate risk limits within the bank's desired risk appetite. Day-to-day management of interest rate or profit rate risk is the responsibility of the treasury.

The treasury manages interest rate or profit rate risk through planning and executing corresponding management strategies and activities (at macro and micro levels). It does so by: providing the risk committee with information on market views on possible interest rate or profit rate fluctuations on a regular basis; reports to the risk committee the status of interest rate or profit rate risk management; and by complying with interest rate or profit rate risk limits.

Monthly interest rate or profit rate exposure reports to the CRO shall, at a minimum, include the following two elements: first, a summary of the bank's aggregate profit-sensitive exposures (assets, liabilities, and off-balance sheet items); and second, the calculation of interest rate or profit rate risk measures (for the banking book as well as all significant currencies), including repricing gap analysis, and adherence to interest rate or profit rate risk limits.

2.7. Foreign Exchange Risk Guidelines

In measuring its market risk, the bank must include the risk of holding or taking positions in foreign currencies (foreign exchange risk). This type of risk may arise from the bank's trading in the foreign exchange market and other markets; it may also arise from non-trading activities that are denominated in a foreign currency.

If foreign currency is to be received or delivered under a binding unilateral promise, the bank must report any interest rate or profit rate exposure from the other leg of the contract in accordance with interest rate and profit rate risk in the trading book.

The RMD ensures that an effective system is in place to identify and forecast foreign exchange exposure positions.

The risk division develops foreign exchange scenario analysis to determine foreign exchange exposures. The bank's approach to foreign exchange risk management includes:

- prompt and timely reporting of open positions and revaluation effects (profit and losses);
- strong monitoring of compliance with the limits approved by the risk committee;
- timely exception reporting to the risk committee, the executive investment committee, and the asset and liability committee;
- coordinating foreign exchange use that arises from different funding needs across the bank.

The bank's approach to foreign exchange risk management also requires:

- anticipating funding needs and currencies involved in order to mitigate currency risk exposures;
- managing foreign exchange risk emanating from other risks (market or credit risk);
- ensuring adequate capital to cover currency risk exposures;
- entering approved hedges to mitigate currency risk exposures.

The bank sets stop-loss levels on a daily and monthly basis for foreign exchange exposures.

Should the monthly stop-loss level be reached, no further proprietary trades are to be undertaken until specific approval as per the delegation of authority structure.

The treasury has the responsibility for the day-to-day management of foreign exchange risk. In addition, it is responsible for planning and executing foreign exchange risk management strategies and activities in line with the BoD-approved policies and risk limits and the risk committee's directives. It also reports to the risk committee the status of foreign exchange risk management programs; and it should comply with foreign exchange risk limits. Foreign exchange risk exposures shall be identified and measured by open position limits, intraday limits, and currency position limits.

Foreign exchange risk includes the following.

In calculating the capital charge for foreign exchange risk, the bank must include in its exposure to each foreign currency:

- the net spot position (that is, assets minus liabilities denominated in the currency, including accrued profit and other accrued income and accrued expenses);

- the net position of binding unilateral promises by the bank to buy or sell currencies on a specified future date (that are not included in the spot position).

Examples of amounts to be received or paid:

- the principal on currency swaps not included in the spot position;
- profit from swaps and other interest rate or profit rate transactions;
- irrevocable guarantees (and similar instruments) that are certain to be called and likely to be irrecoverable;
- any other items representing an exposure to risk in foreign currencies (for example, a specific provision held in the currency in question where the underlying asset is held in a different currency).

The bank includes in its currency exposure any net future income or expenses that are not yet accrued but already fully hedged. If it includes such income or expenses, it must do so consistently and must not select only expected future flows that reduce its position. If the bank has deliberately taken a position to partly or totally protect itself against the adverse effect of a change in an exchange rate on its capital adequacy ratio, it may exclude the position from its currency exposure so far as it relates to that hedge if:

- the position is of a structural and non-trading nature;
- the structural position does no more than protect the bank's capital adequacy ratio;
- the position cannot be traded for speculative or profit-making purposes; and
- the exclusion of the position is done consistently, with the treatment of the hedge remaining the same for the life of the assets or other items.

The bank must calculate its overall foreign currency net open position by:

- calculating the net open position in each foreign currency;
- converting the nominal amount (or net present value) of each such net position into Qatari riyals at the current spot market exchange rate;
- adding all short net positions and adding all long net positions calculated under both the above points; and
- selecting the greater of the absolute values of the two sums in the above point.

The bank must calculate its net position in gold and silver by valuing all gold and silver positions using the US dollar current spot price (regardless of maturity); offsetting long and short positions; and converting the absolute value of the resulting net position into Qatari riyals. To convert the net position in gold and silver into currency, the firm must state the position (spot plus forward) in a standard unit of measurement and then convert the net position at the current spot market exchange rate.

The capital charge for foreign exchange risk held by the bank is 8% of the bank's overall foreign currency net open position in each of the foreign currencies it holds and 8% of its net open position in gold and silver.

2.8. Equity Risk Guidelines

In measuring its market risk, the bank must include the risk of holding or taking positions in equities (equity position risk). If equities are to be received or delivered under a binding unilateral promise, the bank must report any foreign currency or interest rate or profit rate exposure from the other leg of the contract in accordance with interest rate or profit rate guidelines, as the case requires.

Equity risk is handled by the investment function of the bank. The RMD ensures that an effective system to identify and forecast price risk exposure from equity positions is in place. Stop-loss orders should be established to minimize equity risk exposures within the portfolio. Additionally, the investments department sets limits to ensure all equity positions are in accordance with the bank's investment strategy (e.g., country, sector, currency, and instrument).

The bank should use appropriate hedging activities or other market techniques to assist in managing equity price risk. The RMD is also responsible for ensuring that adequate stress testing and scenario analysis are performed and reported to the risk committee on a periodic basis.

The measurement of an equity position risk in the trading book applies to short and long positions in all instruments that exhibit market behavior similar to equities. The bank may report short and long positions in instruments relating to the same issuer on a net basis. It must calculate the long or short position in the equity market on a market-by-market basis. That is, RMD must make a separate capital calculation for each exchange in which it holds equities (whether or not a recognized exchange). In calculating the capital charge for equity position risk, the bank must include equity Shari'a-compliant hedging instruments and off-balance-sheet positions that are affected by changes in equity prices. To calculate the charges for equity position risk in equity Shari'a-compliant hedging instruments and other off-balance-sheet positions, the bank must convert these positions into notional equity positions, so that:

- equity Shari'a-compliant hedging instruments and off-balance-sheet positions relating to individual equities are reported at current market prices;
- equity Shari'a-compliant hedging instruments and off-balance-sheet positions relating to stock indices are reported as the mark-to-market value of the notional underlying equity portfolio; and
- equity swaps are treated as two notional positions.

2.8.1. *Capital charges for specific and general equity risks*

The capital charge for equity position risk consists of two separately calculated charges: first, a charge for the specific risk of holding a long or short position in an individual equity; and second, a charge for the general risk of holding a long or short position in the market (as a whole).

The capital charge for a specific risk is 8% on the gross position in equities listed on a recognized exchange and 12% on the gross position of the bank in other equities.

The gross position in an equity market is the sum of the absolute values of all short equity positions and all long equity positions of the firm. The capital charge for general risk is 8% of the net position.

Net position in an equity market: It is the difference between long equity positions and short equity positions of the firm.

Equity position: It is the net of short and long exposures to an individual company. It is measured on the gross position across the company (rather than individual transactions).

Offsetting positions: If the bank takes a position in depository receipts against an opposite position in the underlying equity (whether or not listed in the same country where the receipts were issued), it may offset the positions only if any costs on conversion are taken into account in full.

The bank may offset matched positions in an identical equity or stock index in each market, resulting in a single net long or short position to which specific and general risk capital charges apply. For this purpose, a future in equity may be offset against an opposite physical position within the same equity.

Charges for index contracts: For an index contract on an index that the bank considers diversified, the risk division must apply a general risk capital charge of 8% and a specific risk capital charge of 2% to the net long or short position in the contract.

For any other index contract, the bank must apply a general risk capital charge of 8% and a specific risk capital charge of 4% to the net long or short position in the contract.

2.9. Commodities and Inventory Risk

In measuring its market risk, the bank has to include the risk of holding or taking positions in commodities and commodity options (commodity risk). Commodities refer to physical or energy products that may be traded. They include precious metals (other than gold and silver), base metals, agricultural products, minerals, oil, gas, and electricity. If a commodity is to be received or delivered under a binding unilateral promise, the firm must report any foreign currency, equity, or interest rate or profit rate exposure from the other leg of the contract in accordance with the respective guidance.

In measuring its market risk, the bank has to include the risk of holding assets in inventory with a view to reselling them under a murabahah contract or for leasing them under an ijarah contract (inventory risk).

Measurement of commodities risk: The bank should use the simplified approach to measure commodities risk. To calculate open positions using this approach, short and long positions in each commodity on a net basis are reported. Positions in the same commodity may be offset. Positions in different commodities must not be offset unless (a) the commodities are deliverable against each other or (b) the commodities are close substitutes for each other and a minimum correlation between price movements of 0.9 can be clearly established over at least the preceding year (subject to regulatory approval in writing). Each commodity position (spot plus forward) has to be reported in terms of the standard unit of measurement for the commodity in dollars, euros, or some other currency.

Inclusion in commodities risk: It includes commodity Sharia-compliant hedging instruments, off-balance-sheet positions affected by changes in commodity prices, commodities risk arising from Salam contracts, and options on commodities for which the options risk is measured using the delta-plus method (with their underlying assets). Options for which the options risk is measured using the simplified approach must be excluded. Commodity Sharia-compliant hedging instruments should be converted into notional commodity positions and assigned to maturities. Binding unilateral promises relating to a particular commodity must be included in the measurement of commodities risk as notional amounts in terms of the standard unit of measurement multiplied by the spot price of the commodity.

Capital charge: It is 15% on the firm's overall net position, long or short, in each commodity and 3% on the firm's gross position (the sum of the absolute values of all short positions and all long positions of the firm, regardless of maturity) in each commodity.

Measurement of inventory risk: The capital charge for inventory risk of an Islamic banking business firm is 15% of the value of assets held by the firm in inventory with a view to resale or lease.

2.10. Options Risk

In measuring its market risk, the bank must include the risk of holding or taking positions in options contracts (options risk). If it does not write options, it must use the simplified approach; otherwise, it must use the delta-plus method to measure options risk. If all the written option positions are hedged by perfectly matched long positions in the same options, no capital charge for options risk is required.

Simplified approach (capital charges for "long cash and long put" or "short cash and long call"): For a position that is "long cash and long put" or "short cash and long call", the capital charge is calculated by multiplying the market value of the underlying security by the sum of the specific and general risk capital charges for the underlying, and then subtracting the amount by which the option is in-the-money (bounded at zero). In the simplified approach, the capital charge is 8% for options on currency and 15% for options on commodities.

For options with a residual maturity of less than six months, the forward price is to be used. For options with a residual maturity of more than six months, the strike price should be compared with the forward price. If this is not possible, the bank takes the in-the-money amount to be zero.

Simplified approach (capital charges for "long put" or "long call"): The capital charge is the lesser of (a) the market value of the underlying security multiplied by the sum of the specific and general risk capital charges for the underlying and (b) the market value of the option. The book value of the option may be used instead of the market value if the position is not included in the trading book.

Delta-plus method: If the bank writes options, it has to calculate specific risk capital charges separately by multiplying the delta-equivalent value of each option by the risk-weight applicable under equity position risk or interest rate or profit rate risk in the trading book. In calculating the general risk capital charge, the bank must enter delta-weighted positions with a debt security or interest rate or profit rate as the underlying into the interest rate or profit rate time bands and risk factors table using a two-legged approach. Under this approach, there is one entry at the time the underlying contract takes effect and a second entry at the time the underlying contract matures. For an option with a debt security as the underlying, the bank must apply a specific risk capital charge to the delta-weighted position based on the issuer's rating and in accordance with interest rate or profit rate risk.

Capital charges under the delta-plus method: The capital charge for an option with equities as the underlying must be based on the delta-weighted positions included in the measurement of specific and general risks in accordance with equity position risk. An Islamic banking business firm writing options must calculate the capital charge for options on foreign exchange and gold and silver positions in accordance with foreign exchange risk. For delta risk, the net delta-based equivalent of the foreign currency, gold, and silver options must be included in the measurement of the exposure for the respective currency, gold, or silver position. The capital charge for an option on commodities must be based on the charge calculated using the simplified approach of commodities risk.

Gamma capital charges: If the bank writes an option, it must calculate the capital charge for gamma risk (gamma capital charge) for each option position separately. To calculate the gamma capital charge, calculate the gamma impact of each option in accordance with the following formula:

$$\text{gamma impact} = 0.5 \times \text{gamma} \times \text{VU}^2,$$

where VU is:

(a) for an interest rate or profit rate option: (i) if the option has a bond as the underlying, the market value of the underlying multiplied by the risk factor applicable from the time bank and risk factor table, or (ii) if the option has an interest rate or profit rate as the underlying, the market value of the underlying multiplied by the assumed changes in yield of the time bank and risk factor table;
(b) for options on equities and stock indices, the market value of the underlying multiplied by 8%;
(c) for options on foreign exchange, gold, and silver, the market value of the underlying multiplied by 8%;
(d) for an option on commodities, the market value of the underlying multiplied by 15%.

In calculating the gamma impact for an option mentioned in the definition of VU, the bank has to treat as the same the underlying: (a) for profit rates, each time band in the time bank and risk factor table (with each position allocated to separate maturity ladders); (b) for equities and stock indices, each recognized exchange; (c) for foreign currencies, gold, and silver, each currency pair, gold, and silver; and (d) for commodities, each individual commodity. Each option on the same underlying described above has a gamma impact that is positive or negative. The bank has to add the individual gamma impacts, resulting in a net gamma impact for each underlying that is either positive or negative. To calculate the total gamma capital charge, exclude positive gamma impacts. The total gamma capital charge is the sum of the absolute values of the net negative gamma impacts.

Vega capital charges: If the bank writes an option, it must calculate the capital charge for vega risk for each option position separately. To calculate the vega capital charge, the firm must multiply the vega for each option mentioned in the definition of VU in rule 12.5.2 by a 25% proportional shift in the option's current volatility. The results must then be summed across each underlying. The total vega capital charge is the sum of the absolute values of the vega capital charges across each underlying.

2.11. Trading Book Guidelines

The bank's trading book consists of the positions held by it (whether on- or off-balance-sheet), which must be included in the book in accordance with the following rules. Other positions held by the bank must be included in its banking book; the bank must have a trading book if it has positions that must be included in the trading book and if the total value of the positions described in the above point has exceeded 5% of the total on- and off-balance-sheet positions at any time in the previous 12 months.

A trading position of an Islamic banking business firm refers to a position held for short-term resale, with the intent of benefiting from actual or expected short-term price movements or to lock in arbitrage profits.

All assets are classified under the banking book unless specifically mentioned as trading positions.

The Basel Committee defines a trading book as

> the bank's proprietary positions in financial instruments which are intentionally held for short-term resale and/or which are taken on by the bank with the intention of benefiting in the short-term from actual and expected differences between their buying and selling prices, or from other price or profit-rate variations, and positions in financial instruments arising from matched principal brokering and market making, or positions taken in order to hedge other elements of the trading book.

All trading book positions in excess of the approved limits would require the risk committees' prior approval.

For each asset acquired under a trading book portfolio, the following information would be required to be presented to the risk division:

nature of the asset and currency; counterparty, rating, and available credit limit; and the holding period; stop-loss; benchmark and exit strategy; sensitivity to market risks; mark-to-market approach; capital adequacy requirements; regulatory limits available; and a statement confirming compliance with market risk policies.

Trading book transactions are limited to counterparties in the approved list and within risk limits approved by the risk committee.

2.12. Investment Management Guidelines

Investment risk is the risk arising from interest rate or profit rate and stock price fluctuations, resulting in asset proceeds being lower than expected. The bank should quantify the risks associated with any investment undertaken. The investment assessment involved in any investment should ensure that the bank only undertakes investments in securities in accordance with its investment strategy and risk profile. The bank can develop an investment strategy that is in line with the bank's risk appetite. The bank should ensure that the following risks are controlled when determining investment decisions: business risk, valuation risk, and liquidity risk.

2.13. Market Risk Identification and Measurement

The identification of market risks must be assured by a continuous survey of the markets.

Macroeconomic developments as well as the business-related political situation in countries should also be taken into consideration. The risk analytics unit works closely with senior management and the treasury unit to provide a "forward-looking" analysis of the economic and financial environment. The information provided is the basis for or input to stress testing. Periodic reports are prepared for the timely identification of market risks and reporting to the risk committee.

Stress tests must be performed on a regular basis in order to identify specific market situations and to assess the maximum loss that could occur in those situations. The bank identifies its market risks in both the banking book and trading book.

The bank must ensure that market risks are promptly identified for all new products and services. New products or services may carry additional market risks directly or indirectly and may require changes to systems, policies, risk limits, and processes.

The risk division should ensure that all new products are reviewed to ensure that all aspects of market risk have been considered prior to the launch of the new product. New products or services should not be launched until the required systems and procedures for managing market risks are in place. Compliance with the bank's guidelines on new products and the new product approval process is mandatory.

Market risk must be calculated daily, and established limits must be adhered to. All functions having market risk exposure must measure and report on market risk.

Stress testing should be performed to determine the effect of abnormal market moves on the market value of the bank's portfolios and the quantum of events lying outside the bounds of value at risk models.

Value-at-risk is defined as an estimate of the potential loss of income over a given time period within a given confidence level due to changes in the market level of profits and foreign exchange rates and prices, and the volatility in prices for financial instruments in which positions are held. The parameter and assumptions for the VaR model must be established by the CRO in consultation with the asset liability management committee and should be approved by the risk committee.

The RMD recommends an approach (historical data, variance-covariance approach, or Monte Carlo simulation) to calculate VaR. The risk committee is responsible for approval.

Stress simulations should be performed regularly to evaluate potential losses resulting from extreme market movements. The frequency of stress testing is set by the risk committee. This should be a dynamic process in order to accommodate the specific types of risk being run by the bank and may be based on historic or potential market shock data using simulations. The CRO should first identify market events and scenarios that could give rise to extreme market exposures for the portfolio as a whole.

A full description of the scenario must include market rates and prices. The results of the stress testing should be reported to the risk committee as and when the test is performed. While these extreme scenarios may have a very small probability of occurring, the intent of stress testing is to identify their impact if they do occur and confirm survivability in the event of such rare occurrences.

2.14. Market Risk Capital Charges for Financial Contracts

This section describes and sets out the market risk capital charges applicable to the main types of financial contracts of the bank.

Capital requirements for murabahah and related contracts: The bank is exposed to market risk under a murabahah contract when the asset is available for sale and on Energy's balance sheet. The capital charge for a murabahah contract is 15% of the position. There is no capital charge for a binding murabahah for purchase order (MPO) contract.

Treatment of salam and related contracts: Under a salam contract, the bank is exposed to market risk after the firm has paid the purchase price to the seller and before the purchased commodity is sold and delivered to a buyer. The capital charge is dependent on the presence or absence of a parallel salam contract. If the bank is the seller under a salam without a parallel salam contract, the capital charge for the contract is 15% of the long salam position. If the bank is the seller under a salam with a parallel salam contract, the capital charge for the contract is 15% of the net position.

Capital requirements for istisna and related contracts: If the bank is the seller under an istisna without a parallel istisna contract, the bank is exposed to market risk when there is unbilled work-in-process inventory. The capital charge for the contract is 1.6% of the bank's unbilled work-in-process inventory. If the bank is the buyer under an istisna without a parallel istisna contract, the bank is exposed to market risk as it makes progress payments to the supplier. The capital charge for the contract is 15% of the work-in-process inventory.

Capital requirements for istisna with a parallel istisna: There is no capital charge for an istisna with a parallel istisna contract if there is no provision in the parallel istisna contract that allows the seller to increase or vary the selling price. Also, there is no capital charge if there is a written undertaking given to the bank that the contractor's performance (including work-in-process) is the responsibility of the ultimate counterparty. However, there is a capital charge of 1.6% of the bank's unbilled work-in-process inventory under two conditions.

The first is there is a provision in the parallel istisna contract that allows the seller to increase or vary the selling price.

The second condition is that there is no written undertaking that the contractor's performance is the responsibility of the ultimate counterparty.

Capital requirements for ijarah and related contracts: There is no market risk capital charge for ijarah contracts, but they are subject to the credit risk capital requirements.

Capital requirements for musharakah: The capital charge for a musharakah contract depends on the category of the enterprise or asset to which the contract relates. If the contract relates to a private commercial enterprise undertaking trading activities in foreign exchange, shares, or commodities, the capital charge depends on the underlying asset as set out in the chapter on credit risk. If the contract relates to joint ownership of real estate or movable assets through musharakah with a murabahah subcontract, the capital charge is 15%. There is no capital charge if the contract relates to joint ownership of real estate or movable assets through musharakah with an ijarah subcontract because there is no charge for the ijarah subcontract.

Capital requirements for mudarabah: The capital charge for a mudarabah contract depends on the category of the enterprise or asset to which the contract relates. If the contract relates to a private commercial enterprise undertaking trading activities in foreign exchange, shares, or commodities, the capital charge depends on the underlying asset. If the contract relates to a placement in the interbank market, there is no capital charge unless the funds are invested in foreign exchange.

Capital requirements for qard: There is no capital charge for a qard contract except if the loan is provided in a foreign currency or in the form of a commodity. For qard-based financing in a foreign currency or commodity, the capital charge is that calculated in accordance with foreign exchange risk or commodities risk, as the case may require.

Capital requirements for wakalah: If a wakalah contract relates to a private commercial enterprise undertaking trading activities in foreign exchange, shares, or commodities, the capital charge depends on the underlying asset as set out in the credit risk chapter. If the contract relates to a placement in the interbank market, there is no capital charge unless the funds are invested in foreign exchange. The capital charge for a wakalah contract where the funds are invested in foreign exchange is calculated in accordance with foreign exchange risk.

2.15. Market Risk Monitoring and Reporting Guidelines

The bank must ensure adherence to the market risk identification, assessment, measurement, and management guidelines set out in the preceding sections. Its market risk monitoring and reporting systems must ensure that both controls and information gathering and reporting are effective and adequate.

The CRO has the primary responsibility to monitor market risk on a day-to-day basis. Market risk reports are generated in accordance with the frequency established by the CRO. The bank can use a variety of methods to monitor identified market risks emanating from its banking and trading books.

The following are examples of reports/tools the bank can employ for monitoring market risks:

> stress testing and scenario analysis; interest rate or profit rate gap analysis; evaluation of fixed income portfolio; evaluation of equity portfolio; monitoring foreign exchange open positions; reviewing exception reports; calculating capital adequacy; monitoring compliance with the governing body's approved limits; and review of exception reports by senior management.

The CRO reviews the market risk status reports, and any exceptions shall be communicated to the risk committee so that corrective action and approval can be taken. The internal audit function must be kept informed about important changes in the market risk management process.

2.16. Risk Reporting

The following non-exhaustive reports (Table 2.1) are published by the risk division and represent a reporting on market risk and exposure.

Table 2.1. A non-exhaustive list of risk reports.

Name of Report	Description	Objective	Reporting Frequency
Investment Portfolio Structure	Analysis of investments held at their net book value, reconciled with the general ledger, by investment category including: share or security; investment issuer or counter-party; industry sector investment type or asset class; currency; maturity; country.	Investment portfolio overview for information and management that enables an assessment of portfolio structure compared with target composition and identifies any portfolio concentrations.	Short-term: Weekly; Long-term: Quarterly
Foreign Exchange Analysis Report	Analysis of foreign exchange exposure held at their estimated value and under future trends.	Evaluate foreign exchange exposure risk due to current and future exchange rate volatilities. Verify adherence to foreign exchange exposure limits.	Weekly
Equity Risk Analysis Report	Analysis of investments held at their estimated market value and future trends. For securities not actively traded (e.g., unlisted shares), estimates may only be possible within a range of values.	Evaluate performance of the portfolio and of individual securities based on changes in current and future market value. Verify adherence to equity exposure limits.	Weekly

(Continued)

Table 2.1. (*Continued*)

Name of Report	Description	Objective	Reporting Frequency
Equity Investment Evaluation Report	Additional financial/narrative analysis for equity investments including: market/industry environment and condition; dividend yield for whole portfolio and for each portfolio company; size, nature, complexity, and risk profile of each portfolio company; recent financial performance of portfolio companies, including historical performance and forecasts.	Additional management information to assist in decision-making for purchase/ disposal of equity investments.	Half-yearly
VaR Report	VaR is based on the probability distribution for a portfolio's market value. All liquid assets have uncertain market values, which can be characterized with probability distributions. VaR is an all-encompassing measure of market risk.	Verify adherence to VaR based limits for desk and dealers.	Daily
Back Testing & P&L Reconciliation Report	Back testing is a process of testing a trading strategy on prior time periods. Instead of applying a strategy for the time period forward, which could take years, a trader can do a simulation of his or her trading strategy on relevant past data in order to gauge its effectiveness.	Back testing using daily profit and losses to uncover cases where the risk measures are not accurately capturing trading volatility.	Daily

Note: The bank uses notional limits and/or VaR. Conditional VaR (CVaR) can also be used according to the context when needed. The bank can also compute potential future exposures (PFEs) for the positions with counterparties when needed.

Summary

This chapter investigates the risk management function within a bank or financial institution. Market risk is the risk of losses in on- and off-balance-sheet positions arising from movements in market prices. Foreign exchange risk is the exposure of a bank's financial condition to adverse movements in foreign exchange rates.

Equity risk is the exposure of the bank's financial condition to adverse movements in equity prices. Equity market risk has two factors. The first is the risk associated with the overall market. The second is the risk associated with a specific security. This risk is captured through a measure called beta, which indicates the relative correlation of a particular security to the market portfolio. Beta measures the covariance of the returns of a given security with a market portfolio divided by the variance of the returns of the market index. Beta is provided by market intelligence systems (such as Bloomberg or Reuters) or can be computed by the risk analytics unit of the bank.

Liquidity risk is the risk that the bank is unable to meet the demands of an unexpected funds outflow caused by the withdrawal of funds by depositors or by the necessity of arranging funds for borrowers. This is covered in greater detail in the liquidity risk management chapter. Interest rate or profit rate risk is the exposure of the bank's financial condition to adverse movements in profit rates. Option risk is the risk arising from open positions in option contracts.

References

Bank for International Settlements, https://www.bis.org (updated 2025).

Bellalah, MO Masood and SM Ghauri (2017). Basel III implementation outcome in Islamic banks. *The Journal of Risk.*

Bellalah, M and F Bouheni (2020). Management et culture risque des Banques des pays émergents. *Revue des Sciences de Gestion.*

Bellalah, B and S Butt (2019). Impact of bank capital regulation and GDP growth on profitability in commercial small and medium banks: Empirical study. *International Journal of Entrepreneurship and Small Business.*

Bellalah, M, FB Bouheni, C Ammi and M Diallo (2022). Digitalisation des Banques françaises et reprise économique. *Revue des Sciences de Gestion*, 311.

Bellalah, M and K Abdel Rahman (2000). Gestion des Risques dans un Cadre International. *Economica.*

Bellalah, M (2004a). Gestion des Risques et Produits Dérivés Classiques et Exotiques. Dunod, Prix Turgot.

Bellalah, M (2004b). *Gestion des Portefeuilles.* Pearson Education.

Bellalah, M and S Zouari (2015). Portfolio credit risk models and name concentration issues: Theory and simulations. *International Journal of Business.*

Bellalah, M and S Zouari and O Levyne (2016). The performance of hybrid models in the assessment of default risk. *Economic Modeling*, 52, 259–265.

Bellalah, M, Z Chayeh and H Miniaoui (2015). Advanced risk profile analysis of Islamic equity investment: Evidence from the American, Asian and European market. *Finance-India.*

Websites

Bank for International Settlements, https://www.bis.org (updated 2025).

Financial Stability Board, https://www.fsb.org Monitoring of Priority Areas (updated 2025).

Chapter 3

Investment Risks Management

Chapter Outline

The chapter is divided into the following sections:

1. Section 3.1 presents an overview of the investment department and its framework.
2. Section 3.2 presents the governing policies for investments.
3. Section 3.3 presents treasury and asset liability management policies and procedures.

Introduction

This chapter focuses on the following two types of investment activities: first, investments associated with the allocation of funds for the extension of financing facilities; second, the other types of investment of funds in capital and money market instruments.

The purpose of the chapter is to assist in creating an efficient process by serving as a point of reference for the policies and procedures followed by various functions within the bank. The chapter ensures consistency in the interpretation and implementation of the procedures throughout the investment department. It defines the interactions between the investment department and other functions within the bank.

The investment department, led by the chief investment officer (CIO), is responsible for spearheading the bank's investment portfolio. This includes providing the bank with strategic direction in terms of lucrative sectors, markets, geographies, etc.

The department plays a key role in ensuring that all investment opportunities are comprehensively evaluated in line with the BoD's approved investment strategy. The investment department has the mandate to execute treasury activities, which primarily pertain to proactively managing the bank's liquidity position and open market operations.

Importantly, this chapter is based on my professional experience in several financial institutions.

All the standard terms (Table 3.1) and abbreviations (Table 3.2) can also be found on the following website: Financial Stability Board: https://www.fsb.org/work-of-the-fsb/implementation-monitoring/monitoring-of-priority-areas/ (updated 2025).

3.1. Investment Framework

The investment department is a fundamental part of each bank and financial institution. There are several investments and financial instruments. The key responsibilities of the investment department are to:

- contribute to the development and refinement of the bank's strategy in coordination with other strategic business units to ensure competitive market positioning;
- monitor and keep abreast of changing trends in the market through proactive market research and analysis;
- research different markets and opportunities in the sector and energy infrastructure investments, focusing on renewables, gas, and transmission;
- coordinate with the business development department for new product development opportunities within the bank;
- spearhead the investment opportunity evaluation process for the bank in line with the BoD's approved investment strategy and objectives;
- facilitate the investment proposal approval process by presenting detailed analysis on potential opportunities to the credit

Table 3.1. Terms

Term	Description
Asset-Liability Committee (ALCO)	A supervisory group comprising senior executives of the bank responsible for coordinating the management of the assets and liabilities with a goal of earning adequate returns.
Closing memorandum	A memorandum that includes a summary of steps to be performed by the bank before the release of funds.
Due diligence	Research conducted prior to executing a business transaction. This includes analyzing financial records and evaluating all possible risks that may affect a business transaction.
EIC approval memo	A formal approval from the executive investment committee (EIC) on an investment opportunity.
Escrow account	An account where funds are held in trust while two or more parties complete a transaction.
Fatwa	A formal ruling or interpretation on a point of Shariah Islamic Law given by a qualified legal scholar (a Mufti).
Funds Release Advice Memorandum (FRAM)	A checklist of requirements to be submitted and completed prior to the disbursement of funds.
Investment Proposal (IP)	A document that consists of detailed and comprehensive analysis undertaken for an investment opportunity, including market and financial analysis and risk assessment.
Investment teaser	A brief summary document that highlights the salient features of an entity to attract potential investment opportunities.
Letter of intent (LOI)	A document which declares the preliminary commitment or interest of a party to pursue a certain opportunity.
Non-disclosure agreement (NDA)	A legally binding contract between two parties that establishes a confidential relationship and prohibits either party from sharing sensitive information that they may obtain with others.
Information memorandum	A package of documents presented to investors, which includes detailed information pertaining to financial standing, assets and liabilities, business description, market position, clients, strategies and promotion methods, markets served, etc.
Request for information (RFI)	A document sent to obtain general information or documentation from a party that the bank may potentially pursue a business relationship with.
Request for proposal (RFP)	A document sent to obtain proposals and bids from potential bidders, some of which might be successful and selected to pursue a certain business opportunity with the bank.
Share purchase agreement (SPA)	A legal contract between an entity and an investor which states the terms and conditions relating to the purchase of shares, and specifically the number of shares the investor intends to sell and at what price.
Short memo note (SMN)	A document that illustrates the high-level analysis of an investment opportunity undertaken by the business development department.

Table 3.2. Abbreviations.

Abbreviation	Description
ALCO	Asset-Liability Committee
ALM	Assets and Liabilities Management
AML	Anti-Money Laundering
ARM	Annual Review Memorandum
BD	Business Development
BoD	Board of Directors
CBO	Chief Business Officer
CC	Credit Committee
CFT	Combating the Financing of Terrorism
CIO	Chief Investment Officer
CRO	Chief Risk Officer
DoA	Delegation of Authority
EIC	Executive Investment Committee
FRAM	Funds Release Advice Memorandum
IP	Investment Proposal
IT	Information Technology
KYC	Know Your Customer
LOI	Letter of Intent
NDA	Non-Disclosure Agreement
PM	Project Management
PRR	Profit Rate Risk
QFCRA	Qatar Financial Centre Regulatory Authority
RFI	Request for Information
RFP	Request for Proposal
RM	Relationship Manager
SMN	Short Memo Note
SPA	Share Purchase Agreement
SSB	Shariah Supervisory Board
SWOT	Strengths, Weaknesses, Opportunities, and Threats

committee (CC), the executive investment committee (EIC), and the Shariah supervisory board (SSB).

The other responsibilities of the investment department are to:

- lead the deal closure process, which involves developing all related transaction documents post-EIC approval in coordination with the respective departments;

- manage the bank's fund disbursement process by ensuring that all prerequisites mentioned by senior management are executed prior to disbursement;
- report periodically on the bank's investment portfolio performance to the EIC;
- lead all deal restructuring initiatives of the bank with respect to distressed investments;
- facilitate the investor onboarding process for the bank in coordination with the respective departments;
- manage all treasury activities, which primarily include proactively managing the liquidity position, open market operations, and bank reconciliations.

3.2. Investment Governing Rules

For an introduction to investments, the reader can refer to Bellalah and Abdel Rahman (2000) and Bellalah (2004a, 2004b).

3.2.1. *Investment strategy development*

All investment department staff should be aware of the rules and comply with them. Any form of breach, willful or accidental, by any staff member should be reported to the compliance department within 24 hours of such occurrence. Failing to report a breach of policy requires initiating disciplinary measures.

The CIO plays a key role in the bank's strategic planning process. He works closely with senior management to contribute to the development of the mission, vision, goals, objectives, and business plan for the bank.

The CIO is responsible for developing the investment strategy. The investment strategy is developed in line with BoD's approved strategic objectives. The CIO coordinates with various departments such as business development, risk management, and compliance. while developing the investment strategy The investment strategy has to be approved by the BoD prior to implementation.

3.2.2. *Investment criteria development*

The CIO is responsible for developing the investment criteria. The investment criteria are developed in line with the BoD's approved investment strategy. The investment criteria have to be approved by the BOD prior to implementation. It is mandatory that all investment opportunities be evaluated in line with the approved investment criteria of the bank.

The investment criteria include the following:

- Strategic fit: Alignment of the investment opportunities with the bank's strategy (as defined and amended by the BoD).
- Shariah compliance: Compliance of investment opportunities (with Shariah laws and principles for Islamic banks.
- Target IRR range expected from the investment opportunities.
- Transaction size range based on the defined concentration limits, i.e., amounts permitted to be invested in a single transaction, in a given asset class, in a single country, etc.
- Target investment horizon.
- Risk appetite indicators as defined by the risk management team within the bank.

3.2.3. *Portfolio performance monitoring*

All investments are subject to an annual investment review conducted by the investment department.

The annual review performed by the investment department is presented in the form of an annual review memorandum (ARM) to the EIC.

Apart from the annual review, the key performance indicators pertaining to each investment are formally evaluated at least once every three months by the investment department.

Although the frequency of formal evaluation of investments is specified above, the investment department is responsible for monitoring the performance of each investment on a regular basis throughout the year.

The performance of an investment is evaluated against the minimum acceptable investment criteria and defined key performance indicators.

3.2.4. *Preparation of investment proposal – INV01*

This process outlines the activities to be undertaken by the investment department to comprehensively evaluate an investment opportunity in line with the BoD's approved investment criteria.

Process owner: The CIO.

Process objectives: The objectives of the preparation of the investment proposal process are to:

- prepare an investment proposal that consists of a comprehensive analysis of an investment opportunity;
- present the investment proposal to the CC, the EIC, and the SSB for their review and approval.

Interrelated processes: Investment opportunity identification (BD01) and deal closure (INV02).

Associated policies:

The CIO initiates the investment opportunity evaluation process only upon receiving an approved short memo note (SMN) from the chief business officer.

The investment manager within the investment department is responsible for undertaking the detailed evaluation of the investment opportunity and preparing the investment proposal.

The CIO, based on his discretion, may choose to engage the services of an external service provider to enhance the evaluation process for the investment opportunity. All investment proposals must be endorsed by the CIO prior to presentation to the CC.

The CIO submits the investment proposal to the CC at least three days prior to the meeting.

For each CC/EIC/SSB meeting conducted, the investment team prepares brief written minutes of the meeting, recording the committee members' concerns, issues, and recommendations, and it provides those minutes to the relevant members within 24 hours of the meeting for agreement.

All investment proposals have to be approved by the CC, EIC, and the SSB prior to initiating deal closure activities. For any additional client information or documentation requirements raised by the committee(s), the CIO should coordinate with the CBO to ensure all such information are duly provided by the client. The investment manager ensures that all information pertaining to the evaluation of an investment opportunity is uploaded.

3.2.5. *Deal closure – INV02*

This process outlines the activities (as in Tables 3.3 to 3.7) to be undertaken by the investment department in coordination with the legal department to prepare all necessary transaction documents in line with the EIC approval memo and the Fatwa issued by the SSB.

Process owner: The CIO.

Process objectives: The objectives of the deal closure process are to:

- prepare transaction documents in line with the approved EIC approval memo and the SSB-issued Fatwa;
- ensure all transaction documents are approved by the legal department, the SSB, and the compliance department prior to signing the agreement with the client.

Interrelated processes: Appointment of external advisors (INV03).

Associated policies:

The investment manager, in coordination with the legal department, is responsible for preparing all transaction documents for an approved investment opportunity. All transaction documents are prepared in accordance with the approval memo issued by the EIC and the Fatwa issued by the SSB.

All transaction documents are approved by the legal department, the SSB, and the compliance department prior to releasing them to the client for signing.

The CBO will be responsible for coordinating with the client for the signing of the relevant financing agreements.

In cases where changes to the SSB-approved deal structure are identified, all such changes require an additional approval from the SSB

Table 3.3. Procedures for INV01.

Step No.	Step	Detailed Procedure	Executed By	Associated Docs
INV01.1	Review Short Memo Note (SMN) provided by the Business Development Department	• The trigger to this process is the receipt of the SMN from the business development department. • The activities pertaining to the development of the SMN are covered in the process "BD01 – Investment Opportunity Identification" within the Business Development chapter. • Review the SMN to ensure that all the necessary information required to evaluate the opportunity is available. The SMN includes: – Brief description of the investment. – Details of the target client. – Details of the shareholding ownership of the target client. – Proposed deal amount. – Preliminary financials. – Preliminary view on the Shariah-compliance of the investment opportunity. – Financials of the target client and other information as required by the credit risk management policy. – Requirement for external advisory assistance (if applicable). – CBO recommendations.	• Investment Manager	• Short Memo Note

(Continued)

Table 3.3. *(Continued)*

Step No.	Step	Detailed Procedure	Executed By	Associated Docs
INV01.2	Additional information required?	• If any information is missing or more documents are required, proceed to step INV01.3. • If no additional information is required, proceed to step INV01.4.	• Investment Manager	• Short Memo Note
INV01.3	Request BD team to provide additional information/ documentation	• Contact the BD team via email to request the missing documents/information. • The application is put on hold until the BD team sends the missing documents/information.	• Investment Manager	• Short Memo Note
INV01.4	Prepare the Investment Proposal (IP) in coordination with the respective departments	• Commence the preparation of the investment proposal (IP). • Request necessary inputs from relevant departments within the bank for the preparation of the IP. • The IP includes the following: – All information contained in the SMN. – Investment background. – Market research. – SWOT (strengths, weaknesses, opportunities, and threats) analysis. – Term sheet (which provides information on the structure of the deal). – Fees to bank (where relevant). – Exit strategy. – Expected investors in the presented deal.	• Investment Manager	• Investment Proposal

		– Risk assessment (market risk, credit risk, and operational risk) – prepared by the CRO. – Financials/return analysis (including financial models/financial assumptions). – Any other project details. – Closing memorandum. – Total anticipated external advisory costs. – Recommendations from CIO and CRO.		
INV01.5	Endorsed by the CIO	• If the IP is endorsed by the CIO, proceed to step INV01.6. • If the IP is not endorsed, revert to step INV01.4 with recommendations on the changes required.	• Chief Investment Officer	• Investment Proposal
INV01.6	Submit the IP and request a meeting with the CC to discuss the transaction	• Submit the IP along with all required documentation to the CC. • Request a meeting with the CC to discuss the IP and the transaction details.	• Chief Investment Officer	• Investment Proposal
INV01.7	Discuss the Investment Proposal	• Discuss the IP and the overall transaction and highlight any clarification requirements, concerns, or issues that need to be further evaluated.	• Credit Committee	• Investment Proposal

(Continued)

Table 3.3. (*Continued*)

Step No.	Step	Detailed Procedure	Executed By	Associated Docs
		• The investment manager prepares brief, written minutes of the meeting, recording the committee members' concerns, issues, and recommendations and provides those minutes to the relevant members within 24 hours of the meeting for agreement. • In cases where additional information/documentation is required from the client, the BD department takes the lead to obtain such information from the client.		
INV01.8	Approved?	• If the IP is approved by the CC, proceed to step INV01.10. • If the IP is not approved by the CC, proceed to step INV01.9.	• Credit Committee	• Investment Proposal
INV01.9	Additional information required	• If any information is missing or more documents are required, proceed to step INV01.10. • If no additional information is required and the IP was not approved, the process ends.	• Credit Committee	• Investment Proposal
INV01.10	Request additional information/ analysis	• Request additional information/analysis from the investment team to be included as part of the IP.	• Credit Committee	• Investment Proposal
INV01.11	Provide recommendations on the opportunity and refer to EIC	• On approval, provide recommendations on the investment opportunity and refer to the EIC for approval.	• Credit Committee	• Investment Proposal

INV01.12	Submit EIC endorsed IP	• Submit the CC-approved IP to the EIC for their review and approval. • The investment manager prepares brief, written minutes of the meeting, recording the committee members' concerns, issues, and recommendations and provides those minutes to the relevant members within 24 hours of the meeting for agreement. • In cases where additional information/documentation is required from the client, the BD department takes the lead to obtain such information from the client.	• Investment Manager	• Investment Proposal
INV01.13	Approved	• If the IP is approved by the EIC, proceed to step INV01.16. • If the IP is not approved by the EIC, proceed to step INV01.14.	• Executive Investment Committee	• Investment Proposal
INV01.14	Additional information required?	• If any information is missing or more documents are required, proceed to step INV01.15. • If no additional information is required and the IP was not approved, the process ends.	• Executive Investment Committee	• Investment Proposal
INV01.15	Request additional information/documentation	• Request additional information/analysis from the investment team to be included as part of the IP.	• Executive Investment Committee	• Investment Proposal

(*Continued*)

Table 3.3. (*Continued*)

Step No.	Step	Detailed Procedure	Executed By	Associated Docs
INV01.16	Approved by the SSB?	• Assess the investment opportunity from a Shariah compliance standpoint. • If the IP is approved, issue a Fatwa and proceed to step INV01.17. • If the IP is rejected, the process ends.	• Shariah Supervisory Board	• Investment Proposal • Fatwa
INV01.17	Receive approval memo on the IP	• Receive the approval memo on the IP from the EIC and the Fatwa from the SSB. • Follow steps as illustrated in the process "INV02 – Deal Closure".	• Investment Manager	• Investment Proposal • Approval memo

prior to finalizing the deal structure and completing the deal closure process.

Such changes are highlighted to the risk management department for their concurrence.

Upon signing the agreement with the customer, the investment manager will be responsible for creating the customer within the bank's core banking system and uploading all related KYC documentation pertaining to the customer.

The investment manager is responsible for creating the facility in the system under each customer account. All facility details are uploaded to the bank's core banking system.

3.2.6. *Appointment of external advisors – INV03*

This process outlines the activities to be undertaken by the investment department to identify, evaluate, and onboard external advisors to assist the investment team during the evaluation and closing phases of an investment opportunity.

Process owner: The CIO.

Process objectives: The objectives of the appointment of external advisors process are to:

- identify aspects requiring external advisory assistance regarding the investment opportunity;
- approve and appoint the most suitable external advisors to assist the investment team;
- ensure that all external advisors have cleared the necessary compliance and anti-money laundering (AML) checks prior to appointment.

Interrelated process: N/A.

Associated policies:

The CIO is responsible for identifying the requirement for external advisors with respect to the evaluation and closure of an investment opportunity.

Table 3.4. Procedures for INV02.

Step No.	Step	Detailed Procedure	Executed By	Associated Docs
INV02.1	Review the approved investment proposal (IP) and memo	• Review the approved IP and approval memo given by the EIC. • Also refer to the SSB-issued Fatwa on the deal. • To engage due diligence advisors for the opportunity, follow steps as illustrated in the process "INV03 – Appointment of External Advisors".	• Investment Manager	• Investment Proposal • Approval memo
INV02.2	Review due diligence reports submitted by external advisors	• Review the due diligence reports submitted to the investment department by the external due diligence advisors. • Based on the review of the due diligence reports, validate all the required elements of the IP.	• Investment Manager	• Due diligence reports
INV02.3	Prepare the transaction documentation	• The investment manager and the legal manager work closely to prepare the transaction documentation for the advisors. • The investment manager also coordinates with the credit administration team within the risk management department for the preparation of collateral documentation pertaining to the deal. • Ensure alignment of the transaction documents with the approval memo and the Fatwa.	• Investment Manager • Legal Manager	• Transaction documentation

INV02.4	Approved by CIO	• If the transaction documentation is approved, proceed to step INV02.5. • If the transaction documentation is not approved, revert to step INV02.3 with recommendations on changes required.	• Chief Investment Officer	• Transaction documentation
INV02.5	Approve transaction documentation	• If the transaction documentation is approved by the legal department, proceed to step INV02.6. • If the transaction documentation is not approved by the legal department, revert to step INV02.3 with recommendations on changes.	• Legal Manager	• Transaction documentation
INV02.6	Approve transaction documentation	• If the transaction documentation is approved by the SSB, proceed to step INV02.7. • If the transaction documentation is not approved by the SSB, revert to step INV02.3 with recommendations on the changes required.	• Shariah Supervisory Board	• Transaction documentation
INV02.7	Approve transaction documentation	• If the transaction documentation is approved by the compliance department, proceed to step INV02.9. • If the transaction documentation is rejected by the compliance department, proceed to step INV02.8.	• Chief Compliance Officer/MLRO	• Transaction documentation

(*Continued*)

Table 3.4. (*Continued*)

Step No.	Step	Detailed Procedure	Executed By	Associated Docs
INV02.8	Request additional information/documentation	• Request the required information and documentation from the investment team to be able to proceed with the approval of the transaction documentation.	• Chief Compliance Officer/MLRO	• Transaction documentation
INV02.9	Share the documentation with the business development team for client signing	• Share the approved transaction documentation with the business development department for client signature. • File and record all relevant information with respect to IP development and deal closure for record-keeping and future reference.	• Investment Manager	• Transaction documentation

The investment manager is responsible for providing all mandatory documentation and information on potential external advisors as per the guidelines stipulated by the compliance department.

The procurement department supports the investment department with respect to the administrative elements of the appointment process. The investment manager ensures that proposals are received from at least three bidders for a particular advisory opportunity.

All external advisors are evaluated based on the following key assessment criteria (note: this list is not exhaustive):

- geographic presence, knowledge, and expertise in the market;
- proven track record and prior experience in executing similar assessments and activities;
- relevant experience in leadership and team members;
- financial strength and health records throughout the years of operation;
- legal health records, in terms of past liabilities or lawsuits;
- the economic cost to the bank for the provision of the contracted services.

The investment manager closely coordinates with the legal department within the bank for the evaluation of bids pertaining to external legal advisors.

All appointments for external legal advisors have to be approved by at least two members of the CC.

The investment manager is responsible for maintaining, updating, and uploading all related documents with respect to the evaluation process to the bank's respective system database.

3.2.7. *Funds disbursement – INV04*

This process outlines the activities to be undertaken by the investment department to ensure that all necessary conditions stipulated in the closing memorandum and the agreement with the customer are executed and complied with prior to authorizing disbursement of funds. This process includes the activities related to the disbursement of the first tranche and subsequent tranches based on drawdown requests received from the customer.

Table 3.5. Procedures for INV03.

Step No.	Step	Detailed Procedure	Executed By	Associated Docs
INV03.1	Identify potential external advisors for the investment opportunity	• Based on the approved investment opportunity, identify the potential external advisors required and most suited for the investment opportunity. • Required advisors could assist in the following areas of specialty: – Legal. – Accounting. – Tax. – Industry. – Technical. – Shariah Law.	• Chief Investment Officer	• Investment Proposal
INV03.2	Request and receive a letter of intent and a non-disclosure agreement from advisors	• Inform external advisors on the external advisory support required and request for an official letter of intent (LOI) from the respective advisory service providers along with signed non-disclosure agreements (NDAs).	• Investment Manager	• LOI • NDA
INV03.3	Submit RFI's to the identified advisors	• Submit requests for information (RFIs) to the interested advisors from each area of specialty and ensure requesting all the mandatory documentation as per the guidelines of the compliance department. • This activity be executed in conjunction with the procurement department at the bank.	• Investment Manager	• RFI • Advisor documentation

INV03.4	Receive and forward documentation to the compliance department for KYC screening	• Receive the requested documentation from the advisors. • Follow up with the advisors to obtain the necessary documents/information wherever required. • Ensure all documents have been received in line with the requirements stipulated in the RFI. • Forward the required documentation to the compliance department for the completion of the necessary KYC screening. • Upload all the relevant documents/information to the system for record keeping and future reference.	• Investment Manager	• Advisor documentation
INV03.5	KYC cleared by and compliance department?	• If the KYC screening is cleared by the compliance department, proceed to step INV03.9. • If not cleared, proceed to step INV03.6.	• Chief Compliance Officer/MLRO	• Advisor documentation
INV03.6	Additional documents required?	• Check for any missing documents, as per the defined requirements. • If any additional documents are required, proceed to step INV03.7 to request documents from the advisors. • If the advisors did not clear the KYC screening, proceed to step INV03.8. • Inform the CIO on the status of the KYC screening process.	• Chief Compliance Officer/MLRO	• Advisor documentation

(*Continued*)

Table 3.5. (*Continued*)

Step No.	Step	Detailed Procedure	Executed By	Associated Docs
INV03.7	Request additional documentation from the advisors	• Based on the additional information requested by the compliance department, coordinate with the advisors to obtain the documentation/information.	• Investment Manager	• Advisor documentation
INV03.8	Send a regret letter to inform the advisor	• Prepare and send a regret letter to inform the advisor that the advisory opportunity cannot be pursued. • Provide the advisor with information on the reasons for the same.	• Investment Manager	• Regret letter
INV03.9	Submit RFPs to the cleared advisors	• Coordinate with the respective department within the bank to develop the respective scope of work for the advisory opportunity. • Develop the request for proposal for the opportunity in conjunction with the procurement department at the bank. • Submit the requests for proposals to the cleared advisors, inviting them to submit their comprehensive bids to provide the respective advisory services.	• Investment Manager	• RFP
INV03.10	Receive, review, and assess bids according to assessment criteria	• Ensure receiving a minimum of three proposals from advisors for the particular advisory opportunity. • Review the received bids to grade and shortlist advisors based on the defined assessment criteria, which includes, but is not limited to, the following aspects:	• Chief Investment Officer	• Proposal

		– geographic presence, knowledge, and expertise in the market; – proven track record and prior experience in executing similar assessments/activities; – relevant experience of leadership and team members; – financial strength and health record throughout the years of operation; – legal health record, in terms of past liabilities or lawsuits.		
INV03.11	Recommend the preferred external advisors and their fees	• Recommend the preferred external advisors and their fees to the credit committee. • Discuss and present the relevant costs and fees associated with the external advisors.	• Chief Investment Officer	• N/A
INV03.12	Approve	• Discuss the recommendations provided on the external advisors. • If the proposed advisor is approved, proceed to INV03.13. • If not approved, the process ends.	• Credit Committee	• N/A

(*Continued*)

Table 3.5. (*Continued*)

Step No.	Step	Detailed Procedure	Executed By	Associated Docs
INV03.13	Complete contractual formalities to onboard external advisor	• Coordinate with the legal department to complete the contractual agreements pertaining to the approved advisors. • Ensure obtaining signoffs on the agreement from all relevant parties, including the CIO and the legal department. • Obtain sign-off on the agreement from the external advisor. • Upload all relevant information on the system and file all necessary documents for record keeping and future reference.	• Investment Manager	• Signed agreement

Process owner: The CIO.

Process objectives: The objectives of the disbursement of funds process are to:

- ensure that all necessary prerequisites recommended by the EIC are complied with prior to disbursement of funds;
- ensure disbursement requests are approved as per the delegation of authority prior to disbursements.

3.2.8. *Investor onboarding – INV05*

This process outlines the activities to be undertaken by the investment department to coordinate with the CBO to identify and onboard potential investors. This includes coordinating with a potential investor and various departments within the bank to seamlessly onboard an investor.

Process owner: The CIO.

Process objectives: The objectives of the investor onboarding process are to:

- identify and contact potential investors who may commit funds for the bank;
- ensure all onboarded investors have cleared the necessary compliance and legal checks.

Interrelated processes: N/A.

Associated policies:

The CBO is primarily responsible for identifying potential investors.

A basic KYC check has to be completed by the compliance department prior to the CBO establishing contact with the potential investor.

It is mandatory to have a signed non-disclosure agreement (NDA) between both parties prior to the bank sharing any information with potential investor(s).

Table 3.6. Procedures for INV04.

Step No.	Step	Detailed Procedure	Executed By	Associated Docs
INV04.1	Review the closing memorandum	• Review the closing memorandum attached in the investment proposal, which includes the steps/activities to be executed prior to the disbursement of funds.	• Investment Manager	• Closing memorandum
INV04.2	Ensure the execution of all conditions as per the closing memorandum	• Ensure that all conditions specified in the closing memorandum are duly executed by the respective stakeholders within the bank.	• Investment Manager	• Closing memorandum
INV04.3	Prepare the funds release advice memorandum (FRAM) and attach all the necessary documentation	• Prepare the FRAM for the first tranche, which is a checklist of requirements to be completed and submitted for approval prior to the disbursement of funds. • Attach all supporting documentation to the FRAM. • Ensure the accuracy and the validity of the information within the attached documentation. • Forward the FRAM for the CIO's approval.	• Investment Manager	• FRAM
INV04.4	Approved by the CIO?	• If the FRAM is approved, proceed to step INV04.6. • If the FRAM is not approved, proceed to step INV04.5 to request additional information.	• Chief Investment Officer	• FRAM

INV04.5	Request additional documentation	• Request additional information/documentation to be included with the FRAM. • Ensure that the required documentation is attached prior to submitting the FRAM to the approving authorities.	• Investment Manager	• FRAM
INV04.6	Approve FRAM?	• If the FRAM is approved by the respective approving authority as per the DoA, proceed to step INV04.7. • If not, revert to step INV04.5 to request additional documentation or information to be included in the FRAM. • The respective approving authority be determined as per the bank's approved delegation of authority.	• Approving Authority (as per DoA)	• FRAM
INV04.7	Forward FRAM to the treasury section for review	• Forward the approved FRAM along with all necessary documentation to the treasury section for their review prior to the disbursement of the first tranche.	• Investment Manager	• FRAM
INV04.8	Review FRAM and send instructions to third party banks for disbursement	• Review the FRAM and the supporting documents to ensure that all terms of the disbursement are fulfilled and required documentation is in place. • Provide the third-party banks with the necessary instructions on the disbursement of funds.	• Treasury and ALM Manager	• FRAM

(Continued)

Table 3.6. (*Continued*)

Step No.	Step	Detailed Procedure	Executed By	Associated Docs
INV04.9	Drawdown request received from client?	• If a subsequent drawdown request is received from the client, proceed to step INV04.10. • If no drawdown request is received, the process ends.	• Chief Business Officer	• Drawdown request
INV04.10	Forward drawdown request and project progress report to the investment department	• Ensure that the drawdown request is clear and contains all necessary information. • Contact the client for any clarifications required. • Forward the drawdown request received from the client, along with the project progress report prepared by the client, to the investment department for their review and analysis.	• Chief Business Officer	• Drawdown request • Project progress report
INV04.11	Analyze drawdown request and project progress report	• Analyze the drawdown request submitted by the client and the project progress report to confirm progress of the works/adherence to conditions as per the contractual agreement. • Ensure that the client drawdown request is line with the drawdown schedule stipulated in the agreement with the customer. • Forward the request and the report to the risk management team for their analysis.	• Investment Manager	• Drawdown request • Project progress report

INV04.12	Conduct a credit review of the facility	• Given the project progress report and other necessary information, conduct a credit review of the facility to identify additional risks associated with the project that would affect the disbursement decision. • Provide recommendations based on the completion of the credit review of the customer.	• Chief Risk Officer	• Drawdown request • Project progress report
INV04.13	Prepare and present a business assessment memorandum to the approving authority	• Prepare a business assessment memorandum, which includes the following: – details pertaining to the independent credit review undertaken by the risk management department; – details on the analysis conducted by the investment department on the project progress. • Present the business assessment memorandum to the approving authority for their review and approval.	• Chief Investment Officer	• Business Assessment Memorandum
INV04.14	Approve disbursement?	• If the disbursement is approved by the respective approving authority, proceed to step INV04.16. • If not, proceed to step INV04.15 to inform the client on the rejection. • The respective approving authority is determined as per the bank's approved delegation of authority matrix.	• Approving Authority (as per DoA)	• Business Assessment Memorandum

(Continued)

Table 3.6. (*Continued*)

Step No.	Step	Detailed Procedure	Executed By	Associated Docs
INV04.15	Inform the client on the reasons for rejection and discuss alternative solutions	• Contact the client to inform him/her of the rejection of the disbursement request and indicate the reasons for this rejection. • Discuss alternative solutions with the client to proceed with disbursement of the funds.	• Chief Business Officer	• N/A
INV04.16	Provide recommendations on the disbursement protocol	• Upon approving the disbursement, provide recommendations on the disbursement protocol, with respect to any additional conditions that need to be considered prior to disbursement.	• Approving Authority (as per DoA)	• N/A
INV04.17	Prepare FRAM and necessary documentation and ensure adherence to additional conditions and recommendations	• Prepare the FRAM for the subsequent tranche. • Obtain the input of relevant departments, if necessary. • Attach all necessary documentation as per the FRAM requirements. • Ensure the accuracy and the validity of information within the attached documentation. • Ensure the adherence to all additional conditions and recommendations as mentioned by relevant departments and approving authorities. • Obtain the CIO's approval before proceeding.	• Investment Manager	• FRAM

INV04.18	Approve FRAM?	• If the FRAM is approved by the respective approving authority, proceed to step INV04.19. • If not approved, revert to step INV04.17 with additional requirements of documentation or information to be included in the FRAM. • The respective approving authority is determined as per the bank's approved delegation of authority matrix.	• Approving Authority (as per the DoA)	• FRAM
INV04.19	Forward FRAM to the treasury section for review	• Forward the FRAM along with all necessary documentation to the treasury section for their review prior to the disbursement.	• Investment Manager	• FRAM
INV04.20	Review FRAM and send instructions to third party banks for disbursement	• Review the FRAM and the supporting documents to ensure that all terms of the disbursement are fulfilled and required documentation is in place. • Provide the third-party banks with the necessary instructions for the disbursement of funds.	• Treasury and ALM Manager	• FRAM

The CBO is required to obtain a letter of intent (LOI) for all potential investors prior to sending the detailed bank information memorandum to the investor.

All investors need to undergo detailed KYC and risk management checks by the compliance and risk management departments, respectively.

The CIO ensures the completeness and authenticity of all documentation/information received from the investor prior to submission to the compliance and risk management departments for KYC and risk checks.

All investors of the bank which have been cleared by the KYC process must be approved by the BoD.

The CIO initiates any contractual formalities with an investor only upon obtaining BoD approval.

For more details about policies and procedures, readers can refer to the updated 2025 websites.

3.3. Treasury and Asset and Liability Management (ALM)

This section gives an introduction to ALM and liquidity management. For further details, the reader can refer to Bellalah *et al.* (2017a, 2017b).

3.3.1. *Functional mandate*

The treasury and the ALM section are responsible for the following three operational activities.

The first is the development of the treasury strategy of the bank for approval by the BoD.

The second is the negotiation of funding from financial institutions and capital markets and ensuring there is sufficient liquidity for the bank's day-to-day requirements as well as unexpected business disruptions.

The third is the management of the bank's liquidity position, including surplus cash and short-term facilities.

Table 3.7. Procedures for INV05.

Step No.	Step	Detailed Procedure	Executed By	Associated Docs
INV05.1	Identify potential investors for the bank	• Identify potential investors for the bank through business relationship networks. • An opportunity could also be identified through strategic alliances developed by the business development department.	• Chief Business Officer	• N/A
INV05.2	Provide details to the compliance department for initial KYC check	• Forward all necessary details pertaining to the potential investor to the compliance team for an initial KYC check on the investor.	• Chief Business Officer	• N/A
INV05.3	Initial go/no-go	• Conduct a basic KYC check on the potential investor. • If the compliance department clears the potential investor, proceed to step INV05.7. • If not cleared, proceed to step INV05.6.	• Chief Compliance Officer	• N/A
INV05.4	Establish contact with the investor and request a signed NDA	• Establish contact with the potential investor and provide a brief summary on the bank and the potential to invest in the bank. • Request for a signed NDA from the potential investor so as to commence sharing information on the investment opportunity. • Provide the investor with the bank's approved NDA template.	• Chief Business Officer	• NDA

(*Continued*)

Table 3.7. (*Continued*)

Step No.	Step	Detailed Procedure	Executed By	Associated Docs
INV05.5	Receive a signed NDA from the investor	• Receive the signed NDA agreement from the investor before proceeding further with the process.	• Chief Business Officer	• NDA
INV05.6	Share a teaser on the bank with the investor and request an LOI	• On receiving a signed NDA from the customer, share an investment teaser with the investor, which includes high-level information on the bank. • The teaser would include: – investment highlights, – bank overview, – customer's overview, – product and service offerings, – financial summary. • Request for an LOI from the investor to proceed with the process.	• Chief Business Officer	• PB teaser • LOI
INV05.7	LOI received	• If an LOI is received from the potential investor, proceed to step INV05.8. • If no, revert to step INV05.1 to identify other potential investors.	• Chief Business Officer	• LOI
INV05.8	Send an information memorandum to the investor	• On receiving the signed LOI from the investor, send an information memorandum that includes all the key information. • The information memorandum covers the following information:	• Chief Business Officer	• PB Information Memorandum

		– executive summary, – investment thesis, – overview of the market, – products and services, – revenue profile, – employee profile, – customer profile, – financials – historical and projections, – management structure. • Ensure that any queries raised by the potential investor are promptly addressed.		
INV05.9	Investor to commit funds	• If the investor commits funds, proceed to step INV05.10. • If the investor is not to commit funds, the process ends.	• Chief Business Officer	• PB Information Memorandum
INV05.10	Obtain the necessary documentation and information from the investor	• Request and obtain the required documentation and information from the investor as per the guidelines stipulated by the compliance department. • Follow up with the investor to obtain the necessary documents/information wherever required.	• Chief Investment Officer	• Investor documentation

(*Continued*)

Table 3.7. (*Continued*)

Step No.	Step	Detailed Procedure	Executed By	Associated Docs
INV05.11	Forward investor details to risk management and compliance departments for risk and KYC screening	• Forward the investor's details and documentation to the risk management and compliance departments for the detailed risk and KYC screening, respectively. • Provide the required support to both departments to effectively undertake the screening of the client.	• Chief Investment Officer	• Investor documentation
INV05.12	KYC cleared by risk and compliance departments?	• If the KYC and risk are cleared by the compliance and risk management departments, proceed to step INV05.15. • If the KYC is not cleared by the compliance department, proceed to step INV05.13.	• Chief Investment Officer	• Investor documentation
INV05.13	Additional information required?	• Communicate with the risk management and compliance departments to check for any missing documents, as per the defined requirements. • If any additional documents are required, revert to step INV05.10 to request those documents. • If the investor did not clear the risk and KYC screening, proceed to step INV05.14.	• Chief Investment Officer	• Investor documentation
INV05.14	Send a regret letter to the investor	• Prepare and send a regret letter to inform the investor that the opportunity cannot be pursued. • Provide the investor with information on the reasons for the same.	• Chief Business Officer	• Regret letter

INV05.15	Present investor to the legal department for clearance	• Present the cleared investor to the legal department for the legal clearance, in terms of any legal liabilities or lawsuits.	• Chief Investment Officer	• N/A
INV05.16	Cleared by legal?	• If the investor is cleared by the legal department, proceed to step INV05.17. • If the investor is not cleared by the legal department, revert to step INV05.14.	• Investment Manager	• N/A
INV05.17	Investor approved?	• The investor is presented to the BoD for the final internal approval. • If the BoD approves the investor, proceed to step INV05.18. • If not approved, revert to step INV05.14.	• Board of Directors	• N/A
INV05.18	Present investor details to QFCRA to obtain clearance	• Present the investor details along with all supporting documentation to QFCRA for clearance. • QFCRA clearance is only required until the bank receives an operating license from QFCRA. • On obtaining an operating license, this step is no longer applicable in the process.	• Executive Investment Committee	• N/A
INV05.19	Cleared by QFCRA?	• If the investor is cleared by the QFCRA, proceed to step INV05.20. • If the investor is not cleared by the QFCRA, revert to step INV05.14.	• Executive Investment Committee	• N/A

(*Continued*)

Table 3.7. *(Continued)*

Step No.	Step	Detailed Procedure	Executed By	Associated Docs
INV05.20	Contact the investor to obtain a signed commitment letter	• Coordinate with the CIO and the legal department to prepare the commitment letter for the approved investor. • The commitment letter includes certain terms and conditions to be fulfilled by both parties. • Obtain investor signature on the commitment letter.	• Chief Business Officer	• Signed commitment letter
INV05.21	Prepare a share purchase agreement (SPA) in coordination with the legal department and share with the BD team	• Coordinate with the legal department to prepare an SPA for the transaction with the investor. • Forward all the relevant information and documentation to the legal department to develop the agreement in line with agreed terms and conditions. • Share the draft SPA with the CBO for investor signing. • Provide the CBO with any required clarifications pertaining to the agreement.	• Chief Investment Officer	• Share purchase agreement
INV05.22	Receive the signed SPA from the investor	• Share the SPA with the investor for signing. • Involve the investment and legal departments for any subsequent discussions pertaining to finalizing the SPA with the investor. • Obtain signed SPA from the investor.	• Chief Business Officer	• Signed share purchase agreement
INV05.23	Receive investor funds in escrow accounts	• Receive investor funds in an escrow account as per the terms and conditions in the SPA.	• Chief Investment Officer	• N/A

The treasury and the ALM section are also responsible for the management of:

- the profit rate risk associated with borrowing and investment of surplus funds;
- foreign currency risks associated with transactional cash flows and translation of overseas net assets;
- credit and operational risks arising from treasury activities;
- bank relationships.

3.3.2. *Asset and liability management*

Liquidity management:

The treasury and ALM manager is responsible for identifying, measuring, managing, and controlling risks related to asset liability bucket mismatch and other factors that may impact the bank's liquidity.

The manager is also responsible for ensuring availability of funds to honor any drawdown requests as per the investment contracts. He works closely with the risk management department to minimize liquidity gaps in accordance with the bank's liquidity policy. The treasury and ALM manager focuses on the strategic positioning of the balance sheet and ensures cash flow mismatches between the assets and liabilities sides are kept within regulatory and BoD-approved limits.

The manager ensures that key liquidity ratios are maintained within regulatory and BoD-approved limits, namely the liquidity coverage ratio (LCR) and net stable funding ratio (NSFR). He closely works with the risk management department for monitoring and reporting credit risk arising from the investment activities undertaken by treasury and ALM functions.

Cash and profitability management:

The treasury and ALM manager manages assets and liabilities in order to maximize shareholder value and to enhance profitability through strategic asset allocation between permissible investment options other than core investments, including investments in Wakala, government and corporate Sukuks, listed equities, commodity markets, foreign exchange markets, derivatives, and alternative investment options.

The list of permissible investment options is approved by the BoD and SSB. The treasury and ALM manager is responsible for regular monitoring and reconciliation of bank accounts (call and current accounts) maintained with third-party banks, including any settlement accounts maintained with other banks internationally.

The manager undertakes activities related to the mitigation of profit rate risk and cash flow risk through the execution of over-the-counter swap contracts. He is responsible for mitigating foreign exchange risk through spot and forward positions.

The treasury and ALM manager also undertakes the responsibility of interbank cash investments and borrowings. In coordination with the risk management team, he ensures that all activities undertaken are within the acceptable and controllable levels of the following risks: price risk (also known as valuation or market risk), foreign exchange risk, and interest or profit rate risk. The treasury and ALM manager tracks the daily cash position and prepares and submits a weekly assets and liabilities report to the ALCO for discussion and action.

Treasury role in ALCO:

The treasury and ALM manager ensures that all treasury activities are executed in line with the BoD-approved short- and long-term strategic goals for the bank. He works closely with the ALCO of the bank. The composition of ALCO is determined by the CEO. It includes representatives or permanent members to be nominated by the CEO, with alternate members to be nominated by the chairman of the ALCO. Other members of the management can be invited on a case-by-case basis; however, they do not constitute a part of the ALCO.

The ALCO has the following duties and responsibilities:

- Define goals and ratios for risks that will be approved by the BoD.
- Analyze and monitor the composition and maintenance of liquid assets in compliance with the regulators' requirements on liquidity and statutory reserve ratios at all times.
- Review and monitor the sources and applications of funds and the maturity gaps of assets and liabilities.
- Monitor the composition and size of risk-weighted assets to ensure that the bank is sufficiently capitalized at all times, as required by the regulatory authority.

- Ensure that the investment portfolio is proactively managed and that resources are appropriately allocated to achieve returns set by the BoD.
- Analyze and project funding requirements of the bank to maintain healthy cash flows and satisfy all financial ratios.
- Monitor market rates and pricing for profit-bearing products and foreign exchange to manage changes and business decisions as and when necessary.
- Monitor and review interbank money market operations, borrowing strategies, and activities.
- Monitor the forex open positions of the bank.
- Proactively formulate or recommend to the BoD regarding the bank's financial market policies, activities, and strategies and ensure timely implementation to manage the bank's assets and liabilities to achieve an optimal balance of risk and reward.
- Monitoring of key limits and reconciliation of externally maintained accounts
- Undertake such other responsibilities as may be directed by the BoD.

Counterparty management:

A counterparty can be defined as a financial institution with which the bank has established an account relationship, involving the lending or borrowing of monies or the buying or selling of currencies for forward delivery. The well-being of counterparties is a concern to the bank as long as contracts with them remain outstanding. Any deterioration in the financial status of a counterparty constitutes a risk and must be monitored very closely by the treasury and ALM manager.

Dealings with counterparties and holdings of financial instruments are subject to pre-approved limits.

The BoD approves these limits, which are recommended by management, after proper credit and other background evaluations have been conducted.

The treasury and ALM manager is responsible for setting up credit lines for certain counterparties to facilitate the bank's business operations. The manager prepares a proposal in this regard and sends it to the CC for their evaluation.

The CC assesses the counterparty based on the following criteria, prior to recommending approval to the BoD:

- current rating by an international rating agency such as Standard & Poor's;
- performance of the last three financial years;
- for foreign counterparties, the country of incorporation – this is a matter of country risk consideration;
- in the case of a correspondent bank, the presence of institutions in foreign locations is useful to the bank.

The treasury and ALM manager alerts the management of any apparent signs of distress suffered by counterparties, regardless of whether presently there are any outstanding contracts. The reason is to allow time for the bank to quickly reassess the validity of existing approved limits.

3.3.3. *Bank relationship management*

The treasury and ALM manager determines (through cost-benefit analysis) the designated banks to serve and satisfy its requirements according to the following elements: competitive pricing of services, the bank's geographical coverage, the bank's automation capabilities, services offered by the bank, response time and periodic reporting, and other criteria identified by the CIO.

The CEO is responsible for approving banking partners.

The CIO is responsible for supervising the opening, closing, and maintenance of all the accounts managed by the bank.

The treasury and ALM manager ensures that the following information is available when the decision to open an account in a selected bank is made:

- instructions regarding the purpose of the account and how it is to be operated and reconciled,
- names of the account signatories,
- approval of the CEO.

The treasury and ALM manager ensures that the following information is available when deciding to close an account in a selected bank:

- reasons for closing account,
- confirmation that the account is zero balanced,
- the last reconciliation of the required closed account.

The manager also reviews periodically (monthly) all open bank accounts maintained by the bank with third-party banks to execute the following:

- the book-to-bank account reconciliation;
- the review of fees and other account-related charges;
- the identification of any redundant or dormant accounts and recommendations to the ALCO/BoD for their closure.

The CIO and the CFO conduct a high-level review of banking partners periodically (at least on a quarterly basis).

Summary

The investment manager ensures compliance with all conditions and prerequisites mentioned in the closing memorandum for disbursement. The investment manager is responsible for preparing the FRAM for all disbursement requests.

Under no circumstances can funds be released to a customer in the absence of a signed financing agreement between the customer and the bank.

The CIO is responsible for preparing a business assessment memorandum for all drawdown requests submitted by a customer. The business assessment memorandum includes details pertaining to an independent credit review undertaken by the risk management department. It also includes details on the analysis conducted by the investment department on project progress.

All business assessment memorandums are approved as per the board-approved delegation of authority.

In exceptional circumstances where a customer requests a variance to the disbursement protocol stipulated in the agreement, such as changes to the geographical location of the account where funds are disbursed, the investment department immediately informs the compliance department of such requests and obtains the necessary clearance.

The CIO ensures that all such requests are explicitly mentioned within the business assessment memorandum with recommendations and approval from the compliance department.

All investment decisions are discussed at the ALCO and evaluated in light of the following:

- movement of interest rates and/or profit rates (deposit and investments);
- inflation rates (current and projected);
- general economic growth and government fiscal policy in markets of interest;
- money supply and market liquidity;
- regulatory and commercial reserve and liquidity requirements;
- rate of appreciation/depreciation of local currency;
- budget surplus usage/deficit financing;
- risks in relation to profit rate, exchange rate, and business environment;
- any other factors that affect risk in managing assets and liabilities.

The treasury and ALM manager informs the ALCO of any risks or issues that have been identified during the execution of treasury operations.

References

Bellalah M and K Abdel Rahman (2000). Gestion des Risques dans un Cadre International. *Economica*, France.

Bellalah M (2004a). *Gestion des Risques et Produits Dérivés Classiques et Exotiques.* Dunod, Prix Turgot.

Bellalah M (2004b). *Gestion des Portefeuilles.* Pearson Education, France.

Bellalah M, O Masood and SM Ghauri (2017a). Basel III implementation outcome in Islamic banks. *Journal of Risk.*

Bellalah M, O Masood, J Younas (2017b). Liquidity Risk management implementation for selected Islamic banks in Pakistan. *Journal of Risk.*

Website

Financial Stability Board: https://www.fsb.org/work-of-the-fsb/implementation-monitoring/monitoring-of-priority-areas/ (updated 2025).

Chapter 4

Managing Banking and Corporate Credit Risks

Chapter Outline

1. Section 4.1 presents the governance structure of credit risk decisions and the abbreviations in Table 4.1.
2. Section 4.2 develops the role of the board of directors and board-level committees in credit decisions.
3. Section 4.3 classifies the types of borrowers and offered products.
4. Section 4.4 develops general granting criteria, borrower granting criteria, and facility/product-level granting criteria.
5. Section 4.5 defines acceptable credit risk mitigations and overarching principles for credit risk mitigants.
6. Section 4.6 describes the credit granting process as well as the management of collateral and guarantees.

Table 4.1. Abbreviations.

Abbreviation	Definition
ALCO	Asset-Liabilities Committee
BCC	Board Credit Committee
BFI	Banks and Financial Institutions
BOD	The Board of Directors

(*Continued*)

Table 4.1. (*Continued*)

Abbreviation	Definition
BRC	Board Risk Committee
BRF	Banking Return Form
CAD	Credit Administration Department
CB	Central Bank
CI	Capital Intelligence
CIB	Corporate and Institutional Banking Group
CCF	Credit Conversion Factor
CCRD	Corporate Credit Risk Department
CEO	The Chief Executive Officer
CFA	Credit Facilities Agreement
CFR	Credit Facilities Review
CRM	Credit Risk Mitigation
DPD	Days Past Due
DVP	Delivery versus Payment
EVP-CRO	Executive Vice President — Chief Risk Officer
SVP-Acting CCO	Senior Vice President — Acting Chief Credit Officer
EVP-CIB	Executive Vice President — Commercial and Institutional Banking
FI	Financial Institution
FX	Foreign Exchange
GCC	Gulf Cooperation Council
GMCC	General Management Credit Committee
GMRC	General Management Risk Committee
HNWI	High Net Worth Individual
KYC	Know Your Customer
LC	Letter of Credit
LG	Letter of Guarantee
LTV	Loan to Value
MIS	Management Information System
NPL	Non-Performing Loan
OD	Overdraft
OECD	Organization for Economic Co-operation and Development
OFAC	Office of the Foreign Assets Control
O.L.E.M.	Other Liabilities Exceptionally Marked
OOT	One Obligor Total
OTC	Over the Counter
PNWS	Personal Net Worth Statement
RAROC	Risk-Adjusted Return on Capital
RAS	Risk Appetite Statement

Table 4.1. (*Continued*)

Abbreviation	Definition
RM	Relationship Manager
RMG	Risk Management Group
SME	Small-to-Medium-sized Enterprise
S&P	Standard & Poor's
TBO	Treasury Back Office
TFD	Trade Finance Dept.
TFO	Treasury Front Office
TWC	Trade Working Capital
BANK	Bank
VP-CCR	Vice President — Corporate Credit Risk

Introduction

The corporate credit guidelines, rules, or simply policies cover the key policies for lending to corporate borrowers across the various stages of the credit lifecycle. The chief risk officer (CRO) is responsible for the corporate credit policy, which is reviewed by the general management risk committee (GMRC) and general management credit committee (GMCC) and approved by the board of directors.

The purpose is to outline the enterprise-wide credit risk management activities of the bank. It details the high-level organization, authorities, and processes relating to credit risk management, which involves processes from origination to approval and ongoing control, review, maintenance, and optimization of credit exposures.

The corporate credit guidelines set out guidelines for the corporate banking business and the bank and financial institution business, aligning with the mission statement, legal and regulatory framework, and the bank's strategic plan and risk appetite. The policy covers the credit risk management framework, credit risk evaluation and mitigation, corporate credit and banks, and financial institution management, as well as the respective roles and responsibilities. It serves as a central policy document, providing employees with a practical account of how the corporate credit risk department and financial institution (FI) credit risk department operate and a best-practice approach to be followed by employees and contractors when performing functions on behalf of the department.

The key features of the chapter are the following:

First, it covers the roles and responsibilities of departments (risk, CIBs, and operations), and the governance of the bank's corporate credit risk is defined.
Second, it gives guidelines on acceptable securities and collaterals, and their mitigation is discussed.
Third, it provides due diligence requirements, and early warning indicators are specified.
Fourth, it covers remedial account management, provisioning, interest reserves, and write-offs.

It may be suitably modified in the future whenever required by the CRO/GMRC in view of changes in broad policy, market conditions, or regulations. In the event of any credit approvals which were approved prior to approval of this policy and are not in line with this document, such events are reviewed on a case-by-case basis to assess the appropriate actions to be undertaken by the bank.

This chapter is designed for the guidance, training, and reference of all staff who are directly and indirectly involved in the corporate credit process.

It is important to note that this chapter is based on my professional experience in several financial institutions. It is also based on several public information sources on Basel III implementation by the Financial Stability Board: https://www.fsb.org/work-of-the-fsb/implementation-monitoring/monitoring-of-priority-areas/ (updated 2025).

4.1. Governance Structure

The bank follows sound risk governance principles, which emphasize clear roles, responsibilities, and reporting lines to ensure adequate segregation of duties, allowing independence and avoiding conflicts of interest in pursuit of the bank's business objectives and strategy.

Adequate segregation of duties should be followed to ensure independence and avoid conflicts of interest in pursuit of the bank's business objectives and strategy. The bank maintains high corporate governance standards and credit principles and adopts industry-accepted practices to avoid undesirable effects of unclear roles and responsibilities.

In line with these risk governance principles, the bank adopts a "three lines of defense" framework for credit risk governance with oversight by the board, as explained in the following.

Lines of defense: CIB acts as the "first line of defense" and is accountable for the results of its businesses, including responsibility for the active and continuous management of corporate credit risk exposures to ensure balanced risks and returns.

RMG, the credit administration department (CAD), and the corporate control desk (CCD), together with the compliance department, represent the "second line of defense". While RMG has functional and management authority over risk control throughout the bank, it also provides independent oversight of credit risk and is responsible for implementing credit risk control processes. Whereas CAD and CCD ensure approval terms are met, documentation is perfected in line with credit terms.

The internal audit department (IAD), the "third line of defense", is responsible for providing reasonable assurance that credit risk management processes are functioning as designed and identifying improvement opportunities.

4.2. Board of Directors and Board-Level Committees

The BoD is responsible for the overall direction, supervision, and control of the bank's banking activities. The BoD reviews and approves strategic initiatives with active participation by the board-level committees. The board risk committee is responsible for maintaining oversight of the risks undertaken by the bank through the CRO, who is responsible for articulating the bank's risk appetite and major portfolio limits, including the allocation of these limits to the CIB in consultation with GMCC and GMRC.

The write-offs are approved by the BRC in consultation with the special advisory committee (SAC), GMCC, CEO, CFO, and head of CIB.

4.2.1. *High-level responsibilities: Management-level committees, CEO, and CRO*

The management-level committees are responsible for implementing the corporate credit strategy, developing policies and procedures, and identifying, measuring, monitoring, and controlling corporate credit risk, as per the mandate from the BoD. The GMCC and GMRC monitor and oversee the bank's risk profile and the implementation of the risk management framework. The GMCC approves the deferment of the primary documents of the customers and also approves the waiver of account opening documents on a case-by-case basis.

The GMCC approves several extensions, such as the extension of the customer file annual review that is above 90 days in consultation with the CCO, CBO, and head of CIB. The GMCC approves the extension of tenor with approved credit limits over 60 days in consultation with the CCO and head of CIB.

It also approves the extension of repayments, drawdowns, moratoriums, and availability of loans and facilities over 120 days in consultation with the CCO and head of CIB.

The CIB policies are approved by the board of directors in consultation with the GMCC, GMRC, and CEO.

The annual plan for corporate and institutional banking is approved by the executive committee of the board in consultation with the BRC, BCC, GMCC, GMRC, and the CEO. The amendments are approved by the GMRC in consultation with the CEO, CRO, CCO, and CBO of the bank. The CEO is informed of the onboarding of high-risk customers and is responsible for approving transactions above 30% of the approved customer limit.

4.2.2. *High-level responsibilities*

- The CCO is responsible for the approval of transactions ranging from 15% to 20% of the approved limit, in consultation with the head of CIB.
- The CCO approves the extension of customer file annual reviews of up to 90 days in consultation with the head of CIB and CBO.
- The CCO approves the extension of the tenor within approved credit limits of up to 60 days in consultation with the head of CIB.
- The CCO approves the extension of repayments, drawdowns, moratoriums, and availability of loans and facilities of up to 120 days in consultation with the head of CIB.
- The CCO approves the reallocation of limits from higher-risk to lower-risk in consultation with the head of CIB.

- The CBO is responsible for developing and implementing the annual business plan of the CIB areas of the bank and is also responsible for implementing the approved business plan within the bank and ensuring that the target market is adhered to.

4.2.3. *Head of corporate and institutional banking*

The head of CIB is responsible for the CIB policies and procedures of the bank.

The head of CIB also approves the onboarding of medium-risk customers and the deferment of secondary documents.

The head of CIB is responsible for approving the execution of transactions without fax/email indemnity, issuance of cheque books on accounts with more than three cheque returns in the past six months, cheque referral due to mismatches, and retention of accounts with four or more returned cheques in the past year.

4.3. Types of Borrowers and Products Offered

4.3.1. *Type of borrowers*

The business unit actively seeks to pursue a diversified portfolio to minimize the effects of accumulated concentration of risk. To this end, the bank's corporate portfolio includes many or all of the following types of counterparties: banks, incorporated corporations, holding companies, and special purpose vehicles (SPVs), such as those for project financing or specific financing.

They also include family-owned/controlled businesses; federal and local government non-commercial and commercial entities; insurance firms; and other commercially viable business entities.

4.3.2. *Products offered*

Credit products offered by the CIB group need to provide the best possible match to the financing requirements of the borrower while taking into account the risks associated with the facility. The CIB group formally approves a set of conventional products applicable for corporate borrowers. The group offers both funded and unfunded products to corporate borrowers for providing facilities for working capital and supporting business expansion and merchandise trade.

4.4. Credit Granting Criteria

The purpose of the credit facility is analyzed with a view to understand whether it aligns with the bank's policies. Exceptions may be considered subject to the approval of the appropriate authority level. Credit risk is difficult to avoid in lending activities. For an analysis of credit risks, the reader can refer to Bellalah (2004a, 2004b), Bellalah and Strtak (2018), Bellalah and ElFarissi (2023), Bellalah and Zouari (2015), Bellalah *et al.* (2015, 2016).

4.4.1. *General granting criteria*

A clearly defined target market must be established. Target market (TM) identifies the acceptable profile of borrowers for the product or range of products offered. Business must not be undertaken outside defined TMs, business strategies, or products/facilities as outlined in the CIB product matrix, except in exceptional cases and with adequate mitigants. Special emphasis is placed on the bank's anti-money laundering (AML) and know-your-customer (KYC) norms when lending to corporate borrowers. It is important to note also that compliance with all applicable statutory and regulatory directives is ensured in all cases, and propriety and ethical standards should be taken into account in all credit decisions.

Credit, whether secured or unsecured, must not be extended to a borrower where the bank lacks an understanding of the borrower or the borrower's business. The borrower should understand the facilities and associated risks and have the authority to enter into the facility.

Credit normally is extended when there are at least two clear alternate sources of repayment. Particular attention should be paid to cash flow projections and to all factors and assumptions that may affect cash flow (the prime source of repayment of such advances), followed by secondary sources of shareholders' means and liquidation of collateral/assets.

The bank extracts a list of all classified borrowers on a monthly basis.

An in-depth analysis of the debtor's age/profile must be made in all cases. Similarly, information on the quality and age of inventories should be commented on. Trade receivables breakdowns, including concentration risk, should be analyzed, and a summary of trade receivables aging should be provided with each proposal. Related party dues should be analyzed and broken down, including the collection timeline, and provided (exceptions or non-availability of this information should be justified in the credit proposal).

The bank will not entertain "name lending" proposals, where credit is solely based on the borrower's reputation. However, lending to well-known HNWIs against adequate tangible securities and repayments from rentals or other income of the borrower is excluded from the definition of name lending. Such lendings are classified under secured lending.

New or prospective customers must be thoroughly investigated by the bank, particularly regarding their banking relationships and market reputation.

Historic and projected cash flows are key criteria for credit evaluation of term loans. The main purpose of risk analysis is to assess the likelihood of repayment of the principal amount and interest within the stipulated period. Forecasts should be based on realistic assumptions and cash flow projections, tied to current and future debt maturities and debt servicing, to measure repayment capacity. In addition, sensitivity analysis should also be performed to assess repayment under downside/stress scenarios.

All relevant central bank circulars and directives must be considered when recommending or deciding on any credit proposal.

Proper credit structuring should be based on realistic requirements and risks with a deeper understanding of the borrower's market and business. The level of facilities should be proposed by CIBs in relation to the borrower's size, equity, leverage, borrowings with other banks, security, and overall financial strength, within the norm of the industry/sector.

Terms of trade and modes should be deeply investigated to assist not only in determining requirements but also in assessing how secure transactions are for the business vis-à-vis its counterparties.

Suitable financial covenants (such as leverage, gearing, current ratio, and minimum net worth) and conditions (e.g., to prevent promoters from selling their shares in the borrower or withdrawals of capital without the bank's consent) should be stipulated where possible or required. Moreover, it is advisable that covenant ratios are computed on a "substance over form" basis (and not solely based on simple balance-sheet ratios); for instance, it should exclude non-trade dues from related parties or non-core investments from net worth while calculating the ratio.

Policies for prohibited credits: Certain credits have been identified as strictly prohibited for the bank as undertaking these exposures can lead to high reputational damage or compliance breaches. These include financing:

- borrowers whose integrity or moral character is questionable;
- money laundering activities;
- credit exposures which lead to breach of regulatory compliance requirements;
- credit exposures to countries sanctioned by the United Nations (UN);
- arms and weapons trade (where such arms and weapons are expected to be used for offensive purposes);
- casinos and gambling equipment, pornography goods and/or stores;
- businesses which are environmentally destructive or engaged in unethical conduct or unethical labor practices;
- speculative transactions;
- hostile takeovers.

Credit risk management, in consultation with the compliance department, updates the list of prohibited credits to ensure that the bank meets all the applicable laws and regulations at all times.

Policies for controlled credits: Certain borrower types and product segments can be identified as "controlled credits", where the bank avoids undertaking credit exposure unless a strong business case is presented and the exposure is expected to result in a highly favorable risk–return trade-off for the bank. The exposures identified as controlled credit by the bank include:

- acquisition financing where the take-out is from the sale of assets of the acquired;
- financing facilities where more than $x\%$ of the principal is a bullet maturity;
- repayments with extended grace periods of more than one year (project finance excluded);

- venture capital or "greenfield" project financing credits or similar transactions where the future cash flow and profitability cannot be reliably forecast and/or credits whose proceeds are substantially used for the acquisition of intangible assets or assets whose value cannot be quantified, unless fully secured by other collateral;
- credits to religious, charitable, or other institutions and to companies or persons where default could be embarrassing to the bank's reputation and image.

The bank should be compliant with all the requirements under the IFRS 9 standards.

The bank's risk management function's involvement in the assessment and measurement of accounting ECL is essential to ensuring adequate allowances in accordance with IFRS 9. For a deep analysis, the reader can refer to Bellalah and Zouari (2015), and Bellalah *et al.* (2016).

4.4.2. *Borrower granting criteria*

This section covers the broad criteria to be adopted by the bank to identify potential borrowers and make credit decisions based on further assessment. Typically, each borrower is assessed based on their ability, i.e., capacity to pay, and character, i.e., ingress to pay, which are governed by the following principles:

Capacity: The borrower must generate adequate cash flows to service the requested debt in a timely manner. The bank must conduct a clear review of the financial standing of the borrowers. The financial standing is evaluated on operational structure, business conditions, and management quality.

Character: The borrower, or the management of the borrower in the event of a corporate or incorporated entity, must be of sound character. This is reflected in the borrower's credit history and reputation in the market.

4.4.2.1. *Lending to corporate borrowers*

The borrower's financial statements must be audited by an auditor approved by the bank.[1]

[1]Please refer to website in the references.

Credit will only be granted upon full and satisfactory completion of all facility documentation and when the bank confidently expects that it will be repaid by the borrower.

Regular site visits are conducted for all borrowers to ascertain more information about the business. The outcome of all such visits must be documented in call reports within seven days of the visit and circulated to senior management in the CIB group.

Corrective actions are taken quickly where deterioration occurs, be it withdrawing a product, tightening acceptance criteria, renegotiating or cancelling credit lines, increasing pricing, or perhaps placing an account on a watchlist.

4.4.2.2. *Lending to government/public sector entities (PSEs)*

For lending to government or PSEs, the above policies for corporate borrowers and any credit to government or PSEs are thoroughly assessed on a standalone basis for repayment capabilities before any credit facility is approved. In the case of exposures (other than those denominated in local currency) to central governments/central banks, the level of exposure is restricted by country limits.

Lending to government or PSEs follows the same normal credit process as other corporate proposals.

4.4.2.3. *Policies for financial institutions including banks*

Lending to banks: The maximum exposure to a country or bank or FI should be in accordance with applicable regulations, if any, and subject to the bank's own risk appetite framework.

Lending to Non-Bank Financial Institutions (NBFIs): Banking relationships with investment banks and other non-bank financial institutions (NBFIs) must be subject to stricter scrutiny and more frequent reviews.

RMs must carefully evaluate the robustness of the AML processes established at the NBFIs.

Generally, credit facilities extended to NBFIs should be for a short term.

Credit applications must be carefully prepared, taking into account the differences in business models applicable to each type of NBFI.

4.4.3. *Facility/product-level granting criteria*

4.4.3.1. *General product level criteria*

The management committee must inform and obtain approval from the board risk committee regarding the introduction of new products and the migration of products undertaken by the bank. Though each credit product or facility varies in its credit risk characteristics, the following criteria must be considered for all credit products and/or facilities:

Purpose: The bank must understand the economic rationale behind all facilities, including those without an explicitly defined purpose. The facility's purpose and features must align with the borrower's sound economic objectives, which the bank must appraise. The actual purpose of the facility is taken into consideration rather than the stated purpose.

Exposure estimation: Situations where a commitment may result in additional future exposure must be considered when estimating the total expected commitment of the bank.

Transparency: Any facilities or transactions intended to alter, in a misleading way, the external perception of borrowers' financial situations will be declined by the bank.

Repayment: It is imperative to always assess the mechanism by which the facility will be repaid, without relying on a future refinancing or an event conditional in nature.

Expertise: The bank will not offer a facility without an in-depth understanding of all aspects of the facility structure or if it is not adequately equipped to monitor it. It must always be ensured that the borrowers share the same understanding of the facilities or transactions and are aware of the monitoring requirements for those facilities or transactions.

Structure: Facilities must be structured considering the impact of all aspects of the underlying transactions as well as the consequences of any of the borrower's known development plans.

Tenor: The tenor of commitments must be in line with projected cash flows and the purpose of the facility.

4.5. Credit Risk Mitigation and Collateral Management

4.5.1. *Acceptable credit risk mitigants*

The following are the acceptable credit risk mitigants acceptable to the bank, subject to legal recognition in the respective jurisdictions and the relevant documentation. being entered into:

- cash and fixed deposits held with the bank against credit facilities;
- guarantees from a bank with an acceptable credit rating and country risk which should be irrevocable, unconditional, payable on demand, and preferably having a tenor of at least one month more than the expiry of the facility sought from the bank or, where the facility (such as a bond) has an auto-renewal clause, the guarantee needs to have an auto-renewal clause as well;
- equities or other marketable securities;
- real estate supported by a professional valuation report;
- assignment over leased premises in free zones, industrial zones, or similar jurisdictions;
- notarized pledge over machinery, plant, or equipment (provided that such pledge is registered with the relevant authority as well), and if the notarized pledge is not registered, then it is not enforceable toward third parties or other creditors of the borrower, whereas in all other circumstances, a notarized pledge does not constitute a perfected, enforceable security, but the CCRD may request it for comfort purposes only;
- commercial mortgage of factory building and business assets;
- any other security, as may be approved on a case-by-case basis by the EVP-CRO on the recommendations of the CCRD.

4.5.2. *Overarching principles for credit risk mitigants*

The bank should verify the credit risk mitigant being offered and ensures the following:

- the credit risk mitigant is materially consistent with its description in the credit proposal package;

- the existence and ownership of the collateral before acceptance are verified;
- any encumbrance, i.e., whether there is any prior claim or claim of equal ranking by another party on the collateral or other type of credit risk mitigant, is verified;
- the legal procedures and documentation for perfecting the collateral or guarantee arrangement must be in strict compliance with local legal requirements;
- the value of the collateral must be appraised and updated on a regular basis, or when circumstances dictate, and independent third-party professional advice may be sought for conducting the valuation exercise;
- all physical collateral accepted by the bank should be insured in line with the bank's policy.

4.5.3. *Management of collateral*

4.5.3.1. *Collateral coverage*

The following policies are applicable with regard to collateral coverage (or LTV) at the bank:

The bank specifies the minimum permissible collateral coverage (or the maximum LTV) for major types of assets that are accepted as collateral. The collateral coverage is commensurate with the relative risk of the assets and is able to provide an adequate buffer against potential losses in realizing the collateral.

The maximum LTVs specified are in line with the requirements set out by the jurisdiction in which the bank operates.

The collateral coverage requirements are a function of the following criteria:

- potential fluctuations in the market value of the collateral;
- currency and maturity of collateral;
- carrying costs of maintaining the repossessed collateral before its disposal and costs incurred for disposing of the collateral (such as auction fees, bid-ask spreads for liquidity adjustment, and repossession charges);

– form of collateral charge, where different forms of legally recognized charges are available.

4.5.3.2. *Collateral haircuts*

The CCRD maintains appropriate haircuts for individual collateral types. As a matter of prudence, the bank applies a conservative haircut to determine the extent to which an exposure is secured. The quantum of that haircut depends on the type of collateral, price volatility of the collateral, term of the exposure, and currency mismatch with the underlying exposure. The haircuts are in line with the requirements of capital adequacy regulations under Basel II. These haircuts are used, as applicable, in determining collateral coverage for the purpose of capital computation.

4.5.3.3. *Use of multiple collateral*

The bank accepts multiple collateral under circumstances where a single collateral does not provide sufficient comfort for the level of risk undertaken. The bank applies the prescribed maximum LTVs for different types of collateral provided by the borrower. The facility documentation clearly specifies the different collateral provided by the borrower and the coverage requirements thereof.

4.5.3.4. *Collateral valuation*

Where the collateral is the sole or primary security and repayment cash flows are not identified, the value of the collateral includes a sufficient margin greater than the loan amount to consider not only the risk that the liquidation value is less than the assessed value but also the unpaid interest that accumulates once the loan begins to deteriorate. Both the market and liquidation values of property collateral are carefully evaluated, and current appraisals of the asset are maintained. The value of marketable securities is determined at least on a weekly basis, with more frequent valuations in case of volatile market movements. Real estate valuations, from agencies acceptable to the bank, are carried out at least once every three years and more frequently if warranted. A request for a current valuation can be a condition for credit approvals.

4.5.3.5. *Collateral top-up*[2]

A collateral call or a request for the top-up of a collateral is initiated under the following circumstances:

- a significant fall in the value of the original collateral due to fluctuations in its market price and where the collateral coverage is less than the stated coverage requirements;
- deterioration in the debt servicing ability of the borrower;
- breach of any financial covenants (covered in the facility documentation) by the borrower.

4.5.4. *Management of guarantees*

The bank provides facilities against the security of a guarantee, subject to the following broad policies:

- The guarantee will continue to be unconditional and irrevocable, representing a direct claim on the guarantor.
- All guarantees must contain indemnity wording, so that if the borrower's primary obligations fall away, the guarantor would allow the bank to be indemnified (i.e., the guarantee remains valid and in full force, notwithstanding the enforceability of the underlying facility or transaction).
- All guarantees are signed in the presence of the bank's representative.
- Where the validity of a guarantee expires before the expiration of the term of the facility, the guarantor is informed in advance to extend the validity of the guarantee or pay prior to the expiry date. This ensures that the facility remains fully secured throughout its term.
- The financial stability and creditworthiness of guarantors are monitored periodically to ensure that the exposure has not deteriorated significantly. The periodic credit review and the rating review process ensure this procedure.

---

[2]Collateral top-up refers to a collateral call or a request made to the borrower to provide additional collateral owing to a fall in the value of the existing collateral or an increase in the collateral coverage based on credit event triggers defined in the facility documentation.

- The bank avoids having significant concentrations in specific forms of guarantees. In this context, the bank avoids accepting guarantees from the same guarantor beyond the specified limit.
- The bank obtains signed personal net worth statements (PNWSs) to assist in assessing the "quality" of the guarantee (although it is highly recommended to obtain PNWSs, as per market practice, shareholders/owners/guarantors do not want to provide them. Furthermore, it is practically impossible to verify the accuracy of the statements in the absence of a tax regime and other similar bodies); nevertheless, the bank should strive to obtain information to assess the estimated net worth.
- Cross-corporate guarantees are obtained from all major operating companies where facilities are provided to a group of borrowers.
- A legal opinion on the enforceability and validity of guarantees from overseas entities must be obtained from the legal department prior to execution.
- Bank guarantees are irrevocable, unconditional, payable on demand, and directly in favor of the bank.

4.6. Credit Granting Process

The sequence of tasks involved in the corporate banking credit granting process is described as follows, indicating individual processes and presenting the cross-functional roles of the various departments within the corporate credit granting process.

The responsibility for initiating credit facilities (via completed credit proposals) lies with the CIB (business unit), whereas the CCRD is responsible for conducting a detailed credit analysis of each borrower. The facilities assessed by the CCRD are submitted to the relevant approval authority along with CCRD's recommendations. Once the facility is approved and disbursed, credit exposures and credit risks are monitored on a regular basis by the business unit and CCRD.

4.6.1. *Credit initiation and initial assessment*

The CIB is primarily responsible as the first line of defense, checking the amount of any financing facility and ensuring it is in line with the customer's needs and the bank's RAS. It is responsible for screening applications for an appropriate amount for the purpose for which they are sought, not the amount the customer expects the bank to finance, as well as conducting a complete and comprehensive initial credit review/analysis and obtaining constitutional documents from the customer and security providers.

The bank proactively monitors the financial performance and conduct of the client/account.

A borrower's credit analysis is carried out by the bank. The CFR, based on the credit analysis, clearly states whether or not the proposed application is in compliance with the bank's credit policies. The completion of a CFR includes a detailed assessment of financial and non-financial analyses. This analysis includes an assessment of the following three elements:

(i) Business and management review (which includes incorporation/years of existence, group companies: size (sales) and profitability (net profits), ownership pattern of the company, ownership pattern of other group firms and key stakeholders, management integrity, experience/track record, and succession issues (if any)).
(ii) Industry review (including size of the industry (in terms of sales volume/value), major players and competitive scenarios, past and projected growth, demand–supply dynamics, and the profitability scenario).
(iii) Financial position (sales growth, gross margins, and profits (comment on gross margins, gross profits, and changes in the same), capital structure (comment on leverage/growth in networth/partners' drawings, if applicable), long-term debt, debt repayment capacity and DSCR, net margin and profits, working capital intensity, debtors, inventory levels and cash conversion cycle, liquidity position (current ratio and cash reserves), contingent liabilities, if any, and cash flow analysis).

For relationships with FIs, RMs perform financial and non-financial analyses using information from the bank's scope and external ratings and analysis provided by rating agencies (e.g., Moody's, Fitch, and Capital Intelligence). The analysis is based on the CAMEL approach, which would include an assessment of: capital adequacy, quality and stability; asset quality; management quality; earnings adequacy and quality; and liquidity.

The non-financial aspects of a client's activities that can be relevant and sometimes decisive to its creditworthiness may not be listed exhaustively or comprehensively, but can include an assessment of one or more of the following: shareholder/partner disputes, management quality, market position and competition, technology support, industry entry and exit barriers, major lawsuits or legal disputes, major new product or market initiatives, major new contracts won or lost, expansion measures or plans, and mergers and acquisitions.

4.6.2. *Appraisal, loan structuring, and pricing*

The CIB is responsible for structuring credit transactions to minimize risk and uncertainty for the bank. This is done through the use of affirmative or negative covenants and the use of collateral. If there are existing credit agreements with other lenders in place, the bank scrutinizes those carefully to determine what rights and remedies the bank would have in view of the terms of those existing agreements.

Proposed facilities: The nature and amount of each proposed facility, with the main and sub-limit, should be mentioned in the credit facility review (CFR).

Purpose of borrowing: The exact purpose of borrowing is ascertained, and the customer's disinclination to supply such information means that such a borrowing request is declined. Investigations are made to ascertain that facilities are to finance the borrower's normal business activities. Where facilities are required to finance a new venture, extreme caution is necessary. Where facilities are required for working capital purposes, the bank ensures that these reflect both the trade cycle and the blend of particular limits. OD lines swing into credit during the cyclical trough.

Amount: The bank assesses that the amount of the facility sought is in line with the stated purpose, after taking into account the borrower's desired equity contribution and any other financing obtained for the same purpose from any other lender. The bank carefully analyzes the data provided by borrowers and assesses the debt/repayment capacity based on the borrower's realistic projected cash flows. For project finance deals, loans are structured with multiple advances based on the attainment of certain milestones, for example, the completion of certain portions of a construction project, and should ideally be in the form of direct payments to suppliers/contractors.

Borrower limits: The bank ensures that the transactions are within approved lending limits. Aggregate funded working capital facilities are proposed at an acceptable level in line with the borrower's business requirements; however, higher amounts should be adequately justified in the CFR. Contract financing requests and adequately secured exposures (secured against tangible securities) may be excluded from this parameter.

Tenor: The tenor of facilities is structured in line with the borrower's needs. Currently, the bank focuses on short-to-medium-term risk exposure. Although RAS allows tenors up to 10 years, those exceeding seven years should be strongly justified in the CFR. In the case of syndicated loans and project finance, the bank may consider a repayment tenor higher than seven years, depending on cash flow projections and subject to the relevant approving authority's decision. Generally, the bank offers credit facilities only for a fixed term. However, all such facilities are payable on demand unless otherwise agreed between the bank and the borrower.

Risk rating: All CFRs must include the risk rating of obligors.

Prudential limits: In addition to the facility limits, the bank also establishes prudential limits detailed in terms of capital utilization, income concentration, and provisioning. These limits should be established as part of the annual risk strategy exercise. The bank ensures that all its exposures are within these prescribed limits.

Repayments and early settlements: The primary source of repayment will be cash flows from operations, followed by secondary sources of shareholders' means and liquidation of collateral/assets. It should be mandatory that borrowers' operating accounts are maintained with the bank (except for the bank's participation in syndicated loans/club deals or where it has provided credit facilities to government-related entities — for these financing types, an operating account is not a mandatory requirement). If the bank is not their main bank, then it remains pari passu with other lenders in terms of routing of cash flows/turnover. The inclusion of an early settlement fee in any funded facility of greater than a 12-month tenor is mandatory (excluding syndicate/club deals). Typically, this fee is 2% payable on the amount prepaid. Any request to waive such a fee requires express written approval of the appropriate authority.

Grace period: The bank may propose a grace period to a borrower on principal loan payments in order to provide enough time to generate revenue and resulting cash. However, if a borrower's existing business is already producing sufficient cash flow to make loan payments, any grace period is clearly inappropriate, yet an exception, if any, should be justified in the CFR with adequate approvals from the designated approval authorities. The grace period is tied strictly to the actual needs of the business and not simply to a borrower's request.

Currency: The appropriate currency is determined by the specific needs of the borrower, as supported by the bank's currency position at the time of borrowing, and it should match the currency of the source of repayment.

Cash flow: There is only one commodity a bank is interested in when it comes to having its loan repaid, and that is cash. Neither reported earnings nor assets (fixed or current) can repay the debt. Reported earnings do not reflect ultimate debt repayment capacity due to the accrual method of income and expense recognition and widely different accounting practices. Cash flow is an indispensable tool for debt settlement, as cash flow statements are relatively inviolable and cannot be window-dressed to the same extent as balance sheets and income statement ratios.

Summary

The risk of financial loss to the bank is primarily dependent on the borrower's willingness and ability to repay, but can be mitigated based on the credit risk mitigants that the bank holds.

As a matter of principle, the bank avoids extending credit facilities to risky borrowers solely based on credit risk mitigants provided.

Lending must not be predicated on credit risk mitigants; these should only be used as a safety net available to the bank.

Where the bank guarantee is the sole or primary consideration for lending, the guarantee must be for an amount at least equal to the facility amount, plus all interest costs and other charges, in the same currency as the facility being provided, and, if not on a continuing basis, then for a validity period at least one month longer than the validity period of the facility so as to enable renewal if necessary (any exceptions to be duly approved by the GMCC).

Bank guarantees from foreign banks incorporate a confirmation that all necessary regulatory permissions to make payment in the event of the guarantee being called have either been obtained or are not required.

In the absence of such confirmation, guidance is sought from the bank's legal department (moreover, all bank guarantees are subject to review and approval by the legal department).

References

Bellalah M (2004a). *Gestion des Risques et Produits Dérivés Classiques et Exotiques*. Dunod, Prix Turgot.

Bellalah M (2004b). *Gestion des Portefeuilles*. Pearson Education.

Bellalah M and S Strtak (2018). Réfexions sur les décisions de Crédit, le risque de défaut et l'évaluation de la perte en cas de défaut, *Revue des Sciences de Gestion*.

Bellalah M and I ElFarissi (2023). Credit risk: Valuation, quality migration, and KMV approach. *International Journal of Strategic Management and Economic Studies*.

Bellalah M and S Zouari (2015). Portfolio credit risk models and name concentration issues: Theory and simulations. *International Journal of Business*.

Bellalah M, M Bellalah and H Heschmi (2015). The recent financial crisis: is there an equity premium puzzle? *Research in International Business and Finance*.

Bellalah M, S Zouari and O Levyne (2016). The performance of hybrid models in the assessment of default risk. *Economic Modeling*, 52, 259–265.

Website

Financial Stability Board: https://www.fsb.org/work-of-the-fsb/implementation-monitoring/monitoring-of-priority-areas/ (updated 2025).

Chapter 5

Credit Risk Management for Islamic Banking

Chapter Outline

1. Section 5.1 presents definitions and governance of credit decisions.
2. Section 5.2 explains credit risk identification, credit risk evaluation, and risk classification.
3. Section 5.3 explains collateral management: eligible collateral, eligible guarantors, collateral haircuts, and collateral valuation.
4. Section 5.4 is devoted to credit risk exposure, expected credit loss and, in particular, the scope of ECL, the staging criteria, and the incorporation of forward-looking information.
5. Section 5.5 discusses the credit risk limit structure.
6. Section 5.6 explains the credit risk capital calculation.
7. Section 5.7 develops the credit risk system and controls.
8. Section 5.8 explains the analysis of concentration risk.
9. Section 5.9 addresses risk monitoring.

Introduction

The risk department/function has the responsibility of identifying and managing the overall credit risk exposure of the bank. The purpose of this chapter is to outline the specific risk management approach to be implemented by the bank in its course of identifying and managing its credit risk exposure.

It addresses the specific approach to mitigate credit risks arising from the bank's financing activities, including credit lines to counterparties, project companies, and other legal entities.

Credit risk management articulates the bank's approach to identifying, measuring, monitoring, and controlling credit risk and administering and managing credit exposures and portfolios, besides providing certain important guidelines for strict adherence in the lending process.

The overall objectives of credit risk management are to ensure orderly growth of the credit portfolio, both qualitatively and quantitatively. The objectives are to ensure adherence to regulatory prudential norms on exposures, classification, and lending restrictions from time to time. They ensure uniformity in lending activity bank-wide, deploy the bank's resources remuneratively, and pursue national priorities.

The overall objectives of credit risk management are also to enable the pricing of various risks within credit exposures, forming a part of an integrated system of management of all risks, encompassing identification, measurement, monitoring, and control.

Importantly, this chapter is based on my professional experience in several financial institutions.

For a review of Islamic finance, the reader can refer to Bellalah and Masood (2015), Bellalah *et al.* (2012a, 2012b, 2012c). The reader can refer to the main updated texts (2025) at the website of the Association Europe Finances Régulations (AEFR): https://www.aefr.eu/en/article/182.

5.1. Definitions and Governance

It is defined as the inability or unwillingness of a borrower or counterparty to meet commitments in accordance with agreed terms in relation to lending, trading, hedging, settlement, and other financial transactions. Also, it is defined as the possibility of losses associated with diminution in the credit quality of borrowers or counterparties.

The bank follows sound risk governance principles, which emphasize clear roles, responsibilities, and reporting lines. The bank follows sound governance principles laid down by local central banks (or regulatory authorities) for corporate governance in its governance structure for credit risk. The following sections in this chapter articulate the bank's governance framework for credit risk management. The governance structure includes various stakeholders such as the board of directors, risk and policy committee, executive investment committee (EIC), credit committee, chief risk officer (CRO), chief investment officer (CIO), and chief business officer (CBO).

Board of directors' responsibilities: The board of directors of the bank has overall responsibility for risk management.

The board approves the framework and guidelines under the bank's credit risk management policy and reviews it periodically. It provides senior management with clear guidance and direction. The board establishes a management structure that can effectively implement the bank's risk management framework, establishing clear lines of management responsibility, accountability, and reporting. It reviews the framework regularly vis-a-vis the market changes, environmental factors, new products, activities, and systems and revises it as necessary based on the analysis.

The board approves risk limits by assessing the bank's risk-bearing capacity, and based on the recommendations of the risk and policy committee, the board ensures the adequacy of the internal audit process to provide quality assurance regarding the implementation of credit risk management policies and procedures.

Risk and policy committee's responsibilities: Monitor the implementation of the credit risk management policy approved by the board.

Ensure compliance with risk parameters and prudential limits approved by the board.

Recommend guidance on the delegation of credit sanctioning, loan collateral, portfolio management, loan review, risk concentrations, risk monitoring and evaluation, regulatory and legal compliance, and prudential limits on large credit, subject to adequate procedures and controls to manage credit risk inherent in new products.

Review and ensure adequate provisions are made for credit risk based on FAS 30 and regulatory guidelines.

The credit committee's responsibilities:

- Evaluate the investment proposals in line with the risk appetite and strategy of the bank.
- Recommend investment proposals to the risk and policy committee for review and ensure adequate mitigation actions are implemented.
- Ensure compliance with risk parameters and prudential limits approved by the board.
- Monitor the implementation of the credit risk management policy approved by the board.
- Review the provisions for key investments.
- Review all past due cases.

Chief risk officer's responsibilities:

- Supervise activities and review and approve recommendations from the credit risk management department before submitting to the credit committee and the risk and policy committee.
- Measure, control, and manage credit risk on a bank-wide basis within the limits set by the board.
- Enforce compliance with the risk parameters and prudential limits approved by the board.
- Create awareness of credit risks and related risk management activities.
- Facilitate the analysis of risks and interrelationships across credit, market, and operational risks.
- Supervise and lead the expected credit loss (ECL)/provisioning activity for the bank.

Credit risk management department's responsibilities:

- Measure, control, and manage credit risk on a bank-wide basis.
- Enforce compliance with the risk parameters and prudential limits.
- Lay down risk assessment systems, develop MIS, guidelines for maintenance of credit quality, identify and analyze deficiencies, if any, and amend policies.

– Be accountable for protecting the quality of the entire loan portfolio.

The department should undertake portfolio evaluations and conduct comprehensive studies on the environment to test the resilience of the loan portfolio. The department should undertake the responsibility for ECL and provision calculations. The department is responsible for credit administration-related activities, such as collateral management and related documentation.

The credit risk management department comprises portfolio management and credit risk analytics, the credit risk rating desk, and the industry research desk; it also includes the credit administration department.

The roles and responsibilities of the EIC, CIO, and CBO are covered in the corporate governance policy, investment manual, and business development manual, respectively.

5.2. Credit Risk Identification

The bank develops a comprchensive credit evaluation framework for identifying credit risk by assigning credit ratings and probability of default to each obligor.

For a comprehensive analysis of credit risk, we refer to Bellalah and Zouari (2015), Bellalah *et al.* (2015, 2016).

5.2.1. *Credit risk evaluation*

The components of the credit evaluation framework are a master rating scale, credit rating model, and early warning indicators.

The master rating scale is used by the bank to establish a master rating scale with probabilities of default (PDs) for each rating grade. The master rating scale consists of a minimum of six performing rating grades, one rating grade for special mention/watchlist, and three rating grades for non-performing obligors.

The credit rating model is used by all banks. The bank develops a comprehensive credit rating model that is used for assigning ratings to each obligor based on financial and qualitative factors. The early warning indicators are fundamental for credit management. The bank establishes an exhaustive list of early warning indicators based on which it classifies obligors to the watch list category.

5.2.2. *Risk classification*

The bank follows the classification shown in Table 5.1 for the purpose of credit risk management.

5.3. Collateral Management

The bank looks for credit risk mitigation measures in the form of collateral as much as possible for all obligors. However, the bank should not solely rely on collateral or guarantees for evaluation of credit risk. While collateral or guarantees may provide secondary protection to the bank if the counterparty defaults, the primary consideration for credit approval should be the counterparty's repayment ability.

As part of the credit evaluation framework, the bank establishes a matrix related to minimum collateral requirements for each rating grade.

5.3.1. *Eligible collateral*

The bank accepts only the following list of eligible collateral as gold bullion; cash and:

- hamish jiddiyah or a refundable security deposit taken by the firm against damages if:
  - a purchase ordered in an MPO contract defaults on its obligation to purchase the asset, or
  - a lease ordered in an ijarah contract defaults on its obligation to lease the asset;
- urban or earnest money held by a firm as collateral to guarantee contract performance;
- sukuk that are assigned, by an ECRA, a rating of:
  - for sovereign or non-commercial public sector enterprise securities that are eligible for zero percent risk weight — at least BB−,
  - for short-term debt securities — at least A-3/P-3, or
  - for any other securities — at least BBB−;

Table 5.1. Credit risk management classification.

Serial Number	Credit Category	Description
1	Performing	In this category, there is no uncertainty about timely repayment of the outstanding amounts. This category comprises credits that are currently in regular payment status with prompt payments.
2	Watchlist	Credits that are 1–30 days in arrears
3	Special mention	This category comprises: – credits with deteriorating or potentially deteriorating credit quality that may adversely affect the counterparty's ability to make scheduled payments on time; – credits that are 30–90 days in arrears; – credits showing weakness arising from the customer's financial position; – credits affected by market circumstances or any other industry-related concerns; and – credits that have been restructured and are not classified into a higher risk category.
4	Substandard	This category comprises: – credits that show definite deterioration in credit quality and impaired repayment ability of the counterparty; and – credits that are 91–180 days in arrears.
5	Doubtful	This category comprises: – credits that show significant credit quality deterioration, worse than those in the substandard category, to the extent that the prospect of full recovery of all the outstanding amounts is questionable and the probability of a credit loss is high (though the exact amount of loss cannot be determined yet); and – credits that are 181–270 days in arrears.
6	Loss	This category comprises: – credits that are assessed as uncollectable; – credits where the probability of recovering the amount due is very low; and – credits that are more than 270 days in arrears.

- sukuk that have not been assigned a rating by an ECRA if:
  - the securities are issued by an Islamic banking business firm (or by a conventional bank that is outside the QFC and that has an Islamic window or subsidiary operation) as senior debt and are listed on a recognized exchange,
  - all rated issues of the same seniority issued by that firm or bank have a credit rating of at least BBB− (for long-term debt instruments) or A-3/P-3 (for short-term debt instruments), and
  - the firm or bank and the holder of the collateral have no information suggesting that the securities should have a rating below BBB− or A-3/P-3;
- Shari'a-compliant equities (including convertible sukuk) that are included in a main index;
- units in Islamic collective investment schemes;
- tracker funds, mutual funds, and undertakings for collective investments in transferable securities (UCITS) if a price for the units is publicly quoted daily, and if the funds or UCITS are limited to investing in instruments listed;
- Shari'a-compliant equities (including convertible sukuk) that are not included in a main index but are listed on a recognized exchange, and funds and UCITS described in point 8 that include such equities.

For collateral to be eligible, it must be pledged for the duration of the exposure and marked-to-market at least once a month. The release of collateral must be conditional on the repayment of the exposure, but collateral may be reduced in proportion to the amount of any reduction in the exposure. Collateral in the form of securities issued by the counterparty or a person connected to the counterparty is not eligible collateral. Takaful contracts, unilateral promises to buy from counterparties (such as put options), and forward sales contracts or agreements (such as salam and istisna contracts) are not eligible collateral.

5.3.2. *Eligible guarantors*

The bank accepts guarantees as collateral from the following entities: the state, any other sovereign, any entity treated as a sovereign, or any other entity (including a public sector enterprise not treated as a sovereign) that has a risk weight of 20% or lower and a lower risk weight than the counterparty.

A parent entity, subsidiary, or affiliate of the counterparty may be an eligible guarantor if it has a lower risk weight than the counterparty.

5.3.3. *Collateral haircuts*

The bank considers recommended haircut rules on collateral for the purpose of capital calculation, ECL calculation, and specific provisions. During the credit approval, the bank considers post-haircut collateral values when making decisions on credit risk mitigation.

5.3.4. *Collateral valuation*

Collateral accepted by the bank must be valued at its net realizable value, taking into account prevailing market conditions. The revaluation of the collateral must be done after at least once every two years or in the event of unexpected market conditions.

5.4. Credit Risk Exposure and Expected Credit Loss — FAS 30

The total exposure to credit risk should be calculated based on the following criteria:

On-balance sheet exposure: The total exposure to credit risk is calculated as the sum of outstanding principal, past due repayments, and accrued profit.

Off-balance sheet exposures and credit commitments: The total exposure to credit risk is calculated based on the credit conversion factors.

FAS 30 should replace the previous FAS 11 loss model with the ECL model for provisioning. Under this methodology, the impairment loss is recognized from the date of origination, depending on the credit quality of the asset at each reporting date.

5.4.1. *Scope of ECL*

The ECL model is applied to the following assets. ECL applies to credit facilities and debt instruments measured at amortized cost. Investment in debt instruments are measured at fair value through other comprehensive income (FVOCI). All credit commitments are not measured at fair value. It refers to off-balance sheet exposure. It concerns all debt-type Islamic products.

5.4.2. *Staging criteria — The three-stage approach*

The FAS 30 ECL model recommends a three-stage approach for calculation of provisions. The stages are based on changes in the credit quality of the asset since its initial recognition. The asset moves through the three stages as credit quality changes, and the level of provision is determined by the stage of the asset.

Stage 1 includes financial assets which have not shown any significant increase in credit risk since initial recognition. The ECLs for the next 12 months are required to be calculated for these exposures.

Stage 2 includes financial assets which have shown a significant increase in credit risk since initial recognition but are not impaired. Calculating ECL for the lifetime of exposures is required. In determining the significant increase in credit risk, the bank considers relative criteria based on movement in credit ratings or absolute criteria based on DPDs and external information.

Stage 3 includes financial assets which have shown objective evidence of impairment as of the reporting date. The entire unsecured amount needs to be set aside as ECL for these exposures.

5.4.3. *Incorporation of forward-looking information*

The ECL is required to be forward-looking and needs to capture the best estimate of future outcomes for systematic risk. The bank incorporates relevant macroeconomic factors and reliable forecasts to ensure the ECL measures are forward-looking.

5.5. Credit Risk Limit Structure

The country limit for credit exposures caps the maximum exposure that the bank may undertake in a particular country as a percentage of its total risk capital allocated to that department or function. Country limits formation takes into account the following considerations:

Country risk ratings (internal): For countries to which significant exposures are intended, exposure limits are based on a risk rating developed internally using the guidelines mentioned here.

Strategic concerns: The governing body may choose to assume exposure in particular countries for long-term strategic motives. Such motives can be for developing market penetration or the existence of positive externalities of investing. The country limits for particular credit exposures aggregate into the total limit for those exposures for the bank.

Product limit formation considers the following considerations:

Product profiling: The level of expected risk and return from an Islamic financial product.

Strategic concerns: Despite the risk considerations mentioned above, certain financial products might be favored over others due to long-term strategic and Shari'a considerations.

Tenor limits are based on the following considerations:

The credit risk associated with a financing facility is affected by the tenor of the facility. Certain financing products might be safer than others for a particular financing term. Tenor limits are therefore based on the past performance and future projections of financing facility portfolios, considering the risk–return profile and the adequacy of the risk management framework to monitor portfolio performance and conduct remedial management.

Concentration of exposures in a particular tenor may lead to liquidity problems despite the risk–return profile of the tenor.

Counterparty limit formation is based on the following considerations:

Counterparty risk ratings: The exposure limit for all customers is based on counterparty risk ratings developed using the counterparty assessment criteria.

A core credit principle whereby lendings to various interrelated clients are combined into "one obligor" due to the high correlation in risk. The bank considers the following as part of an obligor exposure: joint accounts, sole proprietorships, and partnerships; public companies where the client owns 30% or more of the capital and participates in management; limited liability companies whereby the client has 50% or more ownership or influence in;

- credit facilities granted to clients, sponsored by the client of the bank regardless of the legal status of these said clients;
- credit facilities granted to any debtors if it appears to the bank that their credit risks are the same as the client's risks.

5.5.1. *Credit enhancement*

Credit enhancement encompasses a variety of provisions that may be used to reduce the credit risk of an obligation. The two general categories of credit enhancement, reduction and transfer, are described as follows:

- **Credit reduction:** One of the most risk-averse and prudent methods of mitigating credit exposure is reassessing the amount of credit being allocated to counterparties. Sometimes both external and internal conditions of a company make it more prone to default, and thus reassessment of credit limits reduces the risk of this default.
- **Active portfolio management:** A sophisticated credit department or function should be able to provide the organization with real-time advice on how to best manage the selection of counterparties, reducing or optimizing overall portfolio credit exposures.
- **Collateralization:** In collateralization, a party who owes an obligation to another party posts collateral — typically consisting of cash or securities — to secure the obligation and as security for the financing. In the event that the party defaults on the obligation, the secured party may seize the collateral. This arrangement helps the bank reduce its losses in cases of default.
- **Netting agreements:** Netting of cash flows is a means of reducing credit exposure to counterparties. Under a netting agreement, counterparties can net their cash flows between each other into a single payment. This arrangement not only reduces settlement risk but also streamlines processing.

Credit transfers can be third-party financing guarantees. This is a common technique to transfer credit risk in which a third party may be contractually bound to meet the obligations of one party should that party default.

5.6. Credit Risk Capital Calculation

Requirement for risk weights: The bank must apply risk weights to its on-balance-sheet and off-balance-sheet items using the risk-weighted assets approach. Risk weights are based on credit ratings or fixed risk weights and are broadly aligned with the likelihood of counterparty default. The bank may use the ratings determined by an external credit rating agency (ECRA) if deemed appropriate.

The risk management department/function must assess all credit exposures (rated or unrated) to determine whether the risk weights applied to them are appropriate. The determination must be based on each exposure's inherent risk. If there are reasonable grounds to believe that the inherent risk of an exposure is significantly higher than that implied by the risk weight assigned to it, the risk division must consider the higher risk (and apply a higher risk weight) in calculating the credit risk capital requirement.

The risk division will not rely solely on a rating determined by an ECRA to assess the risks associated with an exposure. It must also carry out its own credit risk assessment of each exposure.

Commitments included in calculation: The risk division must take into account all commitments when calculating its credit risk capital requirement, regardless of whether those commitments contain material adverse change clauses or other provisions intended to relieve the bank of its obligations under particular conditions.

Risk weighted assets approach — on balance sheet items: The bank's total risk-weighted on-balance-sheet items is the sum of the risk-weighted amounts of each of its on-balance-sheet items. The risk-weighted amount of an on-balance-sheet item is calculated by multiplying its exposure by the applicable risk weight, as set out in Table 5.2.

Specialized lending (refer to Tables 5.3–5.7): A specialized lending exposure is risk-weighted at one rating less favorable than the rating that would apply, as shown in the above tables, to the

Table 5.2. Risk-weighted amount of an on-balance-sheet item.

Sr. No.	Description of Claim or Asset	Risk Weight (%)
1	Cash:	
	notes, gold bullion	0
	cash items in the process of collection	20
2	Claims on sovereigns:	0
	claims on central bank	0
	claims on sovereigns including respective central banks	0
	claims on other sovereigns including respective central banks	based on ECRA rating
3	Claims on public sector enterprises:	
	claims on non-commercial public-sector enterprises	0
	claims on non-commercial public-sector enterprises in other countries, denominated in the relevant enterprise's domestic currency	0
	claims on non-commercial public-sector enterprises in other countries, not denominated in the relevant enterprise's domestic currency	based on ECRA rating
	claims on other sovereign non-commercial public-sector enterprises	based on ECRA rating
	commercial public-sector enterprises	based on ECRA rating
4	Claims on multilateral development banks:	
	claims on multilateral development banks eligible for 0% risk weight	0
	claims on other multilateral development banks	based on ECRA rating
5	Claims on banks (financial undertakings):	
	claims on banks with an original maturity of more than 3 months	based on ECRA rating
	claims on banks with an original maturity of 3 months or less	based on ECRA rating
6	Claims on securities and investment entities:	
	claims on securities and investment entities that are subject to capital requirements similar to Islamic banks	based on ECRA rating
	claims on securities and investment entities that are not subject to capital requirements similar to Islamic banks	based on ECRA rating
7	Claims on corporates	based on ECRA rating

Table 5.2. (*Continued*)

Sr. No.	Description of Claim or Asset	Risk Weight (%)
8	Claims on small and medium enterprises	100
9	Claims on securitization exposures	based on ECRA rating
10	Claims secured against mortgages:	
	residential mortgages	
	if the loan-to-value ratio is 0–80%	35
	if the loan-to-value ratio is more than 80% but less than 100%	75
	if the loan-to-value ratio is 100% or more	100
	commercial mortgages	100
11	Failed and unsettled transactions — delivery-versus-payment transactions:	
	5–15 days	100
	16–30 days	625
	31–45 days	937.5
	46 or more days	1,250
12	Failed and unsettled transactions — non-delivery-versus-payment transactions	100
13	Investments in funds:	
	rated funds	based on ECRA rating
	unrated funds that are listed	100
	unrated funds that are unlisted	150
14	Equity exposures:	
	equity exposures that are not deducted from capital and are listed on a recognized exchange	300
	equity exposures that are not deducted from capital and are not listed on a recognized exchange	400
15	Investment property (Note: Investment property does not include property held for use in the production or supply of goods or services, for administrative purposes, or for sale in the ordinary course of business. A real estate asset owned by an Islamic banking business firm as a result of a counterparty default is treated as "other item" and risk-weighted at 100% but only for a period of 3 years starting from the date when the firm records the asset on its books.)	150
16	All other items	100

Table 5.3. Risk weights based on ratings determined by ECRAs.

Sr. No.	Description of Claim or Asset	AAA to AA−	A+ to A−	BBB+ to BBB−	BB+ to BB−	B+ to B−	Below B−	Unrated
1	Claims on other sovereigns including respective central banks	0	20	50	100	100	150	100
2	Claims on non-commercial public-sector enterprises in other countries — non-relevant domestic currency	0	20	50	100	100	150	100
3	Claims on other sovereign non-commercial public-sector enterprises	20	50	100	100	100	150	100
4	Claims on commercial public-sector enterprises	20	50	100	100	100	150	100
5	Claims on multilateral development banks not eligible for 0% risk weight	20	50	50	100	100	150	50
6	Claims on banks with an original maturity of more than 3 months	20	50	50	100	100	150	50
7	Claims on banks with an original maturity of 3 months or less	20	20	20	50	50	150	20
8	Claims on securities and investment entities that are subject to capital requirements like Islamic banks	20	50	50	100	100	150	50
9	Claims on securities and investment entities that are not subject to capital requirements like Islamic banks	20	50	100	100	150	150	100
10	Claims on corporates	20	50	100	100	150	150	100
11	Securitization exposures	50	100	100	150	150	250	150
12	Investments in rated funds	20	50	100	100	150	150	N/A

counterparty to the transaction (or to the party to whom that counterparty has the right of recourse). Specialized lending is a lending transaction that complies with the following requirements:

- the purpose of the loan is to acquire an asset;
- the cash flow generated by the collateral is the loan's exclusive (or almost exclusive) source of repayment;
- the loan represents a significant liability in the borrower's capital structure;
- the credit risk is determined primarily by the variability of the cash flow generated by the collateral (rather than the independent capacity of a broader commercial enterprise).

Risk weights for unsecured portions of claims past due for more than 90 days: The risk weight for the unsecured part of a claim (other than a claim secured by an eligible residential mortgage) that is past due for more than 90 days is:

- 150% if the specific provisions are less than 20% of the past due claim;
- 100% if the specific provisions are 20% or more, but less than 50%, of the past due claim; or
- 50% if the specific provisions are 50% or more of the past due claim.

The risk weight for the unsecured part of a claim secured by an eligible residential mortgage that is past due for more than 90 days is:

- 100% if the specific provisions are less than 20% of the past due claim; or
- 50% if the specific provisions are 20% or more of the past due claim.

In this case, "eligible residential mortgage" means a mortgage on a residential property that is, (a) occupied by the counterparty for residential use; or (b) rented out (on a non-commercial basis) for residential use.

Risk-weighted assets approach — off-balance-sheet items: Calculating total risk-weighted items: The bank's total risk-weighted off-balance-sheet items is the sum of the risk-weighted amounts of its market-related and non-market-related off-balance-sheet items. An off-balance-sheet item must be converted to a credit equivalent amount before it can be risk-weighted. The risk-weighted amount of an off-balance-sheet item is calculated as follows:

Firstly, convert the notional principal amount of the item to its on-balance-sheet equivalent (credit equivalent amount).

Secondly, multiply the resulting credit equivalent amount by the relevant risk weights applicable to the claim or asset.

The risk division must include all market-related off-balance-sheet items (including on-balance-sheet unrealized gains on market-related off-balance-sheet items) in calculating its risk-weighted credit exposures. A market-related item must be valued at its current market price.

Risk weightings for Islamic financial contracts: This section describes and sets out the risk weights applicable to the main types of Islamic financial products offered by the bank. The risk weight to be applied to the exposure under a contract of a particular type may differ: (a) at different stages of the contract; or (b) depending on the enterprise or asset to which the contract relates.

Treatment of Murabahah and related contracts: The bank is exposed to credit risk under a murabahah contract if the obligor fails to pay the agreed selling price under the contract. Therefore, the bank is subject to a capital charge for credit risk exposure once the asset is sold and payment is due to the bank.

For a murabahah for purchase order (MPO) contract, the bank is exposed to credit risk if the obligor (purchase order) defaults on its obligation to purchase the asset. Because the bank has recourse against the obligor to purchase the asset at the agreed price, the credit risk exposure commences once the bank acquires the asset. In an MPO contract, the bank is also exposed to credit risk if the obligor fails to pay the agreed price in accordance with the agreed terms.

Treatment of Istisna and related contracts: Under an istisna contract, the bank is exposed to credit risk if the obligor fails to pay the price, whether during the manufacturing or construction stage or upon completion of the asset.

Table 5.4. Credit risk weights for murabahah.

Stage of Contract	Credit Risk Weight
Asset is available for sale and on the bank's balance sheet	N/A
Asset has been sold and title transferred, and selling price is due to the bank	Based on the customer's type and rating

Table 5.5. Credit risk weights for MPO.

Stage of Contract	Credit Risk Weight
Asset available for sale and on the bank's balance sheet	Based on the customer's type and rating, with the applicable risk weight applied to the acquisition cost less any cash collateral
Asset has been sold and title transferred, and selling price is due to bank	Based on the customer's type and rating

Under a parallel istisna contract, the bank, as the purchaser of the asset, is exposed to credit risk if the seller fails to deliver the asset at the agreed time and in accordance with the initial istisna buyer's specifications. The parallel istisna seller's failure to deliver the asset does not discharge the bank's obligation to deliver the asset to the obligor under the initial istisna contract. The bank is also exposed to the potential loss of fulfilling the shortfall or acquiring the asset elsewhere.

The bank will not create an istisna exposure against a parallel istisna exposure.

Treatment of ijarah and related contracts: The bank that is the lessor under an ijarah contract is exposed to credit risk if the lessee fails to pay the rental amount in accordance with the lease agreement. In addition, the bank is exposed to credit risk if the lessee (lease orderer) defaults on its obligation to lease the asset. In this situation,

Table 5.6. Credit risk weights for istisna without parallel istisna.

Stage of Contract	Credit Risk Weight
Unbilled work-in-process	Based on the ultimate counterparty's type and rating
Unpaid billed work-in-process	Based on the ultimate counterparty's type and rating

Table 5.7. Credit risk weights for istisna with parallel istisna.

Stage of Contract	Credit Risk Weight
Unbilled work-in-process	Based on the ultimate counterparty's type and rating
Unpaid billed work-in-process	Based on the ultimate counterparty's type and rating

the bank may lease or dispose of the asset to another party, but it is also exposed to credit risk if the lessee is not able to compensate it for the losses incurred arising from the disposal of the asset.

In an ijarah contract, the underlying asset is not eligible collateral for purposes of credit risk mitigation. An ijarah contract is treated as a financing agreement and must be risk-weighted in accordance with Table 5.8.

An operating ijarah is treated as an investment and must be risk-weighted in accordance with the following sections, depending on the leased asset and how the investment is made.

If the investment is in real estate and the investment is made by the bank itself (direct investment exposure), the risk-weighted amount of the direct investment exposure must be calculated by multiplying the carrying value of the asset by 150%.

If the investment is in real estate and the bank makes it indirectly through a subsidiary, its share of equity investment in the capital of that subsidiary must be risk-weighted at 150%, and any financing provided by the bank to the subsidiary must be risk-weighted at the same rate.

Table 5.8. Risk weights assets for leasing.

Stage of Contract	Credit Risk Weight
Asset available for lease and on the bank's balance sheet	Based on the lessee's type and rating, with the applicable risk weight applied to the acquisition cost
Lease contract has become binding and rental payments due from lessee	Based on the lessee's type and rating, with the applicable risk weight applied to net receivables (that is, the total estimated value of lease receivables for the remaining period plus the residual value of the leased asset at the end of the contract)

If the investment is in real estate and the bank makes it indirectly (indirect investment exposure) through a joint venture or partnership, the indirect investment exposure must be risk-weighted at:

- 300% if the bank has majority ownership over the asset and can exit the investment at any time; or
- 400% if the bank does not have majority ownership over the asset or cannot exit the investment at any time.

If the investment is in physical assets (such as commercial vehicles, passenger cars, ships, aircraft, railway machinery, computers, business machines, and other types of equipment), the exposure must be risk-weighted at:

- 300% if the bank has majority ownership over the asset and can exit the investment at any time; or
- 400% if the bank does not have majority ownership over the asset or cannot exit the investment at any time.

Treatment of mudarabah and related contracts: This rule applies to risk weighting for an exposure arising from a mudarabah contract, except where the regulatory authority examines the exposure and determines it to be an equity investment. Credit risk weights for mudarabah investments (other than project finance):

The reader can refer to Tables 5.9 and 5.10.

Table 5.9. Risk weights for private commercial enterprise.

Enterprise or Asset	Credit Risk Weight
Private commercial enterprise to undertake trading activities in foreign exchange, shares, or commodities	N/A
Private commercial enterprise to undertake a business venture other than trading in foreign exchange, shares, or commodities	Before maturity: 400% of the contributed amount less any specific provisions (or 300% if the funds may be withdrawn by the firm within 5 business days after giving notice of withdrawal) On maturity: after the mudarib has agreed to pay back the firm's initial investment, based on the mudarib's type and rating
Placement in the interbank market	Based on the customer's type and rating

Table 5.10. Credit risk weights for mudarabah investments in project finance.

Stage of Contract	Credit Risk Weight
Before completion: unbilled work-in-process inventory	400% on unbilled inventory less any amount held in the repayment account
On completion: after certification from the ultimate counterparty, where the amount is receivable by the bank from the mudarib (for progress payment to the mudarib from the ultimate counterparty)	Based on the ultimate counterparty's type and rating or Based on the mudarib's type and rating: – for any amount already paid by the ultimate counterparty to the mudarib; or – if the mudarib undertakes to bear the default risk of the ultimate counterparty as part of the mudarabah contract

5.7. Credit Risk System and Controls

The bank has comprehensive credit risk management systems appropriate to the nature, scale, and complexity of its operations. These systems should enable the bank to identify, quantify, monitor, and control credit risks and to ensure that capital resources are available to cover the risks assumed. Credit risk arises from financings, but there are other sources of credit risk such as trade finance and acceptances; interbank transactions; commitments and guarantees; and profit rates, foreign exchange, and equity holdings.

The bank develops, implements, and maintains a written credit risk strategy and policy consistent with its degree of risk tolerance, level of capital available for credit activities, and credit management expertise. This policy must provide sound, well-defined risk management criteria that are to be applied when granting credit. It must clearly indicate the amount and nature of credit risk that the bank wishes to incur.

The policy should set out, where appropriate, the amounts and terms and conditions under which counterparties or clients may be eligible or ineligible for credit. This policy must include a provisioning policy approved by the bank's governing body or other appropriate body to which the governing body has delegated this responsibility, and it must be approved by the governing body. This policy obliges the bank at intervals appropriate to the nature, scale, and complexity of its activities to review and update the credit risk policy.

5.8. Concentration Risk

This section sets out the requirements for the bank's risk division to identify, measure, evaluate, manage, and control or mitigate concentrations of risk. This section also sets limits on the bank's exposures to individual counterparties and connected counterparties.

Connected counterparties: The concept of parties being connected to one another is used in these rules in relation to counterparties or issuers to which the bank has exposures. Connected counterparties are the basis for the measurement of concentration risk and large exposures. It is of course possible for the bank's related parties to be connected counterparties (such as when the bank has exposures to them).

A party is connected to another party if they are linked by cross guarantees, common ownership, common management, or one having the ability to exercise control over the other, whether direct or indirect.

Financial interdependence — that is, the financial soundness of one may affect the financial soundness of the other, or any combination of the factors mentioned above.

A counterparty may be connected to another counterparty by other linkages that, in the risk division's assessment, constitute a single risk. A connected party can be an individual or other entity.

Concentration risk to the bank arises if the bank is exposed to one counterparty or to two or more counterparties that are not truly independent of each other, and the total of the exposures to the counterparty or counterparties is large enough to endanger the firm's liquidity or solvency.

Management of exposures: Large exposure means a gross exposure to a counterparty or connected counterparties that is 10% or greater of the bank's regulatory capital. Gross exposure to a counterparty or connected counterparties is the total of on-balance-sheet and off-balance-sheet exposures, debt securities held by the firm, and equity exposures.

In calculating the gross exposure, the following is to be included:

- the outstanding balances of all loans and advances, including balances with other banks;
- holdings of debt or equity securities;
- unused off-balance-sheet commitments, whether revocable or irrevocable; and
- the credit equivalent amounts of all market-related transactions.

However, when calculating gross exposure, do not include claims, equity investments, or other exposures deducted from the bank's capital; exposures arising in the course of settlement of market-related contracts; and exposures to the extent that they have been written off.

Limits on exposures: The bank must not become exposed without limit to a single counterparty. The bank must not provide a general guarantee of the counterparty's obligations.

The total of the bank's net exposures to any one counterparty or any one group of connected counterparties must not exceed 25% of the bank's regulatory capital. The total of all net large exposures for the bank must not exceed 800% of its capital. The bank may apply to the regulatory authority for approval of a proposed exposure exceeding the limits set forth in the above section. An approval is granted only in exceptional circumstances and only after the bank satisfies the authority that the proposed exposure does not expose the bank to excessive risk. Banks measure, classify, and make provisions for each large exposure individually. Banks notify the regulatory authority if any bank is concerned that risk concentrations or large exposures might significantly affect its capital adequacy. The notice must describe the bank's proposed measures to address its concerns.

5.9. Risk Monitoring

Credit risk must be monitored at the single counterparty and portfolio levels. The details of each component are explained in this section.

5.9.1. *Monitoring single counterparty and portfolio credit*

Monitoring financing on a continual basis is required to obtain "early warning" for any corrective action needed.

Once the bank has granted a financing product, it must be managed actively to ensure that it is repaid. Credit monitoring is one of the most important responsibilities of the credit officer and the front office staff. The customer's credit rating, assigned when granting financing, serves as the benchmark against which the credit officer evaluates the customer's current status.

Credit monitoring by the credit officer includes procedures to:

- ensure that credit risk officers understand the current financial condition of the customer;
- ensure that prior approval of the credit risk team will be mandatory before extending line of credit to new customers;

- ensure that all corporate financing is in compliance with existing covenants;
- ensure that payments are made on time and timely action is taken for non-payments or partial payments;
- ensure that projected cash flows on major financing deals will meet debt servicing requirements;
- ensure that where applicable, collateral provides adequate coverage relative to the borrower's current condition; and
- identify and classify potential problem credits on a timely basis.

Credit officers may use four sources of information to monitor the customer: other departments/functions within the bank that have transactions with the customer; major suppliers of the customer; who may have information on the customer's ability to honor payments for operating activities; other financial institutions; and the customer itself.

Periodic review is important in monitoring and controlling credit risk and should be responsive to indicators of potential or actual deterioration in credit risk. The ratings assigned to single borrowers at the time the credit is granted must be reviewed periodically, and customers should be assigned a new rating when conditions either improve or deteriorate.

Early warning systems: Credit monitoring requires close review of customers to detect signs that the customer may have difficulty repaying the credit. Such early warnings are necessary to maximize the effect of corrective action and to minimize potential losses.

Warning signs: Credit officers should be aware of the following signals that may indicate potential problems:

- delays in the receipt of financial statements, especially if the credit agreement contains a covenant that requires delivery within a specific timeframe;
- abrupt changes in a customer's basic business plans;
- unanticipated changes in the composition of management or the board;
- frequent requests for extensions of the maturity of the credit agreement that may indicate abnormal cash flow situations; and
- delaying payments to suppliers, other creditors, or employees.

Action plan: Early identification allows time to gather the facts and develop a strategy. When a credit officer identifies a problem customer, he or she should take the following steps:

- Further analyze the customer's problem.
- Gather information on total institutional exposure to the customer.
- Review credit documentation, guarantees, and collateral agreements.
- Establish a workout plan for corrective action.

Financing deals identified through the early warning system to be in a deteriorating situation should be subject to additional oversight and monitoring, for example, through more frequent visits from credit officers and inclusion on a "watch list" that is regularly reviewed by the risk and policy committee and CRO.

5.9.2. *Monitoring whole portfolio — Analysis of whole portfolio to identify any concentrations*

The bank also needs to monitor the overall composition and quality of the financing portfolio on a periodic basis.

Credit-related problems can arise due to concentrations within the credit portfolio. Concentrations of risk can take many forms and can arise whenever a significant number of credits have similar risk characteristics. The ability to identify portfolio concentrations, such as those listed above, is contingent on the information available from the bank's information system and whether the exposures can be aggregated across the bank's entire portfolio on a timely and accurate basis.

The bank may need to use alternative strategies to reduce or mitigate concentrations. Actions may include:

- pricing for the additional risk by increasing product prices for those customers where a concentration exists;
- mitigating the risk by seeking additional collateral from those customers where a concentration exists; and
- gradually reducing exposures by not extending, renewing, or rolling over, freezing further lending to this segment until the

concentration is reduced, selling in the secondary markets, or via securitization through Sukuks.

Summary

Credit risk is the risk that a counterparty to a transaction fails to perform according to the terms and conditions of the contract or suffers credit deterioration, thus causing the bank to suffer a loss.

Payment obligations arise principally from traditional on-balance sheet credit business (credit risk). They also arise from settlement risk when payments due are not paid by the third party to the bank on the value date.

The criteria for assessing default are the following:

- facilities within which any repayment or partial repayment is outstanding for a period of more than 90 days;
- all facilities put on non-accrual status (i.e., profit is suspended);
- all facilities designated as non-performing;
- all facilities classified as Stage 3 under FAS 30 by the bank (equivalent to IFRS 9);
- all facilities with a credit rating of default class;
- imminent probability of foreclosure of facility or repossession of collateral due to insolvency or other financial difficulty, which may indicate inability to recover exposure;
- customers against which the bank has taken legal proceedings.

The amount of credit risk principally depends on the probability of default (PD), the probability that the counterparty may default before the asset matures, loss given default (LGD), and the percentage of exposure lost if the counterparty defaults. It also depends on the amount of the exposure at default (EAD) and the potential exposure of the bank to a default on some future date.

Concentration risks may arise on a portfolio level (e.g., geographical, industry/sector). Possible causes for credit losses are a lack of integrity of third parties, diminished repayment ability of third parties, a deteriorating economic situation, and transfer restrictions by actions of foreign states (country risk). Sources of credit risk include accounts receivable in murabahah contracts, counterparty risk in salam contracts, accounts receivable and counterparty risk in istisna contracts, lease payments receivable in ijarah contracts, and capital impairment from investments based on mudarabah or musharakah contracts held in the banking book.

References

Bellalah M and S Zouari (2015). Portfolio credit risk models and name concentration issues: Theory and simulations. *International Journal of Business.*

Bellalah M, M Bellalah and H Heschmi (2015). The recent financial crisis: Is there an equity premium puzzle? *Research in International Business and Finance.*

Bellalah M, S Zouari and O Levyne (2016). The performance of hybrid models in the assessment of default risk. *Economic Modeling*, 52, 259–265.

Bellalah M, C Soke Fun Ho, O Masood and A Abdul Rehman (2012a). Syariah accounting and compliant screening practices. *Qualitative Research in Financial Markets*, 4.

Bellalah M, Z Chayeh and H Miniaoui (2012b). Advanced risk profile analysis of Islamic equity investment: Evidence from the American, Asian and European market. *Finance-India.*

Bellalah M, Z Chayeh and H Miniaoui (2012c). Empirical evidence on Islamic equity investment from the American, Asian and European market. *Finance-India.*

Bellalah M and O Masood (2015). Role of accountants and fair value accounting leading towards the global financial crisis. *International Journal of Business*, 20(1).

Website

Association Europe Finances Régulations | AEFR: https://www.aefr.eu/en/article/182 (2025).

Chapter 6

Managing Retail Lending Credit

Chapter Outline

1. Section 6.1 explains governance structures and the role of corporate remedial and retail collection units, with abbreviations given in Table 6.1.
2. Section 6.2 is devoted to target market and customer segments and products offered.
3. Section 6.3 analyzes the general lending principles and lending principles at the chapter and organizational levels.
4. Section 6.4 studies credit initiation, pricing, credit approval, and the role of documentation and credit administration.

Table 6.1. Abbreviations.

Abbreviation	Definition
The Board	The Board of Directors
BRC	Board Risk Committee
The management	The Executive Management
CEO	The Chief Executive Officer
CB	Central Bank
GMRC	General Management Risk Committee
SOP	Standard Operating Procedure
EOSB	End of Service benefit
AEL	Approved Employer list

(*Continued*)

Table 6.1. (*Continued*)

Abbreviation	Definition
ROD	Revolving overdraft
RCRD	Retail Credit Risk Department
DSR	Debt Servicing Ratio
HO	Head Office
CCD	Credit Control Desk
AML	Anti-Money Laundering
KYC	Know Your Customer
CG	Company Guarantee
T/D	Time Deposits

Introduction

The retail lending credit chapter sets out chapter guidelines for the retail banking business of a bank, aligning with the mission statement, legal and regulatory framework, and the strategic plan and risk appetite of the bank. The head of retail banking is responsible for retail lending credit, which is reviewed by the general management risk committee (GMRC) and general management credit committee (GMCC) and approved by the board of directors (the board) of the bank. The chapter details the high-level organization, authorities, and processes relating to risk management. Risk management covers all risks, including credit, market, and operational risk. It involves processes from origination to approval and ongoing control, review, maintenance, and optimization of exposures.

It is important to note that this chapter is based on my professional experience in several financial institutions. For further analysis, refer to Bellalah and Zouari (2015) and Bellalah *et al.* (2016).

6.1. Governance Structure

The bank follows sound risk governance principles, which emphasize clear roles, responsibilities, and reporting lines to ensure adequate segregation of duties, allowing independence and avoiding conflicts of interest in pursuit of the bank's business objectives and strategy.

The front office and sales teams are the primary point of contact with customers and own the responsibility of evaluating for compliance with credit and approving credit applications for retail customers. Retail lending and sales officers should complete all reasonable checks and enquiries to know their customers and conduct necessary due diligence, including required know your customer (KYC) compliance procedures, prior to extending credit facilities to any customer.

For further analysis, the reader can refer to the following website: https://bankpolicies.com.

The retail credit risk department is entrusted with the primary responsibility of evaluating compliance with credit chapters and approving credit applications for retail customers. Retail credit staff is expected to ensure that parameters as per the chapter are met for all credit approvals.

The department independently assesses all credit proposals and also rechecks the accuracy and completeness of the data. It may recommend amendments to bring the transaction within the bank's risk appetite and then send it to the appropriate higher authority level for approval, as per the DOA manual.

The credit operations department is responsible for ensuring credit facilities are disbursed in accordance with the terms sanctioned by approving authorities. It is therefore expected to exercise the necessary due diligence and to ascertain that all stipulated conditions precedent have been either met or waivers for them have been approved by duly authorized officials prior to enabling the credit facilities for disbursement.

The respective product units in operations are responsible for ensuring standard documentation for the facilities in accordance with the chapter guidelines has been obtained and kept in safe custody in conformity with procedures.

The following measures need to be in place and should be considered at all times:

- monitoring portfolio performance;
- vetting from a credit risk point of view all new product programs proposed by the retail banking group — note that the operational risk assessment process (ORAP) exercises for all new product launches and key process changes will be conducted by operational risk;

- developing standard MIS reports for analyzing the retail portfolio with respect to performance, profitability, and delinquency of individual schemes and on a portfolio level;
- suggesting amendments to policies periodically based on portfolio performance;
- generating and checking transaction activity and identifying potential trends in delinquencies;
- liaison with external agencies for verification of customer details on a case-by-case basis as and when required;
- liaison with law enforcement agencies to prevent fraud and skips.

Corporate remedial and retail collection unit:

Their primary role and responsibility is to monitor and manage delinquent and non-performing accounts, maintain good asset quality, and recover bad debts. A separate section on collections and recovery details the functions, policies, processes, and organization within this department, some of which are summarized as follows:

- The collections unit has the responsibility to track "soft bucket" delinquent accounts (1–90 days overdue installments) and to closely interact and follow up with RBG/branches on prompt follow-up collection efforts by these units to regularize missed payments.
- The collections and recovery unit has the responsibility to pursue defaulting borrowers in the "hard bucket" (90–180 days overdue installments) and non-performing loans, including skip cases, with the assistance of an outsourced third party.
- Apply diligent recovery procedures through contacting employers (for information on employees and release of assigned EOSB), filing police and civil cases against defaulting and absconding borrowers where necessary, and pursuing expatriate absconders/skip cases through overseas collection agencies.
- Maintain follow-up reports of irregular accounts under buckets 1–6 and upgrading/downgrading such accounts based on their performance.
- Submit periodic delinquency analysis reports of the retail portfolio and highlight trends and patterns in delinquency.

- Negotiate, document, and implement (after required level of approval) agreed settlements with defaulters and any associated write-offs on non-performing accounts overdue for more than 180 days, excluding mortgages.
- Ensure that the retail NPL portfolio is covered by an adequate level of specific provisions and satisfies internal and external auditors and central bank examiners on the sufficiency of provisions to cover potential loan losses.
- Recommend required entries for specific provisions on the retail credit portfolio.
- Appoint local and overseas collection agencies and monitor their performance and incentive payment entitlements.
- Process and follow up until receipt of insurance claims and any EOSB for all deceased accounts.
- Coordinate with in-house and external legal counsel on police cases and court litigation under the oversight and supervision of the legal department.

6.2. Types of Borrowers and Products

6.2.1. *Target market and customer segment*

Target market (TM) identifies the acceptable profile of borrowers for a product or a given range of products. The development of TM allows to pre-screen borrowers against prescribed minimum terms of borrower profiles and thereby accelerate the initiation, preparation, and approval process. The TM, lending criteria, pricing, credit terms, and other parameters of each retail credit product are set out in a product program, currently known as retail credit product programs and procedures, and product campaign.

Retail credit is primarily intended to be offered to salaried, self-employed, and high-net-worth individuals (HNIs) to whom the bank extends credit based on their repayment capacity.

The two principal retail banking client segments are individuals who typically require retail credit facilities (personal and vehicle loans, credit cards, etc.) and standard banking services. Salaried individuals service loan repayments through their salary and self-employed via business income.

And HNIs require personalized priority banking services.

A salary transfer and EOSB assignment is a mandatory requirement for personal loans to salaried individuals, except for government employees, short-term loans offered to affluent expatriate salaried employees working for approved employers with specific end uses (e.g., rent or school fees), and disbursement to the end entity and self-employed business owners.

The terms and conditions and eligibility criteria for various retail products are periodically reviewed and, where required, amended by the GMRC.

6.2.2. *Products offered*

The bank offers various retail credit products, which can be either secured or unsecured. Retail banking services are provided to meet the banking and credit needs of individuals (primarily the bank's customers) and include all assets, liabilities, and other revenue-generating activities and services provided to individual customers. As it develops its retail banking capabilities, new retail products are introduced.

The current ranges of retail credit products offered to eligible employees in the list of approved companies and self-employed individuals are outlined as follows:

Personal loans are offered to individuals against assignment of salary and EOSB to meet their needs and to self-employed individuals. This includes cash flow loans for short-term finance requirements.

Vehicle loans are offered to individuals maintaining their current account (with or without a salary transfer through assigned salaries and EOSB) and against the registration/mortgage of vehicles purchased and the assignment of comprehensive insurance.

Credit cards are issued to salaried and self-employed individuals based on their financial status and credit history, as well as other surrogate programs.

Revolving overdraft (ROD) facilities are permitted to salaried individuals employed by a company on the approved list of companies with a good repayment history and excellent conduct of account. ROD limits have validity for one year, and renewal is required annually.

Mortgages in retail, or retail mortgages, are secured loans against completed residential properties offered to salaried and self-employed individuals based on their financial status and credit history.

6.3. Lending Principles

6.3.1. *General lending principles*

All lending to retail borrowers is undertaken as part of the approved product programs and standard operating procedures and is based on several criteria.

A clearly defined TM must be established for relevant approved retail credit products. The TM identifies the acceptable profile of borrowers for the product or range of products offered. Business must not be undertaken outside the defined TM and business strategies — except in exceptional cases and, even then, with adequate mitigants. Facilities are granted to creditworthy individuals who are in regular employment or are self-employed. Facilities are granted only to those individuals who are either nationals or residents, except for mortgage loans, which may be permitted to non-residents.

Credit can only be extended when there is verifiable income. All lending to retail borrowers takes into consideration the repayment capacity of the borrower in line with the following two policies. The first is the total installments of loan repayments, which should be commensurate with monthly income and the borrower's repayment capacity. The second is that income earned and used for the computation of debt burden should be proven, verified, recurring, and non-speculative.

The retail credit department does not extend credit to certain categories of borrowers as defined under the list of non-preferred categories.

Special emphasis is placed on the anti-money laundering and know-your-customer norms when lending to retail borrowers. Compliance with all applicable statutory and regulatory directives is ensured in all cases. Propriety and ethical standards are taken into account in all credit decisions.

Credit risk for all borrowers is assessed using appropriate consumer product parameters. Credit can only be granted upon full and satisfactory completion of all facility documentation and when the bank confidently expects it to be repaid by the borrower.

A signed, undated cheque is required before providing a facility. Any waiver on obtaining undated cheques needs to be explicitly approved by the appropriate authority through the credit application process. Retail credit products are generally structured and offered under principles of criteria-based lending, which involves the evaluation of customer information against prescribed criteria as defined in the product program and retail credit chapter. Individuals and retail customers who meet the criteria are normally eligible for the credit facilities, and requested facilities are processed and approved on a fast-track basis. Where the customer fails to meet all or any of the criteria, exceptional approval must be obtained as per the authorized delegation matrix.

All retail products must be covered by a product program developed by the retail banking group and approved by the GMRC. The product program describes the type of retail credit product, principal terms, target markets, and the credit criteria for the product offering.

SOPs support the functional-level credit policies by setting process standards for the entire credit risk cycle, from initiation and acceptance and loan portfolio management to collection and use of scorecards. The standards set the performance criteria by which actions can be measured for compliance with the stated policies and objectives.

Statistical and behavioral scoring models support new customer acquisitions in a controlled environment with the flexibility to enhance or reduce exposure. The evaluation of customer applications becomes an objective, score-driven exercise, with branch and retail credit staff providing the necessary inputs for exceptions.

The composition of the bank's product portfolio and lending parameters can change from time to time to reflect the prevailing business environment and changes in the bank's resources, structure, and overall strategic focus. However, the guiding principles underlying the extension of any credit remain as follows: mitigation of risk, high asset quality of overall portfolio/risk, maximization of returns, minimization of credit losses, and due diligence and ethical practices.

The primary source of repayment for a salaried individual is through monthly salary and business income for self-employed individuals. Such sources of income should be computed and substantiated via relevant documentation. In the case of government or semi-government departments which do not issue formal assignment letters for EOSB, this requirement may be selectively waived jointly or individually by the EVP of retail banking or the VP of retail credit risk.

Changing circumstances may adversely affect the current primary source of income, which in turn affects repayment capabilities. To mitigate or reduce this risk, secondary sources of repayment, such as financial assets held, spouse income, and other known and verified sources of income free of any commitments (though they cannot be specifically assigned to the bank for repayment of facilities), should be granted while evaluating a case on a best-effort basis.

The bank is compliant with all the requirements under the IFRS 9 standards. The bank's risk management function's involvement in the assessment and measurement of accounting expected losses is essential to ensuring adequate allowances in accordance with IFRS 9.

6.3.2. *Lending principles at the chapter and organization levels*

The management committee must inform and obtain approval from the board risk committee regarding the introduction of new products and the migration of products undertaken by the bank. While developing and offering retail credit products and services to meet customer needs, the safety and protection of the bank's assets and interests, as well as the reputation and image of the bank, should always be kept in focus by retail sales officers in the retail banking group/branches. Retail credit proposals initiated and recommended by the front office sales team are independently reviewed by the retail credit risk department for conformity with policies and any other exceptions or risk factors.

The head of each business unit in the retail banking group has the personal responsibility for identifying and managing the risks within their portfolios. As line managers are closest to their markets, they must understand the risk–reward dynamics of each product offering and manage them effectively. They also ensure adherence to the parameters of the retail credit and individual product programs.

The EVP of retail banking has the responsibility for establishing a risk management culture that promotes sound judgment, awareness of market conditions, and a balance between risk and profitability objectives. This individual ensures that an underlying product program supports all retail credit products. The retail credit risk unit maintains a system of checks and balances for the extension of credit, comprising the four elements.

First, an independent credit risk management function — performed by the VP of retail credit risk, reporting to the chief risk officer. The VP of retail credit risk acts as a counterweight to the sales and marketing functions of the retail banking group and is a major contributor in supporting the financial health and profitability of the retail credit portfolio.

Second, the retail credit risk unit reviews all retail credit transactions and ensures they are in compliance with the product program parameters and highlights exceptions for approval or decline by the VP of retail credit risk, the EVP of retail banking, or other retail credit approvers.

Third, every extension of retail credit must be approved by a proper delegated official who has been delegated retail credit lending approval authority.

Fourth, periodic independent reviews, quality assurance checks, and internal audit inspections must be carried out across all functional units by the concerned authorities.

The CRO, together with the VP of retail credit risk and the EVP of retail banking, establishes and monitors overall lending rules, policies, and guidelines for the retail credit business to ensure credit risk and portfolio composition in all retail business lines are within the bank's risk appetite. They ensure that an effective framework of policies, procedures, and controls is in place to manage operational, legal, regulatory, and compliance risks relating to retail banking activities.

6.4. Credit Granting Process

The sequence of tasks involved in retail's credit granting process indicates the processes and responsibilities of the various departments and personnel involved in the credit process. The credit granting framework applies to new borrowers, existing customers, and repeat customers who use the same credit processes and controls.

6.4.1. *Credit initiation*

The principal acceptance criterion for credit extension is the credit quality of the customer, which is a function of the customer's inherent ability and willingness to fulfill their obligations under the terms and conditions of the credit facilities extended by the bank. The identified source of repayment is of paramount importance. The repayment source is normally the customer's salary in the case of salaried customers, whereas in the case of self-employed individuals it would be their income. However, under certain circumstances, it is also acceptable for the repayment to come from other sources, so long as the source of repayment is clearly identified prior to credit extension and is deemed secure at the bank's primary repayment source.

The process starts with the written retail credit application form from the customer. Designated sales officers and sales staff within the RBG unit/branches originate retail credit applications. These applications should be accompanied by documentation as per chapter parameters supporting the request and credit decisions by the retail credit approvers. Line officers at RBG units are expected to exercise due care to ensure that all material information is disclosed and accuracy is verified. Guidelines for completing the applications must be followed strictly in all cases to prevent rejections due to incomplete data.

Whether the applicant is an existing customer or a new customer, a firm commitment on loan approval should not be made or communicated during the initial contact and before verification of customer data. Customers must be advised of the documentation procedures of the bank and the estimated time required for the final credit decision. All information provided by the customer must be verified and evaluated by the retail banking group to assess the credit risk involved. Some of the common courses and steps of credit verification are mentioned as follows.

First, bank statements and financial documents are used to verify and calculate regular monthly income (according to retail product parameters), recurring monthly debt-related payment obligations, spending and saving patterns, returned cheques, etc. An original sighting by the front office staff of such financial transactions allows one to assess how well the customer manages credit risk.

Second, contact point verification due diligence checks and verification of the customer's employment status and personal data, such as residential and contact details provided by the customer in the application, are done. Third, the central bank report for bounced/returned cheques should be reviewed for the applicant's track record and to ascertain financial discipline, highlighting trends and/or liquidity strains. Fourth, the central bank database for black-listed customers with a default history is checked. Fifth, a credit bureau for customer credit reports is maintained.

Before processing any credit application, adequate knowledge of the customer's/borrower's financial resources and commitments and credit history is essential. Personal identification documents should be obtained. In addition, financial information and net worth statements from borrowers and guarantors (if any) should be collected and verified. Emphasis must be on verifying current personal debt levels and account conduct by checking account activity from recent bank statements and obtaining copies of checks and vouchers (wherever necessary) for further verification of transactions.

Employer history, educational qualifications, length and variety of experience, specializations, and professional accreditations, etc., are recognized as important indicators of the employment stability and prospects of a retail customer. It is necessary for retail sales staff to carefully check the bank's internal database and the central bank's database for any prior negative credit experience or black-listed customers before processing an application for a new customer. The customer's existing debt, monthly commitments, and repayment capacity for proposed facilities have to be carefully assessed. Ensuring the accuracy and consistent determination of the DSR (an individual's total fixed monthly debt service obligations relative to monthly income) must be in line with the credit and product parameters as well as central bank guidelines.

RBG units/branches also ensure that all information available at the point of application is captured accurately in the loan origination system, i.e., application form information and other details. As a general rule, a credit application is appraised and approved by the retail credit risk department if it falls under their credit approval authority. Credit applications requiring exceptional approval should be escalated to relevant approval authorities based on the approval/delegation matrix. Wherever possible, the bank should use the scorecards for assessing the creditworthiness of the applicants.

In the event that no scorecard is implemented and in use for a particular product, the credit appraisal will be solely based on the eligibility criteria and the chapter guidelines.

6.4.2. *Pricing*

Pricing can be determined as per the delegation of authority manual.

6.4.3. *Credit approval*

All verifications and assessments during the process of appraisal, assessment, and recommendations of facilities should be recorded. Besides the documentary information collected from borrowers, the central bank database, etc., any information verbally obtained during discussions and meetings should be recorded in the form of remarks and attachment memos included in the application. Refer the bank's DOA manual for further details on the appropriate approval authorities for all credit transactions.

6.4.4. *Documentation and credit administration*

The respective product units in retail operations have the responsibility to review all retail credit proposals to ensure the bank's procedural requirements are met and disbursement is made only after obtaining properly completed documents. All components of documentation shall be determined by the respective product programs. The respective product units in operations are responsible for the comprehensive review of all facility or guarantee agreements received with respect to a credit application. It ensures that all agreements are executed as per the mandate. The agreements should also be reviewed for accuracy against executed documents to ensure that all compliance requirements have been met.

6.4.5. *Disbursement*

The disbursement of credit facilities should be made only after obtaining properly completed and perfected documentation and registering charges as per the product program guidelines or as approved by the credit department. Creating a loan and/or setting up an overdraft limit and/or setting up a card credit limit constitutes the first act of disbursement. The disbursement of retail credit facilities is centralized at the retail operations, with each retail product handled by the respective unit card operations, operation loans, operation mortgages. Only authorized officials at the centralized unit are authorized to input retail credit limits into the bank's system and disburse the credit facilities as per the terms of approval. The disbursement of the credit facilities should be after the perfection of the security documents.

6.4.6. *Collection management*

The collection phase of the credit cycle covers accounts that have failed to make one or more contractual payments — that is, they have become delinquent and are in default of their contractual obligations to repay.

Collateral risk: The assignment of salaries and EOSB are the main securities and repayment source for retail credit products. It is to be ensured that the calculation of EOSB is completely correct and in line with labor laws and relevant employer policies. One of the most important responsibilities of the RBG is to obtain the salary transfer assignment letter STAL in the bank's standard format and verify the authenticity of the employer's signature.

Mortgage loans on financed properties should be pledged to the bank. Auto loans and vehicles financed should be mortgaged to the bank.

Economic risk: Changes in economic and business cycles may adversely affect sales and profits of a business, which has an effect on our portfolio since retail lending largely caters to salaried employees. This risk can be reduced to some extent by lending only to employees of the bank's approved list of companies.

Periodic risk analysis of sectors of the economy in which approved employers are operating is performed to ensure stability of the business/sector; and periodic review and updating of the list of approved employers are also carried out.

Concentration risk: Diversification in retail products is best achieved by spreading the loan portfolio across markets, organizations, economic sectors, and other key groups of individuals who are important to the demographic profile. The retail strategy endeavors to position our credits predominantly in segments within targeted sectors with the highest potential for stable employment and financial performance over the medium- to long-term.

Operational risk: This is the risk of credit losses due to failure or non-compliance with the bank's credit, operations procedures, and systems relating to the assessment, disbursement, timely follow-up, and administration of credit policies.

Legal and documentation risk: Risk of loss due to incomplete or deficient documents, retail facilities and security documents should always be prepared in line with the bank's approved standard formats, which have been approved by retail credit and legal. The legal department should also approve any new format of standard documents or amendments to standard documents. All required documents should be completed with care and signatures verified.

Fraud/dishonesty risk: This refers to borrowers obtaining a credit facility by providing incorrect or false information deliberately, with the intention of defrauding the bank for the borrowed funds. Here, the branch/retail credit risk staff's maturity and experience, as well as due diligence in checking loan application data, are necessary to help recognize a potential fraud. Timely training of staff, awareness, and communications of fraud risk indicators to staff (payroll/outsource) ensures adequate diligence in the activity performed.

Delinquency analysis: The retail collections and recovery department (whose functions are covered in more detail in the collections chapter) provides a periodic (minimum quarterly) analysis of all retail credit delinquencies and NPLs. The analysis of NPLs is a valuable tool to identify trends, consistent behavioral patterns, and common reasons for default among customer groups and specific product campaigns and to influence appropriate amendments to the chapter and product programs.

It is important to identify potential fraud or probable defaults before a loan is granted. Due diligence verification and validation of key customer and employment-related data, as provided in the loan application form, is an important responsibility and duty of the retail sales team and branches that originate retail credit proposals. This includes information on dependents, confirmation of home country address, telephone number and employment credentials, and ensuring to the extent possible that information and contact details provided by the potential borrower are correct and complete. This is normally easily achieved through independent verification when required.

Summary

This chapter covers the risk management framework, risk evaluation and mitigation, the retail credit management process, and respective roles and responsibilities. It serves as a central document, providing employees with a practical account of how the retail credit risk department operates and a market-leading best-practice approach which should be followed by employees and contractors when performing functions on behalf of the department. The chapter covers all the key policies for lending to retail borrowers, which exposes the bank to credit risk.

The chapter sets out the credit risk management framework for the retail banking business lines. This includes the development of retail credit products and retail business lines (business unit) through a structured lending process and the efficient management of the retail loan assets portfolio to maintain profitability of operations and high asset quality.

The term "risk" means all risks, howsoever arising, that the bank is exposed to in its business, including retail lending activities.

The objective of risk management is to identify, measure, and manage these risks by ensuring that appropriate policies and procedures, proper product parameters, systems support, controls, and review processes are in place in order to minimize risks and business losses to the bank.

The principal risk in retail credit is credit risk, which represents the risk of loss of interest or principal or both, arising out of a lending transaction due to the failure or default by the borrower. Procedures define specific actions or steps that must be completed to ensure that the minimum standards required by these guidelines are met.

References

Bellalah M (2004). *Gestion des Risques et Produits Dérivés Classiques et Exotiques*. Dunod, Prix Turgot.

Bellalah M and S Zouari (2015). Portfolio credit risk models and name concentration issues: Theory and simulations. *International Journal of Business*.

Bellalah M, S Zouari and O Levyne (2016). The performance of hybrid models in the assessment of default risk. *Economic Modeling*, 52, 259–265.

Website

https://bankpolicies.com/bank-policy-manual/ (updated 2025).

Chapter 7

Operational Risk Management

Chapter Outline

This chapter is organized as follows:

1. Section 7.1 investigates the governance structure and, in particular, the roles and responsibilities of the board risk committee, the general risk management committee, the chief risk officer, the head of operational risk, the operational risk manager, and operational risk champions. It provides abbreviations in Table 7.1.
2. Section 7.2 analyzes the operational risk strategy and governance, primarily utilizing the three lines of defense: first line of defense – business units and support functions; second line of defense – operational risk management; and third line of defense.
3. Section 7.3 is about operational risk capital charge.
4. Section 7.4 studies operational risk assessment processes.
5. Section 7.5 investigates risk and control self-assessments.
6. Section 7.6 describes key risk indicators and key risk scenario analysis.
7. Section 7.7 describes internal reporting, action plans of the operational risk assessment processes, etc.
8. Section 7.8 analyzes risk mitigation policies.
9. Section 7.9 studies operational risk event categories: actual losses, potential losses, near misses, boundary events, and credit-related operational losses.
10. Section 7.10 provides guidelines for issue tracking and risk scoring.
11. Section 7.11 discusses Basel II loss event classification and definitions.

Table 7.1. Abbreviations.

Abbreviation	Definition
The Board	The Board of Directors
BCC	Board Credit Committee
BRC	Board Risk Committee
The management	The Executive Management
CEO	The Chief Executive Officer
CB	The Central Bank
GMRC	General Management Risk Committee
GMCC	General Management Credit Committee
CRO	Chief Risk Officer
HO-OR	VP, Operational Risk and Fraud
EVP	Executive Vice President
EXCO	Executive Committee
KRS	Key Risk Scenario
IAD	Internal Audit Department
KRI	Key Risk Indicator
ORAP	Operational Risk Assessment Process
ORD	Operational Risk Department
ORM	Operational Risk Manager
RSA	Risk and Control Self-Assessment
Risk Group	Risk Units headed by the CRO

Importantly, this chapter is based on my professional experience in several financial institutions. We also refer to the principles of the Basel Committee on Banking Supervision.

Introduction

The Basel Committee defines operational risk in Basel II and Basel III as: "The risk of loss resulting from inadequate or failed internal processes, people and systems or from external events. This definition includes legal risk, but excludes strategic and reputational risk".

Operational risk management provides an outline of the various roles performed by the operational risk department of a bank.

Additionally, this chapter provides guidance on the effective and adequate management of operational risk in the bank. This chapter states the bank's approach to the measurement of capital for operational risk and related qualitative and quantitative requirements. The chapter lays out principles for the implementation of the operational risk framework by identifying, measuring, monitoring, and controlling the bank's operational risk exposure.

The chief risk officer (CRO) is responsible for operational risk management, which is reviewed by the board committees (board risk committee and general management risk Committee) and approved by the board of directors of the bank. It provides guidance on the roles and responsibilities exercised within the operational risk department. It sets out the following elements of operational risks: risk and control self-assessments (RSAs), risk events, operational risk assessment process (ORAP), key risk indicators (KRIs), and key risk scenarios (KRSs).

The chapter sets out the operational risk management framework for the bank. This chapter was prepared using regulations set by central banks and the Basel Committee on Banking Supervision. The reader can refer to the following websites for more details (updated 2025): Basel Implementation Guide – Basel 3 Pillars; Wolters Kluwer: https://www.wolterskluwer.com; What is Basel III? cqf.com: https://www.cqf.com; Learn about Basel III – Basel III Finalization: https://www.regnology.net; Basel II Vs Basel III: Key Differences. The reader can also refer to Bellalah *et al.* (2017).

7.1. Governance Structure

7.1.1. *Roles and responsibilities*

The bank follows sound risk governance principles, which emphasize clear roles, responsibilities, and reporting lines. Hence, it ensures adequate segregation of duties. This allows, in turn, independence and avoids conflicts of interest in line with business objectives and strategy.

7.1.1.1. *Board risk committee*

The board risk committee (BRC) plays an important role in risk management. It advises the board on the bank's overall current and future risk tolerance. BRC advises the board on the appetite and strategy. It oversees senior management's implementation of that strategy.

The BRC oversees the risk strategies for credit, market/liquidity, and operational risk, reputational risk, and other risks.

In terms of risk framework, risk strategy/risk appetite, and risk policies, the BRC reviews and recommends the risk charter to the board, approves the risk appetite statement to the board, and reviews and recommends major risk management policies to the board.

In terms of risk profile, the BRC reviews and acknowledges the portfolio risk report submitted to the committee, focuses on current and forward-looking aspects of risk exposure the bank is exposed to, and handles or instructs related committees, functions, and individuals within the bank to implement issues indicated in the risk report.

In terms of risk measurement methodology, the BRC reviews the adequacy of the risk measurement methodologies. It approves risk measurement methodologies, tools, and models for each risk type. This concerns the credit risk, market risk, liquidity risk, and operational risk.

The BRC approves models of scenario analyses, simulations, and stress tests.

In terms of corporate governance, the BRC reviews and recommends to the board for the final approval of the corporate governance charter and framework of the bank. It reviews and recommends to the board for final approval of the bank's policies (including the operational risk management chapter) and chapter governance framework.

7.1.1.2. *General risk management committee*

The GRMC maintains a high-level and broad risk framework within the segments of legal, regulatory, liquidity, credit, market, operational, and financial risks. It reviews the functioning of key business performance and risk functions through periodic reports.

The committee monitors and controls all types of risks to ensure that risk strategies and related policies are approved by the board and are adhered to and implemented.

The committee periodically reviews the risk charter and risk policies as per the mandate and related standards, methodologies, tools, systems, and procedures used or needed in managing the bank's risks.

The committee reviews the bank's policies and governance framework and recommends their approval to the board or relevant board committees.

7.1.1.3. *Chief risk officer*

The CRO is responsible for the bank's overall current and future risk tolerance. He is also in charge of risk appetite and strategy. He facilitates the resolution of any issues escalated by the VP of operational risk and fraud.

CRO elaborates on KRIs, assuming the responsibility to identify, design, capture, and report risk indicators.

He ensures that the operational risk strategies, policies, and management expectations are communicated to all staff.

He ensures adequate communication between the operational risk staff and the staff involved in credit, market, and other risks, as well as those involved in dealing with external agencies such as insurance and outsourcing.

He reviews the ORM reports on a periodic basis.

The CRO is responsible for the business continuity and disaster recovery plans, the systems for periodic testing of those plans, and the corrective actions taken in response to significant BCP incidents.

The CRO monitors the qualitative and quantitative assessment of exposure to all types of operational risk faced by each business line.

He provides assurance that controls are in place to identify and mitigate risks before risks become major issues.

7.1.1.4. *Head of operational risk*

He is in charge of the following tasks:

- Draft specific operational risk policies, standards, procedures, and guidelines, and update them to manage the operational risk cycle (identify, measure, monitor, and mitigate/control), and seek approval as per governance requirements.
- Identify industry best practices, and monitor trends and emerging practices. He is also asked to keep up-to-date on rules and regulations in operational risk and to maintain a repository of all related documents.
- Analyze the operational risks for all existing as well as new products that are being launched by the bank.
- Provide documentation of operational risk policies, procedures, and communication to the appropriate staff.

- Identify technology and consulting requirements and accordingly recommend them by substantiating and justifying the requirements to enhance the operational risk management practices in the bank.
- Identify and procure/develop tools for managing operational risk.
- Undertake enhancements to the operational risk (OR) framework and create an environment for ongoing adaptation.
- Implement recommendations and suggestions made through specific resolutions by the GMRC and BRC.
- Establish operational risk limits (KRI thresholds, loss limits, etc.), seek approval from the GMRC, and monitor and report on an ongoing basis
- Design and implement the risk reporting system for operational risk. The ORM department will collect relevant information from the business units, consolidate the data, and summarize it in reports for submission to the GMRC and other stakeholders. The report should include Basel recommendations, KRIs, loss event data, self-assessment results, and other key observations (see the website links in the references).
- Analyze the adequacy and coverage of insurance to mitigate operational risk and determine the optimal insurance limits and coverage that align with the operational risk profile.

7.1.1.5. *Operational risk manager*

He is in charge of the following tasks:

- Coordinate among their team members for the successful and timely implementation of the OR plans, while also providing the necessary information as part of overall operational risk management driven by ORM.
- Risk and control self-assessments, known as RCSAs, will help facilitate the assessments by active participation and verifying the results of such assessments.
- Loss events: Coordinate the loss event capture process in line with the chapter.
- Risk mitigation plans: Ensure execution of risk mitigation plans originated by ORM and the exception plans for KRI breaches.

- Gaps/Issues: Follow up in a timely manner on all action plans, documentation, and the resolution of open issues from ORM reviews and any inspecting authorities.
- Identify one or more OR coordinators in each of the business units/divisions and departments depending on the size, diversity, and complexity of operations of the unit.
- Facilitate and monitor the qualitative and quantitative assessment of exposure. The latter is related to all types of OR faced by the business lines and branches.
- Document ORM processes (identifying, measuring, and managing/controlling, including monitoring and reporting) within the operational risk chapter.
- Establish communication between ORM and support functions.
- Facilitate RCSAs on a periodic basis.
- Ensure uniform and consistent tracking of operational risk data (losses and near misses) across the bank. The ORM department will monitor reporting of losses across the bank by working closely with business units.
- Periodically monitor KRIs across business units and follow up on exception plans initiated for mitigating the risks identified as a result of KRI breaches. ORM will have the authority to extend the resolution dates at the specific request of the business unit and to coordinate early resolution of the plans.
- Gather information and analyze the risk profile of the business units as well as the bank and communicate the risks to various levels of management.

7.1.1.6. *Operational risk champions*

An operational risk champion is in charge of the following tasks:

- Provide the requisite information and data required for management of operational risks.
- Provide requisite data/information from various sources on a periodic basis for monitoring KRIs.
- Identify appropriate and representative sample data and provide the proof of verifications (stamping) wherever it is mandated (first line of defense activities).

– Input details of loss events identified at the branch/department/division in the respective formats and submit for approvals as per the laid-down risk event procedure. The role also entails timely identification of losses.

7.2. Operational Risk Management Strategy

The ORM strategy takes into account the overall strategy. The strategy is to further enhance and strengthen the ORM framework and the three lines of defense. According to the Basel definition, "operational risk is defined as the risk of loss resulting from inadequate or failed internal processes, people, and systems or from external events. This definition includes legal risk, but excludes strategic and reputational risk". We can refer to the website in the references.

7.2.1. *Governance – Three lines of defense*

Effectively organized and embedded risk management governance is the foundation for all components of ORM. The management of operational risk shall be undertaken at three levels with defined roles and responsibilities.

7.2.1.1. *First line of defense: Business units and support functions*

Heads of businesses have responsibility for the effective control of risks affecting their business (the "first line of defense"). The first line of defense is responsible for executing risk policies. Business units and support functions, e.g., wholesale banking, including commercial banking, group, retail banking, branch services, SME banking, HR, legal, IT, and operations, in the bank are responsible for operational risks. (These risks are inherent in its material products, activities, processes, and systems). They are responsible for implementing the ORM framework in their area of responsibility. They are also responsible for the management of operational risk on a day-to-day basis. This includes risk identification, controls, and managing risks in accordance with risk tolerance and operational risk policies.

7.2.1.2. *Second line of defense: Operational risk management*

Risk management functions (the "second line of defense") support the first line of defense. Risk management functions are "independent" of the management and personnel that originate the risk exposures. Typical second line of defense activities include, for example: overseeing the execution of risk management activities; monitoring key business risks; escalating risk management issues to the next higher level; and vetoing high-risk business activity. The ORM function is part of the second line of defense. ORM is responsible for the risk management of operational risks.

It has direct responsibility for formulating operational risk management frameworks, i.e., methodologies, policies, and procedures approved by the board.

ORM works with the business units and support functions with the objective to ensure that day-to-day operations are in line with the approved ORM policies. The unit provides training to facilitate the implementation of the various ORM programs. The unit monitors the effectiveness and quality of the controls and risk mitigation tools.

7.2.1.3. *Third line of defense: Internal audit*

The mission of internal audit is to provide independent assurance of the effectiveness of internal controls over risks to business performance. In carrying out this task, internal audit provides recommendations for improving governance, risk, and controls.

Its function determines whether the bank's network of risk management, control, and governance processes are adequate.

7.2.2. *Control of operational risk*

Operational risk training, risk education, and enhancement of risk culture at all levels of staff are used as a tool to reduce operational risk.

The bank faces various risks, including legal, regulatory, credit, interest rate, foreign exchange rate, liquidity, equity price, commodity price, reputational, and operational risks. These risks are correlated, i.e., events that affect one area can have ramifications for a range of other risks. The bank tries to improve the ability to identify, measure, monitor, and control the risks undertaken.

Parameters of effective risk management include the bank's organizational structure, the risk measurement approach, risk management policies, and guidelines used to govern risk-taking, including a detailed structure of prudential limits.

Operational risk involves breakdowns in internal controls. Breakdowns lead to financial loss through error, fraud, or failure to perform in a timely manner or compromise the bank's interests. Operational risk represents the risk of loss that stems from different types of errors (human or technical). Operational risk is synonymous with payments risk, business interruption, administrative, and legal risks. Operational risk has a link between credit and market risks. This is due to inadequate or failed internal processes, personnel, and systems, or an external event.

The bank must be compliant with the requirements under the IFRS 9 standards. The involvement of the bank's risk management function in the assessment and measurement of accounting expected credit losses (ECLs) ensures adequate allowances in accordance with IFRS 9.

7.2.3. *Internal controls*

Managing operational risk relies on a control system. The system includes segregation of duties, clear management reporting lines, and adequate operating procedures. Most of the operational risk events are associated with weak links in internal control systems or laxity in complying with existing internal control procedures.

This self-assessment is used to evaluate operational risks along with internal and external audit reports and ratings.

7.3. Operational Risk Capital Charge

For calculating the regulatory operational risk capital charge, banks can use the basic indicator approach.

Under this method, recommended in the Basel report (see the reference to the website in references), the operational risk capital charge is calculated using the average of the positive annual gross income for the last three years. This average is multiplied by a fixed percentage of 15% (alpha factor). The financial control is responsible for calculating regulatory operational risk capital charges.

The bank can use a sophisticated approach for operational risk capital calculation.

7.4. Operational Risk Identification

In line with best practices, for all new products, processes, and system/application implementations, relevant units, along with the risk team, must address the inherent operational risks and document relevant controls to mitigate or minimize this risk.

When inherent risks are not controllable, a decision is taken to proceed with the product or process launch based on the bank's risk appetite. However, the risks are to be clearly documented. The operational risk unit assesses risks in terms of probability and consequence, evaluates reduction and mitigation measures, and allocates ownership.

The unit considers both internal and external factors that could adversely affect the achievement of its objectives.

The operational risk unit ensures a focal point for managing all non-business risks.

7.4.1. *Operational risk assessment process*

The ORAP is designed to ensure that key risks associated with the introduction of new products and services are identified, fully considered, and addressed in a controlled manner prior to the launch of the product or service.

An ORAP is a risk assessment technique to identify risks due to the introduction of new or materially amended products, processes, activities, or systems on an *ad hoc* basis or as directed by senior management. The ORAP process is owned and led at the EVP level and approved by the GMRC.

The ORAP must be applied to the following four areas: new products to the business area and completely new businesses, products, services, or asset classes.

Adaptations to existing products cover significant changes that alter the risk profile or operational processes of the product, new distribution channels (including e-commerce), and new customer segments (e.g., high-net-worth individuals).

New operating models and entities cover strategic alliances and new exchange memberships.

Dormant products and services are reintroduced to cover previously approved products or services that have been dormant for one year.

In the event that an ORAP is not required due to no material process changes in the product/project/system, no new material operational risk exists for the bank. In that case, the head of department/function would approach operational risk with justification and obtain positive affirmation from ORM that an ORAP is not required.

The ORAP shall include the following statements:

Integration: Senior line managers must ensure that an ORAP is an integral part of any materially new or changed products, processes, activities, systems, or organizations under their responsibility. It is the bank's chapter that a discussion takes place between the business unit and risk to determine whether an ORAP is required. While the quality of the process will not be compromised, different circumstances under which a formal risk assessment ORAP shall be required will dictate the composition and timings of the actual ORAP session.

Business cases: Business case proposals related to new or significantly changed products, processes, activities, systems, or organizational setups shall also have an ORAP carried out prior to their implementation/launch.

Accountability: The business case owner and EVP sponsoring the project or material amendment are primarily responsible for the identification of all relevant parties to be involved in the ORAP. ORAP signoff from operations, IT, legal, compliance, and the ORM unit are mandatory, and dependent on the complexity and potential range of impact of the underlying subject matter, additional sign-offs from other related heads of specialist/support functions may be required. It is imperative that all relevant specialist and support parties are identified and involved in the ORAP process at the earliest possible stage to enable a suitably thorough assessment of the potential risks of the business case proposals within their respective areas of responsibility.

Operational risk: The advice of ORM should be sought and included. Depending on the complexity and potential impact of the underlying subject matter, the business unit manager should make a decision on whether or not ORM advice is required.

Review: The ORAP methodology is reviewed at least annually and more frequently as business needs require, with changes approved by the GMRC and/or BRC.

7.5. Operational Risk Assessment

RSA involves assessing each identified operational risk for impact (severity) and likelihood (probability) using risk assessment bands.

The business unit head and ORM will determine whether particular risks are effectively managed within the bank's business risk appetite or otherwise take remedial action after consultation with the head of operational risk and develop specific action plans to further mitigate the bank's exposure to these risks. Business unit representatives will determine the value (threshold) at which they would deem each risk to be unacceptable. The aggregated acceptable level of each business unit's identified risks will be used to determine the risk appetite for that unit.

7.5.1. *Risk and control self-assessment*

According to the operational risk management framework requirements based on the Basel principles (the reader can refer to the websites in the references), the bank must identify, measure, monitor, and report its key operational risks (which the business runs). One of the leading operational risk management tools is risk and control self-assessment (RSA). The RSA methodology helps to review and assess operational risks and to determine the adequacy and effectiveness of internal controls (which are designed to manage those risks).

7.5.1.1. *Definitions*

Risk and control self-assessment: RSA is the process whereby risks inherent in a business unit's strategy, objectives, and activities are identified, and the effectiveness of controls over those risks is evaluated and monitored. The RSA process addresses risks and controls comprehensively. It incorporates the process for evaluating and managing all aspects of risk inherent in how and where the business is done.

Inherent risk: Inherent risk is defined as the risk that an activity would pose before consideration of the effectiveness of the controls or other mitigating factors that were in place.

Residual risk: Residual risk is the risk that is not eliminated by the business control mechanisms or mitigating characteristics of its operating environment.

Key control: The "key control" is defined as any measure that either reduces the likelihood (or frequency) of an incident, mitigates the associated risk, or diminishes the potential damage (or severity) arising from that incident. It includes measures to ensure adherence to management's directives, policies, and procedures, as well as conformity to local laws and regulations.

Probability: The "probability" represents the number or potential number of loss events that the risk event is exposed to.

Impact: The "impact" is the loss amount or the potential loss amount that the operational risk "event" is exposed to if the risk event materializes (happens) in any single year.

7.5.1.2. *Objectives*

The outcome of the "assessment" phase is acceptable risks and unacceptable risks. During the "response" phase, adequate measures are proposed (control, transfer, or avoid) in order to mitigate the unacceptable risk.

The purpose of an RSA is summarized as follows:

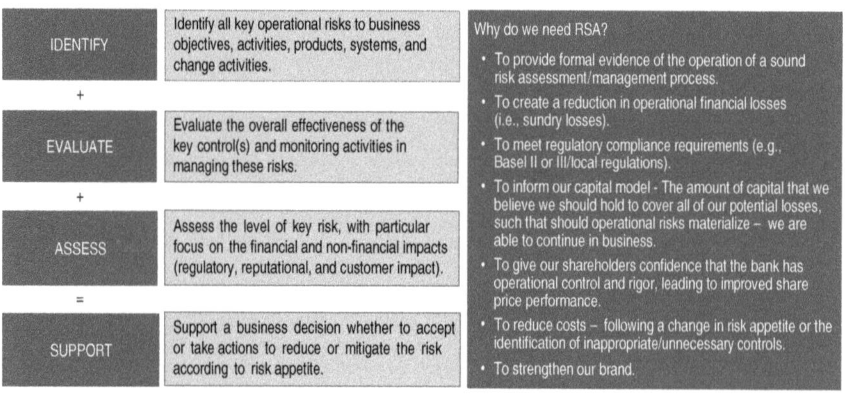

7.5.1.3. *Risks identification*

The RSA plan is preferably based on the outcome of the high-level risk assessment (list of high-risk areas). Additionally, the RSA process can be triggered by one or more of the following criteria:

- after a launch of a product/project;
- incidents occurred;
- deteriorating key risk/performance indicator values;
- increasing risk level due to a changing internal or external environment;
- as a result of a control monitoring exercise and/or management or risk committee decision;
- based on audit findings and recommendations;
- unsatisfactory audit rating;
- program/project or organizational change.

The objective of an RSA workshop or meetings is to agree on and assess the material risks (controlled and uncontrolled) that could threaten business activities and the achievement of defined business objectives.

The bank shall define the possible risks and the associated controls in each of the operational processes across the Basel II-defined eight business lines of the bank (Table 7.2).

All activities of the bank will be invariably classified under any of the above eight business lines that represent the complete operational risk framework of the bank.

7.5.1.4. *Risk assessment*

The activities performed in this phase are based on the results of the phase "risk identification".

Table 7.2 provides risk assessment, the identified risks are to be assessed in detail, preferably in a workshop to ensure joint involvement of relevant business experts (first line of defense) and ORM

Table 7.2. BASEL business lines.

Commercial Banking	Trading & Sales	Payment & Settlement	Retail Banking
Retail Brokerage	Asset Management	Corporate Finance	Agency Services

(second line of defense) by assessing their probability and impact. The risk level is investigated in three steps: inherent risk assessment, control assessment, and residual provides risk assessment.

Inherent risk assessment: Assessment of risk assuming no controls or mitigations are in place. Assessment of inherent risk should be, for example, based on loss event data, lessons learned, and scenario analyses. The inherent risk assessment is particularly applicable for significant new business, regulatory, or external developments (e.g., new markets, products, or regulations) when there is no control environment in place.

The operational risk assessment depends on the probability and impact (represented on a three-point scale) for all activities under each business line. The qualitative and quantitative definitions provide guidance for selecting probability and impact. The "probability" is the number or potential number of loss events that the risk event is exposed to, and the "impact" is the loss amount or the potential loss amount that the operational risk event is exposed to (when the risk event materializes in any single year).

For the measurement of the "probability" of the selected risks, scales of three levels are used: low, medium, and high.

The RSAs are owned by their respective function heads and supported by their risk champions. The function head is responsible for carrying out risk assessments. The same should be shared with ORM for their review.

7.5.1.5. *Identify and evaluate controls*

Once the key risks are identified, key controls and specific control activities in place to reduce vulnerability to each of the key risks are identified.

Probability and impact assessment grid:

For the measurement of the "probability" of the selected risks, scales of three levels are used: low, medium, and high.

For the measurement of the "impact" of the selected risks, scales of three levels are used: low, medium, and high.

There is no predefined minimum or maximum number of risks or controls that should be developed in RSAs, but a limited number of focused key risks and controls will provide value and too many will lose their purpose. Accordingly, RSA should not have more than material risks (for example, 10 risks), and each risk should not have more than key controls (for example, three controls per risk).

Control assessment:

The bank must undertake the control assessment to evaluate the efficiency of controls in terms of consistency with the objectives for implementing such controls. The control assessment will evaluate the controls against relative risks to determine appropriateness, effectiveness, and efficiency, focusing on aspects such as human labor, materials, equipment, money, and time. The following factors that determine the effectiveness of the controls are evaluated for providing ratings to the controls: test of design (ToD) of the controls and test of effectiveness (ToE) of the controls.

ToD and ToE are carried out simultaneously in preparation for risk and control self-assessment by the risk champions and their function head.

The control assessment should aim to identify control gaps and consequently implement appropriate corrective actions within a specified timeframe.

Control design:

All documented controls are required to meet minimum documentation standards as follows:

A control should be "active", i.e., it requires someone to do something specific.

The frequency and timeliness of operating the control are essential.

The control should be performed at a frequency sufficient to provide adequate assurance that the risk is mitigated.

Controls should be clearly defined and should bring out the control activity or control steps clearly (i.e., the description should be clear enough to assist in re-performing the control if required by someone with only indirect knowledge of the control).

The controls should be auditable, and hence evidence of the control operation should be clear from the control description.

A control should always have a control owner who is responsible for its operation.

The person operating the control should be different and independent from the person who prepared the data being controlled.

Controls should have an escalation route for exceptions.

Control operational effectiveness:
RSAs can be finalized only after the operational effectiveness has been assessed for all controls. The assessment results can be one of the following:

Effective (accept): The control is appropriate and operates as intended.

Ineffective (increase controls): Evidence that the control is not operating as intended or is inappropriate and outside of defined business appetite.

Improvement required: If the control has been assessed as anything less than effective, the individual control requires improvement.

For a control to be evaluated as effective, it must operate in accordance with the design, be mature (in terms of operation), and be supported by evidence. If it is not evidenced, there is no proof that the control operated, and the control can only be evaluated as "ineffective".

7.5.1.6. *Residual risk assessment*

Residual risk is defined as the risk that is not eliminated by the business' control mechanisms or mitigating characteristics of its operating environment.

Residual risk focuses on the identification of high-risk profiles that have weak controls. Critical and high residual risks exceed the standard tolerance level, and resources need to be assigned to mitigate these risks. Medium risks do not exceed the tolerance level; if these risks exceed management's own target risk appetite, management shall develop mitigation actions. Low risks are not currently material, but management will monitor these risks and take appropriate action to prevent them from becoming material.

7.6. Operational Risk Monitoring and Control

Prompt detection and mitigation of deficiencies can reduce the potential frequency and/or severity of a loss event. The primary risk owners (business units), in coordination with the risk management group (RMG), determine all material operational risks. They also decide whether to use appropriate procedures to control and/or mitigate the risks or accept them.

Monitoring is assessing whether the organization is in control of its risks. Monitoring is ideally a continuous process (with ongoing or repeated observations) to measure and evaluate the effectiveness of internal controls, to determine whether risks are within the norms of risk appetite and in line with ambition levels, and to determine whether policies, procedures, and regulations are adhered to. Monitoring can be performed through various techniques supported by automated or other tools. Examples are KRI monitoring, action tracking, key control testing, (direct) supervision, quality assurance, backtesting, scorecard review, and chapter review or self-assessment. Common features of all monitoring activities are that they are used to validate a situation, statement, or assumption (risk or control statement); have a sound basis (evidence); are well documented; and lead to conclusions about (risk) controls. The control monitoring aims to identify any material operational risks and ensure mitigating controls are in place. The scope of monitoring and control will generally cover the following:

- review of material risks and key controls with an aim to identify any missing risks in RSAs;
- review department procedures to ensure departmental procedures have been duly approved, and also review such procedures to identify potential operational risk issues;
- review of operational effectiveness of key controls in the department;
- review of closure of audit findings specified in latest internal audit report.

This approach complements other policies and processes for operational risk and will be performed by ORM.

7.6.1. *Key risk indicators*

In an ORM framework, risk indicators (with predictive capabilities) are one of the key tools used to support risk assessment and risk monitoring. Key risk indicators (KRIs) are used as a means to express operational risk appetite and to monitor control effectiveness, risk drivers, and risk exposures.

KRIs are used together with a system of thresholds. When the threshold (or tolerance level) for any KRI is breached, it triggers an immediate review and escalation (or management action).

The key attributes of KRIs are that they provide early warning signals for adverse changes in the risk environment, control effectiveness, and potential risk issues (before they crystallize into an operational loss event).

Also, KRIs highlight current risk profiles by providing a measure of the status of an identified risk and the effectiveness of associated controls. They also highlight trends and changes in risk level by monitoring changes in risk between formal risk and control self-assessments (RSAs).

7.6.1.1. *Definitions*

Key risk indicator: A KRI indicates the risk profile and any change. KRIs act as early warning indicators (EWIs). They are used to monitor potential operational loss events. KRIs can be broadly classified into three types of measures. These include *ex post* (lagging) and *ex ante* (leading) measures of risk) – loss measures, process indicators, and risk environmental indicators.

Loss measure: Loss measures monitor the actual effect of operational loss events. Operational loss events are monitored in accordance with the loss data chapter. By definition, loss measures are *ex post* (lagging) in nature.

Process indicator: Process indicators measure the quality of operations and the effectiveness of controls. Most process indicators measure performance and are *ex post* in nature and do not provide much insight into the future. Process indicators are transformed into leading indicators by making them exception-oriented. (i.e., error rates, limit breach, and outstanding position).

Risk environmental indicator: Environmental indicators are typically *ex ante* (leading) and can have large qualitative components. (i.e., number of customer complaints, employee satisfaction, and training levels).

7.6.2. *Key risk scenario analysis*

Scenario analysis is a process to obtain expert opinion from business managers and risk management experts. The process allows one to derive reasoned assessments of the likelihood (frequency) and impact (severity) of plausible operational losses.

Key risk scenarios (KRSs) are business area-level assessments of material operational risks.

KRSs describe the key risk, the storyline, the applicable key controls, and the effectiveness of these key controls, and they provide estimates of the expected and unexpected losses that could occur in the next year.

Direct loss or impact, for the purpose of this chapter, is defined as a negative financial impact on the profit and loss accounts due to an operational risk event, other than a boundary event resulting in credit risk impairment. An accounting restatement or adjustment without an actual receipt or payment of funds is included in this definition where it relates to an item from a prior accounting period (six months or a full year).

Indirect and non-financial impacts, such as reputational damage, opportunity cost, and loss of potential income, should also be considered in KRSs, though they are not required for capital assessment.

KRSs are informed by risk and control self-assessments (RSAs), internal and external risk events, KRIs, audit findings, and other relevant risk information.

Assessments are validated with the expert opinion and experience of management and the support of the operational risk team.

KRSs facilitate the improved understanding, management, and oversight of material operational risk across the bank and underpin the calculation of operational risk capital requirements and allocation to BUs.

The following methodology is used for scenario analysis. Scenario analysis involves identifying high-impact events that have not occurred to date by using "what-if" questions. Also, any information/data on operational losses that have occurred in other banks shall be used for generating scenarios.

Scenarios are developed taking into account businesses or functions which are subject to higher overall risk to the bank.

Scenarios are developed especially for activities or loss event types where internal data, external data, and self-risk assessments and internal control factors do not provide an estimate of the bank's exposure to operational risk.

Scenario analyses are undertaken every six months to estimate the potential loss severity and frequency. The scenarios are considered to assess the possible impact of significant operational losses on the bank's overall risk exposure.

7.6.2.1. *Annual review requirements*

KRSs must be signed off and validated by each business area and submitted to ORM annually. ORM will provide a timetable for the annual submission each year.

Individual KRS sign-off and acceptance has two aspects.

The first responsibility must be assigned at an appropriate level for the review, sign-off, and acceptance of each KRS assessment. Those assigned this responsibility must have the relevant skills and experience to understand the risk and controls and perform the checks.

The second is that the risk champion is responsible for sign-off and acceptance of a KRS. He must specifically consider whether:

- the risk has been described clearly with realistic example scenarios;
- typical and unexpected assessments are reasonable and are supported by relevant risk data and analysis (including internal and external risk events, KRIs, RSAs, and control issues) and strong, objective rationales;
- projected losses are plausible;
- the maximum probable loss assessment (if any) is reasonable and supported by a strong, objective rationale;
- changes made to KRSs since the previous submission, due to changes in the risk profile, are supported by robust evidence, such as changes in key indicators.

7.7. Operational Risk Reporting

The reporting process ensures relevant information is given to senior management and the board. This allows for the proactive management of operational risk. The process ensures a consistent approach for "information" that allows appropriate decision-making. Reporting can be done in two ways.

7.7.1. *Internal reporting*

The internal monitoring process provides pertinent information for the quick correction of deficiencies in the policies, processes, and procedures (for managing operational risk and regulatory compliance). The business units are required to submit monthly reporting to ORM.

7.7.2. *ORAP action plans*

The head of department/functional unit representative reviews and studies the ORAP initiative and analyzes its potential impact on their areas of responsibility by discussing it with other staff in their unit, if applicable. They also identify and assess the potential impact of operational, legal, and reputational risks associated with the initiative based on the information received from the business case owner. ORM shall circulate the final report and obtain relevant stakeholders' sign-off.

7.7.3. *RSA action plans*

Actions agreed upon and recorded during the RSA must be systematically executed, tracked, and monitored. The ORM unit independently tracks and ensures the execution of agreed action plans and shall report and escalate details regarding any outstanding items as appropriate.

7.7.4. *KRIs*

Performance of KRIs is monitored and reported to the function head and ORM and compared to the target thresholds set during the KRI identification process. The performance against target thresholds will be incorporated into board and senior management reports where the thresholds are exceeded by a fixed percentage. Business unit-level KRI reporting must follow the principle of "one-level-up", i.e., a copy of the KRI report(s) prepared for each function must be sent to the line manager of the immediate head of that function for review. Frequency of reporting each function-specific KRI is determined by the time sensitivity and the potential loss severity of the associated risk.

7.7.5. *Incident reporting*

ORM is responsible for receiving and collating the information contained in the incident reports received each month from the business units.

The information received will be collated into a report that, at a minimum, includes:

- a summary of the major incidents for the period;
- actual losses versus expected or provision for losses;
- a checking process to ensure that all transactions in the general ledger that are defined by the incident/loss chapter are recorded in the appropriate incident management system(s) (at the half-year and year-end).

7.7.6. *Operational loss database*

Business units should routinely collect operational loss data as part of the incident reporting process and provide it to ORM. Collecting operational loss data and reporting operational risk losses is not a goal in itself. It is important to ask the following questions: What went wrong? Which control(s) broke down or were non-existent? Which measures have been or should be taken to avoid recurrence?

7.8. Operational Risk Mitigation

7.8.1. *Treatment of risk/risk response*

The following sections describe the methods that shall be adopted to address risks that have been identified through risk and control self-assessments, KRI monitoring, business process reviews, and loss data collation. The alternatives will be determined based on the bank's individual risk profiles. The choice of the risk treatment measure should essentially depend on the effectiveness of the measure in reducing the probability and impact of a given risk and the cost and time involved in implementing it.

The risk responses are any of the following (or a combination) that will lead to an effective measure. The following "key points" will guide the selection of the risk responses:

Avoid risk:

When the benefit margin is less than the risk cost (considering all types of risk, including operational risk), the bank can consider avoiding such risks. However, the decision to discontinue the activity (or not even introduce it) is given to the GMRC/BRC.

Mitigate risk:

All measures that reduce the frequency or severity of loss occurrences are implemented as part of risk mitigation for the identified risks. The mitigation is done mainly through internal controls. It will have to be prudently applied based on the prioritization of risks: high, medium, or low.

The bank adopts internal controls as risk mitigation techniques: policies, processes, and procedures; the four-eye principle; system access controls; physical access controls; checks and balances; delegation of authority; roles and job responsibilities documented in job descriptions (JDs); limits management; IT disaster recovery; business continuity planning; risk awareness education; and risk and control self-assessments.

All such measures introduced as part of risk mitigation shall be approved by the appropriate authority and adequately documented as part of process documentation and job descriptions.

Transfer risk:

Where the internal control cannot reduce or control the risk, the bank may decide to transfer such risks through insurance and outsourcing.

Further, the above decision shall also take into account the cost associated with such mitigation. Costs should not exceed the expected loss resulting from the activity in which the risk was identified.

The risk appetite of the bank is considered when implementing risk transfer through insurance and outsourcing.

Where it is possible to share the risks between the bank and the third party, the same shall be explored and implemented.

Any undesirable effects that could arise due to risk transfer should also be identified and accounted for at the time of decision by the appropriate authority.

Accept risk:

The acceptance of risk is a process to allow management to document their decision to take no further mitigating actions for a recognized risk. Accepted risks can result from, for example, risk assessment sessions, a product review process, project or other risk and control self-assessments, chapter summaries, KRI reports, audit findings, and incidents. Often, such a risk is a residual risk after mitigating actions have been taken to resolve or control the original risk. Directly reporting to the CEO, the respective EVP/SVP can accept the risk and sign off on the RSA. The head of operational risk may escalate any high-risk issue to the GMRC if deemed fit.

7.8.2. *Risk mitigation policies*

The objective of mitigation is clear in terms of cause-oriented reduction of loss frequency . It is also clear in terms of the effect-oriented reduction of loss severity.

Risk mitigation plans are implemented to reduce exposure to operational risks with low probabilities but potentially large financial impacts.

All risk mitigation decisions are transparent and consistent with the overall business strategy and risk appetite.

Clear responsibilities shall be assigned to the appropriate personnel to implement the risk-mitigating measures and ensure they are initiated within the specified timeframes.

ORM shall assess the effectiveness of operational risk mitigation efforts in terms of quality and appropriateness and report the results and escalate them to senior management/GMRC/BRC as deemed appropriate to address problems before they become major concerns.

The business units should approach ORM for assistance and validation of the design and implementation of the risk mitigation strategies/tools.

For those risks that cannot be mitigated, the bank accepts them, reduces the level of business activity involved, or withdraws from the activity.

7.9. Loss Event Capture

Tracking loss event data is necessary for the development of an operational risk measurement system. The bank intends to systematically capture all operational loss events and allocate them to the specified business lines and loss event types. The bank's operational loss data is considered an integral part of the overall ORM framework. The following are the guiding policies related to ongoing capture of operational events across the bank.

7.9.1. *Definitions*

Operational risk event (internal and external): As it appears on the website of the Basel Committee, an operational risk event is a specific incident that results from the occurrence of one or more causes falling within the definition of operational risk. It gives rise to one or more operational risk effects. Operational risk events are classified into seven event types (operational risk event categories).

Definition of an internal risk event: An internal risk event is any circumstance that has actually or could potentially have resulted in the business unit losing money or incurring a non-financial impact. This includes situations where controls did not operate as intended and the bank could have made a loss, but in fact made a gain, e.g., due to currency movements and also incidents resulting only in reputational damage or regulatory impact. When identifying and measuring operational risk, we have to understand the relationship between causes, events, and effects.

Cause: The proximate cause of an event is the action or set of circumstances that led to the event. Causes seek to identify the action (or inaction) of an individual or institution or the incidence of a natural disaster that triggered, has a direct and substantial impact on, and is a necessary condition for the occurrence of the event.

Event: A malfunction of internal processes, human behavior, or systems or an external factor. It is not certain that an event shall happen. Operational risk is defined in terms of the possibility that a certain event may occur. Events with future impact are events that, at the moment of reporting, cannot be reliably quantified but will most certainly have an impact in the future. Events with a future impact are reportable if an estimated loss is equal to or above a given amount.

Effect: Effects can be described in monetary terms (i.e., profit and loss impact) and/or in qualitative terms (regulatory, reputational, or legal damage).

7.9.2. *Operational risk event categories as defined by the Basel Accord*

The following definitions in Table 7.3 are standards in the Basel Accord (see the updated 2025 website references).

Table 7.3. Definitions of fraud.

Loss Event	Description
Internal fraud	Loss due to criminal and/or fraudulent activities involving at least one person within the firm. An act committed with the intention to defraud, misappropriate property, or circumvent regulations.
External fraud	An act, committed by a third party, with the intention to defraud, misappropriates property, or circumvents regulations.
Employment practices and workplace safety	An act inconsistent with employment, health, or safety related laws and agreements.
Clients products & business practices	An unintentional or negligent act or failure to meet professional obligation to customers.
Damage to physical assets	Loss or damage to physical assets resulting from natural disasters and other events.
Business disruption & system failure	An event that disrupts normal business operations or causes a business or system failure.
Execution delivery and process management	A failure in transaction processing or process management which stems from relations with trade counterparties and vendors.

7.9.3. *Cause categories of operational risk*

People: Insufficient strategies, policies, standards, people management, training, and/or poor staff performance.

Process: Inadequate set up of business processes, poor training of staff in the relevant processes, or poor adherence to controls related to business processes.

Information technology (IT): Inadequate strategy, policies, standards, or shortcomings in the application of IT.

External disruption/event: Unanticipated or uncontrollable external factors, including inadequate business continuity planning, disrupting the bank's operational capability.

7.9.4. *Actual losses*

The operational risk loss event shall be considered a material loss event if it is objective and measurable and there is sufficient evidence that the event has resulted in an operational risk loss (as defined above) to the bank in terms of either a reduction in the value of assets of the bank, both customers and internal, an increase in expenses for the bank, or a quantifiable P&L impact.

For example, a payment instruction was processed to a wrong beneficiary, and the third bank confirms funds already withdrawn, and there is no chance of recovery. The funds need to be written off the profit and loss account.

7.9.5. *Potential losses*

Operational risk event with no immediate impact but where a future negative profit and loss movement and/or indirect impact is probable.

For example, a payment instruction processed to a wrong beneficiary, and the bank is currently in negotiation with the third party to obtain the funds. If the funds are received, they will be classified as a near miss; otherwise, if funds are not received after all recovery efforts, this will be treated as an actual loss.

7.9.6. *Near misses*

Events that have occurred but have not resulted in any financial losses shall be categorized as "near miss" events and captured in the risk event database. While these types of losses do not cause any direct loss, they are indicative of personnel, system, or process shortfalls and could have potentially resulted in losses.

Operational risk event where normal controls did not work as anticipated, but the impact was avoided.

For example, a payment instruction processed to a wrong beneficiary, but the bank was able to recall the funds and there was no loss to the bank.

7.9.7. *Boundary events*

The term "boundary events" is used to refer to events that might be categorized as credit, market, insurance, or strategic/business risk, on the one hand, and/or operational risk, on the other.

7.9.8. *Credit-related operational losses*

Credit-related operational losses (CROLs) are defined as credit losses that are wholly or in part due to an operational risk event.

Examples include failure to perfect security, lending based on fraudulent documents, and ineffective controls or monitoring.

Fraud types that are categorized as CROLs include the following.

Application fraud, where fake documents were used to obtain credit facilities.

Never pays, where a new customer is provided with a credit facility that is fully drawn close to the limit, and the bank has not received a single installment, has had no contact or lost contact with the customer, and the bank has reasons to believe the customer never intended to repay the facility.

7.9.9. *The operational risk database*

All risk events must be reported on an immediate basis to the respective function heads. All risk events must be recorded in the operational risk database (currently maintained in Excel) and, in the future, in the operational risk system.

7.10. Guidelines for Issue Tracking and Risk Scoring

All business and support functions are subject to audits initiated both internally and externally by external auditors and supervisors. Similarly, observations arise as a result of risk assessments, KRIs, loss events, etc. It is important to manage these observations and monitor progress in solving them.

Issues could arise from RSAs: compliance reports, KRI reports, loss events, internal and external audits, scenario analysis, business continuity planning, and ORAP.

To ensure adequate and timely resolution of issues, items, risks, and control/action owners need to appreciate the importance of appropriate responses to issues raised.

The risk and control/action owners shall apply tests on issues raised for compliance with five rules (they may seek advice/assistance of ORM):

Is the resolution correct, or is there a more appropriate, efficient, or effective way to address the shortcoming?

In the event of (IT) solutions which take a long time to implement, how can the risk be mitigated to an acceptable level in the meantime?

Has a specific individual (or identifiable position) been assigned responsibility for carrying out the resolution?

Have appropriate resources been identified and their availability earmarked?

Has a realistic clearance date been assigned based on the above?

Each "open" item is reviewed on a monthly basis by the action owner and updated with the current status and progress. ORM will periodically track to ensure that progress toward a resolution is made on open items by the action owner.

Change of action owner or business unit impacted: The action owner is the named individual responsible for resolving an issue. He should be at an adequate management level. The monitoring entity (usually ORM) can change an action owner or a business unit upon request, in principle after acceptance by the new action owner or business unit.

Due dates: The original target date is set as part of the issue resolution by the action owner or as directed by management or risk committees. If it turns out that the target date cannot be met, it is the duty of the action owner to escalate to the relevant authority who set up the action. The submission should take into account documented rationale for delay, future course of action, mitigating actions until complete resolution is achieved, and a realistic revised target date. The same should be submitted for approval and under intimation to ORM. ORM on its own may escalate to the CRO or risk committees if the action is not closed or the progress is inadequate.

Closing items: Risk champions will be responsible for validating and closing action plans. Validation must be performed prior to closing the items, and closure documents with supporting documentation should be prepared. Following validation by a risk champion and upon receipt of supporting documentation, ORM will either close or reject the closure of an issue. If rejected, the reason will be made clear to the submitter and recorded accordingly in the risk register.

Guidelines for risk champions for validating issues to be submitted for closure to ORM are as follows:

Check that all parts of the original finding/issue are addressed.

Is the issue really valid for closing? For example, if the comment for submission states that a particular action will be performed, this does not indicate closure.

Where precise agreed-upon actions have not been implemented, the action owner should explain and provide evidence that alternative actions address the finding in such a way that identified risks are acceptably mitigated.

7.11. Basel II Loss Event Classification and Definitions

The following definitions (Tables 7.4 and 7.5) are provided by the Basel Committee on Banking Supervision (updated, version 2025). They are provided on websites and books as public information.

They have to be presented as they appear in Basel reports on updated websites (2025) as standard definitions (https://www.wolterskluwer.com, https://www.cqf.com; https://www.regnology.net).

Table 7.4. Basel II loss event classification.

Event Type Category (Level-1)	Categories (Level-2)	Activity Examples (Level-3)	Definition of Activity
Internal Fraud	Unauthorized Activity	Transactions not reported (intentional)	Intentional non reporting of transactions
		Transaction type unauthorized (w/monetary loss)	Transactions that are unauthorized as per the Chapter of the Bank or transactions executed that are not within the delegation powers
		Mismarking of position (intentional)	Intentional mis-marking of positions
	Theft Fraud	Fraud/credit fraud/ worthless deposits	Theft and Fraud perpetrated by any of the employees of the Bank either individually or in collusion with other employee(s) of the Bank. Involves more than one person, at least one of whom is an employee.
		Theft/extortion/ embezzlement/ robbery	The wrongful or willful taking of money or property belonging to someone else after the money or property has lawfully come into the possession or control of the person taking it. Obtaining money by deception; employee effectively steals from a client/customer e.g., raising false loans, altering cheques
		Misappropriation of assets	The intentional, illegal use of the property or funds of another person for one's own use or other unauthorized purpose, particularly by a public official, a trustee of a trust, an executor or administrator of a dead person's estate, or by any person with a responsibility to care for and protect another's assets

(*Continued*)

Table 7.4. *(Continued)*

Event Type Category (Level-1)	Categories (Level-2)	Activity Examples (Level-3)	Definition of Activity
		Malicious destruction of assets	Intentional act of destruction of assets of the Bank for any reason what so ever.
		Forgery	Forgery is the act of counterfeiting or otherwise altering a document, records, identity, signature etc. with an intention to fake the document and draw undue benefit from that act.
		Check kiting	The practice of drawing on uncollected funds during the time needed to clear a check deposited in a Bank esp. if the check is worthless.
		Smuggling	To import or export secretly, contrary to the law; to import or export without paying the duties imposed by law;
		Account take-over/ impersonation/etc.	Purposeful take-over of worthless accounts for individual benefit, impersonation etc. with an intention to defraud the Bank
		Tax non-compliance/ evasion (willful)	Tax avoidance is the legal utilization of the tax regime to one's own advantage, in order to reduce the amount of tax that is payable by means that are within the law. By contrast tax evasion is the general term for efforts to not pay taxes by illegal means.
		Bribes/kickbacks	Kickback A slang term used to describe the payment of something of value to another individual with the goal of persuading or influencing their decision or performance in certain situations. Bribe The offering, giving, receiving, or soliciting of something of value for the purpose of influencing the action of an official in the discharge of his or her public or legal duties.

		Insider trading	Insider trading is the trading of a corporation's stock or other securities (e.g., bonds or stock options) by corporate insiders such as officers, key employees and directors.
External fraud	Theft and Fraud	Theft/Robbery	Theft/Robbery
		Forgery	An illegal modification or reproduction of an instrument, document, signature, or legal tender, or any other means of recording information. An item is also considered forged if it is claimed that it was made by someone who did not make it.
		Check kiting	The practice of drawing on uncollected funds during the time needed to clear a check deposited in a Bank esp. if the check is worthless.
	Systems Security	Hacking damage	Damages caused due to third parties illegally accessing Bank's computer systems for destroying, disrupting or carrying out illegal activities on the network or computer systems.
		Phishing	Phishing is an attempt to criminally and fraudulently acquire sensitive information, such as usernames, passwords and credit card details, by masquerading as a trustworthy entity in an electronic communication.
		Theft of information (w/monetary loss)	Theft of information from the Bank's data bases (physical or electronic).
Employment Practices and Work-place Safety	Employee Relations	Compensation, benefit, termination issues	Losses arising from acts inconsistent with employment, health or safety laws or agreements, from payment of personal injury claims, or from diversity/discrimination events.

(Continued)

Table 7.4. (*Continued*)

Event Type Category (Level-1)	Categories (Level-2)	Activity Examples (Level-3)	Definition of Activity
		Organized labor activity	Strike is a work stoppage caused by the mass refusal by employees to perform work.
	Safe Environment	General liability (slip and fall, etc.)	A liability is defined as an obligation of an entity arising from past transactions or events, the settlement of which may result in the transfer or use of assets, provision of services or other yielding of economic benefits in the future.
		Employee health & safety rules events	Non-compliance to the employee health and safety guidelines issued by the Governmental authorities
		Workers compensation	Workers' compensation provides insurance to cover medical care and compensation for employees who are injured in the course of employment, in exchange for mandatory relinquishment of the employee's right to sue his or her employer for the tort of negligence.
	Diversity & Discrimination	All discrimination types	All discrimination types
Clients, Products & Business Practices	Suitability, Disclosure & Fiduciary	Fiduciary breaches/ guideline violations	Fiduciary breaches/guideline violations
		Suitability/disclosure issues (KYC, etc.)	Suitability/disclosure issues (KYC, etc.)

	Retail customer disclosure violations	Retail customer disclosure violations
	Breach of privacy	Breach of privacy
	Aggressive sales	Aggressive sales
	Account churning	Account churning
	Misuse of confidential information	The duty of confidentiality obliges the Bank to respect the confidentiality of its client's affairs. Information that the Bank obtains about its clients' affairs may be confidential, and must not be used for the benefit of persons not authorized by the client. Confidentiality is a prerequisite for legal professional privilege to hold.
	Lender liability	Lender liability
Improper Business or Market Practices	Antitrust	Antitrust
	Improper trade/market practices	Improper trade/market practices
	Market manipulation	Market manipulation
	Insider trading (on firm's account)	Insider trading (on firm's account)
	Unlicensed activity	Unlicensed activity
	Money laundering	A typical Scheme of bringing the illegal funds into the legal channel where the funds are generally invested in the stock markets and their markets where the yields are lucrative. The performance of diverse transactions to conceal the illegal source of revenue generated by criminal activities.
Product Flaws	Product defects (unauthorized, etc.)	Product defects (unauthorized, etc.)

(*Continued*)

Table 7.4. *(Continued)*

Event Type Category (Level-1)	Categories (Level-2)	Activity Examples (Level-3)	Definition of Activity
		Model errors	Failure of model for intrinsic reasons e.g., inappropriate parameters, incorrect programming, invalid assumptions, mathematical errors.
	Selection, Sponsor-ship & Exposure	Failure to investigate client per guidelines	Failure to investigate client per guidelines
		Exceeding client exposure limits	Exceeding client exposure limits
	Advisory Activities	Disputes over performance of advisory activities	Disputes over performance of advisory activities
Damage to Physical Assets	Disasters and Other Events	Natural disaster losses Human losses from external sources (terrorism, vandalism)	A natural disaster is the consequence of a natural hazard (e.g., volcanic eruption, earthquake and landslide) which moves from potential in to an active phase, and as a result affects human activities.
		Human losses from external sources (terrorism, vandalism)	Human losses from external sources (terrorism, vandalism).
Business disruption and system failures	Systems	Hardware	The physical components of a computer system-the computer, plotters, printers, terminals, digitizers, and so on.
		Software	Various kinds of programs used to operate computers and related devices. It is the term used to describe the instructions that cause the computer system to behave in a given way.

		Telecommunications	Refers to any transmission, emission, or reception of signs, signals, writings, images and sounds or intelligence of any nature by wire, radio, optical, or other electromagnetic systems.
		Utility outage/disruptions	Utility outage/disruptions
Execution, Delivery & Process Management	Transaction Capture, Execution & Maintenance	Miscommunication	Miscommunication
		Data entry, maintenance or loading error	Data entry, maintenance or loading error
		Missed deadline or responsibility	Missed deadline or responsibility
		Model/system mis-operation	Model/system mis-operation
		Accounting error/entity attribution error	Inaccurate measurement or representation of an accounting-related item not caused by intentional Fraud. An error may be due to Negligence or may result from the misapplication of Accounting Principles. Errors may take the form of currency discrepancies or may be compliance errors in employing accounting policies and procedures.
		Other task mis-performance	Other task mis-performance
		Delivery failure	Delivery failure
		Collateral management failure	Collateral management failure

(*Continued*)

Table 7.4. (*Continued*)

Event Type Category (Level-1)	Categories (Level-2)	Activity Examples (Level-3)	Definition of Activity
		Reference Data Maintenance	Reference Data Maintenance
	Monitoring and Reporting	Failed mandatory reporting obligation	Failed mandatory reporting obligation
		Inaccurate external report (loss incurred)	Inaccurate external report (loss incurred)
	Customer Intake and Documentation	Client permissions/ disclaimers missing	A disclaimer is generally any statement intended to specify or delimit the scope of rights and obligations that may be exercised and enforced by parties in a legally-recognized relationship. In contrast to other terms for legally operative language, the term "disclaimer" usually implies situations that involve some level of uncertainty, waiver, or risk.
		Legal documents missing/incomplete	Legal documents missing/incomplete
	Customer/ Client Account Management	Unapproved access given to accounts	Unapproved access given to accounts.
		Incorrect client records (loss incurred)	Incorrect client records (loss incurred)
		Negligent loss or damage of client assets	Negligent loss or damage of client assets

Trade Counterparties	Non-client counterparty mis-performance	Non-client counterparty mis-performance
	Misc. non-client counterparty disputes	The assertion of conflicting claims or rights between parties involved in a legal proceeding, such as a lawsuit, mediation or arbitration.
Vendors & Suppliers	Outsourcing	Outsourcing is the supply to an authorized institution by another entity either intragroup or independent third party) of goods, service or facilities on a structural basis (i.e., the contractual supply of goods, service or failures that form part of the business processes and which are necessary to support the provision of Banking or other financial services). The supplier may itself be an authorized or unauthorized entity.
	Vendor disputes	The assertion of conflicting claims or rights between parties involved in a legal proceeding, such as a lawsuit, mediation or arbitration.

Table 7.5. Risk score.

Risk Rating	Risk Impact			Risk Probability
	Financial	Non-Financial		
Risk Criteria	Direct/Indirect	Customer	Legal, Regulatory and Reputation	Likelihood
High	Financial Impact (Estimated, potential or actual loss from previous or next 12 months)	Significant number of customers impacted	Likely significant regulatory criticism and/or reputational damage and/or serious legal action	Expected/Likely: Will occur in most circumstances in next 12 months.
Medium	Financial Impact (Estimated, potential or actual loss from previous or next 12 months)	Moderate number of customers impacted	Likely moderate regulatory criticism and/or reputational damage and/or moderate legal action	Often: Would occur at some time in next 3 years
Low	Financial Impact (Estimated, potential or actual loss from previous or next 12 months)	Few customers impacted	Likely minor regulatory criticism and/or reputational damage and/or minor legal action	Unlikely: Not likely to occur, or may occur in exceptional circumstances in next 10–20 years

Summary

Operational risk is in charge of the following tasks. The summary shows all that we should know about operational risks.

- Draft specific operational risk standards and guidelines and update them to manage the operational risk cycle.
- Monitor trends and emerging practices and keep up to date on rules and regulations.
- Maintain a repository of related documents.

- Analyze the operational risks for all existing as well as new products.
- Document operational risk management and communication to the appropriate staff.
- Identify technology and consulting requirements and accordingly recommend them by substantiating and justifying the requirements to enhance operational risk management practices.
- Undertake enhancements to the operational risk framework.
- Implement recommendations made through specific resolutions.
- Establish operational risk limits.
- Monitor and report on an ongoing basis.
- Design and implement the risk reporting system.
- Collect relevant information from the business units and consolidate the data.
- Analyze the adequacy and coverage of insurance to mitigate operational risk.
- Determine the optimal insurance limits and coverage that aligns with the operational risk profile of the bank.

Reference

Bellalah M, O Masood and SM Ghauri (2017). Basel III implementation outcome in Islamic banks. *The Journal of Risk.*

Websites

Basel Implementation Guide – Basel 3 Pillars. Wolters Kluwer: https://www.wolterskluwer.com (updated 2025).

What is Basel III? cqf.com: https://www.cqf.com (updated 2025).

https://www.regnology.net.

Basel II Vs Basel III: Key Differences – The Knowledge Academy: https://www.theknowledgeacademy.com/blog/basel-ii-vs-basel-iii/ (updated 2025).

Part II

Capital and Risk Management

Chapter 8

International Financial Reporting Standards 9 (IFRS 9 Impairment)

Chapter Outline

This chapter is organized as follows:

1. Section 8.1 develops IFRS 9 principles, known as the International Financial Reporting Standards. They offer accountability, transparency, and efficiency. This provides a set of worldwide accounting standards.
2. Section 8.2 is devoted to IFRS 9 governance.
3. Section 8.3 explains the provisioning process.
4. Section 8.4 explains the override procedures.
5. Section 8.5 explains the role of the risk management team in reporting and disclosures.

Introduction

The objective of the International Financial Reporting Standards 9, or IFRS 9 impairment, is to establish principles and policies and facilitate implementation of IFRS 9 principles at a bank.

IFRS 9 aims to establish a comprehensive framework to drive the classification of assets and to estimate losses based on portfolio risk. IFRS 9 establishes frameworks to enable the bank to compute provisions in line with the standards stipulated by the IFRS 9 principles.

IFRS 9 principles introduce and maintain related procedures and systems to enable the said objectives.

This chapter provides guidance for impairment computation and related processes. The risk management department (RMD) and the finance department are jointly responsible for the development and maintenance of the IFRS 9 impairment. The board risk committee is the only body within the bank authorized to approve IFRS 9 impairment and any subsequent modifications thereof.

The general management risk committee retains responsibility for implementation, and all modifications and changes must be reviewed by it before submission to the board risk committee. An independent review for overall compliance with IFRS 9 impairment is to be carried out on an annual basis by the audit or risk management departments. The findings of the independent review are to be submitted to the general management risk committee and the board for review and further action, if applicable. Further details of governance are elaborated in a later section.

It is worth mentioning that this chapter is based on my professional experience in several financial institutions. For a detailed analysis, the reader can refer to the two following updated 2025 websites: https://www.insightsoftware.com and https://envoria.com/modules/ifrs-notes.

8.1. IFRS 9 Principles

The IFRS 9 standards have been brought forward by the International Accounting Standards Board (IASB), introducing revised rules for the classification of assets of financial institutions, their accounting, rules for considering provisions, and reporting in accordance with the new standards, with the objective of addressing shortcomings regarding recognition and provisioning for stressed assets. The three main modules of IFRS 9 principles are classification, impairment, and hedge accounting.

The first main module of IFRS 9 is classification and measurement of financial instruments.

The second main module of IFRS 9 concerns impairment of financial assets. The third main module of IFRS 9 is hedge accounting. The standards mandate compliance by January 1, 2018, and the following sections describe the scope of the modules.

8.1.1. *Classification and measurement of financial instruments*

These rules of the IFRS 9 standards aim for the classification and measurement of all financial instruments of the bank across amortized cost, FVOCI, and FVTPL measurement categories. This includes business model identification for all financial instruments at an aggregate level and assessment of cash flow characteristics testing (SPPI) at an individual instrument level.

8.1.2. *Impairment: Stage assessment and loss estimation*

The second dimension of the IFRS 9 requirements is impairment calculation, which entails a focus on models with forward-looking inputs to consider expected losses at three different stages based on their respective credit risk information. This is initiated with the stage assessment exercise to identify the applicability of the assets to the three prescribed stages based on the respective credit risk.

The following Table 8.1 summarizes the stage types and the assessment rules.

The stage assessment is followed by the expected credit loss computation across all stages to arrive at the impairment or provisioning estimate. To comply with IFRS 9 impairment calculations, banks need to estimate forward-looking expected credit losses using methodologies in line with the IFRS 9 principles. This involves extensive risk modeling and analytics expertise to estimate 12-month probabilities of default (PDs), lifetime PDs, loss given defaults (LGDs), model calibrations, and validations.

8.1.3. *Hedge accounting*

IFRS 9 standards provide special rules for hedge instruments and hedge accounting models, allowing entities to better reflect their risk management activities in their financial statements. The hedge accounting documentation elaborates on the risk management strategies considered hedges and the effectiveness of those strategies.

Table 8.1. Impairment stages description.

Stage	Description	Rules
Stage 1	Characterizes low credit risk assets	This stage includes performing assets and would also include newly originated assets, considering assessment in the appraisal process.
Stage 2	Assets where there has been a significant increase in credit risk	The criteria for this stage is "significant increase in credit risk", which is evaluated based on the credit monitoring framework, including internal and macroeconomic factors, and is subject to management overrides. "Significant increase in credit risk" is considered based on a downgrade in the rating scale or other indicators such as 30 DPD, flags of restructuring, selective lending, and the special assets committee.
Stage 3	Asset category of impaired and non-performing assets	Categorization of assets in Stage 3 is based on objective evidence of impairment at the credit monitoring and collateralization levels. Accounts with 90+ DPD or rating grades corresponding to sub-standard, doubtful, or loss portfolios.

8.2. IFRS 9 Governance

The IFRS 9 principles implementation is driven by personnel in the RMD and the finance department, with oversight from the general management risk committee (GMRC) and the board. The governance structure is elaborated in this section.

8.2.1. *Risk management department*

The RMD is the driver for the development and implementation of the stage assessment, loss estimation, and expected credit loss (ECL) computation, as prescribed by IFRS 9 standards, and its responsibilities include:

- the development of a loss estimation methodology, including:
  - development of the stage assessment framework,
  - impairment models for loss estimation and provisioning,

    - considering underlying factors for credit quality monitoring, such as economic factors;

- the review of models and rating systems' results to assess efficacy in estimation and recommend adjustments to the GMRC;
- testing and validation of the loss estimation methodologies on an ongoing basis for ensuring accuracy of provisioning calculation;
- the development of recommended overrides for model outputs in case of counterintuitive results or other forward-looking indicators (including macroeconomic indicators).

8.2.2. *Finance department*

The role of the finance department includes the development of the business model for classifying assets to drive asset classification criteria as per the IFRS 9 principles.

The department also conducts review provisioning results before submission to the GMRC and the board risk committee.

8.2.3. *General management risk committee*

The GMRC is an executive committee comprising three members, including the CEO, CRO, and CFO. The GMRC is responsible for the following activities for IFRS 9 implementation:

- review impairment computation methodology and underlying models to ensure compliance with prescribed standards and to make further recommendations to the board;
- oversee the development of the stage assessment framework and its underlying factors and present recommendations to the board before final implementation;
- assess the loss estimation framework and approve validation results to certify the provisioning computation process;
- assess the applicability of macroeconomic factors on the portfolio(s) for stage assessment and loss estimation;
- review the overrides proposed for model output or stage transfer criteria.
- review the results of validation and findings of independent assessors and audits pertaining to data and framework, and develop an action plan for recommendations to the board.

8.2.4. *General management credit committee*

The general management credit committee (GMCC), which is responsible for all credit approvals within the bank, also assumes the following two responsibilities pertaining to the loss estimation framework. The first is to review stages of assessment on an ongoing basis. The second is the approval for overrides related to stage assessments on a case-by-case basis, based on proposals received from the RMD.

8.2.5. *The board of directors and the board risk committee*

The board of directors retains the responsibility for approval of the IFRS 9 impairment chapter and is the approving authority for instating the framework and any subsequent changes thereto. The board of directors delegates the following three elements to the board risk committee:

- first, ensure the development and implementation of appropriate credit practices, stage criteria, and provision management strategy, including related systems and frameworks, to ensure adherence to the risk management principles prescribed by the central bank, the IFRS, and the Basel committee;
- second, provide oversight for decisions taken by the delegated committees, including the GMRC;
- third, review the recommendations of the GMRC, reports on validation of models, and the findings of the validation exercise with regard to the IFRS 9 framework.

8.2.6. *Validation team*

The internal audit department or risk analytics team is responsible for the review of the credit assessment and loss provisioning framework to ensure compliance with the principles and computation. The responsibilities include independent assessment of the loss estimation process and establishing the integrity of the process. The responsibilities also include presenting the review to senior management, including the GMRC and the board of directors.

8.2.7. *Business units*

The business units are the custodians of portfolio data and provide inputs for the design, inherent factors for the model, and provision computation methodologies. Their key functions for IFRS 9 implementation include the management of portfolio data, as per rules prescribed by the finance and risk management department. Their key functions for IFRS 9 implementation also include providing inputs for the development of the stage assessment and impairment framework, particularly for factors for each portfolio during stage assessment. They also include macroeconomic drivers and forward-looking estimates.

8.3. Provisioning Process

The provisioning rules stipulated by the IFRS 9 standards entail the computation of ECL for pre-defined stages. The loss estimation process is managed by the RMD on a quarterly basis. The process involves the following steps: data extraction, stage assessment, and expected loss calculation.

The following portfolios are categorically considered under the loss estimation computation: corporate, retail, and other applicable portfolios:

- First, corporate portfolios include corporate entities, high-net-worth individuals (HNWIs), banks and financial institutions, sovereign entities, and small- and medium-sized enterprises (SMEs).
- Second, retail includes credit cards, mortgages, and personal loans to self-employed and salaried individuals, car loans, and others.
- Third, other applicable portfolios include investments (which are subject to credit risk) and nostro accounts.

8.3.1. *Data extraction*

A portfolio-level snapshot is to be extracted along with historical data for ECL computation.

The IT team provides access to risk management to the relevant systems and facilitates the data extraction exercise on an ongoing basis.

The extraction parameters include borrower information, exposure values, limits, mapped collateral, utilization, and origin characteristics, including risk rating and interest rate (along with the effective interest rate).

Data cleansing and quality checks will be performed by the IT, business units, and risk team, and the finance team before initiating the ECL computation process. Once the data have been cleansed and reconciled, the ownership of running the estimation process vests with the RMD.

The business units remain the owners of the respective portfolio data and will provide assistance with regard to data validation and transformation, as well as other data adjustments, if required.

The RMD is responsible for preparing for modeling and the estimation process. This includes detecting, investigating, and refining the inaccurate entries from the record set. In the event of model redevelopment or recalibration, the outliers shall be excluded.

In addition to the portfolio data requirement elaborated above, the bank also needs to ensure availability of macroeconomic data for the stage assessment thresholds.

8.3.2. *Stage assessment and credit monitoring*

As per the IFRS 9 standards, it is required to classify all assets within the three stages in accordance with their credit quality. The risk management team will extract the portfolio data and initiate the stage assessment exercise.

On a quarterly basis, the portfolio data are to be extracted by the RMD, and it should carry out the stage assessment based on the criteria mentioned earlier. The staging criterion also considers a comparative analysis from the originating rating grades.

Assets are monitored for any increase in their credit risk levels through a framework comprising portfolio-specific and external macroeconomic factors.

The criterion for transfer between stages for corporate portfolios is as follows:

- The transfer between stages will be considered for each reporting period.
- Transfer from Stage 1 to Stage 2 is applicable based on a "significant increase in credit risk" over the last reporting period, depicted by indicators such as:
  - downgrade by three notches as per the bank's internal 22-point rating scale;
  - the 30 days past due (DPD) condition;
  - the identification of flags for restructuring, selective lending or reference to the special assets committee.

Transfer from Stage 2 to Stage 3 is considered according to the non-performing loans (NPL) identification criteria of the provisioning chapter, with a DPD of 90 days, or if there is objective evidence of impairment recognized by the risk manager and the collateral value is deemed inadequate.

Migration from Stage 2 to Stage 1 is possible if there is adequate information presented by the risk manager highlighting the improvised condition of the said obligor, and such conditions prevail during the six-month cure period.

Direct migration from Stage 1 to Stage 3 may be considered based on non-performance criteria, as per the provisioning chapter or the risk manager's assessment of performance factors and inadequacy of collateral for the coverage of principal loss.

The three criteria for transfer between stages for retail portfolios are as follows.

The first is that transfer from Stage 1 to Stage 2 is applicable based on a "significant increase in credit risk" over the last reporting period, depicted by indicators such as the 30 DPD condition.

It also involves the identification of flags for restructuring (forbearance) or reference to abandon portfolios (non-core).

The second is that migration from Stage 2 to Stage 1 is possible if there is adequate information presented by the risk manager highlighting the improvised condition of the said retail client and such conditions prevail for the cure period specific to each product type.

The third is that transfer from Stage 1 or Stage 2 to Stage 3 is based on the following conditions: accounts with a 90+ DPD, and all accounts with the bank's retail rating grade of RR6, RR7, or RR8.

All overrides will be proposed by the RMD at the reporting date and approved as per the guidelines.

8.3.3. *Loss estimation computation*

The loss estimation computation process is complex. It is to be carried out on a quarterly basis by the RMD. The quality of the portfolios and their staging are also dependent on macroeconomic factors and the underlying collaterals for the portfolio(s). The final loss allowance for each portfolio is computed based on the summation of ECLs from Stage 1, Stage 2, and Stage 3. The finance department reviews the results of ECL computation and reconciles the provisioning numbers.

The key highlights of the process are mainly two points.

The first is that the 12-month ECL is computed for assets in Stage 1 of the portfolio, depicting a low level of credit risk.

The second is that the lifetime ECL is considered for assets under Stage 2 and Stage 3, based on the respective rules.

In the event of counterintuitive results from the ECL output, judgmental overrides are applicable based on approval by senior management.

ECL estimates are computed for each reporting period to reflect changes in credit risk of the portfolio(s) and update the provisioning figure.

ECL is computed considering the applicable models for respective portfolios, using historical data extracted.

In the event that historical data are not available for the portfolios, a judgmental LGD can be considered in discussion with relevant stakeholders and approved by the GMRC.

8.3.4. *Impairment validation*

The validation exercise is carried out independently on an annual basis. The accuracy and consistency of models of the ECL computation will be assessed both on qualitative and quantitative factors, in discussion with the risk management team for input on methodology.

The quantitative considerations include a calibration test, carried out to evaluate the actual performance of model(s) against the expected performance.

In the event that performance thresholds of models are breached significantly, recalibration and redevelopment may be discussed with the risk management team.

The qualitative considerations include portfolio coverage in the computation and their completeness in stage assessments.

It also covers the review of data used for the ECL computation process, along with related processes for transformation or refinement.

It includes model applicability and results in the ECL assessment and measurement estimates. It covers the review of overrides, related approvals, and documentation.

The final validation report is summarized and presented to the GMRC and the board of directors.

8.4. Override Procedures

Overrides to the three stages of assessment or loss estimation computation results should be proposed by the RMD and approved by the relevant authority within the bank when the results of the framework are not considered appropriate.

In the event of any unreasonable and erratic classification, the risk manager shall bring up cases for discussion with the CRO and CFO for their input. Where genuine and reasonable information supports justifying an override of the stage assessment as per the chapter, the risk manager can recommend the change to the GMRC.

The GMCC must review the proposed override, along with the supporting information and approve or reject it. It may also initiate actions for improvisation in stage assessment methodology, if needed.

8.5. Reporting and Disclosures

The risk management team is responsible for computing expected credit losses on a quarterly basis and submitting them to the finance department for review. Provisions in each of the three stages are presented to the GMRC and the board for final approval.

Depending on approval from the board, the final provisioning will be updated in the financial statements of the bank.

The finance department assumes final responsibility for disclosures, including those pertaining to provisioning. Following are the ECL disclosure requirements for provisioning as per IFRS 9 standards:

Qualitative disclosures: Credit risk management practices are to be detailed, including:

- description of the risk management strategy and key processes;
- summary of significant changes and updates to the stage assessment criteria or ECL computation methodology, if any;
- definition of Default;
- grouping criteria for portfolios;
- write-off chapters and factors for write-off categorization.

Quantitative disclosures pertaining to ECL calculations:

- reporting of collaterals and credit enhancements, against credit exposures;
- ECL computation parameters related to macroeconomic scenarios, risk factors, and forward-looking information;
- PDs, LGDs, cure rate, and re-default rates across segments and internal grades.

  Portfolio review, specifying loans, advances, and contingent liabilities across the following overall balance: ECL results based on asset quality; charge to the income statement, and write-offs. Migration across different stages of impairment over the last reporting period, elaborating:

- the transfer to 12-month ECL; transfer to lifetime ECL not credit impaired; and transfer to lifetime ECL credit impaired.

  This also includes the reconciliation of IAS 39 reporting.

Summary

This chapter provided guidance for impairment computation and related processes for a bank or financial institution. The risk management department and the finance department are responsible for the development, implementation, and maintenance of the IFRS 9 impairment.

The board risk committee approves the IFRS 9 impairment.

The general management risk committee implements changes and reviews data before submission to the board risk committee. An independent review for compliance with IFRS 9 impairment is carried out on an annual basis by the audit or risk management departments. The findings of the independent review are submitted to the general management risk committee and the board. The loss estimation computation is carried out on a quarterly basis by the risk management department. The final loss allowance for each portfolio is computed based on the summation of ECL of Stage 1, Stage 2, and Stage 3.

The finance department reviews the results of ECL computation and reconciles the provisioning numbers.

Websites

IFRS Reporting Standards – IFRS Reporting & Analysis: https://www.insightsoftware.com (updated 2025).

IFRS Financial Reporting – IFRS Data Management: https://envoria.com/modules/ifrs-notes (updated 2025).

Chapter 9

Capital Management

Chapter Outline

This chapter is structured as follows:

1. Section 9.1 is about the implementation of capital management.
2. Section 9.2 studies the principles of capital management.
3. Section 9.3 discusses capital measurement.
4. Section 9.4 investigates monitoring and reporting.
5. Section 9.5 studies capital planning and monitoring.

Introduction

Capital management sets out rules within a bank toward capital management and capital planning. The key purpose of this chapter is to provide guidelines to and assist the bank in managing capital efficiently and in compliance with regulatory requirements. The key objective is to outline the measures the bank must comply with regarding capital management and adequacy requirements of all applicable statutory and regulatory laws and regulations and to support the bank in maintaining sufficient funding for its operations and solvency in the long term.

The four specific objectives are as follows.

The first is to ensure the stability of the bank by holding sufficient capital to cover unexpected losses. The second is to enhance the efficiency of the bank by monitoring the risk-adjusted return on regulatory capital at various levels of aggregation. The third is to define the bank's policies and procedures regarding capital adequacy as per the regulatory authority's rules. The fourth is to ensure that the bank complies with principles of conducting business.

Importantly, this chapter is based on my professional experience in several financial institutions. Capital management is based on recommendations, guidelines, and principles of Basel II and Basel III for conventional and Islamic banks.

For an introduction and deep analysis, the reader can refer to the following (updated 2025) websites: https://bankpolicies.com/bank-policy-manual/, https://www.occ.treas.gov/news-events/newsroom/news-issuances-by-year/bulletins/banking-circulars.html, and https://www.wolterskluwer.com.

9.1. Implementation

The scope of implementing guidelines falls within the jurisdiction of the finance department of the bank. The asset liability management committee (ALCO), the supervisory board (SSB), and the board of directors are responsible for approving the capital management policy.

The finance function is responsible for ensuring that capital management policies and procedures are implemented, followed, and updated as needed. All other departments and bank entities are also responsible for coordinating the implementation of this policy.

The chapter incorporates parameters to constantly measure and enhance the effectiveness of the rules contained herein. These measures reflect the improvement in the bank's capital management upon implementation and would enable measurement of the effectiveness of guidelines. For further details, refer to Bellalah *et al.* (2015a, 2015b) and Bellalah and Masood (2015).

The following four measures are used.

The first is the clarity and ease of implementation. The second is the alignment with business needs of the organization. The third is the number of exceptions per year (to be measured based on the creation of policy exceptions). The fourth is noncompliance with regulatory requirements. The results of the key policy effectiveness indicators are discussed in the audit committee meetings.

9.2. Capital Management Principles

9.2.1. *High-level rules*

The risk asset ratio (RAR) of the bank is the ratio of the bank's capital resources to its risk-weighted assets. As a matter of policy, the bank at all times maintains a RAR in excess of 12%, which is higher than the minimum required by the regulator.

The bank has at all times maintained capital resources of at least the amount of its base capital requirement or its risk-based capital requirement, which is the minimum capital requirement to be maintained.

The bank conducts regular scenario analysis and stress testing (at least on a quarterly basis) to ensure that its capital resources are likely to remain above its capital requirement in the near and medium term. The bank must immediately notify of any breach or expected breach of any of the provisions of capital adequacy requirements.

9.2.2. *Principles*

The bank follows the following principles for establishing a good control framework on capital management.

Board and senior management oversight:

The bank's board of directors is responsible for understanding the nature and level of risk being taken by the bank and how this risk relates to adequate capital levels. It is also responsible for ensuring that the formality and sophistication of the risk management processes are appropriate in light of the risk profile and business plan.

The business plan and the strategy of the bank clearly outline the bank's capital needs, anticipated capital expenditures, desired capital level, and external capital sources.

The primary responsibility of the bank's board of directors is to set the bank's tolerance for risks. The bank has a risk management framework for assessing various risks, a system to relate risk to the bank's capital level, and methodologies for monitoring compliance with internal rules.

Sound capital assessment and comprehensive assessment of risks:

The bank has the following documents, which act as overarching principles governing its procedures, and these policy frameworks ensure that the bank identifies, measures, and reports all material risks: risk management, credit risk management, market risk management, liquidity risk management, investment risk management, operational risk management, compliance, anti-money laundering chapter, and capital management.

Each of the risk management sections covers the management of specific risks, including risk identification, measurement, management, and monitoring. Methodologies adopted by the bank, including limit structures, capital requirements, and stress testing requirements, are highlighted in the individual chapters.

Monitoring and reporting:

The bank should set adequate systems and controls in place to enable it to determine and monitor its capital requirements and resources. The finance department generates data and information from an accounting system to calculate the capital adequacy requirements of the bank. This assists in generating MIS reports according to the classification required by categories and also assists in generating numbers which the management can use for capital adequacy reports for the bank.

The risk management framework establishes an adequate system for monitoring and reporting risk exposures.

The reports allow the bank's senior management and board of directors to evaluate the level and trend of material risks and their effect on capital levels. The reports allow evaluation of the sensitivity and reasonableness of key assumptions used in the capital assessment measurement system. The reports allow determining that the bank holds sufficient capital against various risks and follows established capital adequacy goals. They assess future capital requirements based on the bank's reported risk profile and make necessary adjustments to the bank's strategic plan accordingly.

Internal control review:

The bank's risk management organization structure provides for an efficient and independent internal control structure. The risk management department, the risk coordinator within risk management, and the compliance and internal audit functions of the bank are primarily responsible for the internal control review of risks. There are also the risk management committee, asset liability committee, executive investment committee, and audit committee, which oversee the function of internal control. Furthermore, the supervisory board ensures the conduct of business in line with Islamic principles, and the board of directors regularly verifies whether its system of internal controls is adequate to ensure well-ordered and prudent conduct of business.

The bank conducts periodic reviews of its risk management processes to ensure their integrity, accuracy, and reasonableness. Areas that could be reviewed include the appropriateness of the bank's capital assessment process given the nature, scope, and complexity of its activities.

They also include identification of large exposures and risk concentrations. They incorporate accuracy and completeness of data inputs into the bank's assessment process. They cover the reasonableness and validity of scenarios used in the assessment process. They also involve stress testing and analysis of assumptions and inputs.

Follow regulatory requirements:

The bank follows the regulatory requirements from the supervisor. The bank coordinates with the supervisor on a regular basis and also assists the supervisor in their assessment of the bank. The periodic review by the supervisor involves a combination of on-site examinations or inspections, off-site review, discussions with bank management, review of work done by external auditors, and periodic reporting.

The bank facilitates supervision.

The bank must at all times maintain capital resources of at least the amount of its minimum capital requirement or any higher requirement if that has been imposed by the regulator.

The bank has a capital monitoring methodology in place. In the event that unexpected losses are expected to arise for which the bank may not be holding adequate capital, it informs the supervisor about the situation and initiates remedial measures.

9.3. Capital Measurement

The capital available for regulatory purposes is as follows:

(A) **Tier one capital:** Permanent share capital, audited reserves, share premium account, and retained earnings/externally verified interim net profits.
(B) **Deductions from tier one capital:** Investments in own shares, intangible assets, and interim net losses.
(C) Tier one capital after deductions = A – B.
(D) **Upper tier two capital:** Perpetual qualifying hybrid capital instruments, fixed dividend ordinary shares, revaluation reserves, general provisions, profit equalization reserve, and investment risk reserve.
(E) **Lower tier two capital:** Subordinated debt and fixed-term preference shares.
(F) Total tier one capital plus tier two capital = C + D + E.
(G) **Deductions from the total of tier one and two capital:** Connected lending of a capital nature, material holdings of capital instruments issued by regulated financial institutions, qualifying holdings, and liquid assets.
(H) Total tier one capital plus tier two capital after deductions = F – G.

This is the total capital resource.

9.3.1. *Risks measured under the standardized approach*

The bank's capital requirement is measured as the sum of the following components:

(1) **Credit risk capital component:** The bank calculates its credit risk capital requirement as the sum of the credit risk capital component (CRCOM) and the counterparty risk capital component (CPCOM).
(2) **Foreign exchange risk capital:** This is calculated using the standard method as follows:

- calculating its net open position in each currency and in gold;
- calculating its overall net open position; and
- multiplying the overall net open position by the percentage.

(3) **Displaced commercial risk capital:** This is calculated based on 35% of the credit risk and market risk of assets financed by holders, both restricted profit-sharing investment accounts and unrestricted profit-sharing investment accounts, and is calculated using the following formula:

$$\text{PSIACOM} = [\text{PSIACOM } \textit{credit} + \text{PSIACOM } \textit{market}] \times 35\%.$$

- PSIACOM *credit* is the credit risk of assets financed by PSIA holders and is calculated in accordance with and, where applicable, the credit risk requirement.
- PSIACOM *market* is the market risk of assets financed by holders and is calculated in accordance with the market risk requirement section as if the assets were equities.

(4) **Profit rate risk capital requirement:** This is the sum of the two following separate charges. The specific risk of each net position is the sum of the market values of the individual net positions (whether they are long or short), multiplied by the appropriate risk percentage as given in the rulebook. Then, the general market risk uses the simplified framework.
(5) **Equity risk capital requirement:** This is calculated using the standard method. The standard method requires two separate calculations. The first is specific risk, and the second is general market risk.
(6) **Commodities risk capital requirement:** This is obtained by applying the simplified approach to all non-trading and trading book items.
(7) **Option risk:** This needs a capital requirement.
(8) The last is the securities underwriting capital requirement.

9.3.2. *Classification of trading and non-trading books*

Non-trading book capital requirement:

The bank calculates its non-trading book capital requirement as the sum of the following components, regardless of whether they were calculated considering non-trading book items or trading book items: the credit risk capital component, the foreign exchange risk capital requirement, and the commodity risk component.

Trading book capital requirement:

The bank calculates its trading book capital requirement as the sum of the following components:

- the counterparty risk capital component,
- the profit rate risk capital requirement,
- the equity risk capital requirement,
- the foreign exchange risk capital requirement,
- the commodities risk capital requirement,
- the options risk capital requirement, and
- the securities underwriting capital requirement.

9.3.3. *Risks specifically not covered under capital requirements*

The risks for which capital is not directly allocated are as follows:

Reputation risk: Reputation risk is the biggest risk facing the bank and has a far-reaching effect on the bank's operations. The bank is highly sensitive to this risk, and a necessary reputation risk management framework should be in place to ensure the bank does not suffer negative publicity or public opinion, consequently impacting its operations.

Strategic risk: When the bank is in a start-up stage, the presence of a sound market strategy is necessary for the bank. The bank should adopt a market strategy and thus not foresee significant strategic risk impacting it in the near future. While this remains the existing scenario, the likelihood/impact of this risk on the bank is monitored on an ongoing basis.

Liquidity risk: The bank's liquidity risk arises mainly from the funding liquidity risk arising from its inability to meet its obligations when they come due and the trading liquidity risk arising from interest rate, foreign exchange, and equity risk.

9.4. Monitoring and Reporting

The following reports are generated for monitoring regulatory capital requirements:

Quarterly reports as per the standard format prescribed and amended from time to time, a monthly report to the ALCO, and quarterly report to the board executive committee or the board of directors of the bank.

While formal reporting takes place at the end of each calendar quarter, the bank monitors market risk in such a way that the capital requirements for market risk are being met continuously (i.e., at the close of each business day and not merely at the end of each calendar quarter).

The bank's daily compliance with the capital requirements is verified by the finance and risk management department. When the bank fails or is expected to fail to meet the minimum capital requirements on any business day, the authority is informed.

Capital required at the individual transaction level is reported on each investment application and periodic reports.

9.5. Capital Planning and Monitoring

9.5.1. *Capital planning*

The projected balance sheet and projected income statement for each business line are used as the basis to arrive at the projected risk-weighted assets (RWAs) for credit, market, and operational risks, as well as net income for future periods. This information is then used to arrive at the regulatory capital to be allocated to each business line, so as to effectively plan the capital requirement for each business line.

The model supplements the above-mentioned capital requirement planning by allowing the bank to measure and plan the risk-adjusted return on capital for each business line. This is arrived at by computing the return of projected net income on the regulatory capital allocated for each business unit.

The bank decides a benchmark return (hurdle rate) for performance measurement and, ultimately, for capital allocation at the bank level and at the business unit level.

Table 9.1. Illustrative triggers and corrective action strategies under each trigger.

Sr. No.	Illustrative Triggers	Descriptions	Illustrative Corrective Action Strategy
1	Capital ratio of 12%	This represents the minimum capital position which the bank would like to maintain, keeping in mind the regulatory capital requirement of 8%. This would provide the bank the necessary buffer to accommodate any other capital requirements.	None
2	Capital ratio of 8%	The regulatory capital ratio of 8% in normal circumstances is well within the acceptable limits. However, maintaining a capital ratio of 8% means the bank has no buffer under stressed scenarios.	Consider potential liquidation of exposures which yield low-risk-adjusted return on capital and reduce risk-weighted assets to free up capital. Consider measures to increase the capital. Potential liquidation of high-risk-weighted positions to a risk-free position to reduce further stress on the capital. Immediate steps to increase the Tier 1 and Tier 2 capital.
3	Capital ratio of 15% and above	While this situation may reflect the stability of the bank, this could potentially mean that the bank is not efficiently utilizing its capital.	Initiate action to allocate more capital to business units yielding higher risk-adjusted return on capital, thus improving the overall capital utilization position.

9.5.2. *Capital monitoring*

The bank incorporates different capital thresholds, with each threshold having different triggers attached to it. The key purpose of the methodology is to provide an early warning signal regarding capital levels, so corrective measures can be taken before the capital falls below acceptable limits. It also helps the bank to assess whether it is holding excess capital over and above what is required to maintain stability. Table 9.1 provides illustrative triggers and corrective action strategies under each trigger.

Summary

The bank's risk management organization structure provides for an efficient and independent internal control structure.

The risk management department, the risk coordinator within the risk management, and the compliance and internal audit functions of the bank are primarily responsible for the internal control review of risks.

The risk management committee, asset liability committee, executive investment committee, and audit committee oversee the function of internal control.

Furthermore, the supervisory board ensures the conduct of business is in line with Islamic principles, and the board of directors regularly verifies whether its system of internal controls is adequate to ensure well-ordered and prudent conduct of business.

The bank conducts periodic reviews of its risk management process to ensure its integrity.

References

Bellalah M and O Masood (2015). Role of accountants and fair value accounting leading towards the global financial crisis. *International Journal of Business*, 20(1).

Bellalah M, Z Chayeh and H Miniaoui (2015a). Advanced risk profile analysis of Islamic equity investment: Evidence from the American, Asian and European Market. *Finance-India*.

Bellalah M, Z Chayeh and H Miniaoui (2015b). Empirical evidence on Islamic equity investment from the American, Asian and European Market. *Finance-India.*

Websites

BankPolicies.com: https://bankpolicies.com/bank-policy-manual/ (updated 2025).

https://www.occ.treas.gov/news-events/newsroom/news-issuances-by-year/bulletins/banking-circulars.html,

European Banking Authority: Guidelines on internal policies, procedures and controls to ...

Basel Implementation Guide – Basel 3 Pillars: https://www.wolterskluwer.com.

Chapter 10

Internal Capital Adequacy Assessment Process

Chapter Outline

1. Section 10.1 presents definitions and general statements regarding the Internal Capital Adequacy Assessment Process (ICAAP).
2. Section 10.2 investigates the ICAAP.
3. Section 10.3 explains capital computation and minimum capital under ICAAP.
4. Section 10.4 develops stress testing.
5. Section 10.5 is about governance, roles, and responsibilities.

Introduction

The purpose of this chapter is to define and establish guidelines, based on regulatory requirements and industry best practices, for preparing a bank's assessment of internal capital requirements.

This chapter is based on my professional experience in several financial institutions.

Note also that internal capital requirements are key elements under Pillar 2 of Basel II. They are required by regulators globally. All the definitions presented here are public information available in documents on Basel websites (updated 2025).

The scope of this chapter falls within the jurisdiction of the risk division under the direct supervision of the risk committee and the governing body.

The definitions used here are standard. All regulators globally are using the same definitions as in the Basel Accord.

ICAAP: Banks are requested, under Pillar 2 of Basel, to develop internal processes, procedures, and systems. These processes can ensure that the bank has adequate capital resources in the long term with due attention to all material risks. These procedures are known as the Internal Capital Adequacy Assessment Process, or ICAAP.

Risk appetite framework: Risk appetite can be defined as the "amount" or quantity of risk, on a broad level, that a bank is taking on to pursue its strategic objectives. The guidance and framework surrounding it is termed the risk appetite framework.

Credit concentration risk: It refers to the risk of losses arising from concentrations of exposures due to a lack of diversification. This imperfect diversification stems from the small size of a portfolio, a large number of exposures to some specific entities or obligors (which is single customer concentration), or a lack of diversification with respect to general or specific economic sectors.

Interest rate or profit rate risk in the banking book (PRRBB): PRRBB is also a standard definition in Basel that refers to the current (or prospective) risk to both the capital and earnings of a bank (or financial institution) arising from adverse movements in interest rates or risk-free interest (known as profit rates in Islamic banking), which affects the banking book exposures.

Credit residual risk: Credit residual risk is the way banks should ensure that recognized credit risk mitigation (CRM) techniques address and control risk (including by means of written policies and procedures).

Strategic risk: Risk arising due to various effects of administrative or external obstacles. These obstacles can affect the execution of decisions relating to the initiation of banking services, business restructuring, etc.

Reputational risk: Reputational risk considers the current or prospective risk to the bank's earnings, capital, or liquidity. This risk can damage the bank's reputation.

10.1. Definitions and General Statements

10.1.1. *Definitions*

With its three-pillar model, the Basel II capital accord focuses on risk management.

Basel II provides guidelines for the calculation of capital requirements (Pillar 1). It defines extended disclosure requirements (Pillar 3). Under Pillar 2, banks must develop internal processes, procedures, and systems. This ensures that banks possess adequate capital resources in the long term (with due attention to all material risks). These procedures come under ICAAP.

The ICAAP encompasses all bank procedures and measures. They are designed to ensure the appropriate identification and measurement of risks. They also ensure the appropriate level of internal capital in relation to the bank's risk profile. They are conceived to ensure the use of suitable risk management systems.

10.1.2. *Objective*

The implementation of an ICAAP is in the best interest of all stakeholders of the bank (internal and external). Using ICAAP ensures a viable risk position by addressing risk appropriately. Indeed, as a risk management process, the ICAAP aims at assessing the bank's capital adequacy with respect to its risk profile and devising a strategy for maintaining its capital levels.

ICAAP aims at putting in place a risk management system to identify and manage all material risks under Pillar 2. It aims to provide reasonable assurance that achievement of the bank's core purpose will not be threatened by conscious risk-taking in the course of its banking business.

The main objective of the ICAAP is to secure the bank's risk-bearing capacity in relation to capital needed. It aims also to establish a comprehensive risk–return management system.

10.2. ICAAP Overview

The ICAAP ensures that risk management adequately identifies all material risks. The process aims to establish sufficient internal capital relative to the bank's risk profile. The process helps the bank apply and develop proper risk management systems. This helps to improve capital efficiency by mitigating risk exposures. The ICAAP process consists of elements detailed is Table 10.1. In addition, the bank maintains a parallel quality assurance and control process. The ICAAP framework is described as follows.

10.2.1. *Risk appetite*

The first step in linking risk to the strategy is through defining the risk appetite. The bank reviews its risk appetite as per the evolving business plan and changing economic and market scenarios. Risk appetite is the amount of risk, on a broad level, that the bank can take to pursue its strategic objectives. In order to establish a risk appetite framework, key parameters are identified at the group level and for each of the main business lines. The bank's risk limits are defined based on the risk appetite and are monitored at regular intervals.

10.2.2. *Risk identification*

In order to ensure that risks are consciously handled and systematically managed, it is important to identify relevant risk categories. Identifying risks is not sufficient for the bank to manage its risks. Assessing the materiality of the identified risks is vital to help the bank focus its efforts on high-materiality risks. This phase also helps the bank assess the complexity of the risk computation methodology to be used and set up risk limits and escalation criteria for limit breaches. This assessment is reviewed frequently by the risk management team to ensure continuous alignment of the risk management framework (with the evolving business strategy).

Based on Table 10.1, it can be inferred that the following are the key risks being faced by the bank: Risk 1, Risk 2, Risk 3, and Risk 4.

Table 10.1. Relevant risk categories.

Risk Type	Lines of Business (LOB)				Bank-Wide Level
	LOB1	LOB2	LOB3	LOB4	
Credit Risk	–	–	–	–	–
Operational Risk	–	–	–	–	–
Liquidity Risk	–	–	–	–	–
Interest Rate or Profit Rate Risk	–	–	–	–	–
Foreign Exchange Rate Risk	–	–	–	–	–
Concentration Risk	–	–	–	–	–
Strategic and Business Risk	–	–	–	–	–
Reputational Risk	–	–	–	–	–
Other Material Risk	–	–	–	–	–

10.2.3. *Quantifying risk and coverage capital*

This step involves allocating internal capital to each risk. This creates the objective basis for decision-making at the bank. This allows the board and senior management to make decisions regarding the bank's risk-bearing capacity within the ICAAP. Quantification of the capital coverage for various risks is detailed as follows:

Aggregation: Once risks are quantified, individual risks and associated capital requirements are aggregated to determine the capital requirement.

***Ex ante* control:** After the preparation of the bank's strategic plans and associated risk profiles, senior management seeks to evaluate the risk profile. This allows reviewing the level of risks and effects on capital adequacy. The sensitivity of key assumptions used in the capital assessment measurement system would be evaluated. Senior management uses this analysis to determine if the bank holds sufficient capital to meet budgeted plans. Wherever necessary, these risk profiles are either adjusted through prudential steps by minimizing risk exposures through hedging or offloading some risky assets, or the bank's strategic plan needs to be adjusted and additional capital needs to be raised.

Risk monitoring and *ex post* control: The risk monitoring process allows the bank's capital adequacy to remain in line with the

ICAAP. The required information is derived from comparing the bank's ideal position and actual position. The bank includes the results of the monitoring process in (internal) risk reports, which are compiled by the risk management department (RMD).

***Ex post* control:** Reporting is the basis for the measures taken in the *ex post* control stage. *Ex post* controls allow for the exercise of an active influence on risk positions (determined in the preceding stages of risk identification and quantification). The bank's risks are brought in line with its risk preferences. The senior management of the bank chooses the appropriate option from among the following alternatives (based on the specific nature of exceptions to established targets).

Risk mitigation or risk transfer: Risk mitigation reduces the effects of future risks. Such measures can include requesting collateral, diversifying risks, using conventional insurance or risk transfer, or exiting an exposure.

Increasing risk coverage capital: The bank develops emergency plans through discussions with its investors regarding the options of increasing capital. This decision has to be taken by the board.

Quality assurance and control process: The bank's quality assurance and control process runs in parallel with the other processes provided above. These measures are in place to ensure methods are implemented to quantify risks and resulting capital requirements. The control processes cover reviews of responsibilities in risk management. The internal audit department carries out an independent review of the overall ICAAP framework to ensure the implementation of appropriate policies and procedures.

10.3. Capital Computation and Minimum Capital Under ICAAP

The ICAAP exercise is compulsory for every bank. For a detailed analysis, we refer the reader to Bellalah *et al.* (2017a, 2017b).

The ICAAP is based on the following elements of sound capital assessment.

Table 10.2 provides ICAAP & CAR.

Table 10.2. Calculation of ICAAP CAR.

Calculation of ICAAP CAR	
Capital requirement for Pillar 1 risks (regulatory minimum)	10.50%
Capital requirement for Pillar 2 risks	Outcome of ICAAP (minimum of 1%)
Minimum ICAAP CAR	11.50%
Internal additional buffer	To be determined
Internal target CAR	To be determined

First, policies and procedures are designed to ensure that the bank identifies, measures, manages, and reports all material risks.

Second, a process is established between the capital level and the associated risk.

Third, a process is established that describes capital adequacy goals with respect to risk. The process must take into account the bank's strategic focus and business plan.

Fourth, a process of internal controls reviews and audits. This allows ensuring the integrity of the overall management process.

Capital computation methodology:

The following risks are addressed through capital allocation under Pillar l: credit risk, market risk, and operational risk. The ICAAP addresses the following additional risks: business and strategic risk, credit residual risk, liquidity risk, and reputational risk.

The RMD, along with financial control, constantly monitors the bank's CAR. Any transaction that breaches the target CAR is flagged and reported to executive management. The RPC is kept informed by the CRO on a regular basis (at least once monthly) until the bank's CAR remains below the target CAR. All the transactions of the bank (investment and credit) are assessed for the impact on CAR. The target CAR is an ideal situation for the bank to want to be in and work toward maintaining. The bank's minimum CAR as per ICAAP is 11.50%. At no point in time should the bank's CAR drop below 11.50%. If the CAR drops below this value, the CEO and RPC should be immediately notified by risk management. The bank initiates recovery measures under the oversight of RPC to bring the CAR to minimum levels. The bank is also required to inform regulators about the capital breach and the recovery plan on a real-time basis.

10.4. Stress Testing

Stress testing is a process that shows the effects on the bank of low-frequency, high-severity risk events, usually called "tail events", which cannot be captured under "normal" risk measures. Stress testing is considered an integral part of the ICAAP. To that effect, the bank considers the impact of a stressed situation on its capital adequacy.

There are two major stress-testing techniques to assess the impact of stress events on the bank:

Sensitivity analysis provides an estimation of the impact on a portfolio's value of specified movements in a single risk factor (or a set of closely related risk factors). This is a simple technique, but it cannot assess realistic co-variation and co-movements of risk factors.

Scenario analysis measures the effect of adverse movements in a number of risk factors. The stressed scenarios are based on historical (or sometimes hypothetical events), and the correlation between risk factors is taken into account when developing the relevant assumptions used (in the stress scenarios).

10.5. Governance, Roles, and Responsibilities

The bank follows sound risk governance principles, which emphasize clear roles, responsibilities, and reporting lines. The bank follows sound governance principles laid down by local central banks (or regulatory authorities) for corporate governance in its governance structure for market risk. The following sections in this document articulate the bank's governance framework for the ICAAP process. The governance structure includes various stakeholders such as the board of directors (BoD), risk and management committee (RMC), executive investment committee (EIC), asset liability management committee (ALCO), chief risk officer (CRO), chief investment officer (CIO), and chief finance officer (CFO).

The roles and responsibilities of involved authorities and functions with respect to the ICAAP are detailed as follows.

Board of directors: The BoD shall be responsible for periodically reviewing and approving the ICAAP framework. Furthermore, the BoD shall ensure that the ICAAP is subject to comprehensive internal and external audit oversight.

The responsibilities of the BOD include periodically reviewing and approving the ICAAP document framework; reviewing risk profile reports; issuing directions to senior management to address ICAAP issues concerning the bank; and reviewing and approving business strategy and ICAAP capital.

Risk management department: The RMD is responsible for the following:

- facilitating the definition, setup, and implementation of the risk framework across the bank;
- identifying and assessing all inherent and material risks;
- devising appropriate methodologies for measurement of risks;
- measuring the actual and target risk capital in line with the bank's risk capacity;
- devising appropriate methodologies for stress testing the risk factors to measure the stressed capital.

Financial control department: The FCD is responsible for the following three elements:

- coordinating the preparation of a business plan for the next five years based on the strategy approved by the board;
- capital budgeting and capital allocation based on the business plan and risk profile as submitted by the RMD for the next five years;
- recommending appropriate capital instruments for meeting the capital requirements.

Business unit heads (BUHs): The BUHs are responsible for the two following elements:
First, they are responsible for the preparation and provision of business plans for the next five years for their respective units to the FCD.
Second, they support the CRO in the risk assessment process by providing the updated product profile as needed.

Internal audit: The audit exercise is a risk-based process where levels of inherent risk in the entity and the extent, adequacy, and application of mitigating controls are assessed across certain defined risk parameters. The internal audit department is responsible for reviewing the adequacy and appropriateness of the risk measurement process. It is also responsible for ensuring ICAAP adherence to regulatory guidelines.

Summary

The Basel II, Basel III, and soon Basel IV capital accords place greater importance on risk management. Basel II provides guidelines for the calculation of capital requirements under Pillar 1. Basel II defines extended disclosure requirements under (Pillar 3). Banks are requested, under Pillar 2, to develop internal systems in order to ensure adequate capital resources to cover all material risks. These procedures are known as the Internal Capital Adequacy Assessment Process, or ICAAP.

ICAAP is conceived to ensure an appropriate identification and measurement of risks. ICAAP expects an appropriate level of internal capital in relation to the bank's risk profile. Its implementation is in the best interest of all stakeholders of the bank (internal and external).

The risk management process, or ICAAP, aims at assessing the bank's overall capital adequacy in relation to its risk profile. It aims also at putting in place a risk management system to identify and manage all material risks under Pillar 2.

The ICAAP provides reasonable assurance that achievement of the core purpose of the bank will not be threatened by conscious risk-taking in the course of its banking business. The ICAAP secures the bank's risk-bearing capacity and establishes a comprehensive risk–return management system.

References

Bellalah M, O Masood and SM Ghauri (2017a). Basel III implementation outcome in Islamic banks. *The Journal of Risk*.

Bellalah M, O Masood and J Younas (2017b). Liquidity risk management implementation for selected Islamic banks in Pakistan. *The Journal of Risk*.

Websites

World Bank: https://policies.worldbank.org/en/policies (updated 2025).

Independent Community Bankers of America – ICBA: https://www.icba.org/resources (updated 2025).

Part III

Financial Markets and Financial Instruments: Basic Concepts and Strategies

Chapter 11

Financial Markets, Financial Instruments, and Financial Crisis

Chapter Outline

This chapter is organized as follows:

1. Section 11.1 presents the trading characteristics of commodity contracts. The analysis concerns mainly oil markets.
2. Section 11.2 studies the main trading characteristics of commodity markets and instruments. The analysis concerns the instruments in the International Petroleum Exchange.
3. Section 11.3 develops the characteristics of crude oils and the properties of petroleum products.
4. Section 11.4 presents the trading characteristics of another commodity: Cocoa.
5. Section 11.5 illustrates the main trading characteristics of options. The analysis pertains mainly to equity options.
6. Section 11.6 studies the trading characteristics of options on currency forwards and futures.
7. Section 11.7 develops the trading characteristics of options. The analysis pertains mainly to bonds and bond options markets.
8. Section 11.8 provides examples of simple and complex financial instruments.
9. Section 11.9 provides the main reasons behind financial innovations.

10. Section 11.10 provides an overview of derivatives markets in the world: stock options, index options, interest rate and commodity options and futures markets.

Introduction

The main questions regarding the wave of financial innovations are:

What are the specific features of the "new" financial contracts?
Why are there so many financial contracts?
What are the fundamental reasons behind the proliferation of financial assets?

A partial answer to such questions is given in the analysis of Miller (1986), Merton (1988), and Ross (1989), among others. These financial instruments are traded either in organized markets or in non-organized markets, known as over-the-counter markets, or OTC markets. These products are presented either in a straight forward form or in a package. They can be used to create several combinations with different risk and reward trade-offs.

What are derivatives?

A derivative is a generic term to encompass all financial transactions, which are not directly traded in the primary physical market. It refers to a financial instrument to manage a given risk. The term includes forwards, futures, options, commodity contracts, etc.

What is a forward contract?

They are the simplest and most basic hedging instruments. A forward contract is an agreement between two parties to set the price today for a transaction that will not be completed until a specified date in the future. An example is a forward contract for \$1 million, to be delivered in six months, at a price of 5.30 for a dollar. These terms obligate the seller of the contract to deliver \$1 million on the company's account, for the price set today. On the other hand, the buyer has no alternative than to accept delivery under the terms of the contract. The only possibility for the buyer to cancel the contract at a later date, is to enter into a reverse forward contract, with the same bank or another institution, but at the risk of a loss (or a gain) since the new forward rate will be set at a new equilibrium level. Forward rate contracts are flexible and allow for customized hedges since all the terms can be negotiated with the counterparty. However, each side of the contract bears the risk that the other side defaults on the future commitments. That is why futures contracts are often referred to as forward contracts.

What is a futures contract?

A future is an exchange-traded contract between a buyer and seller and the clearinghouse of a futures exchange to buy or sell a standard quantity and quality of a commodity at a specified future date and price. The clearinghouse acts as a counterpart in all transactions and is responsible for holding traders' surety bonds to guarantee that transactions are completed.

Like forward contracts, futures contracts are used to lock in the interest rate, exchange rate, or commodity price. But, futures markets are organized in such a way that the risk of default is always completely eliminated. This is possible by trading futures contracts on an organized exchange with a clearinghouse which steps in between a buyer and a seller, each time a deal is struck in the pit. The clearinghouse adopts the position of the buyer to every seller, and of the seller to every buyer, i.e., the clearinghouse keeps a zero net position. This means that every trader in the futures markets has obligations only to the clearinghouse, and has strong expectations that the clearinghouse will maintain its side of the bargain as well. The credibility of the system is maintained through the requirements of margin and daily settlements. The main purpose of the margin is to provide a safeguard to ensure that traders will perform their obligations. It is usually set to the maximum loss a trader can experience in a normal trading day. Daily settlements or marking to market just consists in a transfer of cash from one account to another. The elimination of default risk has a cost: contracts are standardized in order to bring liquidity to the market, there are only a few financial assets which are traded on futures markets and they do not necessarily correspond to the risk to be hedged. Therefore, there is no perfect hedge with futures contracts. The hedgers keep what is called a basis risk and a correlation risk which cannot be fully eliminated.

What are standard options?

Options are more flexible than forwards and futures in the sense they provide the buyer with the protection needed, and leave him/her with the full benefits associated with a favorable development of the asset price, interest rate, or exchange rate. This nice feature has a price: the option premium. On the contrary, forward and futures prices are set at a level such that the initial price of the contract is exactly zero. A standard or a vanilla option is a security that gives its holder the right to buy or sell the underlying asset within a specified period of time, at a given price, called the strike price, striking price or strike price and no obligation to deliver. A European option can be exercised only on the last day of the contract, called the maturity date or the expiration date. An American option can be exercised at any time during the contract's life.

What are commodity contracts?

Commodity contracts are traded around the world. One of the main examples is oil. Oil has become one of the biggest commodity market in the world. Oil trading evolved from a primarily physical activity into a financial market. The first contract, gas oil futures began trading in 1981. A Brent crude futures contract was launched in 1988. A natural gas futures contract is also traded. A network of Quote Vendors relay information on a real-time basis to end users in several countries worldwide. The Brent crude contract and the gas oil contract are used as benchmarks or price references in trading.

11.1. Trading Characteristics of Commodity Contracts: The Case of Oil

The oil market is ultimately concerned with the transportation, processing, and storage of a raw material. Since oil is a liquid, it requires specialized handling facilities for transportation, processing, and storage. These elements represent the basic building blocks for the physical oil market. The behavior of prices is influenced by the fundamental forces of demand and supply. The demand of oil depends on the state of the global economy.

11.1.1. *Fixed prices*

11.1.1.1. *Outright prices*

A contract for the sale of a cargo of oil must stipulate the basic price, the guaranteed quality, and agreed price adjustment for quality deviations, availability date range, etc. These factors describe the elements of the price of a cargo of oil. Gasoil is sold in Europe at x dollars per metric tonne, based on a specific gravity. The important qualities for crude oil are gravity, measured in API degrees, metals content and sulfur. Crude is in general traded in US dollars per barrel. In Europe, oil products are generally sold in US dollars per metric tonnes. Timing can have an impact on pricing when the market is in backwardation or contango. Backwardation corresponds to a situation in which the price of the commodity available on a prompt basis is higher than that for deferred delivery. Contango corresponds to a situation in which a commodity is cheapest in the prompt position and gets progressively more expensive in the future. Hence, the oil price depends not only on its quality but also on the delivery date range. The location of the oil affects its price.

11.1.2. *Floating prices*

As oil prices became volatile, there was increasing uncertainty about the value of oil at the time it was to be loaded or discharged. As the oil market moved away from fixed prices, oil prices reflected the market value of the oil at the time of moving the oil. The growth of the forward market, futures markets, swaps, and options markets developed the pricing mechanisms.

11.1.3. *Exchange of futures for physical (EFP)*

Exchange of futures for physical (EFP) provide a method of pricing a cargo of oil at a differential to the futures market. The buyer and the seller utilize existing futures positions that match their exposure on the physical oil market.

The buyer of a physical cargo transfers ownership to the seller (of the cargo) of a certain number of futures contracts, equivalent to the volume of the cargo of oil. The value of the futures contract is used to calculate the price of the physical oil. The seller becomes long futures contracts and the buyer short futures contracts at the agreed level.

11.2. Description of Markets and Instruments: The Case of the International Petroleum Exchange

Crude oil trade is a key nexus between the two main centers of activity: upstream exploration and production and downstream refining, and marketing. In this context, the price of crude oil results from the interaction between the signals provided by product markets and the revenue objectives of producers. The growth of the international spot market in crude oil and the ensuing transformation in the structure of oil markets explain the way oil is priced today.

11.3. Characteristics of Crude Oils and Properties of Petroleum Products

Petroleum or crude oil can be described as a viscous brown to black liquid mixture. Petroleum contains a hydrocarbon mixture and non-hydrocarbon compounds such as sulfur, nitrogen, and oxygen compounds.

11.3.1. *Specific features of some oil contracts*

The IPE Brent Crude futures contract is one of the most important energy price indicators in the world. This contract represents the critical part of the Brent Blend complex which represents the benchmark for two thirds of the world's internationally traded crude oil.

11.3.1.1. *Brent crude futures*

There is no maximum price fluctuation imposed upon Brent crude futures. The contract can be settled in cash against a physical price index calculated by the IPE. It can be settled with physical delivery through the EFP mechanism. The unit of trading is one or more lots of 1,000 net barrels (42,000 US gallons) of Brent crude oil. The contract specifies the current pipeline export quality Brent blend as supplied at Sullom Voe. The contract price is in US dollars and cents per barrel. The minimum price fluctuation is one cent per barrel, which gives a tick value of US$10. All open contracts are marked-to-market daily.

11.3.1.2. *Gas oil futures*

The IPE gas oil contract is a benchmark for the physical market in Europe and beyond. This contract is used as a price basis for most middle distillate spot trades in northwest Europe. Companies can use this contract to evaluate arbitrage, storage, and investment opportunities.

11.3.1.3. *Natural gas futures*

The natural gas futures contract was launched in January 1997. Since the launch, many changes to the contract have been made as the industry has uncovered new needs and opportunities. The IPE natural gas futures (NBP) contracts are traded through the IPE automated energy trading system (ETS) or by the EFPs. The contract size corresponds to a minimum of 5 lots of 1,000 therms per lot of natural gas per day during the contract period. The contract price is in Sterling and in pence per therm. If not closed out at expiry, contracts obligate delivery or taking delivery on each day in that contract period of the number of lots remaining open upon expiry.

11.3.1.4. *Options*

The IPE offers American options contracts for Brent crude and gas oil futures. Options enable companies to carry out several complex and hedging techniques. The unit of trading is represented for IPE gas oil options is one IPE gas oil futures contract. The contract price is in US dollars and cents per tonne. The strike price increments are multiples of US$5 per tonne. A minimum of 5 strike prices are listed for each contract month. Due to futures style margining, option premiums are not paid or received at the time of the transaction. Margins are received or paid each day according to the changing value of the option. The total value to be paid or received is only known when the position is closed. This is done by an opposing sale or purchase, the exercise or the maturity of the option. The options can be exercised into gas oil futures contracts.

11.3.2. *Description of markets and trading instruments: The Brent market*

11.3.2.1. *Dated Brent and 15-day Brent*

Two types of transactions can be done in the physical Brent blend market. The first, known as "dated Brent" cargo is a conventional spot transaction which refers to the sale of a specific cargo. The cargo is either available in a specific loading slot or is loaded and in transit to some destination. The second, known as "15-day Brent" is a forward deal, which refers to a standard parcel that will be made available by the seller on an unspecified day of the relevant month. Oil is sold f.o.b. (insurance, freight, and ocean losses are the buyer's responsibility), but demurrage at the terminal is the seller's. For 15-day Brent, the contract is a standard telex and there is no exchange to match sellers and buyers. The clearing of the market involves all participants. The clearing consists of two different operations book-outs and the seller's nominations. A book-out is simply an agreement between some participants to cancel their contracts with a cash settlement procedure for the difference between an agreed reference price and the contract price. The contracts which are not cleared by a book out cancellation are cleared through the nomination process. Sellers through the forward market serve 15-day notices to buyers of cargoes for the relevant month. The 15-day market reveals the buyer's uncertainty regarding the exact date of delivery and it is characterized by a lack of perfect price/volume transparency.

11.3.2.2. *Spread trading*

Forward cargoes can either be traded as single cargoes with an absolute price agreed, or in spread trading. This latter case involves the simultaneous purchase or sale of at least two cargoes and appears in different forms.

11.3.2.3. *Inter-month spreads*

Spread trading in the Brent market appears as transactions of the difference in price between Brent for delivery in different months using two Brent cargoes.

When trader A buys an April/May spread from trader B, then A has bought an April cargo from B and simultaneously sold a May cargo to B.

The inter-month spread is simply a position on the absolute level of the backwardation or contango between the delivery months. In general, a contango appears when prices are higher for more distant delivery months. Backwardation is the reverse.

11.3.2.4. *Inter-crude spreads*

It is possible to trade the differential against another crude oil as Dubai or WTI. When trader A buys an April Brent-Dubai spread, he buys the April Brent cargo and sells the April Dubai cargo. An inter-crude spread is a position taken on the path of the difference in prices between the crude oils. Trader A will gain if the price of the Brent strengthens relative to that of Dubai.

11.3.2.5. *The box trade*

This strategy is implemented by taking a position on the movement of the relative backwardation (or contango) between two crude oil markets. The trader sells and buys simultaneously two inter-crude spreads. The strategy involves the trading of four cargoes. For example, a Brent-Dubai box spread involves the simultaneous purchase of a Brent cargo and the sale of a Dubai cargo for the same delivery month and the purchase of a Dubai cargo for another delivery month.

11.3.2.6. *The IEP Brent futures contract*

The International Petroleum Exchange of London (IEP) trades Brent futures contract on cargoes of 500,000 barrels. The physical base of the New York Mercantile Exchange (NYMEX) contract is pipeline scheduling at Cushing Oklahoma of 1,000 barrel batches.

IPE Brent contracts represent two contracts: one between the buyer and the clearing house and one between the seller and the clearing house. The clearing house is the International Commodities Clearing House Ltd (ICCH).

11.3.2.7. *Exchange of futures for physical (EFPs)*

An EFP is a physical link between the IPE Brent futures contract and North Sea spot market on the 15-day market. This can be used to exchange an IPE position for a spot cargo. It represents, for example, the exchange of a futures market position of 500 IPE lots, (i.e., 500,000 barrels), for a 15-day cargo. It can be viewed as a spread between forward Brent and futures Brent.

11.3.2.8. *IPE Brent options*

The IPE's Brent American options contract was launched on 11 May 1989 trading lots of 1,000 barrels of Brent blend. The IPE Brent futures contract is the underlying asset. The option is exercised, i.e., transferred to a Brent futures contract at any time before maturity. A call gives its holder the right to buy the underlying futures contract at a strike price defined in multiples of 50 cents per barrel. A put gives its holder the right to sell the underlying futures contract at a strike price defined also in multiples of 50 cents per barrel. Options are also traded on Brent delivery month spreads. The over-the-counter (OTC) market represents a series of personalized bilateral trades and provides tailor-made options on deals of any size. This market is used by several large financial institutions.

11.3.2.9. *Swaps*

The swap allows the producer or the consumer of crude oil and oil products to lock in a price or a margin. The main participants are finance houses and the trading departments of large oil companies. A producer can arrange a swap for a given volume over a specified period at a price equating to a "mean" market price over that period. At each agreed settlement period, actual market prices for the agreed volume are compared to the value of that volume under the specified price in the swap transaction. When market prices are higher, the producer pays the swaps provider the difference times the agreed volume. When market prices are lower, the swaps provider pays the producer the difference times the agreed volume. In the swap transaction, there is a physical exchange of oil, but a series of netted transactions or contract for the differences.

11.4. Description of Markets and Trading Instruments: The Case of Cocoa

The International Cocoa Organization (ICCO) was established in 1973 to administer the first International Cocoa Agreement, that of 1972 and its successor Agreements, of 1975, 1980, 1986, and 1993.

For further information, the reader can refer to library@icco.org. The Agreements were concluded among the governments of cocoa producing and consuming countries, under the auspices of the United Nations. As on 13 July 1998, the membership of the ICCO comprised a total of 41 members.

11.4.1. *How do the futures and physicals markets work?*

There are large differences between physical and futures prices. The cocoa trade is based on the actuals market and the futures market. The actuals market is known as thc physical market, the spot market or the cash market.

11.4.2. *Arbitrage*

Arbitrage involves the simultaneous purchase of futures or physical commodities in one market against the sale of the same quantity of futures or physical commodity in a different market. An arbitrage strategy is often implemented to take advantage of differentials in the price of the same instrument on different markets. Cocoa can be traded on CSCE in dollars and LIFFE in pound sterling. The arbitrage price can be derived by subtracting the CSCE price converted to pound sterling from the LIFFE price. In practice, London cocoa sells at a premium over New York cocoa because of a quality in the difference of cocoa.

The arbitrage price is affected by the forces of supply and demand and by exchange rates. Arbitrage allows speculation on whether the premium of London cocoa will increase or decrease over New York.

11.5. Trading Characteristics of Options: The Case of Equity Options

This section describes the specific features of options markets. A call gives the right to its holder to buy the underlying asset at a given price within or at a specified period of time. A put option gives the right to the buyer to sell the underlying asset at the striking price within or at a specified period of time.

Equity warrants are long-term options traded often in securities markets rather than in option markets. Covered warrants are (OTC) long-term options issued by securities houses.

11.5.1. *Options on equity indices*

These options are tin raded on the major indices around the world. Options on the spot index are cash-settled, i.e., there is no physical delivery of the underlying index.

11.5.2. *Options on index futures*

These options require upon exercise a long (a short) position in the future contract for a call (a put) in the same contract.

Index options on stock indexes and stock index futures began trading in the United States in 1983 with the introduction of the S&P 100 contract on the Chicago Board Options Exchange. The 10 largest markets in the FT-Actuaries World Index have listed options (See Table 11.1).

In these countries, index futures are also traded. In general, combined options and futures volumes exceed trading in the underlying stocks. Volume is concentrated in one-month contracts. The volume in options with longer maturities takes place in the OTC. The OTC options market began to develop in 1988.

Table 11.1. Countries in the FT-Actuaries World Index with listed index options.

Country	Index
USA	S&P 500 and S&P 100 since 1983
Japan	Nikkei 225 since 1989
France	CAC 40 since 1988
Germany	DAX since 1991
Switzerland	SMI since 1988
Canada	TSE 35 since 1987
The Netherlands	EOE since 1978
Australia	All ordinaries since 1983

11.5.3. *Index options markets around the world*

In North America, options available are traded on several indices: S&P 100, S&P 500, Major Market, S&P MidCap, NYSE Composite, Value Line, Torento 35, etc. Several listed options exist on indices like Value Line (PHX), National OTC (PHX) indexes, etc. In Japan, the main option contract is the Osaka Nikkei. Options exist also on the Singapore International Monetary Exchange (SIMEX), the Tokyo stock price index (TOPIX), etc. The OTC activity appears on the FT-Actuaries Japan Index. In Europe, several options are listed on European indices.

In Germany, listed DAX options trade on the Deutsche Terminbourde Bourse (DTB) on a screen-based system. Trading in options started in 1991. Investors use also the OTC market for DAX options with maturities greater than three months.

In France, CAC 40 options are traded on the Paris-Bourse. The OTC market is used mainly by large US and European investment banks. In the United Kingdom, FT-SE options are traded on the London International Financial Futures Exchange (LIFFE). The market is dominated by major international banks and UK brokers.

The OTC market is mainly used by global investment banks and the major UK brokers.

11.5.4. *Stock index markets and the underlying indices in Europe*

11.5.4.1. *The CAC 40 index*

The CAC 40 index is computed using 40 stocks in the French market. It does not account for the distributions of dividends. The following formula is used:

$$I_t = \frac{1000 \sum_{i=1}^{N} q_{i,t} S_{i,t}}{K_t C A_0}$$

where:

t: instant at which the index is computed;
N: the number of stocks used (40);
$q_{i,t}$: number of shares of stock i, at date t;

$S_{i,t}$: the price of stock i at date t;
CA_0: market capitalization of the sample used in the reference date (December 1987) and
K_t: an adjustment coefficient at date t.

11.5.4.2. *The STOXX^{SM} 50 and EURO STOXX^{SM}*

The Dow Jones STOXX^{SM} and Dow Jones EURO STOX^{SM} 50 indices are European indices launched on 26 February 1998 by STOXX limited. These indices provide a representative picture of European equity market performance. These indices are composed of 50 industrial, commercial, and financial blue chips. These indices are available on all major information networks and are disseminated every 15 seconds.

The methodology in constructing these indices is based upon a matrix approach that begins with 80% of the investible universe.

Futures on the Dow Jones STOXX^{SM} and Dow Jones EURO STOXX^{SM} 50 indices allow fund managers to insulate the asset value of their European equity portfolios regardless of their performance benchmark. This can be achieved by selling futures contracts in proportion to the sensitivity of these portfolios to fluctuations in the Dow Jones STOXX^{SM} and Dow Jones EURO STOXX^{SM} 50 indices. Selling derivatives allow market participants to stabilize their portfolios. Anticipating a rise (a fall) in prices, investors can buy (sell) index futures and sell at higher (lower) prices at a later date.

Theoretical values of index futures can be calculated at any time using the prices of the equity baskets represented by the Dow Jones STOXX^{SM} and Dow Jones EURO STOXX^{SM} 50 indices. The theoretical value corresponds to the value of the equity basket plus the basis, i.e., the cost of purchasing the index portfolio components, less dividends.

Options on Dow Jones STOXX^{SM} and Dow Jones EURO STOXX^{SM} 50 indices can be used as short hedging instruments, through the purchase of puts.

Derivatives on Dow Jones STOXX^{SM} and Dow Jones EURO STOXX^{SM} 50 indices give investors the tools to pursue simple strategies based on their expectations of market movements. Investors can buy call (put) options or sell put (call) options. Options can be used in arbitrage transactions allowing strategies to be pursued based on comparative fluctuations between equity markets within the Euro zone and the different countries.

The specific features of the Dow Jones Euro STOXX^{SM} 50 index are as follows.

Dow Jones Euro STOXX^{SM} 50 composition:

Basket of 50 highly liquid Euro zone (10 countries) blue chips, belonging to the main business sectors.

Calculation method: The index level is given by: $I = 1{,}000$ (sum of real-time market capitalization for each component stock/adjusted base capitalization). The index is calculated in real-time by STOXX Ltd. Price quotation: The index is disseminated every 15 seconds by ParisBourse (Table 11.2).

Table 11.2. Contract specifications.

Contract specifications	Dow Jones STOXX^{SM} and Dow Jones EURO STOXX^{SM} futures
Underlying index	Dow Jones STOXX^{SM} and Dow Jones EURO STOXX^{SM} indices
Trading unit	Contract valued at EURO 10 times the index quoted in the future
Price quotation	Index without decimal
Minimum price fluctuation (tick)	1 index point equivalent to EURO 10
Contract month	3 spot months, 2 quarterly contract months of the March, June, September, and December cycle
Last trading month	3rd Friday of the contract month at 12:00 p.m.
First trading day	First trading day following the last trading day of the previous contract month
Settlement/exercise	Cash settlement, expiration settlement price = arithmetic mean (with 2 decimals) of each index value calculated and displayed between 11:50 a.m. and 12:00 p.m. (41 values)
Margin	Margin information can be obtained from the MATIF/MONEP information department
Trading hours	NSC day session: 8:00 a.m.–5:00 p.m. NSC evening session: 5:05 p.m.–10:00 p.m

11.6. Trading Characteristics of Options: The Case of Options on Currency Forwards and Futures

These options are traded in the OTC market. The growth of the OTC market is due to its flexibility. In fact, many banks and financial institutions offer options with tailor-made characteristics in order to match the clients needs. Options on the currency futures have been traded since 1982. These options are standardized contracts.

11.7. Trading Characteristics of Options: The Case of Bonds and Bond Options Markets

There are several types of bonds and bond options traded in organized and OTC markets. These financial instruments correspond, for example, to zero-coupon bonds, bonds with call provisions, putable bonds, convertible bonds, bonds with warrants attached, exchangeable bonds, etc.

11.7.1. *The specific features of classic interest rate instruments*

11.7.1.1. *Zero-coupon bonds*

These bonds are bonds with no periodic coupon payments. The interest due to the bond holder is given by the difference between the maturity value and the purchase price. This class of bonds is referred to as zero-coupon bonds and its price is given by the present value of the maturity value.

In the mathematics of bonds, continuous compounded interest rates and/or discrete compounded interest rates can be used.

For continuous trading in derivatives, interest rate is often continuously compounded using the factor e^{-rT} to discount US$ 1 payable in T years at a rate r.

In this case, the value of a zero-coupon bond is computed by discounting its maturity value at this factor. When interest is accumulated annually for T years, discretely compounded interest rate is computed by using $(1/(1+r')^T)$. The equivalence between the two fomulas appears when $r = \log(1+r')$.

11.7.1.2. *A coupon-paying bond*

This bond is often regarded as a portfolio of several cash flows (the coupons) where each cash flow can be seen as a zero-coupon bond. Hence, a coupon-paying bond can be viewed as a package of zero-coupon bonds.

The principal amount of a bond issue can decrease or amortize during the life of the interest-sensitive instrument. The principal is paid back gradually at a given rate and interest is paid on the amount of the principal outstanding.

11.7.1.3. *A corporate bond*

This is a bond issued by a firm. The bond obliges the issuer to pay interest rate charges and the principal amount according to a specified schedule.

If the bond is guaranteed by some assets of the issuer, it becomes a mortgage bond. If the only guarantee is represented by the credibility of the issuer, the bond is a debenture bond. Each bond issue is accompanied with a document known as indenture. It specifies the main features of the issue.

Some bonds are not redeemed before another class of debt. They are referred to as junior or subordinated bonds. The higher priority claims are referred to as senior bonds. A sinking fund provision is often inserted in the bond indenture to describe the way bondholders will be paid.

11.7.1.4. *Bonds with specific features*

A bond with a call provision gives the right to the issuer to call the issue before the specified redemption date. A bond with a put provision gives its holder the right to put the bond back to the issuer at a fixed price.

11.7.1.5. *Indexed bonds*

These bonds are useful when the operating profits of a corporation are exposed to the fluctuations of an index, as with a commodity price like oil, aluminium or inflation. The exposure risk can be partially hedged by issuing bonds whose interest rate payments and/or principal repayment is linked to the index, in such a way that the effective cost of debt is reduced when there is an unfavorable movement in the price index, and is increased to the benefit of the investors when the movement is favorable to the firm. Such a bond issue can be split into parts: the bull and bear tranches, so that investors can choose only one side of the risk exposure. These bonds allow some investors to take risky positions which are not directly available to them, or not allowed, on organized markets. Investors are ready to pay a premium for these opportunities which is translated into a reduced financing cost.

11.7.1.6. *A convertible bond*

Entitles its holder the right to convert the bond into a certain number of units of the equity of the issuing firm or into other bonds.

11.7.1.7. *A bond with an attached warrant*

It is simply a package comprising the bond and a warrant. Most of these bonds are Eurobonds issued in international capital markets.

11.7.1.8. *An exchangeable bond*

It is similar to a convertible bond, with the exception that it gives its holder the right to exchange the bonds for the equity of another company, etc. When a corporation has a low credit rating and must implement a large investment program to survive, it may well be too costly to issue standard debt, while raising equity might dilute considerably the current shareholders' position. Then, warrants (bonds with attached warrants) and convertibles become the only affordable financing instruments.

11.7.1.9. *Floating rate notes, FRN*

The value of an FRN depends mainly on the coupon date payment. The coupon is often determined as a mean of the interest rates applied to three-month treasury bills. A risk premium is added to the mean rate to account for the risk of the issuer.

11.7.1.10. *Floating rate bonds, FRB*

The coupon payments are indexed with reference to a variable interest rate index as the rate on the three-month treasury bills or the rate on 30-year treasury bonds. Several floaters show implicit embedded provisions which have the specific features of call and put options. For example, the provision of the type Floor and Ceiling specifies a minimum coupon rate of $x\%$ and a maximum coupon rate of $y\%$.

11.7.1.11. *Stripped bonds*

The cash flows from treasury bonds can be separated into two assets: an asset corresponding to the principal amount, (principal only, PO), and an asset corresponding to interest rates, (interest only, IO). This type of bond represents a stripped asset and is referred to as treasury-backed stripped. The amount of principal, PO, represents the value of a zero coupon bond. The amount of interest, IO, corresponds to a portfolio of zero coupon bonds. The separation between the cash flows can eliminate the reinvestment risk. It allows the investor to use different IO and PO in hedging strategies.

11.7.1.12. *Strips*

Correspond to an instrument called "Separate Trading of Registered Interest and Principal of Securities". The separation between coupons and principal of a bond allows the creation of artificial zero-coupon bonds of longer maturities than would otherwise exist.

11.7.2. *The specific features of mortgage-backed securities*

These securities are linked to the financial crisis in 2007–2008 and mainly to the subprime. The mortgage is a pledge of real estate which is used to secure the payment of a loan originated for the purchase of a real property. The lender, known as the mortgagee, has the right to foreclose on the loan and to seize the property if the borrower (mortgagor) does not satisfy his contracted obligations.

A mortgage loan is specified by the interest rate of the loan, the number of years to maturity, and the frequency of payments. The mortgage instrument represents an instrument which is guaranteed by a real asset, a land, a building, etc. Mortgages can be divided into different classes according to the nature of the asset used as a guarantee.

Mortgages represent the underlying collateral of mortgage-backed securities. When bonds are guaranteed by the shares of a firm, they are referred to as collateral trust bonds. When the bond is guaranteed by a building for example or other assets of the issuer, it is a mortgage security. If a firm has 100 securities and uses a guarantee of 30, it can issue 30 of mortgage bonds.

In the United States, the Federal National Mortgage Association (FNMA), the Government National Mortgage Association, GNMA, and the Federal Home Loan Mortgage Corporation, (FHLMC) play an important role in the mortgage market. The FNMA introduces mortgage-backed-securities (MBS), which are created by pooling mortgage loans and using this pool of mortgage loans as collateral for the security. The cash flow of an MBS is a function of the cash flows of the underlying mortgage pool.

If you consider an entity that purchases several loans, pools them, and uses them as collateral for issuance of a security, the security created is referred to as a mortgage pass-through security. The security is guaranteed by the GNMA, the FNMA, and the FHLMC.

Pass-through securities can be issued also by private entities. In this case, they are referred to as conventional pass-throughs.

When mortgage loans are used in a pool to create a pass-through security, they are said to be securitized. The process of creating the pass-through security is known as the securitization of mortgage loans.

The FHLMC introduced in 1983, the collaterized mortgage obligations, (CMO). Since an investor in a pass-through security is exposed to the total pre-payment risk due to the pool of mortgage loans underlying the security, it is possible to create three classes of bonds with different par values. This can be done by indicating how the principal is distributed from the pass-through security. In general, there are three classes: A, B, and C. This mortgage-backed security refers to a CMO.

The total pre-payment risk for the CMO remains similar to that of the mortgage loans. The stripped MBS becomes an attractive instrument in managing portfolios of mortgage securities. It is possible to forecast the prepayments from a pass-through security. Therefore, some pre-payment benchmark conventions must be known. In general, the Standard pre-payment model, PSA developed by the public securities association can be used. This benchmark is expressed as a monthly series of annual constant pre-payment rates, CPRs. The CPR is converted into a monthly pre-payment rate, known as the single monthly mortality rate (SMM) where SMM $= 1 - (1 - \text{CPR})^{1/12}$.

The PSA model assumes that pre-payment rates will be low for newly originated mortgages. The rate will speed up as the mortgages become seasoned. For more details, see Fabozzi (1993).

11.7.3. *The specific features of interest rate futures, options, bond options, and swaps*

11.7.3.1. *Interest rate futures contracts*

A futures contract is an agreement between a buyer or a seller and an established exchange to take or make delivery of a given commodity at a specified price at a given delivery or settlement date. An investor can be long (a buyer) or short (a seller). Each investor must deposit an initial margin before trading futures contracts. The margin used to guarantee the transactions can attain a minimum level known as the maintenance margin. The margin varies with the variation in the futures price. The futures contract is marked to market at the end of each trading day and is subject to interim cash flows. The main difference between futures contracts and forward contracts is that forward contracts are OTC instruments which are nonstandardized and are subject to counter-party risk. There are several traded interest rate futures contracts. Interest rate futures contracts are traded on treasury bonds, notes, bills and on the LIBOR rate.

Interest rate futures options are traded on T-bond futures, T-note futures, Eurodollar futures, etc.

11.7.3.2. *Treasury bill futures*

The underlying asset of this contract is a short-term debt obligation. The treasury bill is quoted in the cash market in terms of the annualized yield on a bank discount basis:

$$Y_d = \left(\frac{D}{T}\right)\left(\frac{360}{t}\right)$$

where:

D = difference between the face value and the price of a bill maturing in t days, known also as a dollar discount;
F = face or nominal value and
T = number of days remaining to maturity.

The treasury bill futures contract is quoted in terms of an index associated to the yield as follows: Index = $100 - (Y_d)(100)$.

11.7.3.3. *Eurodollar futures*

Eurodollar represent the liabilities of banks outside the United States of America. The London Interbank offered rate, LIBOR is paid in Eurodollars. The underlying asset of the Eurodollar futures contract is the three-month Eurodollar. The contract is settled in cash.

11.7.3.4. *Treasury bond futures*

Treasury bond futures contracts are traded on several exchanges. The underlying asset of the futures contract traded on the Chicago Board of Trade is 100,000 par value of a hypothetical 20-year, 8% coupon-bond. The futures price is quoted in terms of par being 100. The seller of the futures contract can unwind his position before the maturity date by buying back the contract. If he decides to make delivery, the seller must deliver some treasury bond chosen from the list of specific bonds published by the CBT.

The delivery process allows the seller of the futures contract to choose from one of the acceptable deliverable treasury bonds.

The CBT uses conversion factors for the computation of the invoice price of each deliverable treasury. This factor is determined before a contract with a given settlement date begins trading and it remains constant.

The invoice price indicates the price paid by the buyer when the treasury bond is delivered. It corresponds to the settlement futures price plus accrued interest and is calculated as follows:

$$\text{Invoice price} = \text{Contract size (settlement price of the futures contract times} \times \text{conversion factor)} + \text{accrued interest.}$$

The term accrued interest can be defined as follows:

Accrued interest

Bond market prices are clean prices since they are quoted without any accrued interest. The accrued interest corresponds to the amount of interest since the payment of the last coupon. It is computed as follows:

$$\text{Accrued interest} = \text{interest due in full period } (N_1/N_2)$$

with

N_1 = number of days since the last coupon date and
N_2 = number of days between coupon payments.

The dirty price corresponds to the quoted clean price plus the accrued interest. Upon delivery, the seller will deliver the bond which is cheapest to deliver, also known as the cheapest to deliver (CTD). The seller must compute the return to be earned from buying bonds and delivering them at the settlement date. The return is computed using the price of the treasury issue and the futures price for delivery. This return is referred to as the implied repo rate. The CTD issue corresponds to the issue with the highest implied repo rate since it gives the seller the highest return by buying and delivering the issue.

The delivery process gives the contract seller some options.

The quality option, also known as the swap option, allows the seller to choose among different acceptable treasury issues.

The timing option gives the seller the right to choose the exact time during the delivery month to make delivery. The wildcard option allows the seller to give a notice of intent to deliver up to 8 p.m. Chicago time after the closing of the exchange (3:15 p.m.) on the date when the futures settlement price is scheduled.

11.7.3.5. *Forward rate agreements*

A forward rate agreement (FRA) allows a company to reduce interest rate exposure by locking into a rate of interest. In this contract, the parties agree to exchange, at some future date, interest payments on the notional amount of the contract. The buyer of an FRA contract agrees to pay interest at a specified rate and to receive interest at a floating rate that prevails at a future date T.

11.7.3.6. *Interest rate swaps*

An interest rate swap is an agreement between two counter-parties to exchange periodic interest payments. These interest payments are determined with reference to a pre-determined principal amount known as the notional principal amount. In general, one party, the fixed rate payer, agrees to pay the other party fixed-interest payments with a given frequency at some specified dates. The other party, the floating rate payer, agrees to pay some interest rate payments that vary according to a reference rate. The London Inter-bank Offered Rate, LIBOR, is often used as the reference rate.

11.7.3.7. *Risks in bond investments*

The buyer of a bond faces different risks: an interest rate risk, a re-investment risk, a default or credit risk, an inflation risk, an exchange risk, a liquidity risk, etc.

11.7.3.8. *The interest rate risk*

The variations in interest rates modify the bond price. A higher interest rate leads a lower bond value and a lower interest rate produces a higher bond value.

11.7.3.9. *The re-investment risk*

The return for a bond buyer comes from the perceived interest (the coupons), the capital gain (variation in the bond price), and the interest from the placement of the coupons.

11.7.3.10. *The credit and default risk*

This risk accounts for the possibility of the borrower to honor his liabilities: payments of coupons and principal at their exact timing. The credit crunch in 2008 is largely due to this risk.

11.7.3.11. *The risk to call*

The issuer can insert a provision in the debt contract that allows him to buy back his bonds before the maturity date. In this case, the return for the bondholder can be different from the return anticipated when buying the bond.

11.7.3.12. *The inflation risk*

The variations in inflation rates affect the return from holding the bond. All bonds are expressed in nominal terms. The difference between a nominal return and the inflation rate gives the return in real terms.

11.7.3.13. *The exchange rate risk*

The price of a bond denominated in a foreign currency is affected by the changes in exchange rates. These rates can affect significantly the return from holding the bond.

11.7.3.14. *The liquidity risk*

The liquidity risk reflects the difficulty in selling the bond at a given market price. This risk can be measured by the spread observed in the market place. The higher the spread, the greater is the liquidity risk. The quality of a bond is denoted by a given letter or rating. Rating agencies like Moody and Standard & Poor give their rating to show the risks associated with investments in bonds. The passage from a letter A to B or C and D reflects a higher risk. The risk premium is higher for bonds of type B than type A.

This situation characterises most Islamic bonds or sukuks for which there is often no secondary markets.

11.8. Simple and Complex Financial Instruments

11.8.1. *Forward-start options*

These options give an answer to the following question: how much can one pay for the opportunity to decide after a known time in the future, known as "the grant date", to obtain at the money call with a different time to maturity with no additional cost?

11.8.2. *Pay-later options*

For these options, the premium is paid upon exercise. They are contingent options. In fact, the buyer has the obligation to pay upon exercise when the option is in the money regardless of the amount by which the underlying asset price exceeds the strike price.

11.8.3. *Chooser options*

They are on the holder, immediately after a pre-determined elapsed time, to choose whether the option is to be a call or a put. There are two kinds of chooser options: simple and complex choosers.

11.8.4. *Options on the minimum or the maximum of two or more risky assets*

These options may to be useful in the pricing of a wide variety of contingent claims, traded assets, and financial instruments whose values depend on extreme values. Examples include discount option bonds, compensation plans, risk-sharing contracts, collateralized loans, and growth opportunities among other contracts.

11.8.5. *Two-color rainbow options*

They refer not only to options on the maximum (minimum) of two assets, but also to all options whose pay-off depend on two or more underlying assets: options delivering the best of two assets and cash, spread options, portfolio options, dual-strike options, etc.

11.8.6. *Options with extendible maturities*

They include any financial contract with provisions concerning a re-scheduling of payments and a re-negotiation of terms.

There are many types of exotic and second generation options which take different forms. They include path-dependent options, lookbacks, partial lookbacks, Asian options, shout options, binaries or digitals, knockouts or barriers, ladder, and cliquet options among other things.

11.8.6.1. *Asian options*

Asian options have been in popular in the foreign exchange market, interest rate and commodity markets. These financial innovations are traded in OTC markets and allow investors to accomplish several hedging strategies.

Examples of these options include commodity-linked bond contracts and average currency options. Commodity-linked bond contracts give the right to the holder to receive the average value of the underlying commodity over a certain period or the nominal value of the bond, whichever is higher.

11.8.6.2. *Barrier options*

These belong to the family of path-dependent options. They are in life when they knock-in and are extinguished when they knock-out. They are sometimes referred to as knock-ins or knock-outs when the underlying asset hits (or does not hit) the barrier.

The standard form of barrier options refers to European options which appear or disappear (ins and outs) when the underlying asset reaches a certain level known as the barrier. This barrier or knock-out level is set below the strike price for the call and above it for the put. For example, an in barrier option comes into existence whenever the underlying asset value hits a specified level. The right to exercise an out barrier option is forfeited when the barrier is hit.

11.8.6.3. *Ratio options*

These are options on the ratio of two asset prices, index levels, commodities, etc. An example is given by the dollar-denominated European option on the ratio of the Germain DAX stock index to the French CAC index.

Innovations in OTC options markets not only involve certain relations between the underlying asset price and the strike price but also on the number of time units for which a certain condition is satisfied. This corresponds, for example, to financial assets which are traded within a specified range.

Structured products with embedded digitals are much more interesting than vanilla digitals. There are many types of range structures which may be in the form of range binaries, at maturity range binaries, rebate range binaries, mandarin collars, mega-premium options, limit binary options, boundary options, corridors, wall options, mini-premium options, volatility options, etc.

11.8.6.4. *Complex digitals or binaries*

In their complex forms, complex digitals or binaries may be presented in different forms: compound digitals, boolean digitals, and corridors. Compound digitals obey the same principle as compound options and take different forms: quanto digitals, barriered digitals, and options on digitals.

11.9. The Reasons of Financial Innovations

Financial engineers are working on the design and the valuation of these financial instruments and the new strategies for portfolio and risk management.

The main questions are:

Why there are so many new financial instruments?
Why has the wave of financial innovation not stopped?

The most common explanation often advanced by market authorities is that financial markets are incomplete and that these instruments allow us to complete these markets. However, as noted by Ross (1989), this explanation seems awkward. In fact, the success in valuing these financial instruments comes from the fact that they are regarded as contingent claims or derivative securities which are spanned by the underlying assets on which they are traded and a riskless bond. This allows the derivation of simple valuation formulas in complete markets.

According to Ross (1989), there are two dominant features which contribute to the wave of financial innovation: the role of institutions and the role of marketing. These reasons complement the arguments by Miller (1986) and Merton (1988). Miller's (1986) analysis is based on the role of taxes and regulations in the innovation process.

In his analysis, Miller considers taxes as a source of much of the motivation for financial innovation. Merton (1988) proposes a detailed analysis of the production function underlying the innovation in derivative securities markets. He puts the accent on the role of transaction costs.

The analysis by Ross (1989) ignores production costs and is interested mainly in the role of agency costs and marketing costs, which help to shape the form of the new institutional features. Agency costs and restrictions may arise from monitoring and the regulatory environment. They may result either from the natural needs of market relations between institutions and participants or may be imposed by the government.

The first reason in Ross's analysis is that financial markets become institutional markets since institutions are the most significant participants in these markets. This does not mean that financial markets are solely markets where institutions operate, but rather markets where institutions are significant forces.

Financial institutions range from transparent through translucent to opaque. In this classification, a mutual fund is regarded as a transparent institution and an insurance company is seen as an opaque institution. A pension fund is regarded as a translucent institution. Institutions can be regarded as financial market players whose activities are dominated by agency relations.

11.10. Derivatives Markets in the World: Stock Options, Index Options, Interest Rate and Commodity Options and Futures Markets

11.10.1. *Global overview*

Several institutions produce information regarding futures and options around the world. Often, summary statistics on volume and open interest are given for futures and index options.

Index options on stock indexes and index futures contracts begin trading in the US in 1983. This has been facilitated with the introduction of the SP 100 index contract on the Chicago Board Options Exchange. Today, index futures are traded and are more liquid than index options.

11.10.2. *The main indexes around the world: A historical perspective*

The first options traded on indexes can be traced back to US (SP 500 and SP 100 in 1983), Japan (Nikkei 225 in 1989), UK (FT-SE 100 in 1984), France (CAC 40, 1989), Germany (DAX, 1991), Switzerland, (SMI, 1980), Canada (TSE 35, 1987), Netherlands (EOE, 1978), ...

Options volume in listed markets is mostly concentrated in one month contracts in all markets. For most options, volume with longer maturities take place in OTC markets.

In the OTC market, trading began early in 1988. Several investors buy long-term puts to implement portfolio insurance strategies.

Today, dealers run large OTC options books. This can reduce or eliminate risk in the market.

11.10.2.1. *North America*

US index options trading appear on listed markets and OTC markets with customized features.

Options are traded on SP 100, SP 500, MMI, SPMidCap, options on small capitalization indexes, the NYSE Composite index.

Main information used concerns the average daily volume, Average daily dollar volume (in millions) and Index level.

Options on SP are preferred by retail investors.

MidCap Options and options on SP 500 index attract the interest of institutional money managers and pension funds.

SP 100 are the mostly traded contracts in the US.

SP 500 are the have the greatest open interest in the US.

Hundred billions of dollars are traded.

Institutional use of index options:

Covered call writing: a call is sold and the underlying asset is held. Long index put strategy and collar positions, which is preferred by institutions. The collar can lead to a skew in index options implied volatilities: out of the money puts have higher volatilities than calls. Options are available on National OTC (PHX) indexes.

11.10.2.2. *Stock index markets in North America*

The SP 500 index fluctuated in a band. The move gives a volatility in a range of 10–25%. We can represent a monthly volatility for the year. With its heavier dose of cyclical stocks, the DJIA has been outperforming for some years the broader market.

We can compute historical volatility and implied volatility from at the money options. We should compute the spread.

The following tables shows the volume (number of contracts traded) in several countries.

11.10.2.3. *Japan*

Options exist on Osaka Nikkei, options on TOPIX.

Japanese institutions often use for their long term options exposure or customized strike prices fixed income securities with embedded index options.

Osaka Nikkei options are used by domestic institutional in short term trading. Regulations by the Ministry of Finance prevent pension funds from completely hedging their portfolios (hedging limit 50%).

Hedgers integrated their activities into equity risk management systems.

Life insurance companies focus on using options for directional trading. Offshore hedge funds use the Osaka Nikkei options to take outright short-term trading positions.

The Government intervenes to support the market. Foreign institutions act in the OTC market for different reasons:

They are restricted by regulation from trading listed options.

They do not want to incur the costs of rolling over.

Competition among dealers makes this market very competitive.

Sector options are popular in Japan.

11.10.2.4. *Europe*

In Germany

Listed DAX options are done on a screen-based system.

Major players in this market are the large US and Continental investment banks.

In France

Listed CAC 40 options trade on the French options market where trading is dominated by locals taking speculative positions and by large investment banks.

Institutional users are French insurance companies and fund managers. Players seek leveraged exposures on the market.

Guaranteed funds on the CAC 40 issued by French banks are popular among retail investors. CAC 40 options are used as part of these products. Major participants in the OTC market are large US and European investment banks.

11.10.2.5. *Stock index markets in France*

- An interesting development in the CAC 40 futures is the distribution of open interest across various months.
- Institutions have led to move into the quarterly contracts to eliminate the chore of rolling on a monthly basis.

The lack of a developed stock-borrowing market can reduce trading in futures.

Professional traders can use the futures to hedge OTC options. To hedge collars traders can be short futures.

Arbitrageurs (short stock/long futures) can unwind easily their positions.

11.10.2.6. *United Kingdom*

The market is dominated by major international banks and brokers. Short-term maturities have the most liquidity. End-users are mainly UK institutions for hedging and guaranteed funds.

In OTC markets, the volume is also high because of greater liquidity in the longer-dated contracts. There is flexibility in expiration dates.

11.10.2.7. *Switzerland*

Options are traded on the SOFFEX in an electronic screen system. Active participants are major Swiss and American Banks. End users are a mixture of short-term speculators and international institutions looking for long exposures.

The OTC market is important because there is a need for longer-term strategies on the SMI from pension funds.

Zero premium collars are very popular.

11.10.2.8. *Netherlands*

This market is dominated by locals who service a retail base.

Users are mainly pension funds who hedge equity portfolios.

The index must be compiled using a specific method.

The weighting of the index can overweight smaller, domestically oriented stocks and underweight larger, more internationally oriented stocks. For example, stocks can be weighted using a market capitalization and the maximum weight of a stock in the index will not exceed 10%. This puts a cap on some stocks.

Summary

The last three decades have witnessed a proliferation of financial innovations. Roughly speaking, financial innovations seem to belong to two classes.

First, there are the new securities and their markets such as traded and OTC equity and interest rate derivative assets. Second, there are dynamic trading strategies using these instruments. Traded derivative assets are standardized contracts which are listed on options exchanges. OTC derivative assets are tailor-made to the investor's needs and are often written by investment banks. Examples of classic or standard financial assets and commodity contracts include forward rate contracts, futures contracts, swaps, standard calls and puts, traded stock options, equity warrants, covered warrants, options on equity indices, options on index futures contracts, options on currency forwards or currency futures and bond options. Futures and options market enable investors to manage price risk. The market offers an environment that allows all users to control the price risk. The prices of these financial instruments are fully transparent because they are updated second by second as trading occurs. Examples of commodity contracts are oil and cocoa. The oil market is ultimately concerned with the transportation, processing, and storage of a raw material. Crude oil is traded on world markets using the spot asset, physical forward contracts, futures contracts, options on futures contracts, swaps, warrants, etc. Price information can be obtained from oil and energy pricing information such as Reuters, Bridge Telerate, Platt's, etc. The size and complexity of global crude oil trade are unique among physical commodities. Worldwide crude oil trade in the last 30 years has gone through revolutionary changes that have had large political and economic impact adding to its uniqueness.

References

Fabozzi, F (1993). *Fixed Income Mathematics*, US: Irwin.

Merton, RC (1998). Applications of option pricing theory: twenty five years later. *American Economic Review*, 88(3), 323–345.

Miller, M (1986). Financial innovation: the last twenty years and the next. *Journal of Financial and Quantitative Analysis*, 21 (December), 451–471.

Ross, S (1989). Financial markets, financial marketing and financial innovation. *Journal of Finance*, 44(3), 541–556.

Chapter 12

Risk Management, Derivatives Markets and Trading Strategies

Chapter Outline

This chapter is organized as follows:

1. Section 12.1 gives an overview of futures markets and the trading mechanisms in these markets.
2. Section 12.2 presents the main pricing relationships for forward and futures contracts.
3. Section 12.3 develops the main trading motives in futures markets. Several examples explain strategies with reference to hedging, speculation, and arbitrage.
4. Section 12.4 studies the main bounds on option prices.
5. Section 12.5 illustrates some simple trading strategies for options and their underlying assets.
6. Section 12.6 presents some option combinations involving straddles and strangles.
7. Section 12.7 illustrates some option spreads in bull and bear strategies involving calls and puts.
8. Section 12.8 develops butterfly strategies using put and call options.
9. Section 12.9 presents Condor strategies using put and call options.
10. Section 12.10 studies ratio-spread strategies.

11. Section 12.11 illustrates some combinations of options with bonds and stocks and portfolio insurance strategies.
12. Section 12.12 studies conversion and reversal strategies.
13. Section 12.13 provides a case study: selling calls (without holding the stocks/as an alternative to short selling stocks/the idea of selling calls is also an alternative to buying puts).
14. Section 12.14 studies strategies of buying calls or being long positions.

Introduction

Futures markets are a direct development of traditional agricultural markets, which were initially located in Chicago and London. Chicago is the largest commodity trading center in the world. The standardized futures markets such as the New York Merchantile Exchange (Nymex), the International Petroleum Exchange (IPE), and the Singapore International Monetary Exchange (Simex), or the forward markets like dated Brent, Littlebrook Lottery, or the Russian Roulette have become an important factor in the pricing of crude oil and refined products.

The cost of carry model corresponds to the relation between the futures price and the spot price. It is the basis for the valuation of forward and futures contracts. Futures prices and forward prices are often regarded as being equivalent. However, this is true only if the risk-free interest rate is constant or a known function of time. For the valuation of interest-rate futures contracts, the theoretical futures price can be determined as a function of the underlying asset price (the bond price), the coupon rate, and the financing rate for borrowing and lending during a given period. The fair price of a forward contract is given by the spot price plus the cost of carry until the maturity date of the bond.

A futures contract is, in general, liquidated by offsetting it with a futures contract in the opposite direction. Transactions are done on margin in the futures market. The margin represents a small fraction of the value of the contract. It varies by the type of commodity.

Option prices depend on factors that affect the main elements in computing their prices. These factors concern the volatility in the financial markets, the level of interest rates, the option's maturity date, the exercise price, dividends on the underlying asset, etc. When a derivative asset is about to expire, it is relatively a simple matter to compute its value. In fact, at the option maturity date, the holder can either exercise it or let it expire. Hence, at this date, the option price is given only by the position of the underlying asset price with respect to the option strike price. This position defines the option payoff at this date. At any time, there is a market price for the derivative asset. Models are used to compute the option price at any time. But, this does not mean that the market option price must be equal to the model price. The difference represents the mispricing. Options can be either European or American. A European style-derivative asset cannot be exercised before its maturity date T. An American contract can be exercised at any time t before the maturity date T. At maturity, the European and American derivatives have identical values because it is the last moment to exercise or let expire a contract. A call is in-the-money when the underlying asset price is higher than the strike price. It is out-of-the-money, if the underlying asset price is lower than the strike price. The call is at-the-money if the underlying asset price is equal to the strike price. A put is in-the-money when the underlying asset price is lower than the strike price. It is out-of-the-money if the underlying asset price is higher than the strike price. The put is at-the-money if the underlying asset price is equal to the strike price. These definitions apply at maturity and at each instant before expiration. When a long or a short position is initiated in a derivative contract, the profit or loss is known when an opposite transaction is done or when the option is at its maturity date. The profit or loss is computed with respect to the purchase price or the sale price. It is possible to analyze the profits and losses on options positions by looking at the initial price in the transaction and the maturity price of the derivative contract. This allows the computation of the profit and loss, P&L. This chapter presents in detail the basic theory of commodities, futures, and forward markets. It illustrates the specific features of these markets and the main pricing relationships. It develops the main trading strategies in options markets.

In particular, strategies involving calls and puts, straddles, strangles, conversions and reversals, and the box spread are studied. These trading strategies can be used for most of the derivative assets in this book, since they can be implemented using options with any particular payoff.

12.1. Introduction to Commodity Markets: The Case of Oil

The main commodity exchanges that currently trade oil futures contracts are the Nymex, IPE of London, and the Simex.

12.1.1. *Oil futures markets*

A futures contract is successful when it is based on a volatile price, a standard quality specification, and a wide range of participants in the market. Volatile prices are necessary because they induce investors to use futures markets. In fact, the prime function of a futures market is to provide a hedging mechanism for the related industry. The standard quality specification will attract the whole sector of the industry. The overall volume traded by market participants give a good guide to show how liquid a contract is. A second measure of a successful contract is open interest, i.e., the total number of outstanding bought-and-sold contracts at the close of each trading day. Commercial traders are companies whose business involves handling the physical commodity, i.e., hedgers. Non-commercial traders are mainly financial companies, i.e., speculators.

12.1.2. *Oil futures exchanges*

The most successful oil futures market is the Nymex. The success of this market is largely due to the importance of its West Texas Intermediate (WTI) crude contract.

The IPE of London trades only energy contracts. Unlike the Nymex, the IPE has now chosen the cash settlement procedure rather than physical delivery for the Brent crude contract. However, there is a physical delivery option. The Simex offers an oil futures contract.

12.1.3. *Delivery procedures*

In general, futures contracts are almost never delivered since participants prefer to close out (or roll over) their positions before the last trading day for each delivery month. The main reason is that futures contracts are either traded in conjunction with a position in the physical market (hedging) or used in a speculative strategy. Physical delivery ensures that the futures prices remain anchored to the underlying physical market. The physical delivery of the standardized commodity specified in the futures contract or its cash equivalent are not the only delivery mechanisms. Other procedures are used like the exchange for physical (EFP), exchange for swaps (EFS), and alternative delivery procedure (ADP).

12.1.4. *The long-term oil market*

The standardized futures markets such as the Nymex, the IPE, and the Simex, or the forward markets like dated Brent, Littlebrook Lottery, or the Russian Roulette have become an important factor in the pricing of crude oil and refined products. The emergence of a long-term oil market allows one to meet specific requirements in the industry. This market provides new opportunities for speculators. The participants in this new over-the-counter (OTC) market are highly ranked oil companies, banks, and traders.

12.2. Pricing Models

The futures price, F can be described using different parameters: the spot price S, the risk-less interest rate r, the cost of carrying the stocks b, and the convenience yield cy. The cy represents short- to medium-term effects related to physical supply and demand unbalance. It can be measured using futures prices. For the case of oil, this yield indicates the intrinsic oil interest rate.

12.2.1. *The pricing of forward and futures oil contracts*

Forward and futures contracts enable firms to determine a price for future delivery. Most forward and futures contracts are traded for a few months ahead. In the refined products markets, trading extends to a year. The futures contract, Nymex and WTI can be traded up to four years ahead.

12.2.1.1. *Relationship to physical market*

Forward and futures prices can differ from the spot price of the commodity. However, as the expiration date approaches, the prices must converge. However, there are occasional squeezes on forwards and futures. When the nearby contract is at a premium to the later month, the market is in backwardation. When the nearby month is at a discount, the market is in contango.

12.2.1.2. *Term structure of prices*

Changes in demand and in stock levels held by the industry affect forward and futures prices. There is a limit on the size of the contango imposed by the cash and carry arbitrage. In fact, buying the oil for one month, paying for it, moving it into storage, insuring it, and delivering it back to the market one month later at profit represent the cash and carry arbitrage.

Example. A trader implements the following transactions:

- Buys heating oil at 60 cents/gallon in March
- Sells heating oil at 63 cents/gallon in April

In March, he takes delivery of the heating oil futures at 60 cents/ gallon
He pays storage costs for 6 weeks, at 2.50 cents/gallon
The interest costs and product losses are 0.25 cents/gallon
The total cost in March is 62.75 cents/gallon
In April, he delivers the heating oil at 63 cents/gallon
The net profit is 0.25 cents/gallon

12.2.2. *Pricing swaps*

The price of a swap can be determined using the arbitrage relationships between the swap and the forward or the futures markets.

A swap agreement can be replicated by a position in a portfolio of futures or forward contracts.

Example. Consider a swap agreement between a producer of oil and a swap provider. The swap allows the producer to sell a specified quantity of crude oil at a fixed price over a period of one year. The swap can be reproduced as a portfolio of short futures or forward contracts on the same volume of oil for each delivery month.

12.2.3. *The pricing of forward and futures commodity contracts: General principles*

The proposed relation between the futures price and the spot price, $F = Se^{bT}$ is useful. Re-call that F is the future price, S is the spot price, b corrresponds to the carrying cost, and T is the time to maturity. This relationship applies to futures prices and forward prices as well.

12.2.3.1. *Forward prices and futures prices: Some definitions*

Futures prices and forward prices are often regarded as being equivalent. However, this is true only if the risk-free interest rate is constant or a known function of time. The proof of this equivalence is based on a roll-over strategy proposed in Cox *et al.* (1981). In this strategy, the investor buys every day a specific amount of futures so that he/she holds e^r futures contracts at the end of the first day of trading (initial time, day 0), e^{2r} futures contracts at the end of the day 1, e^{3r} futures contracts at the end of the day 2, etc., and e^{ir} futures contracts at the end of the day $i - 1$, where r corresponds to the daily interest rate.

Since at the beginning of day i, the investor has e^{ir} contracts in his/her position, the position on that day shows a profit (loss) of $(F_i - F_{i-1})e^{ir}$.

When this amount is invested until the day N corresponding to the contract's maturity date, where the number of days i is between 0 and N, this amount will be $(F_i - F_{i-1})e^{ir}e^{(N-i)r} = (F_i - F_{i-1})e^{Nr}$.

The sum of the amounts of profit (loss) from the day 0 until day N turns out to be $(F_N - F_0)e^{Nr}$. However, since at the contract's maturity date, the futures price F_N is equal to the spot price, S_T, the terminal value of this investment strategy is $(F_N - F_0)e^{Nr} = (S_T - F_0)e^{Nr}$. Using a portfolio which corresponds to this strategy and an investment of an amount F_0 in a risk-free bond, gives the following payoff at time T:

$$(S_T - F_0)e^{Nr} + F_0e^{Nr} = S_Te^{Nr}$$

Since for a strategy in futures contracts no funds are invested, the result S_Te^{Nr} corresponds to the investment of F_0 in the risk-free bond.

Another strategy can be constructed to give the same pay-off as the preceding one. In fact, if f_0 stands for the forward price at the end of day 0, then a strategy which consists in investing this amount in a risk-less bond and an amount e^{Nr} in forward contracts also gives a final payoff at T equal to $S_T e^{Nr}$. Since the two strategies require an investment of an amount $F_0, (f_0)$ and yield the same result, $S_T e^{Nr}$, they must have the same value in efficient capital markets. In the absence of profitable arbitrage opportunities, the futures price F_0 must be equal to the forward price f_0. Hence, the proposed relation applies for both futures and forward prices and we have $F = f = Se^{bT}$. Some examples are given below to illustrate the use of this relationship in the determination of forward and futures prices on some securities.

12.2.3.2. *Futures contracts on commodities*

When the cost of carrying an asset refers to the storage costs of a commodity such as silver or gold and when these costs are proportional to the commodity price, the futures price is given by $F = Se^{(r+a)T}$, where "a" stands for the storage costs.

12.2.3.3. *Futures contracts on a security with no income*

When there are no distributions from the underlying asset, the cost of carry is equal to the risk-less interest rate. The future price is given by $F = Se^{rT}$. More generally, this relation represents the forward or futures price F as a function of the spot price S. It applies to the valuation of forward or futures contracts on a security that provides no income.

Example. Consider the valuation of a forward contract on a non-dividend paying stock. Suppose the maturity date is in three months, the current asset price is 100, and the three-month risk-free rate is 7% per annum.

In this case, $S = 100$, $T = 0.25$ year, $r = 0.07$, so the futures or forward price is 101.765 or $F = 100e^{(0.07)0.25} = 101.765$.

12.2.3.4. *Futures contracts on a security with a known income*

For dividend-paying assets, the cost of carrying the stocks is given by the difference between the risk-less rate and the dividend yield,

d. This gives the following relation $F = Se^{(r-d)T}$. This relationship gives the forward price F as a function of the spot price S for a forward contract on a security that provides a known dividend yield.

Example. Consider the valuation of a three-month forward or futures contract on a security that provides a continuous dividend yield of 5% per annum. Suppose that the current asset price is 100 and the risk-free rate is 7% per annum. In this case, $S = 100$, $T = 0.25$ year, $r = 0.07$, and $d = 5\%$, so the futures or forward price is 100.501: $F = 100e^{(0.07-0.05)0.25} = 100.501$.

12.2.3.5. *Futures contracts on foreign currencies*

The cost of carrying a foreign currency is given by the difference between the domestic risk-less rate and the foreign risk-less rate, r^*. This gives the following relation between the futures price and the spot price of the currency: $F = Se^{(r-r^*)T}$. This relationship also gives the forward price F (or foreign exchange rate F) as a function of the spot price S for a forward contract on a currency. This is often known in international finance as the interest-rate parity theorem.

Example. Consider the valuation of a three-month forward or futures contract on a foreign currency. If the spot price is 180, the domestic risk-free rate is 6% per annum and the foreign risk-free rate is 7% per annum, then: $S = 180, T = 0.25$ year, $r = 0.07$, and $r^* = 6\%$ per annum. The future or forward price is 180.45.

$$F = 180e^{(0.07-0.06)0.25} = 180.45$$

12.2.3.6. *Futures contracts on a security with a discrete income*

When the cost of carrying the commodity is not a constant proportional rate, the formulae discussed above must be slightly modified. In the case of stocks paying known dividends, coupon-bearing bonds and some commodities for which there are storage costs, the formula for future prices becomes $F = (S - I)e^{rT}$. where I is the discounted value of the cash-flow between t and t^*. It is positive when it corresponds to an income and is negative when it refers to a cost.

Example. Consider the valuation of a one-year forward contract on a two-year bond. The two-year bond's price is 800, the delivery price is 820, and two coupons of 50 will be paid in 6 and 12 months, respectively. The risk-less interest rate is 8% per annum for 6 months and 9% per annum, for 12 months. In order to apply the formula, the value of I must be discounted to the present at an appropriate interest rate. In this case, I is given by:

$$I = 50e^{-0.08(0.5)} + 50e^{-0.09(1)} = 48.039 + 45.696 = 93.735$$

and the forward price is: $F = (800 - 93.735)e^{0.09(1)} = 706.265e^{0.09(1)} = 772.777$.

Example. Consider now the valuation of a one-year forward contract on a stock with a price equal to 100. When the dividend is two and the interest paid at the end of the year is 10% per annum, the present value of dividends is $I = 2e^{-0.01(1)} = 1.8096$ and the forward price is given by $F = (100 - 1.8096)e^{0.1(1)} = 108.516$.

Example. Consider the valuation of a one-year futures contract on gold. If the cost of carry is 3 per ounce paid at the end of the year, the spot price is 500, and the risk-free rate is 10% per annum, the value of I is given by $I = 3e^{-0.1(1)} = 2.7145$ and the futures price is $F = (500 + 2.7145)e^{0.1(1)} = 555.585$.

12.2.3.7. *Valuation of interest rate futures contracts*

The theoretical futures price can be determined as a function of the underlying asset price (the bond price), the coupon rate, and the financing rate for borrowing and lending during a given period. We denote these by:

P: bond price in the cash market;
F: futures price;
T: time to maturity (the delivery date);
r: financing cost or rate and
c: coupon rate divided by the market bond price, known also as the current yield.

Consider the following strategy: sell a futures contract at F, buy the bond at P, and borrow an amount P at the rate r until the date T. At the contract's delivery date, the investor receives F plus the accrued interest cTP. He must re-pay the loan P and the interest-rate charges, rTP. The profit is given by the difference between the amount received and the outlay or: Profit $= F + cTP - (P + rTP)$. At equilibrium, in an efficient market, the fair futures price must be:

$$0 = F + cTP - (P + rTP)$$

or: $F = P(1 + T(r - c))$. This price allows to avoid a cash and carry arbitrage. Consider now the following strategy: buy a futures contract at F, sell (short) the bond at P, and lend (invest) an amount P at the rate r until the date T. At the contract's delivery date, the investor pays F plus the accrued interest cTP. He/she receives P and the interest earned, rTP. The profit is given by the difference between the amount received and the outlay or:

$$\text{Profit} = P + rTP - (F + cTP)$$

At equilibrium, in an efficient market, the fair futures price must be:

$$0 = P + rTP - (F + cTP)$$

Hence: $F = P(1 + T(r - c))$. If this equation is not satisfied, then a reverse cash and carry arbitrage can be implemented. The difference $(r-c)$ refers to the net financing cost or the cost of carry. The futures price is at a discount with respect to the cash price $(F < P)$ when $(c > r)$. The futures price is at a premium with respect to the cash price $(F > P)$ when $(c < r)$. The futures price is equal to the cash price $(F = P)$ when $(c = r)$.

Using the cash and carry arbitrage and the reverse cash and carry arbitrage, it is possible to derive the theoretical fair price of a forward or a futures contract. Our analysis assumes that there is only one deliverable bond. However, in practice, futures contracts on treasury bonds are issued on a number of deliverable issues and the futures price tracks in general, the price of the bond which is the cheapest to deliver. Since the cheapest to deliver is unknown before the delivery date, the futures price must account for the price of the quality option: $F = P + P(r - c)$ – quality option premium. Since the exact delivery date is also unknown and the seller has delivery options, the fair futures price must be:

$$F = P + P(r - c) \text{ — delivery option premiums}$$

12.2.3.8. *The pricing of future bond contracts*

The fair price of a forward contract is given by the spot price plus the cost of carry until the maturity date of the bond:

$$F = S + cp$$

In general, the futures contract is traded at a price which accounts for the implicit options. Its price must satisfy the following relationship:

$$F = S + cp - O + e$$

where: F = futures price, S = spot price for the cheapest bond, cp = cost of carry, O = value of the embedded options, and e = a white noise.

The process for the pricing of a futures contract must account for the following relationship:

$$F(fc) = S + cp - O + e$$

Hence, its theoretical fair price must be:

$$F = (S + cp - O)/(fc) + e$$

12.3. Trading Motives: Hedging, Speculation, and Arbitrage

Futures markets are used for hedging, speculation, and arbitrage motives. The main question for the producer is to implement the appropriate hedging strategies in response to the changes in backwardation or contango.

Backwardation: When spot prices are higher than long-term prices, any hedge using a future maturity will be equivalent to a forward sale below the spot price. This can lead to a loss if the market prices do not fall at the same rate. Careful long-term analysis may provide good hedging opportunities.

Contango: When spot prices are lower than long-term prices, the producer can sell the futures market at a higher price. So, he/she can fix his/her hedge or future sales at a better price than the spot market. In this case, hedging can generate profits if prices are not increasing at the same rate.

12.3.1. *Hedging using futures markets*

Companies using the physical oil market can hedge themselves against adverse price movements by taking an opposite position on the futures or the forward market. The potential loss in the physical market can be offset by an equivalent gain in the futures or the forward market. In practice, the hedge is rarely perfect.

The futures market offers a facility for hedging price risks. Hedging price risk can be regarded as a trading operation allowing one to transform a less acceptable risk into a more acceptable risk by engaging in an offsetting transaction in a similar commodity under roughly the same terms as the original transaction. In this spirit, a futures purchase, which is equal and opposite to the physical trading contract is made with an idea that any loss in the first transaction will be compensated by an equal gain in the offsetting operation.

12.3.1.1. *Hedging: The case of cocoa*

12.3.1.1.1. The selling hedge

A company holding stocks of a commodity can protect itself against the risk that the value of the unsold products will depreciate if the commodity price falls. This risk is offset by a forward sale of the same tonnage on the futures market. The hedge is based on the assumption that futures prices decline as physical prices fall.

12.3.1.1.2. The buying hedge

Manufacturers of chocolate, exporters selling cocoa do not actually possess, and manufacturers who fix selling prices and current contracts for future delivery based on the current costs, etc. can implement a buying hedge. These agents would suffer if the costs of the raw material rise. Therefore, they can purchase the required tonnage on the futures market using a long hedge. When the price falls by the time of shipment, the hedger will lose on the futures market and profit from a cheaper purchase on the spot market. The hedging strategy needs some funds to cover for the security deposits and margins and any commission paid to brokers.

12.3.1.2. *Hedging: The case of oil*

Example (A short hedge). An oil trader who buys a cargo of physical oil while oil is in transit, can protect himself/herself, by selling an equivalent volume of oil futures or forward contracts. When the physical cargo is sold, the hedger can lift his/her hedge by buying back the futures contract.

Example (A short hedge). Consider a company A buying 500,000 barrel cargo of crude oil for US$ 28/barrel when futures price is US$ 28.50/barrel. The manager decides to use the futures market to implement a hedging strategy by selling futures contracts. A week later, the manager sells the physical cargo for US$ 27.00/barrel. He/she decides to lift the hedge by buying back the futures contracts at their market price of US$ 27.40/barrel (Table 12.1).

The profit on the futures position is larger than the loss on the physical market. This result can be explained by this basis. It corresponds to the differential between the futures and the spot price.

Example (A long hedge). Consider a company B which is short of oil in the spot market. A gasoil distributor agrees to sell oil to a customer at a fixed price for some months ahead. The manager decides to use the futures market to implement a hedging strategy by buying futures contracts in order to protect himself/herself against a rise in price (Table 12.2).

This result can also be explained by this basis. It corresponds to the differential between the futures and the spot price.

12.3.1.3. *Hedging: The case of petroleum products futures contracts*

When the futures markets tend to move parallel to the spot (cash) market, a hedge can be implemented by buying or selling futures

Table 12.1. Short hedge using futures contracts.

Period	Physical Market	US$/bl	Futures Market	US$/bl
$t = 0$	bought at	28.00	futures sold at	28.50
$t = +6$	sold at	27.00	futures bought at	27.40
	loss	−1.00	profit	+1.10

Table 12.2. Long hedge using futures contracts.

Period	Physical Market	US$/tonne	Futures Market	US$/tonne
$t = 1$	sold at	200	futures bought at	199
$t = 3$	bought at	210	futures sold at	208
	loss	−10	profit	+9

contracts. This is possible because a loss due to an adverse price change in the cash market can be offset by a gain in the futures market. Also, a loss in the futures market can be offset by a gain in the cash market.

12.3.1.3.1. Using a short hedge

A short (selling) hedge is implemented when a decline in cash market prices is expected. This is the case for a refiner or a distributor who is holding an inventory. The short hedger forgoes the opportunity of additional profits in a rising cash market.

12.3.1.3.2. Hedging by a petroleum marketer – Hedge of a fixed price purchase commitment

Consider a marketer who is committed to buy a certain quantity of a product at a given price. He/she expects a price decline and enters into a short futures contract to protect his/her normal gross profit margin.

If the cash price of heating oil declines, the futures price can also decline. Hence, the marketer will realize a loss or less of a gain on physical sale and a profit on his/her futures position.

If the oil price increases, the resulting profit from the physical sale will be offset by a loss on the futures market. In both cases, the marketer will have protected his/her normal gross profit margin.

12.3.1.3.3. Hedging by a petroleum refiner

Consider a refiner who has not a firm sales commitment. Since there is a time lag between the time the refiner purchased crude oil and delivers the refined oil to the consumer, the price of oil can decline during this time period. He/she can implement a hedge by selling futures contracts.

If the oil price declines, the resulting loss in the value of the inventory will be offset by a gain on the futures market. In the same way, if the oil price increases, the loss on the futures market will be offset by an increase in inventory value.

12.3.1.3.4. Using a long hedge

A long (buying) hedge is implemented when a rise in cash-market prices is expected. This is the case for a consumer of petroleum products.

The long hedger gives up the opportunity of increased profits should the price of the physical asset decline. The hedger forgoes this opportunity for the protection of his/her operating margins.

12.3.1.3.5. Hedging by a petroleum marketer – Hedge of a fixed-price sale commitment

Consider a marketer who enters into long-term contracts to deliver products to customers in the futures at a fixed price. His/her profit margin will be at risk since the oil prices may increase before delivery. The marketer can implement a hedge against price risk (a rise in the price in excess of the contracted sale price) by buying futures contracts for the month of delivery.

He/she expects a price rise and enters into a long futures contract to protect his/her portfolio.

If the cash price of heating oil increases, the marketer will realize a loss on the physical sale to customers because he/she will have to buy oil at a higher price in the cash market to satisfy his/her sales commitment. However, the cash loss would be offset by a futures profit on his/her futures position.

If the oil price decreases, the resulting profit from the physical sale will be offset by a loss on the futures market.

12.3.1.3.6. Hedging by a petroleum consumer to protect against rising prices

Consider a petroleum consumer who expects an increase in petroleum product prices. He/she can implement a hedge by buying futures contracts.

If the oil price increases, the consumer will have to pay the higher market price at the time of purchase. The increased cost can be offset by a gain on the futures market. In the same way, if the oil price decreases, the gain on the physical transaction will be offset by a loss on the futures market.

12.3.1.4. *The use of futures contracts by petroleum products marketers, jobbers, consumers, and refiners*

Example A (Hedge by a petroleum products marketer against a fixed-price purchase commitment). This example shows how a marketer can maintain his/her normal gross profits in the physical market, regardless of the dynamics of the oil prices.

A marketer is commited to buy a fixed quantity at 90 cents per gallon. He/she expects a price decline and implements a hedge by selling futures contracts. In September, the marketer enters into a contract with a company to supply 420,000 gallons of heating oil for delivery the following December.

If the current price of US$ 1 per gallon is expected to prevail at delivery, the marketer expects a profit of 10 cents. The marketer can protect this profit margin against a decline in oil prices by December. He/she can sell 10 heating oil contracts at US$ 1 per gallon for delivery in December (the contract is equivalent to 42,000 gallons).

If the cash price declines to 80 cents, the marketer will realize a loss of 10 cents (90–80) on the physical sale.

However, a profit of 20 cents is achieved in the futures market since the short futures contract is sold at US$ 1 and the investor bought it back at 80 cents.

The net effect of 10 cents corresponds to the original expected profit of 10 cents.

If oil prices rise, the resulting profit from the physical sale will be offset by an equivalent loss on the futures market.

Example B (Hedge by a petroleum products marketer against a fixed-price sales commitment). A marketer is committed to sell to customers a fixed quantity at US$ 1.30 per gallon. In June, the marketer enters into a sales contract to deliver 420,000 gallons of heating oil in December.

He/she expects a price decline from US$ 1.3 to US$ 1 in December. The profit margin will be eroded if the marketer is forced to buy the heating oil at a price in excess of the contract price of US$ 1.3.

The marketer can protect his/her position against the price risk by buying 10 futures contracts at US$ 1 for delivery in December.

In December, he/she can accept the delivery or close out the position by selling an identical futures contract.

If the oil price is US$ 1.4 per gallon, the marketer will lose 10 cents on the physical market (to honor his/her sales contract price of 1.3). The marketer can close his/her futures long position by selling a futures contract at 1.4. A profit of 40 cents is achieved in the futures market since the long futures contract is bought at US$ 1 and it is sold at US$ 1.4.

The net effect of 30 cents corresponds to the original expected profit of 30 cents.

If oil prices decrease to 90 cents, the resulting profit from the physical sale is 40 cents, (selling at 1.3 minus cost of 90 cents).

Example C (Hedge of an existing asset (inventory) position by a refiner). This example shows how a refiner can protect his/her inventory from an erosion in value when prices fall, using the futures market.

A refiner has a risk resulting from the time lag between the time of buying crude oil and the time of delivery to the consumer. When the oil price declines during this time period, the value of his/her inventory will decline.

Consider a refiner who holds 420,000 gallons of uncommitted refined inventory at an average cost of 90 cents per gallon at first in September. He/she expects to sell his/her inventory in the cash market in December. Expecting a possible decline below 90 cents, he/she sells 10 futures contracts maturing in December at US$ 1.

At maturity, if the price declines to 80 cents, he/she loses 10 cents on his/her inventory. When closing his/her futures position, he/she will realize a gain of 20 cents (US$ 1 less 80 cents). This reduces the basis of his/her inventory to 70 cents. In this context, he/she can sell the inventory in the cash market at a lower cash price, and preserving a profit margin. If the oil prices increase, this would be offset by a corresponding loss on the futures position.

Table 12.3. Speculating on a price rise.

Period	Physical Market	US$/bl	Futures Market	US$/bl
$t = 0$	nothing	–	futures bought at	26.50
$t = +6$	nothing	–	futures sold at	25.00
		–	profit	+1.50

12.3.2. *Speculation using futures markets*

The main objective of speculators is profit. Speculators take on the risk which hedgers try to lay off. Speculators hold onto their positions for a very short time. They are sometimes in-and-out of the market several times a day.

Example (Speculation on a price rise). Consider a speculator who expects prices to rise and buys consequently IPE Brent futures contracts. A week later, the speculator closes out his/her position in the futures market before the prices can fall back again. The two trades are regarded as purely speculative because there is no physical transaction in the spot market (Table 12.3).

12.3.3. *Arbitrage and spreads in futures markets*

Arbitrage keeps prices in line since the arbitrageur buys the asset in one market and sells it in other market. When prices move out of line, the arbitrageur buys the under-priced asset in one market and sells the over-priced asset in another market.

We give an example using IPE gasoil contracts and the Nymex heating-oil contracts. IPE gasoil contracts are 100 tonnes and Nymex heating-oil contracts are 1,000 gallons. The relationship shows the trading of three Nymex contracts for every four IPE contracts.

Besides, since IPE gasoil prices are quoted in US$/tonne and Nymex heating-oil prices are quoted in cents/gallon, a conversion factor must be used. Assuming a specific gravity for gasoil of 0.845 kg/liter and since there are 313 gallons of heating oil in a tonne, the conversion factor is 3.13.

Table 12.4. Heating-oil arbitrage.

Period	Nymex Heating Oil	Price cts/gall	Price US$/tonne	IPE Gasoil	Price US$/tonne	Price Differential
$t = 0$	Buy 3 at	62.00	170	Sell 4 at	170.10	−0.10
$t = +1$	Sell 3 at	61.50	169	Buy 4 at	164.00	+5.00
	Loss	−0.50	−1	Profit	+6.10	+5.10

12.3.3.1. *Heating-oil arbitrage*

Consider a trader who expects Nymex heating oil to move to a premium over the IPE. He/she buys the Nymex heating-oil contracts and sells IPE gasoil contracts.

The total profit of US$ 5.10/tonne comes from the change in the differential regardless of the market direction (Table 12.4). Other types of spreads can be implemented. The analysis can be extended to the valuation of these contracts in the presence of information costs in supplementary material.

The financial crisis in 2008 reveals the importance of hedging strategies in a risk framework.

12.4. The Main Bounds on Option Prices

The option value before maturity is a function of five parameters: the price of the underlying asset, the strike price, the risk-free rate of interest, the movements in the underlying asset prices (volatility), and the time remaining to maturity. Option prices move at each instant of time as a reaction to the changes in the above parameters. Since we know the option pay-off at maturity, it is possible to determine some main relationships before the maturity date. Hence, we can give minimum and maximum values of calls and puts as well as the behavior of the option price in response to the changing parameter values.

The two following main relationships apply for the European and American calls (c and C, respectively) and European and American puts payoffs (p and P, respectively) at maturity:

$$C_T = c_T = \max[0, S_T - K], \quad P_T = p_T = \max[0, K - S_T]$$

where K is the strike price and T is the option's maturity date. The boundary space refers to the largest range of possible option prices before expiration.

12.4.1. *Boundary conditions for call options*

When the call holder exercises his/her option, he/she receives the difference between the underlying asset price and the strike price.

When the strike price is zero and the maturity date is infinite, the call can be exercised with zero cost. This gives the call holder the right to receive the underlying asset with zero cost. The value of this option must be equal to that of its underlying asset. Hence, the call price must be between these two limits.

12.4.2. *Boundary conditions for put options*

When the put holder exercises his/her option at maturity, he/she receives the difference between the strike price and the underlying asset price. This is the minimum value for the put.

When the underlying asset price tends to become zero, the put holder can receive at maximum the value of the strike price. Hence, the maximum value of the American put, which can be exercised at any time before maturity must be the option's strike price. However, the maximum value for a European put must be the present value of the strike price since the put holder must wait until expiration to exercise his option. Hence, the minimum put price must be $\max[0, K - S_T]$. The maximum price for an American put is K and for a European put is $Ke^{-r(T-t)}$, where t is the current time and r is the risk-free interest rate.

12.4.3. *Some relationships between call options*

We define some main relationships which hold good for European and American calls.

The call payoff shows that the lower the strike price, the higher is the call value. This property can be shown using no-arbitrage arguments. Hence, if you consider two calls with different strike prices, then the call with the lower strike price must be at least equal to the call price with the higher strike price.

It can also be shown that the call value must be at least equal to the stock price minus the present value of the strike price or $C_t \geq S_t - Ke^{-r(T-t)}$. This relationship holds good at any time before expiration.

Example. Consider a call trading at 3 when $S_t = 105$, $K = 100$, $r = 7\%$, and $T = 0.5$ years. These data violate the previous relationship and give rise to an arbitrage opportunity because the call is undervalued. In this case, an investor can implement the following strategy: sell the underlying asset at 105, buy the option at -3, and buy the bond with the remaining funds at -102.

The investor can exercise immediately the option, pay 100, return the stock, and keep 2.

The investor can also wait for the maturity date. At this date, the bond price is $102e^{0.07(0.5)} = 105.6332$.

If the stock price is 97 at expiration, the option expires worthless and the investor pays 97 for the share to re-pay the obligation. The profit in this case is $102e^{0.07(0.5)} - 95 = 10.6332$.

Even, if we consider other levels of the underlying asset, the investor can re-pay with profit. Hence, the option value must be at least equal to $105 - 100e^{-0.07(0.5)} = 8.435$.

All the prices below this allow arbitrage profits.

The call price is an increasing function of time until expiration. In fact, if we consider two calls with the same characteristics, except for maturity, then the price of the call with a longer maturity must equal or exceed the price of the call with a shorter maturity. If this principle is violated, arbitrage can be implemented with risk-less profits.

In the absence of dividend or cash distributions to the underlying asset, there is no reason to exercise a call on a non-dividend paying asset. In fact, a call on a non-dividend paying asset is always worth more than its intrinsic value $S_t - K$. Since before expiration, the call value must be at least worth $S_t - Ke^{-r(T-t)}$, exercising the call before expiration discards at least the option time value, i.e., the difference between K and $Ke^{-r(T-t)}$. Early exercise is never optimal for an American call on a non-dividend paying asset. Since European calls cannot be exercised before expiration, this makes an equivalence between the European call price and the American call price in the absence of distributions to the underlying asset.

Example. Consider a call when $S_t = 110$, $K = 100$, $r = 7\%$, and $T = 0.5$ years. In this case, the call's intrinsic value is 10, $S_t - K$. But, the call market price must be at least $C_t \geq S_t - Ke^{-r(T-t)} \geq 110 - 100e^{-0.07(0.5)} \geq 13.4395$. The investor can exercise immediately the option of throwing away at least the difference $K - Ke^{-r(T-t)} = 100 - 100e^{-0.07(0.5)} = 3.435$.

The investor discards also the difference between $13.4395 - 10 = 3.4395$.

12.4.4. *Some relationships between put options*

We define some main relationships, which hold good for European and American puts.

The put payoff shows that the put must be worth at expiration the difference between the strike price and the underlying asset value.

The put payoff reveals that before maturity, the put value must be worth at least the difference between the strike price and the underlying asset value. This is because the American put holder can exercise his/her option at any instant before maturity. It can also be shown that the European put value must be at least equal to the present value of the strike price minus the underlying asset price. Since the American put value must be at least equal to $K - S_t$ because of the possibility of an early exercise, the European put value must verify the following relationship:

$$p_t \geq Ke^{-r(T-t)} - S_t$$

This relationship holds good at any time before expiration since the put holder cannot exercise his/her put before expiration.

Example. Consider a European put trading at 2.5 when $S_t = 95$, $K = 100$, $r = 7\%$, and $T = 0.5$ years. Using this information, the put value satisfying the following relationship: $p_t \geq Ke^{-r(T-t)} - S_t = 100e^{-0.07(0.5)} - 95 = 1.5605$, must be worth 1.5605.

Since the actual price is 2.5, the investor can implement a trading strategy to generate risk-less profits. In this case, he/she can buy the put at 2.5 and buy the stock at 95. The strategy can be implemented by borrowing at 97.5 or (95+2.5) at 7% for six months. The net cash-flow of this strategy is zero.

At maturity, the investor exercises his/her put option, (receives the strike price of 100 and delivers the stock). He re-pays the borrowed amount $97e^{0.07(0.5)}$. The net cash-flow from this strategy is 100.45511. This is the risk-less arbitrage profit. Hence, with zero investment, the strategy guaranteed a risk-less arbitrage profit. Therefore, the above inequality must hold good.

The put price is an increasing function of time until expiration. In fact, if we consider two puts with the same characteristics, except for maturity, then the price of the put with a longer maturity must equal or exceed the price of the put with the shorter maturity. If this principle is violated, arbitrage can be implemented with risk-less profits.

The put price is a decreasing function of the strike price. In fact, if we consider two American puts with the same characteristics, except for the strike price, then the price of the put with a higher strike price must be higher than the price of the put with the lower strike price.

If we consider two European puts with the same characteristics, except for the strike price, then the price of the put with a higher strike price must be higher than the price of the put with the lower strike price.

If we consider two American puts with the same characteristics, except for the strike price, then the difference between their prices must be less than the difference in their strike prices.

If we consider two European puts with the same characteristics, except for the strike price, then the difference between their prices must be less than the difference in the present value of their strike prices.

12.4.5. *Other properties*

12.4.5.1. *Interest rate and option prices*

Call prices are an increasing function of the interest rate. This is not the case for put options.

12.4.5.2. *Interest rate and call prices*

The price of a European or an American call must satisfy the following relationship:

$$C_t \geq S_t - Ke^{-r(T-t)}$$

This equation shows that the higher the interest rates, the smaller is the present value of the strike price $Ke^{-r(T-t)}$. Hence, higher interest rates give a higher value for the difference $S_t - Ke^{-r(T-t)}$.

12.4.5.3. *Interest rate and put prices*

The price of a European put must satisfy the following relationship:

$$p_t \geq Ke^{-r(T-t)} - S_t$$

Since the put holder receives a maximum value of the strike price (a potential cash inflow), the higher the present value of this cash inflow, the higher is the put value. Therefore, the put must be higher for lower interest rates. The above relationship can be used in this context to show the presence of a profitable arbitrage opportunity when the put fails to adjust to the changing interest rates.

12.4.5.4. *Risk and option prices*

Call and put prices are increasing functions of the risk of the underlying asset.

Risk is measured by the standard deviation or the volatility of the underlying asset's returns.

With 25 years of experience with financial markets, I have learnt that options are to be bought, not sold.

12.5. Simple Trading Strategies for Options and Their Underlying Assets

12.5.1. *Trading the underlying assets*

The value of any option underlying asset such as a stock, a default-free bond, a futures or a forward contract is determined in a market place. In general, there are two prices quoted: the bid and the ask price. These two prices define a spread. In theory, there is only one price for each asset, but in practice, these two prices are observed in financial markets. An investor can buy (long position) or sell (short position) a financial instrument. It is possible to represent the gain or loss from a transaction at a given date in the future. If one buys a stock at 100 and sells it in a year at 110, the profit is 10. If one buys a bond at 90 and sells it in a year at 100, the profit is 10. The graph of the profit and loss as a function of the stock price at a given date (one year, for example) is diagonal. For a bond, the graph of the profit and loss is a straight line because the bond value is known with certainty at maturity.

12.5.2. *Buying and selling calls*

Buying a call gives the right to the option holder to pay the strike price K at maturity and to receive the value of an underlying asset S_T. He/she can also let the option expire. In this case, the call option is worth zero. The positive difference between $(S_T - K)$ refers to the intrinsic value or exercise value. Hence, at maturity, the value of a European or an American call is given by $C_T = c_T = \max[0, S_T - K]$. This represents the value of a long call position at expiration, where C_T and c_T refer respectively to the American and European call values.

The profit for the option buyer represents exactly the loss of the option seller and vice versa.

Example. Consider a call with $K = 100$ when $S_T = 90$. At maturity, the call buyer does not exercise his/her option because he/she pays 100 and receives an underlying asset that is worth 90. He/she allows the option to expire to avoid losing 10 since the option is worthless.

$$S_T - K = 90 - 100 = -10 < 0$$

Hence, the payoff for the call buyer is:

$$C_T = \max[0, S_T - K] = \max[0, 90 - 100] = \max[0, -10] = 0$$

However, if $S_T = 110$, this gives an immediate payoff of 10 exercise, or:

$$C_T = \max[0, S_T - K] = \max[0, 110 - 100] = \max[0, 10] = 10$$

The call seller implements a short position in the call. The value of a short call position at expiration is:

$$-C_T = -c_T = -\max[0, S_T - K]$$

It is clear that the value of the short position is always negative. This is because at initial time, the option seller receives the premium option.

Example. Consider a call with $K = 100$ when $S_T = 110$. In this case, upon exercise by the call holder, the option seller delivers a stock worth $S_T = 110$ and receives the strike price $K = 100$. Hence, the value of the call position for the seller is -10 or:

$$-C_T = -c_T = -\max[0, S_T - K] = -\max[0, 110 - 100] = -10$$

As we compute the payoffs at maturity, we can determine the profit or loss P&L from holding long and short positions in options. If we denote the value of the purchased call at time t or the cost of the call by C_t, then the profit or loss on a long call position held until maturity is:

$$C_T - C_t = \max[0, S_T - K] - C_t$$

In the same way, if we denote the value of the sold call at time t by C_t, then the profit or loss on a short call position held until maturity is:

$$C_t - C_T = C_t - \max[0, S_T - K]$$

Example. Consider a call with $K = 100$ when $S_T = 110$. The investor paid 10 for this call at time $t = 0$. In this case, if at the maturity date T, $S_T \leq 110$, the option buyer loses his/her option premium. However, when $100 < S_T < 110$, the call holder loses less than the purchase price 10. When $S_T = 105$, the call holder loses 5. In fact, he/she receives 5 upon exercise, i.e., $(105 - 100)$, coupled with the 10 paid for the option, his/her net loss is 5. If $S_T = 110$, he/she receives 10 upon exercise coupled with the 10 paid for the option, gives a zero profit.

It is important to note that, in any case, the profits from the buyer and the seller of the option sum up always to zero since the gains for the buyer are the losses of the seller and vice versa. If an investor buys and sells calls on the same underlying asset for the same maturity date, then the profits and losses from the two operations are equal to zero at the call's maturity date. In fact, derivatives markets are zero-sum games because they do not lead to net profits and losses. What the buyer wins is lost by the seller and vice versa.

If one computes the sum of gains and losses from the long and short call positions, the result is zero. In fact:

$$(C_T - C_t) + (C_t - C_T) = 0$$

since

$$(\max[0, S_T - K] - C_t) + (C_t - \max[0, S_T - K]) = 0$$

A trader buys, in general, a call when he/she expects the underlying asset price to rise. He/she shorts a call when he/she expects a stability or a decline in the /sheunderlying asset price.

12.5.3. *Buying and selling puts*

Buying a put gives the right to the option holder to sell at maturity the underlying asset S_T at the strike price K. He/she can also let the option expire. In this case, the put option is worth zero. The positive difference between $(K - S_T)$ refers to the intrinsic value or an exercise value. Hence, at maturity, the value of a European or an American call is given by $P_T = p_T = \max[0, K - S_T]$. The value of a short put position at expiration is $-P_T = -p_T = -\max[0, K - S_T]$.

Example. Consider a put with $K = 100$ when $S_T = 105$. At maturity, the put buyer does not exercise his/her option because he/she receives 100 and delivers an underlying asset that is worth 105. He/she allows the option to expire to avoid losing 5 since the option is worthless. Hence, the payoff for the put buyer is:

$$P_T = \max[0, K - S_T] = \max[0, 100 - 105] = \max[0, -5] = 0$$

If $S_T = 100$, this gives an immediate payoff of zero upon exercise, or:

$$P_T = \max[0, K - S_T] = \max[0, 100 - 100] = \max[0, 0] = 0$$

The holder of the put receives nothing upon exercise when $S_T \geq K$.

However, if $S_T < K$, the put value is positive for any value of the stock. If $S_T = 85$, we have:

$$P_T = \max[0, K - S_T] = \max[0, 100 - 85] = \max[0, 15] = 15$$

If the put holder had paid 10 at time zero, his/her net profit is 5 or $(15 - 10)$.

The previous analysis shows that the payoffs of calls and puts depend on the position of the option's underlying asset with respect to the strike price. A trader buys, in general, a put when he/she expects the underlying asset price to fall. He/she shorts a put when he/she expects a stability or an appreciation in the underlying asset price.

12.6. Some Option Combinations

It is possible to use calls or puts in different simple strategies. We can combine calls and puts in order to create some option combinations that are discussed below.

12.6.1. *The straddle*

The straddle is one of the simplest option strategies. An investor buying a straddle buys simultaneously a call and a put on the same underlying asset with the same strike price and maturity date.

An investor selling a straddle sells simultaneously a call and a put on the same underlying asset with the same strike price and maturity date.

Example. Consider a call and a put on the same underlying asset and maturity date. The call costs 10 and the put's value is 8. The strike price is 100. The P&L of the straddle corresponds to the combined profits and losses from buying or selling both options.

Let us denote the current option prices by C_t and P_t and the option prices at maturity by C_T and P_T. At maturity, the long straddle position is worth:

$$C_T + P_T = \max[0, S_T - K] + \max[0, K - S_T]$$

The cost of the long straddle is $C_t + P_t$. The maximum loss of this strategy corresponds to the costs necessary to its implementation. A trader buys, in general, a straddle when he/she expects erratic movements in the underlying asset price. This refers to a very volatile market for the underlying asset. At maturity, the short straddle position is worth:

$$-C_T - P_T = -\max[0, S_T - K] - \max[0, K - S_T]$$

A trader shorts a straddle when he/she expects a stability in the underlying asset price. The cost of the short straddle is $-C_t - P_t$.

12.6.2. *The strangle*

The strangle is one of the simplest option strategies. An investor buying a strangle (long a strangle) buys simultaneously a call and a put on the same underlying asset with different strike prices K_1 and K_2 at the same maturity date. The call with a strike price K_1 and the put with a strike price K_2 are both out-of-the money with $K_1 > K_2$. An investor selling a strangle (short a strangle) sells simultaneously a call and a put on the same underlying asset with two strike prices. The only difference with the straddle is the presence of two different strike prices.

The long strangle is worth at maturity:

$$C_T(S_T, K_1, T) + P_T(S_T, K_2, T) = \max[0, S_T - K_1] + \max[0, K_2 - S_T]$$

The cost of the long strangle is $C_t(S_t, K_1, T) + P_t(S_t, K_2, T)$. A trader buys, in general, a strangle when he/she expects erratic movements in the underlying asset price. The short strangle is worth at maturity:

$$\begin{aligned} &-C_T(S_T, K_1, T) - P_T(S_T, K_2, T) \\ &= -\max[0, S_T - K_1] - \max[0, K_2 - S_T] \end{aligned}$$

The cost of the short strangle is $-C_t(S_t, K_1, T) - P_t(S_t, K_2, T)$. A trader sells, in general, a strangle when he/she expects some stability in the underlying asset price.

12.7. Option Spreads

12.7.1. *Bull and bear spreads with call options*

A spread consists in buying an option and selling another option. A bull spread corresponds to a combination of options with the same underlying asset and the same maturity, but different strike prices. When it is implemented with two calls, it is designed to have a profit from a rise in the underlying asset price. This strategy limits the risks and the potential of profits.

The bull spread buyer buys an in-the-money call and sells an out-of-the-money call. At maturity, the long bull spread is worth:

$$C_T(S_T, K_1, T) - C_T(S_T, K_2, T) = \max[0, S_T - K_1] - \max[0, S_T - K_2]$$

The cost of the long bull spread is $C_t(S_t, K_1, T) - C_t(S_t, K_2, T)$.

A bear spread corresponds to a combination of options with the same underlying asset and the same maturity, but different strike prices. When it is implemented with two calls, it is designed to profit from falling underlying asset prices. This strategy with calls corresponds to the short position to the bull spread. The bear spread buyer buys the call with the higher strike price and sells the call with a lower strike price. At maturity, the long bear spread is worth:

$$\begin{aligned}&-C_T(S_T, K_1, T) + C_T(S_T, K_2, T)\\&\quad = -\max[0, S_T - K_1] + \max[0, S_T - K_2]\end{aligned}$$

The cost of the long bear spread is $-C_t(S_t, K_1, T) + C_t(S_t, K_2, T)$.

A trader implements a bull spread with calls when he/she expects the underlying asset price to rise. He/she implements a bear spread with calls when he/she expects the underlying asset price to fall.

12.7.2. *Bull and bear spreads with put options*

A bull spread corresponds to a combination of puts with the same underlying asset and the same maturity, but different strike prices. When it is implemented with two puts, the trader buys a put with a lower strike price and sells a put with a higher strike price. The bear spread trader buys a put with a higher strike price and sells a put with a lower strike price. At maturity, the bull spread is worth:

$$P_T(S_T, K_1, T) - P_T(S_T, K_2, T) = \max[0, K_1 - S_T] - \max[0, K_2 - S_T]$$

The cost of the long bull spreads is $P_t(S_t, K_1, T) - P_t(S_t, K_2, T)$ with $K_1 < K_2$. At maturity, the bear spread with puts is worth:

$$\begin{aligned}&-P_T(S_T, K_1, T) + P_T(S_T, K_2, T)\\&\quad = -\max[0, K_1 - S_T] + \max[0, K_2 - S_T]\end{aligned}$$

The cost of the bear spread is $-P_t(S_t, K_1, T) + P_t(S_t, K_2, T)$.

A trader implements a bull spread with puts when he/she expects the underlying asset price to rise. He/she implements a bear spread with puts when he/she expects the underlying asset price to fall.

12.7.3. *Box spread*

12.7.3.1. *Definitions and examples*

A box spread corresponds to a combination of a bull spreads with calls and a bear spread with puts. It is implemented using two spreads with two strike prices. Since at maturity, the long bull spread is worth:

$$C_T(S_T, K_1, T) - C_T(S_T, K_2, T) = \max[0, S_T - K_1] - \max[0, S_T - K_2]$$

and at the same date, the bear spread with puts is worth:

$$\begin{aligned} &-P_T(S_T, K_1, T) + P_T(S_T, K_2, T) \\ &\quad = -\max[0, K_1 - S_T] + \max[0, K_2 - S_T] \end{aligned}$$

then at maturity, the box spread is worth:

$$C_T(S_T, K_1, T) - C_T(S_T, K_2, T) - P_T(S_T, K_1, T) + P_T(S_T, K_2, T)$$

This is equal to:

$$\begin{aligned} &\max[0, S_T - K_1] - \max[0, S_T - K_2] \\ &\quad - \max[0, K_1 - S_T] + \max[0, K_2 - S_T] \end{aligned}$$

This strategy is "neutral" since it produces a return equal to the risk-less rate of interest.

Example. Consider the following four legs of a transaction: a long call with $K_1 = 90$, a short call with $K_2 = 100$, a long put with $K_2 = 100$, and a short put with $K_1 = 90$.

At maturity, the box spread is worth:

$$\max[0, S_T - 90] - \max[0, S_T - 100] + \max[0, 100 - S_T] - \max[0, 90 - S_T]$$

When the underlying asset $S_T = 98$, the payoff is:

$$\max[0, 98 - 90] - \max[0, 98 - 100] + \max[0, 100 - 98] - \max[0, 90 - 98]$$

or

$$8 - 0 + 2 - 0 = 10.$$

When the underlying asset $S_T = 70$, the payoff is:

$$\max[0, 70-90] - \max[0, 70-100] + \max[0, 100-70] - \max[0, 90-100]$$

or

$$0 - 0 + 30 - 20 = 10.$$

Note that in all the cases, the box spread is worth 10. This corresponds to the difference between the strike prices. Hence, the strategy appears equivalent to a risk-less investment. Therefore, to avoid profitable arbitrage opportunities, the box-spread value at time zero must be the discounted value of the difference between the two strike prices. Hence, its initial cost must be $\frac{K_2-K_1}{(1+r)(T-t)}$.

12.7.3.2. *Trading a box spread*

The box-spread strategy can be implemented with options on spot or options on futures. In the following discussion, $c(K_1), c(K_2), p(K_1)$, and $p(K_2)$ denote respectively, the prices of calls and puts with strike prices K_1 and K_2 with $K_2 > K_1$.

Consider a portfolio corresponding to the following strategy:

a long bullish call spread: buy $c(K_1)$ and sell $c(K_2)$
a long bearish put spread: buy $p(K_2)$ and sell $p(K_1)$

This strategy is a box spread which costs $c(K_1) - c(K_2) - p(K_1) + p(K_2)$.

The following non-arbitrage condition must be satisfied:

$$c(K_1) - c(K_2) - p(K_1) + p(K_2) \leq (K_2 - K_1)e^{-rT}$$

At the maturity date, the result of the strategy is always $(K_2 - K_1)$. In fact, the pay-off of each option is:

$$\max[S_T - K_1, 0] - \max[S_T - K_2, 0] - \max[K_1 - S_T, 0] + \max[K_2 - S_T, 0]$$

This shows that the box is worth $(K_2 - K_1)$ at the maturity date. If its value is less than the discounted value of $(K_2 - K_1)$, then risk-less arbitrage would be possible.

Consider the two following two relationships between the European options c and p and the American options C and P:

$$C(K_1) - c(K_1) \geq C(K_2) - c(K_2), P(K_2) - p(K_2) \geq P(K_1) - p(K_1)$$

These relations account for the value of the early exercise premium for calls and puts with different strike prices. If the first condition was not satisfied, then selling the American call and buying the European call (with a strike price K_2) and buying the American call and selling the European call (with a strike price K_1), would allow an immediate profit. If the American call with a strike price K_2 is not exercised before the maturity date, the position produces a zero cash-flow at this date. If the call with a strike price K_2 is exercised, the option with a strike price K_1 can be exercised to generate a cash-flow $(K_2 - K_1)$, which will be invested until the maturity date T.

If the option with a strike price K_2 is exercised before the maturity date at a date $t_1 < T$, the result at maturity is $(K_2 - K_1)e^{r(T-t_1)} > K_2 - K_1$. Tests of the box strategy for options traded on the Chicago Board Options Exchange (CBOE) over eight years reveal some violations of the non-arbitrage condition. However, the profitable opportunities disappeared when transaction costs were taken into account. Hence, the market is globally efficient.

12.8. Butterfly Strategies

12.8.1. *Butterfly spread with calls*

A butterfly spread corresponds to a combination using three calls with three strike prices $K_1 < K_2 < K_3$. The calls have the same underlying asset and maturity date. An investor long the butterfly buys the call with the lowest strike price K_1, buys the call with the highest strike price K_3, and sells two calls with an intermediate strike price K_2. At maturity, the long butterfly spread is worth:

$$\begin{aligned} &C_T(S_T, K_1, T) - 2C_T(S_T, K_2, T) + C_T(S_T, K_3, T) \\ &\quad = \max[0, S_T - K_1] - 2\max[0, S_T - K_2] + \max[0, S_T - K_3] \end{aligned}$$

The cost of a long butterfly spread is:

$$C_t(S_t, K_1, T) - 2C_t(S_t, K_2, T) + C_t(S_t, K_3, T)$$

An investor short the butterfly sells the call with the lowest strike price K_1, sells the call with the highest strike price K_3, and buys two calls with intermediate strike price K_2. This strategy tends to be profitable when the underlying asset at maturity is at the intermediate strike prices. At maturity, the short butterfly spread with calls is worth:

$$\begin{aligned}&-C_T(S_T, K_1, T) + 2C_T(S_T, K_2, T) - C_T(S_T, K_3, T)\\&\quad = -\max[0, S_T - K_1] + 2\max[0, S_T - K_2] - \max[0, S_T - K_3]\end{aligned}$$

The cost of the short butterfly spread with calls is:

$$-C_t(S_t, K_1, T) + 2C_t(S_t, K_2, T) - C_t(S_t, K_3, T)$$

A trader implements a long butterfly spread with calls when he/she expects the underlying asset price to be relatively stable. He/she implements a short butterfly spread with calls when he/she expects strong movements in the underlying asset price.

12.8.2. *Butterfly spread with puts*

A butterfly spread corresponds to a combination using three puts with three strike prices $K_1 < K_2 < K_3$. The calls have the same underlying asset and maturity date. An investor long the butterfly buys the put with the lowest strike price K_1, buys the put with the highest strike price K_3, and sells two puts with an intermediate strike price K_2. At maturity, the long butterfly spread with puts is worth:

$$\begin{aligned}&P_T(S_T, K_1, T) - 2P_T(S_T, K_2, T) + P_T(S_T, K_3, T)\\&\quad = \max[0, K_1 - S_T] - 2\max[0, K_2 - S_T] + \max[0, K_3 - S_T]\end{aligned}$$

The cost of a long butterfly spread with puts is:

$$p_t(S_t, K_1, T) - 2P_t(S_t, K_2, T) + P_t(S_t, K_3, T)$$

An investor short the butterfly sells the put with the lowest strike price K_1, sells the put with the highest strike price K_3, and buys two puts with an intermediate strike price K_2. At maturity, the short butterfly spread with puts is worth:

$$
\begin{aligned}
&-P_T(S_T, K_1, T) + 2P_T(S_T, K_2, T) - P_T(S_T, K_3, T) \\
&\quad = -\max[0, K_1 - S_T] + 2\max[0, K_2 - S_T] - \max[0, K_3 - S_T]
\end{aligned}
$$

The cost of the short butterfly spread is:

$$-P_t(S_t, K_1, T) + 2P_t(S_t, K_2, T) - P_t(S_t, K_3, T)$$

A trader implements a long butterfly spread with puts when he/she expects the underlying asset price to be relatively stable. He/she implements a short butterfly spread with puts when he/she expects strong movements in the underlying asset price.

12.9. Condor Strategies

12.9.1. *Condor strategy with calls*

A condor corresponds to a combination using four calls with four strike prices $K_1 < K_2 < K_3 < K_4$. The calls have the same underlying asset and maturity date. An investor long the condor buys the call with the lowest strike price K_1, sells the call with a somewhat higher strike price K_2, sells the call with the yet higher strike price K_3, and buys the calls with the highest strike price K_4. At maturity, the long condor with calls is worth:

$$
\begin{aligned}
&C_T(S_T, K_1, T) - C_T(S_T, K_2, T) - C_T(S_T, K_3, T) + C_T(S_T, K_4, T) \\
&\quad = \max[0, S_T - K_1] - \max[0, S_T - K_2] - \max[0, S_T - K_3] \\
&\qquad + \max[0, S_T - K_4]
\end{aligned}
$$

The cost of a long condor with calls is:

$$C_t(S_t, K_1, T) - C_t(S_t, K_2, T) - C_t(S_t, K_3, T) + C_t(S_t, K_4, T)$$

An investor short the condor sells the call with the lowest strike price K_1, buys the call with a somewhat higher strike price K_2, buys the call with the yet higher strike price K_3, and sells the calls with the highest strike price K_4.

At maturity, the short condor with calls is worth:

$$-C_T(S_T, K_1, T) + C_T(S_T, K_2, T) + C_T(S_T, K_3, T) - C_T(S_T, K_4, T)$$
$$= -\max[0, S_T - K_1] + \max[0, S_T - K_2] + \max[0, S_T - K_3]$$
$$- \max[0, S_T - K_4]$$

The cost of a short condor with calls is $-C_t(S_t, K_1, T) + C_t(S_t, K_2, T) + C_t(S_t, K_3, T) - C_t(S_t, K_4, T)$.

A trader implements a long condor with calls when he/she expects the underlying asset price to be relatively stable. He/she implements a short condor with calls when he/she expects strong movements in the underlying asset price.

12.9.2. *Condor strategy with puts*

A condor corresponds to a combination using four puts with four strike prices $K_1 < K_2 < K_3 < K_4$. The puts have the same underlying asset and maturity date. An investor long the condor buys the put with the lowest strike price K_1, sells the put with a somewhat higher strike price K_2, sells the put with the yet higher strike price K_3, and buys the put with the highest strike price K_4.

At maturity, the long condor with puts is worth:

$$P_T(S_T, K_1, T) - P_T(S_T, K_2, T) - P_T(S_T, K_3, T) + P_T(S_T, K_4, T)$$
$$= \max[0, K_1 - S_T] - \max[0, K_2 - S_T] - \max[0, K_3 - S_T]$$
$$+ \max[0, K_4 - S_T]$$

The cost of a long condor with puts is:

$$P_t(S_t, K_1, T) - P_t(S_t, K_2, T) - P_t(S_t, K_3, T) + P_t(S_t, K_4, T)$$

An investor short the condor sells the put with the lowest strike price K_1, buys the put with a somewhat higher strike price K_2, buys the put with the yet higher strike price K_3, and sells the put with the highest strike price K_4. At maturity, the short condor with puts is worth:

$$-P_T(S_T, K_1, T) + P_T(S_T, K_2, T) + P_T(S_T, K_3, T) - P_T(S_T, K_4, T)$$
$$= -\max[0, K_1 - S_T] + \max[0, K_2 - S_T] + \max[0, K_3 - S_T]$$
$$- \max[0, K_4 - S_T]$$

The cost of a short condor with puts is:

$$-P_t(S_t, K_1, T) + P_t(S_t, K_2, T) + P_t(S_t, K_3, T) - P_t(S_t, K_4, T)$$

A trader implements a long condor with puts when he/she expects the underlying asset price to be relatively stable. He/she implements a short condor with puts when he/she expects strong movements in the underlying asset price.

12.10. Ratio Spreads

A ratio spread is a strategy involving two or more related options in a given proportion. A trader can buy a call with a lower strike price and sell a higher number of calls with a higher strike price. A 2:1 ratio spread corresponds, for example, to a strategy in which the trader buys two options and sells an option. It is possible to use options with different maturities.

A spread based on options with different times to maturity is referred to as a calendar spread. The investor can implement different combinations of options with different strikes and time to maturity in order to construct a wide range of profit and loss profiles. These strategies can also be implemented in connection with the underlying assets and in particular with stocks, bonds, foreign currencies, commodities, etc.

Using simultaneously options and their underlying assets allows one to adjust payoff patterns to fit the attitude of investors toward the risk-return profile.

A trader implements ratio spreads with calls and puts in different contexts according to his/her future expectations about the underlying asset price and his/her risk-return profile.

12.11. Some Combinations of Options with Bonds and Stocks

12.11.1. *Covered call: Short a call and hold the underlying asset*

This strategy is implemented by selling the call and buying a certain quantity of the underlying asset. This strategy corresponds to a covered strategy since the investor owns the underlying asset. This asset covers the obligation inherent in selling the call. This strategy enhances income.

12.11.2. *Portfolio insurance*

Portfolio insurance is an investment-management technique that protects a portfolio from drops in value. This technique proposes some simple concepts allowing one to insure a stock portfolio. The strategy can be implemented using options, futures contracts, and other financial products. Consider, for example, a well-diversified portfolio of stocks. Portfolio insurance can be implemented in its basic form by buying a put on the owned portfolio of assets. At maturity or the horizon date, the value of the insured portfolio corresponds to the sum of the stock portfolio S_T and the put P_T written on this portfolio. The value of the insured portfolio can be written as:

$$S_T + P_T = S_T + \max[0, K - S_T]$$

The cost of the insured portfolio at initial time t corresponds to the sum of the stock portfolio S_t and the put price P_t or $(S_t + P_t)$.

The profit (or loss) on an uninsured portfolio is simply the difference between its final value and initial value or $S_T - S_t$. The insured portfolio has a superior performance only when:

$$\max[0, K - S_T] - P_t - S_t > 0$$

This strategy pays when markets are down, as in the year 2008.

12.11.3. *Mimicking portfolios and synthetic instruments*

A trader can use European options in connection with other instruments to create some specific payoff patterns at expiration. Two main relationships are often used: mimicking portfolios and synthetic instruments.

A mimicking portfolio: It shows the same results (profits and losses) as the instrument it mimics, but it might not have the same value.

A synthetic instrument: It exhibits the same results and value as the instrument it synthetically replicates.

12.11.3.1. *Mimicking the underlying asset*

An investor who buys a European call and sells a European put on the same underlying asset creates a position that exhibits the same payoff pattern as the underlying asset. At maturity, the payoff of this position is:

$$c_T - p_T = \max[0, S_T - K] - \max[0, K - S_T]$$

The initial cost of this position is $c_t - p_t$. Assume that at time t, $K = S_t$. In this setting, the value of the portfolio comprising a long call and a short put is obtained by replacing K with S_t in the previous equality:

$$\max[0, S_T - S_t] - \max[0, S_t - S_T]$$

If the underlying asset price rises with respect to the initial level S_t, then $S_T > S_t$ and the call is worth $S_T - S_t$. The put value is zero.

If the underlying asset price falls with respect to the initial level S_t, then $S_T < S_t$, the call is worth zero and the put value is $S_t - S_T$.

Note that this result is equivalent to that of the stock portfolio. Hence, the value of a portfolio comprising a long call and a short put is equivalent to that of the underlying asset or portfolio. This result is always verified when the option's strike price corresponds to the value of the underlying asset when this strategy is implemented.

12.11.3.2. *Synthetic underlying asset: Long call plus a short put and bonds*

A portfolio with a long European call and a short European put shows a profit (loss) pattern that can mimic the result of the underlying asset. Using a risk-free bond (as a proxy for investing a certain amount K at the risk-free interest rate r), it is possible to create a portfolio that synthesizes the option's underlying asset. The synthetic underlying asset has the same value and exhibits the same profit (loss) pattern as the underlying asset (or stock).

The value of the synthetic underlying asset at time t can be written as $S_t = c_t - p_t + Ke^{-r(T-t)}$.

The investor invests an amount $Ke^{-r(T-t)}$ in risk-free bonds at time t. This amount grows at the rate $e^{r(T-t)}$. At maturity, the value of the investment in risk-free bonds is exactly K. This corresponds also to the face value of the discount bonds at maturity.

At the option's maturity date, the value of the portfolio comprising a long call, a short put, and a certain amount K is:

$$c_T - p_T + K = \max[0, S_T - K] - \max[0, K - S_T] + K$$

In the absence of an early exercise, this equality is also verified for American options at expiration:

$$C_T - P_T + K = \max[0, S_T - K] - \max[0, K - S_T] + K$$

At maturity, if $S_T > K$, the call's value is $S_T - K$. The put value is zero. The value of the portfolio is simply that of the call and the bond or $S_T - K + K = S_T$.

At maturity, if $S_T < K$, the call's value is zero and the put's value is $K - S_T$. The value of the portfolio simply corresponds to that of the short position in the put and the bond or $-(K - S_T) + K = S_T$. Hence, as discussed before, the value of a portfolio comprising a long call and a short put and the bond is equivalent to that of the underlying asset.

Buying a call, selling a put, and investing in a risk-free discount bond is a strategy equivalent to an investment in the option's underlying asset.

12.11.3.3. *The synthetic put: Put-call parity relationship*

The put-call parity relationship stipulates simply that buying a call, selling a put, and investing in a risk-free discount bond is a strategy equivalent to an investment in the option's underlying asset. Hence, using three of these four instruments allows one to synthesize the fourth instrument. The put-call parity relationship is often presented in the following form:

$$p_t = c_t - S_t + Ke^{-r(T-t)}$$

It stipulates that the put can be duplicated by a short position in the stock, a long position in the call, and an investment in risk-free bonds paying the strike price at the option's common maturity date.

When at initial time t, $S_t = K$, then the call price must be higher than the put price. In fact, the relationship can also be presented in the following form: $c_t - p_t = S_t + Ke^{-r(T-t)}$. Since $S_t = K$, the right-hand side must be positive. Therefore, $c_t - p_t$ must be positive. Therefore, the call price must be higher than the put price.

12.12. Conversions and Reversals

A strategy can be implemented by going long a call and short a put. If the underlying asset price is above the strike price at the option's maturity date, the put is worthless and the call's value corresponds to the intrinsic value. The position will behave exactly as the value of the underlying asset. However, if the underlying asset price is below the strike price, the call is worthless and the put's value is its intrinsic value. The position will again behave exactly as the value of the underlying asset.

Buying the call and selling the put is a position equivalent to buying the underlying asset. More generally, the following no-arbitrage between a call c, a put p, the underlying asset price S, and the strike price K must hold:

$$c - p = S - Ke^{-rT}$$

where r stands for the risk-less interest rate and T is the option's maturity date.

A conversion is a strategy based on the above relationship. It can also be written as: short a call + long a put + long the underlying asset = short a synthetic underlying asset+long the underlying asset.

A reversal corresponds simply to a reverse conversion: long a call+ short a put+short the underlying asset = long a synthetic underlying asset + short the underlying asset.

If we substitute the underlying asset by a synthetic underlying asset in the conversion strategy for a different strike price, this eliminates the risks associated with the variations of the underlying asset price and gives the well-known strategy, the box spread. The box spread is simply a strategy equivalent to borrowing or lending money for a certain period. For an analysis of financial markets, volume, volatility, and spreads, readers can refer to Hong and Wang (2000), French (1980), and Gibbons and Hess (1981).

12.13. Case Study: Selling Calls (Without Holding the Stocks/as an Alternative to Short Selling Stocks/the Idea of Selling Calls Is Also an Alternative to Buying Puts)

12.13.1. *Data and assumptions*

We consider a **Risk capital of 100,000** to invest for 3 months.

When the stock is at 15 and the strike price at 15, using option valuation procedure and assuming a volatility of **20%**, the interest rate at 5%, the call price is 0.69.

If we change the volatility to **45%**, the option price is 1.5.

The results show a profit in each scenario.

12.13.1.1. *Selling calls (without holding the stock)*

The investor (DC) sells (short) 6,666 calls.

This is **a covered position** because its aggregate underlying value is no greater than **the risk capital** that would have gone into buying stocks instead of selling calls: 100,000.

Aggregate underlying value = stock price × number of options sold × contract multiplier

$$\mathbf{100{,}000 = 15 \times 6{,}666 \times 1}$$

The short sale of 6,666 calls would result in proceeds of 4,599.54, which would be invested in T-bills during the holding period:

Proceeds of call short sale = call price × number calls × multiplier

$$4{,}599.54 = 0.69 \times 6{,}666 \times 1$$

The pattern of risk return associated with this strategy is as follows:

If the stock price is unchanged or down at expiration, the investment profit is 4,657.03.

If the stock is up by 10%, from 15 to 16.5, each option has an exercise value of 1.5 for an aggregate exercise value of 9,999.

Offset by the initial proceeds of the short sale and income from T-bills, the investor's loss is 4,542.05. Recall, if the investor sold a portfolio of stocks short, his loss was 9,750.

Tables 12.5–12.22 provide simulation results.

Table 12.5. Results at the maturity date in three months of the strategy of selling 6,666 calls at 0.69 when volatility is at 20%.

	Stock Unchanged: 15	Stock + 10%: 16.5	Stock – 10%: 13.5
Initial proceeds from calls: 6,666 × 0.69	4,599.54	4,599.54	4,599.54
Exercise value of calls	0	(9,999) 1.5 × 6,666	0
Profit (loss) from calls	4,599.54	(5,399.46)	4,599.54
Interest income on T-bills: 5% × 4,599.54 × 0.25	57.49	57.49	57.49
Total profit (loss)	4,657.03: maximum gain	(4,542.05)	4,657.03: maximum gain
Return on risk capital	4.65%	(4.54%)	4.65%

Notes: No initial capital to use.
Profit if the stock is less than 15.6986, otherwise losses appear.

Comparison with selling short the stock:

– When the investor *short sells calls*, with the stock unchanged, he experiences a profit of 4,657.03 and this is *his maximum gain.*

No matter how far the underlying asset may fall by expiration, the calls he sold short will still expire worthless and the most he can hope to collect on them is what he initially sold them for 4,599.54, *no matter what happens* to the stock, the T-bills will still yield 57.49.

We can calculate the *up-side tolerance point for a short sale* of 6,666 calls, 15.6986.

Below this stock price level, the premium initially received from the short sale of calls and the interest income from his T-bills is sufficient to repay the exercise value of the short calls.

Case 1: $C = 0.69$

$$\textit{Proceeds per contract} = (\text{proceeds from calls} + \text{T-bills}) / (\text{Number contracts} \times \text{multiplier})$$

$$0.6986 = (4{,}599.54 + 57.49)/(6{,}666 \times 1)$$

Table 12.6. Results at the maturity date in three months of the strategy of selling 6,666 calls at 1.5 when volatility is at 47%.

	Stock Unchanged: 15	Stock + 10%: 16.5	Stock − 10%: 13.5
Initial proceeds from calls: 6,666 × 1.5	9,999	9,999	9,999
Exercise value of calls	0	(9,999) 1.5 × 6,666	0
Profit (loss) from calls	9,999	(0)	9,999
Interest income on T-bills: 5%×9,999×0.25	124.98	124.98	124.98
Total profit (loss)	10,123: maximum gain	124.98	10,123: maximum gain

Notes: No initial capital to use.
Profit in each scenario if call sold at this price of 1.5.
Profit in every scenario for IC.
If the stock is higher than **16.518**, losses appear.

$$\textit{Upside tolerance point} = \text{Proceeds per contract} + \text{strike price}$$
$$15.6986 = 0.6986 + 15$$

Above this point, the exercise value of the calls becomes great enough *to cause a net loss.*

The 15.6986 in the price at which the risk return line crosses down through the center of the chart into the region representing losses.

Case 2: $C = 1.5$

$$\textit{Proceeds per contract} = (\text{proceeds from calls} + \text{T-bills}) / (\text{Number contracts} \times \text{multiplier})$$
$$1.5187 = (9{,}999 + 124.98)/(6{,}666 \times 1)$$
$$\textit{Upside tolerance point} = \text{Proceeds per contract} + \text{strike price}$$
$$16.518 = 1.5187 + 15$$

Above this point, the exercise value of the calls becomes great enough *to cause a net loss.*

The 16.518 in the price at which the risk return line crosses down through the center of the chart into the region representing losses.

12.13.1.2. *Comparing the strategy of selling calls (with a short portfolio of stocks): The extreme case*

Comparing covered short calls with a short portfolio of stocks, the short calls are less risky.

The extreme case: In theory, there is no limit to how far the stock might rise over a given holding period, but as an extreme example, let's see what would happen if the stock doubled from 15 to 30.

The portfolio would show a **loss of 100,000**, offset by 1,250 in interest income – a net loss of 98,750. **The position with 6,666 calls, *fares* somewhat better.**

The investor must pay an aggregate exercise value of 99,990, but this is offset by the initial proceeds from the calls and the interest income — the net loss is (95,332.97), an improvement of 3,417.03. (98,750–95,332.97)

12.13.1.3. *Selling calls (holding the stock)*

The investor sells short 6,666 calls.
What must be the position **in the stock**:
To cover the position, we buy **Delta units** of the underlying asset.
Assume that the call's delta is about **0.55** and that the option is on one share.
At time zero, we sell the calls and we buy: $0.55 \times 6{,}666 \times 15 = 55{,}000$ stocks.
The pattern of **risk return** associated with this strategy is as follows:

Table 12.7. Extreme case: Stock up by 100%.

Proceeds from short sale of stocks	100,000
Repurchase of stocks	(200,000)
Loss from stocks	(100,000)
Interest income on T-bills 5% × 100,000 × 0.25	1,250
Total loss	(98,750)

Table 12.8. Stock up by 100%: Position in the short calls: Case 1.

Proceeds from sale of calls 6,666 × 0.69	4,599.54
Exercise value of calls 6,666 × 15 × 1	(99,990)
Loss from calls	(95,390.46)
Interest income on T-bills 5% × 4,599.54 × 0.25	57.49
Total loss	(95,332.97)

Table 12.9. Stock up by 100%: Position in the short calls: Case 2.

Proceeds from sale of calls 6,666 × 1.5	9,990
Exercise value of calls 6,666 × 15 × 1	(99,990)
Loss from calls	(90,000)
Interest income on T-bills 5% × 9,990 × 0.25	124.875
Total loss	(89,875)

Note: **Position in calls**: shows a net loss of (89,875).

12.13.2. *Leverage in selling call options (without holding the stocks)*

If the investor of the previous example were willing to lower his *upside tolerance* point in *exchange for higher profits* with the stock unchanged or down, he could sell a larger number of calls.

12.13.2.1. *Selling call options (without holding the stocks)*

If the investor wished to commit all of his *100,000 dollars to margining short calls* he could sell:

$$\text{Net requirement} = 5\% \text{ of stock price} \times \text{contract multiplier}$$

$$0.75 = 5\% \times 15 \times 1$$

Table 12.10. Results at the maturity date in three months of the strategy of selling calls and buying the underlying stock for a hedge: Delta stocks: 0.55 stocks.

	Stock Unchanged	Stock + 10%	Stock – 10%
Total profit (loss) on options	4,657.03	(4,542.05)	4,657.03
Portfolio of Stock's ending value	55,000	60,500 (55,000 × 1.1)	49,500
Profit (loss) from stocks	0	5,500	(5,500)
Total profit (loss) from options and stocks	4,657.03	958	(843)
Return on risk capital (in stocks)	8.46%	1.74%	(1.53%)
	= 4,657.03/55,000	= 958/55,000	= (843)/55,000

Note: If we account for dividends of 1%, about 549 dollars, all the results may become positive.

Table 12.11. Results at the maturity date in three months of the strategy of selling calls and buying the underlying stock for a hedge: Delta stocks: 0.55 stocks.

	Stock Unchanged	Stock + 10%	Stock – 10%
Profit (loss) from calls	9,999	(0)	9,999
Portfolio of Stock's ending value	55,000	60,500 (55,000 × 1.1)	49,500
Profit (loss) from stocks	0	5,500	(5,500)
Total profit (loss) from options and stocks	9,999	5,500	4,499
Return on risk capital (in stocks)	18%	10%	8.2%
	= 9,999/55,000	= 5,500/55,000	4,499/55,000

$$\text{Maximum contracts to Margin} = \text{Total Margin deposit}/\text{Net requirement per contract}$$

$$133{,}333 = 100{,}000/0.75$$

At 0.69, the proceeds from selling 133,333 calls would be:

$$\textbf{Proceeds of call short sale} = \text{call price} \times \text{number} \times \text{contract multiplier}$$

$$91{,}999 = 0.69 \times 133{,}333 \times 1$$

The patterns of risk and return associated with this strategy shows that with the stock unchanged or down, the investor's profit would be the *initial proceeds* from the sale plus interest from the T-bills, a total of 93,148.98.

This will be the maximum profit (as other short positions).

But, if the stock rises, he is exposed to unlimited losses.

If the stock rises 10%, the aggregate exercise value is (199,999).

Offset by the initial proceeds from the sale of calls and the interest on the TB, the investor total loss is (98,850).

The investor loss can be more than the *100,000 margin deposit.*

Losses in short calls are almost limitless. (Unlike the case with short puts, in which losses are limited by the fact that the stock cannot trade below zero.)

12.13.2.2. *Leverage in selling call options (without holding the stocks): The extreme case*

Extreme case: Stock up by 100%

Consider the limiting case in which the stock doubles from 15 to 30, the aggregate exercise value the call seller would have to pay totals (1,999,990).

Offset by the initial proceeds from sale of the calls and the interest on the T-bills, the investor's total loss is (1,906,849).

12.13.2.3. *Selling calls using leverage (and holding the stock)*

The investor sells short 133,3333 calls.

What must be the position in the stock?

Table 12.12. Results at the maturity date in three months of the strategy using leverage in selling calls.

	Stock Unchanged	Stock + 10%	Stock − 10%
Initial proceeds from calls: 133,333 × 0.69	91,999	91,999	91,999
Exercise value of calls	0	(199,999) 1.5 × 133,3333	0
Profit (loss) from calls	91,999	(100,000)	91,999
Interest income on T-bills: 5% × 91,999 × 0.25	1,149.98	1,149.98	1,149.98
Total profit (loss)	93,148.98	(98,850)	93,148.98
Return: Profit/initial proceeds	1,012 = 93,148.98/ 91,999	(1,074) = (98,850/ 91,999)	1.012 = (93,148.98/ 91,999)

Table 12.13. Results at the maturity date in three months of the strategy using leverage in selling calls.

	Stock Unchanged	Stock + 10%	Stock − 10%
Initial proceeds from calls: 133,333 × 1.5	199,999	199,999	199,999
Exercise value of calls	0	(199,999) 1.5 × 133,3333	0
Profit (loss) from calls	199,999	(000)	199,999
Interest income on T-bills: 5% × 199,999 × 0.25	2,499.98	2,499.98	2,499.98
Total profit (loss)	202,498	2,499.98	202,498
Return: Profit/initial proceeds	101.2% = 202,498 /199,999	1.02% = (2,499.98 /199,999)	101.2% = (202,498 /199,999)

To **cover the position**, we buy **Delta units** of the underlying asset. Assume that the call's delta is about **0.55** and that the option is on one share.

At time zero, we sell the calls and we buy stocks: **0.55** × **133,3333** × **15** = **1,099,997**.

Table 12.14. Case 1. Leverage in selling call options (without holding the stocks): The extreme case stock up by 100%.

Proceeds from sale of calls 133,3333 × 0.69	91,999
Exercise value of calls 133,3333 × 15 × 1	(1,999,990)
Loss from calls	(1,907,999)
Interest income on T-bills 5% × 91,999 × 0.25	1,149.875
Total loss	(1,906,849)

Table 12.15. Case 2. Leverage in selling call options (without holding the stocks): The extreme case stock up by 100%: Call: 1.5.

Proceeds from sale of calls 133,3333 × 1.5	199,999
Exercise value of calls 133,3333 × 15 × 1	(1,999,995)
Loss from calls	(1,799,996)
Interest income on T-bills 5% × 199,999 × 0.25	2,499.9875
Total loss	(1,7907,496)

Table 12.16. Results at the maturity date in three months of the strategy of selling calls and buying the underlying stock.

	Stock Unchanged	Stock + 10%	Stock − 10%
Total profit on options (loss)	93,148.98	(98,850)	93,148.98
Portfolio of Stock's ending value	1,099,997 **0.55 × 133,3333 × 15(1,099,997)**	1,209,996 **0.55 × 133,3333 × 15(1,099,997) × 1.1**	989,997 **0.55 × 133,3333 × 15(1,099,997) × 0.9**
Profit (loss) from stocks	0	109,999	(109,999)
Total profit (loss) from options and stocks	93,148.98	11,149	(16,851)
Return on options	100%	−100%	100%
Return on stocks	0	10%	(−10%)

The pattern of risk return associated with this strategy is as follows:

12.13.3. *Short sale of the stocks without options*

An investor (DC) buys stocks in anticipation of a rise in the market.

An investor (DC) can sell stocks short in anticipation of a decline.

Table 12.17. Results at the maturity date in three months of the strategy of selling calls and buying the underlying stock.

	Stock Unchanged	Stock + 10%	Stock − 10%
Profit (loss) from calls	199,999	(000)	199,999
Portfolio of Stock's ending value	1,099,997 **0.55 × 133,3333 × 15(1,099,997) × 1**	1,209,996 **0.55 × 133,3333 × 15 × 1.1**	989,997
Profit (loss) from stocks	0	109,999	(109,999)
Total profit (loss) from options and stocks	93,148.98	109,999	90,0000
Return on options	100%	0%	100%
Return on stocks	0	10%	(−10%)

If an investor sells short a stock, another who already owns the stock (IC) has to be willing to lend it to DC to sell.

First, if the lender (IC) suddenly requires (DC) to immediately return the borrowed stock, forcing DCG to buy it in the open market, prices may be far from favorable.

Second, If IC accepts to lend the stock, DC must put collateral to guarantee the loan (apart from the margin DC must put with broker), tying up some of the proceeds of the sale.

This creates an *economic asymmetry between buying and short selling.*

Buying stocks ties up funds that could otherwise be invested to earn interest and although the proceeds from selling stocks one already owns can be fully reinvested to earn interest only on a portion of the proceeds from short-selling stocks can be reinvested.

In the US, New York Exchange rules plus-tick rule, permits short sales to be executed only at prices representing a plus tick from the previous different price.

If we sold the portfolio of stocks short, the loss is:

As the long stock has a downside tolerance point, the short stock has an upside tolerance point.

Table 12.18. Short selling stocks (stock lending).

Stocks	Stock Unchanged	Stock + 10%	Stock − 10%
Short sale stocks	100,000	100,000	100,000
Repurchase of stocks	100,000	110,000	90,000
Profit(loss) from stocks	0	(10,000)	10,000
Interest income from T-bills (5%100,000 × 0.25)	1,250	1,250	1,250
Restitution of dividends: 1%	(1,000)	(1,000)	(1,000)
Total profit or loss	250	(9,750)	10,250

Table 12.19. Short selling stocks (stock lending) example: Double the dividend payment.

Stocks	Stock Unchanged	Stock + 10%	Stock − 10%
Short sale stocks	100,000	100,000	100,000
Repurchase of stocks	100,000	110,000	90,000
Profit(loss) from stocks	0	(10,000)	10,000
Interest income from T-bills (5%100,000 × 0.25)	1,250	1,250	1,250
Restitution of dividends: 1%	(2,000)	(2,000)	(2,000)
Total profit or loss	(750)	(10,750)	9,250

Net percentage interest income from T-bills: offset by the restitution of dividends/**Holding period net interest yield** = (Interest income − dividends)
Value of T-bills

$$0.25\% = (1{,}250 - 1{,}000)/100{,}000 = 0.0025$$

The upside tolerance point is:

Upside tolerance point = stock price + holding period net interest yield.

$$15.0025 = 15 + 0.0025$$

If restitution of dividend payments through expiration is greater than the interest income from the reinvestment of the proceeds of the short sale, the investor will show a loss if the stock is unchanged.

The short position shows a loss if the index is unchanged, rather than a profit.

Performance is also degraded when the stock is down.

The question is how low the stock must fall before the position fails to show a loss?

Holding period interest yield = (Interest income − dividends)/Value of T-bills

$$0.75\% = (1{,}250 - 2{,}000)/100{,}000 = -0.0075$$

The upside tolerance point is:

Downside breakeven point = stock price + holding period interest yield

$14.9925 = 15 - 0.0075$

A position of US$ 100 millions.

How options can be used as alternatives to a direct investment in stocks?

12.14. Buying Calls on EMA

12.14.1. *Buying a call as an alternative to buying the stock (also as an alternative to short sell put options)*

Buying calls can be a unique managerial alternative to buying stocks. Another alternative is to short sell put options.

12.14.1.1. *Data and assumptions*

An investor with 100,000 to invest for 3 months in the call. When the stock is at 15, he can either buy the stock or invest in T-bills. This leads to symmetrical risk and return pattern, profit or loss dollar for dollar plus income from dividends.

12.14.1.2. *Pattern of risk and return*

Consider the pattern of risk and return with a purchase of 3 month call option with a strike price of 15. We selected at the money so

that at expirations, appreciation in the underlying will be reflected in the exercise value of calls.
To scale the position in calls to the investor **Risk capital** of 100,000, we begin by calculating the value of one contract.
The stock price times the multiplier.

$$\textbf{Call's underlying value} = \text{asset price} \times \text{contract multiplier}$$
$$= 15 \times 1$$

Number of calls to buy:
To determine the number of calls to buy, we divide the risk capital of 100,000 by call's underlying value of 15:

$$\textbf{Contracts required} = \text{risk capital: call's underlying value}$$
$$6{,}666 = 100000\text{: } 15$$

Valuation:
Using option valuation procedure and assuming a volatility of 30%, the interest rate at 5%, the call price is 0.98746. Assuming options can be purchased at theoretical value, the investor would have to spend to buy 6,666 contracts:

$$\textbf{Investment required to buy} = \textbf{call price} \times \textbf{number} \times \textbf{contract multiplier}$$
$$\textbf{US\$ 6,583.608} = \textbf{0.98764} \times \textbf{6,666} \times \textbf{1}$$

The balance of the 100,000 risk capital that could be invested in T-bills would be:
Remaining capital in T-bills = total capital − investment required to buy calls

$$\textbf{93,416,391} = \textbf{100,000} - \textbf{6,583}$$

Strategy: invest an amount in options and the balance in T-bills.
Buy calls, strike 15, stock initially at 15 at 0.98746.
Invest: 93,416,391 in 3 month TB, Hold for 3 months, Collect interest.

12.14.2. *Compare buying calls (as an alternative to portfolio of stocks)*

Here we compare **buying calls** as an alternative to portfolio of stocks.

At maturity after 3 months:
If the asset price does not change:
Initial cost of calls (6,583.6080)
Exercise value: 0
Loss from calls (6,583.6080)
Interest income on T-bills
(5% on 93,416,391 for 3 months: 1,167.704)
Total loss: (5,415.903)
If we examine the outcomes of investing directly in stock, the return is zero.

Return in stock: 0

12.14.2.1. *Risk return in options*

If the investor uses options to take a position in the market, the position is not profitable unless the **asset is high enough to give options** sufficient exercise value to repay their initial cost.

The upside break even point can be computed as follows.

$$\textbf{Cost per contract} = \textbf{(invt to buy calls-T-bill income)}$$
$$\textbf{/(number of contracts}$$
$$\times\ \textbf{multiplier contract)}$$
$$= (6{,}583.608 - 1{,}167.704)/(6{,}666 \times 1)$$
$$0.8124 = 5{,}415.904/6{,}666$$

Upside break-even point = Net cost per contract + call's strike price

$$\text{US\$ } 15.8124 = 0.8124 + 15$$

The Upside break-even point is US$ 15.8124.

Each call at this point would has an exercise value of 0.8124.

The aggregate exercise value of the position would be 5,415.455 just above the amount required to repay the cost less the offsetting treasury bill income:

$$0.8124 \times 6{,}666 = 5{,}415.455$$

Exercise value of call = stock price upside − option strike price × contract multiplier

$$\mathbf{0.8124 = (15.8124 - 15) \times 1}$$

Aggregate exercise value of position = exercise value of call × number of calls in position

$$\mathbf{5{,}415.455 = 0.8124 \times 6{,}666}$$

If the stock rallies beyond the upside break even point, the position will show a healthy profit.
For example, If the stock rallies by 10%, from 15 to 16.5, each option will have an exercise value of 1.5
Exercise value of call = (stock − call's strike) × contract multiplier

$$1.5 = (16.5 - 15) \times 1$$

Aggregate Exercise value of position = Exercise value of call × number of calls

$$9{,}999 = 1.5 \times 6{,}666$$

Including the interest income from T-bills, the investor's total profit with the stock up 10% is 4,584.26.

At maturity after 3 months:
If the asset price up by 10%:
Initial cost of calls (6,583.6080)
Exercise value: 1.5 × **6,666** × **1** = **9,999**
Profit from calls 3,415.4
Interest income on T-bills
(5% on 93,416,391 for 3 months: 1,167.704) 1,167.704
Total profit: 4,584.26

Return from options and T-bills: 4.58%
This profit is less than a direct investment in the stock:
If the asset price up by 10%:
Initial cost of stocks = 100,000
Sale of stocks = 110,000
Profit = 10,000
Return from the stock: 10%

When the investor established his position in stocks, he earned a profit of 10,000.
With options, he can not break even until the stock rises to US$ 15.8124.

With stocks, his profit with the stock up by 10% was 10,000, with options only 4,584.26.

Advantages: The advantages gained for these handicaps are that the option buyer is assured that his investment cannot do any worse than a known maximum loss equal to the costs of the options, minus any interest earned on the leftover cash invested in T-bills.

Maximum loss in position = cost of calls – interest on T-bills

$$5{,}415.904 = 6{,}583.608 - 1{,}167.704$$

This example is done to replicate a position in the stock.
When the investor chooses to buy options, he is making a different kind of investment.
The tradeoff is: in exchange of a known maximum loss (the option premium), he sacrifies performance.
The tradeoff is equitable.
This is a managerial choice driven by the attitude toward the pattern of risk and returns.

12.14.3. *Example by changing volatility to 20%*

12.14.3.1. *Data and assumptions*

An investor with 100,000 to invest for 3 months in the call.
When the stock is at 15.
He can either buy the stock or invest in T-bills. This leads to symmetrical risk and return pattern, profit or loss dollar for dollar plus income from dividends.

12.14.3.1.1. Pattern of risk and return

Consider the pattern of risk and return with a purchase of 3 month call option with a strike price of 15.
We selected at the money so that at expiration any appreciation in the underlying will be reflected in the exercise value of calls.
To scale the position in calls to the investor **Risk capital** of 100,000, we begin by calculating the value of one contract.
The stock price times the multiplier.

Valuation:
Using option valuation procedure and assuming a volatility of 30%, the interest rate at 5%, the call price is 0.96.

Call's underlying value = asset price × contract multiplier

$$15 = 15 \times 1$$

Number of calls to buy:
To determine the number of calls to buy, we divide the risk capital of 100,000 by call's underlying value of 15:
Contracts required = Risk capital: call's underlying value
6,666 = 100,000: 15
Assuming options can be purchased at theoretical value, the investor would have to spend to buy 6,666 contracts:

$$\textbf{Investment required to buy} = \textbf{call price} \times \textbf{number} \times \textbf{contract multiplier}$$

$$\textbf{US\$ 4,599} = \textbf{0.69} \times \textbf{6,666} \times \textbf{1}$$

The balance of the 100,000 Risk capital that could be invested in T-bills would be:
Remaining capital in T-bills = total capital − investment required to buy calls

$$\textbf{95,400.46} = \textbf{100,000} - \textbf{4,599}$$

Strategy: Buying calls and investing balance in T-bills
Buy calls, strike 15, stock initially at 15 at 0.69
Invest: 95,400.46 in 3 month TB

12.14.3.2. *Compare buying calls (as an alternative to portfolio of stocks)*

Here we compare **buying calls** as an alternative to portfolio of stocks.

At maturity: after 3 months:
If the asset price does not change:
Initial cost of calls (**4,599**)

Exercise value: 0
Loss from calls (**4,599**)
Interest income on T-bills
(5% on **95,400.46** for 3 months: 1,192.575)
Total loss: (3,406.425)
Return from investment is stocks: 0%

Return using call options:
If the investor uses options to take a position in the market, the position is not profitable unless the **asset is high enough to give options** sufficient exercise value to repay their initial cost.
The upside break even point can be computed as follows.

Cost per contract = (invt to buy calls − T-bill income)/ (number of contracts × multiplier contract)

$$0.5110 = (4{,}599 - 1{,}192.575)/(6{,}666 \times 1)$$

Upside break-even point = net cost per contract + call's strike price

$$\text{US\$ } 15.511 = 0.5110 + 15 = 15.511$$

The Upside break-even point is US$ 15.511.
Each call at this point would has an exercise value of 0.511.
The aggregate exercise value of the position would be 3,406.42 just above the amount required to repay the cost less the offsetting treasury bill income:

$$0.511 \times 6{,}666 = 3{,}406.42$$

Exercise value of call = stock price upside-option strike price × contract multiplier

$$\mathbf{0.5111 = (15.511 - 15) \times 1}$$

Aggregate exercise value of position = exercise value of call × number of calls in position:

$$\mathbf{3{,}406.42 = 0.511 \times 6{,}666}$$

If the stock rallies by 10%, from 15 to 16.5, each option will have an exercise value of 1.5.

Exercise value of call = (stock − call's strike) × contract multiplier

$$\mathbf{1.5 = (16.5 - 15) \times 1}$$

Aggregate Exercise value of position = Exercise value of call × number of calls

$$\mathbf{9{,}999 = 1.5 \times 6{,}666}$$

Including the interest income from T-bills, the investor's total profit with the stock up 10% is 6,592.57.

At maturity after 3 months:
If the asset price up by 10%:
Initial cost of calls (**4,599**)
Exercise value: **1.5 × 6,666 × 19,999**
Profit from calls 5,400
Interest income on T-bills
(5% on **95,400.46** for 3 months: 1,192.575) 1,192.575
Total profit: 6,592.57
Return from options and T-bills: 6.59%
This profit is less than a direct investment in the stock:
If the asset price up by 10%:
Initial cost of stocks = 100,000
Sale of stocks = 110,000
Profit = 10,000
Return from stock: 10%

- When the investor established his position in stocks he earned a profit of 10,000.
- With options, he cannot break even until the stock rises to US$ 15.511.
- With stocks, his profit with the stock up by 10% was 10,000, with options only 6,592.57.

Advantages: The advantages gained for these handicaps are that the option buyer is assured that his investment cannot do any worse than a known maximum loss equal to the costs of the options, minus any interest earned on the leftover cash invested in T-bills.
Maximum loss in position = cost of calls − interest on T-bills

$$\mathbf{5{,}391.04 = 6{,}583.608} - 1{,}192.575$$

This example is done to replicate a position in the stock.

When the investor chooses to buy options, he is making a different kind of investment. The tradeoff is: in exchange of a known maximum loss (the option premium), he sacrifies performance. The tradeoff is equitable

This is a managerial choice driven by the attitude toward the pattern of risk and returns.

Buy calls, strike 15, stock initially at 15 at 0.69
Invest: 95,400.46 in 3 month TB

12.14.3.3. *Leverage in buying call options (without selling the underlying)*

What happens if the investor devotes the risk capital to buy calls? With this capital, the investor can buy 145,000.

To determine the number of calls to buy, we divide the risk capital of 100,000 by call's underlying value of 15:

Number of contracts = risk capital/(cost per contract × contract multiplier)

$$145{,}000 = 100{,}000/(0.69 \times 1)$$

If the asset declines or is unchanged, the calls expire worthless.
The investor will lose 100,000.

In the previous example, with the purchase of 6,666 contracts, the loss was 3,406.

Table 12.20. Results at the maturity date in three months of the strategy of buying calls and holding the underlying stock.

	Stock Unchanged	Stock + 10%	Stock − 10%
Investment required to buy calls: 0.69 × 6,666 × 1	(4,599)	(4,599)	(4,599)
Exercise value of calls	0	**9,999 (1.5 × 6,666)**	0
Profit (loss) from calls	0	**5,400**	0
Interest income on T-bills: **5% on** 95,400.46	**1,192.575**	**1,192.575**	**1,192.575**
Total profit (loss)	(3,406.425)	**6,592.57**	(3,406.425)

This reflects the smaller initial cost of the position and the interest income from T-bill. He can no longer afford not to buy.
If the asset rises by 10%, from 15 to 16.5, the investor profit will be 117,500.
With options, the investor has the benefit of an assured maximum loss-no matter how much the stock declines, the loss can never be greater than the price paid for options.
Using the procedure developed before, the break even point is:
Upside break-even point = net cost per contract + call's strike price

$$\text{US\$ } 15.69 = 0.69 + 15.$$

The investor is assured of a maximum loss of 100,000 with the possibility of upside rewards that could potentially be greater than those of other strategies with other instruments.

Table 12.21. Leverage in buying call options (without selling the underlying).

Asset Level	Unchanged	Stock + 10%	Stock − 10%
Initial cost of calls	(100,000)	(100,000)	(100,000)
Exercise value of calls	0	217,500	0
		1.5 × (145,000 calls)	
Profit (loss) from calls	(100,000)	117,500	(100,000)
Total profit and loss	(100,000)	117,500	(100,000)
Return/initial calls	(100%)	117.5%	(100%)

Table 12.22. Hedging: buying call options (selling the underlying).

Asset Level	Unchanged	Stock + 10%	Stock − 10%
Total profit and loss from calls	(100,000)	117,500	(100,000)
Initial stock position sell: 0.55 × 15 × 145,000	1,196,250	1,196,250	1,196,250
Ending stock position	1,196,250	1,315,875	1,076,625
Profit and loss from stock position	(000)	(119,625)	119,625
Total profit and loss from calls and stocks	(100,000)	(2,125)	19,625

Summary

A forward contract or a futures contract is an agreement between two parties to buy or sell a specific asset at a specified price at a given time in the future. Futures contracts are traded on an exchange and have standardized features. They are settled on a daily basis while the forward contracts are settled at the end of the contract. Besides, for most futures contracts, delivery is never actually made. Futures markets are used for hedging, speculation, and arbitrage motives. Futures and forward contracts are priced using the cost of carry model. Petroleum futures contracts (or other commodity contracts) can be used as specific hedges when they are associated with a planned cash transaction. The benefit to a company using petroleum products futures is to "lock in" profit margins and/or to protect inventory against falling prices. When spot prices are higher than long-term prices, any hedge using a future maturity will be equivalent to a forward sale below the spot price. This can lead to a loss if market prices do not fall at the same rate. When spot prices are lower than long-term prices, the producer can sell on the futures market at a higher price. So, he/she can fix his/her hedge or future sales at a better price than the spot market. Companies using the physical oil market, for example, (or other commodities) can hedge themselves against adverse price movements by taking an opposite position on the futures or the forward market. The potential loss in the physical market can be offset by an equivalent gain on the futures or the forward market. The futures market offers a facility for hedging price risks. Hedging price risk can be regarded as a trading operation allowing to transform a less acceptable risk into a more acceptable risk by engaging into an offsetting transaction in a similar commodity under roughly the same terms as the original transaction. Futures markets are often used for speculation. The main objective for speculators is to accomplish profit. Speculators take on the risk, which hedgers try to lay off. Speculators hold onto their positions for a very short time. They are sometimes in and out of the market several times a day. Arbitrage keeps prices in line since the arbitrageur buys the assets in one market and sells it in other market. When prices move out of line, the arbitrageur buys the under-priced asset in one market and sells the over-priced asset in another market.

The option value before maturity is a function of five parameters: the price of the underlying asset, the strike price, the risk-free rate of interest, the movements in the underlying asset prices (volatility), and the time remaining to maturity.

The value of any option underlying asset such as a stock, a default-free bond, or a futures or a forward contract is determined in a market place. In general, there are two prices quoted: the bid and the ask price. These two prices define a spread. In theory, there is only one price for each asset, but in practice, two prices are observed in financial markets.

Buying a call gives the right to the option holder to pay the strike price K at maturity and to receive the value of an underlying asset S_T. Buying a put gives the right to the option holder to sell at maturity, the underlying asset S_T at the strike price K. The most frequent strategies consist in buying and selling calls and puts with or without using the underlying asset. Several other strategies can be implemented as a function of the risk-reward profile. An investor selling a straddle sells simultaneously a call and a put on the same underlying asset, with the same strike price and maturity date.

The strangle is one of the simplest option strategies. An investor buying a strangle (long a strangle) buys simultaneously a call and a put on the same underlying asset with different strike prices K_1 and K_2 and at the same maturity date. The call with a strike price K_1 and the put with a strike price K_2 are both out-of-the money with $K_1 > K_2$.

A spread consists in buying an option and selling another option. A bull spread corresponds to a combination of options with the same underlying asset and the same maturity, but different strike prices. A bear spread corresponds to a combination of options with the same underlying asset and the same maturity, but different strike prices. When it is implemented with two calls, it is designed to profit from falling underlying asset prices. This strategy with calls corresponds to the short position to the bull spread.

A box spread corresponds to a combination of a bull spreads with calls and a bear spread with puts. It is implemented using two spreads with two strike prices. A butterfly spread corresponds to a combination using three calls with three strike prices $K_1 < K_2 < K_3$. The calls have the same underlying asset and maturity date. A condor corresponds to a combination using four calls with four strike prices $K_1 < K_2 < K_3 < K_4$. The calls have the same underlying asset and maturity date.

A ratio spread is a strategy involving two or more related options in a given proportion. A trader can buy a call with a lower strike price and sell a higher number of calls with a higher strike price. Portfolio insurance is an investment-management technique that protects a portfolio from drops in value. This technique proposes some simple concepts allowing to insure a stock portfolio.

An investor who buys a European call and sells a European put on the same underlying asset creates a position that exhibits the same payoff pattern as the underlying asset. A portfolio with a long European call and a short European put shows a profit (loss) pattern that can mimic the result of the underlying asset. This chapter develops some of the most frequent strategies used in the market place.

References

French K (1980). Stock returns and the weekend effect. *Journal of Financial Economics*, 8 (March), 55–69.

Gibbons MR and P Hess (1981). Day of the week effects and asset returns. *Journal of Business*, 54, 579–596.

Hong H and J Wang (2000). Trading and returns under periodic market closures. *Journal of Finance*, 55(1) (February), 297–354.

Chapter 13

Trading Options and Their Underlying Asset: Risk Management in Discrete Time

Chapter Outline

This chapter is organized as follows:

1. Section 13.1 develops the basic strategies using calls and puts.
2. Section 13.2 illustrates several combined strategies.
3. Section 13.3 explains the way traders use option pricing models to compute option prices and to estimate the market volatility.

Introduction

Using the definition of a standard or a plain vanilla option, it is evident that the higher the underlying asset price, the greater the call's value. When the underlying asset price is much greater than the strike price, the current option value is nearly equal to the difference between the underlying asset price and the discounted value of the strike price. The discounted value of the strike price is given by the price of a pure discount bond, maturing at the same time as the option, with a face or nominal value equal to the strike price. Hence, if the maturity date is very near, the call's value (put's value) is nearly equal to the difference between the underlying asset price and the strike price or zero. If the maturity date is very far, then the call's value is nearly equal to that of the underlying asset since the bond's price will be very low. The call's value can not be negative and can not exceed the underlying asset price. Options enable investors to customize cash-flow patterns. We present some of the most common used option strategies, which apply to options on a spot asset, to options on a futures contract and in general to options with any particular payoff. These strategies are illustrated with respect to the diagram payoffs or the expected return and risk trade-off of standard options. The understanding of option strategies is based on the use of synthetic positions. This chapter provides several illustrations of the main strategies provided in the previous chapter. In particular, we develop the basic strategies and synthetic positions: long or short the underlying asset, long a call, long a put, and short a put. Then, we present some combinations and more elaborated strategies as: long a straddle, short a straddle, long or short a strangle, long a tunnel, short a tunnel, long a call or put bull spread, long a call or a put bear spread, long or short a butterfly, long or short a condor, etc. Finally, we show how traders and market participants use option pricing models and estimate model parameters. We introduce the concepts of Greek letters or the sensitivities of the option price or position with respect to some parameters.

13.1. Basic Strategies and Synthetic Positions

This section develops the main option strategies and synthetic positions.

13.1.1. *Options and synthetic positions*

Synthetic positions can be constructed by options on spot assets, options on futures contracts, and their underlying assets. If we use the symbol 0 to denote a horizontal line, the symbol -1 for the slope under 0 and the symbol 1 for the slope above 0, then it is possible to represent the diagram pay offs of a long call by $(0, 1)$, a short call by $(0, -1)$, a long put by $(-1, 0)$, and a short put by $(1, 0)$.

Adopting this notation for the basic option pay offs, it is possible to construct all the synthetic positions as well as most elaborated diagram strategies using this representation. We denote by:

$S, (F)$: price of the underlying asset, which may be a spot asset, S (or a futures contract F);
K: strike price;
C: call price and
P: put price.

We use the following symbols: 0, /: 1, \: −1.

The results of the basic strategies can be represented as follows: Long a call: $(0, 1)$: , Short a call: $(0, -1)$: , Long a put: $(-1, 0)$: 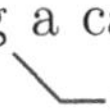, Short a put: $(1, 0)$: .

Long the underlying asset: $(1, 1)$: , Short the underlying asset: $(-1, -1)$: .

The symbols $(-1, 0, 1)$ refer to a downward movement, (-1), a flat position (0) or an upward movement (1). The risk-return trade-off of the basic strategies can be represented using the different symbols.

Using the above notations, it is possible to construct the risk-reward trade-off of any option strategy.

For example, long a call $(0, 1)$ and short a put $(1, 0)$ is equivalent to long the underlying asset $(1, 1)$. Also, short a call $(0, -1)$ and long a put $(-1, 0)$ is equivalent to a short position in the underlying asset $(-1, -1)$.

We give the basic synthetic positions when the options have the same strike prices and maturity dates.

Long a synthetic underlying asset = long a call + short a put.

$$(1, 1) = (0, 1) + (1, 0)$$

Short a synthetic underlying asset = short a call + long a put.

$$(-1, -1) = (0, -1) + (-1, 0)$$

Long a synthetic call = long the underlying asset + long a put.

$$(0, 1) = (1, 1) + (-1, 0)$$

Short a synthetic call = short the underlying asset + short a put.

$$(0, -1) = (-1, -1) + (1, 0)$$

Long a synthetic put = short the underlying asset + long a call.

$$(-1, 0) = (-1, 1) + (0, 1)$$

Short a synthetic put = long the underlying asset + short a call.

$$(1, 0) = (1, 1) + (0, -1)$$

The knowledge of synthetic positions is necessary for market participants since it allows the implementation of hedged positions. Hedged positions are often implemented by traders and market makers who follow delta-neutral strategies. For example, when managing an option position, buying a call or a put with the same strike price are two equivalent strategies since when buying a call, the trader or the market maker hedges his transaction by the sale of the underlying asset and when buying a put, he hedges his transaction by the purchase of the underlying asset. Buying the call and selling the put is equivalent to a long put with the same strike price. This transaction enables the trader or market maker to make a direct sale of the put since a position in a long call and a short put is equivalent to a long position in the underlying asset.

13.1.2. *Long or short the underlying asset*

The risk-return profile for a position which is long or short the underlying asset (for example a futures contract) shows unlimited profit or loss. If we put on a horizontal line the underlying asset price and on a vertical line the profit or loss, the payoff to a long or a short position in the underlying asset can be easily represented. If the asset price rises or falls by one point, the profit or loss will be of the same amount.

13.1.3. *Long a call*

Expectations: The trader expects a rising market and (or) a high volatility until the maturity date.

Definition: Buy a call, c with a strike price K.

Specific features: The potential gain is not limited but the potential loss is limited to the option premium.

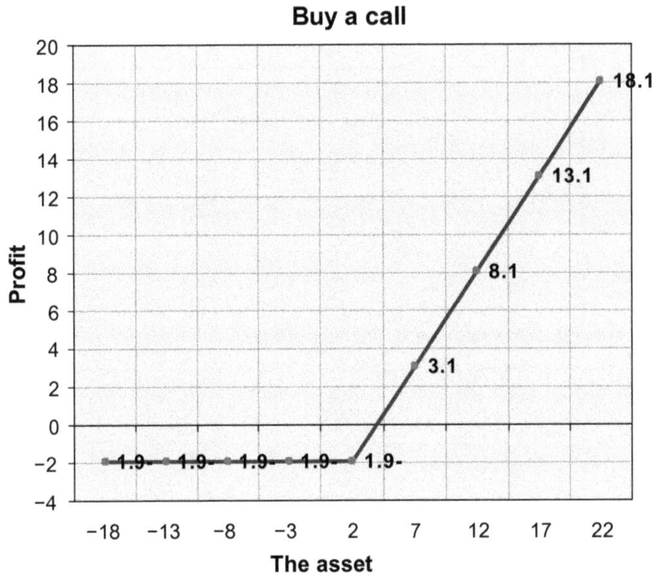

Figure 13.1. Long a call.

Table 13.1. Long a call: $S = 102$, $r = 5\%$, volatility $= 20\%$, and $T = 100$ days.

Type	Point	Value
Break-even point	A	$K + c$
Maximal loss		c
Maximal gain		Not limited, if $S > K$

Buying the call at 1.9, reveals the risk-reward profile as shown in Fig. 13.1 at expiration.

If $S = 111.9$ at maturity; $(110 + 1.9)$, the profit is zero. This is the break-even point of the position. Beyond this level, the profit is not limited. The maximum loss or performance corresponds to 1.9 or 100% (Table 13.1). In Fig. 13.1, the break-even point is given by the sum of the strike price and the option premium.

13.1.4. *Short call*

Expectations: The trader expects a falling market and (or) a lower volatility until the maturity date.

Table 13.2. Short a call: $S = 102$, $r = 5\%$, volatility $= 20\%$, $T = 100$ days.

Type	Point	Value
Break-even point	A	$K + c$
Maximal loss		Not limited
Maximal gain		Premium

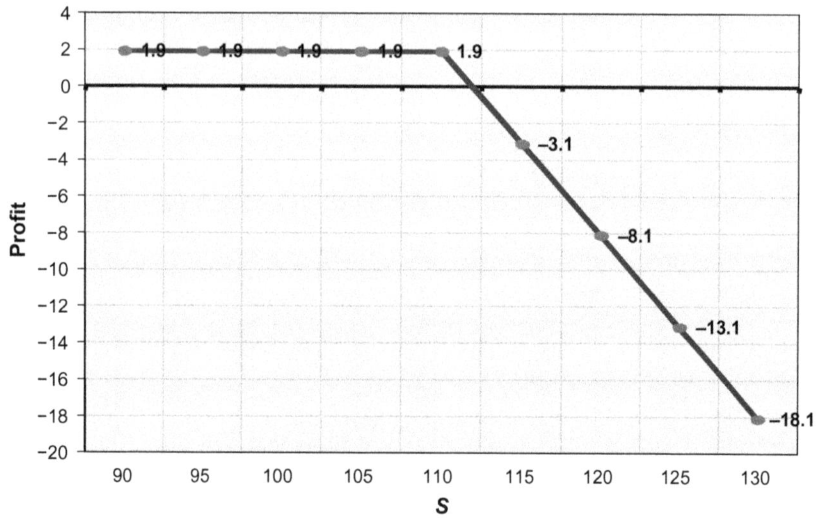

Figure 13.2. Short a call.

Definition: Sell a call, c with a strike price K.

Specific features: The potential gain is limited to the perceived premium and the potential loss is not limited.

The risk-reward trade-off is inverted when selling calls (Table 13.2). The results of the strategy are given in Fig. 13.2 (Tables 13.3 and 13.4).

In Fig. 13.2, the break-even point is given by the sum of the strike price and the option premium.

13.1.5. *Long a put*

Expectations: The trader expects a falling market and (or) a higher volatility until the maturity date.

Table 13.3. Short a call.

Short a call
Strike price = 110 Premium = 1.9 Profit for a multiple of 10: 19 Break-even point = 111.9

Table 13.4. Short a call.

S	Variation (%)	Call	Performance (%)
90	−12	1.9	100
95	−7	1.9	100
100	−2	1.9	100
105	3	1.9	100
110	8	1.9	100
115	13	−3.1	−165
120	18	−8.1	−430
125	23	−13.1	−696
130	27	−18.1	−961

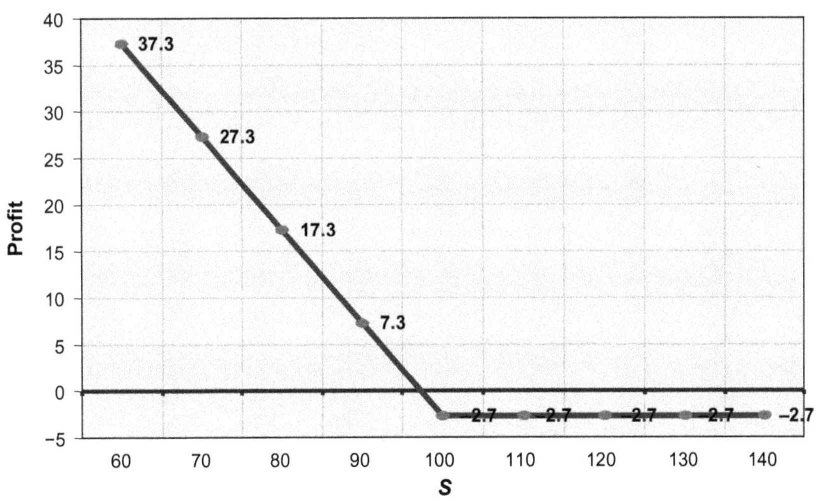

Figure 13.3. Long a put.

Table 13.5. Long a put.

Long a put
Strike price = 100 Premium = 2.7 Profit for a multiple of 10: 27 Break-even point = 97.28

Table 13.6. Long a put.

S	Variation (%)	Put	Performance (%)
60	−41	37.3	1,371
70	−31	27.3	1,003
80	−22	17.3	635
90	−12	7.3	268
100	−2	−2.7	−100
110	8	−2.7	−100
120	18	−2.7	−100
130	27	−2.7	−100
140	37	−2.7	−100

Table 13.7. Long a put: $S = 102$, $r = 5\%$, volatility = 20%, and $T = 100$ days.

Type	Point	Value
Break-even point	A	$K - p$
Maximal loss		Premium
Maximal gain		Not limited

Definition: Buy a put p with a strike price K

Specific features: The potential gain is not limited and the potential loss is limited to the option premium.

In Figure 13.3 (Tables 13.5 and 13.6), the break-even point is given by the algebraic sum of the strike price and the option premium (Table 13.7).

13.1.6. *Short a put*

Expectations: The trader expects a stable and (or) a rising market.

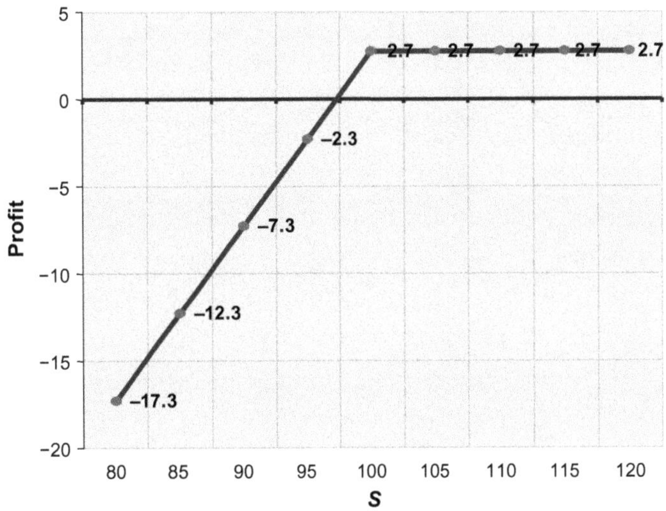

Figure 13.4. Short a put.

Table 13.8. Short a put.

	Short a put
Strike price	100
Premium	2.7
Profit	27
Break-even point	97.28

Definition: Sell a put p with a strike price K.

Specific features: The potential gain is limited to the option premium and the potential loss is unlimited (Fig. 13.4, Tables 13.8 and 13.9).

Figure 13.3 represents in a certain way the opposite of the risk-reward profile in Fig. 13.2. The profit is limited when the underlying asset price increases and the risk is unlimited when the underlying asset price is decreasing (Table 13.10).

13.2. Combined Strategies

This section illustrates several combined strategies involving call and put options.

Table 13.9. Short a put.

S	Variation (%)	Put	Performance (%)
80	−22	−17.3	−635
85	−17	−12.3	−451
90	−12	−7.3	−268
95	−7	−2.3	−84
100	−2	2.7	100
105	3	2.7	100
110	8	2.7	100
115	13	2.7	100
120	18	2.7	100

Table 13.10. Short a put: $S = 102$, $r = 5\%$, volatility $= 20\%$, and $T = 100$ days.

Type	Point	Value
Break-even point	A	$K - p$
Maximal loss		Not limited
Maximal gain		Premium

13.2.1. *Long a straddle*

This strategy is perfect during the 2008 financial crisis.

Expectations: The trader expects a high volatility until the maturity date.

Definition: Buy a call, c and simultaneously buy a put, p on the same underlying (for the same maturity date and the same strike price).

Specific features: The initial investment is important since the investor buys simultaneously the call and the put.

- The loss is limited to the initial cost (c and p).
- The maximum potential gain is not limited when the market goes up or down.

Buying a straddle needs a simultaneous purchase of call and a put with the same strike price for the same maturity (Fig. 13.5,

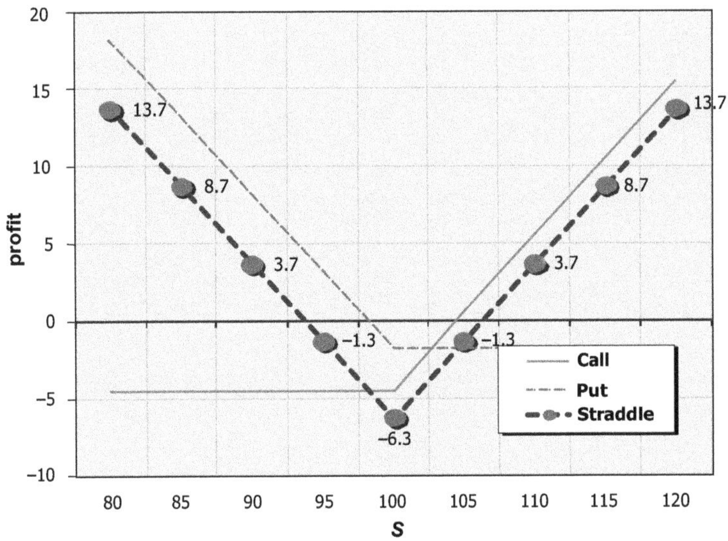

Figure 13.5. Buying a straddle.

Table 13.11. Long a straddle.

	Long a Call	Long a Put	Strategy
Strike price	100	100	
Premium	4.5	1.8	6.3
Cost	45	18	63
Break-even point	104.50	98.18	5

Tables 13.11 and 13.12). When the put is worthless, the call is deep-in-the money. When the call is worthless, the put is in-the-money (Table 13.13).

Notes: The strike price is chosen according to the trader expectations about the future market direction.

Simulation: Underlying asset $S = 102$, Interest rate r (%) = 5%, Volatility (%) = 20%, and Maturity (in days) = 50.

13.2.2. *Short a straddle*

Expectations: The trader expects a low volatility until the maturity date.

Table 13.12. Long a straddle.

S	Variation (%)	Call	Put	Straddle	Performance (%)
80	−22	−4.5	18.2	13.7	216
85	−17	−4.5	13.2	8.7	137
90	−12	−4.5	8.2	3.7	58
95	−7	−4.5	3.2	−1.3	−21
100	−2	−4.5	−1.8	−6.3	−100
105	3	0.5	−1.8	−1.3	−21
110	8	5.5	−1.8	3.7	58
115	13	10.5	−1.8	8.7	137
120	18	15.5	−1.8	13.7	216

Table 13.13. Long a straddle.

Type	Point	Value
Break-even point	A	$S = K - (c + p)$
	B	$S = K + (c + p)$
Maximal loss	C	$(c + p)$ if $S = K$
Maximal gain		$K - (c + p)$, if S tends toward 0
		Unlimited, if S is beyond the limits

Definition:

- Sell a call c and simultaneously.
- Sell a put, p on the same underlying for the same maturity date and the same strike price.

Specific features:

- The initial revenue is limited to the option premiums.
- The loss is not limited when the market goes up or down.
- The maximum potential gain is limited to the initial premium (c and p).

When the underlying asset price is expected to be in a specified interval at maturity, the trader can sell simultaneously a call and a put. The profit is limited to the premium received and the risk may be unlimited (Fig. 13.6).

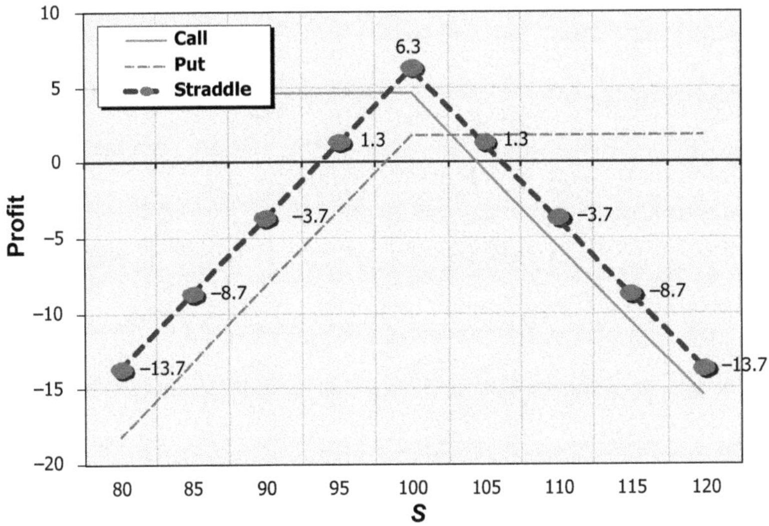

Figure 13.6. Short a straddle.

Table 13.14. Shorting a straddle.

S	Variation (%)	Call	Put	Straddle	Performance (%)
80	−22	4.5	−18.2	−13.7	−216
85	−17	4.5	−13.2	−8.7	−137
90	−12	4.5	−8.2	−3.7	−58
95	−7	4.5	−3.2	1.3	21
100	−2	4.5	1.8	6.3	100
105	3	−0.5	1.8	1.3	21
110	8	−5.5	1.8	−3.7	−58
115	13	−10.5	1.8	−8.7	−137
120	18	−15.5	1.8	−13.7	−216

If the underlying asset is not expected to move much either side, the investor can sell the put and the call. The maximum profit at expiration is obtained when S is in a given interval (Table 13.14).

13.2.3. *Long a strangle*

Expectations: The trader expects a high volatility during the options' life.

Definition: Buy a call with a strike price K_c and buy a put with a strike price K_p where the $K_p < K_c$.

Specific features:

- This strategy costs less than the straddle.
- The maximum loss is limited to the initial cost of $(c + p)$.
- The net result is a profit only when the market movement is important (Fig. 13.7). In this example, the market must increase by 5%, (107.49 – 102)/102 or decrease by 9%, (92.41 – 102)/102 (Table 13.15).

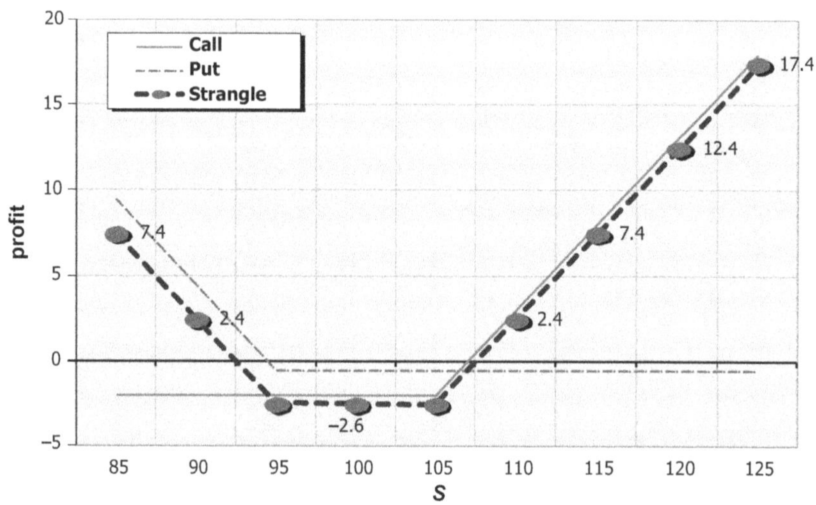

Figure 13.7. Profit (per unit) of a long strangle strategy.

Table 13.15. Long a strangle.

Type	Point	Value
Break-even point	A	$S = K_p - (c + p)$
	B	$S = K_c + (c + p)$
Maximal loss		$(c + p)$, if $K_p < S < K_c$
Maximal gain	A	$K_p - (c + p)$, if S tends toward 0
	B	Unlimited, if S is higher

Table 13.16. Profit (per unit) of a long strangle strategy.

S	Variation (%)	Call	Put	Strangle	Performance (%)
85	−17	−2	9.5	7.4	287
90	−12	−2	4.5	2.4	93
95	−7	−2	−0.5	−2.6	−100
100	−2	−2	−0.5	−2.6	−100
105	3	−2	−0.5	−2.6	−100
110	8	3	−0.5	2.4	93
115	13	8	−0.5	7.4	287
120	18	13	−0.5	12.4	480
125	23	18	−0.5	17.4	674

Notes: The trader buys the 105 call and the 95 put. The theoretical prices of these options, respectively are 2.04 and 0.55, or a total of 2.58. The quantity is 10, and the total cost of the strategy is 25.8.

The two break-even points are computed as follows (Table 13.17):

- $105 + (2.04 + 0.55) = 107.59$ or a variation of 5.38%.
- $95 - (2.04 + 0.55) = 92.41$ or a variation of −9.40%.

If the underlying asset price is between the two strike prices at expiration, the maximum loss is reduced to the initial cost of 25.8. The net result is a loss, if the underlying asset price is between the two break-even points, 92.41 and 107.59. This loss is less than the initial cost. However, if the underlying asset price is above the break-even points, on either side, the trader benefits from the leverage effect (Table 13.16). For example, if the underlying asset price is 90 at expiration, or a variation of 12%, the net result is 93%. If the underlying asset goes up by 18% to attain a level of 120, the net profit of 12.4, compared to 2.58, represents a performance of 480%.

Simulation: The parameters used in the simulation are: $S = 102$, $r = 5\%$, Volatility = 20%, and Maturity = 50 days.

13.2.4. *Short a strangle*

Expectations: The trader expects a low volatility during the options' life.

Table 13.17. Long a straddle.

	Long a call	Long a put
Strike price	105	95
Premium	2.04	0.55
Cost for 10	20.4	5.5
Break-even point	107.59	92.41

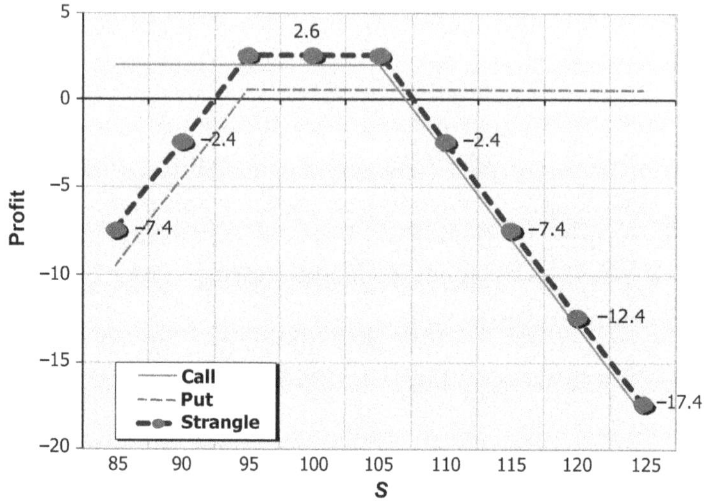

Figure 13.8. Short a strangle.

Definition: Sell a call with a strike price K_c and Sell a put with a strike price K_p where the $K_p < K_c$ (Fig. 13.8).

Specific features:

- The maximum gain is limited to the initial premium of $(c + p)$.
- The strategy can show a loss (Table 13.18).

The reader can make the specific comments by comparing this strategy with the long strangle.

13.2.5. *Long a tunnel*

Expectations: The trader expects a high volatility during the options' life.

Table 13.18. Short a strangle.

S	Variation (%)	Call	Put	Strangle	Performance (%)
85	−17	2	−9.5	−7.4	−287
90	−12	2	−4.5	−2.4	−93
95	−7	2	0.5	2.6	100
100	−2	2	0.5	2.6	100
105	3	2	0.5	2.6	100
110	8	−3	0.5	−2.4	−93
115	13	−8	0.5	−7.4	−287
120	18	−13	0.5	−12.4	−480
125	23	−18	0.5	−17.4	−674

Table 13.19. Long a tunnel.

	Long a Call	Short a Put	
Strike price	570	550	
Premium	22.3	15.3	7
Cost for 10	223	153	−70
Break-even point	592.32	534.68	10

Definition: Buy an out-of-the money call and sell out-of-the money put as in Table 13.19 (Fig. 13.9, Table 13.20).

13.2.6. *Short a tunnel*

This is the opposite of the previous strategy (Fig. 13.10, Tables 13.21 and 13.22).

13.2.7. *Long a call bull spread*

A strategy can be implemented by buying a call with a lower strike price and selling a call with a higher strike price (Fig. 13.11).

If the underlying asset price is below the lower strike price at expiration, the maximum loss is limited to the difference between the two option premiums.

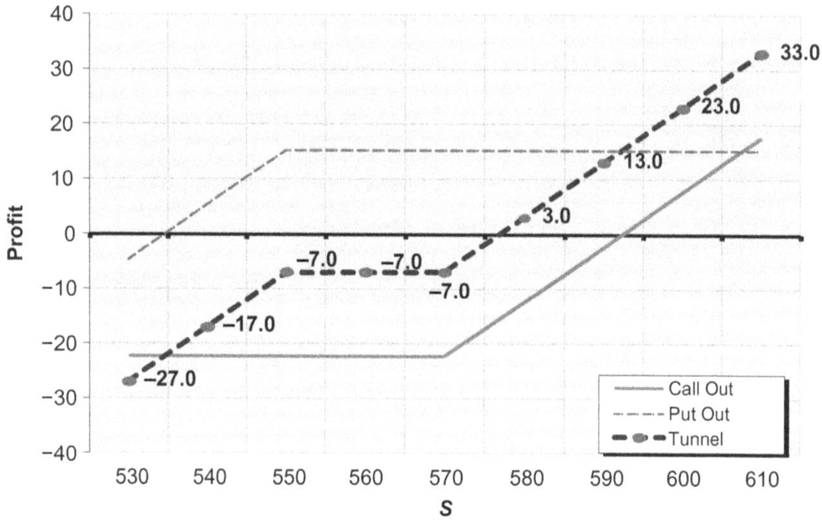

Figure 13.9. Long a tunnel (Buy an out-of-the money call and sell an out-of-the money put).

Table 13.20. Long a tunnel.

Underlying Asset S	Variation (%)	Call out-of-the Money	Put out-of-the Money	Tunnel	Performance (%)
530	−5	−22.3	−4.7	−27	−386
540	−4	−22.3	5.3	−17	−243
550	−2	−22.3	15.3	−7	−100
560	0	−22.3	15.3	−7	−100
570	2	−22.3	15.3	−7	−100
580	4	−12.3	15.3	3	43
590	5	−2.3	15.3	13	186
600	7	7.7	15.3	23	329
610	9	17.7	15.3	33	471

If the underlying asset price is above the higher strike price at expiration, the lower strike price call is worth the intrinsic value. This strategy shows a limited profit (a loss) (Table 13.23).

Long a Bull Spread with Calls for the following parameters: $S = 102$, $r = 5\%$, volatility $= 20\%$, $T = 100$ days.

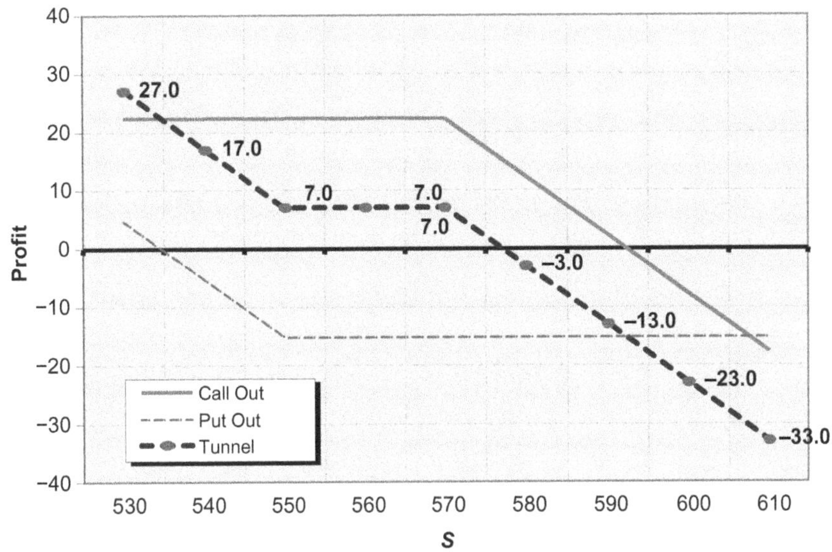

Figure 13.10. Short a tunnel (Sell an out-of-the money call and buy an out-of-the money put).

Table 13.21. Short a tunnel.

Underlying Asset	Variation (%)	Call Out	Put Out	Tunnel	Performance (%)
530	−5	22.3	4.7	27	386
540	−4	22.3	−5.3	17	243
550	−2	22.3	−15.3	7	100
560	0	22.3	−15.3	7	100
570	2	22.3	−15.3	7	100
580	4	12.3	−15.3	−3	−43
590	5	2.3	−15.3	−13	−186
600	7	−7.7	−15.3	−23	−329
610	9	−17.7	−15.3	−33	−471

13.2.8. *Long a put bull spread*

Expectations: Buying a put spread is equivalent to buying the higher strike price put and selling the lower strike price put (Fig. 13.12).

Table 13.22. Long bull spread.

$Q = 10$	Short a Call	Long a Put	
Strike price	570	550	
Premium	22.3	15.3	7.0
Cost	223	153	−70
Break-even point	592.32	534.68	10

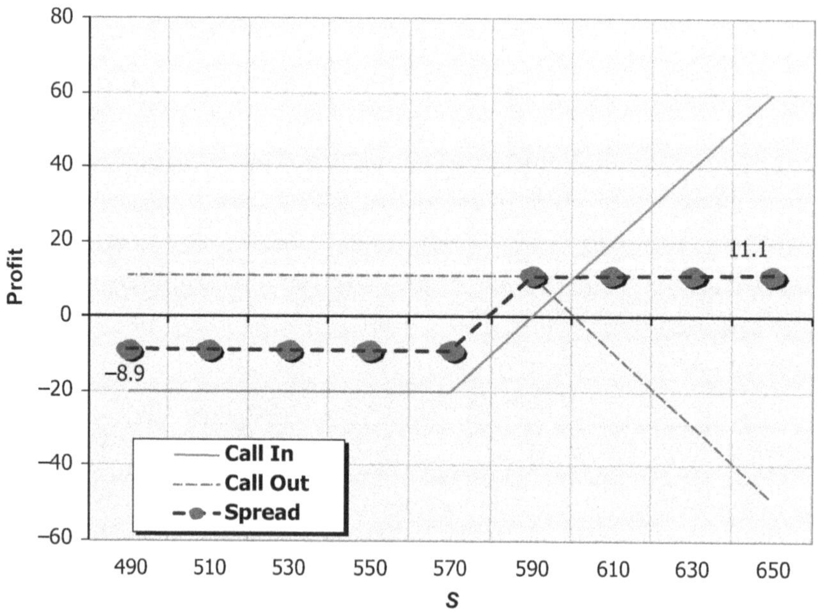

Figure 13.11. Buying a bull spread with calls.

If the underlying asset is around the lower strike price at maturity, the higher strike price put is worth the intrinsic value and the lower strike price is worthless. The maximum profit is given by the difference between the two option premiums. The strategy is done with a debit (Table 13.24).

The trader can sell the put spread by selling the higher strike price put and buying the lower strike price put. The strategy is done with a credit.

Table 13.23. Bull spread with calls: $S = 102$, $r = 5\%$, volatility $= 20\%$, and $T = 100$ days.

S	Variation (%)	Call In	Call Out	Spread	Performance (%)
490	−14	−19.9	11	−8.9	−100
510	−11	−19.9	11	−8.9	−100
530	−7	−19.9	11	−8.9	−100
550	−4	−19.9	11	−8.9	−100
570	0	−19.9	11	−8.9	−100
590	3	0.1	11	11.1	125
610	7	20.1	−9	11.1	125
630	10	40.1	−29	11.1	125
650	14	60.1	−49	11.1	125

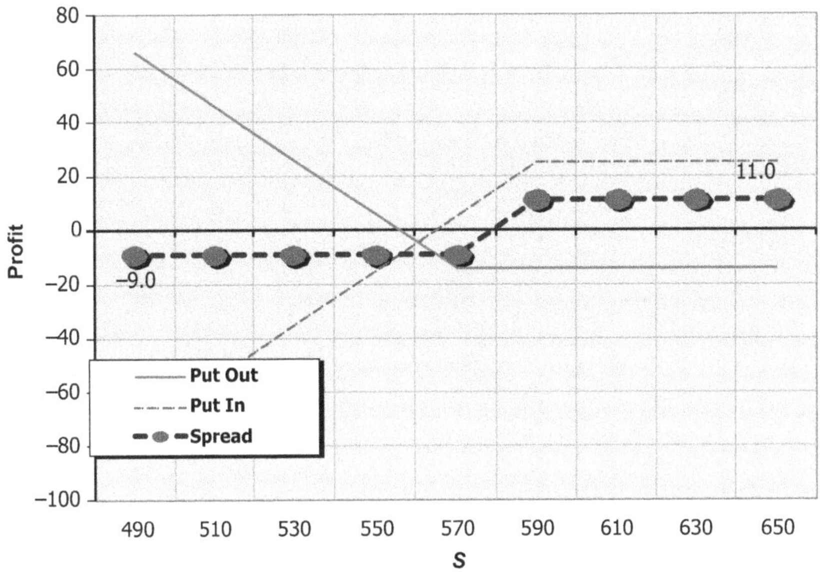

Figure 13.12. Buying a bull spread with puts.

13.2.9. *Long a call bear spread*

The reader can refer to the previous chapter for more details and make the necessary comments (Fig. 13.13 and Table 13.25).

Table 13.24. Buying a bull spread with puts.

S	Variation (%)	Put Out	Put In	Spread	Performance (%)
490	−14	66	−75	−9	82
510	−11	46	−55	−9	82
530	−7	26	−35	−9	82
550	−4	6	−15	−9	82
570	0	−14	5	−9	82
590	3	−14	25	11	−100
610	7	−14	25	11	−100
630	10	−14	25	11	−100
650	14	−14	25	11	−100

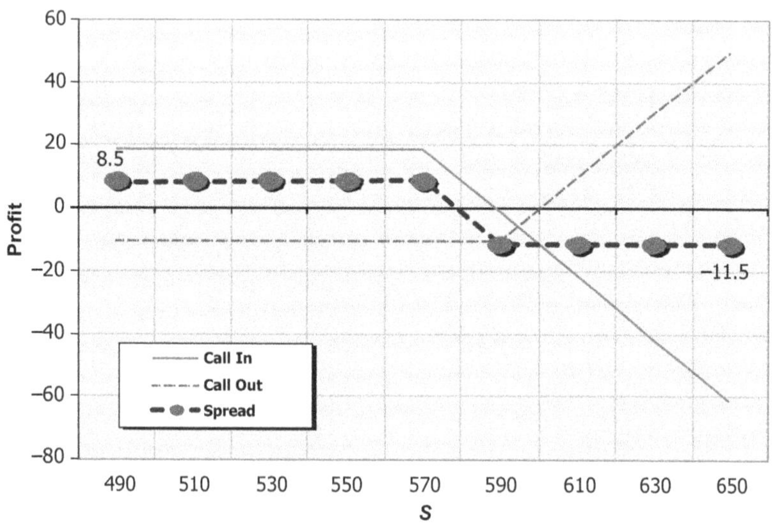

Figure 13.13. Selling a call bear spread.

13.2.10. *Selling a put bear spread*

Refer Fig. 13.14 and Table 13.26. This is best understood from Fig. 13.14 and Table 13.26.

13.2.11. *Long a butterfly*

Expectations: The reader can refer to the previous chapter for more details and make the necessary comments (Fig. 13.15 and Table 13.27).

Table 13.25. Selling a call bear spread.

S	Variation (%)	Call In	Call Out	Spread	Performance (%)
490	−14	18.8	−10.3	8.5	100
510	−11	18.8	−10.3	8.5	100
530	−7	18.8	−10.3	8.5	100
550	−4	18.8	−10.3	8.5	100
570	0	18.8	−10.3	8.5	100
590	4	−1.2	−10.3	−11.5	−134
610	7	−21.2	9.7	−11.5	−134
630	11	−41.2	29.7	−11.5	−134
650	14	−61.2	49.7	−11.5	−134

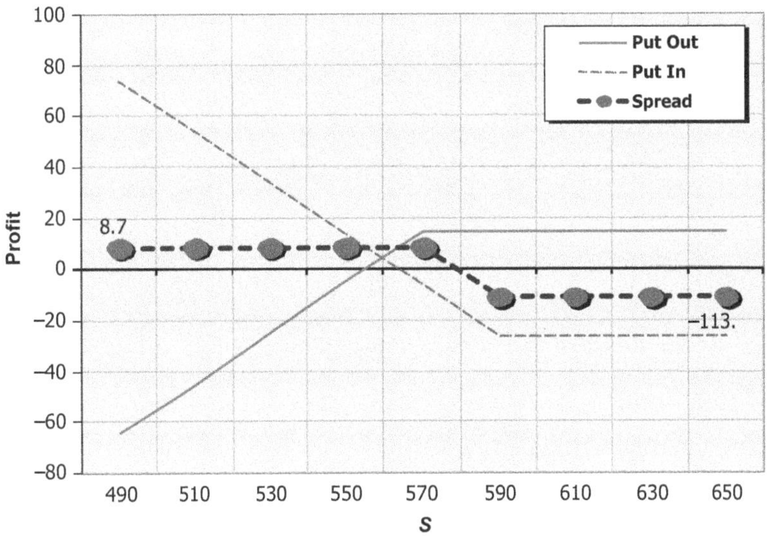

Figure 13.14. Selling a put bear spread.

13.2.12. *Short a butterfly*

Expectations: The reader can refer to the previous chapter for more details and make the necessary comments (Table 13.28).

13.2.13. *Long a condor*

Expectations: The reader can refer to the previous chapter for more details and make the necessary comments (Fig. 13.16 and Table 13.29).

Table 13.26. Selling a put bear spread.

S	Variation (%)	Put Out	Put In	Spread	Performance (%)
490	−14	−65.1	73.8	8.7	−77
510	−11	−45.1	53.8	8.7	−77
530	−7	−25.1	33.8	8.7	−77
550	−4	−5.1	13.8	8.7	−77
570	0	14.9	−6.2	8.7	−77
590	4	14.9	−26.2	−11.3	100
610	7	14.9	−26.2	−11.3	100
630	11	14.9	−26.2	−11.3	100
650	14	14.9	−26.2	−11.3	100

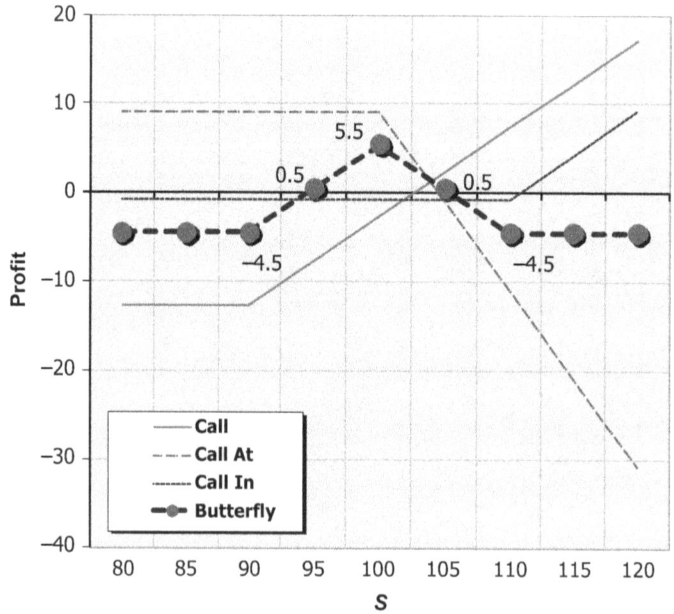

Figure 13.15. Long a butterfly.

13.2.14. *Short a condor*

Expectations: The reader can refer to the previous chapter for more details and make the necessary comments (Fig. 13.17 and Table 13.30).

Table 13.27. Long a butterfly.

S	Variation (%)	Call out	Call at	Call in	Butterfly	Performance (%)
80	−22	−12.7	9	−0.7	−4.5	−20
85	−17	−12.7	9	−0.7	−4.5	−20
90	−12	−12.7	9	−0.7	−4.5	−20
95	−7	−7.7	9	−0.7	0.5	2
100	−2	−2.7	9	−0.7	5.5	25
105	3	2.3	−1	−0.7	0.5	2
110	8	7.3	−11	−0.7	−4.5	−20
115	13	12.3	−21	4.3	−4.5	−20
120	18	17.3	−31	9.3	−4.5	−20

Table 13.28. Short a butterfly.

S	Variation (%)	Call out	Call at	Call in	Butterfly	Performance (%)
80	−22	12.7	−9	0.7	4.5	20
85	−17	12.7	−9	0.7	4.5	20
90	−12	12.7	−9	0.7	4.5	20
95	−7	7.7	−9	0.7	−0.5	−2
100	−2	2.7	−9	0.7	−5.5	−25
105	3	−2.3	1	0.7	−0.5	−2
110	8	−7.3	11	0.7	4.5	20
115	13	−12.3	21	−4.3	4.5	20
120	18	−17.3	31	−9.3	4.5	20

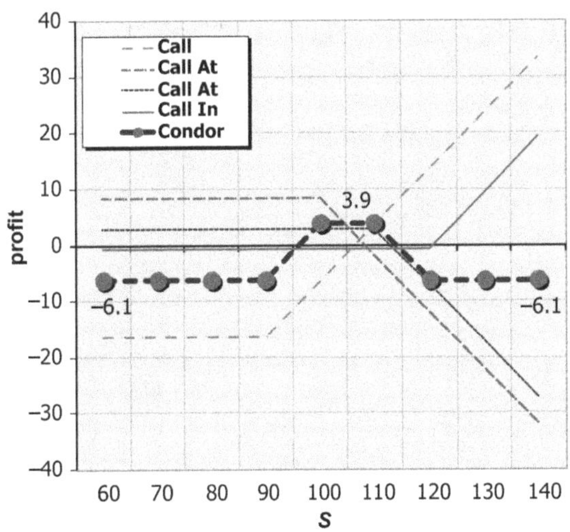

Figure 13.16. Long a condor.

Table 13.29. Long a condor.

S	Variation (%)	Call out	Call at	Call at	Call in	Condor	Performance (%)
60	−43	−16.5	8.2	2.9	−0.7	−6.1	−22
70	−33	−16.5	8.2	2.9	−0.7	−6.1	−22
80	−24	−16.5	8.2	2.9	−0.7	−6.1	−22
90	−14	−16.5	8.2	2.9	−0.7	−6.1	−22
100	−5	−6.5	8.2	2.9	−0.7	3.9	14
110	5	3.5	−1.8	2.9	−0.7	3.9	14
120	14	13.5	−11.8	−7.1	−0.7	−6.1	−22
130	24	23.5	−21.8	−17.1	9.3	−6.1	−22
140	33	33.5	−31.8	−27.1	19.3	−6.1	−22

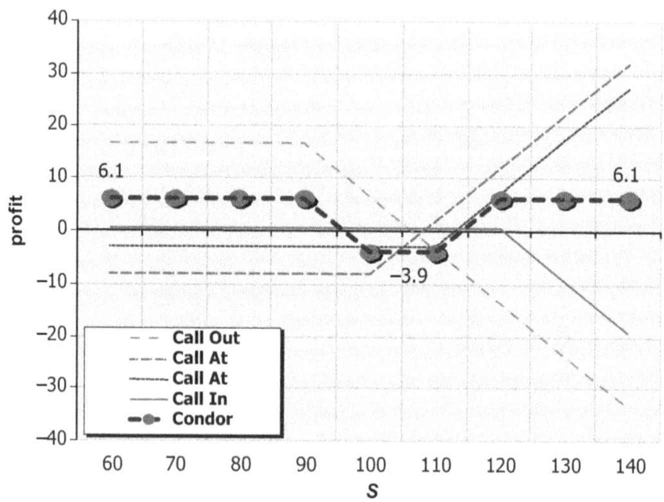

Figure 13.17. Short a condor.

Table 13.30. Short a condor.

S	Variation (%)	Call out	Call at	Call at	Call in	Condor	Performance (%)
60	−43	16.5	−8.2	−2.9	0.7	6.1	22
70	−33	16.5	−8.2	−2.9	0.7	6.1	22
80	−24	16.5	−8.2	−2.9	0.7	6.1	22
90	−14	16.5	−8.2	−2.9	0.7	6.1	22
100	−5	6.5	−8.2	−2.9	0.7	−3.9	−14
110	5	−3.5	1.8	−2.9	0.7	−3.9	−14
120	14	−13.5	11.8	7.1	0.7	6.1	22
130	24	−23.5	21.8	17.1	−9.3	6.1	22
140	33	−33.5	31.8	27.1	−19.3	6.1	22

13.3. How Traders Use Option Pricing Models: Parameter Estimation

The option price depends on the underlying asset price S, the strike price K, the interest rate r, the time to maturity, T, the volatility σ, and the dividend payouts. The option maturity corresponds to the number of days until expiration. It is often given in a fraction of a year or in days. The dividends must be known or estimated before using an option pricing model.

13.3.1. *Estimation of model parameters*

We explain briefly how the model parameters are obtained when trading options. The interest rates must be estimated during the option's life. Volatility is a measure of risk and is a fundamental element in the computation of the option premium. It can be computed using historical prices of the underlying asset. This refers to the historical volatility. It can also be calculated using the observed option prices in the market place and an option pricing model. This refers to the implicit volatility. The effect of the parameters on the option value can be appreciated using Table 13.31.

There are at least two ways to estimate the volatility: the historical volatility and the implied volatility.

13.3.1.1. *Historical volatility*

The return on an asset can be computed using three measures for the variations of its price.

Table 13.31. The effect of the parameters on option prices.

Parameters	Call	Put
Underlying asset, S	+	−
Strike price, K	−	+
Dividends	−	+
Interest rates	+	−
Maturity	+	+
Volatility	+	+

The first direct measure of return is given by the difference between the asset prices at two dates as:

$$R_{i,t}^{(1)} = S_{i,t+1} - S_{i,t}$$

The second measure allows the computation of a compound return as:

$$R_{i,t}^{(2)} = \mathrm{Log}(S_{i,t+1}) - \mathrm{Log}(S_{i,t})$$

The third method uses the relative variations in the underlying asset prices.

$$R_{i,t}^{(3)} = \frac{S_{i,t+1} - S_{i,t}}{S_{i,t}}$$

Historical volatility can be estimated using historical returns as follows:

$$\hat{\sigma}_H^2(t, N_j) = \sqrt{\frac{\sum_{\tau=1}^{N_j}(R_{t-\tau} - \bar{R})^2}{N_j - 1}}$$

where the mean return is given by,

$$\bar{R} = \frac{1}{N_j}\sum_{\tau=1}^{N_j} R_{t-\tau}$$

where N_j corresponds to the number of observations. In general, historical volatilities are computed using a period of nearly 20 days for short-term options and a period of 250 trading days for long-term options.

Example. Consider the computation of the historical volatility for the CAC40 (Table 13.32). Computations are done on 11 July 2003. The volatility is computed for a 20-day period using closing prices for the CAC40 over the past 21 days (between lines −1 and −21). The logarithmic formula giving the compound return is used in the computation of the return. For example, the relative variation of prices on 7 July 2003 is computed using the prices of the 4 and 7 July as: 0.45% = Ln(2947.66) − Ln(2934,48) where Ln(.) corresponds to the Neperian logarithm.

Table 13.32. Computation of the historical volatility for the CAC40 index.

No	Date	CAC40	$Rt = \text{Ln}(S_t) - \text{Ln}(S_{t-1})(\%)$	$(R_t - R)^2$
0	11/07/03			
−1	10/07/03	2929.09	−0.73	0.00010550
−2	09/07/03	2950.56	0.71	0.00001672
−3	08/07/03	2929.81	−0.61	0.00008176
−4	07/07/03	2947.66	0.45	0.00000229
−5	04/07/03	2934.48	−0.09	0.00001459
−6	03/07/03	2936.98	0.94	0.00004160
−7	02/07/03	2909.45	−1.18	0.00021865
−8	01/07/03	2944.04	2.96	0.00070764
−9	30/06/03	2858.26	−1.14	0.00020654
−10	27/06/03	2891.04	−0.09	0.00001495
−11	26/06/03	2893.64	0.91	0.00003755
−12	25/06/03	2867.44	2.93	0.00069115
−13	24/06/03	2784.76	0.81	0.00002669
−14	23/06/03	2762.20	0.18	0.00000125
−15	20/06/03	2757.10	0.63	0.00001133
−16	19/06/03	2739.69	−0.44	0.00005412
−17	18/06/03	2751.74	−0.39	0.00004771
−18	17/06/03	2762.60	−1.20	0.00022318
−19	16/06/03	2795.87	−0.45	0.00005599
−20	13/06/03	2808.52	1.73	0.00020624
−21	12/06/03	2760.27		
		Mean	0.30	0.00276546
				0.00014555
			1.21	1.21%
			Volatility	23.05%

Other methods can be used in the computation of historical volatilities. These methods use opening prices, closing prices, opening and closing prices, high and low prices during a trading period, etc. The estimated volatility using closing prices is given by the following formula:

$$\hat{\sigma}_0^2(t) = (S_t^{(f)} - S_{t-1}^{(f)})^2$$

where (f) refers to closing prices.

The estimated volatility using opening prices is given by:

$$\hat{\sigma}_0^2(t) = (S_{t+1}^{(o)} - S_t^{(o)})^2$$

where (o) refers to opening prices.

The estimated volatility using opening and closing prices is given by:

$$\hat{\sigma}_1^2(t) \equiv \frac{(S_t^{(o)} - S_{t-1}^{(f)})^2}{2f} + \frac{(S_t^{(f)} - S_t^{(o)})^2}{2(1-f)} \quad 0 < f < 1$$

This estimated volatility is two times more efficient than $\hat{\sigma}_0^2$.

The estimated volatility using high and low prices is given by the following formula:

$$\hat{\sigma}_2^2(t) \equiv \frac{(H_t - B_t)^2}{4\text{Ln}(2)}$$

where H refers to the high price and B refers to the low price. This estimated volatility is 5.2 times more efficient than $\hat{\sigma}_0^2$.

The estimated volatility using high and low prices is given by the following formula:

$$\hat{\sigma}_3^2(t) \equiv a\frac{(S_t^{(o)} - S_{t-1}^{(f)})^2}{f} + (1-a)\frac{(H_t - B_t)^2}{4\text{Ln}(2)(1-f)} \quad 0 < f < 1$$

This estimated volatility is 6.2 times more efficient than $\hat{\sigma}_0^2$ when the coefficient $a = 0.17$.

13.3.1.2. *Implied volatilities and option pricing models*

Using an option pricing model, (for example the Barone–Adesi and Whaley, 1987; Black and Scholes, 1973; Merton, 1973), the call price can be computed using the different parameters: the underlying asset price S, the strike price K, the interest rate r, the time to maturity T and the volatility σ. Using the market price, and the inputs S, K, r, and T, the following relationship is used to compute the implied volatility:

$$f(\sigma) = \text{Call market price}$$

The implied volatility is estimated by,

$$\hat{\sigma} = f^{-1}[f(\sigma)] = f^{-1}(\text{Call})$$

Several numerical approximations can be used in the computation of the solution to the function $F(x) = 0$. It is possible to aggregate different implicit volatilities each day to get a significant number.

Hence, we can compute an arithmetic mean of the implied standard deviations (AISD) as:

$$\sigma^{(1)}_{\mathrm{AISD}}(t) = \frac{1}{N(t)} \sum_{j=1}^{N(t)} \sigma_{\mathrm{IMP}}(t, j)$$

We can compute a weighted average of implied standard deviations (WISD).

13.3.2. *Trading and Greek letters*

It is important for traders to follow the changes in their portfolios of options. It is not sufficient to buy and sell options because the risk inherent to these operations must be managed. The management is facilitated by the use of an option pricing model and some of its partial derivatives, often known as Greek-letter risk measures. The most widely used measures are known as the delta, gamma, vega, and theta.

The delta shows the absolute change in the option price with respect to a small variation in the underlying asset price. It is given by the option's partial derivative with respect to the underlying asset price. It represents the hedge ratio, or the number of options to write in order to create a risk-free portfolio. Figure 13.18 shows the dynamics of the delta for the call and the put as a function of the underlying asset price.

The gamma gives the change in the delta, or in the hedge ratio as the underlying asset price changes. The gamma measures the change in delta, or in the hedge ratio, as the underlying asset price changes The gamma is given by the derivative of the hedge ratio with respect to the underlying asset price. As such, it is an indication of the vulnerability of the hedge ratio. Figure 13.19 shows the dynamics of the gamma for the call and the put as a function of the underlying asset price.

The vega or lambda is a measure of the change in the option price for a small change in the underlying asset's volatility. The vega or lambda measures the change in the option price for a change in the underlying's asset volatility. It is given by the first derivative of the option premium with respect to the volatility parameter.

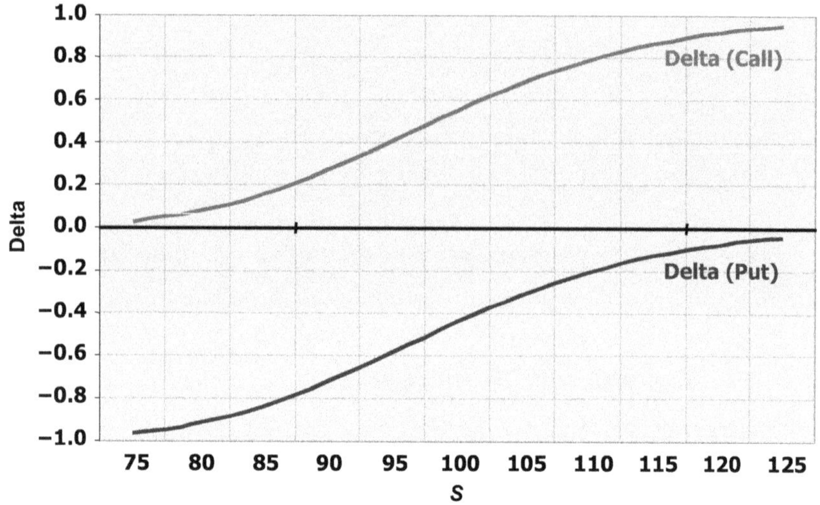

Figure 13.18. Evolution of the delta as a function of the underlying asset price.

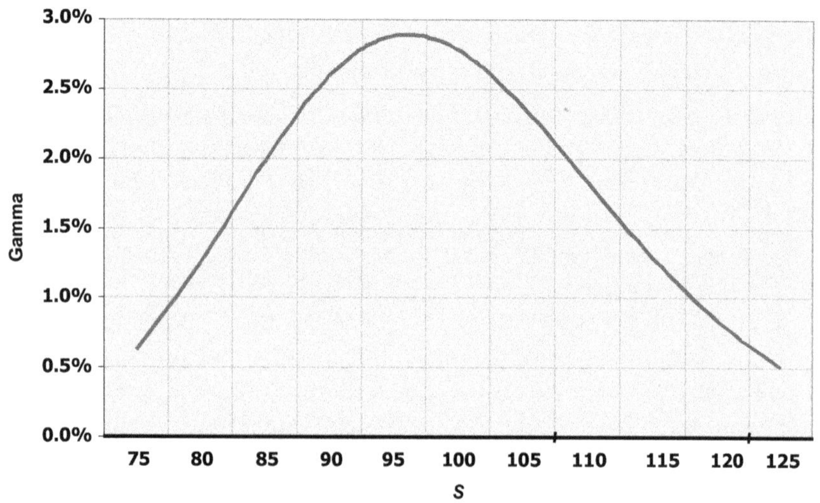

Figure 13.19. Evolution of the gamma as a function of the underlying asset price.

Figure 13.20 shows the dynamics of the vega for the call and the put as a function of the underlying asset price.

The theta measures the change in the option price as time elapses. The theta measures the change in the option price as time elapses

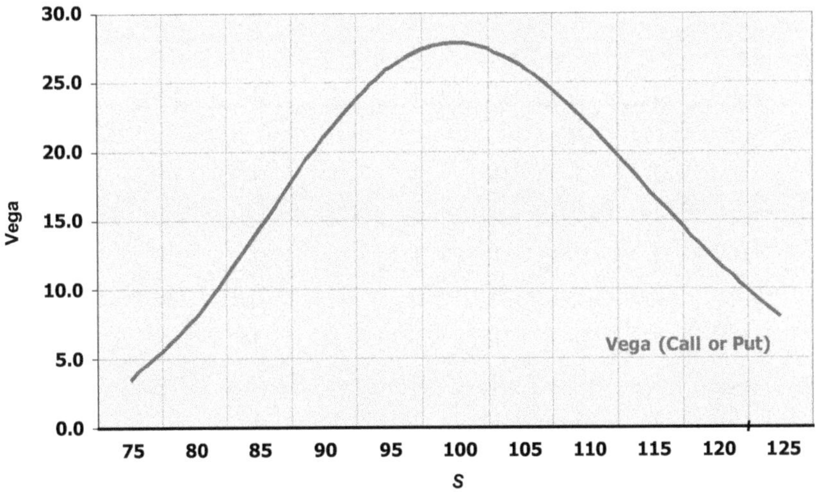

Figure 13.20. Evolution of the vega as a function of the underlying asset price.

since time decays presents a negative impact on option values. The theta is given by the first partial derivative of the option premium with respect to time.

Figures 13.21 and 13.22 shows the dynamics of the theta for the call and the put as a function of the underlying asset price and the days to maturity.

A chapter is devoted to the use of these parameters in the monitoring and the management of an option position. This is because of the importance of the sensitivity parameters in the management of portfolios of derivatives.

Figure 13.19 shows the shape of the option's gamma as a function of the underlying asset price. The gamma is the same for call and put options.

Figure 13.20 shows the shape of the option's vega as a function of the underlying asset price.

Figure 13.21 shows the shape of the option's theta as a function of the underlying asset price.

Figure 13.22 shows the shape of the option's theta as a function of the number of days until maturity.

It is important for any head of trading to compare the notional amount of the position with respect to the capital of the institution.

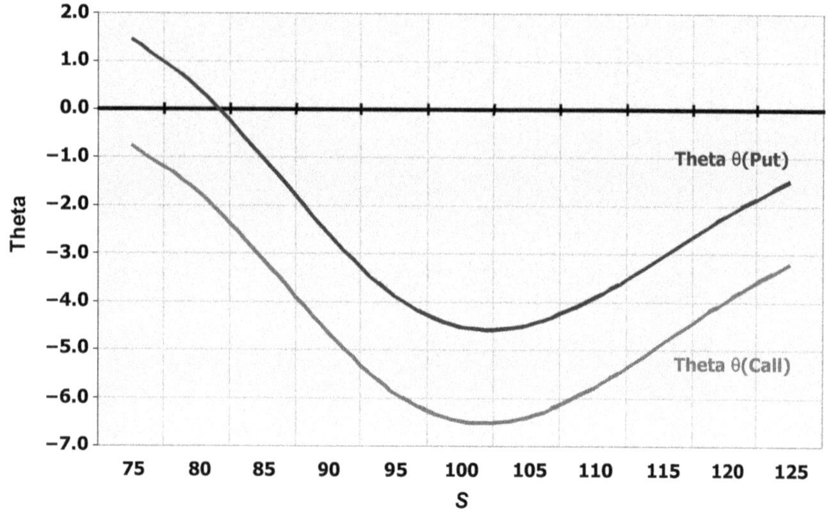

Figure 13.21. Evolution of the theta as a function of the underlying asset price.

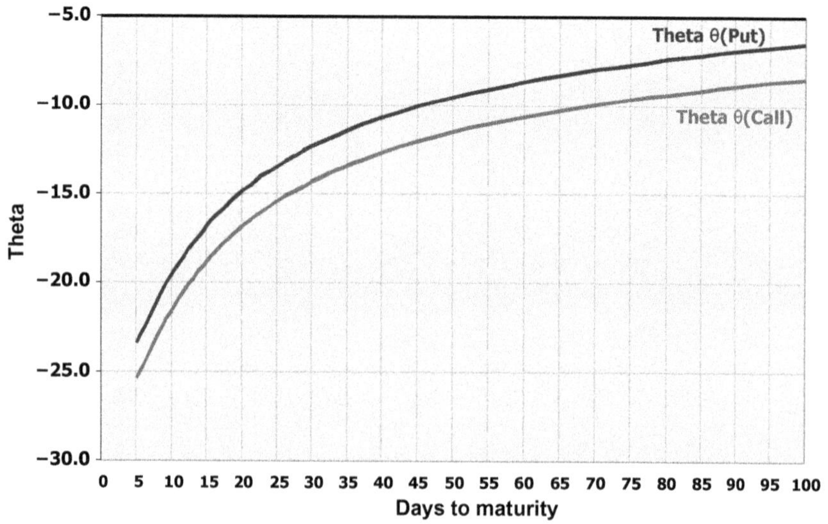

Figure 13.22. Evolution of the theta as a function of the number of days until maturity.

Summary

Since there are at least three maturity dates and three to sometimes twelve strike prices, the fundamental question is to determine which option to trade. The most well-known strategies in portfolio management involve combinations of options. They include vertical spreads, calendar spreads, diagonal spreads, ratio spreads, volatility spreads, and synthetic contracts.

A vertical spread involves the purchase of an option and the sale of an other with the same time to maturity and a different strike price. When the strategy produces a cash-out flow, we say that the investor is long the spread. When the strategy generates a cash-inflow, the investor is said short the spread. The strategy can be implemented by calls or puts using different strike prices.

A vertical bull spread is implemented when an at-the-money option is bought and an out-of-the-money option is sold. A calendar-spread strategy represents a position where the investor is long an option with a longer term and short an option with a short term for the same strike price.

A diagonal spread involves the purchase of an option with a longer term and the sale of an other with a short term where both options have different strike prices.

A bullish diagonal spread is implemented when the purchased option is at parity and the short option is out-of-the-money.

Volatility strategies are often based on the option implicit volatility.

Examples of volatility strategies include straddles and combinations. A straddle corresponds to the purchase of a call and a put with the same strike price and the same maturity date. A combination is a straddle for which the options exercise prices are out-of-the money. When the strategy implies a cash-outflow, the investor is long the strategy and when it involves a cash-inflow, the investor is short the strategy.

A synthetic forward contract can be created by the purchase of a call and the sale of a put with the same strike price. In this case, the investor is long the synthetic forward contract.

The main difference between futures contracts and option contracts is that the investor pays a premium for options but nothing to establish a futures position.

The option price depends on the underlying asset price S, the strike price K, the interest rate r, the time to maturity, T, the volatility σ, and dividend payouts. The option maturity corresponds to the number of days until expiration. It is often given in a fraction of a year or in days. The dividends must be known or estimated before using an option pricing model. Volatility is the most difficult parameter to estimate. It is a measure of risk and is a fundamental element in the computation of the option premium. It can be computed using historical prices of the underlying asset. This refers to the historical volatility. It can be also calculated using the observed option prices in the market place and an option pricing model. This refers to the implicit volatility.

Using an option pricing model, for example the Black and Scholes model, the call or model, it is possible to compute an option-implied volatility. We have also introduced the main concepts governing the management of a portfolio of options: the delta, the gamma, the theta, and the vega. These parameters enable market participants and option users to manage their portfolios of options.

References

Barone-Adesi G and RE Whaley (1987). Efficient analytic approximation of American option values. *Journal of Finance*, 42 (June), 301–320.

Black F and M Scholes (1973). The pricing of options and corporate liabilities. *Journal of Political Economy*, 81, 637–654.

Merton R (1973). Theory of rational option pricing. *Bell Journal of Economics and Management Science*, 4, 141–183.

Part IV

Pricing Derivatives and Their Underlying Assets in a Discrete-Time Setting

Chapter 14

Option Pricing: The Discrete-Time Approach for Stock Options

Chapter Outline

This chapter is organized as follows:

1. Section 14.1 presents the Cox, Ross and Rubinstein (CRR) model for the valuation of standard equity options (Cox *et al.*, 1979).
2. Section 14.2 extends the standard binomial model of Cox *et al.* (1979), to account for the effects of distributions to the underlying asset.

Introduction

This chapter deals with the valuation of derivative assets using the binomial or the lattice approach. Ironically enough, however, the more complex approach, namely the Black–Scholes (1973) one, was discovered before the simple binomial approach. Even if the discrete-time approach is not always computationally efficient, option valuation with the lattice approach is very flexible. It can handle many situations where no analytical solutions are possible. This is the case, for example, for the valuation of stock options and index options, when there are several discrete cash payouts made by the underlying asset, such as cash dividends on a stock.

Various numerical procedures have been proposed by researchers for the pricing of derivative securities. These procedures include the lattice approach, finite difference schemes, and the Monte-Carlo method, among others. When pricing European options, these procedures are asymptotically equivalent to closed-form solutions *à la* Black and Scholes (1973). However, binomial methods may be more practical for the pricing of American options and complex derivative securities. In fact, these approaches can handle more complex situations such as cash dividend payouts.

In this chapter, we are interested in the lattice approach pioneered by Cox *et al.* (1979). These authors proposed a binomial model in a discrete-time setting for the valuation of options. Using the risk-neutral framework, their approach is based on the construction of a binomial lattice for stock prices. They applied the risk-neutral valuation argument, pioneered by Black and Scholes (1973), which simply means that one can value the option at hand as if investors were risk-neutral. With an appropriate choice of the binomial parameters, they established a convergence result of their model to that of Black–Scholes. Since then, the CRR approach was extended and extensively used for the valuation of many contingent claims and options.

14.1. The CRR Model for Equity Options

Cox *et al.* (1979), proposed the first discrete-time model for the pricing of stock options. Rendleman and Bartter (1980), developed a similar model for the pricing of interest rate sensitive instruments.

14.1.1. *The mono-periodic model*

To illustrate the foundations of the binomial model, consider the following data:

- Underlying asset price: $S = 40$;
- Strike price: $K = 40$;
- Riskless interest rate: $r = 10\%$ or $R = 1 + r = 1.1$ and
- Time to maturity: 1 year.

At the end of the year, the underlying stock can increase by 20%, from 40 to (40×1.2), or 48, as it can decrease by the same amount from 40 to (40×0.8), or 32 as in Fig. 14.1.

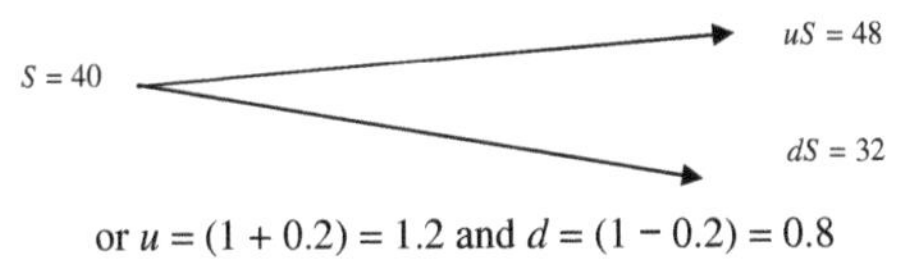

Figure 14.1. One period binomial model.

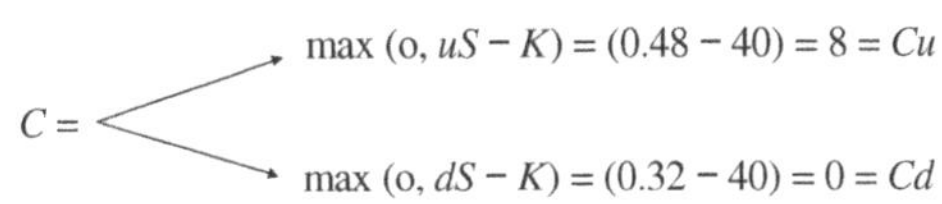

Figure 14.2. Pricing a call.

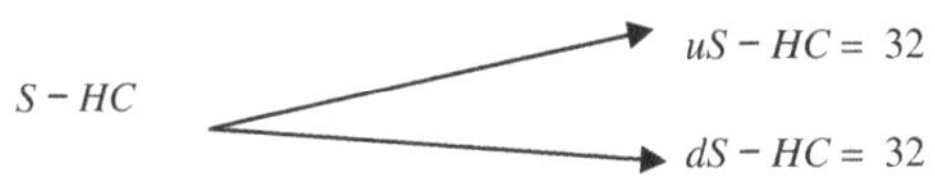

Figure 14.3. Dynamics of the ⟨⟨hedge⟩⟩ portfolio.

The dynamics of the option is nearly similar to that of the underlying asset. The call option price at the maturity date is given by the greater of zero and the intrinsic value. As in Fig. 14.2, the option price can go up to C_u or down to C_d.

It is possible to construct an initial hedge portfolio using the underlying asset S and a certain number H of options as $(S - HC)$. If this portfolio ⟨⟨hedges⟩⟩ the investor against risk, it must lead to the same result at the maturity date as in Fig. 14.3.

The possible change in the underlying asset price at maturity is given by:

$$(uS - dS) = 48 - 32 = S(u - d) = 16, \quad \text{or} \quad 40(1.2 - 0.8) = 16.$$

The possible change in the option price at maturity is given by:

$$(C_u - C_d) = (8 - 0) = 0.$$

Using this information, it is possible to compute the number H as follows:

$$H = S(u - d)/(C_u - C_d) = 40(1.2 - 0.8)/(8 - 0) = 16/8 = 2.$$

When the stock price increases, the value of the ⟨⟨hedge⟩⟩ portfolio is:

$$uS - HC_u = 1.2(40) - 2(8) = 48 - 16 = 32.$$

When the stock price decreases, the value of the ⟪ hedge ⟫ portfolio is:

$$dS - HC_d = 0.8(40) - 2(0) = 32.$$

What is the option price at time 0 in this simple binomial model?

Since the initial portfolio value is $(S - HC)$, its final value must be multiplied by the risk-less rate since it is a hedge portfolio. The value of the hedged portfolio at the maturity date becomes $R(S - HC)$. In order to avoid risk-less arbitrage, we must have $R(S - HC) = (uS - HC_u)$, which gives:

$$C = \frac{S(R-u) + Hc_u}{HR}$$

Since the value of H is given by $H = \frac{S(u-d)}{C_u - C_d}$, then

$$C = \left[C_u \frac{(R-d)}{(u-d)} + C_d \frac{(u-R)}{(u-d)}\right] \Big/ R$$

This is the option price in a mono-periodic binomial model.

Example. Using the following data:

$$C_u = 8, \quad C_d = 0, \quad u = 1.2, \quad d = 0.8, \quad R = 1.1$$

The option price is:

$$C = \left[8 \frac{(1.1 - 0.8)}{(1.2 - 0.8)} + 0 \frac{(1.2 - 1.1)}{(1.2 - 0.8)}\right] \Big/ 1.1 = (6 + 0)/1.1 = 5.4545$$

The call price can also be written as:

$$C = [pC_u + (1-p)C_d]/R$$

with

$$p = (R - d)/(u - d) \quad \text{and} \quad (1 - p) = (u - R)/(u - d)$$

where p refers to the probability of an increase in the underlying asset price.

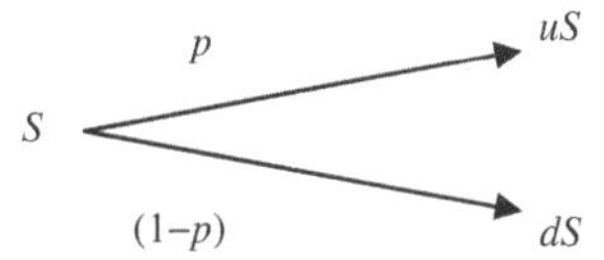

Figure 14.4. Dynamics of the underlying asset price.

14.1.2. *The multiperiodic model*

This simple mono-periodic model can be repeated N times to construct the multiperiodic binomial option pricing model. Time to maturity T is divided into N intervals of length Δt, where the underlying asset price increases from S to uS or decreases from S down to dS with a probability p and $(1-p)$ as in Fig. 14.4.

In a risk-neutral world, the expected value of S is $Se^{r\sqrt{\Delta t}}$. The expected value can also be calculated as follows:

$$pSu + (1-p)Sd \tag{14.1}$$

The equality between the two expected values gives:

$$Se^{r\sqrt{\Delta t}} = pSu + (1-p)Sd \tag{14.2}$$

Simplifying by S gives:

$$e^{r\sqrt{\Delta t}} = pu + (1-p)d \tag{14.3}$$

The variance of S over the same time interval Δt is $\sigma^2 S^2 \ \Delta t$, since the variance of a random variable X is given by:

$$E(X^2) - E(X)^2$$

Calculating the variance and simplifying gives:

$$\sigma^2 \Delta t = pu^2 + (1-p)d^2 - [pu + (1-p)d]^2 \tag{14.4}$$

Using Eqs. (14.3), (14.4), and $u = 1/d$, it is possible to show that the following relationships are verified:

$$u = e^{r\sqrt{\Delta t}}, \quad d = e^{r\sqrt{\Delta t}}, \quad m = e^{r\sqrt{\Delta t}}, \quad p = (m-d)/(u-d) \tag{14.5}$$

At each node, the underlying asset value can be written as $Su^j d^{i-j}$, for j varying from 0 to i. The first index i corresponds to the period and the second index j indicates the position. For example, when the option's maturity date is in one period, $i = 1$ and j varies from 0 to i, i.e., 0 to 1. Using 0 for the lowest position at each period, when the underlying asset value decreases, we have $Su^0d^{1-0} = Sd$. When it increases, we have $Su^1d^{1-1} = Su$. The value of an European or an American option at each pair (i, j) is denoted by $F_{i,j}$. The option price at time 0 can be computed by a recursion starting from the maturity date T. The option price is given by its expected future value discounted to the present at the appropriate risk-less rate. At maturity, the payoff from an European call is:

$$F_{N,j} = \max[0, Su^j d^{N-j} - K]$$

The payoff from an European put:

$$F_{N,j} = \max[0, K - Su^j d^{N-j}]$$

where K is the strike price. Authors use E or K to denote the strike price. We use both E and K for the strike price.

The option value at each node can be computed using the two immediate successive nodes. The expected value must be discounted using the risk-less rate as follows:

$$F_{i,j} = e^{r\sqrt{\Delta t}}[pF_{i+1,j+1} + (1-p)F_{i+1,j}] \tag{14.6}$$

for $0 \leq i \leq M - 1$ and $0 \leq j \leq i$.

Since the value of an American call option must be at least equal to its intrinsic value, the following condition must be satisfied:

$$F_{i,j} = \max[Su^j d^{i-j} - K, e^{r\sqrt{\Delta t}}(pF_{i+1,j+1} + (1-p)F_{i+1,j})] \tag{14.7}$$

The value of an American put option must satisfy the following condition:

$$F_{i,j} = \max[K - Su^j d^{i-j}, e^{r\sqrt{\Delta t}}(pF_{i+1,j+1} + (1-p)F_{i+1,j})] \tag{14.8}$$

This model appears in Cox *et al.* (1979), Cox and Rubinstein (1985), Boyle (1986, 1988) and Hull and White (1993) etc.

14.1.3. *Applications and examples*

14.1.3.1. *Applications of the CRR model within two periods*

Consider the following data for the pricing of an European call:

$$S = 100, \quad K = 100, \quad T = 1\,\text{year}, \quad N = 2, \quad \sigma = 0.2, \quad r = 0.1.$$

In the first step, the values of the model parameters must be computed:

$$u = e^{-\sigma\sqrt{\Delta t}} = 1.1519, \quad d = e^{-\sigma\sqrt{\Delta t}}, = e^{-0.2\sqrt{1/2}} = 0.8681,$$
$$m = e^{r\sqrt{\Delta t}} = e^{-0.1\sqrt{1/2}} = 1.0732, \quad p = (m - d)/(u - d) = 0.7227.$$

For an initial value of $S = 100$, the two possible values in the next period are:

$$Su = 100(1.1519) = 115.19, \quad Sd = 100(0.8681) = 86.81.$$

These two values of the underlying asset price lead to three possible values, as shown in Fig. 14.5:

$$Suu = 115.19(1.1519) = 132.68, \quad Sud = 115.19(0.8681) = 100$$
$$\text{and} \quad Sdd = 86.81(0.8681) = 75.36.$$

Using the index representation, (i, j), we have (Fig. 14.6):

In the above representation, $S_{0,0}$ refers to the initial time 0 and the lowest position 0. $S_{1,0}$ corresponds to the period 1 and the lowest

$Suu = 132.68$

$Su = 115.19$

$S = 100$ $\qquad$ $Sud = 100$

$Sd = 86.81$

$Sdd = 75.36$

Figure 14.5. Dynamics of the underlying asset price.

$S_{2,2} = 132.68$

$S_{1,1} = 115.19$

$S_{0,0} = 100$ $\qquad$ $S_{2,1} = 100$

$S_{1,0} = 86.81$

$S_{2,0} = 75.36$

Figure 14.6. Dynamics of the underlying asset price.

$C_{2,2} = 132.68 - 100 = 32.68$

$C_{1,1} = ?$

$C_{0,0} = ?$

$C_{2,1} = 100 - 100 = 0$

$C_{1,0} = ?$

$C_{2,0} = 75.36 - 100 = 0$

Figure 14.7. Dynamics of the option price.

position 0. $S_{1,1}$ refers to the period 1 and the first position after 0, i.e., 1. The dynamics of the option price are given in Fig. 14.7.

The option value can be computed by using a simple application of the following formula:

$$F_{i,j} = e^{-r\sqrt{\Delta t}}[pF_{i+1,j+1} + (1-p)F_{i+1,j}].$$

The option value at node (1,1), i.e., $C_{1,1}$ is given by:

$$C_{1,1} = e^{-r\sqrt{\Delta t}}[pC_{2,2} + (1-p)C_{2,1}],$$

or

$$C_{1,1} = e^{-0,1(1/2)}[0.7227(32.68) + (1-0.7227)0] = 22.465.$$

The option value at node $(1,0)$, i.e., $C_{1,0}$ is:

$$C_{1,0} = e^{-r\sqrt{\Delta t}} = [pC_{2,1} + (1-p)C_{2,0}], \quad \text{or}$$

$$C_{1,0} = e^{-0,1(1/2)}[0.7227(22.465) + (1-0.7227)0] = 0$$

Using the possible values in one period, what is the option price at time 0?

Using the same formula, $C_{0,0}$ is given by:

$$C_{0,0} = e^{-r\sqrt{\Delta t}}[pC_{1,1} + (1-p)C_{1,0}], \quad \text{or}$$

$$C_{0,0} = e^{-0,1(1/2)}[0.7227(0) + (1-0.7227)0] = 15.443$$

The option value at time 0 is 15.443. The same method is used by Rendleman and Bartter (1979) for the valuation of interest rate options.

14.1.3.2. *Other applications of the binomial model of CRR for two periods*

Consider the following data for the valuation of European and American call and put options:

$$S = 100, \quad K = 100, \quad r = 5\%, \quad \sigma = 30\%, \quad N = 2, \quad T = 1\,\text{year}.$$

14.1.3.2.1. Computation of the European call price

Using the above date, the dynamics of the underlying asset are given by:

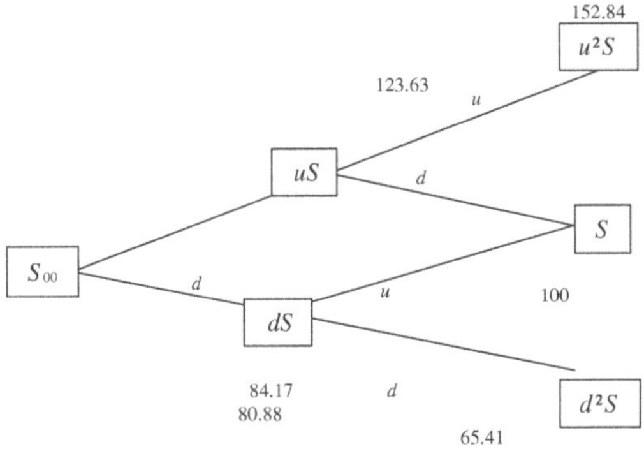

The dynamics of the option price are given by:

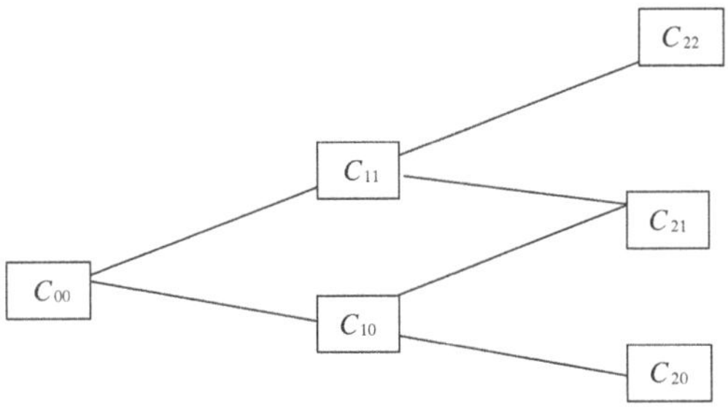

In this case, option values are given by:

$$C_{2,2} = 52.84, \quad C_{1,1} = 0, \quad C_{2,0} = 0$$

$$C_{1,1} = \frac{0.5064 * 52.84 + 0 * (1 - 0.5064)}{1.025} = 26.105, \quad C_{1,0} = 0$$

$$C_{0,0} = \frac{0.5064 * 26.105 + 0}{1.025} = 12.897.$$

Hence, the option price is 12.897.

14.1.3.2.2. Computation of the European put price

The dynamics of the put price are given by:

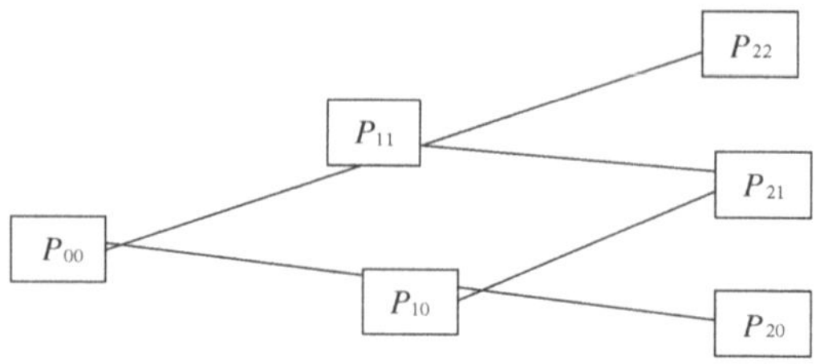

Option prices are given by:

$$P_{2,2} = 0, \quad P_{2,1} = 0, \quad P_{2,0} = 100 - 65.41 = 34.59$$

$$P_{1,1} = \frac{0.5064 * 0 + 0}{1.025} = 0$$

$$P_{1,0} = \frac{0.5064 * 0 + 0.4936 * 34.59}{1.025} = 16.657$$

$$P_{0,0} = \frac{0 + 0.4936 * 16.657}{1.025} = 8.021$$

Hence, the option price is 8.021. We can check that the put–call parity theorem is verified.

$$P = C + Ke^{-rt} - S = 12.897 + 100e^{-0.05*1} - 100 = 8.02$$

Computation of the American call price

Option prices are computed as:

$$C_{1,1} = \max\left(\frac{0.5064 * 52.84 + 0.4936 * 0}{1.025}; \quad 23.63\right) = 26.105$$

$$C_{1,0} = \max\left(\frac{0.5064 * 0 + 0}{1.025}; \quad 0\right) = 0$$

$$C_{0,0} = \frac{0.5064 * 26.105}{1.025} = 12.88$$

14.1.3.2.3. Computation of the American put price

Option prices are computed as:

$$P_{1,1} = \max\left(\frac{0.5064 * 0 + 0.4936 * 0}{1.025}; \quad 100 - 80.88\right) = 0$$

$$P_{1,0} = \max\left(\frac{0.5064 * 0 + 0.4936 * 34.59}{1.025}; \quad 100 - 80.88\right) = 19.12$$

$$P_{0,0} = \frac{0.5064 * 0 + 0.4936 * 19.12}{1.025} = 9.2$$

14.1.3.3. *Applications of the binomial model of CRR for three periods*

Consider the following data for the valuation of European and American call and put options: $S = 100, K = 100, r = 5\%, \sigma = 30\%, N = 3, T = 1$ year.

14.1.3.3.1. Computation of the European call price

Using the above data, we have $u = e^{\sigma\sqrt{\Delta t}}$ with $N\Delta t = T$. Hence,

$$\Delta t = \frac{1}{3} = 0.33, \quad u = e^{0.30\sqrt{0.33}} = 1.1881, \quad d = \frac{1}{u} = \frac{1}{1.1881} = 0.8417$$

$$p = \frac{e^{r\Delta t} - d}{u - d} = \frac{e^{0.05*0.33} - 0.8417}{1.1881 - 0.8417} = 0.5050$$

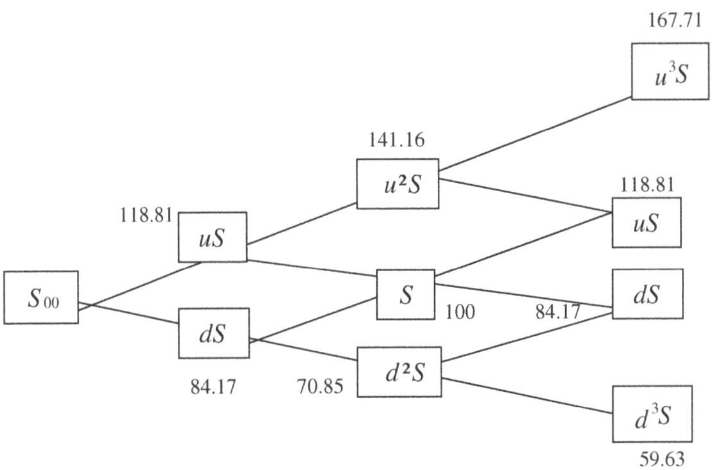

The option payoff at maturity is:

$$C_{3,3} = 167.71 - 100 = 67.71, \quad C_{3,2} = 118.81 - 100 = 18.81$$
$$C_{3,1} = 84.17 - 100 = 0, \quad C_{3,0} = 59.63 - 100 = 0.$$

Before maturity, option prices are computed as:

$$C_{2,2} = \frac{0.5050 * 67.71 + 0.495 * 18.81}{1.017} = 42.78$$
$$C_{2,1} = \frac{0.5050 * 18.81 + 0.495 * 0}{1.017} = 9.34$$
$$C_{2,0} = \frac{0.5050 * 0 + 0.495 * 0}{1.017} = 0$$
$$C_{1,1} = \frac{0.5050 * 42.78 + 0.495 * 9.34}{1.017} = 25.79$$
$$C_{1,0} = \frac{0.5050 * 9.34 + 0.495 * 0}{1.017} = 4.64$$
$$C_{0,0} = \frac{0.5050 * 25.79 + 0.495 * 4.64}{1.017} = 15.06$$

The option price is $C_{0,0} = 15.06$.
The option payoff at maturity is given by:

$$P_{3,3} = 100 - 167.71 = 0, \quad P_{3,2} = 100 - 118.81 = 0$$
$$P_{3,1} = 100 - 84.17 = 15.83$$
$$P_{3,0} = 100 - 59.63 = 40.37$$

Before maturity, option prices are given by:

$$P_{2,2} = \frac{0.5050 * 0 + 0.495 * 0}{1.017} = 0$$
$$P_{2,1} = \frac{0.5050 * 0 + 0.495 * 15.83}{1.017} = 7.70$$
$$P_{2,0} = \frac{0.5050 * 15.83 + 0.495 * 40.37}{1.017} = 27.51$$

$$P_{1,1} = \frac{0.5050 * 0 + 0.495 * 7.70}{1.017} = 3.75$$

$$P_{1,0} = \frac{0.5050 * 7.70 + 0.495 * 27.51}{1.017} = 17.21$$

$$P_{0,0} = \frac{0.5050 * 3.75 + 0.495 * 17.21}{1.017} = 10.24$$

We can check the put–call parity relationship in this context:

$$P = C + Ke^{-rt} - S = 15.06 + 100e^{-0.05*1} - 100 = 10.2$$

14.1.3.3.2. Computation of the American call price

American call option prices are computed as follows:

$$C_{2,2} = \max\left(\frac{0.5050 * 27.71 + 0.495 * 18.81}{1.017}; \quad 141.16 - 100\right) = 42.78$$

$$C_{2,1} = \max\left(\frac{0.5050 * 18.81 + 0.495 * 0}{1.017}; \quad 100 - 100\right) = 9.34$$

$$C_{2,0} = \max\left(\frac{0.5050 * 0 + 0.495 * 0}{1.017}; \quad 0\right) = 0$$

$$C_{1,1} = \max\left(\frac{0.5050 * 42.78 + 0.495 * 9.34}{1.017}; \quad 118.8 - 100\right) = 25.79$$

$$C_{1,0} = \max\left(\frac{0.5050 * 9.34 + 0.495 * 0}{1.017}; \quad 84.17 - 100\right) = 4.64$$

$$C_{0,0} = \frac{0.5050 * 25.79 + 0.495 * 4.64}{1.017} = 15.06$$

14.1.3.3.3. Computation of the American put price

American put prices are computed as follows:

$$P_{2,2} = \max\left(\frac{0.5050 * 0 + 0.495 * 0}{1.017}; \quad 100 - 141.16\right) = 0$$

$$P_{2,1} = \max\left(\frac{0.5050 * 0 + 0.495 * 15.83}{1.017}; \quad 100 - 100\right) = 7.70$$

$$P_{2,0} = \max\left(\frac{0.5050 * 15.83 + 0.495 * 40.37}{1.017}; \quad 100 - 70.85\right) = 29.15$$

$$P_{1,1} = \max\left(\frac{0.5050 * 0 + 0.495 * 7.70}{1.017};\quad 100 - 118.8\right) = 3.75$$

$$P_{1,0} = \max\left(\frac{0.5050 * 7.70 + 0.495 * 29.15}{1.017};\quad 100 - 84.17\right) = 18.01$$

$$P_{0,0} = \frac{0.5050 * 3.75 + 0.495 * 18.01}{1.017} = 10.63$$

14.1.3.4. *Examples with five periods*

Example 1. Consider the valuation of European and American options in the following context:

Underlying asset, $S = 100$, strike price $K = 100$, interest rate $= 0.1$, volatility $= 0.4$, $T = 5$ months, and $N = 5$. In this case, we have $p = 0.5073$, $d = 0.8909$, and $u = 1.1224$.

Dynamics of the underlying asset price					
					178.1312
				158.7055	
			141.3982		141.3982
		125.9784		125.9784	
	112.2401		112.2401		112.2401
100		100		100	
	89.0947		89.0947		89.0947
		79.3787		79.3787	
			70.7222		70.7222
				63.0098	
					56.1384

The valuation of European put options					
					0
				0	
			0		0
		1.2720		0	
	4.2282		2.6033		0
8.6380		7.3442		5.3282	
	13.3256		12.3506		10.9053
		19.7110		19.7914	
			27.6249		29.2778
				36.1603	
					43.8616

The valuation of American put options					
					0
				0	
			0		0
		1.2720		0	
	4.3250		2.6033		0
8.9769		7.5423		5.3282	
	13.9195		12.7561		10.9053
		20.7226		20.6213	
			29.2778		29.2778
				36.9902	
					43.8616

The valuation of European call options					
					78.1312
				59.5354	
			43.0511		41.3982
		29.7194		26.8082	
	19.7467		16.4963		12.2401
12.7191		9.8132		6.1581	
	5.6987		3.0982		0
		1.5587		0	
			0		0
				0	
					0

The valuation of American call options					
					78.1312
				59.5354	
			43.0511		41.3982
		29.7194		26.8082	
	19.7467		16.4963		12.2401
12.7191		9.8132		6.1581	
	5.6987		3.0982		0
		1.5587		0	
			0		0
				0	
					0

Example 2. Consider the valuation of European and American options in the following context:

Underlying asset, $S = 100$, strike price $K = 80$, interest rate $= 0.1$, volatility $= 0.4$, $T = 5$ months, and $N = 5$. In this case, we have $p = 0.5073$, $d = 0.8909$, and $u = 1.1224$.

Dynamics of the underlying asset price					
					142.5050
				126.9644	
			113.1186		113.1186
		100.7827		100.7827	
	89.7921		89.7921		89.7921
80		80		80	
	71.2758		71.2758		71.2758
		63.5030		63.5030	
			56.5778		56.5778
				50.4078	
					44.9107

The valuation of European put options					
					0
				0	
			2.4369		0
		7.0283		4.9875	
	12.9178		11.8756		10.2079
19.3423		19.2016		19.1701	
	26.2863		27.0714		28.7242
		34.0280		35.6672	
			41.7694		43.4222
				48.7623	
					55.0893

Valuation of American put options					
					0
				0	
			2.4369		0
		7.2265		4.9875	
	13.5117		12.2811		10.2079
20.8323		20.2132		20	
	28.7242		28.7242		28.7242
		36.4970		36.4970	
			43.4222		43.4222
				49.5922	
					55.0893

The valuation of European call options					
					42.5050
				27.7943	
			17.2083		13.1186
		10.2801		6.6001	
			3.3206		0
3.4234		1.6706		0	
	0.8405		0		0
		0		0	
			0		0
				0	
					0

The valuation of American call options					
					42.5050
				27.7943	
			17.2083		13.1186
		10.2801		6.6001	
			3.3206		0
3.4234		1.6706		0	
	0.8405		0		0
		0		0	
			0		0
				0	
					0

14.2. The Binomial Model and the Distributions to the Underlying Assets

Let us denote by:

$C(.)$, $c(.)$: prices of American and European call options and
$P(.)$, $p(.)$: prices of American and European put options.

14.2.1. *The put-call parity in the presence of several cash-distributions*

The traditional put–call parity can be easily adapted to account for the cash income paid (or received) at the end of each month on the underlying stock. Consider the two following portfolios:

Portfolio A: one call option plus a discount bond that will be worth K at time T and
Portfolio B: one put option plus one share.

At the maturity date, both portfolios are worth $\max(K, S_T)$. If the options are European, the portfolios must have identical values at time $t : [c + Ke^{-r(T-t)} = p + S]$.

The two most basic forms of arbitrage are the conversion and the reverse conversion or reversal. Since the value of the stock must be discounted by the amount of the cash received, R, or paid, D, the conversion ought to net a profit when:

$$c - p + (-\text{ call parity or } +\text{ put parity}) > R - D$$

The reverse is profitable when:

$$c - p - (-\text{ call parity or } + \text{ call parity}) < R - D$$

These relationships must hold independently from the option-valuation model. To prevent risk-less free arbitrage in efficient markets, we must have:

$$c - p \pm (\text{put–call parity}) = R - D$$

14.2.2. *Early exercise of American stock options*

The argument of Merton (1973) and Jarrow and Rudd (1983) can be extended to early exercise of American calls when there are several cash payments at different dates t_i. When the amounts of cash distributions are accounted for, it can be shown that a sufficient condition for optimal exercise is:

$$(D_i + R_i) > K[1 - e^{-r(t_i+1-t_i)}]$$

with $(D_i + R_i) \geq 0$. Generally, a put is exercised when it is in the money and the call price is less than the cash amount. Formally, the put is exercised at time t_i if:

$$(D_i + R_i) < K[1 - e^{-r(t_i+1-t_i)}]$$

with $(D_i + R_i) \geq 0$.

14.2.3. *The model*

When there is just one ex-cash income date τ, during the option's life and $k\,\Delta t \leq \tau \leq (k+1)\Delta t$, then at time x, the value of the random component S is:

$$S^*(x) = S(x) \quad \text{when } x > \tau$$

$$S^*(x) = S(x) - (D_i + R_i)e^{-r(\tau - x)} \quad \text{when } x \leq \tau$$

Assume σ^* is the constant volatility of S^*. Using the parameters p, u, and d, at time $t + i\Delta t$, the nodes on the tree define the stock prices:

$$\text{If } i\Delta t < \tau : S^*(t)u^j d^{i-j} + (D_i + R_i)e^{-r(\tau - i\Delta t)} \quad j = 0, 1, \ldots, i$$

$$\text{If } i\Delta t \geq \tau : S^*(t)u^j d^{i-j} \quad j = 0, 1, \ldots, i$$

14.2.4. *Simulations for a small number of periods*

Example 1. Applications of the CRR model for five periods with dividends

Consider the following data for the valuation of European and American call and put options: $S = 110$, $K = 115$, $r = 10\%$, $\sigma = 40\%$, $N = 0.5$, $t = 5$ months, $\Delta t = 1$ month date of dividend: 105 days, dividend amount: $D = 10$.

14.2.4.1. *The European call price*

Using the above data, the dynamics of the underlying asset are computed using:

$$u = e^{\sigma\sqrt{\Delta t}}, \quad u = e^{0.4\sqrt{1/2}}, \quad \text{or}$$

$$u = 1.1224, \quad d = \frac{1}{u} = 0.8909, \quad p = \frac{e^{r\Delta t} - d}{u - d} = 0.5073$$

$$S^* = S - D = 110 - 10 = 100$$

$$S_{0,0} = S^* u^0 d^0 + De^{-r(105/365)} = 109.7164$$

$$S_{1,1} = S^* u^1 d^0 + De^{-r((105/365)-(1/12))}$$

$$= 100(1.1224) + 10De^{-r((105/365)-(1/12))} = 122.0377$$

$$S_{1,0} = S^* u^0 d^1 + De^{-r((105/365)-(1/12))} = 98.8925$$

$$S_{2,2} = S^* u^2 d^0 + De^{-r((105/365)-(2/12))} = 135.8579$$

$$S_{2,1} = S^* u^1 d^1 + De^{-r((105/365)-(2/12))} = 109.8797$$

$$S_{2,0} = S^* u^0 d^2 + De^{-r((105/365)-(2/12))} = 89.2586$$

$$S_{3,3} = S^* u^3 d^0 + De^{-r((105/365)-(3/12))} = 151.3603$$

$$S_{3,2} = S^* u^2 d^1 + De^{-r((105/365)-(3/12))} = 122.2024$$

$$S_{3,1} = S^* u^1 d^2 + De^{-r((105/365)-(3/12))} = 99.0572$$

$$S_{3,0} = S^* u^0 d^3 + De^{-r((105/365)-(3/12))} = 80.6848$$

$$S_{4,4} = S^* u^4 d^0 = 158.7050, \quad S_{4,3} = S^* u^3 d^1 = 125.782$$

$$S_{4,2} = S^*u^2d^2 = 100.00, \quad S_{4,1} = S^*u^1d^3 = 79.3788,$$
$$S_{4,0} = S^*u^0d^4 = 63.0100, \quad S_{5,5} = S^*u^5d^0 = 178.1305,$$
$$S_{5,4} = S^*u^4d^1 = 141.3979, \quad S_{5,3} = S^*u^3d^2 = 112.2400,$$
$$S_{5,2} = S^*u^2d^3 = 89.0948, \quad S_{5,1} = S^*u^1d^4 = 70.7224,$$
$$S_{5,0} = S^*u^0d^5 = 56.1386$$

The dynamics of the underlying asset are represented in the following way.

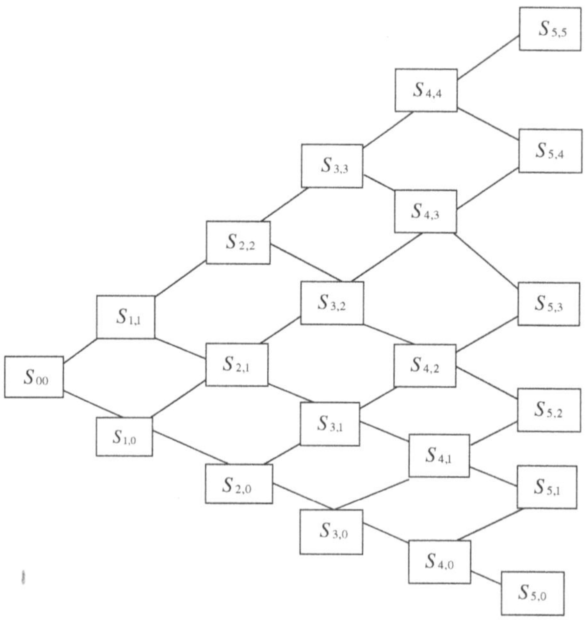

The option's maturity value is computed as:

$$C_{5,5} = \max[0;\ S_{5,5} - K] = 63.1305$$
$$C_{5,4} = \max[0;\ S_{5,4} - K] = 26.3979$$

$$C_{5,3} = \max[0;\ \ S_{5,3} - K] = 0,\ \ C_{5,2} = \max[0;\ \ S_{5,2} - K] = 0$$
$$C_{5,1} = \max[0;\ \ S_{5,1} - K] = 0,\ \ C_{5,0} = \max[0;\ \ S_{5,0} - K] = 0$$

The American call option price is computed as:

$$\begin{aligned}
C_{4,4} &= \max\left[\frac{p \cdot C_{5,5} + q \cdot C_{5,4}}{e^{r\Delta t}};\ \ VI\right] \\
&= \max[44.6586;\ \ S_{4,4} - K] = \max[44.6586;\ \ 43.7050] \\
&= 44.6586 \quad \text{where VI stands for the option intrinsic value.}
\end{aligned}$$

$$\begin{aligned}
C_{4,3} &= \max\left[\frac{p \cdot C_{5,4} + q \cdot C_{5,3}}{e^{r\Delta t}};\ \ S_{4,3} - K\right] \\
&= \max[13.2805;\ \ 10.9782] = 13.2805
\end{aligned}$$

$$C_{4,2} = \max\left[\frac{p \cdot C_{5,3} + q \cdot C_{5,2}}{e^{r\Delta t}};\ \ \max[0;\ \ S_{4,2} - K]\right] = 0$$

$$C_{4,1} = \max\left[\frac{p \cdot C_{5,2} + q \cdot C_{5,1}}{e^{r\Delta t}};\ \ \max[0;\ \ S_{4,1} - K]\right] = 0$$

$$C_{4,0} = \max\left[\frac{p \cdot C_{5,1} + q \cdot C_{5,0}}{e^{r\Delta t}};\ \ \max[0;\ \ S_{4,0} - K]\right] = 0$$

$$\begin{aligned}
C_{3,3} &= \max\left[\frac{p \cdot C_{4,4} + q \cdot C_{4,3}}{e^{r\Delta t}};\ \ S_{3,3} - K\right] \\
&= \max[28.9563;\ \ 36.3603] = 36.3603
\end{aligned}$$

$$\begin{aligned}
C_{3,2} &= \max\left[\frac{p \cdot C_{4,3} + q \cdot C_{4,2}}{e^{r\Delta t}};\ \ S_{3,2} - K\right] \\
&= \max[6.6813;\ \ 7.2024] = 7.2024
\end{aligned}$$

$$C_{3,1} = \max\left[\frac{p \cdot C_{4,2} + q \cdot C_{4,1}}{e^{r\Delta t}};\ \ S_{3,1} - K\right] = 0$$

$$C_{3,0} = \max\left[\frac{p \cdot C_{4,1} + q \cdot C_{4,0}}{e^{r\Delta t}};\ \ S_{3,0} - K\right] = 0$$

American call option prices are computed as follows:

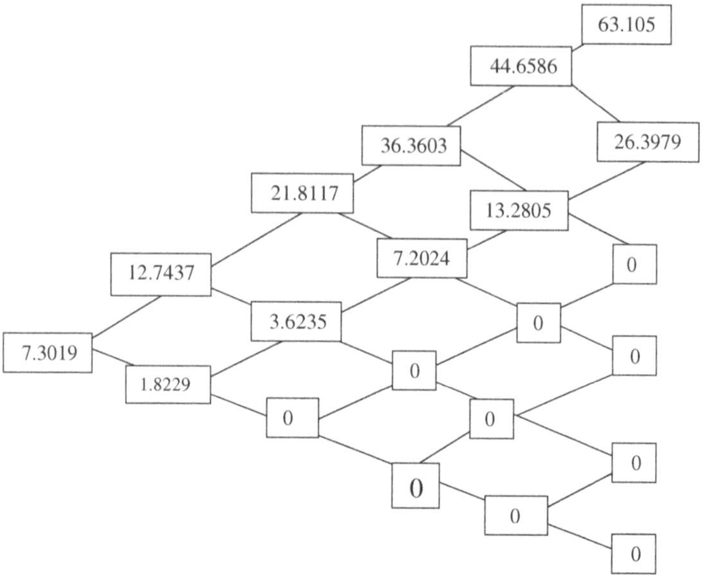

$$C_{2,2} = \max\left[\frac{p \cdot C_{3,3} + q \cdot C_{3,2}}{e^{r\Delta t}};\;\; S_{2,2} - K\right]$$

$$= \max[21.8117;\;\; 20.8579] = 21.8117$$

$$C_{2,1} = \max\left[\frac{p \cdot C_{3,2} + q \cdot C_{3,1}}{e^{r\Delta t}};\;\; \max[0;\;\; S_{2,1} - K]\right]$$

$$= \max[3.6235;\;\; 0] = 3.6235$$

$$C_{2,0} = \max\left[\frac{p \cdot C_{3,1} + q \cdot C_{3,0}}{e^{r\Delta t}};\;\; \max[0;\;\; S_{2,0} - K]\right] = 0$$

$$C_{1,1} = \max\left[\frac{p \cdot C_{2,2} + q \cdot C_{2,1}}{e^{r\Delta t}};\;\; \max[0;\;\; S_{1,1} - K]\right]$$

$$= \max[12.7437;\;\; 7.0377] = 12.7437$$

$$C_{1,0} = \max\left[\frac{p \cdot C_{2,1} + q \cdot C_{2,0}}{e^{r\Delta t}};\;\; \max[0;\;\; S_{1,0} - K]\right]$$

$$= \max[1.8229;\;\; 0] = 1.8229$$

$$C_{0,0} = \max\left[\frac{p \cdot C_{1,1} + q \cdot C_{1,0}}{e^{r\Delta t}};\ \ \max[0;\ \ S_{0,0} - K]\right]$$
$$= \max[7.3019;\ \ 0] = 7.3019$$

14.2.4.2. *The American put price*

Using the above data, the American put price is computed as follows at different nodes.

$$P_{5,5} = \max[0;\ \ K - S_{5,5}] = 0, \quad P_{5,4} = \max[0;\ \ K - S_{5,4}] = 0,$$
$$P_{5,3} = \max[0;\ \ K - S_{5,3}] = 2.76,$$
$$P_{5,2} = \max[0;\ \ K - S_{5,2}] = 25.9052,$$
$$P_{5,1} = \max[0;\ \ K - S_{5,1}] = 44.2776,$$
$$P_{5,0} = \max[0;\ \ K - S_{5,0}] = 58.8614$$

Before maturity, the option price is computed as:

$$P_{4,4} = \max\left[\frac{p \cdot P_{5,5} + q \cdot P_{5,4}}{e^{r\Delta t}};\ \ \max[0;\ \ K - S_{4,4}]\right] = 0$$
$$P_{4,3} = \max\left[\frac{p \cdot P_{5,4} + q \cdot P_{5,3}}{e^{r\Delta t}};\ \ \max[0;\ \ K - S_{4,3}]\right]$$
$$= \max[1.3486;\ \ 0] = 1.3486$$
$$P_{4,2} = \max\left[\frac{p \cdot P_{5,3} + q \cdot P_{5,2}}{e^{r\Delta t}};\ \ \max[0;\ \ K - S_{4,2}]\right]$$
$$= \max[14.0461;\ \ 0] = 15$$
$$P_{4,1} = \max\left[\frac{p \cdot P_{5,2} + q \cdot P_{5,1}}{e^{r\Delta t}};\ \ \max[0;\ \ K - S_{4,1}]\right]$$
$$= \max[34.6672;\ \ 35.6212] = 35.6212$$
$$P_{4,0} = \max\left[\frac{p \cdot P_{5,1} + q \cdot P_{5,0}}{e^{r\Delta t}};\ \ \max[0;\ \ K - S_{4,0}]\right]$$
$$= \max[51.0360;\ \ 51.9900] = 51.9900$$

Option prices are reported in the following figure.

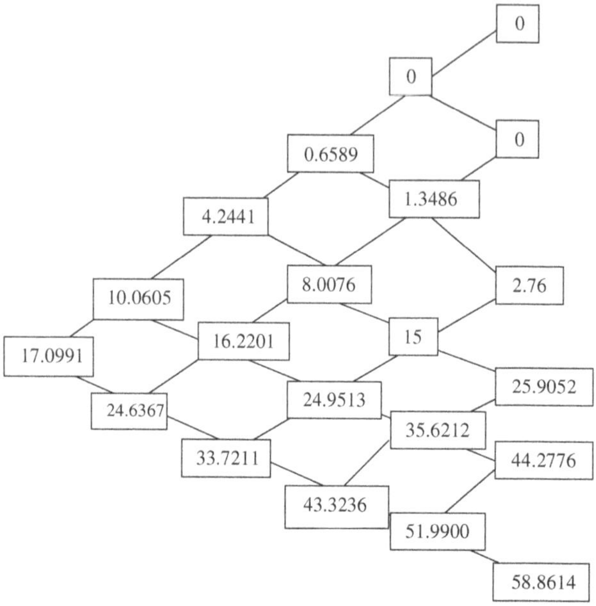

$$P_{3,3} = \max\left[\frac{p \cdot P_{4,4} + q \cdot P_{4,3}}{e^{r\Delta t}};\ \max[0;\ K - S_{3,3}]\right]$$
$$= \max[0.6589;\ 0] = 0.6589$$

$$P_{3,2} = \max\left[\frac{p \cdot P_{4,3} + q \cdot P_{4,2}}{e^{r\Delta t}};\ \max[0;\ K - S_{3,2}]\right]$$
$$= \max[8.0076;\ 0] = 8.0076$$

$$P_{3,1} = \max\left[\frac{p \cdot P_{4,2} + q \cdot P_{4,1}}{e^{r\Delta t}};\ \max[0;\ K - S_{3,1}]\right]$$
$$= \max[24.9513;\ 15.9428] = 24.9513$$

$$P_{3,0} = \max\left[\frac{p.P_{4,1} + q \cdot P_{4,0}}{e^{r\Delta t}};\ \max[0;\ K - S_{3,0}]\right]$$
$$= \max[43.3236;\ 34.3152] = 43.3236$$

$$P_{2,2} = \max\left[\frac{p \cdot P_{3,3} + q \cdot P_{3,2}}{e^{r\Delta t}};\ \max[0;\ K - S_{2,2}]\right]$$
$$= \max[4.2441;\ 0] = 4.2441$$

$$P_{2,1} = \max\left[\frac{p \cdot P_{3,2} + q \cdot P_{3,1}}{e^{r\Delta t}};\ \ \max[0; K - S_{2,1}]\right]$$

$$= \max[16.2201;\ \ 5.1203] = 16.2201$$

$$P_{2,0} = \max\left[\frac{p \cdot P_{3,1} + q \cdot P_{3,0}}{e^{r\Delta t}};\ \ \max[0;\ \ K - S_{2,0}]\right]$$

$$= \max[33.7211;\ \ 25.7414] = 33.7211$$

$$P_{1,1} = \max\left[\frac{p \cdot P_{2,2} + q \cdot P_{2,1}}{e^{r\Delta t}};\ \ \max[0;\ \ K - S_{1,1}]\right]$$

$$= \max[10.0605;\ \ 0] = 10.0605$$

$$P_{1,0} = \max\left[\frac{p \cdot P_{2,1} + q \cdot P_{2,0}}{e^{r\Delta t}};\ \ \max[0;\ \ K - S_{1,0}]\right]$$

$$= \max[24.6367;\ \ 16.1075] = 24.6367$$

$$P_{0,0} = \max\left[\frac{p \cdot P_{1,1} + q \cdot P_{1,0}}{e^{r\Delta t}};\ \ \max[0;\ \ K - S_{0,0}]\right]$$

$$= \max[17.0991;\ \ 5.2836] = 17.0991$$

Example 2. Consider the valuation of European and American options in the following context:

Underlying asset, $S = 100$, strike price $K = 100$, interest rate $= 0.1$, volatility $= 0.4$, $T = 5$ months, $N = 5$, dividend $= 10$, and dividend date $= 105$. In this case, we have:

$$p = 0.5073, \quad d = 0.8909, \quad \text{and} \quad u = 1.1224.$$

Dynamics of the underlying asset for five periods					
					178.1312
				158.7055	
			151.3606		141.3982
		135.8581		125.9784	
	122.0378		122.2025		112.2401
110		109.8797		100	
	98.8925		99.0571		89.0947
		89.2584		79.3787	
			80.6846		70.7222
				63.0098	
					56.1384

The valuation of European put options

					0
				0	
			0		0
		1.2720		0	
	4.2282		2.6033		0
8.6380		7.3442		5.3282	
	13.3256		12.3506		10.9053
		19.7110		19.7914	
			27.6249		29.2778
				36.1603	
					43.8616

The valuation of American put options

					0
				0	
			0		0
		1.2720		0	
	4.3250		2.6033		0
8.8801		7.5423		5.3282	
	13.7214		12.7561		10.9053
		20.3171		20.6213	
			28.4479		29.2778
				36.9902	
					43.8616

The valuation of European call options

					78.1312
				59.5354	
			43.0511		41.3982
		29.7194		26.8082	
	19.7467		16.4963		12.2401
12.7191		9.8132		6.1581	
	5.6987		3.0982		0
		1.5587		0	
			0		0
				0	
					0

The valuation of American call options

					78.1312
				59.5354	
			51.3606		41.3982
		36.6880		26.8082	
	24.6554		22.2025		12.2401
15.8944		12.6840		6.1581	
	7.1430		3.0982		0
		1.5587		0	
			0		0
				0	
					0

14.2.5. *Simulations in the presence of two dividend dates*

We consider the valuation of a stock option using the binomial model. The option is priced as of 15/06/2002. The maturity date is 15/06/2004. The following strike prices are used: 22, 23, 24, 25, 26, 27, 28, 29, 30. The following dates and amounts of dividends are available:

For 2003, 0.35 and for 2004, 0.35. We used a historical simulation to estimate the volatility parameter. Dividends are distributed at the end of May each year. The interest rate is 5%. The annualized volatility is between 45% and 50%. In this analysis, a dividend rate is used by dividing the dividend amount by the initial underlying asset price. The annualized volatility is 45% (Tables 14.1–14.4).

We consider the same valuation problem, except that the volatility used is 50%.

14.2.6. *Simulations for different periods and several dividends: The general case*

Tables 14.5 and 14.6 present the simulation results of the model proposed for American long-term call and put values by taking into account the magnitude of cash distributions and their timing. Simulations are run as of 11/05/2002 for a stock price of 423. Each share entitles the holder on 05/06/2002, a net dividend of 12.

The following dates and amounts for the cash distributions are retained: 24/05/2002: −3.08, 24/06/2002: −3.08, 24/07/2002: −2.99, 24/08/2002: −2.98, 24/09/2002: −2.99, 24/10/2002: −2.82, 24/11/2002: −2.82, 24/12/2002: −2.82.

These amounts correspond to interest rates of 8.75% for options maturing in June, 8.5% for options maturing in September, and 8% for the maturity date of December. For example, when the stock price equals 423, the interest rate is 8.75%, the cash amount is 3.08.

Cox *et al.* (1979) indicates the prices obtained from a modified version of the CRR model. The following dates and amounts for the cash distributions are retained: 24/05/2002: −3.08, 24/06/2002:

Table 14.1. Simulations in the presence of two dividends using the binomial model.

Call price	$S = 18$	$S = 19$	$S = 20$	$S = 21$
$K = 22$	3.49	4.09	4.71	5.33
$K = 23$	3.25	3.76	4.38	5.00
$K = 24$	3.03	3.50	4.05	4.67
$K = 25$	2.82	3.29	3.76	4.33
$K = 26$	2.60	3.07	3.55	4.03
$K = 27$	2.38	2.86	3.33	3.80
$K = 28$	2.19	2.64	3.11	3.58
$K = 29$	2.06	2.42	2.89	3.37
$K = 30$	1.93	2.26	2.68	3.15

Table 14.2. Simulations in the presence of two dividends using the binomial model.

Call price	$S = 22$	$S = 25$	S = 28	$S = 30$
$K = 22$	5.95	8.13	10.38	12.05
$K = 23$	5.61	7.67	9.90	11.46
$K = 24$	5.28	7.21	9.44	10.94
$K = 25$	4.95	6.80	8.98	10.47
$K = 26$	4.62	6.47	8.52	10.01
$K = 27$	4.29	6.14	8.06	9.55
$K = 28$	4.06	5.81	7.66	9.09
$K = 29$	3.84	5.47	7.33	8.63
$K = 30$	3.62	5.14	6.99	8.23

Table 14.3. Simulations in the presence of two dividends using the binomial model.

Call price	$S = 18$	$S = 19$	$S = 20$	$S = 21$
$K = 22$	3.99	4.61	5.23	5.86
$K = 23$	3.71	4.30	4.92	5.54
$K = 24$	3.51	4.00	4.60	5.23
$K = 25$	3.30	3.78	4.29	4.92
$K = 26$	3.10	3.58	4.06	4.60
$K = 27$	2.90	3.38	3.86	4.34
$K = 28$	2.70	3.18	3.66	4.14
$K = 29$	2.49	2.97	3.45	3.93
$K = 30$	2.36	2.77	3.25	3.73

Table 14.4. Simulations in the presence of two dividends using the binomial model.

	$S = 22$	$S = 25$	$S = 28$	$S = 30$
$K = 22$	6.48	8.68	10.94	12.56
$K = 23$	6.17	8.24	10.50	12.01
$K = 24$	5.85	7.80	10.06	11.56
$K = 25$	5.54	7.41	9.61	11.12
$K = 26$	5.23	7.10	9.17	10.68
$K = 27$	4.90	6.79	8.73	10.23
$K = 28$	4.60	6.47	8.34	9.79
$K = 29$	4.42	6.16	8.03	9.35
$K = 30$	4.21	5.84	7.72	8.96

Table 14.5. Simulations of the American long-term equity call values: $S = 423$, $K = 360$ to 460, $r = 0.08$, $D = 12$, $T = 233$ days, number of iterations: 233, and dividend date: 25 days.

	CRR	
K	$\sigma = 0.244$	$\sigma = 0.304$
360	86.11	94.01
380	70.88	80.70
400	57.22	68.58
420	45.29	57.91
440	35.14	48.50
460	26.82	40.29

Table 14.6. Simulations of the American long-term equity option values.

	CRR	
K	$\sigma = 0.244$	$\sigma = 0.304$
360	5.52	13.71
380	9.62	19.74
400	15.50	27.12
420	23.42	36.10
440	33.49	46.51
460	45.77	58.33

−3.08, 24/07/2002: −2.99, 24/08/2002: −2.98, 24/09/2002: −2.99, 24/10/2002: −2.82, 24/11/2002: −2.82, 24/12/2002: −2.82.

Table 14.5 shows the American call prices for different strike prices varying from 360 to 460. The volatility parameter takes two values 24.4% and 30.4%. Table 14.6 presents the American put prices for the same parameters as in Table 14.5. The number of iterations used for the CRR model corresponds to the number of days to maturity (233). The dividend is paid in 25 days.

Summary

Cox *et al.* (1979) proposed the first discrete-time model for the pricing of stock options. This binomial model is used for the valuation of options on different underlying assets.

References

Black F and M Scholes (1973). The pricing of options and corporate liabilities. *Journal of Political Economy*, 81, 637–654.

Boyle P (1986). Option valuation using a three jump process. *International Options Journal*, 3, 7–12.

Boyle PP (1988). A lattice framework for option pricing with two state variables. *Journal of Financial and Quantitative Analysis*, 23 (March), 1–12.

Briys E, M Bellalah, F de Varenne and H Mai (1998). *Options, Futures and Other Exotics*. John Wiley and Sons, New York.

Cox, J, S Ross and M Rubinstein (1979). Option pricing: A simplified approach. *Journal of Financial Economics*, 7, 229–263.

Hull J and A White (1993). Efficient procedures for valuing European and American path dependent options. *Journal of Derivatives*, 1 (Fall), 21–31.

Hull J and A White (1988). An analysis of the bias in option pricing caused by a stochastic volatility. *Advances in Futures and Options Research*, 3, 29–61.

Hull J (2000). *Options, Futures, and Other Derivative Securities*. Prentice Hall International Editions, New Jersey.

Jarrow RA and A Rudd (1983). *Option Pricing*. Homewood, IL: Irwin.

Merton R (1973). Theory of rational option pricing. *Bell Journal of Economics and Management Science*, 4, 141–183.

Rubinstein M (1994). Implied binomial trees. *Journal of Finance*, 3, 771–818.

Whaley RE (1986). Valuation of American futures options: Theory and empirical tests. *Journal of Finance*, 41 (March), 127–150.

Chapter 15

Credit Risks, Pricing Bonds, Interest Rate Instruments, and the Term Structure of Interest Rates

Chapter Outline

This chapter is organized as follows:

1. Section 15.1 is an introduction to the main concepts in discounting and factors.
2. Section 15.2 develops the main concepts for the pricing of bonds.
3. Section 15.3 presents some simple measures to calculate the yield on bonds.
4. Section 15.4 develops the main concepts in the analysis of bonds: duration and convexity.
5. Section 15.5 is an introduction to the yield curve and the theories of interest rates.
6. Section 15.6 presents a simple analysis of the yield to maturity and the theories of the term structure of interest rates.
7. Section 15.7 reviews the specific features of spot and forward interest rates.
8. Section 15.8 presents a simple analysis of mortgage-backed securities.
9. Section 15.9 is an introduction to swaps.

Introduction

The price of a bond depends on the future coupons and the notional amount. The price corresponds to the present value of all the future cash flows discounted to the present at the appropriate discount rate. The yield on a bond can be determined by calculating the interest rate that makes the present value of all future cash flows equal to the initial bond price. The management of a portfolio of bonds needs the knowledge of the main yield measures: the current yield (CY), yield to maturity (YTM), and the yield to call (YTC).

The duration of a bond is a measure of the bond price volatility. The concept of duration is introduced by Macaulay (1938) as a proxy for the length of time a bond investment is outstanding. The yield curve corresponds to the graphical relationship between the YTM of a security and the corresponding maturity date. This curve is often constructed using the maturities and the observed yield on Treasury securities.

An interest rate swap is an agreement between two counter-parties to exchange periodic interest payments. These payments are computed with reference to a pre-determined amount known as the notional principal amount. In general, one party, the fixed rate payer, agrees to pay the other party fixed-interest payments with a given frequency at some specified dates. The other party, the floating rate payer, agrees to pay some interest rate payments that vary according to a reference rate.

15.1. Time Value of Money and the Mathematics of Bonds

We use the following symbols:

I: value or sum of money at the present (a present sum);
F: value or sum of money in the future (future sum);
A: series of equal end-of-period amounts of money (a uniform series);
n: number of periods and
r: interest rate per interest period.

While I and F occur at one time, the fixed amount A occurs at each interest period for a given or a specified number of periods. A net cash flow refers to the difference between receipts (income) and cash disbursements (costs).

15.1.1. *Single payment formulas*

Simple interest is computed using the principal amount by ignoring interest accrued in previous interest periods. Simple interest is computed using the formula: Interest $= I(n)r$. Example: When $I = 100$, $r = 10\%$, and $n = 1$ year, the formula shows an interest of 10, or 100(0.1)(1).

The compound interest is used when more than one interest period is used.

When an amount I is invested at time 0, it becomes in one period (a year), F_1 or:

$$F_1 = I + rI = I(1 + r)$$

At the end of the second period, the amount accumulated corresponds to the amount accumulated after the first period plus the interest from the end of period 1 to the end of period 2, or:

$$F_2 = F_1 + F_1 r = I(1 + r) + I(1 + r)r = I(1 + 2r + r^2) = I(1 + r)^2$$

It is straight forward to generalize this formula for n periods as:

$$F_n = I(1 + r)n$$

or

$$F = I(1 + r)^n \tag{15.1}$$

The term $(1 + r)^n$ is often referred to as the single-payment compound-amount factor (SPCAF). It is denoted by $(F/I, r\%, n)$. It provides the future value F of an initial investment I, after n periods (years) for a given interest rate r. Formula (15.1) can be used to generate the present worth I of a future amount F after n years at the rate r as:

$$I = F\frac{1}{(1+r)^n} \tag{15.2}$$

The term $1/(1 + r)n$ is referred to as the single-payment present worth factor (SPPWF). It is denoted by $(I/F, r\%, n)$. When there is a single payment (or receipt), the formulas allow the derivation of future and present values.

15.1.2. *Uniform-series present worth factor (USPWF) and the capital recovery factor (CRF)*

The present worth of uniform series can be computed by assimilating each given A as a future worth F in formula (15.2). The present value is:

$$I = A\frac{1}{(1+r)} + A\frac{1}{(1+r)^2} + A\frac{1}{(1+r)^3} + \cdots + A\frac{1}{(1+r)^n}$$

or:

$$\begin{aligned} I &= A\left[\frac{1}{(1+r)} + \frac{1}{(1+r)^2} + \frac{1}{(1+r)^3} + \cdots + \frac{1}{(1+r)^n}\right] \\ &= A\left[\sum_{i=1}^{n}\frac{1}{(1+r)^i}\right] \end{aligned}$$

Multiplying both sides by $(1/(1+r))$ gives:

$$\frac{I}{(1+r)} = A\left[\frac{1}{(1+r)^2} + \frac{1}{(1+r)^3} + \frac{1}{(1+r)^4} + \cdots + \frac{1}{(1+r)^{n+1}}\right]$$

The difference between the last two equations gives:

$$I\left(\frac{1}{1+r} - 1\right) = A\left[\frac{1}{(1+r)^{n+1}} - \frac{1}{(1+r)}\right]$$

or:

$$I\frac{-r}{1+r} = A\left[\left(\frac{1}{(1+r)^n} - 1\right)\right]\left(\frac{1}{1+r}\right)$$

Dividing by $-r/(1+r)$ yields:

$$I = A\left[\frac{((1+r)^n - 1)}{r(1+r)^n}\right] = A\left[\sum_{i=1}^{n}\frac{1}{(1+r)^i}\right] \tag{15.3}$$

The term or factor:

$$\sum_{i=1}^{n}\frac{1}{(1+r)^i} = \left[\frac{(1+r)^n - 1}{r(1+r)^n}\right] = \frac{1-(1+r)^{-n}}{r}$$

is the USPWF. It is denoted by $(I/A, r\%, n)$. It allows the computation of the present worth I of an equivalent uniform annual series A that starts at the end of the first period (year 1), for n years.

Equation (15.3) can be written as:

$$A = I\left[\frac{r(1+r)^n}{((1+r)^n - 1)}\right] = I\sum_{i=1}^{n}(1+r)^i = \frac{r}{1-(1+r)^{-n}} \tag{15.4}$$

The term $\left[\frac{r(1+r)^n}{((1+r)^n-1}\right]$ corresponds to the capital-recovery factor (CRF). It is denoted by $(A/I, r\%, n)$. It provides the equivalent uniform annual worth A over n years of a given amount I at the rate r.

15.1.3. *Uniform-series compound-amount factor (USCAF) and the sinking fund factor (SFF)*

Re-call that the present worth is given by:

$$I = F\frac{1}{(1+r)^n}$$

If I is substituted in Eq. (15.4), this yields:

$$A = F\left[\frac{1}{(1+r)^n}\right]\left[\frac{r(1+r)^n}{((1+r)^n - 1)}\right]$$

or:

$$A = F\sum_{i=1}^{n}\frac{(1+r)^i}{(1+r)^n} = F\left[\frac{r}{(1+r)^n} - 1\right] \tag{15.5}$$

The discounting factor $[r/((1+r)^n - 1)]$ is the sinking fund factor (SFF). It is denoted by $(A/F, r\%, n)$. This equation allows the computation of the uniform series A that starts at the end of period 1 and continues through the period of a specified F. Equation (15.5) can also be written in the following way:

$$F = A\frac{((1+r)^n - 1)}{r} = A\frac{(1+r)^n}{\sum_{i=1}^{n}(1+r)^i} \tag{15.6}$$

The term in brackets refers to the USCAF. It is denoted by $(F/A, r\%, n)$. When this factor is multiplied by a given uniform amount A, this gives the future worth of the uniform series. The factors $(a/b, r, n)$ in formulas (15.1)–(15.6) allows one to find the value of (a) when (b) is given for a specified interest rate at a given number of periods.

Table 15.1 provides the necessary formulas.

15.1.3.1. *Applications*

Using Eq. (15.1), when $r = 6\%$, $n = 8$ years, formula (15.1) gives the factor:

$$(I/F, 6\%, 8) = 1/(1+0.06)^8 = 0.6274126$$

When $F = 1000$, the initial value I is 627.4126.

Using Eq. (15.3), when $r = 6\%(8\%, 11\%)$, $n = 11(20, 14)$ years, formula (15.3) gives the value of the uniform series A:

$$(I/A, 6\%, 11) = (1+0.06)^{11} - 1/0.06(1+0.06)^{11} = 7.886869$$

$$(I/A, 8\%, 20) = (1.08)^{20} - 1/0.08(1.08)^{20} = 9.81815$$

$$(I/A, 11\%, 14) = (1.11)^{14} - 1/0.11(1.11)^{14} = 6.981866.$$

Using Eqs. (15.4), (15.5), (15.6), we obtain:

$$(A/I, 6\%, 5) = 0.06(1.06)^5/(1.06)^5 - 1 = 0.2373966$$

$$(A/F, 6\%, 5) = 0.06/(1.06)^5 - 1 = 0.1773966$$

$$(F/A, 6\%, 5) = (1.06)^5 - 1/0.06 = 5.637087.$$

Table 15.1. Computations with reference to standard notations.

To Find (*a*) for a Given (*b*)	Appropriate Factor	Equation	Formula (15.1)–(15.6)
I, F	Simple discounting $\left[\frac{1}{(1+r)^n}\right]$	$(I/F, r, n)$: SPPWF	Formula (15.1): $I = F\left[\frac{1}{(1+r)^n}\right]$
F, I	Simple capitalization $(1+r)^n$	$(F/I, r, n)$: SPCAF	Formula (15.2): $F = I(1+r)^n$
I, A	Factor providing I as a function of an equivalent annuity. It is denoted sometimes by $I = A\sum_{i=1}^{n}\frac{1}{(1+r)^i}$	$(I/A, r, n)$: USPWF	Formula (15.3): $I = A\left[\frac{((1+r)^n-1)}{r(1+r)^n}\right]$ $= A\left[\frac{1-(1+r)^{-n}}{r}\right]$
A, I	Factor of an annuity equivalent to I $\sum_{i=1}^{n}(1+r)^i$	$(A/I, r, n)$: CRF	Formula (15.4): $A = I\left[\frac{r(1+r)^n}{(1+r)^n-1)}\right]$ $= J\left[\frac{r}{1-(1+r)^{-n}}\right]$
A, F	SFF $\sum_{i=1}^{n}\frac{(1+r)^i}{(1+r)^n}$	$(A/F, r, n)$: SFF	Formula (15.5): $A = F\left[\frac{r}{((1+r)^n-1)}\right]$
F, A	Factor providing the future value of a constant annuity $\frac{(1+r)^n}{\sum_{i=1}^{n}(1+r)^i}$	$(F/A, r, n)$: USCAF	Formula (15.6): $F = A\left[\frac{((1+r)^n-1)}{r}\right]$

15.1.4. *Nominal interest rates and continuous compounding*

A nominal interest rate is the usual interest rate which accounts for the effects of inflation. In fact, the real rate plus inflation define the nominal interest rate. When an individual deposits an amount of 1,000 in a bank account, for an interest rate of 12% per year (compounded annually), the future worth is:

$$F = 1000(1.12) = 1120$$

If the bank pays an interest computed for every six months, the future value must account for the interest on the interest earned. When the annual interest rate is 12%, this means that the bank will pay 6% interest two times a year. In the presence of a 6% effective semi-annual interest rate, the future value is: $1000(1 + 0.06)^2 = 1123.6$. Hence, the effective annual interest rate is 12.36% rather than 12%. The following relationship shows the link between nominal interest rates and effective interest rates:

$$r = (1 + i_m)^m - 1$$

or:

$$r = (1 + (12\%/2))^2 - 1 = 12.36\%$$

where r is the effective interest rate per period, i is the nominal interest rate per period, and m stands for the number of compounding periods. This relation represents the effective interest rate equation. This equation can be approximated by: $r' + 1 = (1 + mi_m)$ or $r' = m(i_m)$ where r' is the effective global interest rate. When the number of compounding periods m increases, m approaches infinity, and we must use continuous compounding. Re-call the definition of the natural logarithm base e:

$$\lim_{h\to\infty} (1 + 1/h)^h = e$$

When $i_m = (i/m) = (1/h)$, $(m = hi)$ in Eq. (15.1), we have:

$$\lim_{m\to\infty} r = \lim_{m\to\infty} (1 + i/m)^m - 1 = \lim_{m\to\infty} [(1 + 1/h)^h]^i - 1$$

We have: $r = e^i - 1$.

Example. If $i = 20\%$ (annual), the effective continuous rate is: $r = e^{0.2} - 1 = 22.1408\%$.

For more details, see Blanck and Tarquin (1989) and Bellalah (1991, 1998a, 1998b).

15.2. Pricing Bonds

15.2.1. *A coupon-paying bond*

The price of a bond depends on the future coupons and the notional amount.

The price of a bond is given by the present value of all the future cash flows discounted to the present as follows:

$$B = \sum_{t=1}^{n} \frac{c}{(1+r)^t} + \frac{M}{(1+r)^n}$$

where:

B: bond price at time 0;
c: coupon payments;
r: periodic interest rate;
M: par or maturity value of the bond and
n: number of periods.

The coupon corresponds to the interest rate times, the nominal value of the bond. In several countries, semi-annual coupons are paid every six months. In other countries, coupons are paid annually. For semi-annual coupon payments, the periodic interest rate used in the discounting procedure must be the required yield divided by two. Using standard formulas for the annuity, it is possible to write the bond price in the following form:

$$B = c\left(\frac{\left\{1 - \left[\frac{1}{(1+r)^n}\right]\right\}}{r}\right) + \frac{M}{(1+r)^n}$$

When calculating the time value of money, the following equality is often used to facilitate the computations:

$$\sum_{t=1}^{n} \frac{1}{(1+r)^t} = \frac{\left\{1 - \left[\frac{1}{(1+r)^n}\right]\right\}}{r}$$

The interest rate used in the discounting procedure is referred to as the required yield. The following example illustrates the use of the formula in the computation of the bond price.

Example. Consider the pricing of a bond in the following context.

Time to maturity = 10 years, coupon rate = 10%, maturity value of the bond = 1000, and periodicity of coupons = 20. The annual coupon is 100 or 10% (1000). The semi-annual coupon is 50 or (100/2). Since there are 20 coupons and M is 1000, we need the required yield to compute the bond price. If the yield on a comparable bond (with the same characteristics and risk) is 11%, then the required yield for six months is 5.5% or (11%/2). Using this discount rate, the present value of the coupons is 597,519 or:

$$c(\{1 - [1/(1 + r)^n]\}/r) = 50(\{1 - [1/(1 + 0.055)^{20}]\}/0.055)$$

The present value of the nominal amount is 342.298 or $1000/(1.055)^{20}$. Hence, the bond price is 940.247 or (597.519 + 342.298).

15.2.2. *Zero-coupon bonds*

A zero-coupon bond pays no periodic coupons. However, the investor gains interest from the difference between the purchase price and the maturity value. Using zero coupons, the bond pricing formula becomes:

$$B = \frac{M}{(1 + r)^n}$$

It shows that the zero-coupon bond price is given by the discounting of its final value to the present.

15.3. Computation of the Yield or the Internal Rate of Return

15.3.1. *How to measure the yield*

The yield on an investment can be computed by determining the interest rate that makes the present value of all future cash flows equal to the initial price. It is calculated from the following equality:

$$B = \sum_{t=1}^{n} \frac{CF_t}{(1+y)^t}$$

where CF_t refer to the cash flows, y to the yield and t denotes the number of years from year 1 to n. The yield y is calculated in general using a trial and error procedure.

Example. Consider a financial instrument which offers the following annual payments in Table 15.2.

Suppose that the price of this instrument is 931. What is the yield or the internal rate of return on this instrument?

If we use an interest rate of 10%, we have:

$$120(3.169) + 1000(0.6209) = 1001.18 \text{ Euros}$$

If we use an interest rate of 12%, we get:

$$120(3.0373) + 1000(0.5674) = 931 \text{ Euros}$$

This computation is done with reference to the following identity:

$$P = \sum_{t=1}^{n} \frac{1}{(1+y)^t} = \frac{(1-(1+y)^{-n})}{y}$$

Hence, the internal rate of return, y is 12%. In general, people annualize interest rates multiplying by the frequency of payments per year. If, for example, the semi-annual interest rate is 4%, then the annual interest rate is 8% and vice versa. This is not always

Table 15.2. The promised annual payments for a financial instrument.

Number of Years from Now	Promised Annual Payments
1	120
2	120
3	120
4	120
5	1,000

correct because interest can also be earned when compounding the interest. To obtain the effective annual yield, which is associated with a given periodic interest rate, the following formula can be used:

$$\text{Effective annual yield} = (1 + \text{periodic interest rate})^m - 1$$

where m stands for the frequency of payments each per year.

$$\text{Periodic interest rate} = (1 + \text{effective annual yield})^{1/m} - 1$$

The management of a portfolio of bonds requires the knowledge of the main yield measures: CY, YTM, and YTC.

Very high yield bonds are regarded as junk bonds.

15.3.2. *The CY*

The CY gives an indication of the relation between the annual coupon interest and the market bond price as:

$$\text{CY} = \text{Annual coupon payments/market bond price}$$

15.3.3. *The YTM*

The YTM is calculated in the same way as the internal rate of return for an investor holding the bond until maturity.

For a semi-annual coupon paying bond, the YTM is obtained by solving the following equation:

$$B = \sum_{t=1}^{n} \frac{C}{(1+y)^t} + \frac{M}{(1+y)^n}$$

or:

$$B = C\left(\frac{\{1 - [1/(1+y)^n]\}}{y}\right) + \frac{M}{(1+y)^n}$$

where B is the bond price, C is the semi-annual coupon, y is half of the YTM, M is the maturity value of the bond and n the number of periods.

For a semi-annual coupon paying bond, it is sufficient to double the interest rate or the discount rate to get the YTM. The YTM accounts for the current coupons, their timing and the capital gain or loss from holding the bond until maturity.

15.3.4. *The YTC*

Some bonds have embedded options. These options allow the issuer to call the bond at some specified points in time. The cash flows for the calculation of the yield to call correspond to those appearing before the first call date.

Hence, the yield to call can be calculated as the interest rate that would make the present value of the cash flows, if the bond is held until the first call date equal the bond price. The following formula is used to calculate the YTC:

$$B = \sum_{t=1}^{n} \frac{C}{(1+y)^t} + \frac{CP}{(1+y)^n}$$

where

B: the bond price;
y: one-half the yield to call;
c: semiannual coupon interest;
n: the number of periods until the first call and
CP: the call price used to redeem the bond.

15.3.5. *The potential yield from holding bonds*

Investors can calculate the potential yield from holding a bond. This is done using the potential sources of dollar return which must be converted in a yield measure. An investor holding a bond portfolio can expect to receive a given return from the coupons perceived, the capital gain or loss and from the re-investment of the periodic coupons.

The coupons received by the investor can be re-invested at a given rate, giving rise to a dollar return from coupon interest and interest on interest.

This component of return can be calculated using the formula for the future value of an annuity.

The interest on interest can be an important source of potential return for an investor holding the bond.

$$\begin{aligned}&\text{Coupon interest and interest on interest}\\&\quad = \text{Coupons} + \text{interest on interest}\end{aligned}$$

or:

$$Ip = \frac{C[(1+r)^n - 1]}{r}$$

where the total coupon amount is given by the semi-annual coupon interest times the number of periods or:

$$\text{Total coupon amount} = nC$$

The formula for Ip corresponds to the future value of an annuity where C corresponds to the amount of the annuity, r is the annual interest rate divided by the number of payments per year and n corresponds to the number of periods.

It is possible to compute just the interest on interest by subtracting from the Ip formula the amount of the total coupon interest as:

$$\text{Interest on interest} = \frac{C[(1+r)^n - 1]}{r} - nC$$

This analysis assumes that re-investment of the coupons is done at the YTM.

15.4. Price Volatility Measures: Duration and Convexity

15.4.1. *Duration*

The duration of a bond is a measure of the bond price volatility.

The concept of duration is introduced as a proxy for the length of time, a bond investment is outstanding. It is given by the weighted average term-to-maturity of the cash flows of a bond. It is often computed using the first derivative of the bond price with respect to the yield y. Re-call that the bond price is given by the following relationship:

$$B = \frac{c}{(1+y)} + \frac{c}{(1+y)^2} + \cdots + \frac{c}{(1+y)^n} + \frac{M}{(1+y)^n}$$

where c and M stand respectively for the coupon amount and the principal.

To compute the duration of a bond one needs to examine the sensitivity of the bond price to the yield. This variation is given by:

$$\frac{dB}{dy} = c\left[\frac{-1}{(1+y)^2}\right] + c\left[\frac{-2}{(1+y)^3}\right] + \cdots + c\left[\frac{-n}{(1+y)^{n+1}}\right] + M\left[\frac{-n}{(1+y)^{n+1}}\right]$$

or:

$$\frac{dB}{dy} = -\frac{1}{(1+y)}\left[\frac{1c}{(1+y)} + \frac{2c}{(1+y)^2} + \cdots + \frac{nc}{(1+y)^n} + \frac{nM}{(1+y)^n}\right] \tag{15.7}$$

The term between brackets shows that each cash flow is weighted by its "maturity". If both sides of Eq. (15.7) are divided by the bond price P, we obtain the percentage price change for a small variation in y:

$$\frac{dB}{dy}\left(\frac{1}{B}\right) = -\frac{1}{(1+y)} \times \left[\frac{c}{(1+y)} + \frac{2c}{(1+y)^2} + \cdots + \frac{nc}{(1+y)^n} + \frac{nM}{(1+y)^n}\right]\left(\frac{1}{P}\right)$$

The term between brackets divided by the bond price is known as the duration of Macaulay. The amounts of the coupons can be variable with different amounts of ci. In this case, the bond duration can be written as:

$$D = 1\frac{\frac{c_1}{(1+y)^1}}{B} + 2\frac{\frac{c_2}{(1+y)^2}}{B} + 3\frac{\frac{c_3}{(1+y)^3}}{B} + \cdots + n\frac{\frac{c_n+M}{(1+y)^n}}{B}$$

Each coupon payment date (including the principal) is multiplied by the present value of the cash flow in period t. The formula for the bond duration multiplies the present value of each cash flow in period t by the period, when the cash flow is expected to be received. The resulting amount is divided by the total present value of the cash flow of the bond using the prevailing yield to maturity. The formula for the duration can be written as:

$$D_m = \frac{\frac{1c}{(1+y)^1} + \frac{2c}{(1+y)^2} + \cdots + \frac{nc}{(1+y)^n} + \frac{nM}{(1+y)^n}}{B}$$

or:

$$D_m = \frac{\sum_{t=1}^{n} \frac{tc}{(1+y)^t} + \frac{nM}{(1+y)^n}}{B}$$

When the Macaulay duration (in periods) is divided by the number of payments per year ($k = 2$ for semi-annual-pay bonds), this gives the Macaulay duration in years:

$$\text{Macaulay duration (in years)} = \text{Macaulay duration (in periods)}/k$$

15.4.2. *Duration of a bond portfolio*

A portfolio duration can be computed using the weighted average of the duration of the bonds in the portfolio as:

$$D_p = w_1 D_1 + w_2 D_2 + w_n D_n$$

or:

$$D_p = \sum_i D_i w_i$$

where:

$$w_i = \frac{Pv_i}{\sum_i Pv_i}$$

where

D_p: Macaulay duration for a portfolio of bonds;
N: number of bonds in the portfolio;
Pv_i: present value (market price) of the ith bond and
w_i: market value of bond i divided by the market value of the portfolio.

15.4.3. *Modified duration*

Substituting for Macaulay duration for a bond gives:

$$\frac{dB}{dy}\left(\frac{1}{B}\right) = -\frac{1}{(1+y)}(\text{Macaulay duration}) \qquad (15.8)$$

This relationship allows the definition of the Modified duration:

$$\text{Modified duration} = \frac{\text{Macaulay duration}}{(1+y)}$$

where y is one-half the YTM.

Replacing this expression in the previous relationship gives:

$$\frac{dB}{dy}\left(\frac{1}{B}\right) = -\text{Modified duration}$$

It is possible to show that the approximate percentage change in price is given by:

$$= -(1/(1+y)) \times \text{Macaulay duration} \times \text{Yield change}$$

$$= -\text{Modified duration} \times \text{Yield change}$$

There is a relationship between duration and the bond price volatility. In fact, using a Taylor series of the price function, it is possible to show that:

$$\text{Approximate percentage change in price}$$
$$= -(1/(1+y)) \times \text{Macaulay duration} \times \text{Yield change}$$

where y corresponds to one-half the YTM.

The modified duration is given by:

$$\text{Modified duration} = \text{Macaulay duration}/(1+y)$$

which can also be written as:

$$\text{Approximate percentage change in price}$$
$$= -\text{Modified duration} \times \text{Yield change}$$

The modified duration can be used to approximate the percentage change in the bond price per basis point change.

The dollar price change per 100 dollars of par value can be computed as:

Approximate dollar price change
= −(Modified duration) × (Initial price) × (Yield change)

The dollar duration is given by:

Dollar duration = (Modified duration) (Initial price)

So, we have:

Approximate dollar price change = −(Dollar duration) (Yield change)

15.4.4. *Price volatility measures: Convexity*

It is possible to use a Taylor series to approximate the price change of a bond for a given change in the required yield by the following relationship:

$$dB = \frac{dB}{dy}dy + 0.5\frac{d^2B}{dy^2}(dy^2) + \epsilon$$

where ϵ is an error term. When both sides of this equality are divided by the bond price, this allows to express the percentage price change as:

$$dB = \frac{dB}{dy}\left(\frac{1}{B}\right)dy + 0.5\frac{d^2B}{dy^2}(dy^2)\left(\frac{1}{B}\right) + \left(\frac{\epsilon}{B}\right)$$

The first term of this equation refers to the dollar price change based on dollar duration. The second term corresponding to the second derivative can be used as a proxy for the convexity of the price-yield relationship. The dollar convexity of the bond is given by:

$$\text{Dollar convexity} = 0.5\frac{d^2B}{dy^2}$$

The approximate change in the bond price due to convexity is:

$$dB = (\text{dollar convexity})(dy)^2$$

When the second derivative of the bond price is divided by the price, this gives a measure of the percentage change in the bond price due to convexity:

$$\text{Convexity} = \frac{d^2B}{dy^2}\left(\frac{1}{B}\right)$$

This refers also to convexity.

The percentage price change for the bond, which results from its convexity can be written as:

$$\frac{dB}{B} = (\text{convexity})(dy)^2$$

In practice, using the second derivative of the bond price with respect to y gives the following equation which is used to compute the convexity:

$$\frac{d^2B}{dy^2} = \sum_{t=1}^{n} \frac{ct(t+1)}{(1+y)^{t+2}} + \frac{n(n+1)M}{(1+y)^{n+2}}$$

For more details, see Fabozzi (1996) and Briys *et al.* (1998).

15.5. The Yield Curve and the Theories of Interest Rates

The yield curve corresponds to the graphical relationship between the YTM of a security and the corresponding maturity date. This curve is often constructed using the maturities and the observed yield on Treasury securities.

15.5.1. *The shapes of the yield curve*

Different shapes of the yield curve are observed over time.

When the yield increases with maturity, the relationship corresponds to an upward sloping or normal yield curve.

When the yield decreases with maturity, the relationship corresponds to a downward sloping or an inverted yield curve.

When the yield increases and then decreases with maturity, this pattern indicates a humped yield curve. When the yield is constant for all maturities, the yield curve is flat (see Capie, 1991).

15.5.2. *Theories of the term structure of interest rates*

15.5.2.1. *The pure expectations theory*

This theory asserts that the entire term structure is explained by the market's expectations of the future short-term rates of different maturities. Hence, a rising term structure can be explained by the fact that the market participants expect a rise in short-term rates in the future. An inverted term structure can be explained by the fact that the market participants expect a decline in short-term rates in the future. A flat term structure can be explained by the fact that the market participants expect constant and stable short-term rates in the future.

The pure expectations theory is based on the assumption that forward rates are affected systematically by the expected future short-term rates. The main drawback of the pure expectations theory is that it does not account for the risks inherent in investing in bonds. By assuming that forward rates are perfect predictors of future interest rates, then the bond future prices would be certain. It ignores the uncertainty about the bond's price at the end of the investment horizon as well as the re-investment risk.

The first interpretation of the **pure expectations theory**, according to Cox *et al.* (1985a, b), is that the expected return for any investment horizon is the same regardless of the maturity. The second interpretation given by the local expectations theory assumes that the return over very short-term intervals of time must be equal to the short-term risk-less rate of interest. The third interpretation of the pure expectations theory is that the return from a roll-over short-term strategy is equivalent to holding a zero-coupon bond with a maturity equal to that of the investment horizon. This is referred to as the return-to-maturity expectations.

15.5.2.1.1. Biased expectations theories

The liquidity theory and the **preferred habitat theory**, referred to **as biased expectations theories**, assume that other factors affect the forward rates.

The liquidity theory: According to this theory, forward interest rates account for interest rate expectations and a liquidity premium or a risk premium. Investors expect to hold bonds for longer maturity dates for higher risk premiums. Hence, the presence of a risk premium implies that the implied forward rates will not be an unbiased estimate of the expectations of future interest rates. The shape of an upward sloping of the yield curve can reflect expectations about a rise, a stable or a fall in the expected future rates, where the liquidity premium can increase fast enough to conserve an upward-sloping yield curve.

The preferred habitat theory: This theory shows that the expectations of future interest rates account for a risk premium where this premium (positive or negative) does not necessarily rise uniformly with maturity. According to this theory, for a given imbalance between the supply and demand for funds within a maturity range, investors will not be reluctant to shift their portfolios out of their preferred maturity sector. Investors require a yield premium to move out of their preferred sector. This theory can then explain different shapes of the yield curve.

Market segmentation theory: This theory supports the "preferred habitat" and explains the yield curve shape by asset and liability management constraints. This theory assumes that investors are not willing to shift from one maturity to another, to take advantages from the differences in expectations and forward rates. Hence, the yield curve is explained by the supply and demand within each maturity sector (see Carleton and Cooper, 1976).

15.6. The YTM and the Theories of the Term Structure of Interest Rates

15.6.1. *Computing the YTM*

The YTM, refers to the average annual rate of return expected from the purchase of a bond. This is a promised return rather than an actual return. The YTM can be computed using one of the following three methods: the arithmetic mean, the geometric mean, and the internal YTM.

15.6.1.1. *The arithmetic mean YTM*

This method computes the arithmetic mean of the expected future rates of return on a bond. It uses the expected rates of return over the next years. The arithmetic mean corresponds to the sum of the expected returns on the bond over its life, which is divided by the number of years until maturity. The resulting figure corresponds to the arithmetic mean YTM or the expected average annual percentage increase in the capital invested. This method assumes that the dollar investment in the bond remains constant.

15.6.1.2. *The geometric mean YTM*

This method adds 1.00 to each expected annual return on the bond. All the converted returns are multiplied and the nth root of the product is computed, where n refers to the number of years until maturity. Subtracting one from the root gives the geometric mean YTM. This method is based on the assumption that all profits are re-invested by buying more bonds. The geometric mean YTM reflects in this context, the average percentage increase in the capital over the bond's life.

15.6.1.3. *The internal YTM*

The equality between the current bond market price and the discounted value of all cash flows of the investment gives an internal YTM. This method assumes the re-investment of coupons at the internal yield without any re-investment risk.

15.6.2. *Market segmentation theory of the term structure*

The market segmentation theory assumes that the market is composed of extremely risk averse investors whose objective is portfolio "immunization". Immunization is achieved when the effective maturity of assets is perfectly matched up with the effective maturity of liabilities. In this theory, the survival of an institution is an objective function. The yield of each segment in the market corresponds to the intersection of supply and demand.

15.7. Spot Rates and Forward Interest Rates

15.7.1. *The theoretical spot rate*

The theoretical spot rate for an nth six-month period can be calculated using the following equation:

$$B_n = \frac{C}{(1+y_1)} + \frac{C}{(1+y_2)^2} + \frac{C}{(1+y_3)^3} + \cdots + \frac{(C+100)}{(1+y_n)^n}$$

where

B_n: price of a coupon Treasury security with n periods to maturity (per 100 dollar of value);
C: semi-annual coupon for the coupon Treasury security with n periods to maturity (per 100 dollar of par value) and
y_t: $t = 1, \ldots, (n-1)$: known theoretical spot rates.

This equation can also be written as:

$$y_n = \left[\frac{(C+100)}{B_n - \left[C - \sum_{t=1}^{n-1} \frac{1}{(1+y_t)^t}\right]}\right]^{\frac{1}{n}} - 1$$

When y_n is multiplied by two, this gives the theoretical spot rate on a bond-equivalent basis.

15.7.2. *Forward rates*

Consider the two following investment opportunities:

Strategy 1: Invest in a one-year Treasury bill,
Strategy 2: Invest in a six-month Treasury bill and buy another six-month Treasury bill at the maturity date of the first Treasury bill.

These two strategies are equivalent if they give the same result over the one-year investment horizon. The knowledge of the spot rates on a six-month and a one-year Treasury bills allows the computation of the yield on a six-month Treasury bill, six months from now or the forward rate.

An investor buying a one-year Treasury bill maturing in a year with a maturity value of 100, pays a price B:

$$B = 100/(1+Y_2)2$$

where Y_2 represents one-half the bond-equivalent yield of the one-year spot rate.

If the investor buys the six-month Treasury bill, the value of his investment in six months would be:

$$B(1+Y_1)$$

where Y_1 represents one-half the bond-equivalent yield of the six-month spot rate.

In the same context, if we denote by f_2 one-half the forward rate on a six month Treasury bill available six months from now, then the P dollars in one year becomes:

$$B(1+Y_1)(1+f_2)$$

The result of investing in an asset that gives 100 in one year can be written as:

$$B(1+Y_1)(1+f_2) = 100$$

or:

$$B = 100/[(1+Y_1)(1+f_2)]$$

The two strategies are equivalent for the investor if they lead to the same result or:

$$100/(1+Y_2)^2 = 100/[(1+Y_1)(1+f_2)]$$

Hence, the value of the implied forward rate is given by:

$$f_2 = [(1+Y_2)^2/(1+Y_1)] - 1$$

Example. When the six-month and the one-year Treasury bill rates are respectively equal to 8.5% and 8.9%, then $Y_1 = 4.25\%$, $Y_2 = 4.45\%$, and the implied forward rate is 4.65%, or:

$$f_2 = [(1.0445)2/1.0425] - 1 = 4.65\%$$

Hence, the forward rate for a six-month instrument on a bond-equivalent basis is 9.3% or 2(4.65%). The formula can be generalized to compute implicit forward rates from theoretical spot rates as follows:

$$f_{nt} = \left[\frac{(1+y_{n+t})^{n+t}}{(1+y^n)n}\right]^{1/t} - 1$$

where

f_{nt}: forward rate n periods from now for t periods,
y_n: semi-annual spot rate.

The implied forward rate on a bond-equivalent basis is obtained by multiplying f_{nt} by two.

15.8. Mortgage-Backed Securities: The Monthly Mortgage Payments for a Level-Payment Fixed-Rate Mortgage

When determining the monthly mortgage payments, the formula for the present value of an ordinary annuity is used. The mortgage payment for each month is defined with respect to a level-payment fixed-rate mortgage. The monthly mortgage payment is due in the beginning of each month. It consists of two elements. The first corresponds to interest of 1/12th of the fixed annual interest rate times the outstanding mortgage balance amount at the beginning of the previous month. The second element corresponds to the re-payment of a fraction of the outstanding mortgage balance or the principal. The mortgage payment is defined in a way such that after the last fixed monthly payment, the amount of the outstanding mortgage balance is zero.

Example. Consider a mortgage loan of 150,000 Euros with maturity in 15 years (180 months), the mortgage rate is 10%. Table 15.3 shows the amortization schedule for a level-payment fixed-rate mortgage for the period of 180 months. Each monthly mortgage payment comprises interest and re-payment of principal.

The first month, the mortgage balance corresponds to the interest rate for the month on the 150,000 Euros borrowed or (10%/12) 150,000 = 1,250 Euros. The monthly mortgage payment that represents re-payment of the principal corresponds to the difference between the monthly mortgage payment and the interest rate. The last monthly mortgage payment is sufficient to pay off the remaining mortgage balance.

Table 15.3. Amortization schedule for a level-payment fixed-rate mortgage using the following parameters: term of loan $n = 180$, mortgage loan = 150,000 Euros, and mortgage rate = 0.1/12.

Month	Beginning Mortgage Balance	Monthly Mortgage Payment	Interest for Month	Principal Re-payment	Ending Mortgage Balance (2)−(5)
1	150000	1611.907677	1250	361.9076766	149638.0923
2	149638.0923	1611.907677	1246.984103	364.9235739	149273.1687
3	149273.1687	1611.907677	1243.943073	367.9646036	148905.2041
4	148905.2041	1611.907677	1240.876701	371.0309753	148534.1732
5	148534.1732	1611.907677	1237.784776	374.1229001	148160.0503
6	148160.0503	1611.907677	1234.667086	377.240591	147782.8097
7	147782.8097	1611.907677	1231.523414	380.3842626	147402.4254
8	147402.4254	1611.907677	1228.353545	383.5541314	147018.8713
9	147018.8713	1611.907677	1225.157261	386.7504158	146632.1209
10	146632.1209	1611.907677	1221.934341	389.973336	146242.1475
11	146242.1475	1611.907677	1218.684563	393.2231138	145848.9244
12	145848.9244	1611.907677	1215.407703	396.4999731	145452.4244
13	145452.4244	1611.907677	1212.103537	399.8041395	145052.6203
14	145052.6203	1611.907677	1208.771836	403.1358407	144649.4845
15	144649.4845	1611.907677	1205.412371	406.495306	144242.9892
16	144242.9892	1611.907677	1202.02491	409.8827669	143833.1064
17	143833.1064	1611.907677	1198.60922	413.2984566	143419.8079
18	143419.8079	1611.907677	1195.165066	416.7426104	143003.0653
...			...		
74	113834.9611	1611.907677	948.624676	663.2830006	113171.6781
75	113171.6781	1611.907677	943.0973176	668.8103589	112502.8678
76	112502.8678	1611.907677	937.523898	674.3837786	111828.484
77	111828.484	1611.907677	931.9040332	680.0036434	111148.4803
78	111148.4803	1611.907677	926.2373361	685.6703404	110462.81
86	105500.4334	1611.907677	879.1702784	732.7373982	104767.696
87	104767.696	1611.907677	873.0641334	738.8435431	104028.8525
88	104028.8525	1611.907677	866.9071039	745.0005727	103283.8519
89	103283.8519	1611.907677	860.6987658	751.2089108	102532.643
90	102532.643	1611.907677	854.4386915	757.468985	101775.174
...			...		
175	9395.51514	1611.907677	78.2959595	1533.611717	7861.903423
176	7861.903423	1611.907677	65.51586186	1546.391815	6315.511609
177	6315.511609	1611.907677	52.6292634	1559.278413	4756.233195
178	4756.233195	1611.907677	39.63527663	1572.2724	3183.960795
179	3183.960795	1611.907677	26.53300663	1585.37467	1598.586126
180	1598.586126	1611.907677	13.32155105	1598.586126	0

The following formula is used to compute the monthly mortgage payment for a level-payment fixed-rate mortgage.

$$PV = A\left\{\frac{\left[1-\left(\frac{1}{(1+r)^n}\right)\right]}{r}\right\}$$

where:

PV: present value of an annuity or the original mortgage balance;
A: amount of the annuity (monthly mortgage payment);
n: number of periods or months and
r: periodic interest rate (annual interest rate/12).

The formula corresponds to the present value of an ordinary annuity formula.

The equality can also be written as:

$$\text{Monthly payment} = \frac{\text{Amount due to be paid}}{\text{Present value of an annuity of 1 Euro/month}}$$

Using the above PV formula and the data in the example, we have $n = 180$, $VA = 150{,}000$ Euros, $r = 0.1/12$, the monthly mortgage payment is 1611.907677:

$$\left[\frac{150{,}000}{\frac{1-\frac{1}{(1.00833)^{180}}}{0.008333}}\right] = 1611.907677.$$

It is assumed in the above analysis of fixed-rate mortgages, that the level homeowner would not pay any fraction of the mortgage balance before the fixed date. We refer to the payments made in excess of the fixed principal payments as pre-payments. The amount and the timing of the pre-payment are uncertain and define the pre-payment risk.

15.9. Interest Rate Swaps

15.9.1. *The pricing of interest rate swaps*

Example. Consider the following interest rate swap between two firms A and B in the presence of a commercial bank (Fig. 15.1).

	9.6%		9.5%	
Firm A	$\rightleftharpoons$	Commercial bank	$\rightleftharpoons$	Firm B
	LIBOR		LIBOR	

Figure 15.1. An interest rate swap.

The bank pays the six-month LIBOR rate to the firm A and receives a fixed rate of 9.6%. The bank pays to firm B a fixed rate of 9.5% and receives the LIBOR. A notional amount No is used. The bank benefits from a commission of 0.10% per year on the notional amount. If the LIBOR rate is 11%, firm B pays the bank: $1/2(0.11 - 0.095) = 0.0075$ No and the bank pays A: $1/2(0.11 - 0.096) = 0.0070$ No.

The bank gains 0.005 No for six months. This swap can be assimilated to two default bonds since the bank borrows from A at the six-month LIBOR and lends to A at a rate of 9.6%.

15.9.2. *The swap value as the difference between the prices of two bonds*

Let us denote by Sw, the value of the swap for the bank, B_1 the value of bond paying a coupon at 9.6% per year, and by B_2 the value of a bond paying the six-month LIBOR. The value of the swap for the bank is:

$$Sw = B_1 - B_2$$

The value of the bond B_1 is given by:

$$B_1 = \sum_{i=1}^{n} Ce^{-r_i t_i} + Ne^{-r_n t_n}$$

where

C: semi-annual coupon;
T_i: time until the ith coupon payment where $1 \leq i \leq n$;
r_i: risk-less rate for t_i and
N: the notional amount.

Since the value of B_2 is based on a variable interest rate, its price after each coupon date must be equal to the discounted value of the notional amount and the last coupon. Hence, the value B_2 between two payment dates is:

$$B_2 = Ne^{-r_1 t_1} + C_1 e^{-r_1 t_1}$$

where C_1 is the certain coupon at date t_1.

15.9.2.1. *The swap as a series of forward contracts*

A swap position can be seen as a package of forward or futures contracts. In fact, firm A has agreed to pay 9.6% and receive six-month LIBOR. Assuming a 100 million dollars NO, A has agreed to buy the six-month LIBOR for 48 million dollars. This represents a six-month forward contract, where A agrees to pay 48 million in exchange for delivery of six-month LIBOR. An interest rate swap can be assimilated to a portfolio of forward contracts. In fact, firm A receives each six month an amount equal to 0.5 No (LIBOR−0.096) where the LIBOR rate corresponds to the previous period. This is a forward contract on the six-month LIBOR rate.

15.9.3. *The valuation of currency swaps*

Example 1. Consider a firm A borrowing 600,000 units of currency A at a fixed rate of 8% for five years. The firm must convert this in a currency B.

A firm B enters into a five-year swap with firm A at a rate of 9.5% for an amount of 2,200,000 of currency B. The principal amount is exchanged for an exchange rate equal to 3.666, (the day of the swap implementation). At each payment date, firm A pays B interest charges in the currency of B using a rate of 9.5% on the principal amount of 2,200,000 units of currency B. The firm B pays A at a rate of 8% on the principal amount of 600,000 units of currency A. Each six months, A pays 104,500 units of currency B, or (9.5%) (2,200,000)/2, and B pays 88,000 units of currency B, or (8%) (2,200,000)/2. At the swap term, A pays 2,200,000 units of currency B to B and B pays 600,000 units of currency A to A. This swap operation is equivalent to a position in a currency forward contract.

	(dollars)8%		(dollars)7.75%	
Firm A	⇌	Bank	⇌	Firm B
	11%(pound)		11%(pound)	

Figure 15.2. Foreign currency swap.

	(dollars)8%		(dollars)9%	
Firm A	⇌	Bank	⇌	Firm B
	11%(sterling)		12.25%(sterling)	

Figure 15.3. The foreign currency swap.

Example 2. Two firms A and B are engaged in a swap. The bank receives a commission of 25 basis points on the principal amount denominated in dollars as in Fig. 15.2.

Firm A pays in dollars and receives sterling. If the NA is 30 million dollars and 20 million sterling, each year, A pays 2.4 million dollars (8%) (30 million) and receives 2.2 million sterling (11%) (20 million). At the swap term, firm A pays 30 million dollars of principal and 20 million sterling. The swap allows A to convert a fixed-rate loan denominated in sterling, (11% per year) into a fixed-rate loan denominated in dollars (8% per year). Firm B converts a fixed-rate loan in dollars (7.75% per year) into a fixed-rate loan in sterling (11% per year).

If, for example, the loan for A (in sterling) is at a rate of 11% and B (in dollars) at 9%, the swap can be presented as in the Fig. 15.3.

The loan at 11% for A is converted into a dollar loan at 8% and the loan for B in dollars at 9% is converted into a loan in sterling at 12.25%. If the exchanged amounts are 20 million dollars and 30 million sterling, the bank loses 300,000 dollars per year and gains 250,000 sterling. The bank can implement a hedge against exchange rate risk by selling forward the 250,000 sterling against dollars.

15.9.4. *Computing the swap*

Since the parties in an interest swap agree to exchange future interest payments with no upfront payment, this means that the present value of the cash flows for the payments must be equal. This equivalence allows the computation of the swap rate. Hence, the swap rate corresponds to an interest rate that makes equal the present value of the payments on the fixed side, with the present value of the payments on the floating rate side.

Each cash-flow in a swap must be discounted at a unique theoretical spot rate. This spot rate is obtained from forward rates. The following example illustrates the procedure for the computation of the swap rate.

Summary

The yield on an investment can be computed by determining the interest rate that makes the present value of all future cash flows equal to the initial price. The YTM is calculated in the same way as the internal rate of return for an investor, holding the bond until maturity. In bond analysis, the coupons received by the investor can be re-invested at a specified rate giving rise to a dollar return from coupon interest and interest on interest. The concept of duration is introduced by Macaulay (Bellalah *et al.*, 1998) as a proxy for the length of time a bond investment is standing. It is given by the weighted average term-to-maturity of the cash flows of a bond. A portfolio duration can be computed using the weighted average of the duration of the bonds in the portfolio.

Several theories are developed to explain the shape of the yield curve. The main theories explaining the behavior of interest rates are the expectations theory and the market segmentation theory. The expectations theory has several variations: the pure expectations theory, the liquidity theory, and the preferred habitat theory. In these theories, the market expectations about future short-term rates can explain the forward rates in current long-term bonds.

The YTM, corresponds to the average annual rate of return expected from the purchase of a bond. The YTM refers to a promised return rather than an actual return. It can be computed using one of the following three methods: the arithmetic mean, the geometric mean and the internal YTM.

The shape of the yield curve is affected by market expectations about future interest rates. The relationship between the yield on zero-coupon Treasury securities and maturity is referred to as the

Treasury spot-rate curve where the yield on a zero-coupon bond refers to the spot rate.

Several types of bonds and mortgage securities are issued in the market place.

When determining the monthly mortgage payments, the formula for the present value of an ordinary annuity is used. The mortgage payment for each month is defined with respect to a level-payment fixed-rate mortgage.

A swap position can be seen as a package of forward or futures contracts.

Since the parties in an interest swap agree to exchange future interest payments with no upfront payment, this means that the present value of the cash flows for the payments must be equal. This equivalence allows the computation of the swap rate. Hence, the swap rate corresponds to an interest rate that makes equal, the present value of the payments on the fixed side with the present value of the payments on the floating rate side.

A swaption gives the right to assume a position in an underlying interest rate swap with a given maturity. In swaptions, the right to pay the fixed component is equivalent to the right to receive the floating component and vice versa. Swaptions are offered as receiver swaptions and payer swaptions. Receiver swaption gives the right to receive a fixed interest rate and payer swaption gives the right to pay a fixed interest rate.

Using coupon paying bonds with different maturity dates in the presence of different taxation rates (for capital gains), it is difficult to observe the term structure of interest rates. Therefore, several techniques are proposed to estimate the term structure of interest rates. Several methods are proposed in the literature for the estimation of forward interest rates. Empirical methods are continuous or discrete.

References

Bellalah M (1991). *Gestion Quantitative du Portefeuille et nouveaux marchs financiers*. Editions Nathan, Paris.

Bellalah M (1998a). *Gestion financire: diagnostic, valuation et choix des investissements*. Editions Economica, Paris.

Bellalah M (1998b). *Finance d'entreprise: stratgies et politiques financires*. Editions Economica, Paris.

Blanck LT and A Tarquin (1989). *Engineering Economy*. McGraw-Hill, New York.

Briys E, M Bellalah *et al.* (1998). *Options, Futures and Exotic Derivatives*. En collaboration avec E. Briys, *et al.*, John Wiley & Sons.

Capie F (1991). *Major inflations in History*. Edward Elgar, Vermont.

Carleton W and I Cooper (1976). Estimation and uses of the term structure of interest rates. *Journal of Finance*, 31, 1067–1083.

Cox J, I Ingersoll and S Ross (1985a). An intertemporal general equilibrium model of asset prices. *Econometrica*, 53, 363–384.

Cox J, I Ingersoll and S Ross (1985b). A theory of the term structure of interest rates. *Econometrica*, 53, 385–407.

Fabozzi F (1996). *Bond Markets, Analysis and Strategies*. Prentice Hall, New Jersey.

Chapter 16

Extensions of Simple Binomial Option Pricing Models to Interest Rates and Credit Risk

Chapter Outline

This chapter is organized as follows:

1. Section 16.1 extends the standard binomial model of Cox *et al.* (1979) for the valuation of interest-rate sensitive instruments. It develops the Rendleman and Bartter (for details, refer to Bellalah *et al.*, 1998) model for the pricing of bonds and bond options.
2. Section 16.2 studies the Ho and Lee (1986) model for the valuation of bonds and bond options.
3. Section 16.3 shows how to construct interest-rate trees and how to price bonds and options.
4. Section 16.4 presents a simple derivation of the Black–Derman–Toy model.

Introduction

This chapter extends the basic lattice approach to the pricing of interest-rate sensitive instruments and options in the presence of several distributions to the underlying asset. We are interested in the lattice approach pioneered by Cox *et al.* (CRR) (1979). These authors proposed a binomial model in a discrete-time setting for the valuation of options. Using the risk-neutral framework, their approach is based on the construction of a binomial lattice for stock prices. They applied the risk-neutral valuation argument, pioneered by Black and Scholes (1973), which simply means that one can value the option at hand as if investors were risk-neutral. With an appropriate choice of the binomial parameters, they established a convergence result of their model to that of Black and Scholes. Since then, the CRR approach was extended and extensively used for the valuation of many contingent claims and options.

Rendleman and Bartter (for details, refer to Bellalah *et al.*, 1998) applied this methodology to the pricing of options on debt instruments. They proposed a binomial approach similar to that of the CRR for the pricing of derivative assets. The bond's value at a given node can be computed using the immediate next two nodes since at a given node, the bond's value will depend on the future cash flows. The future cash flows correspond to the bond value of one year from now and the coupon payments. The binomial model is based on the recursive procedure starting from the last year and working backward through the tree till the initial time. The value at each node is given by the expected cash flows under the appropriate discount rate.

Ho and Lee (1986) proposed a model for the pricing of bonds and options. However, their model allows for the possibility of negative interest rates. Ritchken and Boenewan (1990) developed a simple approach to eliminate the possibility of observing negative interest rates. This analysis is extended by Pederson *et al.* (for details, refer to Bellalah *et al.*, 1998). Bliss and Ronn (for details, refer to Bellalah *et al.*, 1998) and Hull and White (1988) developed a trinomial model for the pricing of interest-rate sensitive instruments. An alternative to the Ho and Lee model was proposed by Black *et al.* (1990), and Hull and White (1993) among others. Black *et al.* (1990) used a binomial tree to construct a one-factor model of the short rate that fits the current volatilities of all discount bond yields as well as the current term structure of interest rates.

Rubinstein (1994) developed a new method for inferring risk-neutral probabilities or option prices from observed market prices. These probabilities were used to infer a binomial tree by implementing a simple backward recursive procedure. However, this approach is restricted to the European options, and future research must be done with regard to the pricing of the American options.

16.1. The Rendleman and Bartter Model (For Details, Refer to Bellalah *et al.*, 1998) for Interest-Rate Sensitive Instruments

The CRR (1979) approach can be applied to the valuation of interest-rate sensitive instruments. It can be presented in the form developed by Rendleman and Bartter (for details, refer to Bellalah *et al.*, 1998). This model is used for the pricing of bonds and interest-rate instruments.[1] The dynamics of the interest rate are described by a two-state process with the following parameters:

$$u = e^{\sigma\sqrt{dt}}, \quad d = 1/u, \quad q = e^{(a-\sigma\theta)\Delta t}, \quad \text{and} \quad p = (q-d)/(u-d)$$

To illustrate the Rendleman and Bartter (for details, refer to Bellalah *et al.*, 1998) model over a period of six years when the current interest rate is equal to 11%, consider the following data:

$$a = 0, \quad \sigma = 0.2, \quad \theta\sigma = -0.03, \quad \Delta t = 1, \quad n = 6.$$

Using these parameters, we have: $u = 1.2214$, $d = 0.8187$, $q = 1.03045$, and $p = 0.5257$.

Figure 16.1 describes the dynamics of interest rates in this context.

Starting from an interest rate of 11%, the next rate in an upstate 13.43 is given by 11 times u or 11(1.2214). The rate 16.41% is given by 13.43 times u, or 13.43(1.2214). In each upstate, this operation is repeated until the rate 36.52% given by 29.9(1.2214) is obtained at the end. Starting from a rate of 11%, the rate 9% is obtained from the product of 11 by d, or 11(1/1.2214). The rate 7.36 corresponds to 9 times d, or 9(1/1.2214). This operation is repeated till the end. The rate 3.31 is obtained by 4.04(1/1.2214).

---

[1] In this model, the dynamics of the short-term rate are described by:

$$dr = (a - \theta\sigma)rdt + \sigma rdz$$

where a, θ and σ are constants and dz is a Wiener process. The term $(a - \theta\sigma)$ represents the drift in the short-term rate.

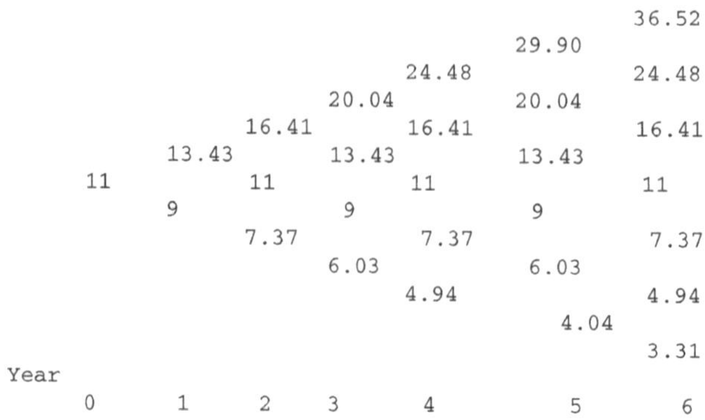

Figure 16.1. Rendleman and Bartter model for the dynamics of interest rates.

16.1.1. *Using the model for coupon-paying bonds*

Consider a 8.5%, six-year bond with a maturity value equal to 1000 paying an annual coupon of 85.

In the first step, the bond price must be computed at each node in the binomial tree.

The bond value can be calculated using the following relationship:

$$B_{ij} = [pB_{i+1,j+1} + (1-p)B_{i+1,j} + \text{coupon})]/e^{r}ij^{\Delta t}$$

with:

r_{ij}: interest rate at position j and time i;
B_{ij}: corresponding to the bond price at state j and time i; and
p: the probability corresponding to an upstate.

The bond price at any position is given by the expected values in an upstate $pB_{i+1,j+1}$ plus the expected value in a down state $(1-p)$ $B_{i+1,j}$, discounted to the present using the corresponding interest rate $e^{r}ij^{\Delta t}$. Using this recursive procedure, the bond price at time 0 is 846,869 (Fig. 16.2).

Since the bond price at maturity is 1000, the price one period before the maturity date is 804,580. It is calculated using the relation above for the bond value as follows:

$$[0.5257(1000) + (1-p)(1000) + 85)]/e^{0.299(1)} = 804.58$$

The same formula can be applied until the initial time 0.

Year 0	1	2	3	4	5	6
						1000
					804,580	
				727,350		1000
			712,44		887,930	
		734,740		850,100		1000
	781,824		856,54		948,590	
846,869		891,855		944,170		1000
	947,400		970,45		991,550	
		1018,02		1013,19		1000
			1055,8		1021,43	
				1062,34		1000
					1041,97	
						1000

Figure 16.2. Dynamics of the bond price.

16.2. Ho and Lee Model for Interest Rates and Bond Options

Ho and Lee (1986) assumed the existence of a zero-coupon bond for each maturity, n, $(n = 0, 1, 2, \ldots)$. They denoted by $P_i^{(n)}(T)$ the equilibrium price of a zero-coupon bond at time n and state i. Hence, the price $P_i^{(n)}(.)$ is a function relating each bond price with its corresponding maturity date or a discount function. The price of a bond maturing instantaneously is 1 or:

$$P_i^{(n)}(0) = 1 \quad \text{for all } i, n$$

The price of a long-lived bond is nearly zero since:

$$\lim_{T\to\infty} P_i^{(n)}(T) = 0 \quad \text{for all } i, n$$

16.2.1. *The binomial dynamics of the term structure*

At time zero, the discount function is observed and is denoted by: $P(.) = P_0^{(0)}(.) = 1$.

At time 1, the discount function is specified by two $P_1^{(1)}(0)$ and $P_0^{(1)}(0)$ for an upstate and a down state, respectively. The discount function at the second period between two dates 1 and 2 leads to two possible functions. Hence, at time 1, $P_1^{(1)}(.)$ leads to the functions

$$P_{i+1}^{(n+1)}(.) \quad : \text{up}$$

$$P_i^{(n)}(.)$$

$$P_i^{(n+1)}(.) \quad : \text{down}$$

Figure 16.3. The discount function in the Ho-Lee model.

$P_2^{(2)}(.)$ and $P_1^{(2)}(.)$ at time 2. We denote the discount function at time n by $P_i^{(n)}(.)$ after i ups and $(n-i)$ downs, at period $(n+1)$ between the dates n and $(n+1)$ (Fig. 16.3).

Given the discount function $P(T)$, the yield curve can be written as:

$$r(T) = -\ln(P(T))/T$$

where $r(T)$ is the continuous yield for a bond maturing in T.

16.2.2. *The binomial dynamics of bond prices*

When the term structure is described by a binomial model, the same dynamics applies for zero-coupon bonds $P(N)$ with a maturity date N at an initial time. When it remains at $(N-1)$ periods, the discounting functions in upstates and down states allow the computation of $P_1^{(1)}(N-1)$ and $P_0^1(N-1)$.

This model is similar to the binomial model of CRR (1979) and Rendleman and Bartter (for details, refer to Bellalah *et al.*, 1998). Ho and Lee (1986) introduced two perturbation functions $h(T)$ and $h^*(T)$. The discount function at period n and state i is $P_1^{(n)}(.T)$. The details are provided in the supplementary material of this chapter. They developed a non-arbitrage condition, that ensures that:

$$\pi h(T) + (1-\pi)h^*(T) = 1 \quad \text{for } n, i > 0$$

where π corresponds to the implied binomial probability. Hence, we have:

$$P_i^{(n)}(T) = \left[\pi P_{i+1}^{(n+1)}(T-1) + (1-\pi)P_i^{(n+1)}(T-1)\right] P_i^{(n)} \qquad (1)$$

This equation gives the bond price at a given node where the probability is given by:

$$\pi = (r-d)/(u-d)$$

with:

r: return for one period, u return in an upstate, d return in a down state. Ho and Lee (1986) showed that:

$$h(T) = \frac{1}{\pi + (1-\pi)\delta^T} \quad \text{for } T \geq 0 \quad \text{and} \quad h^*(T) = \frac{\delta^T}{\pi + (1-\pi)\delta^T}$$

where the term δ corresponds to the spread between the two perturbation functions.

The dynamics of interest rates is completely specified by π and δ.

16.2.3. *Computation of bond prices in the Ho and Lee model*

Example 1: Consider the following parameters in the Ho and Lee model: $n = 4$, $\delta = 0.994$, $\pi = 0.5$, and $t = 365$ days. The term structure is specified by the following discount function observed at initial time and applying for periods 1 to 5: $P_{00}(0) = 1$, $P_{00}(1) = 0.9826$, $P_{00}(2) = 0.9651$, $P_{00}(3) = 0.9474$, $P_{00}(4) = 0.9296$, and $P_{00}(5) = 0.9119$. Results are reproduced in Table 16.1.

Table 16.1. Discount function and bond prices in the Ho and Lee model.

Period $TP_{ij}(k)$	0	1	2	3	4	5
$P_{00}(K)$	1	0.98260	0.96510	0.94740	0.92960	0.9119
$P_{10}(K)$	1	0.97923	0.95837	0.93752	0.91687	–
$P_{11}(K)$	1	0.98514	0.96997	0.95460	0.93921	–
$P_{20}(K)$	1	0.9757	0.95164	0.9278	–	–
$P_{21}(K)$	1	0.98164	0.96316	0.94477	–	–
$P_{22}(K)$	1	0.98756	0.97482	0.96198	–	–
$P_{30}(K)$	1	0.97235	0.94520	–	–	–
$P_{31}(K)$	1	0.97822	0.95664	–	–	–
$P_{32}(K)$	1	0.98412	0.96823	–	–	–
$P_{33}(K)$	1	0.99006	0.97995	–	–	–
$P_{40}(K)$	1	0.96915	–	–	–	–
$P_{41}(K)$	1	0.97500	–	–	–	–
$P_{42}(K)$	1	0.98088	–	–	–	–
$P_{43}(K)$	1	0.98680	–	–	–	–
$P_{44}(K)$	1	0.99276	–	–	–	–

Table 16.2. Discount function and bond prices in the Ho and Lee model.

Period $P_{ij}(k)$	0	1	2	3	4	5
$P_{00}(K)$	1	0.98200	0.96100	0.94100	0.92100	0.91100
$P_{10}(K)$	1	0.97567	0.95248	0.92941	0.91653	–
$P_{11}(K)$	1	0.98155	0.96604	0.94634	0.93886	–
$P_{20}(K)$	1	0.9732	0.9468	0.9309	–	–
$P_{21}(K)$	1	0.97917	0.95832	0.94786	–	–
$P_{22}(K)$	1	0.98508	0.96992	0.96513	–	–
$P_{30}(K)$	1	0.96991	0.95069	–	–	–
$P_{31}(K)$	1	0.97576	0.96220	–	–	–
$P_{32}(K)$	1	0.98165	0.97385	–	–	–
$P_{33}(K)$	1	0.98758	0.98564	–	–	–
$P_{40}(K)$	1	0.9772	–	–	–	–
$P_{41}(K)$	1	0.98313	–	–	–	–
$P_{42}(K)$	1	0.98907	–	–	–	–
$P_{43}(K)$	1	0.99504	–	–	–	–
$P_{44}(K)$	1	1	–	–	–	–

Example 2: Consider the following parameters to compute the discount functions in the Ho and Lee model: $n = 4$, $\delta = 0.994$, $\pi = 0.5$, and $t = 365$ days. The present term structure is specified by the following discount function:

$P_{00}(0) = 1$, $P_{00}(1) = 0.982$, $P_{00}(2) = 0.961$, $P_{00}(3) = 0.941$, $P_{00}(4) = 0.921$, and $P_{00}(5) = 0.911$. Results are reproduced in Table 16.2.

16.2.4. *Option pricing in the Ho and Lee model*

Consider the pricing of an option on an interest-rate instrument, with a maturity T and a final payoff $X(n, i)$ such that: $C(T, i) = X(n, i)$ $0 \leq i \leq T$.

The underlying asset may be a bond, an interest rate, or a futures contract. The option price at moment n and position i can be located between a lower value L and an upper bound U. The possible prices of the option at instant n and position i satisfy the following relationship: $L(n, i) \leq C(n, i) \leq U(n, i)$.

The option holder receives at instant n and state i, the payoff $X(n, i)$ for i in the interval $1 \leq n < T$. Ho and Lee (1986) showed that a hedged portfolio comprising options and zero-coupon bonds allowed the elimination of profitable arbitrage opportunities and leads to the following equation:

$$C(n,i) = [\pi\{C(n+1,i+1) + X(n+1,i+1)\} + (1-\pi)\{C(n+1,i) + X(n+1,i)\}]P_i^{(n)}(1)$$

where $P_i^{(n)}(1)$ is the price of a zero-coupon bond at the node (n,i) and π corresponds to the implied binomial probability. The option price must satisfy the condition: $C(T-1,i) = \max[L(T-1,i), \min(C^*(T-1,i), U(T-1,i)]$.

The application of this model to the pricing of any type of interest-contingent claim requires the estimation of the probability π and the spread δ between the two perturbations functions.

First, the discount function at the time of pricing must be estimated. Then, the parameters π and δ are estimated using a non-linear procedure like that in Ho and Lee (1986) or Whaley (1986).

The estimation approach uses observed contingent claim prices and a pricing model in order to imply the parameters in the same way as we calculate an implied volatility for stock options.

Example 3: Consider the pricing of a one-year put option on a Treasury bill. The option's strike price is 980. The three-month T-bill has a face value of 1000 euros. The term structure is defined by the following parameters: $n = 4$, $\delta = 0.99$, $\pi = 0.5$, and $\Delta t = 3$ months. The discount function is: $P_{00}(0) = 1$, $P_{00}(1) = 0.992$, $P_{00}(2) = 0.975$, $P_{00}(3) = 0.957$, $P_{00}(4) = 0.939$, and $P_{00}(5) = 0.921$, where $P_{00}(1)$ is the price of a default-free bond paying 1 in 3 months. Figure 16.4 shows the dynamics of the Treasury bond.

At maturity, the option price is calculated using the following condition:

$$P = \max[980 - 1000P4j(1),\ \ 0] \quad \text{for } j = 0,1,2,3,4.$$

Using the recursive procedure, the put option price in period 3, position 1 is 4.477, or $(0.5(0) + 0.5(9.173))0.976 = 4.477$.

At period 2, the put price at the pair (2,0) is:

$$(0.5(4.477) + 0.5(13.556))0.9716 = 8.761.$$

As in Fig. 16.5, the option price at initial time is 3.196.

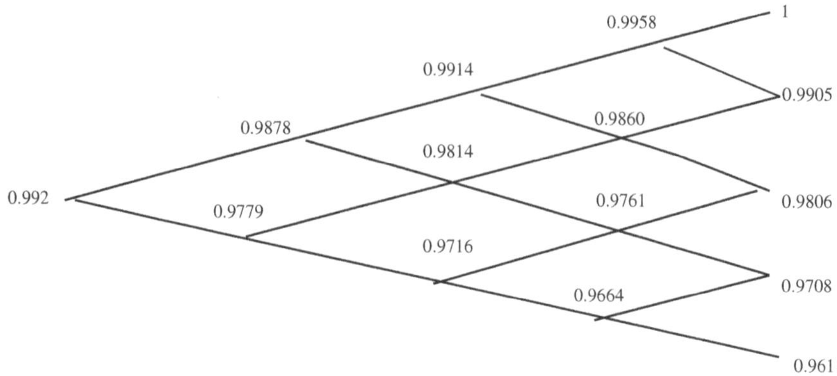

Figure 16.4. Dynamics of the Treasury bond.

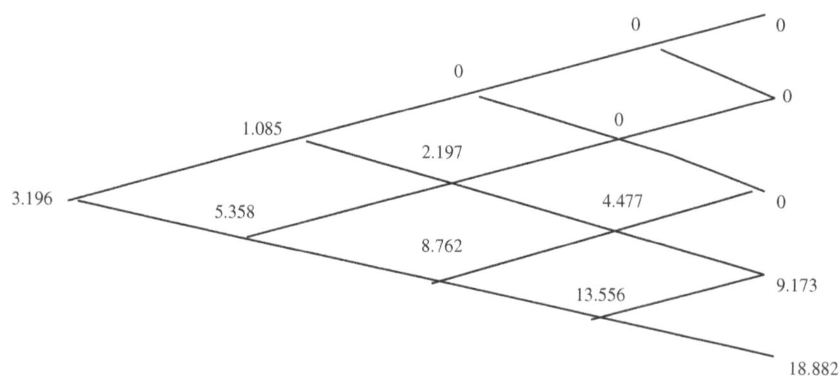

Figure 16.5. Dynamics of the option price for the following parameters $n = 4$, $\delta = 0.99$, $\pi = 0.5$, and $K = 980$.

Ritchken and Boenawen (1990) showed that the Ho and Lee model does not completely prevent the possibility of negative interest rates. These negative rates disappear when the following constraint is used: $P_n^{(n)}(1) < 1$.

To illustrate this point, consider the following parameters: $\delta = 0.9$, $\pi = 0.5$, and $n = 4$. The observed initial term structure of interest rates for the following five periods is specified by:

$r_0(1) = 9.531\%$, $r_0(2) = 8.6178\%$, $r_0(3) = 7.696\%$, $r_0(4) = 7.2321\%$, $r_0(5) = 7.2321\%$, which gives: $p(1) = e^{-r_0(1).1}$, $p(2) = e^{-r_0(2).2}$, $p(3) = e^{-r_0(3).3}$, $p(4) = e^{-r_0(4).4}$, and $p(5) = e^{-r_0(5).5}$

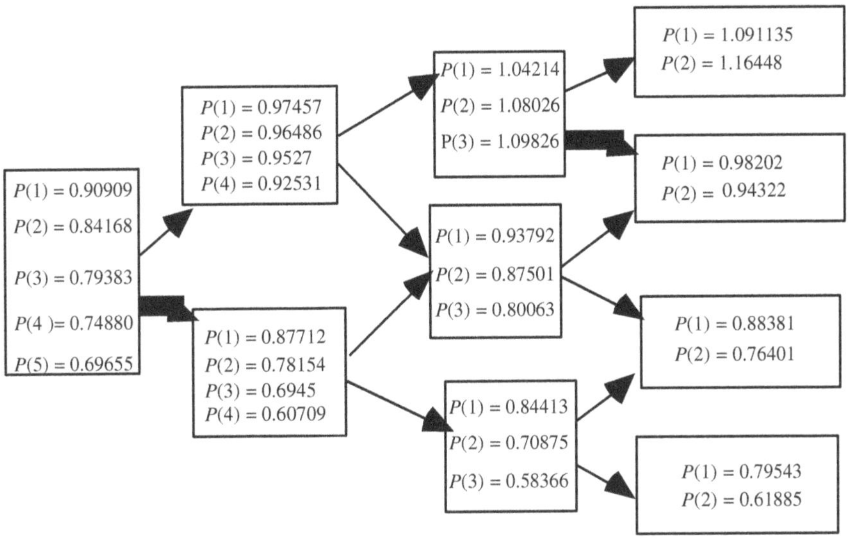

Figure 16.6. Possibility of negative interest rates in the Ho and Lee model.

Figure 16.6 reveals the possibility of negative interest rates in the Ho and Lee model.

16.2.5. *Deficiency in the Ho and Lee model*

Ho and Lee model presents a deficiency. In fact, the constraints imposed on movements of the entire discount function are not sufficient to eliminate negative interest rates. This deficiency has been recognized by Heath *et al.* (1987), and Ritchken and Boenawen (1990) among others. These authors generalized the Ho and Lee model and provided the necessary adjustments in order to obtain an economically meaningful model. Ritchken and Boenawen (1990) showed that the restrictions imposed by Ho and Lee imply that bonds are priced by a model characterized by a "risk neutral" probability parameter π and an "interest-rate spread", δ. However, the evolution of the discount function, namely the default-free zero-coupon bond prices, may not be bounded in the interval. To show this, they developed an example where $\pi = 0.4$, and $\delta = 0.8$. They generated prices of pure discount bonds at all the vertices and found that some prices exceeded one. This indicates the presence of negative interest rates in the lattice. In fact, if one modifies their δ from 0.8 to 0.9 and generates bond prices, it is clear that some bond prices exceed one. To avoid negative interest rates, the constraint $P_n^n(1) < 1$, must be added for each time period in the lattice.

16.3. Binomial Interest-Rate Trees and the Log-Normal Random Walk

Consider a binomial interest-rate tree where the interest rate moves up (u) or down (d). The initial interest rate r_0 corresponds to the current one-year interest rate when the length of each period is one year. It also corresponds to the one-year forward rate.

The initial rate or the one-year forward rate can take on two possible values in the next period with the same probability of occurring. Hence, one rate results from a rise in rates and the other results from a fall in rates. Assume that the dynamics of interest rates are specified by a log-normal random walk process with a given volatility (Fig. 16.7). For the sake of clarity, let us denote respectively by:

- σ: assumed volatility for the one-year forward rates;
- $r_{1,u}$: one-year forward rate, one year from now if rates rise and
- $r_{1,d}$: one-year forward rate, one year from now if rates fall.

Hence, in the first year, there are two possible rates. We specify the following relationship between rising and falling rates as follows:

$$r_{1,u} = r_{1,d}e^{2\sigma}.$$

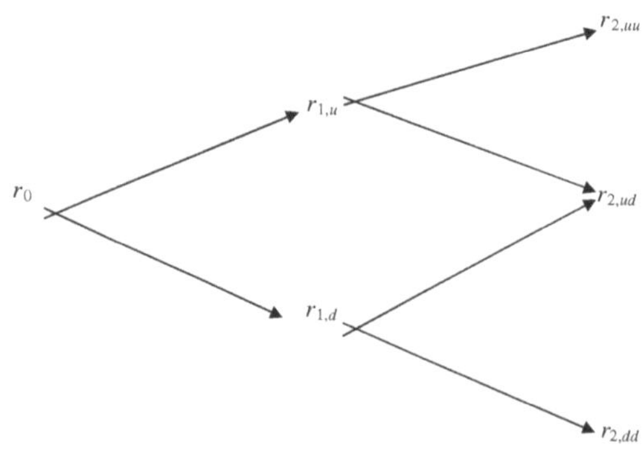

Figure 16.7. Dynamics of interest rates.

In the second year, there are three possible values for the one-year forward rates:

$$r_{2,uu}, r_{2,ud}, r_{2,dd}$$

where:

$r_{2,uu}$: one-year forward rate in the second year if the interest rate rises in the first and the second year;

$r_{2,ud}$: one-year forward rate in the second year if the interest rate rises in the first year and falls in the second year or vice versa and

$r_{2,dd}$: one-year forward rate in the second year if the interest rate falls in the first and the second year.

The same relationship between rising and falling interest rates is maintained. Hence, we have:

$$r_{2,ud} = r_{2,dd}e^{2\sigma} \quad \text{and} \quad r_{2,uu} = r_{2,dd}e^{4\sigma}$$

Let us denote simply by r_t the one-year forward rate t years from now if the rates decline.

The volatility of the one-year forward rate is equal to $r_0\sigma$. It is possible to see this result by noting that $e^{2\sigma}$ is nearly equal to $(1 + 2\sigma)$. In this case, the volatility of the one-period forward rate can be written as:

$$(re^{2\sigma} - r)/2 \quad \text{which is nearly equal to } (r + 2r\sigma - r)/2 \text{ or } \sigma r.$$

The process generating the interest-rate tree or the forward rates implies that volatility is measured with respect to the current level of rates. For example, if $\sigma = 20\%$ and the one-year rate is 3%, then the volatility of the one-year forward rate is 20% (3%) or 6% or 60 basis points. Hence, when the current one-year rate is 10%, the volatility of the one-year forward rate would be $10\% \times 20\%$ or 200 basis points. The bond's value at a given node can be computed using the immediate next two nodes since at a given node, the bond's value will depend on the future cash flows. The future cash flows correspond to the bond value one year from now and the coupon payments. The binomial model is based on the recursive procedure starting from the last year and working backward through the tree until the initial time. The value at each node is given by the expected cash flows under the appropriate discount rate. The one-year forward rate at this node must be used. We denote these values by:

V_u: value of the bond if the one-year interest rate rises;
V_d: value of the bond if the one-year interest rate falls;
C: amount of the coupon payment and
r: one-year forward rate at the node where valuation is sought.

Hence, the value of the bond at a given node is:

$$\text{Bond value} = p(V_u + c)/(1 + r^-) + (1 - p)(V_d + c)/(1 + r^-)$$

How to construct a binomial interest-rate tree?

Consider the valuation of a two-year bond with a coupon rate of 4.5% when σ is 10%. Figure 16.8 shows the cash flows at each node. The initial interest rate is equal to 4.5%.

Figure 16.9 shows how to calculate the one-year forward rates for the first year by a trial-and-error method.

The model is based on an iterative process that allows the computation of the forward rates $r_{1,d}$ and $r_{1,d}$, which are consistent with the volatility assumption and the observed market value of the bond. This can be done in different steps as shown below.

- **Step 1:** A value of r_1 (the one-year forward rate, one year from now) is set arbitrarily to 3.9%.
- **Step 2:** Since the one-year forward rate, if rates, rise corresponds to $r_1 e^{2\sigma}$, then $r_{1,u} = r_{1,d}e^{2\sigma} = 4.7634\% = 3.9\%e^{(2\times 0.1)}$.
- **Step 3:** The bond's value is computed for one year from now.

The two-year bond's value is given by its maturity value (100) plus the coupon payment at the same date (4.5), or 104.5.

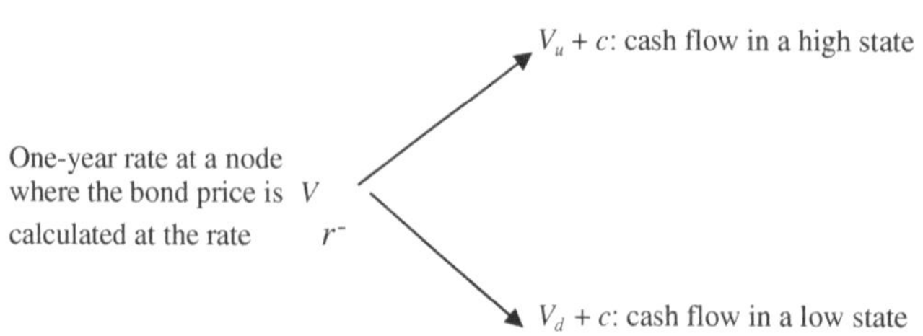

Figure 16.8. Computing the bond value at a given node.

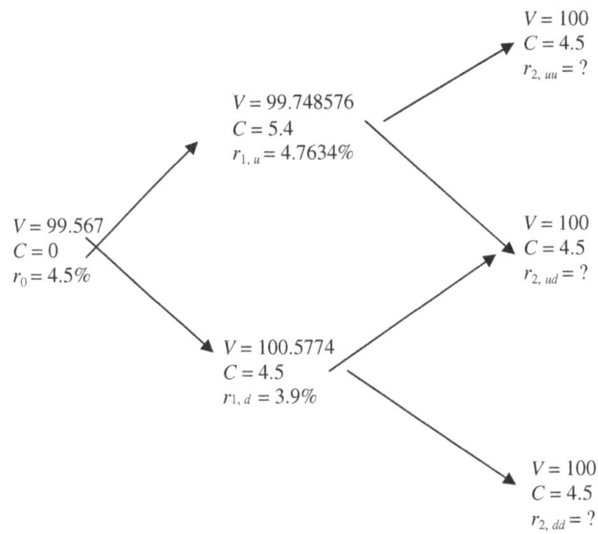

Figure 16.9. Computing the one-year forward rates for year 1 using a two-year 4.5% on-the-run issue: first trial.

When interest rates rise, the present value is $V_u = 99.748576 = 104.5/1.047634$.

When interest rates fall, the present value is $V_d = 100.5774 = 104.5/1.039$.

At time 0, the present value resulting from a rise in the interest rate is computed as:

$$(V_u + c)/1.045 = (99.748576 + 4.5)/1.045 = 99.7594.$$

The present value resulting from a fall in the interest rate is computed as:

$$(V_d + c)/1.045 = (100.5774 + 4.5)/1.045 = 100.5525.$$

Using an equal probability, the value at time 0 is:

$$\text{Value} = 0.5(99.113 + 100.021) = 100.15596.$$

Since the observed market value of the bond at time 0 is 100, the computed value of 100.15596 is not the correct one. This means that the one-period forward interest rate used (r_1) is not consistent with the volatility assumption of 10% and the process used to generate the one-year forward rate.

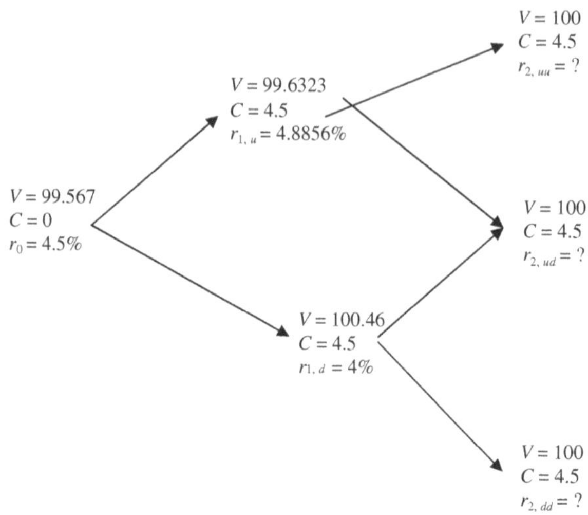

Figure 16.10. Computing the one-year forward rates for year 1 using a two-year 4.5% on-the-run issue: second trial.

Hence, the 3.9% rate is low and a higher rate must be used in the same procedure.

If we use an interest rate of 4% for r_1, this leads to a bond price equal to 100 at time 0. Figure 16.10 is based on a second trial in the computation of the interest rate.

- **Step 1:** A value of r_1 (the one-year forward rate one year from now) is set arbitrarily to 4%.
- **Step 2:** Since the one-year forward rate, if rates rise corresponds to $r_1 e^{2\sigma}$, then $r_{1,u} = r_{1,d} e^{2\sigma} = 4.8856\% = 4\% e^{(2\times 0.1)}$
- **Step 3:** The bond's value is computed one year from now.

The two-year bond's value is given by its maturity value (100) plus the coupon payment at the same date (4.5), or 104.5.

When interest rates rise, the present value is $V_u = 99.6323 = 104.5/1.048856$.

When interest rates fall, the present value is $V_d = 100.48076 = 104.5/1.04$.

At time 0, the present value resulting from a rise in the interest rate is computed as:

$$(V_u + c)/1.045 = (99.6323 + 4.5)/1.045 = 99.6481.$$

The present value resulting from a fall in the interest rate is computed as:

$$(V_d + c)/1.045 = (100.48076 + 4.5)/1.045 = 100.46.$$

Using an equal probability, the value at time 0 is:

$$\text{Value} = 0.5(99.6481 + 100.46) = 100.$$

Since the observed market value of the bond at time 0 is 100, the computed value of 100 is the correct one. This means that the one-year forward interest rate used (r_1) is consistent with the volatility assumption of 10% and the process used to generate the one-year forward rate. Hence, the current one-year forward rate is 4.5% and the forward rate one year from now is 4%. It is possible to extend the analysis to three periods using a 5% three-year bond. The same method can be used in the computation of one-year forward rate, two years from now. This analysis allows to obtain the value of r_2 that leads to a bond value of 100. We let this as an exercise for the interested reader.

16.4. The Black–Derman–Toy Model (BDT)

This model is consistent with the observed term structure of interest rates. The volatility of the short rate is time dependent. The continuous process of the short rate is given by:

$$d\ln r = [\theta(t) + (\delta\sigma(t)/\delta t)/\sigma(t)\ln(r)]dt + \sigma(t)dz$$

where $(\delta\sigma(t)/\delta t)/\sigma(t)$ corresponds to the speed of mean-reversion.

The following example calibrates the BDT model to the current term structure of zero-coupon rates and volatilities.

16.4.1. *Examples and applications*

Example 4: Consider the following sample current data (Table 16.3): Consider the following tree for bond prices (Fig. 16.11).

The price of a zero-coupon bond maturing in one year is given by:

$$92.59259 = [100(0.5) + 100(0.5)]/1.08.$$

Table 16.3. Current data for zero-coupon bonds.

Years to Maturity	Zero-Coupon Rates (in %)	Zero-Coupon Volatilities (in %)
1	8	20
2	8.5	18
3	9	16
4	9.5	14
5	10	12

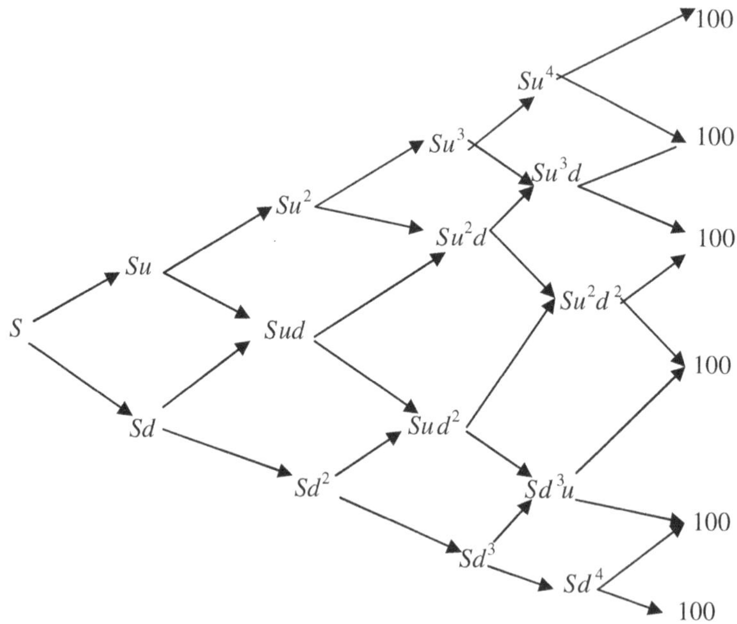

Figure 16.11. Binomial tree for bond prices.

This allows the description of a one-period price tree:

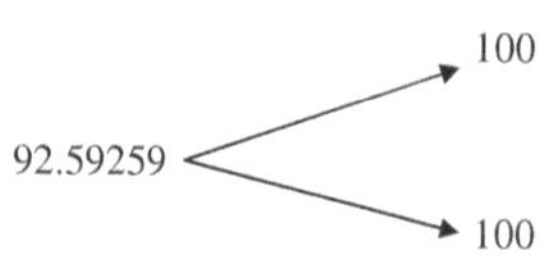

The price today of a two-year zero-coupon bond maturing in two years can be computed as:

$$84.945528 = 100/1.085^2 = 100/1.177225.$$

This second step allows to build a two-period price tree. The second-year bond prices at year one can be computed using the short rates at step one:

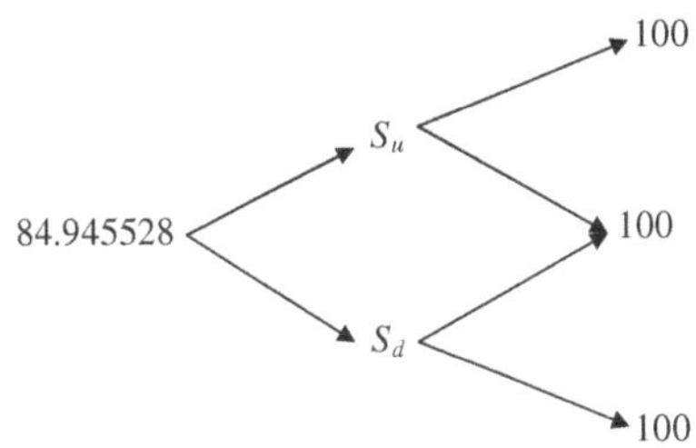

The following relationship must be verified:

$$84.945528 = [0.5S_u + 0.5S_d]/1.08.$$

The standard relationships in the binomial models apply also in the BDT model.

In fact, remember that in the standard binomial analysis, we have:

$$u = e^{\sigma\sqrt{T/N}}, \quad d = 1/u, \quad u/d = e^{2\sigma\sqrt{T/N}},$$
$$\ln(u/d) = 2\sigma\sqrt{T/N} \quad \text{and} \quad \sigma = [1/2\sqrt{T/N}]\ \ln(u/d).$$

In the BDT model, rates follow a log-normal distribution, so we have:

$$\sigma_N = [1/2\sqrt{T/N}]\ln(r_u/r_d) = 0.18$$

or

$$\sigma_N = [1/2]\ln(r_u/r_d) = 0.18 \quad \text{and} \quad S_d = 100/(1 + r_u),$$
$$S_u = 100/(1 + r_d).$$

Substituting these expressions, it gives:

$$84.945528 = [0.5\{100/(1 + r_u)\} + 0.5\{100/(1 + r_d)\}]/1.08.$$

We can use the previous equations to determine the two values of the interest rate (Fig. 16.12).

Since $r_u = r_d e^{0.18(2)}$, this gives the following quadratic equation:

$$84.945528 = [0.5\{100/(1 + r_d e^{0.18(2)})\} + 0.5\{100/(1 + r_d)\}]/1.08.$$

Solving this equation gives the following two rates: $r_d = 7.4\%$, $r_u = 10.60\%$.

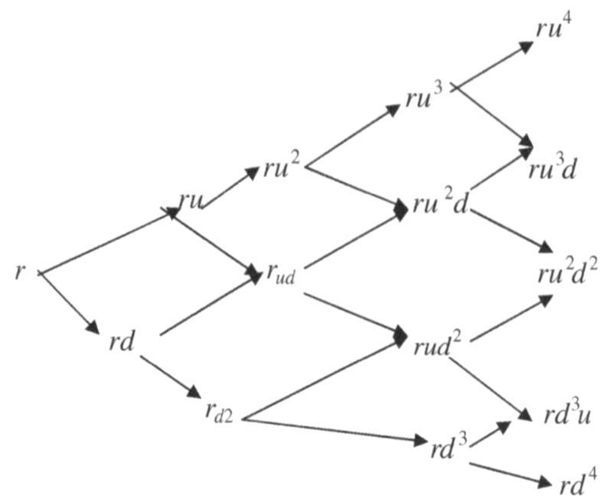

Figure 16.12. Binomial tree for interest rates.

Since these two rates are known, it is possible to use these rates to compute the corresponding bond prices, i.e., 93.11 = (100/1.074) and 90.41 = (100/1.1060). The tree becomes:

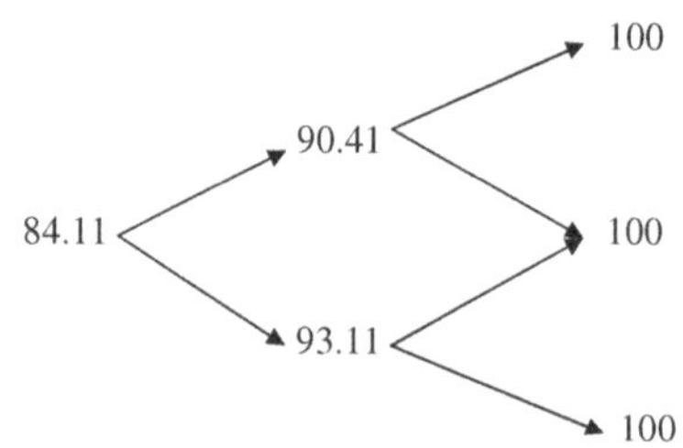

The next step gives the following exhibit.

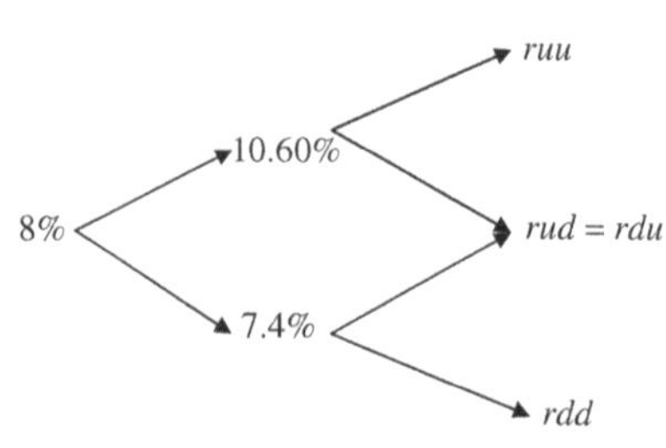

In order to find the rates at the end of period 2, we use the fact that rates are log-normally distributed and that volatility is time dependent. In this case, we have:

$$0.5 \ln(ruu/rud) = 0.5 \ln(rud/rdd) \quad \text{or} \quad rdd = r^2ud/ruu.$$

As before, the price today of a bond maturing in three years is:

$$77.22 = 100/(1 + 0.09)^3$$

Using the risk-neutral valuation principle, we have:

$$Suu = 100/(1 + ruu), \quad Sud = 100(1 + rud), \quad Sdd = 100/(1 + rdd)$$
$$Su = [0.5\,Suu + 0.5\,Sdd]/(1 + 0.1060),$$
$$Sd = [0.5\,Sdd + 0.5\,Sud]/(1 + 0.074),$$
$$77.22 = [0.5\,Su + 0.5\,Sd]/(1 + 0.08).$$

If the bond's maturity is in two years, its yield must satisfy the following:

$$Su = 100/(1 + y_u)^2, \quad Sd = 100/(1 + y_d)^2$$

or

$$y_u = \sqrt{}(100/Su) - 1, \quad y_d = \sqrt{}(100/Sd) - 1$$

We have: $\ln(y_u/y_d) = 0.16$ or $\ln(y_u/y_d) = 0.32$, which gives: $y_u/y_d = e^{0.32}$.

Using these last two equations, it is possible to obtain:

$$y_u = (y_u/y_d)y_d \quad \text{or} \quad y_u = e^{0.32}(\sqrt{}(100/Sd) - 1).$$

In this case, Su can be written as:

$$Su = 100/[1 + e^{0.32}(\sqrt{}(100/Sd) - 1)]^2.$$

This equation can be solved using the Newton–Raphson algorithm. The solution gives the values of Su, Sd, rdd, rud, and ruu.

Summary

Rendleman and Bartter (for details, refer to Bellalah *et al.*, 1998; Bellalah 2018a, 2018b; Bellalah 2025a, 2025b) developed a similar model for the pricing of interest-rate sensitive instruments. Ho and Lee (1986) extended the binomial model for the valuation of interest-rate options and bond options. This model presents some deficiencies. In fact, the constraints imposed on movements of the entire discount function are not sufficient to eliminate negative interest rates. This deficiency has been recognized by Heath, *et al.* (1987), Pedersen *et al.* (for details, refer to Bellalah *et al.*, 1998), and Ritchken and Boenawen (1990) among others. These authors proposed other specific models.

Trigeorgis (1993) applied the methodology to the valuation of investments with multiple real options and to the pricing of managerial flexibility implicit in investment opportunities.

Hull and White (1988,1993) provided a modified binomial lattice model for the valuation of stock options and interest-rate options.

Boyle (1986) proposed a trinomial option-pricing model in which the stock price can move either upwards or downwards or stay unchanged at a given time period. In another paper, Boyle (1988) showed how a five-jump, three-dimensional lattice can be used for the valuation of options on two underlying assets.

Omberg (1988) studied a family of discrete-time jump processes and applied a Gauss-Hermite quadrature technique to derive the prices of options on options or compound options.

Yisong (1993) modified Boyle's approach by presenting a general methodology that can be applied to any multidimensional lattice approach. He proposed a modified approach to the selection of lattice parameters including probabilities and jumps using additional restrictions.

Sandmann (1993) developed a model for the pricing of European options under the assumption of a stochastic interest rate in a discrete time setting. He used a combination of the binomial model for a stock with a binomial model for the spot interest rate.

Derivative securities can be valued using the recursive method through the trinomial tree in the same way, as in the binomial model. This model also applies to discount bonds. Using bond prices, it is also possible to determine the complete yield curve at any given node of the trinomial lattice.

References

Black F and M Scholes (1973). The pricing of options and corporate liabilities. *Journal of Political Economy*, 81, 637–654.

Black F, E Derman and W Toy (1990). A one factor model of interest rates and its application to treasury bond options. *Financial Analysts Journal*, 46 (January–February), 33–39.

Bellalah M (2018a). On information costs, short sales and the pricing of extendible options, steps and Parisian options. *Annals of Operations Research*, 262(2) (March), 361–387.

Bellalah M (2018b). Pricing derivatives in the presence of shadow costs of incomplete information and short sales. *Annals of Operations Research*, 262(2) (March).

Bellalah,M, D Zhang and K Zhang (2025a). On optimal carbon tax in China: Implications for net-zero emissions and development. *Annals of Operations Research* (May).

Bellalah M, D Zhang and K Zhang (2025b). Dynamic stochastic optimization strategies for green production of enterprises in discrete time. *Annals of Operations Research* (May).

Boyle P (1986). Option valuation using a three jump process. *International Options Journal*, 3, 7–12.

Boyle PP (1988). A lattice framework for option pricing with two state variables. *Journal of Financial and Quantitative Analysis*, 23 (March) 1–12.

Briys E, M Bellalah, F de Varenne and H Mai (1998). *Options, Futures and Other Exotics.* Chichester, UK: John Wiley and Sons.

Cox J, S Ross and M Rubinstein (1979). Option pricing: A simplified approach. *Journal of Financial Economics*, 7, 229–263.

Heath D, R Jarrow and A Morton (1987). Bond pricing and the term structure of interest rate: A new methodology for contingent claims valuation. Working paper, Ithaca, NY: Cornell University (Revised edition, 1989).

Ho T and S Lee (1986). Term structure movements and pricing interest rate contingent claims. *Journal of Finance*, 41, 1011–1029.

Hull J and A White (1988). An analysis of the bias in option pricing caused by a stochastic volatility. *Advances in Futures and Options Research*, 3, 29–61.

Hull J and A White (1993). Efficient procedures for valuing European and American path dependent options. *Journal of Derivatives*, 1 (Fall 1993), 21–31.

Omberg E (1988). Efficient discrete time jump process models in option pricing. *Journal of Financial and Quantitative Analysis*, 23(2), 161–174.

Rendleman RJ and BJ Bartter (1980). The pricing of options on debts securities. *Journal of Financial and Quantitative Analysis*, 15 (March), 11–24.

Ritchken P and K Boenawen (1990). On arbitrage free pricing of interest rate contingent claims. *Journal of Finance*, 55(1), 259–264.

Rubinstein M (1994). Implied binomial trees. *Journal of Finance*, 49(3), 771–818.

Sandmann K (1993). The pricing of options with an uncertain interest rate: A discrete time approach. *Mathematical Finance*, 3 (April), 201–216.

Trigeorgis L (1993). The nature of option interactions and the valuation of investments with multiple real options. *Journal of Financial and Quantitative Analysis*, 28, 1–20.

Whaley RE (1986). Valuation of American futures options: Theory and empirical tests. *Journal of Finance*, 41 (March), 127–150.

Yisong T (1993). A modified lattice approach to option pricing. *Journal of Futures Markets*, 13, 563–577.

Chapter 17

Derivatives and Path-Dependent Derivatives: Extensions and Generalizations of the Lattice Approach by Accounting for Information Costs and Illiquidity

Chapter Outline

This chapter is organized as follows:

1. Section 17.1 presents the lattice approach and the binomial model for the valuation of equity and futures options.
2. Section 17.2 presents a simple extension of the lattice approach to account for the effects of information costs.
3. Section 17.3 develops some important results regarding the binomial model and the risk neutrality.
4. Section 17.4 presents the Hull and White's interest-rate trinomial model for the valuation of interest-rate derivatives.
5. Section 17.5 develops a simple context for the pricing of path-dependent interest-rate contingent claims using a lattice.

Introduction

This chapter deals with the valuation of derivative assets using the binomial or the lattice approach. The lattice approach was initiated by Cox *et al.* (CRR) (1979). CRR approach considers the situation where there is only a single underlying asset: the price of a non-dividend paying stock. The time to maturity of the option is divided into several equal small intervals during which the underlying asset price moves from its initial value to one of the two new values up or down. In a risk-neutral world, it is possible to obtain the values corresponding to an upward or downward movements and the corresponding probabilities. The valuation of options in a binomial framework starts at the maturity date since at this date, the option payoff is known. Then, we proceed backward through the binomial tree from the maturity to the initial time. In a risk-neutral world, the option value at each time can be calculated as the expected value at the maturity date discounted at the risk-less rate of interest.

The lattice approach can be easily extended to account for the effects of a continuous dividend yield. If a security pays a dividend yield, then the expected return on the underlying asset is given by the difference between the risk-less rate and the continuous dividend yield. The extension of the lattice approach in the presence of discrete dividends to the valuation of options on stocks paying a known dividend can be easily implemented. In the presence of a discrete dividend, the pricing problem can be simplified as in Hull (2000) by assuming that the implicit spot stock price has two components: a part which is stochastic and a part which is the present value of all future cash payments during the option's life.

The lattice approach has also been used by several authors to model the dynamics of the term structure of interest rates and to value bonds and bond options. There have been many attempts and approaches to describe yield-curve movements using a one-factor model. The approach presented by Ho and Lee (1986), in the form of a binomial tree for discount bonds, provides an exact fit to the current-term structure of interest rates. Their model is interesting since it takes the market data such as the current-term structure of interest rates as given. In this respect, it is close to a binomial stock option pricing approach where the current stock price is taken as an input to the model. Unlike most interest-rate contingent claims models, this model uses full information on the current-term structure. In fact, using an ingenious discrete-time approach for pricing bonds and interest-rate contingent claims, Ho and Lee (1986) succeeded in incorporating all information about the yield curve in their model.

Hull and White (1993) presented a general numerical procedure involving the use of trinomial trees for constructing one-factor models where the short rate is Markovian and the models are consistent with initial market data. Their procedure is efficient and provides a convenient way of implementing models already suggested in the literature. In this respect, their contribution is more a numerical one than a financial one. This chapter covers binomial and more general lattice approaches for the pricing of equity and interest-rate dependent claims.

Dharan (1997) developed a simple framework for the valuation of path-dependent interest-rate claims such as index-amortizing swaps or mortgage-backed securities with a simple pre-payment function for which there is no analytical solution. Dharan (1997) showed how to construct a lattice to value a mortgage-backed security when the pre-payment function is linear. The different models are illustrated in detail using several numerical examples.

17.1. The Standard Lattice Approach for Equity Options: The Standard Analysis

We re-call the standard lattice approach here in order to allow its extension to account for the effects of information costs on the pricing of derivatives.

17.1.1. *The model for options on a spot asset with any pay outs*

The lattice approach can be introduced by first looking at a stock option whose underlying asset does not pay any dividend. Let T be the option's maturity date, which is divided into N reasonably small intervals of length Δt, so that $T = N\Delta t$. In this world, the expected return on the underlying asset in time Δt is $r\Delta t$. The variance of this underlying asset on the same interval is $\sigma^2\Delta t$. For the valuation of derivative assets, re-call that the expected value of the underlying asset in a risk-neutral world is $Se^{r\Delta t}$. In this context, we can write the equality between this expected value and the one given by the binomial model as:

$$pSu + (1-p)Sd = Se^{r\Delta t} \quad \text{or} \quad pu + (1-p)d = e^{r\Delta t} \tag{17.1}$$

Since the variance of a variable X is given by $E(X^2) - E(X)^2$, we can write the equality between this variance and $S^2\sigma^2\Delta t$:

$$S^2\sigma^2\Delta t = S^2(pu^2 + (1-p)d^2) - S^2(pu + (1-p)d)^2$$

or

$$\sigma^2\Delta t = pu^2 + (1-p)d^2 - (pu + (1-p)d)^2 \tag{17.2}$$

If we use Eqs. (17.1), (17.2) and suppose that $u = \frac{1}{d}$, then we have:

$$u = e^{\sigma\sqrt{\Delta t}}, \quad d = e^{-\sigma\sqrt{\Delta t}}, \quad \text{and} \quad p = \frac{a-d}{u-d}, \quad a = e^{r\Delta t}.$$

The expected return on the stock can be written as $pSu + (1-p)Sd = Se^{r\Delta t}$. The variance on the stock can be written for the same interval Δt as:

$$pS^2u^2 + (1-p)S^2d^2 - (Se^{r\Delta t})^2.$$

This last expression can be written as $S^2(e^{r\Delta t}(e^{\sigma\sqrt{\Delta t}} + e^{-\sigma\sqrt{\Delta t}}) - 1 - e^{2r\Delta t})$.

Now, using the expansion of e^x in series form as $e^x = 1 + x + \frac{x^2}{2} + \frac{x^3}{6} + \cdots$ It is clear that when terms of order Δt^2 and higher are ignored, the variance of the stock price is $S^2\sigma^2\Delta t$. This shows that we have the appropriate values for u, d, and p. The nature of the lattice of stock prices is completely specified and the nodes correspond to:

$$Su^jd^{i-j} \quad \text{where } j = 0, 1, \ldots, i.$$

The option is evaluated by starting at time T and working backward.

17.1.2. *The model for futures options*

Merton (1973), Black (1976), and Barone-Adesi and Whaley (1987) among others, showed that futures contracts, stock index options, and currency options may be assimilated to options on a stock that pays a continuous dividend. In a risk-neutral economy, the expected return on an asset paying a continuous dividend yield δ is $(r - b)$ so that we can write $e^{(r-b)\Delta t} = pu + (1 - p)d$ and $a = e^{(r-b)\Delta t}$. Hence, the model for futures options is completely specified using the following equations:

$$u = e^{\sigma\sqrt{\Delta t}}, \quad d = e^{-\sigma\sqrt{\Delta t}}, \quad p = \frac{a-d}{u-d}, \quad \text{and} \quad a = e^{(r-b)\Delta t}.$$

For a futures contract, $r = b$ so that $a = 1$.

17.1.3. *The model with dividends*

We study three cases: a known dividend yield, a known proportional dividend yield, and a discrete dividend.

17.1.3.1. *A known dividend yield*

The extension of the lattice approach in the presence of a continuous dividend yield is simple. If a security pays a dividend yield q, then the expected return on the underlying asset is $(r-q)$. In this case, we can write the equality between the expected value of the underlying asset and the one given by the binomial model as $pSu + (1-p)Sd = Se^{(r-q)\Delta t}$ or $pu + (1-p)d = e^{(r-q)\Delta t}$.

In this case, using the same procedure as before, it can be shown that the parameters for the binomial model are:

$$u = e^{\sigma\sqrt{\Delta t}}, \quad d = e^{-\sigma\sqrt{\Delta t}}, \quad p = \frac{a-d}{u-d}, \quad a = e^{(r-q)\Delta t}.$$

The value of a European contingent claim $F_{i,j}$ at time $(t + i\Delta t)$ when the underlying asset is $Su^j d^{i-j}$ can be calculated using the following equation:

$$F_{i,j} = e^{(-r)\Delta t}[(pF_{i+1,j+1} + (1-p)F_{i+1,j})]$$

In the same context, at time $t + i\Delta t$, the American call option value is:

$$F_{i,j} = \max[Su^j d^{i-j} - K, e^{-r\Delta t}(pF_{i+1,j+1} + (1-p)F_{i+1,j})]$$

At each node, at time $t + i\Delta t$, the American put value is given by,

$$F_{i,j} = \max[K - Su^j d^{i-j}, e^{-r\Delta t}(pF_{i+1,j+1} + (1-p)F_{i+1,j})].$$

It is convenient to note that these formulas apply to index options, currencies, and futures contracts.

17.1.3.2. *A known proportional dividend yield*

The extension of the lattice approach in the presence of discrete dividends to the valuation of options on stocks paying a known dividend is as follows. Assume that a known proportional dividend yield δ is to be paid at a certain date. When there is only one dividend at the time $(t + i\Delta t)$, the nodes correspond to the stock prices $Su^j d^{i-j}$ for $j = 0, 1, \ldots, i$ where the time $(t + i\Delta t)$ is prior to the stock going ex-dividend.

The values of u, d, and p are $u = e^{\sigma\sqrt{\Delta t}}$, $d = e^{-\sigma\sqrt{\Delta t}}$, and $p = \frac{a-d}{u-d}$ respectively. When the time $(t + i\Delta t)$ is after the underlying stock goes ex-dividend, then the nodes give the following prices $S(1-\delta)u^j d^{i-j}$ for $j = 0, 1, \ldots, i$. The same analysis applies when there are several dividends. In this case, the total dividend yield δ_i corresponding to all ex-dividend dates between t and $(t + i\Delta t)$ is accounted for using the following values of the stock at different nodes: $S(1-\delta_i)u^j d^{i-j}$ for $j = 0, 1, \ldots, i$.

17.1.3.3. *A known discrete dividend*

In general, the dividend amount D is known, rather than the dividend yield. Assume that there is only one dividend date, τ, between an instant $k\Delta t$ and $(k+1)\Delta t$. When there is just one ex-cash income date τ, during the option's life, then the nodes on the tree at time $(t + i\Delta t)$ are $Su^j d^{i-j}$ for $i \leq k$ with $j = 0, 1, 2, \ldots, i$. The nodes on the tree at time $i = (k+1)$ are: $(Su^j d^{i-j} - D)u$ and $(Su^j d^{i-j} - D)d$ for $j = 0, 1, 2, \ldots, i$. The analysis can be simplified as before.

17.1.4. *Examples*

In these examples, we use the following parameters for the valuation of a European and an American put option on a stock paying a dividend of 2.05 in three months and a half: $S^* = 40$, $S = 42$,

$K = 45$, $r = 0.1$, $N = 5$, $T = 5$ months, $\Delta t = 1$ month, and $\sigma = 0.4$. The first step is the calculation of the parameters u, d, a, and p using $u = e^{\sigma\sqrt{\Delta t}}$, $d = e^{-\sigma\sqrt{\Delta t}}$, $p = \frac{a-d}{u-d}$, $q = 1 - p$, $a = e^{r\Delta t}$. This gives $u = 1.1224, d = 0.8909, a = 1.0084, p = 0.5073$, and $q = 0.4927$.

Using these parameters, it is possible to generate the dynamics of the underlying asset. The values of the underlying asset at different nodes are:

$S_{0,0} = 42;$

$S_{1,1} = 46.9136, \quad S_{1,0} = 37.6556;$

$S_{2,2} = 52.4256, \quad S_{2,1} = 42.0344, \quad S_{2,0} = 33.7859;$

$S_{3,3} = 58.6107, \quad S_{3,2} = 46.9475, \quad S_{3,1} = 37.6893, \quad S_{3,0} = 30.3403;$

$S_{4,4} = 63.4822, \quad S_{4,3} = 50.3914, \quad S_{4,2} = 40, \quad S_{4,1} = 31.7515,$

$S_{4,0} = 25.2039$ and

$S_{5,5} = 71.2525, \quad S_{5,4} = 56.5593, \quad S_{5,3} = 44.8960, \quad S_{5,2} = 35.6379,$

$S_{5,1} = 28.2289,$ and $S_{5,0} = 22.4554.$

The indices (i, j) correspond respectively to the period and the position. The lowest position on a tree is indexed by zero. For example, the values of the underlying asset in the nodes following nodes are generated as follows:

$$S_{0,0} = S^*(u^0d^0) + De^{-r\frac{\tau}{12}}, \qquad S_{1,1} = S^*(u^1d^0) + De^{-r\frac{(\tau-1)}{12}}$$
$$S_{1,0} = S^*(u^0d^1) + De^{-r\frac{(\tau-1)}{12}}, \quad S_{2,2} = S^*(u^2d^0) + De^{-r\frac{(\tau-2)}{12}}$$
$$S_{2,1} = S^*(u^1d^1) + De^{-r\frac{(\tau-2)}{12}}, \quad S_{2,0} = S^*(u^0d^2) + De^{-r\frac{(\tau-2)}{12}}$$
$$S_{3,3} = S^*(u^3d^0) + De^{-r\frac{(\tau-3)}{12}}, \quad S_{3,0} = S^*(u^0d^3) + De^{-r\frac{(\tau-3)}{12}}$$

When $y > \tau$, we do not discount the dividends and the above values are generated as follows: $S_{4,4} = S^*(u^4d^0)$, $S_{4,3} = S^*(u^3d^1)$, $S_{4,0} = S^*(u^0d^4)$, and $S_{5,0} = S^*(u^0d^5)$.

17.1.4.1. *The European put price with dividends*

The values are computed by starting at the maturity date. At this date, the possible option values are: $P_{5,5} = 0, P_{5,4} = 0, S_{5,3} = 0.104, P_{5,2} = 9.3621, P_{5,1} = 16.7111$, and $P_{5,0} = 22.5446$.

Using the recursive procedure, the European put values are: $P_{4,4} = 0$, $P_{4,3} = 0.0508$, $P_{4,2} = 4.6266$, $P_{4,1} = 12.8751$, $P_{4,0} = 19.4226$, $P_{3,3} = 0.0248$, $P_{3,2} = 2.2861$, $P_{3,1} = 8.6183$, $P_{3,0} = 15.9673$, $P_{2,2} = 1.1294$, $P_{2,1} = 5.3610$, $P_{2,0} = 12.1375$, $P_{1,1} = 3.1876$, and $P_{1,0} = 8.6274$. The European put price with dividends is equal to 5.8190.

For example, at the nodes (5,0) and (4,0), the European put price is computed as: $P_{5,0} = \max[0, K - S_{5,0}]$, $P_{4,0} = [pP_{5,1} + qP_{5,0}]/a$.

17.1.4.2. *The American put price with dividends*

For the put, we have $P_{i,j} = \max[[pP_{i+1,j+1} + qP_{i+1,j}]/a; \max[0, K - S_{i,j}]]$.

The values are computed by starting at the maturity date. At this date, the possible option values are $P_{5,5} = 0$, $P_{5,4} = 0$, $S_{5,3} = 0.104$, $P_{5,2} = 9.3621$, $P_{5,1} = 16.7111$, and $P_{5,0} = 22.5446$. These values are the same for both European and American options. Using the recursive procedure, the European put values are $P_{4,4} = 0$, $P_{4,3} = 0.0508$, $P_{4,2} = 5$, $P_{4,1} = 13.2485$, $P_{4,0} = 19.7961$, $P_{3,3} = 0.0248$, $P_{3,2} = 2.4685$, $P_{3,1} = 8.9887$, $P_{3,0} = 16.3377$, $P_{2,2} = 1.2186$, $P_{2,1} = 5.6337$, $P_{2,0} = 12.5047$, $P_{1,1} = 3.3657$, and $P_{1,0} = 8.9441$.

For example, the values $P_{4,4}$ and $P_{4,3}$ are calculated as follows:

$$P_{4,4} = \max(0.0508; \max[0; 45 - 50.3914]) = \max(0.0508; 0) = 0.0508.$$

$$P_{4,3} = \max(4.6266; \max[0; 45 - 40]) = \max(4.6266; 5) = 5.$$

The price of the American put is 6.0633 when there are dividends. The difference between the American price and the European price corresponds to the early exercise premium. The lattice can be used to estimate the hedge ratio Δ from the nodes at time $t + \Delta t$ as:

$$\Delta = \frac{F_{1,1} - F_{1,0}}{Su - Sd}.$$

We can obtain a more accurate estimate at time $t - 2\Delta t$ by assuming a stock price S at this time. In this case, the Δ is

$$\Delta = \frac{F_{2,2} - F_{2,0}}{Su^2 - Sd^2}$$

The Γ is given by:

$$\Gamma = \frac{\frac{F_{2,2} - F_{2,1}}{Su^2 - S} - \frac{F_{2,1} - F_{2,0}}{S - Sd^2}}{\frac{1}{2}(Su^2 - Sd^2)}$$

The Greek-letter delta corresponds to the option partial derivative with respect to the underlying asset price. The gamma indicates the partial derivative of the delta with respect to the underlying asset price. The theta indicates the option partial derivative with respect to time. The vega indicates the option partial derivative with respect to the volatility parameter. The following Tables 17.1–17.8 show the simulations of binomial option prices using 150 periods for different parameters. The reader can see at the same time the sensitivities of the option price to different parameters (the Greek letters). These parameters are provided for illustrative purposes.

Table 17.1. Simulations of European binomial call prices, $S = 100$, $K = 100$, $t = 22/12/2003$, $T = 22/12/2004$, $r = 2\%$, and $\sigma = 20\%$.

S	Price	Delta	Gamma	Vega	Theta
80	1.43986	0.18415	−0.00000	0.21391	−0.00656
85	2.54367	0.24220	0.06668	0.26153	−0.00827
90	4.17276	0.38248	−0.00000	0.34631	−0.01107
95	6.29601	0.46056	0	0.37528	−0.01239
100	8.91144	0.61818	−0.00000	0.39070	−0.01336
105	12.06935	0.69165	0	0.37547	−0.01345
110	15.63786	0.75817	0	0.34667	−0.01313
115	19.55770	0.81605	0	0.30750	−0.01246
120	23.76469	0.86445	0	0.26200	−0.01154

Table 17.2. Simulations of American binomial call prices, $S = 100$, $K = 100$, $t = 22/12/2003$, $T = 22/12/2004$, $r = 2\%$, and $\sigma = 20\%$.

S	Price	Delta	Gamma	Vega	Theta
80	1.43986	0.18415	−0.00000	0.21391	−0.00656
85	2.54367	0.24220	0.06668	0.26153	−0.00827
90	4.17276	0.38248	−0.00000	0.34631	−0.01107
95	6.29601	0.46056	0	0.37528	−0.01239
100	8.91144	0.61818	−0.00000	0.39070	−0.01336
105	12.06935	0.69165	0	0.37547	−0.01345
110	15.63786	0.75817	0	0.34667	−0.01313
115	19.55770	0.81605	0	0.30750	−0.01246
120	23.76469	0.86445	0	0.26200	−0.01154

Table 17.3. Simulations of European binomial put prices, $S = 100$, $K = 100$, $t = 22/12/2003$, $T = 22/12/2004$, $r = 2\%$, and $\sigma = 20\%$.

S	Price	Delta	Gamma	Vega	Theta
80	19.45436	−0.81585	0	0.21391	−0.00119
85	15.55817	−0.75780	0.06668	0.26153	−0.00289
90	12.18726	−0.61752	0	0.34631	−0.00570
95	9.31050	−0.53944	−0.00000	0.37528	−0.00702
100	6.92594	−0.38182	0	0.39070	−0.00799
105	5.08385	−0.30835	−0.00000	0.37547	−0.00808
110	3.65236	−0.24183	−0.00000	0.34667	−0.00776
115	2.57220	−0.18395	−0.00000	0.30750	−0.00709
120	1.77919	−0.13555	−0.00000	0.26200	−0.00617

Table 17.4. Simulations of American binomial put prices, $S = 100$, $K = 100$, $t = 22/12/2003$, $T = 22/12/2004$, $r = 2\%$, and $\sigma = 20\%$.

S	Price	Delta	Gamma	Vega	Theta
80	20.32877	−0.88286	0.01314	0.14678	−0.00244
85	16.16444	−0.79424	0.05407	0.23133	−0.00417
90	12.58896	−0.65043	0.00726	0.32805	−0.00657
95	9.58087	−0.55677	0.00338	0.36977	−0.00777
100	7.10987	−0.43411	0.03640	0.39021	−0.00857
105	5.19837	−0.31985	0.00356	0.37831	−0.00853
110	3.72566	−0.24764	0.00126	0.34991	−0.00807
115	2.61920	−0.18740	0.00100	0.31041	−0.00731
120	1.80907	−0.13757	0.00057	0.26443	−0.00633

Table 17.5. Simulations of European binomial call prices, $S = 100$, $K = 100$, $t = 22/12/2003$, $T = 22/06/2004$, $r = 2\%$, and $\sigma = 20\%$.

S	Price	Delta	Gamma	Vega	Theta
80	0.36079	0.08693	0	0.09055	−0.00526
85	0.93264	0.16894	−0.00000	0.15281	−0.00903
90	2.00036	0.28849	−0.00000	0.21932	−0.01322
95	3.70780	0.43730	0	0.26800	−0.01658
100	6.11625	0.59557	−0.00000	0.27901	−0.01794
105	9.25379	0.67066	0.06878	0.26813	−0.01807
110	12.96246	0.80000	0	0.21954	−0.01604
115	17.11629	0.85123	0.04165	0.18706	−0.01475
120	21.61974	0.92542	0	0.12028	−0.01144

Table 17.6. Simulations of American binomial call prices, $S = 100$, $K = 100$, $t = 22/12/2003$, $T = 22/06/2004$, $r = 2\%$, and $\sigma = 20\%$.

S	Price	Delta	Gamma	Vega	Theta
80	0.36079	0.08693	0	0.09055	−0.00526
85	0.93264	0.16894	−0.00000	0.15281	−0.00903
90	2.00036	0.28849	−0.00000	0.21932	−0.01322
95	3.70780	0.43730	0	0.26800	−0.01658
100	6.11625	0.59557	−0.00000	0.27901	−0.01794
105	9.25379	0.67066	0.06878	0.26813	−0.01807
110	12.96246	0.80000	0	0.21954	−0.01604
115	17.11629	0.85123	0.04165	0.18706	−0.01475
120	21.61974	0.92542	0	0.12028	−0.01144

Table 17.7. Simulations of European binomial put prices, $S = 100$, $K = 100$, $t = 22/12/2003$, $T = 22/06/2004$, $r = 2\%$, and $\sigma = 20\%$.

S	Price	Delta	Gamma	Vega	Theta
80	19.36306	−0.91307	0	0.09055	0.00017
85	14.93492	−0.83106	0	0.15281	−0.00360
90	11.00263	−0.71151	−0.00000	0.21932	−0.00779
95	7.71007	−0.56270	0	0.26800	−0.01115
100	5.11852	−0.40443	0	0.27901	−0.01252
105	3.25606	−0.32934	0.06878	0.26813	−0.01265
110	1.96473	−0.20000	−0.00000	0.21954	−0.01061
115	1.11857	−0.14877	0.04165	0.18706	−0.00933
120	0.62201	−0.07458	−0.00000	0.12028	−0.00602

Table 17.8. American binomial – CRR, put $S = 100$, $K = 100$, $t = 22/12/2003$, $T = 22/06/2004$, $r = 2\%$, and $\sigma = 20\%$.

S	Price	Delta	Gamma	Vega	Theta
80	20.00779	−0.97909	0.01600	0.02403	−0.00077
85	15.33467	−0.87409	0.01205	0.11948	−0.00456
90	11.24360	−0.73921	0.00890	0.20431	−0.00862
95	7.85080	−0.58226	0.00764	0.26240	−0.01179
100	5.20147	−0.45140	0.03865	0.27868	−0.01303
105	3.30000	−0.33283	0.06361	0.26892	−0.01297
110	1.98701	−0.20271	0.00120	0.22094	−0.01083
115	1.13111	−0.14941	0.04099	0.18764	−0.00943
120	0.62757	−0.07518	0.00028	0.12100	−0.00609

Table 17.9. CRR binomial call currency price, $S = 1$, $K = 1$, $t = 07/02/2003$, $T = 07/02/2004$, $r = 3\%$, $r^* = 4\%$, and $\sigma = 20\%$.

S	Price	Delta	Gamma	Vega	Theta
0.96	0.05371	0.45561	0.50475	0.00356	0.00008
0.97	0.05826	0.46131	0.49915	0.00374	0.00008
0.98	0.06288	0.46131	0.49921	0.00377	0.00009
0.99	0.06749	0.46131	0.49921	0.00380	0.00009
1	0.07210	0.53768	0.42285	0.00382	0.00009
1.01	0.07748	0.53768	0.42285	0.00385	0.00008
1.02	0.08286	0.53768	0.42285	0.00388	0.00008
1.03	0.08823	0.53768	0.42285	0.00391	0.00008
1.04	0.09361	0.60551	0.35503	0.00394	0.00008

The binomial model can also be used for the pricing of foreign currency options. In this case, the cost of carry or the risk-free rate is replaced by the difference between the domestic risk-less rate r and the foreign risk-less rate r^*. In this case, the underlying asset price S indicates the exchange rate (Table 17.9).

17.2. A Simple Extension to Account for Information Uncertainty in the Valuation of Futures and Options

We can extend the previous analysis to account for the effects of information costs. Information costs can be used in the valuation of futures and options. For introduction, we refer to supplementary material. For the analysis of information costs and valuation, we can refer to Bellalah (2001, 2018), Bellalah *et al.* (2001a, 2001b), Bellalah and Prigent (2001), Bellalah and Selmi (2001) and so on.

17.2.1. *On the valuation of derivatives and information costs*

An important question in financial economics is how frictions affect equilibrium in capital markets since in a world of costly information, some investors will have incomplete information. Merton (1987) developed a simple model of capital market equilibrium with incomplete information, CAPMI. The CAPMI model can explain several anomalies in financial markets.

Merton (1987) advanced the investor recognition hypothesis (IRH) in a mean-variance model. This assumption explains the portfolio formation of informationally constrained investors (ICI). The IRH in Merton's context states that investors buy and hold only those securities about which they have enough information. Merton (1987) adapted the rational framework of the static CAPM to account for incomplete information. The premise in Merton's (1987) model and Shapiro's (2000) extension is that the costs of gathering and processing data lead some investors to focus on stocks with high visibility and also to entrust a portion of their wealth to money managers employed by pension plans.

In this context, a trading strategy shaped by real-world information costs should incorporate an investment in well-known, visible stocks, and an investment delegated to professional money managers. In this theory, an investor considers only the stocks visible to him/her, i.e., those about which he/she has sufficient information to implement the optimal portfolio re-balancing. In general, information about larger firms is likely to be available at a lower cost. The claim that large firms are more widely known is consistent with the empirical evidence that large firms have more shareholders as in Merton (1987). For these reasons, it is important to account for information costs in the pricing of assets and derivatives. The works of Markowitz (1952), Sharpe (1964), and Lintner (1965) on the capital asset pricing model provided the general equilibrium model of asset prices under uncertainty. This model represents a fundamental tool in measuring the risk of a security under uncertainty. The CAPM model can be applied to the valuation of options and futures contracts.

Merton's model is a two-period model of CAPM in an economy where each investor has information about only a subset of the available securities. The main assumption in the Merton's model is that an investor includes an asset S in his/her portfolio only if he/she has some information about the first and second moment of the distribution of its returns. In this model, information costs have two components: the costs of gathering and processing data for the analysis and the valuation of the firm and its assets, and the costs of information transmission from an economic agent to another. Merton's model may be stated as follows:

$$\bar{R}_S - r = \beta_S[\bar{R}_m - r] + \lambda_S - \beta_S\lambda_m$$

where:

- $\bar{R}_S$: the equilibrium-expected return on security S;
- $\bar{R}_m$: the equilibrium-expected return on the market portfolio;
- R: one plus the risk-less rate of interest, r;
- $\beta_S = \frac{\text{cov}(\tilde{R}_S/\tilde{R}_m)}{\text{var}(\tilde{R}_m)}$: the beta of security S;
- λ_S: the equilibrium aggregate "shadow cost" for the security S and
- λ_m: the weighted average shadow cost of incomplete information over all securities in the market place.

The CAPM of Merton (1987), referred to as the CAPMI is an extension of the standard CAPM to a context of incomplete information. Note that when $\lambda_m = \lambda_S = 0$, this model reduces to the standard CAPM of Sharpe (1964).

Since the publication of the pioneering papers by Black and Scholes (1973) and Merton (1973), three industries have blossomed: an exchange industry in derivatives, an OTC industry in structured products, and an academic industry in derivative research. As it appears in Scholes (1998), derivative instruments provide low-cost solutions to investor problems than that of competing alternatives. Differences in information are important in both financial and real markets (see the models in Bellalah, 1999a, 1999b; Bellalah and Jacquillat, 1995).

17.2.2. *The valuation of forward and futures contracts in the presence of information costs*

17.2.2.1. *Forward, futures, and arbitrage*

We denote respectively by:

- t: current time;
- T: maturity date of the contract in years;
- $(T-t)$: time remaining until the maturity of the contract in years;
- S: spot price of the asset;
- K: delivery price for a forward contract;
- f: value of a long position in a forward contract;

- F: forward price at time t;
- r: risk-free rate at time t for maturity T;
- r_f: risk-free rate at time t for maturity T in a foreign country and
- λ_S: information cost for the asset S.

For an introduction to information costs and their use in the valuation of derivatives, we can refer to Bellalah and Jacquillat (1995, 2018) and Bellalah (2000a, 2000b, 2001). It is important to make a difference between the price and value of a contract. The forward price of a contract corresponds to its delivery price that would make its value equal to zero. When a contract is initiated, the delivery price is fixed equal to the forward price in such a way that $f = 0$ and $K = F$. Bellalah shows that these costs of information explain to a large extent the financial crisis of 2008 because of a lack of information transmission between economic agents.

17.2.2.2. *The valuation of forward contracts in the absence of distributions to the underlying asset*

The underlying asset may be a non-dividend paying stock or a non-coupon-bearing bond. Consider an investment in two portfolios.

Portfolio A corresponds to a long position in a forward contract and a cash amount equal to $Ke^{-r(T-t)}$.

Portfolio B contains the underlying security of the forward contract.

At maturity, cash can be used to pay for the security. However, before buying the security, an investor pays information costs and therefore needs an additional return of λ_S before investing in the asset.

To implement arbitrage, the investor must be informed about the markets and pays information costs. Hence, arbitrage considerations imply that the real discount rate must be $e^{-(r+\lambda_S)(T-t)}$ rather than $e^{-r(T-t)}$. The equivalence between these values of the two portfolios at each time implies that

$$f + Ke^{-(r+\lambda_S)(T-t)} = S \quad \text{or} \quad f = S - Ke^{-(r+\lambda_S)(T-t)}.$$

Re-call that when a contract is initiated, its forward price must be equal to the delivery price, which is chosen in such a way that the contract's value is zero. The forward price F corresponds to the value of K for which, $f = 0$. Using the last equation, the forward price $F = Se^{(r+\lambda_S)(T-t)}$.

17.2.2.3. *The valuation of forward contracts in the presence of a known cash income to the underlying asset*

The underlying asset may be a dividend-paying stock or a coupon-bearing bond. Consider an investment in two portfolios.

Portfolio A corresponds to a long position in a forward contract and a cash amount equal to $Ke^{-r(T-t)}$.

Portfolio B contains the underlying security of the forward contract plus borrowings of an amount I corresponding to the known income.

Since income can be used to re-pay the loan, portfolio B has the same value as one security or portfolio A at T. However, before using the security, an investor pays information costs and therefore needs an additional return of λ_S before investing in the security. Both portfolios must have the same initial value and $f + Ke^{-(r+\lambda_S)(T-t)} = S - I$ or $f = S - I - Ke^{-(r+\lambda_S)(T-t)}$.

As before, the forward price F can be computed as the value of K for which, $f = 0$, or $F = (S - I)e^{(r+\lambda_S)(T-t)}$.

17.2.2.4. *The valuation of forward contracts in the presence of a known dividend yield to the underlying asset*

The underlying asset may be a stock index or a currency. A known dividend yield corresponds to an income expressed as a percentage of the security price. Consider an investment in two portfolios A and B. Portfolio A is conserved and portfolio B contains an amount $e^{-q(T-t)}$ of the security with income re-invested. Hence, the fraction of the security in B will grow as a result of the dividends so that at maturity, one security is held.

At T, portfolios A and B have the same value and this must be true at time t to give:

$$f + Ke^{-(r+\lambda_S)(T-t)} = Se^{-q(T-t)} \quad \text{or} \quad f = Se^{-q(T-t)} - Ke^{-(r+\lambda_S)(T-t)}.$$

As before, the forward price F can be computed as the value of K for which $f = 0$, or $F = Se^{(r-q+\lambda_S)(T-t)}$.

17.2.2.5. *The valuation of stock index futures*

A stock index is constructed using some fixed number of stocks. The stocks can have equal weights or weights that change over time. The stock index can be seen as the price of an asset that pays dividends. In general, it is a reasonable approximation for some indices to assume that they pay a continuous dividend yield. In this case, it is possible to use arbitrage arguments as before to show that the futures price must satisfy the following relationship:

$$F = Se^{(r-q+\lambda_S)(T-t)}.$$

17.2.2.6. *The valuation of forward and futures contracts on currencies*

Currency forward and futures contracts can be analyzed using arbitrage arguments. Consider as before two portfolios A and B. The first portfolio A corresponds to a long position in a forward contract plus an amount of cash, which is equal to $Ke^{-r(T-t)}$. Portfolio B contains an amount $e^{-r_f(T-t)}$ of the foreign currency. The value of the two portfolios at time T is equivalent to one unit of the foreign currency. Portfolios A and B must have the same value at time t to give:

$$f + Ke^{-(r+\lambda_S)(T-t)} = Se^{-r_f(T-t)}$$

or

$$f = Se^{-r_f(T-t)} - Ke^{-(r+\lambda_S)(T-t)}.$$

As before, the forward price F or the forward exchange rate can be computed as the value of K for which $f = 0$ in this last equation, or:

$$F = Se^{(r-r_f+\lambda_S)(T-t)}.$$

This corresponds to the interest-rate parity theorem in international finance in the presence of information uncertainty. These last equations are identical to those for stock indices, where q is replaced by r_f. This result reveals that a foreign currency is similar to a security paying a continuous dividend yield. The latter corresponds to the foreign risk-free interest rate.

17.2.2.7. *The valuation of futures contracts on silver and gold*

The underlying assets of these contracts are held by several investors for investment purposes. This is not the case for several other commodities. When storage costs are neglected, silver and gold can be seen as securities paying no income. In this case, the futures price must satisfy the following relationship:

$$F = Se^{(r+\lambda_S)(T-t)}$$

where λ_S corresponds to information costs on the security. We denote by G the present value of the storage costs. In the same context, we have $F = (S + G)e^{(r+\lambda_S)(T-t)}$.

When storage costs are proportional to the commodity price, then $F = Se^{(r+g+\lambda_S)(T-t)}$ where g corresponds to the storage cost per annum.

17.2.2.8. *The valuation of futures on other commodities*

Several commodities are held by investors for some reasons other than investment purposes. This is the case for commodities held in inventory because of their consumption values. In this case, investors conserve the commodity and do not buy futures contracts because they cannot be consumed. This is one of the reasons given to explain the decrease in futures prices for longer maturities. In general, holders of commodity positions feel some benefits from holding physical commodities such as the ability to keep a production process running. These benefits are not available for the holder of a futures contract. The benefits are referred to as the convenience yield (cy). In the presence of information uncertainty, the cy can be defined as:

$$Fe^{cy(T-t)} = (S + G)e^{(r+\lambda_S)(T-t)}.$$

When storage costs are expressed as a constant proportion, g, then y is defined so that: $Fe^{cy(T-t)} = Se^{(r+g+\lambda_S)(T-t)}$ or $F = Se^{(r+g-cy+\lambda_S)(T-t)}$.

When a commodity is held only for investment purposes, the cy is zero and we have $F = (S+G)e^{(r+\lambda_S)(T-t)}$ or $F = Se^{(r+g+\lambda_S)(T-t)}$.

17.2.3. *Arbitrage and information costs in the lattice approach*

The lattice approach can be introduced with reference to a stock option in the absence of payments to the underlying asset.

Let T be the option's maturity date which is divided into N reasonably small intervals of length, so that $T = N\Delta t$. During each time interval, the stock price moves either upwards from S to Su or downwards from S to dS. This movement in the stock price is binomial with a probability p attached to an upward jump and a probability $(1-p)$ to a downward movement. The parameters u, d, and p are functions of the mean and variance of the rates of return on S during the interval. The basic lattice approach as suggested by CRR considers the situation where there is only one state variable: the price of a non-dividend paying stock. The time to maturity of the option is divided into N equal intervals of length Δt during which the stock price moves from its initial value S to one of the two new values Su and Sd with probabilities p and $(1-p)$, respectively.

It is a simple matter to extend the binomial approach to account for information costs. The acquisition of information and its dissemination are central activities in finance, and especially in capital markets. Merton (1987) provided a model of CAPMI to provide some insights into the behavior of security prices. From Merton's model (1987), it appears that taking into account the effect of incomplete information on the equilibrium price of an asset is similar to applying an additional discount rate to this asset's future cash flows. In fact, the expected return on the asset is given by the appropriate discount rate that must be applied to its future cash flows. In fact, in a risk-neutral world, it is possible to show that we have the appropriate value for u, d, and p. In this world, the expected return on the underlying asset in time Δt is $(r + \lambda_S)\Delta t$. The variance of this underlying asset on the same interval is $\sigma^2\Delta t$.

The term λ_S indicates the shadow cost of incomplete information for the asset S. Consider the previous analysis in the presence of an information cost λ. This cost can be seen as a shadow cost or a marginal cost reflecting the return required by market participants to include some assets in their portfolios. It is well known that there are thousands of financial assets in financial markets. However, investors decide to include only some of these assets in their portfolios. They suffer “a sunk cost” in collecting data, analyzing financial products and implementing financial models. These costs are necessary in the choice of financial assets and the implementation of some strategies. Therefore, investors need to be compensated by a return corresponding to these costs as it appears in Merton’s (1987) model. Consider, for example, a financial institution using a given market. If the costs of portfolio selection and models conception, etc. are computed, then it can require at least a return of say, for example $\lambda = 3\%$, before acting in this market. This cost represents its minimal cost before acting in a given market. It is in some way, its minimal return required before implementing a given strategy.

The expected return on the stock can be written as:

$$pSu + (1 - p)Sd = Se^{(r+\lambda_S)\Delta t}.$$

The variance on the stock can be written for the same interval Δt as:

$$pS^2u^2 + (1 - p)S^2d^2 - (Se^{(r+\lambda_S)\Delta t})^2.$$

The last expression can be written as:

$$S^2(e^{(r+\lambda_S)\Delta t}(e^{\sigma\sqrt{\Delta t}} + e^{-\sigma\sqrt{\Delta t}}) - 1 - e^{2(r+\lambda_S)\Delta t}).$$

For the valuation of derivative assets, the expected value of the underlying asset in a risk-neutral world of Merton (1987) is $Se^{(r+\lambda_S)\Delta t}$. In this context, we can write the equality between this expected value and the one given by the binomial model: $pSu + (1 - p)Sd = Se^{(r+\lambda_S)\Delta t}$ or: $pu + (1 - p)d = e^{(r+\lambda_S)\Delta t}$.

If we use the above equations and assume that $u = \frac{1}{d}$, then we have:

$$u = e^{\sigma\sqrt{\Delta t}}, \quad d = e^{-\sigma\sqrt{\Delta t}}, \quad p = \frac{a - d}{u - d}, \quad a = e^{(r+\lambda_s)\Delta t}.$$

In a risk-neutral world, the option value at time $T - \Delta t$ can be calculated as the expected value at the maturity date T discounted at $(r + \lambda_c)$ for the time Δt. In the same way, the values of the derivative security can be calculated at time $T - 2\Delta t$ as the expected value at time $T - \Delta t$ discounted at $(r + \lambda_c)$ for the time Δt and so on. If we define the value of a contingent claim as $F_{i,j}$ at time $t+i\Delta t$ when the underlying asset is $Su^j d^{i-j}$, then the value of a European option with information costs can be computed using the following equation:

$$F_{i,j} = e^{-(r+\lambda_c)\Delta t}[(pF_{i+1,j+1} + (1-p)F_{i+1,j})].$$

At each node, at time $t + i\Delta t$, the American call option value is given by:

$$F_{i,j} = \max[Su^j d^{i-j} - K, e^{-(r+\lambda_c)\Delta t}(pF_{i+1,j+1} + (1-p)F_{i+1,j})].$$

At maturity, the value of a European put on a non-dividend paying asset is:

$$F_{N,j} = \max[K - Su^j d^{N-j},\ 0]$$

This terminal value gives the option values for the $(N + 1)$ terminal nodes. Then at each node, at time $t + i\Delta t$, the American put value is given by:

$$F_{i,j} = \max[K - Su^j d^{i-j}, \quad e^{-(r+\lambda_c)\Delta t}(pF_{i+1,j+1} + (1-p)F_{i+1,j})].$$

17.2.4. *The binomial model for options in the presence of a continuous dividend stream and information costs*

The extension of the lattice approach in the presence of information costs and a continuous dividend yield is simple. If a security pays a dividend yield q, then the expected return on the underlying asset is $(r + \lambda_c - q)$. In this case, we can write the equality between the expected value of the underlying asset and the one given by the binomial model as: $pSu + (1-p)Sd = Se^{(r+\lambda_S-q)\Delta t}$ or: $pu + (1-p)$ $d = e^{(r+\lambda_S-q)\Delta t}$. In this case, using the same procedure as before, it can be shown that the parameters for the binomial model are:

$$u = e^{\sigma\sqrt{\Delta t}}, \quad d = e^{-\sigma\sqrt{\Delta t}}, \quad p = \frac{a-d}{u-d}, \quad \text{and} \quad a = e^{(r+\lambda_s-q)\Delta t}.$$

The value of a European contingent claim $F_{i,j}$ at time $t + i\Delta t$ when the underlying asset is $Su^j d^{i-j}$, in the presence of information uncertainty can be calculated using the following equation:

$$F_{i,j} = e^{-(r+\lambda_c)\Delta t}[(pF_{i+1,j+1} + (1-p)F_{i+1,j})].$$

In the same context, at time $t + i\Delta t$, the American call option value is given by:

$$F_{i,j} = \max[Su^j d^{i-j} - K, e^{-(r+\lambda_c)\Delta t}(pF_{i+1,j+1} + (1-p)F_{i+1,j})].$$

At each node, at time $t + i\Delta t$, the American put value is given by:

$$F_{i,j} = \max[K - Su^j d^{i-j}, e^{-(r+\lambda_c)\Delta t}(pF_{i+1,j+1} + (1-p)F_{i+1,j})].$$

17.2.5. *The binomial model for options in the presence of a known dividend yield and information costs*

The lattice or binomial approach can be easily modified when the underlying asset pays a known dividend yield, δ.

At an instant $t + i\Delta t$, prior to the ex-dividend date, stock prices are given by: $Su^j d^{i-j}$ for $j = 0, 1, \ldots, i$. At an instant $(t + i\Delta t)$, just after the ex-dividend date, stock prices are given by:

$$S(1-d)u^j d^{i-j} \quad \text{for } j = 0, 1, \ldots, i.$$

17.2.6. *The binomial model for options in the presence of a discrete dividend stream and information costs*

When there is just one ex-cash income date τ, during the option's life and $k\Delta t \leq \tau \leq (k+1)\Delta t$, then at time y, the value of the stochastic component S is given by:

$$S^*(y) = S(y) \quad \text{when } y > \tau,$$

and

$$S^*(y) = S(y) - D_i e^{-(r+\lambda_c)(\tau - y)} \quad \text{when } y \leq \tau.$$

Assume σ^* is the constant volatility of S^*. Using the parameters p, u, and d, at time $t + i\Delta t$, the nodes on the tree define the stock prices:

$$\text{If } i\Delta t < \tau\text{: } S^*(t)u^j d^{i-j} + De^{-(r+\lambda_c)(\tau - i\Delta t)} \quad j = 0, 1, \ldots, i$$

$$\text{If } i\Delta t \geq \tau\text{: } S^*(t)u^j d^{i-j} \quad j = 0, 1, \ldots, i.$$

17.2.7. *The binomial model for futures options in the presence of information costs*

In a risk-neutral economy, the expected return on an asset paying a continuous dividend yield q is $(r - q)$.

In this context, the equations:

$$u = e^{\sigma\sqrt{\Delta t}}, \quad d = e^{-\sigma\sqrt{\Delta t}}, \quad p = \frac{a-d}{u-d},$$

are used, except for a, which must be re-written as: $a = e^{(r-q+\lambda_c)\Delta t}$. For a futures, contract, $r + \lambda_c = b$ and $a = 1$. When information costs are equal to zero, then $r = b$ and $a = 1$.

17.2.8. *The lattice approach for American options with information costs and several cash distributions*

17.2.8.1. *The model*

When the amounts of payments are accounted for, it can be shown that a sufficient condition for optimal exercise is:

$$(D_i + R_i) > K[1 - e^{-(r+\lambda_S)(t_{i+1}-t_i)}]$$

with $(D_i + R_i) \geq 0$. When there are no dividends, the American put may be exercised because interest can be earned on the exercisable proceeds of the option. The put is exercised at time t_i if:

$$(D_i + R_i) < K[1 - e^{-(r+\lambda_S)(t_{i+1}-t_i)}]$$

with $(D_i + R_i) \geq 0$. It is a simple matter to extend this approach to account for information uncertainty. When $u = 1/d$, it can be shown that:

$$p = \frac{a-d}{u-d}, \quad u = e^{\sigma\sqrt{\Delta t}}, \quad d = e^{-\sigma\sqrt{\Delta t}}, \quad \text{and} \quad a = e^{(r+\lambda_S)\Delta t}.$$

The term λ_S appears because of the duplication portfolio. The nature of the lattice of stock prices is completely specified and the nodes correspond to:

$$Su^j d^{i-j} \quad \text{where } j = 0, 1, \ldots, i.$$

The option is evaluated by starting at time T and working backward. Let us denote by $F_{i,j}$, the option value at time $t + i\Delta t$ when the stock price is $Su^j d^{i-j}$. At time $t + i\Delta t$, the option holder can choose to exercise the option and receives the amount by which K (or S) exceeds the current stock price (or K) or wait. The American call is given by:

$$F_{i,j} = \max[Su^j d^{i-j} - K, e^{-(r+\lambda_c)\Delta t}(pF_{i+1,j+1} + (1-p)F_{i+1,j})].$$

The discounting factor is adjusted by information costs in the option market to reflect sunk costs paid in this market. The American put is given by:

$$F_{i,j} = \max[K - Su^j d^{i-j}, e^{-(r+\lambda_c)\Delta t}(pF_{i+1,j+1} + (1-p)F_{i+1,j})].$$

When there is just one ex-cash income date τ, and $k\Delta t \leq \tau \leq (k+1)\Delta t$, then at time y, the value of the stochastic component S is given by:

$$S^*(y) = S(y) \quad \text{when } y > \tau$$
$$S^*(y) = S(y) - (Di + Ri)e^{-(r+\lambda_S)(\tau - y)} \quad \text{when } y \leq \tau$$

Assume σ^* is the constant volatility of S^*. Using the parameters p, u, and d, at time $t + i\Delta t$, the nodes on the tree define the stock prices:

$$\text{If } i\Delta t < \tau\text{: } S^*(t)u^j d^{i-j} + (Di + Ri)e^{-(r+\lambda_S)(\tau - i\Delta t)} \quad j = 0, 1, \ldots, i$$
$$\text{If } i\Delta t \geq \tau\text{: } S^*(t)u^j d^{i-j} \quad j = 0, 1, \ldots, i.$$

17.3. The Binomial Model and Risk Neutrality: Some Important Details

Nawalkha and Chambers (1995) re-examine the consistency of the binomial option pricing model with the risk-neutrality argument of

Cox and Ross (1976). They show that risk neutrality in discrete time is a consequence of a specific choice of binomial parameters by Cox *et al.* (CRR) (1979).

17.3.1. *The binomial parameters and risk neutrality*

The original discrete-time binomial model of CRR, can be presented as follows. Consider at time $t = 0$, a call option with a maturity date T. Let T be divided into N number of sub-intervals. Denote the current time by $t = \frac{T}{N}(N-1)$. At the current time, the option is $\frac{T}{N}$ periods from the expiration date. In the next period, the stock S goes up to uS or down to dS with $u \geq d$. The probability of an upward movement is q. The probability of a downward movement is $(1-q)$.

As shown by CRR (1979), the call price at the current time is:

$$C = [p_u C^u + p_d C^d]/r^h \tag{17.3}$$

where,

$$p_u = \frac{r^h - d}{u - d'} \quad p_d = \frac{u - r^h}{u - d'}$$
$$C^u = \max[0,\ uS - K]$$
$$C^d = \max[0,\ dS - K]$$

and $r = 1+$ the risk-less rate over a single period and $h = \frac{T}{N}$ periods.

The binomial parameters specified by CRR are:

$$u = \exp(\sigma(T/N)^{0.5})$$
$$d = \exp(-\sigma(T/N)^{0.5})$$
$$q = (1/2)[1 + (\mu/\sigma)(T/N)^{0.5}).$$

In this expression, the term μ indicates the preference parameter. In this model, the probability q is between 0 and 1, so $-\sigma(T/N)^{0.5} < \mu(T/N)^{0.5} < \sigma(T/N)^{0.5}$. Since the expressions of u and d do not contain μ, the risk-neutral probabilities p_u and p_d and the call prices C^u and C^d are independent of preferences. The choice of binomial parameters is not unique. For example, Jarrow and Rudd (1983) specify u, d, and q as:

$$u = \exp[\mu(T/N) + \sigma(T/N)^{0.5}] \tag{17.4}$$

$$d = \exp[\mu(T/N) - \sigma(T/N)^{0.5}] \tag{17.5}$$

$$q = (1/2).$$

Jarrow and Rudd (1983) showed that the first three parameters for the stock's return are consistent with the log-normal process. The three moments are the mean $\mu(T/N)$, the variance $\sigma^2(T/N)$, and the skewness, which equal zero. However, the three moments for the log-normal process using the CRR parameters are inconsistent with the corresponding moments of the log-normal process. In fact, using the CRR parameters, the moments are: the mean $\mu(T/N)$, the variance $\sigma^2(T/N) - \mu^2(T/N)^2$, and the skewness which equals $2\mu[\mu^2(T/N)^3 - \sigma^2(T/N)^2]$. This simple analysis shows that the CRR parameters imply a level of skewness, which is different from zero. The variance and the skewness of the binomial model of CRR converge to the variance and the skewness of the log-normal process only in the continuous time limit. This is the case since $(T/N)^2$ and $(T/N)^3$ become insignificant in comparison to (T/N) as N tends to infinity. The Jarrow and Rudd (1983) parameters are inconsistent with the risk-neutral approach in discrete time. In fact, if one replaces the values of u and d from Eqs. (17.4) and (17.5) in Eq. (17.3), we see that the probabilities and option values depend on the preference parameter μ.

Consider the general form of the binomial model parameters:

$$\begin{aligned} u &= \exp[m(T/N) + \sigma(T/N)^{0.5}] \\ d &= \exp[m(T/N) - \sigma(T/N)^{0.5}] \\ q &= (1/2)[1 + ((\mu - m)/\sigma)(T/N)^{0.5}] \end{aligned} \tag{17.6}$$

with

$$-\sigma(T/N)^{0.5} < (\mu - m)(T/N) < \sigma(T/N)^{0.5}.$$

This choice of the binomial parameters leads to the following three moments over a discrete subinterval: a mean $\mu(T/N)$, a variance $\sigma^2(T/N) - (\mu - m)^2(T/N)^2$ and the skewness which equals

$2(\mu - m)[(\mu - m)^2(T/N)^3 - \sigma^2(T/N)^2]$. Again, the terms $(T/N)^2$ and $(T/N)^3$ become insignificant in comparison to (T/N) as N tends to infinity.

In this case, the variance and the skewness of the binomial process implied by these parameters converge to the variance and skewness of the log-normal process in the continuous time limit.

Equation (17.6) and other equations given under Eq. (17.6) imply that the probabilities and option prices depend upon m. Investors may disagree about the preference parameter μ and agree on m.

In the CRR model, the parameter $m = 0$.

In the Jarrow and Rudd (1983) model, the parameter $\mu = m$.

A unique equivalent probability measure à la Harrison and Kreps (1979) exists and implies that the stock price discounted at the riskless rate is a martingale under this measure. In this setting, the risk-neutral probabilities must be greater than zero in Eq. (17.3). Hence, we must have for the CRR choice that:

$$\exp[-\sigma(T/N)^{0.5}] < r^h < \exp[\sigma(T/N)^{0.5}].$$

We must have for the Jarrow and Rudd (1983) choice that:

$$\exp[\mu(T/N) - \sigma(T/N)^{0.5}] < r^h < \exp[\mu(T/N) + \sigma(T/N)^{0.5}].$$

We must have for the revealed preference parameters in Nawalkha and Chambers (1995) choice that:

$$\exp[m(T/N) - \sigma(T/N)^{0.5}] < r^h < \exp[m(T/N) + \sigma(T/N)^{0.5}].$$

The analysis shows that when $m = \mu$, the binomial model is inconsistent with the risk-neutrality argument of Cox and Ross (1976) and the model is preference dependent. When m differs from μ, the risk neutrality can still hold because investors are allowed to disagree with μ. In this case, different values of m can generate different option prices in discrete time. These limitations disappear in the continuous time limit. In fact, when N tends to infinity, the Black and Scholes (1973) formula is obtained. Hence, the binomial model is independent of the parameter m only in the continuous time limit.

17.3.2. *The convergence argument*

We use the binomial equation for the general choice of binomial parameters. The call price at time t between 0 and T is given by:

$$C_t = [p_u C^u_{t+h} + p_d C^d_{t+h}]/r^h \tag{17.7}$$

where the different parameters are given in Eq. (17.6). We can write that: $C_t = C(S_t, T-t), C^u_{t+h} = C(uS_t, T-(t+h)), C^d_{t+h} = C(dS_t, T-(t+h))$.

By appropriate substitutions, we can write (17.7) as:

$$\begin{aligned}
&\left[\frac{r^h - \exp[mh - \sigma(h^{0.5})]}{\exp[mh + \sigma(h^{0.5})] - \exp[mh - \sigma(h^{0.5})]}\right] \\
&\quad \cdot C(\exp[mh + \sigma(h^{0.5}] \cdot S_t, T - (t+h)) \\
&\quad + \left[\frac{\exp[mh + \sigma(h^{0.5})] - r^h}{\exp[mh + \sigma(h^{0.5})] - \exp[mh - \sigma(h^{0.5})]}\right] \\
&\quad \cdot C(\exp[mh + \sigma(h^{0.5}] \cdot S_t, T - (t+h)) \\
&\quad - r^h C(S_t, T-t) = 0
\end{aligned}$$

Using Taylor series expansions of $C(\exp[mh + \sigma(h^{0.5})]S_t, T - (t+h))$ and $C(\exp[mh - \sigma(h^{0.5})]S_t, T - (t+h))$ around the point $(S_t, (T-t))$ gives:

$$\begin{aligned}
C(\exp[mh + \sigma(h^{0.5})]S_t, T - (t+h)) &= C_t \\
&+ [\exp[mh + \sigma(h^{0.5})] - 1]S_t \frac{\partial C_t}{\partial S_t} \\
&+ \frac{1}{2}[\exp[mh + \sigma(h^{0.5})] - 1]^2 S_t^2 \frac{\partial^2 C_t}{\partial^2 S_t} + h\frac{\partial C_t}{\partial t} + \cdots +
\end{aligned} \tag{17.8}$$

A similar expression can be obtained for $C(\exp[mh - \sigma(h^{0.5})]S_t, T - (t+h))$ with $-\sigma(h^{0.5})$ instead $+\sigma(h^{0.5})$. Using Taylor series for:

$$\begin{aligned}
\exp[mh + \sigma(h^{0.5})] &= 1 + [mh + \sigma(h^{0.5})] \\
&+ \frac{1}{2}[mh + \sigma(h^{0.5})]^2 + \cdots +
\end{aligned} \tag{17.9}$$

A similar expression can be obtained for $\exp[mh - \sigma(h^{0.5})]$. A Taylor series expansion of r^h gives:

$$r^h = \exp(h \cdot \mathrm{logr}) = 1 + h \cdot \mathrm{logr} + \frac{1}{2}(h \cdot \mathrm{logr})^2 + \cdots + \qquad (17.10)$$

Substituting Eqs. (17.8), (17.9), (17.10) gives:

$$\frac{1}{2}\sigma^2 S_t^2 \frac{\partial^2 C_t}{\partial^2 S_t} h + (\mathrm{logr}) S \frac{\partial C_t}{\partial S_t} \cdot h + \frac{\partial C_t}{\partial S_t} \cdot h - (\mathrm{logr}) C_t h + Z = 0$$

where Z contains all terms of higher order of h. Dividing this last equation by h gives:

$$\frac{1}{2}\sigma^2 S_t^2 \frac{\partial^2 C_t}{\partial^2 S_t} h + (\mathrm{logr}) S \frac{\partial C_t}{\partial S_t} + \frac{\partial C_t}{\partial t} - (\mathrm{logr}) C_t + Z/h = 0.$$

The solution to this equation depends on the revealed preference parameter contained in the term Z/h. However, when the number of sub-intervals tend to infinity, the term Z/h goes to zero. This last equation converges then to the Black and Scholes (1973) partial differential equation. This equation is independent of m.

17.4. The Hull and White Trinomial Model for Interest Rate Options

Hull and White (1993) presented a general numerical procedure involving the use of trinomial trees for constructing one-factor models, which are consistent with initial market data where the short rate follows a Markovian process. Their procedure is efficient and provides a convenient way of implementing models already suggested in the literature. It should be noted in passing that a one-period trinomial tree is somehow equivalent to a standard two-period binomial tree. For example, they studied the case where the process for $r(t)$ has the general form considered by Hull and White (1990), also called the extended Vasicek model:

$$dr = \mu[\theta, r, t]dt + \sigma dW(t)$$

In this model, the volatility σ is a known constant and the functional form of μ is known. The value of θ_t is unknown.

The short interest rate r corresponds to the continuously compounded yield on a discount bond maturing at date Δt. When the tree is constructed, the values of r are equally spaced and have the following form: $T_\theta + j\Delta t$. Note that r_0 is the current interest-rate value and j is an integer, which may be positive or negative. Also, the values of Δt are equally spaced with a positive integer i. As shown in Hull and White (1990), the variables Δt and Δr must be chosen in such a way that Δr lies in an interval between $\frac{\sigma}{2}\sqrt{3\Delta t}$ and $2\sigma\sqrt{\Delta t}$.

We use the following notation:

(i,j): a node on the tree for the values of $t = i\Delta t$, and $r_j = r_0 + j\Delta r$ with $i \geq 2$;
$R(i)$: yield at time zero on a discount bond maturing at time $i\Delta t$;
$\mu(i,j)$: drift rate of r at node (i,j) with $r_j = r_0 + j\Delta r$ and
$P_k^{(i,j)}$: for $k = 1, 2, 3$, the probabilities corresponding respectively to the upper, middle, and lower branches emanating from node (i,j).

If the tree constructed up to time $n\Delta t, (n \geq 0)$ is consistent with the observed $R(i)$ and the interest rate r at time $i\Delta t$ applies to the interval time between $i\Delta t$ and $(i+1)\Delta t$, then the tree reflects the values of $R(i)$ for $i \leq (n+1)$. Note that between times $n\Delta t$ and $(n+1)\Delta t$, the value of $\theta(n\Delta t)$ must be chosen in such a way that the tree is consistent with $R(n+2)$.

Once the value of $\theta(n\Delta t)$ is known, then it is possible to calculate the drift rates $\mu_{n,j}$ for r at time $n\Delta t$ using:

$$\mu_{n,j} = \mu[\theta(n\Delta t), r_0 + j\Delta r, n\Delta t)]. \tag{17.11}$$

The three nodes from node (n,j) are: $(n+1, k+1)$, $(n+1, k)$, and $(n+1, k-1)$, where k must be chosen in such a way that r_k, (the value of the interest rate reached by the middle branch) is very close to the expected value of the interest rate, $r_j + \mu_{n,j}\Delta t$.

Hull and White (1993) gave the following probabilities:

$$P_1(n,j) = \frac{\sigma^2\Delta t}{2\Delta r^2} + \frac{\eta^2}{2\Delta r^2} + \frac{\eta}{2\Delta r}$$

$$P_2(n,j) = 1 - \frac{\sigma^2\Delta t}{\Delta r^2} + \frac{\eta^2}{\Delta r^2}$$

$$P_3(n,j) = \frac{\sigma^2\Delta t}{2\Delta r^2} + \frac{\eta^2}{2\Delta r^2} - \frac{\eta}{2\Delta r^2}$$

with

$$\eta = \mu_{n,j}\Delta t + (j - k)\Delta r.$$

This general procedure for fitting a one-factor model of the short rate to the initial yield curve using a trinomial interest-rate tree can be used to test the effect of a wide range of assumptions about the interest-rate process on the prices of interest-rate derivatives. However, much research remains to be done to obtain better models for interest rates. Anyway, this model also allows for negative interest rates.

17.5. Pricing Path-Dependent Interest Rate Contingent Claims Using a Lattice

Dharan (1997) proposed a framework for the pricing of path-dependent interest rate derivatives such as index-amortizing swaps or mortgage-backed securities with a simple pre-payment function for which there is no analytical solution. He showed how to construct a lattice to value a mortgage-backed security when the pre-payment function is linear. This model and several of its applications to the pricing of path-dependent claims are provided by Dharan (1997).

Summary

The lattice approach for the pricing of options can be specified with respect to stock options in the absence of payments to the underlying asset. The option's maturity date is divided into several reasonably small intervals of time. During each time interval, the underlying asset price moves either upward or downward. This movement in the stock price is binomial with a probability p attached to an upward jump and a probability $(1-p)$ to a downward movement. The parameters corresponding to the up, down, and the probability are functions of the mean and variance of the rates of return on S during the interval. The basic lattice approach suggested by CRR considers the situation where there is only one state variable: the price of a non-dividend paying stock. The time to maturity of the option is divided into equal intervals. It is a simple matter to extend this approach to account for the effects of a continuous dividend yield, a discrete dividend, information costs, etc. The valuation of options in a binomial model is easy to implement since we start at the maturity date, where the payoff is known, and then proceed backward through the tree. In a risk-neutral world, the option value at a given time can be calculated as the expected value at the maturity date discounted at the appropriate rate.

The valuation of European options is slightly different from that of the American options. For the American options, the holder can exercise his/her option at any instance before the maturity date. Therefore, at each node, the option value must be at least equal to its intrinsic value. The extension of the lattice approach in the presence of information costs and a continuous dividend yield is simple.

This chapter shows that the consistency of the discrete-time binomial option pricing model of Cox *et al.* (1979) with the risk-neutrality argument depends heavily on the appropriate choice of its parameters. In fact, for a certain choice of the parameters, the option prices can depend on investor preferences. This preference dependence diminishes as the number of sub-intervals become large. This dependence disappears only in the continuous time limit when the binomial model converges to the Black and Scholes (1973) model. Risk neutrality is obtained when the CRR model assumes a very specific behavior regarding the price changes of the underlying asset. Hence, in general, risk neutrality is not obtained in discrete time in some cases.

Hull and White (1993) developed a numerical procedure that is based on the use of trinomial trees for constructing one-factor models of interest rates. The models are consistent with initial market data where the short rate follows a Markovian process. The procedure adopted by Hull and White (1993) is efficient and provides a convenient way of implementing several other models in the literature.

This chapter presents the basic concepts and techniques underlying the derivative assets pricing problem within the context of binomial models and lattice approaches. The lattice approach is applied to the valuation of European and American equity options when the underlying asset is traded in a spot or in a futures market. The approach is extended to the valuation of options by taking into account several cash distributions to the underlying assets. It is convenient to note that lattice approaches can be easily implemented and adapted to different derivative asset payoffs. This approach is more pedagogical than the continuous time approach. However, it takes some time to offer accurate option prices, which is not a major handicap when there is no closed form or analytic solutions.

References

Barone-Adesi G and RE Whaley (1987). Efficient analytic approximation of American option values. *Journal of Finance*, 42 (June), 301–320.

Bellalah M (1999a). The valuation of futures and commodity options with information costs. *Journal of Futures Markets*, 19 (September), 645–664.

Bellalah M (1999b). Les biais des modeles d'options revisites. *Revue Francaise de Gestion* (Juin), 94–100.

Bellalah M (2000a). A risk management approach to options trading on the Paris Bourse. *Derivatives Strategy*, 5(6), 31–33.

Bellalah M (2000b). Valuation of American CAC 40 index options and wildcard options. *International Review of Economics and Finance.*

Bellalah M (2001). Market imperfections; information costs and the valuation of derivatives: Some general results. *International Journal of Finance*, 13(3), 1895–1927.

Bellalah M and B Jacquillat (1995). Option valuation with information costs: Theory and tests. *The Financial Review*, 30(3), 617–635.

Bellalah M and J-L Prigent (2001). Pricing standard and exotic options in the presence of a finite mixture of Gaussian distributions. *International Journal of Finance*, 13(3), 1975–2000.

Bellalah M and F Selmi (2001). On the quadratic criteria for hedging under transaction costs. *International Journal of Finance*, 13(3), 2001–2020.

Bellalah M, JL Prigent and C Villa (2001a). Skew without skewness: Asymmetric smiles; information costs and stochastic volatilities. *International Journal of Finance*, 13(2), 1826–1837.

Bellalah M, M Bellalah and R Portait (2001b). The cost of capital in international finance. *International Journal of Finance*, 13(3), 1958–1973.

Black F (1976). Studies of stock price volatility changes. In *Proceedings of the 1976 Meeting of the Business Economics Statistics Section.* American Statistical Association, pp. 177–181.

Black F and M Scholes (1973). The pricing of options and corporate liabilities. *Journal of Political Economy*, 81, 637–659.

Cox JC and SA Ross (1976). The valuation of options for alternative stochastic processes. *Journal of Financial Economics*, 3, 145–166.

Cox J, S Ross and M Rubinstein (1979). Option pricing: A simplified approach. *Journal of Financial Economics*, 7, 229–263.

Dharan VG (1997). Pricing path-dependent interest rate contingent claims using a lattice. *Journal of Fixed Income*, 6 (March), 41–49.

Harrison JM and D Kreps (1979). Martingales and arbitrage in multiperiod securities markets. *Journal of Economic Theory*, 20, 381–408.

Ho I and S Lee (1986). Term structure movements and pricing interest rate contingent claims. *Journal of Finance*, 41, 1011–1029.

Hull J (2000). *Options, Futures, and Other Derivative Securities*. 4th edn. Prentice Hall, Englewood Cliffs, NJ.

Hull J and A White (1990). Pricing interest rate derivative securities. *Review of Financial Studies*, 3, 573–592.

Hull J and A White (1993). Efficient procedures for valuing European and American path dependent options. *Journal of Derivatives*, 1 (Fall), 21–31.

Jarrow RA and A Rudd (1983). *Option Pricing*. Irwin, Homewood, IL.

Lintner J (1965). Security prices, risk and maximal gains from diversification. *Journal of Finance*, 20, 587–616.

Markowitz HM (1952). Portfolio selection. *Journal of Finance*, 7(1), 77–91.

Merton R (1973). Theory of rational option pricing. *Bell Journal of Economics and Management Science*, 4, 141–183.

Merton RC (1987). A simple model of capital market equilibrium with incomplete information. *Journal of Finance*, 42(3), 483–510.

Nawalkha SK and DR Chambers (1995). The binomial model and the risk neutrality: Some important details. *Financial Review*, 30(3) (August), 605–615.

Scholes M (1998). Derivatives in a dynamic environment. *American Economic Review*, 88(2), 350–370.

Shapiro A (2000). The investor recognition hypothesis in a dynamic general equilibrium: Theory and evidence. Working Paper, Stern School of Business, New York University.

Sharpe WF (1964). Capital asset prices: A theory of market equilibrium under conditions of risk. *Journal of Finance*, 19, 425–442.

Part V

Option Pricing in a Continuous-Time Setting: Basic Models, Extensions and Applications

Chapter 18

European Option Pricing Models: The Precursors of the Black–Scholes–Merton Theory and Holes During Market Turbulence

Chapter Outline

This chapter is organized as follows:

1. Section 18.1 gives an overview of the option pricing theory in the pre-Black–Scholes period.
2. Section 18.2 presents the story and the main results in the breakthrough work of Black–Scholes for the pricing of derivative assets when the underlying asset is traded in a spot market. It proposes the story until the publication of the original formula.
3. Section 18.3 develops the foundations of the Black–Scholes–Merton Theory.
4. Section 18.4 presents two alternative derivations of the Black–Scholes model. The formula is derived using equilibrium market conditions and arbitrage theory.
5. Section 18.5 reviews the main results in Black's (1976) model for the pricing of derivative assets when the underlying asset is traded on a forward or a futures market. Some applications of the model are also given.

6. Section 18.6 applies the capital-asset pricing model (CAPM) to the valuation of forward contracts, futures, and commodity options.
7. Section 18.7 studies the "holes" in the Black–Scholes–Merton theory.

Introduction

Numerous researchers have worked on building a theory of rational option pricing and a general theory of contingent claims valuation. The story began in 1900, when the French mathematician, Louis Bachelier, obtained an option pricing formula. His model is based on the assumption that stock prices follow a Brownian motion. Since then, numerous studies on option valuation have blossomed. The proposed formulas involve one or more arbitrary parameters. They were developed by Sprenkle (1961), Ayres (1963), Boness (1964), Samuelson (1965), Thorp and Kassouf (1967), and Chen (1970) among others. The Black and Scholes (1973) formulation, hereafter called as B–S, solved a problem, which has occupied the economists for at least three-quarters of a century. This formulation represented a significant breakthrough in attacking the option pricing problem. In fact, the Black–Scholes theory is attractive since it delivers a closed-form solution to the pricing of European options. Assuming that the option is a function of a single source of uncertainty, namely the underlying asset price, and using a portfolio which combines options and the underlying asset, Black and Scholes constructed a risk-less hedge, which allowed them to derive an analytical formula. This model provides a no-arbitrage value for European options on shares. It is a function of the share price S, the strike price K, the time to maturity T, the risk-free interest rate r, and the volatility of the stock price, σ. This model involves only observable variables to the exception of volatility and it has become the benchmark for traders and market makers. It also contributed to the rapid growth of the options markets by making a brand new pricing technology available to market players.

About the same time, the necessary conditions to be satisfied by any rational option pricing theory were summarized in Merton's (1973) theorems. The post-Black–Scholes period has seen many theoretical developments. The contributions of many financial economists to the extensions and generalizations of Black–Scholes type models has enriched our understanding of derivative assets and their seemingly endless applications.

The first specific option pricing model for the valuation of futures options is introduced by Black (1976). Black (1976) derived the formula for futures and forward contracts and options under the assumption that investors create risk-less hedges between options and the futures or forward contracts. The formula relies implicitly on the capital asset pricing model (CAPM). Futures markets are not different in principal from the market for any other asset. The returns on any risky asset are governed by the asset contribution to the risk of a well-diversified portfolio. The classic CAPM is applied by Dusak (1973) in the analysis of the risk premium and the valuation of futures contracts.

Black's (1976) model is used in Barone-Adesi and Whaley (1987) for the valuation of American commodity options. This model is referred to as the BAW (1987) model. It is helpful, as in Smithson (1991), to consider the Black–Scholes model within a family tree of option pricing models. This allows the identification of three major tribes within the family of option pricing models: analytical models, analytic approximations, and numerical models. Each analytical tribe can be further divided into three distinct lineages: precursors to the Black–Scholes model, extensions of the Black–Scholes model, and generalizations of the Black–Scholes model.

This chapter presents in detail the basic theory of rational option pricing of European options and its applications along the Black–Scholes lines and its extensions by Black (1976) for options on futures, and European commodity options. The question of dividends, stochastic interest rates, and stochastic volatilities are left to other chapters since the main concern in this chapter is about analytical models under the Black and Scholes' (1973) assumptions. There is usually a difference between model values and options market prices. There are three possible reasons for the difference between the theoretical value and the market price. The first is that the model gives the correct value and the option price is out of line. In this case, it may be possible to trade profitably using this model. The second reason is that the wrong inputs are used in the formula. The main input is the volatility of the underlying asset over the life of the option that must be estimated. The third reason is that the formula is wrong because of its assumptions. These three reasons can explain the difference between model values and market prices.

18.1. Precursors to the Black–Scholes Model

The story began in 1900 with a doctoral dissertation at the Sorbonne in Paris, France, in which Louis Bachelier gave an analytical valuation formula for options.

18.1.1. *Bachelier formula*

Using an arithmetic Brownian motion for the dynamics of share prices and a normal distribution for share returns, Bachelier obtained the following formula for the valuation of a European call option on a non-dividend paying stock:

$$c(S,T) = SN\left(\frac{S-K}{\sigma\sqrt{T}}\right) - KN\left(\frac{S-K}{\sigma\sqrt{T}}\right) + \sigma\sqrt{T}n\left(\frac{K-S}{\sigma\sqrt{T}}\right) \tag{18.1}$$

where

S: underlying common stock price;
K: option's strike price;
T: option's time to maturity;
σ: instantaneous standard deviation of return;
$N(.)$: cumulative normal density function and
$n(.)$: density function of the normal distribution.

As pointed out by Merton (1973) and Smith (1976), this formulation allows for both negative security and option prices and does not account for the time value of money. Sprenkle (1961) re-formulated the option pricing problem by assuming that the dynamics of stock prices are log-normally distributed. By introducing a drift in the random walk, he ruled out negative security prices and allowed risk aversion. By letting asset prices to have multiplicative, rather than additive fluctuations, the distribution of the option's underlying asset at maturity is log-normal rather than normal.

18.1.2. *Sprenkle formula*

Sprenkle (1961) derived the following formula:

$$c(S,T) = Se^{\rho T}N(d_1) - (1-Z)KN(d_2)$$

$$d_1 = \frac{\ln\left(\frac{S}{K}\right) + \left(\rho + \frac{\sigma^2}{2}\right)T}{\sigma\sqrt{T}}, \quad d_2 = \frac{\ln\left(\frac{S}{K}\right) + \left(\rho - \frac{\sigma^2}{2}\right)T}{\sigma\sqrt{T}} \tag{18.2}$$

where ρ is the average rate of growth of the share price and Z corresponds to the degree of risk aversion. As it appears in this formula, the parameters corresponding to the average rate of growth of the share price and the degree of risk aversion must be estimated. This reduces considerably the use of this formula. Sprenkle (1961) tried to estimate the values of these parameters, but he was unable to do so.

18.1.3. *Boness formula*

Boness (1964) presented an option pricing formula accounting for the time value of money through the discounting of the terminal stock price using the expected rate of return to the stock. The option pricing formula proposed is:

$$c(S,T) = SN(d_1) - e^{-\rho T}KN(d_2)$$

$$d_1 = \frac{\ln\left(\frac{S}{K}\right) + \left(\rho + \frac{\sigma^2}{2}\right)T}{\sigma\sqrt{T}}, \quad d_2 = \frac{\ln\left(\frac{S}{K}\right) + \left(\rho - \frac{\sigma^2}{2}\right)T}{\sigma\sqrt{T}} \tag{18.3}$$

where ρ is the expected rate of return to the stock.

18.1.4. *Samuelson formula*

Samuelson (1965) allowed the option to have a different level of risk from the stock. Defining ρ as the average rate of growth of the share price and w as the average rate of growth of the call's value, he proposed the following formula:

$$c(S,T) = Se^{(\rho - w)T}N(d_1) - e^{-wT}KN(d_2)$$

$$d_1 = \frac{\ln\left(\frac{S}{K}\right) + \left(\rho + \frac{\sigma^2}{2}\right)T}{\sigma\sqrt{T}}, \quad d_2 = \frac{\ln\left(\frac{S}{K}\right) + \left(\rho - \frac{\sigma^2}{2}\right)T}{\sigma\sqrt{T}}. \tag{18.4}$$

Note that all the proposed formulas show one or more arbitrary parameters, depending on the investors' preferences towards risk or the rate of return on the stock. Samuelson and Merton (1969) proposed a theory of option valuation by treating the option price as a function of the stock price. They advanced the theory by realizing that the discount rate must be determined in part by the requirement that investors hold all the amounts of stocks and the option. Their final formula depends on the utility function assumed for a "typical" investor. Black and Scholes (1973) used a formula that was derived in Thorp and Kassouf (1967), who presented an empirical formula for warrants. This formula determines the ratio of shares of stocks needed to construct a hedged position. This position is constructed by buying an asset and selling another. However, Thorp and Kassouf did not realize that in equilibrium, the expected return on a hedged position must be the return on a risk-less asset. This concept is due to Black and Scholes as we will see in the derivation of their model.

18.2. How the Black–Scholes Option Formula Is Obtained

18.2.1. *The short story*

The main idea behind the Black–Scholes formula is the existence of a relationship among a call price, its underlying asset, the volatility, the strike price, the maturity date, and the interest rate. This relationship indicates how much the option value will change when the underlying asset changes by a small amount within a short time. Assume that the option price increases by US$ 0.5 when the underlying asset increases by US$ 1 and that the option price decreases by US$ 0.5 when the underlying asset decreases by US$ 1. In this context, it is possible to create a hedged position by selling two options and buying one round lot of stock. For small changes in the underlying asset price, the losses on one side will be nearly offset by gains on the other side. Hence, at first, a hedged position is created by selling two options and holding the underlying asset. When the underlying asset price increases, the position shows a loss on the option and a profit on the underlying asset. When the underlying asset price decreases, the position shows a gain on the option and a loss on the underlying asset. A neutral hedge can be maintained by modifying the position in the option, in the stock, or in both. The principle leading to the option formula is that a hedged position should yield an amount equal to the short-term interest rate on close-to-risk-less securities. A "reverse hedge" can also be implemented to generate the Black and Scholes (1973) formula by selling short the stock and buying the option (in the right ratio).

The formula can also be derived by assuming that a neutral spread must earn the interest rate. In fact, selling an option and buying another option on the same underlying asset in the right ratio is a neutral spread. The formula can be obtained even without the assumption of hedging or spreading. In this case, a comparison is done between a long stock position with a long option position that has the same action as the stock. In the above example, the investor compares a long position of one round lot of stock and the purchase of two option contracts. These two positions show the same movements for very small changes in the stock prices, so their returns must differ only by an amount equal to the interest rate times the difference in the total values of both positions. At equilibrium, investors are indifferent between the two positions. This leads to the same valuation formula.

18.2.2. *The differential equation*

The notion of equilibrium in the market for risky assets implies that riskier securities must have higher expected returns, or investors will not hold them – except that investors do not count the part of the risk they are able to diversify away.

Black (1976) applied the CAPM to the valuation of warrants in 1969. The method used at that time was based on the discounted expected value of the warrant at expiration. This method has two problems. First, the warrant price depends on the stock's expected return. Second, an appropriate discount rate must be chosen.

One key to solve this problem is to write the warrant formula as a function of the stock price and other factors. This approach was adopted by Black (1998) and Samuelson and Merton (1969). Black's unpublished formula shows that the expected return on a warrant depends on the risk of the warrant in the same way that a common stock's expected return depends on its risk.

Black used the CAPM to write down how the discount rate for a warrant varies with time and the stock price. This gave a differential equation for the warrant formula. Black did not recognize the equation as a version of the "heat equation". Therefore, he did not write down its solution. Besides, he did not note that the warrant value did not depend on the stock's expected return or any other asset's expected return.

18.2.3. *The derivation of the formula*

In 1969, Scholes and Black started working on the option problem at Massachusetts Institute of Technology (MIT). They concentrated on the fact that the option price depends on the volatility rather than the expected return. They assumed that the stock's expected return was equal to the constant interest rate. This assumption is equivalent to the fact that the stock's beta is zero, so all of its risk can be diversified away. They assumed also that the stock's volatility was constant and the terminal stock price "fits" into a log-normal distribution. Sprenkle used the same assumptions, except that he allowed the stock to have any constant expected return. The problem was to find the present value of the option rather than its expected terminal value.

The main idea to derive the formula was as follows: If the stock had an expected return equal to the interest rate, so would the option. Hence, all the stock's risk could be diversified away, so could all the option's risk. In other terms, if the stock's beta were zero, the option's beta would have to be zero too.

Hence, the expected terminal option's value must be discounted at the constant interest rate. The Black and Scholes (1973) formula can be obtained using Sprenkle's formula by putting in the interest rate for the expected return on the stock and putting in the interest rate again for the discount rate for the option.

18.2.4. *Publication of the formula*

Several discussions are done with Merton (1973) who was also working on option valuation. Merton (1973) pointed out that assuming continuous trading in the option or its underlying asset can preserve a hedged portfolio between the option and its underlying asset. Merton was able to prove that in the presence of a non-constant interest rate, a discount bond maturing at the option expiration date must be used.

Black and Scholes (1973) and Merton (1973) worked separately on the application of the formula to the valuation of risky corporate bonds and common stock. Black and Scholes gave an early version of their paper at a conference on capital market theory during summer 1970. Black and Scholes sent their article to the *Journal of Political Economy, the Review of Economics and Statistics* and it was rejected even without a review. The paper was sent again in 1971 to the *Journal of Political Economy* after accounting for the comments and suggestions by Merton, Miller, and Fama. The final draft of the paper dated May 1972 appeared in the May/June 1973 issue of the *Journal of Political Economy.* However, a paper on the results of some empirical tests appeared in the May 1972 issue of *Journal of Finance.*

18.2.5. *Testing the formula*

The formula was first tested on warrants. Black and Scholes estimated the volatility of the stock of each of a group of companies with warrants. Black, Scholes, and Merton found the best to buy be National General new warrants. They bought a bunch of these warrants. The formula and the volatility estimates were always based on the information at hand. Using the premiums received by a broker's option-writing customers in the over-the-counter (OTC) option market for a period of several years, some trading rules were tested by Black and Scholes. The formula was used to find out how much money could one have made if he had bought the options whose prices seemed lower than the formula values and sold the options whose prices seemed higher than the formula values. When transaction costs are ignored, this trading rule seemed to generate substantial profits. The second test was to assume buying the underpriced options and selling the overpriced options at the values given by the formula. Galai (for more details, refer to Bellalah *et al.*, 1998) tested the formula using listed options traded in the Chicago Board Options Exchange (CBOE) and found profits which are much larger than those found in the OTC market. He tested the profitability of spreads that are kept neutral continuously. A neutral spread corresponds to a strategy of buying an option and selling another option on the same underlying asset. A neutral spread is maintained when the long or short positions are changed for every change in the underlying asset price and time to maturity. This strategy involves buying one contract of the underpriced option and selling either more or less than one contract of the overpriced option. This strategy seemed to generate a consistent profit if transaction costs and other trading costs were ignored. Today, traders use the formula so much that the market prices are usually close to formula values even in the presence of a cash takeover.

18.3. Financial Theory and the Black–Scholes–Merton Theory

18.3.1. *The Black–Scholes–Merton theory*

Black and Scholes (1973) and Merton (1973) showed that the construction of a risk-less hedge between the option and its underlying asset, allows the derivation of an option pricing formula regardless of investor's risk preferences. The main intuition behind the risk-free hedge is simple. Consider an at-the-money European call giving the right to its holder to buy one unit of the underlying asset in one month at a strike price of US$ 100. Assume that the final asset price is either 105 or 95. An investor selling a call on the unit of the asset will receive either 5 or 0. In this context, selling two calls against each unit of the asset will create a terminal portfolio value of 95. The certain terminal value of this portfolio must be equal today to the discounted value of 95 at the risk-less interest rate. If this rate is 1%, the present value is (95/1.01). The current option value is (100 – (95/1.01))/2. If the observed market price is above (or below) the theoretical price, it is possible to implement an arbitrage strategy by selling the call and buying (selling) a portfolio comprising a long position in a half unit of the asset and a short position in risk-free bonds. The Black–Scholes–Merton model is the continuous-time version of this example. The theory assumes that the underlying asset follows a geometric Brownian motion and is based on the construction of a risk-free hedge between the option and its underlying asset. This implies that the call payout can be duplicated by a portfolio consisting of the asset and risk-free bonds. In this theory, the option value is the same for a risk-neutral investor and a risk-averse investor. Hence, options can be valued in a risk-neutral world, i.e., expected returns on all assets are equal to the risk-free rate of interest.

18.3.2. *Analytical formulas*

The main and general result in the Black–Scholes–Merton theory is that if a risk-free hedge can be implemented using the option and its underlying asset, then risk-neutral valuation may be applied. This means that the theory applies in the presence of simple and complex options payouts. The Black–Scholes and Merton formula for a European call follows directly from the work of Sprenkle and Samuelson. In a risk-neutral world, all assets show an expected rate of return equal to the risk-free interest rate. This does not mean that all assets have the same expected rate of price appreciation. If the asset income which may be a dividend, a coupon, etc. is modeled as a constant continuous proportion of the asset price, then the expected rate of price appreciation must be equal to the interest rate less than the cash distribution rate. The theory covers a wide range of underlying assets.

For non-dividend-paying stock options: When there are no dividends on the underlying stock, the expected price appreciation rate of the stock is the risk-free interest rate.

For constant-dividend-yield stock options: When stocks pay dividends at a constant and a continuous dividend yield, Merton (1973) derives the option valuation formula. In his formula, the cost of carrying the underlying asset corresponds to the difference between the risk-free rate and the stock's dividend-yield rate.

Futures options: In a risk-neutral world with constant interest rates, the expected rate of price appreciation on a futures contract is zero. This is because the futures contract does not involve any cash outlay.

Foreign currency options: Garman and Kohlhagen (1983) value options on foreign currency. The expected rate of price appreciation of a foreign currency equals the domestic rate of interest less than the foreign rate of interest.

18.4. The Black–Scholes Model

Under the following assumptions, the value of the option will depend only on the price of the underlying asset S, time t, and on other variables that are assumed constants. These assumptions or "ideal conditions" as expressed by Black–Scholes are the following:

- The option is European;
- The short-term interest rate is known;
- The underlying asset follows a random walk with a variance rate proportional to the stock price. It pays no dividends or other distributions;
- There is no transaction costs and short selling is allowed, i.e., an investor can sell a security that he/she does not own and
- Trading takes place continuously and the standard form of the capital market model holds at each instant. The main attractions of the Black–Scholes model are that their formula is a function of "observable" variables and that the model can be extended to the pricing of any type of option.

18.4.1. *The Black–Scholes model and CAPM*

The CAPM of Sharpe (1964) can be stated as follows:

$$\overline{R}_S - r = \beta_S[\overline{R}_m - r] \tag{18.5}$$

where,

$\overline{R}_S$: equilibrium-expected return on security S;
$\overline{R}_m$: equilibrium-expected return on the market portfolio;
r: 1 + the risk-less rate of interest and
$\beta_S = \frac{\text{cov}(\tilde{R}_S/\tilde{R}_m)}{\text{var}(\tilde{R}_m)}$: the beta of security S, that is the covariance of the return on this security with the return on the market portfolio, divided by the variance of market return.

This model gives a general method for discounting future cash flows under uncertainty. Denote the value of the option by $C(S, t)$ as a function of the underlying asset and time. To derive their valuation formula, B–S assumed that the hedged position was continuously re-balanced in order to remain risk-less. They found that the price of a European call or put must verify a certain differential equation, which is based on the assumption that the price of the underlying asset follows a geometric Wiener process:

$$\frac{\Delta S}{S} = \alpha dt + \sigma \Delta z \tag{18.6}$$

where α and σ refer to the instantaneous rate of return and the standard deviation of the underlying asset, and z refers to Brownian motion. The relationship between an option's beta and its underlying security's beta is:

$$\beta_C = S\left(\frac{C_S}{C}\right)\beta_S \tag{18.7}$$

where,

β_c: the option's beta;
β_S: the stock's beta;
C: the option value;
C_S: the first derivative of the option with respect to its underlying asset. It is also the hedge ratio or the option's delta in a covered position. According to the CAPM, the expected return on a security should be:

$$\bar{R}_S - r = \beta_S[\bar{R}_m - r]$$

where $\bar{R}_S$ is the expected return on the asset S and $\bar{R}_m$ is the expected return on the market portfolio. This equation may also be written as:

$$E\left(\frac{\Delta S}{S}\right) = [r + \beta_S(\bar{R}_m - r)]\Delta t \tag{18.8}$$

Using the CAPM, the expected return on a call option should be:

$$E\left(\frac{\Delta C}{C}\right) = [r + \beta_C(\bar{R}_m - r)]\Delta t \tag{18.9}$$

Multiplying (18.8) and (18.9) by S and C yields:

$$E(\Delta S) = [rS + S\beta_S(\bar{R}_m - r)]\Delta t \tag{18.10}$$

$$E(\Delta C) = [rC + C\beta_C(\bar{R}_m - r)]\Delta t. \tag{18.11}$$

When substituting for the option's elasticity from Eq. (18.7), Eq. (18.11) becomes after transformation:

$$E(\Delta C) = [rC + SC_S\beta_S(\bar{R}_m - r)]\Delta t \tag{18.12}$$

Assuming a hedged position is constructed and "continuously" re-balanced, and since ΔC is a continuous and differentiable function of two variables, it is possible to use Taylor's series expansion to expand ΔC.

$$\Delta C = \frac{1}{2}C_{SS}(\Delta S)^2 + C_S\Delta S + C_t\Delta t \tag{18.13}$$

This is just an extension of simple results to get Ito's lemma. Taking expectations of both sides of Eq. (18.13) and replacing ΔS, we obtain:

$$E(\Delta C) = \frac{1}{2}\sigma^2 S^2 C_{SS}\Delta t + C_S E(\Delta S) + C_t\Delta t \tag{18.14}$$

Replacing the expected value of ΔS from Eq. (18.8) gives,

$$E(\Delta C) = \frac{1}{2}\sigma^2 S^2 C_{SS}\Delta t + C_S[rS + S\beta_S(\bar{R}_m - r)]\Delta t + C_t\Delta t \tag{18.15}$$

Combining Eqs. (18.11) and (18.15) and re-arranging yields:

$$\frac{1}{2}\sigma^2 S^2 C_{SS} + rSC_S - rC + C_t = 0. \tag{18.16}$$

This partial differential equation corresponds to the Black–Scholes valuation equation. Let T be the maturity date of the call and E be its strike price. Equation (18.16) subject to the boundary condition at maturity:

$$C(S,T) = S - K, \quad \text{if } S \geq K$$
$$C(S,T) = 0 \quad \text{if } S < K$$

is solved using standard methods for the price of a European call, which is found to be equal to:

$$C(S,T) = SN(d_1) - Ke^{-rT}N(d_2) \tag{18.17}$$

with

$$d_1 = \left[\ln\left(\frac{S}{K}\right) + \left(r + \frac{1}{2}\sigma^2\right)T\right] \Big/ \sigma\sqrt{T}, \quad d_2 = d_1 - \sigma\sqrt{T}$$

and where $N(.)$ is the cumulative normal density function.

It may be shown that Eq. (18.16) applies to both European and American options.

18.4.2. *An alternative derivation of the Black–Scholes model*

Assuming that the option price is a function of the single source of uncertainty, namely stock price and time to maturity, $c(S,t)$ and that over "short"-time intervals, Δt, a hedged portfolio consisting of the option, the underlying asset, and a risk-less security can be formed, where portfolio weights are chosen to eliminate "market risk" Black–Scholes expressed the expected return on the option in terms of the option price function and its partial derivatives. In fact, following Black–Scholes, it is possible to create a hedged position consisting of a sale of $\frac{1}{\left[\frac{\partial c(S,t)}{\partial S}\right]}$ options against one share of stock long. If the stock price changes by a small amount ΔS, the option changes by an amount $\left[\frac{\partial c(S,t)}{\partial S}\right]\Delta S$. Hence, the change in value in the long position (the stock) is approximately offset by the change in $\frac{1}{\left[\frac{\partial c(S,t)}{\partial S}\right]}$ options. This hedge can be maintained continuously so that the return on the hedged position becomes completely independent of the change in the underlying asset value, i.e., the return on the hedged position becomes certain.

The value of equity in a hedged position, containing a stock purchase and a sale of $\frac{1}{\left[\frac{\partial c(S,t)}{\partial S}\right]}$ options is:

$$S - \frac{C(S,t)}{\left[\frac{\partial c(S,t)}{\partial S}\right]} \tag{18.18}$$

Over a short interval Δt, the change in this position is:

$$\Delta S - \frac{\Delta c(S,t)}{\left[\frac{\partial c(S,t)}{\partial S}\right]} \tag{18.19}$$

where, $\Delta c(S,t)$ is given by $c(S+\Delta S, t+\Delta t) - c(S,t)$.

Using stochastic calculus for $\Delta c(S,t)$ gives,

$$\Delta c(S,t) = \frac{\partial c(S,t)}{\partial S}\Delta S + \frac{1}{2}\frac{\partial^2 c(S,t)}{\partial S^2}\sigma^2 S^2 \Delta t + \frac{\partial c(S,t)}{\partial t}\Delta t. \tag{18.20}$$

The change in the value of equity in the hedged position is found by substituting $\Delta c(S,t)$ from Eq. (18.20) in Eq. (18.19).

$$-\frac{\left(\frac{1}{2}\sigma^2 S^2 \frac{\partial^2 c(S,t)}{\partial S^2} + \frac{\partial c(S,t)}{\partial t}\right)\Delta t}{\frac{\partial c(S,t)}{\partial S}}. \tag{18.21}$$

Since the return to the equity in the hedged position is certain, it must be equal to $r\Delta t$ where r stands for the short-term interest rate. Hence, the change in the equity must be equal to the value of the equity times $r\Delta t$, or:

$$-\frac{\left(\frac{1}{2}\sigma^2 S^2 \frac{\partial^2 c(S,t)}{\partial S^2} + \frac{\partial c(S,t)}{\partial t}\right)\Delta t}{\frac{\partial c(S,t)}{\partial S}} = \left[S - \frac{c(S,t)}{\frac{\partial c(S,t)}{\partial S}}\right] r\Delta t. \tag{18.22}$$

Dropping the time and re-arranging gives the Black–Scholes partial differential equation:

$$\frac{1}{2}\sigma^2 S^2 \frac{\partial^2 c(S,t)}{\partial S^2} - rc(S,t) + \frac{\partial c(S,t)}{\partial t} + rS\frac{\partial c(S,t)}{\partial S} = 0. \tag{18.23}$$

This partial differential equation must be solved under the boundary conditions expressing the call's value at maturity date: $c(S,t^*) = \max[0, S_{t^*} - K]$ where K is the option's strike price.

For the European put, the above equation must be solved under the following maturity date condition: $P(S,t^*) = \max[0, K - S_{t^*}]$.

To solve this differential equation, under the call-boundary condition, Black–Scholes made the following substitution:

$$c(S,t) = e^{r(t-t^*)}y\left[\frac{2}{\sigma^2}\left(r-\frac{\sigma^2}{2}\right)\left(\ln\frac{S}{K}-\left(r-\frac{1}{2}\sigma^2\right)(t^*-t)\right),\right.$$
$$\left.-\frac{2(t^*-t)}{\sigma^2}\left(r-\frac{1}{2}\sigma^2\right)^2\right] \tag{18.24}$$

Using this substitution, the differential equation becomes:

$$\frac{\partial y}{\partial t} = \frac{\partial^2 y}{\partial S^2}.$$

This differential equation is the heat transfer equation in physics. The boundary condition is re-written as $y(u,0)=0$, if $u<0$ otherwise,

$$y(u,0) = K\left[e^{\left(\frac{\frac{1}{2}u\sigma^2}{r-\frac{1}{2}\sigma^2}\right)}-1\right].$$

The solution to this problem is the solution to the heat transfer equation given in Churchill (1963):

$$y(u,s) = \frac{1}{\sqrt{2\Pi}}\int_{\frac{-u}{\sqrt{2s}}}^{\infty} K\left[e^{\left(\frac{\frac{1}{2}(u+q\sqrt{2s})\sigma^2}{r-\frac{1}{2}\sigma^2}\right)}-1\right]e^{\left(-\frac{q^2}{2}\right)}dq.$$

Substituting from this last equation in Eq. (18.24) gives the following solution for the European call price with $T=t^*-t$

$$c(S,T) = SN(d_1) - Ke^{-rT}N(d_2)$$

$d_1 = \frac{\ln\left(\frac{S}{K}\right)+\left(r+\frac{\sigma^2}{2}\right)T}{\sigma\sqrt{T}}$, $d_2 = d_1-\sigma\sqrt{T}$ where $N(.)$ is the cumulative normal density function given by:

$$N(d) = \frac{1}{\sqrt{2\Pi}}\int_{-\infty}^{d} e^{\left(-\frac{x^2}{2}\right)}dx.$$

It is important to note that the option value is independent of its underlying asset-expected return. This may sound rather strange. One intuitive way to account for this is to say the expected return on the stock is already embedded into the stock price itself. It is also worth noting that the option price rises when the asset price, the time to maturity, the interest rate, and the variance increase. The partial derivative $\left[\frac{\partial c(S,t)}{\partial S}\right]$, which is equal to $N(d_1)$ gives the ratio of the underlying asset to options in the hedged position. It also refers to what is known as the option's delta. Since $\frac{S}{c(S,t)}\left[\frac{\partial c(S,t)}{\partial S}\right]$ is always greater than one, the option is more volatile than its underlying asset. The value of the put option can be obtained from that of the call option using the put-call parity relationship.

18.4.3. *The put-call parity relationship*

The put-call parity relationship can be derived as follows. Consider a portfolio A which comprises a call option with a maturity date t^* and a discount bond that pays K dollars at the option's maturity date. Consider also a portfolio B, with a put option and one share.

The value of portfolio A at maturity is $\max[0, S_{t^*} - K] + K = \max[K, S_{t^*}]$. The value of portfolio B at maturity is $\max[0, K - S_{t^*}] + S_{t^*} = \max[K, S_{t^*}]$. Since both these portfolios have the same value at maturity, they must have the same initial value at time t, otherwise arbitrage will be profitable. Therefore, the following put-call relationship must hold $c_t - p_t = S_t - Ke^{-r(t^*-t)}$ with $t^* - t = T$.

If this relationship does not hold, then arbitrage would be profitable. In fact, suppose for example, that $c_t - p_t > S_t - Ke^{-r(t^*-t)}$.

At time t, the investor can construct a portfolio by buying the put and the underlying asset and selling the call. This strategy yields a result equal to $c_t - p_t - S_t$. If this amount is positive, it can be invested at the risk-less rate until the maturity date t^*, otherwise it can be borrowed at the same rate for the same period. At the option maturity date, the options will be in-the-money or out-of-the money according to the position of the underlying asset S_{t^*} with respect to the strike price K. If $S_{t^*} > K$, the call is worth its intrinsic value. Since the investor sold the call, he/she is assigned on this call. He/she will receive the strike price, delivers the stock, and closes his/her position in the cash account. The put is worthless. Hence, the position is worth $K + e^{r(t^*-t)}[c_t - p_t - S_t] > 0$. If $S_T < K$, the put is worth its intrinsic value. Since the investor is long the put, he/she exercises his/her option. He/she will receive upon exercise the strike price, delivers the stock, and closes his/her position in the cash account. The call is worthless. Hence, the position is worth $K + e^{r(t^*-t)}[c_t - p_t - S_t] > 0$.

In both cases, the investor makes a profit without an initial cash outlay. This is a risk-less arbitrage, which must not exist in efficient markets. Therefore, the above put-call parity relationship must hold good. Using this relationship, the European put option value is given by:

$$p(S,T) = -SN(-d_1) + Ke^{-rT}N(-d_2) \tag{18.25}$$

$$d_1 = \frac{\ln\left(\frac{S}{K}\right) + \left(r + \frac{\sigma^2}{2}\right)T}{\sigma\sqrt{T}}, \quad d_2 = d_1 - \sigma\sqrt{T},$$

where $N(.)$ is the cumulative normal density function. We illustrate by the following examples, the application of the Black and Scholes (1973) model for the determination of call and put prices.

18.4.4. *Examples*

Example 1. When the underlying asset $S = 18$, the strike price $K = 15$, the short-term interest rate $r = 10\%$, the maturity date $T = 0.25$, and the volatility $\sigma = 15\%$, the call price is calculated as follows.

First, we compute the discounted value of the strike price,

$$Ke^{-rT} = 15e^{-0.1(0.25)} = 14.6296.$$

Second, the values of d_1 and d_2 are calculated as:

$$\begin{aligned} d_1 &= \frac{1}{0.15\sqrt{0.25}}\left[\ln\left(\frac{18}{15}\right) + \left(0.1 + \frac{1}{2}0.15^2\right)0.25\right] \\ &= \frac{0.21013}{0.075} = 2.8017 \\ d_2 &= 2.8017 - 0.5\sqrt{0.25} = 2.7267. \end{aligned}$$

Substituting d_1 and d_2 in the call price formula gives:

$$C = 18N(2.8017) - 15e^{-0.1(0.25)}N(2.7267).$$

Using the approximation of the cumulative normal distribution in the points 2.8017 and 2.7267, the call price is 3.3659 or:

$$C = 18(0.997) - 14.6296(0.996) = 3.3659$$

The following (Tables 18.1–18.4) provide simulation results for a European call and put prices using the Black–Scholes model. The tables also provide the Greek letters.

Table 18.1. Simulations of Black and Scholes put prices, $S = 100$, $K = 100$, $t = 22/12/2003$, $T = 22/12/2004$, $r = 2\%$, and $\sigma = 20\%$.

S	Price	Delta	Gamma	Vega	Theta
80	19.44832	−0.81955	0.01676	0.21155	−0.00575
85	15.56924	−0.72938	0.01967	0.28240	−0.00769
90	12.17306	−0.62762	0.02105	0.34124	−0.00931
95	9.29821	−0.52216	0.02086	0.37895	−0.01035
100	6.94392	−0.42055	0.01933	0.39156	−0.01069
105	5.07582	−0.32847	0.01692	0.38031	−0.01038
110	3.63657	−0.24939	0.01412	0.35019	−0.00955
115	2.55742	−0.18449	0.01130	0.30789	−0.00838
120	1.76806	−0.13331	0.00871	0.26002	−0.00707

Table 18.2. Simulations of Black and Scholes call prices, $S = 100$, $K = 100$, $t = 22/12/2003$, $T = 22/12/2004$, $r = 2\%$, and $\sigma = 20\%$.

S	Price	Delta	Gamma	Vega	Theta
80	1.43382	0.18045	0.01676	0.21155	−0.00575
85	2.55474	0.27062	0.01967	0.28240	−0.00769
90	4.15856	0.37238	0.02105	0.34124	−0.00931
95	6.28371	0.47784	0.02086	0.37895	−0.01035
100	8.92943	0.57945	0.01933	0.39156	−0.01069
105	12.06132	0.67153	0.01692	0.38031	−0.01038
110	15.62208	0.75061	0.01412	0.35019	−0.00955
115	19.54292	0.81551	0.01130	0.30789	−0.00838
120	23.75356	0.86669	0.00871	0.26002	−0.00707

Table 18.3. Simulations of Black and Scholes call prices, $S = 100$, $K = 100$, $t = 22/12/2003$, $T = 22/06/2004$, $r = 2\%$, and $\sigma = 20\%$.

S	Price	Delta	Gamma	Vega	Theta
80	0.36459	0.07582	0.01332	0.08172	−0.00442
85	0.93156	0.15729	0.02070	0.14559	−0.00791
90	1.99540	0.27358	0.02656	0.21252	−0.01158
95	3.70489	0.41284	0.02900	0.26201	−0.01429
100	6.12966	0.55640	0.02763	0.27966	−0.01526
105	9.24535	0.68669	0.02332	0.26377	−0.01439
110	12.95409	0.79246	0.01781	0.22359	−0.01218
115	17.12243	0.87053	0.01245	0.17279	−0.00939
120	21.61673	0.92356	0.00807	0.12322	−0.00668

Table 18.4. Simulations of Black and Scholes put prices, $S = 100$, $K = 100$, $t = 22/12/2003$, $T = 22/06/2004$, $r = 2\%$, and $\sigma = 20\%$.

S	Price	Delta	Gamma	Vega	Theta
80	19.36686	−0.92418	0.01332	0.08172	−0.00442
85	14.93383	−0.84271	0.02070	0.14559	−0.00791
90	10.99767	−0.72642	0.02656	0.21252	−0.01158
95	7.70716	−0.58716	0.02900	0.26201	−0.01429
100	5.13193	−0.44360	0.02763	0.27966	−0.01526
105	3.24762	−0.31331	0.02332	0.26377	−0.01439
110	1.95636	−0.20754	0.01781	0.22359	−0.01218
115	1.12471	−0.12947	0.01245	0.17279	−0.00939
120	0.61900	−0.07644	0.00807	0.12322	−0.00668

18.5. The Black Model for Commodity Contracts

Using some assumptions similar to those used in deriving the original B–S option formula, Black (1976) presented a model for the pricing of commodity options and forward contracts.

18.5.1. *The model for forward, futures, and option contracts*

In this model, the spot price $S(t)$ of an asset or a commodity is the price at which an investor can buy or sell it for an immediate delivery at current time, t. This price may rise steadily, fall, and fluctuate randomly.

The futures price $F(t, t^*)$ of a commodity can be defined as the price at which an investor agrees to buy or sell at a given time in the future, t^*, without putting up any money immediately. When $t = t^*$, the futures price is equal to the spot price.

A forward contract is a contract to buy or sell at a price that stays fixed until the maturity date, whereas the futures contract is settled every day and re-written at the new futures price.

Following Black (1976), let v be the value of the forward contract, u be the value of the futures contract, and c be the value of an option contract. Each of these contracts is a function of the futures price $F(t, t^*)$ as well as other variables. So, we can write at an instant t, the values of these contracts, respectively as $V(F, t), u(F, t)$, and $c(F, t)$. The value of the forward contract also depends on the price of the underlying asset, K at time t^* and can be written $V(F, t, K, t^*)$. It is important to distinguish between the price and the value of the contract. The futures price is the price at which a forward contract presents a zero current value. It is written as:

$$V(F, t, F, t^*) = 0 \tag{18.26}$$

Equation (18.26) implies that the forward contract's value is zero when the contract is initiated and the contract price, K, is always equal to the current futures price $F(t, t^*)$. The main difference between a futures contract and a forward contract is that a futures contract may be assimilated to a series of forward contracts. This is because the futures contract is re-written every day with a new contract price equal to the corresponding futures price. Hence, when F rises, i.e., $F > K$, the forward contract has a positive value and when F falls, $F < K$, then the forward contract has a negative value. When the transaction takes place, the futures price equals the spot price and the value of the forward contract equals the spot price minus the contract price or the spot price:

$$V(F, t^*, K, t^*) = F - K. \tag{18.27}$$

At maturity, the value of a commodity option is given by the maximum of zero and the difference between the spot price and the contract price. Since at this date, the futures price equals the spot price, it follows that if $F \geq K$, then $c(F, t^*) = F - K$ otherwise,

$$c(F, t^*) = 0. \tag{18.28}$$

In order to value commodity contracts and commodity options, Black (1976) assumed that:

- The futures price changes are distributed log-normally with a constant variance rate σ^2;
- All the parameters of the CAPM are constant through time and
- There are no transaction costs and no taxes.

Under these assumptions, it is possible to create a risk-less hedge by taking a long position in the option and a short position in the futures contract.

Let $\left[\frac{\partial c(F,t)}{\partial F}\right]$ be the weight affected to the short position in the futures contract, which is the derivative of $c(F, t)$ with respect to F. The change in the hedged position may be written as:

$$\Delta c(F, t) - \left[\frac{\partial c(F, t)}{\partial F}\right] \Delta F. \tag{18.29}$$

Using the fact that the return to a hedged portfolio must be equal to the risk-free interest rate and expanding $\Delta c(F, t)$ gives the following partial differential equation:

$$\frac{\partial c(F, t)}{\partial t} = rc(F, t) - \frac{1}{2}\sigma^2 F^2 \left[\frac{\partial^2 c(F, t)}{\partial F^2}\right]$$

or

$$\frac{1}{2}\sigma^2 F^2 \left[\frac{\partial^2 c(F, t)}{\partial F^2}\right] - rc(F, t) + \frac{\partial c(F, t)}{\partial t} = 0 \tag{18.30}$$

Denoting $T = t^* - t$ and using Eqs. (18.28) and (18.30), the value of a commodity option is:

$$\begin{gathered} c(F, T) = e^{-rT}[FN(d_1) - KN(d_2)] \\ d_1 = \frac{\ln\left(\frac{F}{K}\right) + \frac{\sigma^2}{2}T}{\sigma\sqrt{T}}, \quad d_2 = d_1 - \sigma\sqrt{T}. \end{gathered} \tag{18.31}$$

It is convenient to note that the commodity option's value is the same as the value of an option on a security paying a continuous dividend. The rate of distribution is equal to the stock price times the interest rate. If Fe^{-rT} is substituted in the original formula derived by Black and Scholes, the result is exactly the above formula. In the same context, the formula for the European put is:

$$p(F,T) = e^{-rT}[-FN(d_1) + KN(-d_2)]$$

$$d_1 = \frac{\ln\left(\frac{F}{K}\right) + \frac{\sigma^2}{2}T}{\sigma\sqrt{T}}, \quad d_2 = d_1 - \sigma\sqrt{T} \tag{18.32}$$

where $N(.)$ is the cumulative normal density function given by:

$$N(d) = \frac{1}{\sqrt{2\Pi}} \int_{-\infty}^{d} e^{\left(-\frac{x^2}{2}\right)} dx.$$

The value of the put option can be obtained directly from the put-call parity.

18.5.2. *The put-call relationship*

The put-call parity relationship for futures options is:

$$p - c = e^{-rT}(K - F). \tag{18.33}$$

This relationship can be explained as follows. Consider a portfolio where the investor is long a future contract, long a put on the future contract, and short a call with the same time to maturity and strike price. Note that the combination of the call and the put is equivalent to a short synthetic future. At expiration, the payoff is given by the difference between the options strike prices and the current futures price. Hence, the current value of this portfolio must be equal to the present value of this difference. Since these options are European, they have the same cash flows as options on the spot asset. This is because at the maturity date, the futures price is equal to the spot price. We now give some examples for the calculation of option prices using Black's formula.

18.6. Application of the CAPM Model to Forward and Futures Contracts

The major difficulty arising from the application of the CAPM to the risk-return relationship on a capital asset comes from the definition of the appropriate rate of return. More specifically, the CAPM cannot be directly applied to the futures contract because the initial value of the contract is zero.

18.6.1. *An application of the model to forward and futures contracts*

Following the work of Dusak (1973), when applying the classic CAPM, the percentage change in the futures price is used as a candidate since it can always be computed. However, the percentage change in the futures price cannot be interpreted as a rate of return comparable to the $\tilde{R}_S$ value, since the holder of the position does not invest current resources in the contract. It can be rather seen as a risk premium, $(\tilde{R}_S - r)$ on the underlying spot assets. In fact, the buyer of the futures contract takes the risk and has no capital on his/her own invested. Hence, he/she earns no interest on the capital.

The CAPM equilibrium conditions can then be re-stated by saying that the expected return on any asset S, is written as $E(\tilde{R}_S) = r(1 - \beta_S) + \beta_S(E(\tilde{R}_m))$ where $E(\tilde{R}_S)$ can be represented in terms of periods 0 and 1 prices for the asset S as: $\frac{E(S_1 - S_0)}{S_0}$.

The equilibrium risk-return relationship on asset S can then be expressed as $S_0 = E(S_1) - \beta_S(E(\tilde{R}_m) - r)S_0$, where S_0 is the price of asset S in the start of period and S_1 is the asset's price at the end of the period. In present-value form, the above equation is equivalent to $S_0 = \frac{E(S_1) - \beta_S(E(\tilde{R}_m) - r)S_0}{(1+r)}$.

On the other hand, the current price for asset S under an agreement to buy the asset at time 0 but with payment deferred to time 1 is $S_0(1 + r)$.

This can be seen as the current futures price for payment of the spot price in a period. The term $E(S_1)$ is interpreted as the spot price expected to prevail at time 1. Multiplying the above equation by $(1+r)$ gives:

$$(1+r)S_0 = E(S_1) - \beta_S(E(\tilde{R}_m) - r)S_0.$$

Setting $F_0 = (1+r)S_0$ and re-arranging the terms gives:

$$\frac{E(S_1) - F_0}{S_0} = \beta_S(E(\tilde{R}_m) - r).$$

This equation can be interpreted as expressing the risk premium on the underlying spot asset as the change in the futures price divided by the period zero spot price. The analysis in Black (1976) can be implemented in this context. In fact, let us re-write the CAPM in the following form:

$$E(\tilde{R}_S) - r = \beta_S[E(\tilde{R}_m) - r].$$

Writing S_0 and S_1 as the start and end-of-period prices of an asset i and using the definition of β_i, the CAPM can be written as:

$$E\left(\frac{(S_1 - S_0)}{S_0}\right) - r = \frac{\operatorname{cov}\left(\frac{S_1 - S_0}{S_0}, \tilde{R}_m\right)}{\operatorname{var}(\tilde{R}_m)}[E(\tilde{R}_m) - r]. \tag{18.34}$$

If we multiply by S_0, we obtain the expected dollar return on asset i as:

$$E(S_1 - S_0) - rS_0 = \frac{\operatorname{cov}((S_1 - S_0), \tilde{R}_m)}{\operatorname{var}(\tilde{R}_m)}[E(\tilde{R}_m) - r]. \tag{18.35}$$

The price S_0 can be set equal to zero since the futures contact's value at this time is zero. Ignoring daily limits, we set S_1 equal to ΔS. In fact, if we apply this equation to a futures contract, the change in the futures price over the period is $E(\Delta S) = \frac{\operatorname{cov}(\Delta S, \tilde{R}_m)}{\operatorname{var}(\tilde{R}_m)}[E(\tilde{R}_m) - r]$.

Equation (18.34) can be written for the futures prices as:

$$E(\Delta S) = \beta^*[E(\tilde{R}_m) - r]. \tag{18.36}$$

Equation (18.35) shows that the expected change in the futures price is proportional to the dollar "beta" of the futures price. The expected change in the futures price may be zero, positive, or negative. Also, the expected change in the futures price is zero when the covariance of the change in the futures price with the market portfolio is zero, i.e., $E(\Delta S) = 0$ when $\operatorname{cov}(\Delta S, \tilde{R}_m) = 0$.

18.6.2. *An application to the derivation of the commodity option valuation*

Black (1976) showed that in the absence of interest-rate uncertainty, a European commodity option on a futures (or a forward) contract can be priced using a minor modification of the Black and Scholes (1973) option pricing formula. In deriving expressions for the behavior of the futures price, he assumed that both taxes and transaction costs are zero and that the CAPM applies at each instance of time. Following Black (1976), we assume that the fractional change in the futures price is distributed log-normally, with a known constant variance rate, σ. We also assume that all the parameters of the CAPM are constant through time. Under these assumptions, the value of the futures commodity option, $C(S,t)$, can be written as a function of the underlying futures price and time. In this context, it is possible to create a risk-less hedge by taking a long position in the option and a short position in the futures contract with the same transaction date. Black (1976) assumed that a continuously re-balanced self-financing portfolio of the underlying futures contracts and the risk-less asset can be constructed to duplicate the payoff of the futures option. The relationship between a commodity option's beta and its underlying security's beta is given by $\beta_C = S\left(\frac{C_S}{C}\right)\beta_S$, where β_c and β_S refer respectively, to the betas of the commodity option and its underlying commodity contract. The expected return on a security in the context of the CAPM is:

$$\bar{R}_S - r = \beta_S[\bar{R}_m - r]$$

or

$$\bar{R}_S - r = a\beta_S \quad \text{with } a = [\bar{R}_m - r].$$

This equation can be written for the expected return on the spot asset and the option as:

$$E\left(\frac{\Delta S}{S}\right) = r\Delta t + a\beta_S\Delta t$$

$$E\left(\frac{\Delta C}{C}\right) = r\Delta t + a\beta_C\Delta t.$$

Multiplying this last equation by C and substituting for β_C gives:

$$E(\Delta C) = rC\Delta t + aS\beta_S C_S \Delta t.$$

Taking the expected value and replacing $E(\Delta S)$ gives:

$$E(\Delta C) = rSC_S\Delta t + aS\beta_S C_S\Delta t + C_t\Delta t + \frac{1}{2}C_{SS}S^2\sigma^2\Delta t.$$

Making the equality between this equation and

$$E(\Delta C) = rC\Delta t + aS\beta_S C_S \Delta t.$$

Simplification gives:

$$\frac{1}{2}C_{SS}S^2\sigma^2 + rSC_S - rC + C_t = 0.$$

This equation is the Black and Scholes (1973) equation.

Since the value of a futures contract is zero, the equity in the position is just the value of the option. In this context, the system:

$$E(\Delta C) = rSC_S\Delta t + aS\beta_S C_S\Delta t + C_t\Delta t + \frac{1}{2}C_{SS}S^2\sigma^2\Delta t$$
$$E(\Delta C) = rC\Delta t + aS\beta_S C_S \Delta t,$$

becomes:

$$E(\Delta C) = C_t\Delta t + \frac{1}{2}C_{SS}S^2\sigma^2\Delta t$$
$$E(\Delta C) = rC\Delta t,$$

which gives:

$$\frac{1}{2}C_{SS}S^2\sigma^2 - rC + C_t = 0.$$

This equation is the Black (1976) equation.

$$\frac{1}{2}C_{SS}S^2\sigma^2 - rC + C_t = 0. \tag{18.37}$$

Let T be the maturity date of the call and K be its strike price. The equation must be solved under the boundary condition at maturity:

$$C(S,T) = S - K \quad \text{if } S \geq K$$
$$C(S,T) = 0 \quad \text{if } S < K.$$

There is a simple relationship between the future price and the spot price $F = Se^{bT}$. The value of a European commodity call is:

$$C(F,T) = e^{-rT}[FN(d_1) - KN(d_2)]$$

with

$$d_1 = \frac{\ln\left(\frac{F}{K}\right) + \frac{\sigma^2}{2}T}{\sigma\sqrt{T}}, \quad d_2 = d_1 - \sigma\sqrt{T}.$$

The solution for a European futures put is:

$$P(F,T) = e^{-rT}[-FN(-d_1) + KN(-d_2)].$$

The term $FN(d_1) - KN(d_2)$ shows that the expected value of the futures call at expiration, is the expected difference between the futures price and the strike price conditional upon the option being in-the-money times the probability that it will be in-the-money. The term e^{-rT} is the appropriate discount factor by which the expected expiration value is brought to the present. It is possible to use directly the put-call parity to write down the put formula. Re-call that the put-call parity relationship between puts and call with identical strike prices is an arbitrage-based relationship, which holds regardless of the distribution of financial asset prices. More general results about calls and puts with different strike prices can be written down for both symmetric and asymmetric processes using the propositions in Bates (1997).

18.6.3. *An application to commodity options and commodity futures options*

A commodity call gives the right to its holder to buy a specific commodity at a specified price within a specified period of time. A commodity put gives the right to its holder to buy a specific commodity at a specified price within a pre-determined period of time. A commodity futures option is an option on the futures contract having a commodity as an underlying asset.

The commodity may be a precious metal such as either silver or gold. It may be a financial instrument such as a common stock, a treasury bond, or a foreign currency. For example, if the commodity option is written on a foreign currency, the option refers to a currency option. If the commodity option is written on a stock index, the option is an index option.

Since all the analytical models for European options presented in this chapter can be obtained by modifying the parameters in the Merton (1973) and BAW (1987) model, all the applications presented here are also true for this model.

For example, when the option's underlying asset is an index, which is constructed to pay continuous dividends, this version is a particular case of the Merton's and BAW's model for commodity options.

When the continuous dividend yield is d, the formula for European commodity options is re-written for index options with $b = (r - d)$. For a European index call, the formula is:

$$c(S,T) = Se^{-dT}N(d_1) - Ke^{-rT}N(d_2) \tag{18.38}$$

with

$$d_1 = \frac{\ln\left(\frac{Se^{-dT}}{K}\right) + \frac{\sigma^2}{2}T}{\sigma\sqrt{T}}, \quad d_2 = d_1 - \sigma\sqrt{T}.$$

For a European index put, the formula becomes:

$$p(S,T) = -Se^{-dT}N(-d_1) + Ke^{-rT}N(-d_2)$$

with

$$d_1 = \frac{\ln\left(\frac{Se^{-dT}}{K}\right) + \frac{\sigma^2}{2}T}{\sigma\sqrt{T}}, \quad d_2 = d_1 - \sigma\sqrt{T}.$$

18.7. The Holes in the Black–Scholes–Merton Theory and the Financial Crisis

Black (1998) examined the assumptions of the Black and Scholes (1973) model and suggested some modifications to improve the model.

In the original formula, it is assumed that:

- the volatility of the underlying asset is known;
- investors can either borrow or lend at a single interest rate;

- the short seller of the underlying asset can use the proceeds of the sale even if they are used as collateral;
- there are no transaction costs;
- there are no dividends and no taxes and
- there are no takeovers or other events that end the life of the option early.

18.7.1. *Volatility changes*

In practice, volatility is not constant. It can change and affect especially far-out-of-the-money options.

For example, if the formula is computed for an out-of-the-money option with a volatility of 20% when $S = 28$ and $K = 40$, the option price is 0.0088. Doubling the volatility to 40%, this can give a new option value of 0.46, which is more than 50 times higher than in the first case.

In this case, it is possible to assign probability estimates to various volatility figures and to use the probabilities to weigh the resulting option values. For example, if there is a 0.5 chance that the volatility will be 0.2 and a 0.5 chance that it will be 0.4, then the option value will be 0.23. This procedure increases out-of-the-money option values. It is true that volatility changes in an unexplainable way, but there is a relationship between the stock price and volatility. In general, the stock price and the volatility change in opposite directions, i.e., when the stock price increases, the volatility decreases and vice versa. Cox and Ross (1976) used different formulas to explain the deviations between model values and option prices by accounting for this fact. The Cox and Ross (1976) formula gives lower values for out-of-the-money options than the Black–Scholes formula. Merton (1976) accounted for jumps to increase the relevant values of both out-of-the-money and in-the-money options. His formula decreases at the same time the values of at-the-money-options.

Jumps affect the underlying asset price and can be viewed as momentary large increases in the volatility of the underlying asset. The formula handles only jumps and does not account for stock-price related changes in volatility. The changing character of volatility does not lead to a "close-to-riskless" hedge. Consider an initial position in which the investor is short two calls and long one round lot of the underlying asset. If the stock moves by US$ 1 and the call by

US$ 0.5, the position is protected against stock-price movement but not against changes in volatility. In practice, it is impossible to diversify away this risk so that investors do not care about it.

18.7.2. *Interest rate changes*

As volatility changes over time, interest rates also move with a main difference so that interest rates can be observed. Merton (1973) has shown that the random character of interest rates can be accounted for by substituting the interest rate on a zero-coupon bond and a maturity equal to the option expiration for the short-term interest rate in the formula. This is possible when the volatility is constant. The effect of changing interest rates on option values do not seem as great as the effects of changes in volatility.

18.7.3. *Borrowing penalties*

In general, investors borrow at a higher rate than the rate at which they can lend. High-borrowing rates may increase option values. This is because options can provide leverage that can substitute for borrowing.

18.7.4. *Short-selling penalties*

Short-selling leads the investor to borrow the stock and to put up a cash collateral with the person who lends the stock. This cash does not produce an interest. In general, professional option traders find that the penalties to writing naked options do not affect them. However, there are often penalties on short selling of the stock.

Since buying a put option is equivalent to selling stock short, penalties on short selling of stock can increase the prices of put options.

18.7.5. *Transaction costs*

Transaction costs paid in the form of brokerage charges and clearing charges can affect the hedging strategy. It is not possible to maintain a neutral hedge continuously, by changing the ratio of option position to stock position as the parameters change. Stock prices can also jump without a chance for trades to take place. This makes the strategy impossible to maintain a neutral hedge.

18.7.6. *Taxes*

The existence of different tax rates for institutions and individuals can affect option values. The exact rules used to restrict tax arbitrage will affect option values. For example, index option positions are taxed, in general, partly at short-term capital gains rates and partly at long-term capital gains rates. This depends on whether the position has been closed out each year. If several investors pay taxes on gains and cannot deduct losses, they want to limit the volatility of their positions and have the freedom to control the timing of their gains and losses. This can affect the use of options and the option values.

18.7.7. *Dividends*

Dividends reduce call-option values and increase put-option values. Several formulas are proposed in the literature to handle dividends, but the exact solution, needs the knowledge of how the amount of future unknown dividends depends on the factors affecting the stock price.

18.7.8. *Takeovers*

The Black–Scholes model assumes that the stock will continue trading for the option's life. If, for example, firm A takes over firm B through an exchange of stock, options on B's stock will expire early. However, the stock value is higher than before. The premium of the tender offer will increase the call value and reduce the put value.

Summary

"Because options are specialized and relatively unimportant financial securities, the amount of time and space devoted to the development of a pricing theory might be questioned", said Professor Merton (1973), in *Bell Journal of Economics and Management Science.* Thirty years ago, no one could have imagined the changes that were about to occur in finance theory and the financial industry. The seeds of change were contained in option theory being conducted by the Nobel Laureates Black, Scholes, and Merton. Valuing claims to future income streams is one of the central problems in finance. The first known attempt to value options appeared in Bachelier (1900) doctoral dissertation using an arithmetic Brownian motion. This process amounts to negative asset prices. Sprenkle (1961) and Samuelson (1965) used a geometric Brownian motion that eliminated the occurrence of negative asset prices. Samuelson and Merton (1969) proposed a theory of option valuation by treating the option price as a function of the stock price. They advanced the theory by realizing that the discount rate must be determined in part by the requirement that investors hold all the amounts of stocks and the option. Their final formula depends on the utility function assumed for a "typical" investor. Several discussions are done with Merton (1973) who was also working on option valuation. Merton (1973) pointed out that assuming continuous trading in the option or its underlying asset can preserve a hedged portfolio between the option and its underlying asset. Merton was able to prove that in the presence of a non-constant interest rate, a discount bond maturing at the option expiration date must be used. Black and Scholes (1973) and Merton (1973) showed that the construction of a risk-less hedge between the option and its underlying asset, allows the derivation of an option pricing formula regardless of investors' risk preferences. The main attractions of the Black–Scholes model are that their formula is a function of "observable" variables and that the model can be extended to the pricing of any type of option. Using some assumptions similar to those used in deriving the original B–S option formula, Black (1976) presented a model for the pricing of commodity options and forward contracts. Black (1976) showed that in the absence of interest-rate uncertainty, a European commodity option on a futures (or a forward) contract can be priced using a minor modification of the Black and Scholes (1973) option pricing formula. In deriving expressions for the behavior of the futures price, he assumed that both taxes and transaction costs are zero and that the CAPM applies at each instant of time. This chapter presented in detail the basic concepts and techniques underlying rational derivative asset pricing in the context of analytical European models along the lines of Black and Scholes (1973), Black (1976), and Merton (1973). First, an overview of the analytical models proposed by the precursors is given. Second, the simple model of Black and Scholes (1973) is derived in detail for the valuation of options on spot assets and some of its applications are presented. Third, the Black model, which is an extension of the Black–Scholes model for the valuation of futures contracts and commodity options, is analyzed. Also, applications of the model are proposed. Fourth, the basic limitations of the Black–Scholes–Merton theory are studied and the models are applied to the valuation of several financial contracts. The Black–Scholes hedge works in the real, discrete, and frictionful world when the hedger uses the correct volatility of the prices at which he/she actually trades and when the asset prices do not jump too much. The assumptions of the Britten-Jones and Neuberger (1996) model provided a framework in which a trader can avoid jumps and in which total variance can be estimated perfectly. The model transforms the question of pricing and hedging options into how well investors can predict the total variance of returns of the associated hedging strategy. The Black–Scholes formula gives a rough approximation to the formula investors would use, if they knew how to account for the above factors. Modifications of the Black–Scholes formula can move it to the hypothetical perfect formula.

References

Ayres HF (1963). Risk aversion in the warrants market. *Industrial Management Review*, 4 (Fall), 497–505.

Bachelier L (1900). Theorie de la speculation. Ph.D. Thesis in Mathematics, *Annales de l'Ecole Normale Superieure*, III.17, 21–86.

Barone-Adesi G and RE Whaley (1987). Efficient analytic approximation of American option values. *Journal of Finance*, 42 (June), 301–320.

Bates DS (1997). Jumps and stochastic volatility: Exchange rate processes implicit in Deutsche mark options. *Review of Financial Studies*, 9, 69–107.

Black F (1976). The pricing of commodity contracts. *Journal of Financial Economics*, 3 (January/March), 167–179.

Black F (1998). The holes in Black–Scholes. *Risk*, 1(4), 6–8.

Black F and M Scholes (1973). The pricing of options and corporate liabilities. *Journal of Political Economy*, 81, 637–659.

Boness AJ (1964). Elements of a theory of stock option value. *Journal of Political Economy*, 72 (April), 163–175.

Britten-Jones M and A Neuberger (1996). Arbitrage pricing with incomplete markets. *Applied Mathematical Finance*, 3(4), 347–363, 11–13.

Chen A (1970). A model of warrant pricing in a dynamic market. *Journal of Finance*, 25, 1041–1060.

Churchill RV (1963). *Fourier Series and Boundary Value Problems*, 2nd edn. McGraw–Hill, New York.

Cox JC and SA Ross (1976). The valuation of options for alternative stochastic processes. *Journal of Financial Economics*, 3, 145–166.

Dusak K (1973). Futures trading and investor returns: An investigation of commodity market risk premiums. *Journal of Political Economy*, 81, 1387–1406.

Garman M and S Kohlhagen (1983). Foreign currency option values. *Journal of International Money and Finance*, 2, 231–237.

Merton R (1973). Theory of rational option pricing. *Bell Journal of Economics and Management Science*, 4, 141–183.

Merton RC (1976). Option pricing when underlying stock returns are discontinuous. *Journal of Financial Economics*, 3, 125–144.

Samuelson PA (1965). Rational theory of warrant pricing. *Industrial Management Review*, 6, 13–31.

Samuelson P and RC Merton (1969). A complete model of warrant pricing that maximises utility. *Industrial Management Review*, 10, 17–46.

Sharpe WF (1964). Capital asset prices: A theory of market equilibrium under conditions of risk. *Journal of Finance*, 19, 425–442.

Smith CW (1976). Option pricing: A review. *Journal of Financial Economics*, 3 (January/March 1976), 3–52.

Smithson C (1991). Wonderful life. *Risk*, 4(9) (October), 50–51.

Sprenkle C (1961). Warrant prices as indications of expectations. *Yale Economic Essays*, 1, 179–232.

Thorp E and S Kassouf (1967). *Beat the Market*. Random House, New York.

Chapter 19

Simple Extensions and Applications of the Black–Scholes Type Models in Valuation and Risk Management

Chapter Outline

This chapter is organized as follows:

1. Section 19.1 gives some applications of the Black and Scholes (1973) option pricing theory.
2. Section 19.2 presents the main applications of the Black's (1976) model.
3. Section 19.3 develops the main results in Garman and Kohlhagen's (1983) model for the pricing of currency options.
4. Section 19.4 presents the main results in the models of Merton (1973) and Barone-Adesi and Whaley (1987) model for the pricing of European commodity and commodity futures options. Some applications of the model are also proposed.
5. Section 19.5 compares the Black–Scholes world with the real world.

Introduction

Broadly speaking, there are four groups of equity options: traded options, over-the-counter (OTC) options, equity warrants, and covered warrants. Traded options are standardized contracts which are listed on options exchanges. These options are not protected against dividend and their strike prices and maturity dates are set by the exchange. Stock index options and futures markets have experienced remarkable growth rates. Stock index options are of the European or the American type and often involve cash settlement procedure upon exercise. The Black and Scholes (1973) model can be used in the valuation of options for which the underlying asset is a fixed-income instrument. However, this model presents some limitations in the valuation of interest rate options. The standard binomial models can also be applied for the valuation of interest rate options. Since the Black and Scholes formula is valid for a non-cash paying security, it can be used for the pricing of a zero-coupon bond. The Black and Scholes (1973) model is universally applied by market participants even though several other alternative models exist. The main question is why the Black–Scholes model successful and how to apply the model when the imperfections of the real world loom large.

This chapter presents the theory of European options and its applications along the Black–Scholes lines and its extensions by Black (1976) for options on futures, Garman and Kohlhagen (1983) for options on currencies and indirectly by Merton (1973), and Barone-Adesi and Whaley (1987) for European commodity and futures options. These models and especially the Black's (1976) model apply for commodity options. Commodity markets can be traced back to the corn markets of the Middle Ages when farmers, merchants, and end-users would all meet in a specific place. The term "commodity" refers, today, to a variety of products, ranging from the traditional agricultural crops to oil and financial instruments. Since the main concern in this chapter is about analytical models under the Black–Scholes (1973) assumptions, the question of dividends, stochastic interest rates, and stochastic volatilities are discussed in other chapters.

19.1. Applications of the Black–Scholes Model

Equity options can be used in several ways in portfolio management. Buying or selling options involves the payment or the receipt of the option premium at the initial time when the transaction is done.

19.1.1. *Valuation and the role of equity options*

Since the option payoff is asymmetric, this gives rise to an asymmetric distribution of returns. Hence, options can be used in portfolio management to structure the distribution of expected returns. The best-known strategies in portfolio management involve combinations of options. They include vertical spreads, calendar spreads, diagonal spreads, ratio spreads, volatility spreads, and synthetic contracts. The main difference between futures contracts and option contracts is that the investor pays a premium for options and nothing to establish a futures position.

Calls and puts are bought or sold in anticipation of future cash flows, for defensive purposes, and speculative reasons. The investor must choose the appropriate options to be bought or sold. Therefore, the question of the management of an option position is as important as the question of option valuation and strategies.

Over-the-counter (OTC) options are tailor-made to the investor's needs and are often written by investment banks.

Equity warrants are long-term options and are often traded in securities markets rather than in option markets. When these options are exercised, new shares are issued by the company.

Covered warrants are OTC long-term options issued by securities houses. These equity options can be valued using the Black–Scholes model. However, the following specificities of these instruments imply some extensions of the Black–Scholes model.

First, these options are frequently traded on an asset, which distributes dividends and they are of the American type, i.e., they can be exercised before maturity.

Second, the assumed diffusion process may not represent reality since equity prices may jump downward or upward in response to either bad or good news.

Third, it is more dificult to justify a constant volatility for the underlying asset when the option maturity is long. The same argument applies for the risk-less interest rate. In this chapter, we restrict our analysis to the assumptions of the Black–Scholes model, which will be relaxed afterwards when studying the extensions and generalizations of the model.

Many strategies can be implemented with equity derivatives. These strategies are obviously not specific to equities. They also apply to options on other types of underlying assets.

19.1.2. *Valuation and the role of index options*

Stock index options and futures markets have experienced remarkable growth rates. Stock index options are either of the European or the American type and often involve cash settlement procedure upon exercise.

19.1.2.1. *Analysis and valuation*

Stock index options are traded on the major indices around the world. These options are of the European or American-type. Options on the spot index are cash-settled and there is no physical delivery of the underlying index, i.e., of a weighted average of prices of the stocks that constitutes the index.

There are several weighting schemes. The most commonly used is the market capitalization where each equity price is weighted by the market capitalization of the firm, i.e., the number of shares times the share price.

Two alternative methods are sometimes used: equal weighting and price weighting. The last two methods assign greater relative weight to small-company constituents than do capitalization-weighted indices. Index options are also sold in the OTC market as OTC warrants. In this case, they refer to long-term options on the spot index. Because they are traded on OTC markets, they are subject to credit risk. When the option underlying index is constructed to pay continuous dividends, the index price is adjusted by the discounted value of the continuous dividend yield. The appropriately adjusted Black–Scholes (1973) version when the continuous dividend yield d corresponds to the following formula for a European index call is:

$$c(S,T) = Se^{-dT}N(d_1) - Ke^{-rT}N(d_2)$$

$$d_1 = \frac{\ln\left(\frac{Se^{-dT}}{K}\right) + \left(r + \frac{\sigma^2}{2}\right)T}{\sigma\sqrt{T}}, \quad d_2 = d_1 - \sigma\sqrt{T},$$

where $N(.)$ is the cumulative normal density function given by:

$$N(d) = \frac{1}{\sqrt{2\Pi}}\int_{-\infty}^{d} e^{\left(-\frac{x^2}{2}\right)}dx.$$

The European index put formula is given by:

$$p(S,T) = -Se^{-dT}N(-d_1) + Ke^{-rT}N(-d_2)$$

$$d_1 = \frac{\ln\left(\frac{Se^{-dT}}{K}\right) + \left(r + \frac{\sigma^2}{2}\right)T}{\sigma\sqrt{T}}, \quad d_2 = d_1 - \sigma\sqrt{T}.$$

19.1.2.2. *Arbitrage between index options and futures*

It is convenient to note that the same strategies for stock options can also be used in portfolio management with index options. Also, these options can be used in asset allocation and portfolio insurance. Since these instruments are based on the same underlying index, their prices must be interrelated. If this is not the case, the relative mispricing should instantaneously disappear given the variety of cross-market strategies. These strategies include arbitrage between index options and index futures, and between index futures and the stocks comprising the index. Many researchers have studied these arbitrages which imply that significant deviations from prices dictated by the relevant market interrelationships should disappear. It is often found that there are some violations of the no-arbitrage bounds. However, when taking into account the transaction costs, the future price lies often between the no-arbitrage bounds.

Even if all tests and published studies are in favor of market efficiency and integrated markets, it is often reported that relative mispricing does exist between index options and futures contracts. For more details, see for example, Evnine and Rudd (1985) and Brennan and Schwartz (1990), among others. On the other hand, despite the controversy about index arbitrage and program trading, these financial instruments are beneficial to stock portfolio managers and institutional investors. Before the emergence of these contracts, market participants cannot hedge and control the market risk of their portfolios. Even if there is some evidence that trading in index futures increases cash-market volatility, arbitrage activities via program trading may cause prices to adjust more rapidly to new information. This helps to keep the movements of index futures price and the stock index more synchronous. The deviations of futures prices from their "fair" value result from various considerations including imperfect substitutability between spot and futures markets, the speed with which information is incorporated in prices in the different markets, and market imperfections including transaction costs and regulatory constraints, among other things.

19.1.3. *Valuation of options on zero-coupon bonds*

The Black and Scholes (1973) model can be used in the valuation of options for which the underlying asset is a fixed-income instrument. However, this model presents some limitations in the valuation of interest rate options.

The standard binomial models can also be applied for the valuation of interest rate options. Since the Black and Scholes formula is valid for a non-cash paying security, it can be used for the pricing of a zero-coupon bond. When using the Black and Scholes formula, the underlying asset is the bond price. The bond price can be observed in the market place, as it can be calculated by discounting its maturity value at the appropriate risk-free rate. The underlying bond price can have a maturity of five years for example and the option time to maturity is in five months. The underlying asset (the bond) has, in principle, a maximum value. It is given by the sum of the coupon payments plus the maturity value. If the bond price is greater than this maximum value, this means that interest rates are negative. Re-call that the bond price is higher, if higher is the interest rate. Or, in the Black and Scholes model for stock options, the underlying stock does not have a maximum value. Hence, applying the Black–Scholes model for an interest rate option can lead to nonsensical option prices. Besides, the Black–Scholes model assumes that interest rates are constant during the option's life. This is clearly an inappropriate assumption for interest rate options since interest rates change every day and affect the option price. Finally, the Black–Scholes model assumes a constant variance for the underlying asset. This assumption is inappropriate for interest rates since the bond-price volatility declines as the bond approaches the maturity date. In fact, the bond price tends to reach its face value at the maturity date. When there is no coupon payment, the Black–Scholes model is applied as follows for bond calls:

$$c(B,T) = BN(d_1) - Ke^{-rT}N(d_2)$$

$$d_1 = \frac{\ln\left(\frac{B}{K}\right) + \left(r + \frac{\sigma^2}{2}\right)T}{\sigma\sqrt{T}}, \quad d_2 = d_1 - \sigma\sqrt{T}.$$

The Black–Scholes model is applied as follows for bond puts:

$$p(B,T) = -BN(-d_1) + Ke^{-rT}N(-d_2)$$

$$d_1 = \frac{\ln\left(\frac{B}{K}\right) + \left(r + \frac{\sigma^2}{2}\right)T}{\sigma\sqrt{T}}, \quad d_2 = d_1 - \sigma\sqrt{T}.$$

19.1.4. *Valuation and the role of short-term options on long-term bonds*

Short-term options on long-term bonds are often traded on OTC markets. These options may be of the European or the American type. There is a traded option on the Chicago Board Options Exchange (CBOE), which is based upon the yield to maturity on a portfolio of bonds. The yield to maturity is driven by the changes in the term structure of interest rates.

The Black–Scholes model is sometimes used to price short-term European options on zero-coupon bonds. In this context, the call's value is given by:

$$c(B,T) = BN(d_1) - Ke^{-rT}N(d_2),$$

where

$$d_1 = \frac{\ln\left(\frac{B}{K}\right) + \left(r + \frac{\sigma^2}{2}\right)T}{\sigma\sqrt{T}}, \quad \text{and} \quad d_2 = d_1 - \sigma\sqrt{T},$$

where

B: price of the bond;
K: strike price of the option;
T: time to maturity of the option;
σ: instantaneous standard deviation of the bond price and
r: spot rate on a risk-free investment with a maturity date T.

Using the put-call parity relationship, the put's value is given by:

$$p(B,T) = -BN(-d_1) + Ke^{-rT}N(-d_2)$$

$$d_1 = \frac{\ln\left(\frac{B}{K}\right) + \left(r + \frac{\sigma^2}{2}\right)T}{\sigma\sqrt{T}}, \quad d_2 = d_1 - \sigma\sqrt{T}.$$

However, other European models, which are extensions or generalizations of the Black–Scholes model like Merton's (1973) model, are more appropriate for the pricing of these options.

19.1.5. *Valuation of interest rate options*

Interest rate options are often used in the management of interest-rate risk in the same way as equity options. A direct implication is that option strategies for equity options apply directly to interest rate options.

The most common and specific strategies based on short-term interest rate options are caps and floors. These strategies place either a cap on the future level of interest rates on a floating instrument or a floor on the interest rate receivable on deposits.

A cap: It is an option strategy which protects from a rise in interest rates and allows a profit when interest rates are falling.

A floor: It is an option strategy which protects from a decrease in interest rates at the time when the deposit rate is re-set.

A collar: When an investor buys a cap (floor) and sells the floor (cap), this strategy is known as the collar.

The cap, the floor, and the collar can be valued using standard formulas for call and put options.

19.1.6. *Valuation and the role of bond options: The case of coupon-paying bonds*

The price of any financial asset is given by the present value of its expected cash flows. The first step in determining the bond's price is to determine its cash flows, i.e., the periodic coupon interest payments until the maturity date and the par value at maturity. Since the bond price is given by the present value of the cash flows, its price is given by adding all the discounted future payments at the appropriate interest rates. Some bonds do not make any periodic coupon payments and the interest due to the difference between the maturity value and the purchase price given by the bond holder. This class of bonds is referred to as zero-coupon bonds. It is convenient to note that there are several types of bonds: bonds with call provisions, putable bonds, convertible bonds, bonds with warrants attached, exchangeable bonds, etc.

A bond with a call provision gives the right to the issuer to call the issue before the specified redemption date. The call price is different from par and is specified at the bond issue.

A bond with a put provision gives its holder the right to put the bond back to the issuer at a fixed price. It is a putable bond.

A convertible bond entitles its holder the right to convert the bond into a certain number of units of the equity of the issuing firm or into other bonds. This number is often called the rate of conversion which is specified when the bond is issued.

A bond with an attached warrant is simply a package comprising the bond and a warrant. It allows the holder to purchase the equity of the issuing firm. Most of these bonds are Eurobonds issued in international capital markets.

An exchangeable bond is similar to a convertible bond, with the exception that it gives its holder the right to exchange the bonds for the equity of other company. The call or the put provision in these bonds can be valued using the Black–Scholes model. However, the model is not appropriate if there are many call or put dates and if the embedded options in the bonds are of the American type. We give an application of this model to options on zero-coupon bonds and options on coupon-paying bonds under the Black–Scholes assumptions. If the bond is a coupon-paying bond, then the present value of all coupons due during the option's life must be substracted from the bond's price.

Example. Consider a European call for which the underlying asset is a coupon bond with the following characteristics:

- Bond's price = 96 Euro;
- One year interest rate = 10%;
- Time to maturity = 10 years;
- Volatility of the bond's price = 8%;

- Coupon payments = 5 Euros in 3 months and 9 months;
- Three-month interest rate = 8% and
- Nine-month interest rate = 8.5%.

The option has a strike price equal to 100 Euro and its maturity date is in one year. The present value of coupon payments is 9.59 Euro, or:

$$5e^{-0.25x0.08} + 5e^{-0.75x0.085} = 4.9 + 4.69 = 9.59.$$

Applying the Black–Scholes formula gives:

$$B = 96 - 9.59 = 86.41 \text{ Euro},$$
$$d_1 = \frac{1}{0.080}\left[\ln\left(\frac{86.41}{100}\right) + 0.1 + 0.0032\right]$$
$$d_2 = d_1 - 0.08 \times 1 = -0.6158$$
$$c = 86.41N(-0.5358) + 100e^{-0.1}N(-0.6158)$$

or $c = 1.25$ Euro.

It is convenient to note the "incoherence" with this model since it assumes constant interest rates and at the same time a stochastic bond price.

19.1.7. *The valuation of a swaption*

A swaption: It is the right to assume a position in an underlying interest-rate swap with a given maturity. In swaptions, the right to pay the fixed component is equivalent to the right to receive the floating component and vice versa. Swaptions are offered as receiver swaptions and payer swaptions. Receiver swaption gives the right to receive a fixed interest rate and payer swaption gives the right to pay a fixed interest rate.

The buyer of a receiver swaption benefits when the interest rate falls because he/she is guaranteed to receive a fixed rate, which is higher than the floating rate. If interest rates rise, the swaption can be ignored because the buyer can get a higher fixed rate in the market. The seller of the receiver swaption is obliged to pay the fixed rate and to receive the floating rate in the swap context. Most swaptions are of the European style.

Interest-rate swap agreements are second-order derivatives. Interest-rate swaps reflect an equilibrium rate that equates a floating-rate stream of payments with a fixed-rate stream of payments at the present date. A swaption price can be computed using an option pricing model where the underlying market input is the rate on the swap. The forward rate for the expiry date of the swaption can be used for a swaption with a European exercise. The following formula is often used to determine forward/forward rates:

$$F = (T-t)\sqrt{\left[\frac{(1+S_T)^T}{(1+r_t)}\right]} - 1,$$

where:

F: forward swap rate;
S: spot swap rate;
r: deposit rate for time t (the time to swaption expiration) and
T: term of the swap in years.

Swaption pricing is based on a model allowing the computation of the value of the option to exchange one asset for another as given by the formula in Margrabe (1978):

$$W(x_1, x_2, t) = x_1 N(d_1) - x_2 N(d_2)$$

$$d_1 = \frac{(\ln(x_1/x_2) + 0.5\sigma^2(t^* - t))}{\sqrt{(t^* - t)}}$$

$$d_2 = d_1 - v\sqrt{(t^* - t)}$$

$$\sigma^2 = \sigma_1^2 + \sigma_2^2 - 2\sigma_1\sigma_2\rho_{1,2},$$

where:

W: price of receivers/payers option;
x_1, x_2: the prices of assets 1 and 2;
$\sigma_1(\sigma_2)$: the volatility of assets 1 (asset 2);
$\rho_{1,2}$: correlation coefficient;
t: current date and
t^*: expiration date.

This formula is derived in the last chapter (Chapter 8). Tompkins (for more details, refer to Bellalah *et al.*, 1998) proposed the following put-call relationship for swaptions expressed in annual terms:

Payer swaption − receiver

$$\text{swaption} = \sum_{t=i}^{T} \frac{(\textit{prevailing swap rate} - \textit{swaption strike})}{(1+r^t)^t},$$

where:
r: discount rate for the time period t;
T: term of the interest rate swap and
t: first exchange date of coupons.

19.2. Applications of the Black's Model

19.2.1. *Options on equity index futures*

Options on index futures require upon exercise the exchange of a long position in the future contract for a call and a short position in the future contract for the put. Hence, a call is exercised into a long position in the future contract and a put is exercised into a short position in the same contract. The underlying futures contract does not require a physical delivery but is rather settled in cash. The amount received corresponds to the difference between the current and the future level of the underlying index. In this context, the futures contract is regarded as an agreement to either pay or receive a cash payment based upon the difference between the current and the future values of a specified index.

Options on index futures are often treated as options on an asset paying a continuous stream of dividends, regardless of whether the underlying spot index pays a continuous or a discrete dividend.

Since the assumptions used by Black are similar to those in Black–Scholes, some of them are also questionable, such as the constant volatility and the certainty of interest rates. In fact, the non-stationarity of volatility causes some problems in the pricing of options on index futures. As we will see later, some extensions on the Black's model are more appropriate for the valuation of these options. However, when these options are of the European type, Black's model is often used in the pricing of these options.

The various strategies applied with options on individual assets can be used as well for options on index futures.

Index futures and options on index futures are often used in asset allocation and portfolio insurance. Asset allocation refers to the structuring of a multiasset portfolio with respect to the type and the weighing scheme of asset classes. Strategic asset allocation is the construction of a portfolio such that long-run objectives are attained when different classes of assets are transacted at their long-run equilibrium values.

Tactical asset allocation, also known as market timing involves short-term allocations toward rising markets and away from falling markets.

Portfolio insurance refers to a group of techniques that insure a portfolio against falling in value below a certain specified level, the floor level. This level does not eliminate the potential profits from a rise in the asset value.

19.2.2. *Options on currency forwards and options on currency futures*

19.2.2.1. *Options on currency forwards*

They are traded in the OTC market. This market is regarded as the major market for currency options. The growth of the OTC market is due to its flexibility, since many banks and financial institutions offer options with tailor-made characteristics in order to match the clients' needs.

19.2.2.2. *Options on currency futures*

These options have been traded since 1982. These options are standardized contracts and can be inflexible. They are priced off the underlying futures contract. When exercised, the call buyer receives a long position in one futures contract marked-to-market at the current price. In the same way, when exercised, the put holder receives a short position in one futures contract.

These options must have the same value as European options on the spot currency since they are not exercised before the maturity date, at which the futures price is equal to the spot price.

The similarity between forward and futures prices suggests the use of Black's model for the valuation of these options.

Currency futures and currency forwards are often used to hedge currency risks. Options on currency futures are applied in the currency-risk management. The basic strategies of buying and selling calls and puts, the vertical, diagonal, calendar, and volatility spreads are also applied in the currency futures options markets. They can also be used in portfolio insurance.

Several other applications of currency futures and options are used to manage currency risks. Examples include basket options, average rate options, cylinder options, and many other exotic options.

19.2.3. *The Black's model and valuation of interest rate caps*

An interest rate cap: It is defined as an agreement or a contractual arrangement where the seller known as the grantor is obliged to pay cash to the buyer whenever the interest rate exceeds or is less than a pre-specified agreed level at some future time. When the grantor pays cash to the cap holder, this latter's net position is equivalent to borrowing at a fixed rate at this specified level. Hence, an interest rate cap can be seen as an option where the holder pays a premium upfront. The well-known forms of interest rate cap agreements are the floor and ceiling agreements. The floor holder can establish a minimum level for his/her floating-rate deposits over a given period. If at future dates the interest rate falls below the floor rate, the seller makes good the holder's interest income shortfall. However, if rates are higher than the floor rate, the buyer receives nothing, but has the possibility to place his/her deposit at a higher market rate. The ceiling agreement gives the right to the buyer to establish a maximum interest-rate level for borrowing over a given period. If rates turn to be higher than the ceiling rate, the buyer receives cash to exactly offset the additional interest-rate charge due because of higher rates. However, if rates fall in the future, the holder can borrow at a rate lesser than the ceiling rate. Therefore, the Black's model can be used for the pricing of the caps. The model requires five variables: time to maturity, the price of the underlying futures, the strike price or cap level, the risk-free rate for the option maturity, and the volatility.

19.3. The Extension to Foreign Currencies: The Garman and Kohlhagen Model and Its Applications

Garman and Kohlhagen (1983) provided a formula for the valuation of foreign currency options. These options are traded on the foreign exchange market, which is fundamentally an inter-bank market where transactions are conducted over the telecommunications system. The foreign exchange market called also the FX market operates internationally 24 hours a day where the major participants are commercial banks around the world and treasury departments of large companies. As in other markets, the various participants search for hedging exchange risks, speculation, and the implementation of arbitrage strategies. Foreign currency options satisfy some of the needs of these participants and the important volume of transactions implies the use of an option pricing model. A simple and an interesting analytic model is provided by Garman and Kohlhagen (1983). Foreign currency options are priced along the lines of Black and Scholes (1973) and Merton (1973). Specifically, Garman and Kohlhagen (1983) and Grabbe (1983) presented models for currency options, which are based on the assumption that a risk-less hedge portfolio can be formed by investing in foreign bonds, domestic bonds, and the option.

19.3.1. *The currency call formula*

Using the same assumptions as in the Black and Scholes (1973) model, Garman and Kohlhagen (1983) presented the following formula for a European currency call:

$$c(S,T) = Se^{-r^*T}N(d_1) + Ke^{-rT}N(d_2)$$

$$d_1 = \frac{\ln\left(\frac{S}{K}\right) + (r - r^* + \frac{\sigma^2}{2})T}{\sigma\sqrt{T}}, \quad d_2 = d_1 - \sigma\sqrt{T}.$$

19.3.2. *The currency put formula*

The formula for a European currency put is:

$$p(S,T) = -Se^{-r^*T}N(-d_1) - Ke^{-rT}N(-d_2)$$

$$d_1 = \frac{\ln\left(\frac{S}{K}\right) + (r - r^* + \frac{\sigma^2}{2})T}{\sigma\sqrt{T}}, \quad d_2 = d_1 - \sigma\sqrt{T}.$$

Note that the main difference between these formulae and those of B–S model for the pricing of equity options is that the foreign risk-free rate is used in the adjustment of the spot rate. The spot rate is adjusted by the known "dividend", i.e., the foreign interest earnings, whereas the domestic risk-free rate enters the calculation of the present value of the strike price since the domestic currency is paid over on exercise.

Examples. Assume that the US dollar/sterling spot rate is 1.8, the time to maturity is three months, the three-month dollar interest rate is 7%, and the sterling interest rate is 10%. When the volatility is 20%, the option price is 6.3817, or:

$$C = 180e^{-(0.1)(0.25)}N(d_1) - 180e^{-(0.07)(0.25)}N(d_2)$$

$$d_1 = [\ln(180/180) + (0.06 - 0.10 + 0.5(0.2)^2)0.25]/0.2\sqrt{0.25} = -0.05$$

$$d_2 = d_1 - 0.2\sqrt{0.25} = -0.15$$

$$N(d_1) = 0.4801, N(d_2) = 0.4404$$

$$C = 84.284 - 77.896 = 6.3817.$$

Note that the value of $N(d_1)$ is discounted to the present using the foreign interest rate. This is because this rate is assumed to correspond to a continuous dividend stream on the underlying asset. In the same way, we can calculate risk parameters of other options.

19.3.3. *The interest-rate theorem and the pricing of forward currency options*

The interest-rate parity theorem states that the forward rate is equal to the spot rate compounded by the differential between the foreign and domestic interest rates. Using continuously compounded interest rates, the forward exchange rate is:

$$f = Se^{(r-r^*)T}$$

which means simply that the formula for the pricing of a European call on a spot currency can be re-written as:

$$c(F,T) = e^{-rT}[fN(d_1) - KN(d_2)]$$

$$d_1 = \frac{\ln\left(\frac{f}{K}\right) + \frac{\sigma^2}{2}T}{\sigma\sqrt{T}}, \quad \text{and} \quad d_2 = d_1 - \sigma\sqrt{T}.$$

The formula for the European currency put is:

$$p(F,T) = e^{-rT}[-fN(-d_1) + KN(-d_2)]$$

$$d_1 = \frac{\ln\left(\frac{f}{K}\right) + \frac{\sigma^2}{2}T}{\sigma\sqrt{T}}, \quad \text{and} \quad d_2 = d_1 - \sigma\sqrt{T}$$

where all the parameters have the same meaning as before, except for the spot exchange rate S, which is replaced by the forward exchange rate f. Note that the interest-rate differential is not explicitly taken into account in the above formula. This is because all the available information about spot rates and the interest-rate differential is integrated in the forward exchange rate via the interest-rate parity theorem. The following tables provide simulation results for option prices using the Garman-Kohlhagen model (Tables 19.1–19.4). The tables also give the Greek letters. The reader can make comments about the values of the Greek letters.

These tables provide the risk matrix for managing and monitoring options positions. The head of trading and the asset risk officer must continuously control these risk parameters.

19.4. The Extension to Other Commodities: The Merton, Barone-Adesi and Whaley Model, and Its Applications

The model presented in Barone-Adesi and Whaley (1987) is a direct extension of the models presented by Black and Scholes (1973), Merton (1973), and Black (1976).

Table 19.1. Simulations of Garman-Kohlhagen call prices. $S = 1$, $K = 1$, $t = 07/02/2003$, $T = 07/02/2004$, $r = 3\%$, $r^* = 4\%$ and $\sigma = 20\%$.

S	Price	Delta	Gamma	Vega	Theta
0.96	0.05384	0.43109	0.52931	0.00364	0.00008
0.97	0.05815	0.45081	0.50961	0.00370	0.00008
0.98	0.06266	0.47042	0.49003	0.00376	0.00009
0.99	0.06737	0.48984	0.47063	0.00380	0.00009
1	0.07227	0.50904	0.45145	0.00383	0.00009
1.01	0.07736	0.52798	0.43253	0.00386	0.00008
1.02	0.08264	0.54661	0.41391	0.00387	0.00008
1.03	0.08810	0.56492	0.39562	0.00388	0.00008
1.04	0.09375	0.58286	0.37769	0.00387	0.00008

Table 19.2. Simulations of Garman-Kohlhagen call prices. $S = 1.1$, $K = 1$, $t = 07/02/2003$, $T = 07/02/2004$, $r = 3\%$, $r^* = 4\%$ and $\sigma = 20\%$.

S	Price	Delta	Gamma	Vega	Theta
1.06	0.10315	0.61071	0.34986	0.00385	0.00008
1.07	0.10988	0.62921	0.33137	0.00382	0.00008
1.08	0.11680	0.64714	0.31345	0.00378	0.00007
1.09	0.12392	0.66449	0.29611	0.00373	0.00007
1.10	0.13123	0.68123	0.27937	0.00368	0.00007
1.11	0.13872	0.69736	0.26325	0.00362	0.00007
1.12	0.14639	0.71287	0.24775	0.00355	0.00006
1.13	0.15423	0.72774	0.23289	0.00347	0.00006
1.14	0.16224	0.74198	0.21865	0.00339	0.00006

19.4.1. *The model*

The absence of risk-less arbitrage opportunities imply that the following relationship exists between the futures contract, F, and the price of its underlying spot commodity, S: $F = Se^{bT}$, where T is the time to expiration and b is the cost of carrying the commodity. When the underlying commodity dynamics are given by:

$$\frac{dS}{S} = \alpha dt + \sigma dW,$$

Table 19.3. Simulations of Garman-Kohlhagen put prices. $S = 1$, $K = 1$, $t = 07/02/2003$, $T = 07/02/2004$, $r = 3\%$, $r^* = 4\%$ and $\sigma = 20\%$.

S	Price	Delta	Gamma	Vega	Theta
0.96	0.10195	−0.52960	0.52931	0.00364	0.00011
0.97	0.09666	−0.50987	0.50961	0.00370	0.00011
0.98	0.09156	−0.49027	0.49003	0.00376	0.00011
0.99	0.08666	−0.47084	0.47063	0.00380	0.00011
1	0.08195	−0.45164	0.45145	0.00383	0.00011
1.01	0.07744	−0.43271	0.43253	0.00386	0.00011
1.02	0.07311	−0.41407	0.41391	0.00387	0.00011
1.03	0.06896	−0.39577	0.39562	0.00388	0.00011
1.04	0.06500	−0.37783	0.37769	0.00387	0.00011

Table 19.4. Simulations of Garman-Kohlhagen put prices and the Greek letters. $S = 1.1$, $K = 1$, $t = 07/02/2003$, $T = 07/02/2004$, $r = 3\%$, $r^* = 4\%$ and $\sigma = 20\%$.

S	Price	Delta	Gamma	Vega	Theta
1.06	0.05904	−0.34997	0.34986	0.00385	0.00011
1.07	0.05519	−0.33148	0.33137	0.00382	0.00011
1.08	0.05155	−0.31354	0.31345	0.00378	0.00011
1.09	0.04810	−0.29620	0.29611	0.00373	0.00011
1.10	0.04484	−0.27945	0.27937	0.00368	0.00011
1.11	0.04177	−0.26332	0.26325	0.00362	0.00010
1.12	0.03887	−0.24781	0.24775	0.00355	0.00010
1.13	0.03615	−0.23294	0.23289	0.00347	0.00010
1.14	0.03358	−0.21870	0.21865	0.00339	0.00010

where α is the expected instantaneous relative price change of the commodity and σ is its standard deviation, then the dynamics of the futures price are given by the following differential equation:

$$\frac{dF}{F} = (\alpha - b)dt + \sigma dW.$$

Assuming that a hedged portfolio containing the option and the underlying commodity can be constructed and adjusted continuously, the partial differential equation that must be satisfied by the option price, c, is:

$$\frac{1}{2}\sigma^2 S^2 \left[\frac{\partial^2 c(S,t)}{\partial S^2}\right] - rc(S,t) + bS\left[\frac{\partial c(S,t)}{\partial S}\right] + \left[\frac{\partial c(S,t)}{\partial t}\right] = 0.$$

This equation first appeared indirectly in Merton (1973).

When the cost of carry b is equal to the risk-less interest rate, this equation reduces to that of the equation in B–S (1973) model.

When the cost of carry is zero, this equation reduces to that of the equation given in Black (1976).

When the cost of carry is equal to the difference between the domestic and the foreign interest rate, this equation reduces to that in Garman and Kohlhagen (1983).

It is convenient to note that the short-term interest rate r, and the cost of carrying the commodity, b, are assumed to be constant and proportional rates.

Using the terminal boundary condition: $c(S,T) = \max[0, S_T - K]$.

Merton (1973) showed indirectly that the European call price is:

$$c(S,T) = Se^{(b-r)T}N(d_1) - Ke^{-rT}N(d_2)$$

$$d_1 = \frac{\ln\left(\frac{S}{K}\right) + (b + \frac{\sigma^2}{2})T}{\sigma\sqrt{T}}, \quad \text{and} \quad d_2 = d_1 - \sigma\sqrt{T}.$$

Using the boundary condition for the put $p(S,T) = \max[0, K - S_T]$, the European put price is given by:

$$p(S,T) = -Se^{(b-r)T}N(-d_1) + Ke^{-rT}N(-d_2)$$

$$d_1 = \frac{\ln\left(\frac{S}{K}\right) + \left(b + \frac{\sigma^2}{2}\right)T}{\sigma\sqrt{T}}, \quad d_2 = d_1 - \sigma\sqrt{T}.$$

The call formula provides the composition of the asset-bond portfolio that mimics exactly the call's payoff. A long position in a call can be replicated by buying $e^{(b-r)T}N(d_1)$ units of the underlying asset and selling $N(d_2)$ units of risk-free bonds, each unit with strike price Ke^{-rT}. When the asset price varies, the units invested in the underlying asset and risk-free bonds will change. Using a continuous re-balancing of the portfolio, the pay* outs will be identical to those of the call. The same strategy can be used to duplicate the put's payoff.

19.4.2. *An application to portfolio insurance*

Dynamic portfolio insurance strategies are based on a dynamic replication argument. The nontrading of the long-term index put options in the 1980s led stock portfolio managers to create their own insurance using a dynamic re-balancing portfolio-containing stocks and risk-free bonds. The portfolio weights in a dynamically re-balancing portfolio are determined using the put option formula:

$$p(S,T) = -Se^{(b-r)T}N(-d_1) + KN(-d_2)$$

$$d_1 = \frac{\ln\left(\frac{S}{K}\right) + (b + \frac{\sigma^2}{2})T}{\sigma\sqrt{T}} \quad \text{and} \quad d_2 = d_1 - \sigma\sqrt{T}.$$

The objective of portfolio insurance is to create an "insured" portfolio whose pay outs mimic the portfolio $Se^{(b-r)T} + p$. The strategy is equivalent to:

$$Se^{(b-r)T} + p = Se^{(b-r)T} - Se^{(b-r)T}N(-d_1) + Ke^{-rT}N(-d_2)$$

or $Se^{(b-r)T}N(d_1) + Ke^{-rT}N(-d_2)$, in this context, a dynamically insured portfolio shows an investment of $Se^{(b-r)T}N(d_1)$ units of stocks and $N(-d_2)$ units of risk-free bonds. When the stock price increases, funds are transferred from bonds to stocks and vice versa.

19.5. The Real World and the Black–Scholes Type Models

The Black and Scholes (1973) type model is universally applied by market participants even though several other alternative models exist. The main question is why the Black–Scholes model successful and how to apply the model when the imperfections of the real world loom large.

19.5.1. *Volatility*

The historical volatility can be used as a proxy of the future volatility of the underlying asset. For example, it is possible to consider the prices of the asset every day for the last 200 days and compute the standard deviation of log returns on this arbitrary time interval. This gives a good estimate of volatility with a standard error of around 5%. There are several other ways of predicting volatility. In any case, the assumption of a constant volatility is violated in the real world.

19.5.2. *The hedging strategy*

In the Black–Scholes (1973) theory, the more frequently the hedge is adjusted, the more precise is the hedge. This assumes that the volume of trading will also increase without limit as the portfolio is re-balanced more frequently. The model seems to break down when frictions are introduced into the trading process.

19.5.3. *The log-normal assumption*

This model assumes that the log returns are normally distributed. However, for several underlying assets, returns seem to be fat-tailed. Besides, this model assumes that the dynamics of the underlying asset are almost continuous, however prices tend to move discretely and jump. Despite its simplifying assumptions, the model seems to give "good" results because it represents the limiting case for option price bounds that exist in more general models.

19.5.4. *A world of finite trading*

Britten-Jones and Neuberger (1998) developed a model of finite trading to analyze trading costs, hedging strategies, and the effect of price jumps. Consider the pricing and the hedging of a short position in a European call option on a non-dividend paying asset. The model assumes that the trader can trade when he/she wants and not continuously as in the Black–Scholes model. Denote the net prices by $P_0, P_1, \ldots, P_N$ (after taking account of market impact, spreads, commissions, etc.) used by the trader to re-balance the hedge. The price P_0 corresponds to the initial price when the option is sold and P_N is the price at the option maturity. The trader increases the hedge when prices increase and reduces the hedge when the prices decrease. P_{i+1} is the total cost of buying (ask price plus commissions) when $P_{i+1} > P_i$ and it represents the net revenue from selling (bid price minus commissions) when $P_{i+1} < P_i$. The model assumes that jumps in prices are less than some amount d with: $d \geq \log \frac{P_i}{P_{i-1}}$ with $i = 1, \ldots, N$.

19.5.5. *Total variance*

The total variance in this model is given by: $\nu = \Sigma_1^N \left[\log \frac{P_i}{P_{i-1}}\right]^2$. This total variance is a function of transaction prices.

19.5.6. *Black–Scholes as the limiting case*

Britten-Jones and Neuberger (1996) have shown that when there is an upper bound on total variance and when asset prices do not jump too much, it is possible to place an upper bound on the call price $\overline{C}(\nu, d)$. This upper bound depends on the total variance and the maximum jump size. In the same way, it is possible to place a lower bound on the option price $\underline{C}(\nu, d)$. If the trader has a view that the jump size will not exceed d and the total variance will not be higher than ν, then he/she can sell the option at $\overline{C}(\nu, d)$ confident that at worst he/she will break even. When d tends to zero, the option price in this model tends to be the Black–Scholes price. If the trader is confident that the total variance will lie somewhere between $\underline{\nu}$ and $\overline{\nu}$ and the maximum jump will be less than d, then it is possible to place bounds on the option price $\underline{C}(\underline{\nu}, d)$ and $\overline{C}(\overline{\nu}, d)$. These two bounds allow the trader to buy the option for less than the lower bound and to sell it for more than the upper bound. In this limit, when ν is known and d is very small, the two bounds coalesce and become equal to the Black–Scholes price. If the trader could predict the total variance exactly and if prices do not jump, the options can be priced exactly.

19.5.7. *Using the model to optimize hedging*

How often a hedge should be re-balanced for a sold call?

This question can be turned into an empirical issue about forecasting the total variance of returns. Britten-Jones and Neuberger (1998) give an example to illustrate the answer to this question.

Consider a trader who believes that the volatility of the asset price is 15%. Transaction costs are five basis points.

If the hedge is re-balanced 10 times for a three-month maturity call, this leads to low transaction costs. Selling an option at a volatility of 15.3% can lead to profits. However, because of infrequent re-balancing, this situation can lead to losing money. The trader can be sure to make money at 99% if the option priced at three standard deviations away from the mean is sold on a volatility of 23%. If the position is re-balanced about 300 times, the investor can make money when the option is sold at a volatility of 18.3%.

Summary

Stock index options and futures markets have experienced remarkable growth rates. Stock index options are either of the European or the American type and often involve cash settlement procedure upon exercise. Stock index options are traded on the major indices around the world. These options are of the European or American type. Options on the spot index are cash-settled and there is no physical delivery of the underlying index. The price of any financial asset is given by the present value of its expected cash flows. Options on index futures require upon exercise the exchange of a long position in the future contract for a call and a short position in the future contract for the put. Options on currency forwards are traded in the OTC market. This market is regarded as the major market for currency options. The growth of the OTC market is due to its flexibility, since many banks and financial institutions offer options with tailor-made characteristics in order to match the clients' needs. Garman and Kohlhagen (1983) provided a formula for the valuation of foreign currency options. These options are traded on the foreign exchange market, which is fundamentally an inter-bank market where transactions are conducted over the telecommunications system. The foreign exchange market also called the FX market operates internationally 24 hours a day where the major participants are commercial banks around the world and treasury departments of large companies. Currency options were traded on the spot currency for the first time in 1982 at the Philadelphia Stock Exchange. Since this date, currency options are traded on many other financial places. However, the trading on the OTC market seems to be more important. The strategies discussed for stock options also apply to currency options and currency futures options. This chapter presented in detail the basic concepts and techniques underlying rational derivative asset pricing in the context of the analytical European models along the lines of Black–Scholes and Merton. First, some applications of the Black–Scholes (1973) model are provided. Second, applications of the Black (1976) model are presented. Third, applications of the Garman and Kohlhagen model are presented for the valuation of currency options. Fourth, the Merton (1973) and Barone-Adesi and Whaley (1987) model is proposed for the valuation of European commodity contracts, commodity options, and commodity futures options. Some applications of the model are given. Note that this model reduces to the models in Black–Scholes, Black and Garman and Kohlhagen for some values of its parameters. Since all these models (except Arone-Adesi and Whaley (1987)) are interested in the valuation of European style options in a continuous time framework, (without discrete distributions to the underlying asset), a natural extension of these models must introduce the possibility of an early exercise and discrete distributions. However, before making some extensions of the basic analytical models, it is useful to study in this simple context, the option price sensitivities and the use of these Greek-risk measures in the monitoring and the management of an option position. The question of managing an option position is as important as some issues regarding the option pricing. The Black–Scholes hedge works in the real, discrete, and frictionful world when the hedger uses the correct volatility of the prices at which he/she actually trades and when the asset prices do not jump too much. The assumptions of the Britten-Jones and Neuberger (1998) model provide a framework in which a trader can avoid jumps and in which total variance can be estimated perfectly. The model transforms the question of pricing and hedging options into how well investors can predict the total variance of returns of the associated hedging strategy.

References

Barone-Adesi G and RE Whaley (1987). Efficient analytic approximation of American option values. *Journal of Finance*, 42 (June), 301–320.

Black F (1976). The pricing of commodity contracts. *Journal of Financial Economics*, 3, 167–179.

Black F and M Scholes (1973). The pricing of options and corporate liabilities. *Journal of Political Economy*, 81, 637–659.

Brennan MJ and ES Schwartz (1990). Arbitrage in stock index futures. *Journal of Business*, 63, 7–31.

Britten-Jones M and AF Neuberger (1996). Arbitrage pricing with incomplete markets. *Applied Mathematical Finance*, 3(4), 347–363, 11–13.

Britten-Jones M and AF Neuberger (1998). Welcome to the real world. *Risk* (September), 11–13.

Evnine J and A Rudd (1985). Index options: The early evidence. *Journal of Finance*, 40(3), 743–756.

Garman M and S Kohlhagen (1983). Foreign currency option values. *Journal of International Money and Finance*, 2, 231–237.

Grabbe JO (1983). The pricing of call and put options on foreign exchange. *Journal of International Money and Finance*, 2, 239–253.

Merton R (1973). Theory of rational option pricing. *Bell Journal of Economics and Management Science*, 4, 141–183.

Chapter 20

Applications of Option Pricing Models to the Monitoring and the Management of Portfolios of Derivatives in the Real World

Chapter Outline

This chapter is organized as follows:

1. In Section 20.1, option price sensitivities are presented and the formulas are applied.
2. In Section 20.2, the Greek-letter risk measures are simulated for different parameters. The question of monitoring and managing an option position in real time is studied for the different risk measures with respect to an option pricing model.
3. In Section 20.3, some of the characteristics of volatility spreads are presented.

Introduction

As seen during the financial crisis 2008–2009, risk appears as a major concern for the financial system and defies all that has been written by academics in this area. The sensitivity parameters or Greek-letter risk measures are important in managing an option position.

The delta measures the absolute change in the option price with respect to a small change in the price of the underlying asset. It is given by the option's partial derivative with respect to the underlying asset price. It represents the hedge ratio, or the number of options to write in order to create a risk-free portfolio.

Call buying involves the sale of a quantity delta of the underlying asset in order to form the hedging portfolio.

Call selling involves the purchase of a quantity delta of the asset to create the hedging portfolio.

Put buying requires the purchase of a quantity delta of the underlying asset to hedge a portfolio.

Put selling involves the sale of delta stocks to create a hedged portfolio.

The delta varies from zero for deep out-of-the-money (OTM) options to one for deep in-the-money (ITM) calls. This is not surprising, since by definition, the delta is given by the first partial derivative of the option price with respect to the underlying asset. For example, the value of a deep ITM call is nearly equal to the intrinsic value for which the first partial derivative with respect to the underlying asset is one.

Charm is a risk measure that clarifies the concept of carry in financial instruments. The concept of carry refers to the expenses due to the financing of a deferred delivery of commodities, currencies, or other assets in financial contracts. Even though charm is used by market participants as an ad hoc measure of how delta may change overnight, it is an important measure of risk since it divides the theta into its asset-based constituents.

The gamma measures the change in delta, or in the hedge ratio, as the underlying asset price changes. The gamma is the greatest for at-the-money (ATM) options. It is nearly zero for deep ITM and deep OTM options. Approximately, the gamma is to the delta what convexity is to duration. The gamma is given by the derivative of the hedge ratio with respect to the underlying asset price. As such, it is an indication of the vulnerability of the hedge ratio. The gamma is very important in the management and the monitoring of an option position. It gives rise to two other measures of risk: speed and color.

Speed is given by the gamma's derivative with respect to the underlying asset price.

Color is given by the gamma's derivative with respect to the time remaining to maturity.

The theta measures the change in the option price as time elapses since time decays presents a negative impact on option values. Theta is given by the first partial derivative of the option premium with respect to time.

The vega or lambda measures the change in the option price for a change in the underlying asset's volatility. It is given by the first derivative of the option premium with respect to the volatility parameter.

The knowledge of the "true" option price is not sufficient for the monitoring and the management of an option position. Therefore, it is important to know the option-price sensitivities with respect to the parameters entering the option formula. We begin our discussion with the delta. In this chapter, we show how to calculate some of these parameters within the context of each analytical model presented in Chapter 9. Also, we develop some examples to show how to use the Greek-letter risk measures in the monitoring and the management of an option position in response to the changing market conditions.

20.1. Option-Price Sensitivities: Some Specific Examples

20.1.1. *Delta*

The delta is given by the option's first partial derivative with respect to the underlying asset price. It represents the hedge ratio in the context of the Black–Scholes model (B–S model).

20.1.1.1. *The call's delta*

The call's delta is given by $\Delta_c = N(d_1)$. The use of this formula requires the computation of d_1 given by:

$$d_1 = \frac{\ln \frac{S}{K} + \left(r + \frac{1}{2}\sigma^2\right) T}{\sigma\sqrt{T}}.$$

Example. Let the underlying asset price $S = 18$, the strike price $K = 15$, the short-term interest rate $r = 10\%$, the maturity date $T = 0.25$, and the volatility $\sigma = 15\%$, the option's delta is given by $\Delta_c = N(d_1)$.

To apply this formula, the calculation of d_1 is:

$$d_1 = \frac{1}{0.15\sqrt{0.25}}\left[\ln\left(\frac{18}{15}\right) + \left(0.1 + \frac{1}{2}0.5^2\right)0.25\right] = 2.8017.$$

Hence, the delta is $\Delta_c = N(2.8017) = 0.997$. This delta value means that the hedge of the purchase of a call needs the sale of 0.997 units of the underlying asset. When the underlying asset price rises by 1 unit, from 18 to 19, the option price rises from 3.3659 to approximately $(3.3659 + 0.997)$, or 4.3629. When the asset price falls by 1 unit, the option price changes from 3.3659 to approximately $(3.3659 - 0.997)$, or 2.3689.

20.1.1.2. *The put's delta*

The put's delta has the same meaning as the call's delta. It is also given by the option's first derivative with respect to the underlying asset price. When selling (buying) a put option, the hedge needs selling (buying) delta units of the underlying asset. The put's delta is given by: $\Delta_p = \Delta_c - 1 = 0.0997 - 1 = -0.003$. The hedge ratio is -0.003. When the underlying asset price rises from 18 to 19, the put price changes from 0.0045 to approximately $(0.0045 - 0.003)$, or 0.0015. When it falls from 18 to 17, the put price rises from 0.0045 to approximately $(0.0045 + 0.003)$, or 0.0075. Supplementary material provides the derivation of the Greek letters in the context of analytical models. Supplementary material provides a detailed derivation of these parameters.

20.1.2. *Gamma*

The option's gamma corresponds to the option's second partial derivative with respect to the underlying asset or to the delta partial derivative with respect to the asset price.

20.1.2.1. *The call's gamma*

In the B–S model, the call's gamma is given by $\Gamma_c = \frac{\partial \Delta_c}{\partial S} = \frac{1}{S\sigma\sqrt{T}}n(d_1)$ with $n(d_1) = \frac{1}{\sqrt{2\pi}}e^{-\frac{1}{2}d_1^2}$. Using the same data as in the example, $n(d_1) = \frac{1}{\sqrt{6.2831}}e^{-\frac{1}{2}(2.8017)^2} = 0.09826$ and $\Gamma_c = \frac{1}{18(0.15)\sqrt{0.25}}0.09826 = 0.0727$. When the underlying asset price is 18 and its delta is 0.997, a fall in the asset price by 1 unit yields a change in the delta from 0.997 to approximately $(0.997 - 0.0727)$, or 0.9243. Also, a rise in the asset price from 18 to 19, yields a change in the delta from 0.997 to $(0.997 + 0.0727)$, or 1. This means that the option is deeply ITM, and its value is given by its intrinsic value $(S - K)$. The same arguments apply to put options. The call and the put have the same gamma.

20.1.2.2. *The put's gamma*

The put's gamma is given by $\Gamma_p = \frac{\partial \Delta_p}{\partial S} = \frac{1}{S\sigma\sqrt{T}}n(d_1)$ with $n(d_1) = \frac{1}{\sqrt{2\pi}}e^{-\frac{1}{2}d_1^2}$ or $\Gamma_p = \frac{1}{18(0.15)\sqrt{0.25}}0.09826 = 0.0727$.

When the asset price changes by one unit, the put price changes by the delta amount and the delta changes by an amount equal to the gamma.

20.1.3. *Theta*

The option's theta is given by the option's first partial derivative with respect to the time remaining to maturity.

20.1.3.1. *The call's theta*

In the B–S model, the theta is given by:

$$\Theta_c = \frac{\partial c}{\partial T} = \frac{-S\sigma n(d_1)}{2\sqrt{T}} - rKe^{-rT}N(d_2).$$

Using the same data as in the example above, we obtain:

$$\Theta_c = -0.2653 - 1.4571 = -1.1918.$$

When the time to maturity is shortened by 1% per year, the call's price decreases by 0.01 (1.1918), or 0.011918 and its price changes from 3.3659 to approximately (3.3659 – 0.01918), or 3.3467.

20.1.3.2. *The put's theta*

In the B–S model, the put's theta is given by:

$$\Theta_p = \frac{\partial p}{\partial T} = -\frac{S\sigma n(d_1)}{2\sqrt{T}} + rKe^{-rT}N(d_2)$$

or $\Theta_p = -0.2653 + 0.0058 = -0.2594$.

Using the same reasoning, the put price changes from 0.0045 to approximately (0.0045 – 0.0025), or 0.002.

20.1.4. *Vega*

The option's vega is given by the option's price derivative with respect to the volatility parameter.

20.1.4.1. *The call's vega*

In the B–S model, the call's vega is given by $v_c = \frac{\partial c}{\partial \sigma} = S\sqrt{T}n(d_1)$ or using the above data $v_c = 18\sqrt{0.25}(0.09826) = 0.88434$. Hence, when the volatility rises by 1 point, the call price increases by 0.88434. The increase in volatility by 1% changes the option price from 3.3659 to (3.3659 + 1%(0.88434)), or 3.37474. In the same context, the put's vega is equal to the call's vega. The put price changes from 0.0045 to (0.0045 + 1%(0.88434)), or 0.0133434. When the volatility falls by 1%, the call's price changes from 3.3659 to (3.3659 – 1%(0.88434)), or 3.36156 . In the same way, the put price is modified from 0.0045 to approximately (0.0045 – 1%(0.88434)), or zero since option prices cannot be negative.

20.1.4.2. *The put's vega*

In the B–S model, the put's vega is given by:

$$v_p = \frac{\partial p}{\partial \sigma} = S\sqrt{T}n(d_1)$$

or $v_p = 18\sqrt{0.25}(0.09826) = 0.88434$ and it has the same meaning as the call's vega.

20.1.5. *Rho*

20.1.5.1. *The call's rho*

The option's rho is given by the option's first partial derivative with respect to interest rates. In the B–S model, the call's rho is given by $Rho_c = \frac{\partial c}{\partial r} = KTe^{-rT}N(d_2)$.

Using the above data $Rho_c = e^{-0.1(0.25)}(0.996)(0.25) = 3.64$.

The Rho does not affect the call and put prices in the same way. In fact, a rise in the interest rate yields higher call price (positive Rho) and reduces the put price (negative Rho).

20.1.5.2. *The put's rho*

In the B–S model, the put's rho is given by:

$$Rho_p = \frac{\partial p}{\partial r} = -KTe^{-rT}N(-d_2)$$

or $Rho_p = -15e^{-0.1(0.25)}(0.996)(0.25) = -3.64$.

20.1.6. *Elasticity*

20.1.6.1. *The call's elasticity*

For a call option, this measure is given by Elasticity $= S\frac{\Delta c}{c} = \frac{S}{c}N(d_1)$ or using the above data:

$$\text{Elasticity} = \frac{18}{3.3659}0.997 = 5.3317.$$

The elasticity shows the change in the option price when the underlying asset price varies by 1%. Hence, a rise in the asset price by 1%, i.e., 0.18, induces an increase in the call price by 5.33%. The put price decreases by 12%. Hence, when the asset price changes from 18 to 18.18, the call's price is modified from 3.3659 to approximately (3.3659 (1+5.33%)), or 3.545. In the same way, the put price changes from 0.0045 to (0.0045(1 – 12%)), or 0.00396.

20.1.6.2. *The put's elasticity*

The put's elasticity is given by:

$$\text{Elasticity} = S\frac{\Delta p}{p} = \frac{S}{p}[N(d_1) - 1]$$

or Elasticity $= \frac{18}{0.0045}[0.997 - 1] = -12$.

The knowledge of the variations in these parameters is fundamental for the monitoring and the management of an option position. Supplementary material provides the relationship between these hedging parameters.

20.2. Monitoring and Managing an Option Position in Real Time

Since option prices change in an unpredictable way in response to the changes in market conditions, traders, market makers, and all option users must rely upon some model to monitor the evolution of their profit and loss accounts. Such a model allows them to know the variations in option price sensitivities and their risk exposure. With such quantities, the monitoring and the management of option positions are more easily achieved. We illustrate the management of an option position in real time using the model proposed indirectly in Merton (1973) and derived afterwards in Black (1975) and Barone-Adesi and Whaley (1987) for the valuation of European futures options. First, option prices are simulated and the sensitivity parameters are calculated. Second, we study the risk-management problem in real time with respect to option price sensitivities.

20.2.1. *Simulations and analysis of option price sensitivities using Barone-Adesi and Whaley model*

Re-call that the commodity call price and the commodity futures call price in the context of Merton's (1973) and Barone-Adesi and

Whaley's (1987) model is given by:

$$c(S,T) = Se^{(b-r)T}N(d_1) - Ke^{-rT}N(d_2),$$

$$d_1 = \frac{\left[\ln\left(\frac{S}{K}\right) + \left(b + \frac{1}{2}\sigma^2\right)T\right]}{\sigma\sqrt{T}}, \quad d_2 = d_1 - \sigma\sqrt{T},$$

where b stands for the cost of carrying the underlying commodity.

By the put-call parity relationship or by a direct derivation, the put's value is given in the same context by:

$$p(S,T) = -Se^{(b-r)T}N(-d_1) + Ke^{-rT}N(-d_2),$$

$$d_1 = \frac{\left[\ln\left(\frac{S}{K}\right) + \left(b + \frac{1}{2}\sigma^2\right)T\right]}{\sigma\sqrt{T}}, \quad d_2 = d_1 - \sigma\sqrt{T},$$

where all the parameters have the same meaning as before.

For a non-dividend paying asset, $b = r$. For a dividend-paying asset, $b = r - d$ where d stands for the dividend yield.

For a currency option, $b = r - r^*$, where r^* stands for the foreign risk-less rate.

Tables 20.1–20.12 simulate option values and sensitivity parameters for calls and puts in the context of the above model.

20.2.1.1. *Sensitivity parameters for call options*

Table 20.1 gives call prices, delta, gamma, theta, and vega when the underlying commodity price varies from 75 to 110 in steps of 5. For example, when the volatility $\sigma = 20\%$, $r = 8\%$, $b = 10\%$, and $T = 3$ months (0.25 year), the price of an ATM call for $K = 90$ is 5.07.

The call has a delta of 0.64, a gamma of 0.04, a theta of 0.17, and a vega of 1.94. Note that an ATM call has more theta and vega than an ITM and an OTM call.

Using the same data except for the strike price, which is modified from 90 to 100, Table 20.2 shows that an ATM call ($K = 100, S = 100$) has more gamma, theta, and vega than ITM, and OTM calls.

Table 20.3 shows call prices and sensitivity parameters for European calls when the time to maturity varies from 0.05 to 0.75 year.

Note that the call price, the vega, and the theta increase with the time to maturity. However, the delta falls when the time to maturity is longer.

Table 20.1. Changing the underlying asset prices for European calls. $\sigma = 0.2$, $r = 0.08$, $b = 0.10$, $T = 0.25$, and $K = 90$.

Call	Asset	Delta	Gamma	Theta	Vega
0.23	75	0.07	0.02	0.05	0.47
0.88	80	0.21	0.03	0.11	1.10
2.42	85	0.42	0.04	0.17	1.71
5.07	90	0.64	0.04	0.17	1.94
8.76	95	0.82	0.03	0.13	1.78
13.17	100	0.93	0.02	0.08	1.46
17.44	105	0.97	0.01	0.04	1.05
22.37	110	0.99	0.01	0.02	0.89

Table 20.2. Changing the underlying asset prices for European calls. $\sigma = 0.2$, $r = 0.08$, $b = 0.10$, $T = 0.25$, and $K = 100$.

Call	Asset	Delta	Gamma	Theta	Vega
0.01	75	0.01	0	0.01	0.06
0.09	80	0.03	0.01	0.03	0.25
0.40	85	0.10	0.02	0.08	0.71
1.23	90	0.24	0.03	0.14	1.37
2.92	95	0.44	0.04	0.19	1.94
5.64	100	0.64	0.04	0.19	2.16
8.87	105	0.79	0.03	0.15	1.89
13.11	110	0.90	0.02	0.10	1.56

Table 20.3. Changing time to maturity for European calls. $\sigma = 0.2$, $r = 0.08$, $b = 0.10$, $S = 100$, and $K = 90$.

Call	Maturity	Delta	Gamma	Vega	Theta
10.47	0.05	0.99	0	0	0.83
11.00	0.10	0.97	0.01	0.02	1.03
12.71	0.25	0.91	0.02	0.08	1.34
15.44	0.50	0.88	0.01	0.14	1.45
17.98	0.75	0.88	0.01	0.19	1.46

Table 20.4 gives call prices and sensitivity parameters for ATM calls when ($S = K = 100$) and the time to maturity varies from 0.05 to a year. Note that the call price, its delta, and vega are increasing functions of the time to maturity. However, the gamma and the theta are more important on near maturities.

Table 20.5 gives ITM call prices ($S = 100, K = 90$) for different levels of the volatility parameter. When the delta is equal to 1, the gamma is nearly equal to zero. Also, the vega is nearly nil and the theta is weak.

Table 20.6 gives the same information as Table 20.5, except that calculations are done for ATM options ($S = K = 100$).

20.2.1.2. *Sensitivity parameters for put options*

Table 20.7 gives put prices and the sensitivity parameters when: $\sigma = 0.2$, $r = 0.08$, $b = 0.1$, $T = 0.25$, and $K = 90$.

Table 20.4. Changing time to maturity for European calls. $\sigma = 0.2$, $r = 0.08$, $b = 0.10$, $S = 100$, and $K = 100$.

Call	Maturity	Delta	Gamma	Vega	Theta
2.04	0.05	0.55	0.08	0.09	2.09
3.05	0.10	0.58	0.06	0.12	2.09
5.32	0.25	0.62	0.04	0.20	2.05
8.36	0.50	0.67	0.03	0.26	1.98
11.04	0.75	0.71	0.02	0.31	1.91
13.53	1.00	0.74	0.02	0.34	1.84

Table 20.5. Changing the volatility for European calls. $T = 0.25$, $r = 0.08$, $b = 0.10$, $S = 100$, and $K = 90$.

Call	Volatility	Delta	Gamma	Vega	Theta
12.29	0.05	1	0	0	0.76
12.29	0.10	1	0.025	0.01	0.78
12.71	0.20	0.92	0.01	0.08	1.34
13.78	0.30	0.85	0.01	0.13	2.18
15.19	0.40	0.78	0.01	0.15	3.02

Table 20.6. Changing the volatility for European calls, $T = 0.25$, $r = 0.08$, $b = 0.10$, $S = 100$, and $K = 100$.

Call	Volatility	Delta	Gamma	Vega	Theta
2.69	0.05	0.85	0.09	0.12	0.94
3.46	0.10	0.70	0.06	0.17	1.28
5.32	0.20	0.62	0.03	0.19	2.05
7.26	0.30	0.60	0.02	0.19	2.84
9.21	0.40	0.59	0.01	0.20	3.64

Table 20.7. Changing the underlying asset prices for European puts. $\sigma = 0.2$, $r = 0.08$, $b = 0.10$, $T = 0.25$, and $K = 90$.

Put	Asset	Delta	Gamma	Vega	Theta
13.04	75	−0.89	0.02	0.05	0.83
8.61	80	−0.81	0.03	0.11	0.96
5.04	85	−0.61	0.04	0.16	1.01
2.55	90	−0.38	0.04	0.17	0.88
1.12	95	−0.26	0.03	0.13	0.61
0.43	100	−0.08	0.02	0.08	0.34

For an ATM put, $(K = 90, S = 90)$, the gamma and the vega are important.

The put's theta increases when the option tends to parity and decreases afterwards.

The same behavior applies for the put's gamma and vega.

Table 20.8 gives the same information as Table 20.7, except for the strike price which is changed from 90 to 100. For ITM puts, the delta approaches -1, the gamma and vega are not important, and the theta is very weak.

Table 20.9 gives OTM put prices $(S = 100, K = 90)$ and the put price sensitivities when the time to maturity varies from 0.05 to a year. The values of the delta and gamma are weak. However, there is more vega and theta for longer maturities.

Table 20.10 shows the same information for ATM put prices $(S = K = 100)$. Note that the deltas and gammas are decreasing functions of the time to maturity. For an ATM put, there

Table 20.8. Changing the underlying asset prices for European puts. $\sigma = 0.2$, $r = 0.08$, $b = 0.10$, $T = 0.25$, and $K = 100$.

Put	Asset	Delta	Gamma	Vega	Theta
22.65	75	−1.00	0	0	0.79
17.69	80	−0.97	0.01	0.02	0.85
12.94	85	−0.91	0.02	0.07	0.97
8.69	90	−0.73	0.03	0.14	1.09
5.26	95	−0.48	0.04	0.19	1.12
2.84	100	−0.38	0.04	0.19	0.98

Table 20.9. Changing time to maturity for European puts. $\sigma = 0.2$, $r = 0.08$, $b = 0.10$, $S = 100$, and $K = 90$.

Put	Asset	Delta	Gamma	Vega	Theta
0.01	0.05	−0.01	0	0	0.07
0.08	0.10	−0.04	0.01	0.02	0.22
0.43	0.25	−0.08	0.02	0.08	0.34
0.91	0.5	−0.12	0.01	0.14	0.35
1.23	0.75	−0.13	0.01	0.19	0.32
1.45	1.00	−0.13	0.01	0.22	0.30

Table 20.10. Changing time to maturity for European puts. $\sigma = 0.2$, $r = 0.08$, $b = 0.10$, $S = 100$, and $K = 100$.

Put	Asset	Delta	Gamma	Vega	Theta
1.54	0.05	−0.45	0.09	0.09	1.85
2.04	0.10	−0.42	0.06	0.12	1.40
2.84	0.25	−0.38	0.04	0.14	0.98
3.43	0.50	−0.34	0.03	0.27	0.74
3.71	0.75	−0.31	0.02	0.31	0.62
3.83	1.00	−0.28	0.02	0.34	0.54

is more theta on short maturities and more vega on longer maturities.

Table 20.11 gives OTM put prices when the volatility varies from 0.05 to 0.4.

Table 20.11. Changing time to maturity for European puts. $T = 0.25$, $r = 0.08$, $b = 0.10$, $S = 100$, and $K = 90$.

Put	Volatility	Delta	Gamma	Vega	Theta
0	0.05	−0.00	0	0	0
0.01	0.10	−0.00	0	0.01	0.01
0.43	0.20	−0.09	0.02	0.08	0.34
1.50	0.30	−0.17	0.02	0.13	0.80
2.91	0.40	−0.23	0.02	0.15	1.22

Table 20.12. Changes in volatility, TM puts. $T = 0.25$, $r = 0.08$, $b = 0.10$, $S = 100$, and $K = 100$.

Put	Volatility	Delta	Gamma	Vega	Theta
0.21	0.05	−0.16	0.10	0.12	0.23
0.98	0.10	−0.30	0.07	0.17	0.55
2.84	0.20	−0.38	0.04	0.19	0.97
4.78	0.30	−0.41	0.03	0.19	1.34
6.73	0.40	−0.41	0.02	0.20	1.69

When the volatility is respectively equal to 0.05 and 0.1, the put price is nil and so are the sensitivity parameters as well.

Table 20.12 shows ATM put prices ($S = K = 100$) for different levels of the volatility, parameter. Note that the put price, the delta (in absolute value), the vega, and the theta are increasing functions of the volatility parameter.

Note that the negative sign for the delta concerns only the put option.

20.2.2. *Monitoring and adjusting the option position in real time*

20.2.2.1. *Monitoring and managing the delta*

The call's delta is between zero and one and the put's delta is between 0 and −1. When the delta is 0.5, the call price rises (falls) by 0.5 point for each increase (decrease) in the asset price by 1 point. A delta of 0.5 corresponds to an ATM call.

For a deep ITM call, the variation in the asset price by one unit implies an equivalent variation in the option price. The delta of an OTM call is almost zero and of a deep ITM call is almost 1.

Since the put's delta lies in the interval -1 and 0, a rise in the underlying asset price implies a fall in the put price and vice versa.

The delta is -0.5 for an ATM put, -1 for a deep ITM put and 0 for a deep OTM put.

The call delta is often assimilated to the hedge ratio. Since the underlying asset delta is 1 and that of an ATM call is 0.5, the hedge ratio is (1/0.5) or 2/1. Hence, we need two ATM calls to hedge the sale of the underlying asset. Note that the delta is calculated in practice using the observed volatility or the implicit volatility.

Delta-neutral hedging requires the adjustment of the option position according to the variations in the delta. When buying or selling a call (put), the investor must sell or buy (buy or sell) delta units of the underlying asset to represent a hedged portfolio.

In practice, the hedged portfolio is adjusted nearly continuously to account for the variations in the delta's value. An initially hedged position must be re-balanced by buying and selling the underlying asset as a function of the variations in the delta through time.

The delta changes as the value of the underlying asset, the volatility, the interest rate, and the time to maturity are modified.

Table 20.13 shows how to adjust a hedged portfolio in order to preserve main characteristics of delta-neutral strategies.

It is important to note that delta-neutral hedging strategies do not protect completely the option position against the variations in the volatility parameter (Table 20.14).

It is also important to note that delta-neutral hedging does not protect the option position against the variations in the time

Table 20.13. Adjustment of the hedged portfolio as a function of the underlying asset price.

Options	Delta Hedging When S Rises	Delta Hedging When S Falls
Long a call	Delta increases: short more S	Delta decreases: buy more S
Short a call	Delta increases: buy more S	Delta decreases: sell more S
Long a put	Delta decreases: sell more S	Delta increases: buy more S
Short a put	Delta decreases: buy more S	Delta increases: sell more S

Table 20.14. Adjustment of a hedged position when the volatility changes.

Options	Volatility Increases	Volatility Decreases
Long a call		
ITM	Delta decreases: buy more S	Delta increases: sell more S
ATM	Delta nonadjusted	Delta nonadjusted
OTM	Delta decreases: sell more S	Delta decreases: buy more S
Short a call		
ITM	Delta decreases: re-sell of S	Delta increases: buy more S
ATM	Delta nonadjusted	Delta nonadjusted
OTM	Delta increases: buy more S	Delta decreases: sell more S
Long a put		
ITM	Delta decreases: re-sell of S	Delta increases: buy more S
ATM	Delta nonadjusted	Delta nonadjusted
OTM	Delta increases: buy more S	Delta decreases: sell more S
Short a put		
ITM	Delta increases: buy more S	Delta increases: sell more S
ATM	Delta nonadjusted	Delta nonadjusted
OTM	Delta decreases: sell more S	Delta decreases: buy more S

remaining to maturity. The adjustment of the position when the time to maturity changes can be done as explained in Table 20.15.

Note that the deltas are additive. For example, when buying two calls having respectively, a delta of 0.2 and 0.7, the investor must sell 0.9 units of the underlying asset in a delta-neutral strategy.

Option market-makers implement often delta-neutral hedging strategies in order to maintain a nil delta (in monetary unit). When the delta of an option position is positive, this means that the market-maker is long the underlying asset. If the asset price rises, he/she makes a profit since he/she will be able to sell it at a higher price. However, if the asset price decreases, he/she will lose money since he/she will sell the underlying asset at a lower price. When the delta is positive, the investor is over-hedged with respect to delta-neutral strategies.

When the delta (in monetary unit) is negative, the investor is shorting the underlying asset. If the underlying asset price rises, the investor loses money since he/she adjusts his/her position by buying more units of the underlying asset. However, when the asset price falls, he/she makes a profit since he/she pays less for the underlying asset.

Table 20.15. Adjustment of a hedged position as a function of time.

Options	Adjustment of the Hedged Position as a Function of Time
Long a call	
ITM	Delta rises: sell more S
ATM	Delta nonmodified
OTM	Delta decreases: buy more S
Short a call	
ITM	Delta rises: buy more S
ATM	Delta nonmodified
OTM	Delta decreases: sell more S
Long a put	
ITM	Delta rises: buy more S
ATM	Delta nonmodified
OTM	Delta decreases: sell more S
Short a put	
ITM	Delta rises: sell more S
ATM	Delta nonmodified
OTM	Delta decreases: buy more S

When a portfolio is constructed by buying (selling) the securities and derivative assets vj, the portfolio value is given by:

$$P = n_1 v_1 + n_2 v_2 + n_3 v_3 + \cdots + n_j v_j,$$

where n_j stands for the numbers of units of the assets bought or sold.

The delta's position, or its partial derivative with respect to the securities and derivative assets is:

$$\begin{aligned}\Delta_{\text{position}} &= \left(\frac{\partial v_1}{\partial S}\right) + n_2\left(\frac{\partial v_2}{\partial S}\right) + n_3\left(\frac{\partial v_3}{\partial S}\right) + \cdots + n_j\left(\frac{\partial v_j}{\partial S}\right)\\ &= n_1\Delta_1 + n_2\Delta_2 + n_3\Delta_3 + \cdots + n_j\Delta_j.\end{aligned}$$

Delta-neutral hedging is convenient for an investor who does not have prior expectations about the market direction. However, if the investor expects a rising market, he/she can have a positive delta, i.e., long the underlying asset, so he/she can sell at a higher price when the market effectively rises.

If the investor expects a down market, he/she can have a negative delta, i.e., short the underlying asset, so he/she can buy it at a lower price when the market effectively goes down.

20.2.2.2. *Monitoring and managing the gamma*

The gamma is given by the second derivative of the option price with respect to the underlying asset price. A high value of gamma (either positive or negative) shows a higher risk for an option position. The gamma shows what the option gains (loses) in delta when the underlying asset price rises (falls).

For example, when the option's gamma is 4 and the option's delta is zero, an increase by 1 point in the underlying asset price allows the option to gain 4 points in delta, i.e., the delta is equal to 4.

When the delta is constant, the gamma is zero. The gamma varies when the market conditions change. The gamma is the highest for an ATM option and decreases either side when the option gets ITM or OTM. The gamma of an ATM option rises significantly when the volatility decreases and the option approaches its maturity date.

When the gamma is positive, an increase in the underlying asset price yields a higher delta. The adjustment of the position entails the sale of more units of the underlying asset. When the asset price falls, the delta decreases and the adjustment of the option position requires the purchase of more units of the underlying asset. Since the adjustment is done in the same direction as the changes in the market direction, this monitoring of an option position with a positive gamma is easily done.

When the gamma is negative, an increase in the underlying asset price reduces the delta. The adjustment of a delta-neutral position needs the purchase of more units of the underlying asset. When the asset price decreases, the delta rises. The adjustment of the option position requires the sale of more units of the underlying asset. Hence, the adjustment of the position implies a re-balancing against the market direction which produces some losses (Table 20.16).

In general, the option's gamma is a decreasing function of the time to maturity. The longer is the time to maturity, the weaker is the gamma and vice versa.

When the option approaches its maturity date, the gamma varies significantly (Table 20.17).

Table 20.16. The adjustment of a hedged position and the gamma.

Position	Gamma	Adjustment of the Position	Effect on the Position
Long options	Positive	Market up: sell more S	Easy adjustment, yields profits
Long options	Positive	Market down: buy more S	Easy adjustment, yields profits
Short options	Negative	Market up: buy more S	Difficult adjustment, yields losses
Short options	Negative	Market down: sell more S	Easy adjustment, yields losses

Table 20.17. The variations in gamma and the time to maturity.

	Longer T	Short T	Near T
Gamma	Low	High	High for ATM
Gamma	Low	High	Very low for OTM
Effect on position	Low	Easy adjustment	Delta is very sensitive to S
Effect on position	Low	Easy adjustment	Gamma is used with care

Table 20.18. Effect of the gamma on an option position.

	OTM	ATM	ITM
Gamma	Near zero	High for a shorter T	Near zero for a near T
Gamma	Near zero	Stable for a longer T	Near zero for a near T
Effect	Weak	Gamma is fundamental	Weak

The variations in the gamma for ITM, ATM and OTM options is explained below in Table 20.18.

The management of an option position with a positive gamma is simple. When the market rises, the investor becomes long and must sell some quantity of the underlying asset to re-establish his/her delta-neutral position. This produces a gain.

When the underlying asset decreases, the investor becomes short and must buy more units of the underlying asset to re-establish his/her delta-neutral position. This yields a profit.

The management of an option position with a negative gamma is more difficult when the underlying asset's volatility is high. When the market rises, the investor becomes short and must buy some quantity of the underlying asset to re-establish his/her delta-neutral position. This produces a loss. When the underlying asset decreases, the investor becomes long and must sell more units of the underlying asset to re-establish his/her delta-neutral position. This yields a loss.

In general, one should be careful when adopting a positive gamma since the option position loses from its theta when the market is not volatile. In this context, it is better to have a negative gamma. However, when the market is volatile, a position with a positive gamma allows profits, since the adjustment requires buying the underlying asset when the market falls and selling it when the market rises. The gamma of an option position with several assets is given by:

$$\begin{aligned}\Gamma_{\text{position}} &= \frac{\partial \Delta_{\text{position}}}{\partial S}\\ &= n_1\left(\frac{\partial \Delta_1}{\partial S}\right) + n_2\left(\frac{\partial \Delta_2}{\partial S}\right) + n_3\left(\frac{\partial \Delta_3}{\partial S}\right) + \cdots + n_j\left(\frac{\partial \Delta_3}{\partial S}\right).\end{aligned}$$

For delta-neutral strategies, a positive gamma allows profits when the market conditions change rapidly and a negative gamma produces losses in the same context.

20.2.2.3. *Monitoring and managing the theta*

The theta is given by the option's partial derivative with respect to the remaining time to maturity. As maturity date approaches, the option loses value. The theta is often expressed as a function of the number of points lost each day. A theta of 0.4, means that the option loses US$ 0.4 in value when the maturity date is reduced by one day.

In general, the gamma and the theta are of opposite signs. A high positive gamma is associated with a high negative theta and vice versa.

By analogy with the gamma, as a high gamma is an indicator of a high risk associated with the underlying asset price, a high theta is an indicator of a high exposure to the passage of time. An ATM option with a short maturity loses value much more than a corresponding option on a longer term. The theta of an ATM option is often higher

Table 20.19. The option value and the theta for an ATM option.

	Longer Maturity	Shorter Maturity	Near Maturity
Loss in time value	Low	High	Very high
Effect on position	Needs passive monitoring	Profit for seller	Profit for seller
Effect on position	Needs passive monitoring	Loss for buyer	Loss for buyer

than that of an equivalent ITM or an OTM option having the same maturity date. The option buyer loses the theta value and the option writer "gains" the theta value (Table 20.19).

Example. A theta of US$ 1000 means that the option buyer pays US$ 1000 each day for the holding of an option position. This amount profits to the option writer. The theta remains until the last day of trading. When a position shows a positive gamma, its theta is negative. In general, a high gamma induces a high theta and vice versa. For example, when $\Gamma = 1500$, theta may be US$ 10,000, i.e., a loss of US$ 10,000 each day for the option position. This loss is compensated by the profits on the positive gamma since the adjustments of the position imply selling (buying) more units of the underlying asset when the market rises (falls).

When the $\Gamma = -1500$ for an option position, theta may be 10,000 i.e., a gain of US$ 10,000 each day. However, the position implies a loss on the underlying asset since the adjustments are done against the market direction when the gamma is negative.

The theta of an option position is:

$$\Theta_{\text{position}} = n_1\left(-\frac{\partial v_1}{\partial t}\right) + n_2\left(-\frac{\partial v_2}{\partial t}\right) + n_3\left(-\frac{\partial v_3}{\partial t}\right) + \cdots + n_1\left(-\frac{\partial v_j}{\partial t}\right).$$

20.2.2.4. *Monitoring and managing the vega*

The vega is given by the option's derivative with respect to the volatility parameter. It shows the induced variation in the option price when the volatility varies by 1%.

The vega is always positive for call and put options since the option price is an increasing function of the volatility parameter.

A vega of 0.6 means that an increase in the volatility by 1% increases the option price by 0.6. For a fixed time to maturity, the vega of an ATM option is higher than that of an ITM or an OTM option.

Since all the option pricing parameters are observable, except the volatility, buying (selling) options is equivalent to buying (selling) the volatility.

When monitoring an option position, a trade off must be realized between the gamma and the vega. Buying options and hence having a positive gamma is easy to manage. However, when the implicit volatility falls, the investor must adopt one of the two following strategies.

He/she can either preserve a positive gamma, if he/she thinks that the loss due to a decrease in volatility will be compensated by adjusting the gamma in the market direction.

He/she can sell the volatility (options) and re-establish a position with a negative gamma.

In this case, the losses due to the adjustments of the delta must be sufficient to compensate for the decrease in volatility (Tables 20.20 and 20.21).

The impact of the vega on ATM option is the highest and is summarized in Table 20.22.

Table 20.20. Effect of the volatility on a portfolio of options.

Options	Volatility	Effect
Long	Long	Profit (loss) when the volatility rises (falls)
Short	Short	Loss (profit) when the volatility rises (falls)

Table 20.21. Effect of the vega with respect to time to maturity.

	Longer Maturity	Shorter Maturity	Near Maturity
Vega	High	Low	Implicit volatility depends on other factors
Effect	Very sensitive	Little sensitivity	Implicit volatility depends on other factors

Table 20.22. Effect of the vega on the option price.

	OTM	ATM	ITM
Vega	Depends on T	For a given T, vega is higher	Depends on T
Option position	Low	High	Low

When the vega is US$ 50,000, this means that a rise in the volatility by 1% produces a profit of US$ 500. However, when the volatility decreases by 1%, this implies a loss of US$ 500.

When the vega is US$ 50,000, an increase in the volatility by 1% implies a loss of US$ 500 and a decrease by 1% yields a profit of US$ 500.

The vega of an option position is given by:

$$\begin{aligned}\text{Vega}_{\text{position}} &= n_1\left(-\frac{\partial v_1}{\partial \sigma}\right) + n_2\left(-\frac{\partial v_2}{\partial \sigma}\right)\\ &\quad + n_3\left(-\frac{\partial v_3}{\partial \sigma}\right) + \cdots + n_1\left(-\frac{\partial v_j}{\partial \sigma}\right)\end{aligned}$$

20.3. The Characteristics of Volatility Spreads

As a simple standard option, a spread is also characterized by its delta, gamma, theta, and vega. These sensitivity parameters allow the investor to manage his/her, option positions as a consequence of the changes in the market conditions. The implementation of strategies based on volatility spreads, implies often the use of delta-neutral strategies to be able to predict the variations in the market conditions.

When the changes in the underlying asset value give more value to the spread, the gamma is positive. On the other direction, the spread's gamma exhibits is negative when the variations in the underlying asset price reduce the spread value. Since the effects of these changes in the underlying asset price and the time to maturity operate in the opposite side, a spread with a positive gamma shows a negative theta and vice versa. Table 20.23 summarizes the effect of the sensitivity parameters on various spread strategies.

Table 20.23. Characteristics of volatility spreads.

Strategy, Position	Δ	Γ	Θ	Vega
Short a call ratio spread	0	+	−	+
Short a put spread	0	+	−	+
Long a straddle	0	+	−	+
Long a strangle	0	+	−	+
Short a butterfly	0	+	−	+
Long call ratio spread	0	−	+	−
Long a put ratio spread	0	−	+	−
Short a straddle	0	−	+	−
Short a strangle	0	−	+	−
Long a butterfly	0	−	+	−

The investor can implement delta-neutral strategies when he/she has no prior anticipations as to where the market is going. However, he/she can resort to bullish and bearish spreads when he/she is confident about the market timing. This leads him/her to be long or short the underlying asset.

When the options used are overvalued, (according to the investor), for instance, when the implied volatility is high (with respect to the historical volatility and its normal level), the investor can sell some puts if the market rises and some calls if the market falls.

When the options are undervalued, (according to the investor), for instance, when the implied volatility is low (with respect to the historical volatility and its normal level), the investor can be long calls and puts when the market falls.

Summary

It is important to monitor the variations in a derivative asset price with respect to its determinants or the parameters, which enter the option formula. These variations are often known as Greek-letter risk measures. The most widely used measures are known as the delta, charm, gamma, speed, color, theta, vega, rho, and elasticity.

The delta shows the absolute change in the option price with respect to a small variation in the underlying asset price. Charm corresponds to the partial derivative of the delta with respect to time.

The gamma gives the change in the delta, or in the hedge ratio as the underlying asset price changes.

Color corresponds to the gamma's derivative with respect to the time remaining to maturity.

The theta measures the change in the option price as time elapses.

The vega or lambda is a measure of the change in the option price for a small change in the underlying asset's volatility.

This chapter presented the main Greek-letter risk measures, i.e., the delta, the gamma, the theta, and the vega in the context of the European analytical models. These risk measures are simulated for different parameters, which enter the option formulas. Then the magnitude of these risk measures is appreciated in connection with the management and the monitoring of an option position.

The knowledge of the changes in these risk parameters is necessary for the management of an option position and the determination of the profits and losses associated with the portfolio. To put it differently, the pricing of a European call option can be viewed as requiring inputs (the underlying asset and the Treasury bill) and a production technology (the hedge portfolio and the Greek-letter risk measures). In a B–S world, by tracking continuously the hedge ratio (being delta-neutral), the investor makes sure that the duplicating portfolio does mimic the call option, namely does "produce" the option. In the course of doing so, the investor controls his/her production costs and protects his/her mark up on the option. However, these risk measures depend on the theoretical model used for the valuation and the management of the option position. This is why, one could call such a risk measure as a technological risk. This position must be adjusted nearly continuously, in response to the changes in the market conditions.

References

Barone-Adesi G and RE Whaley (1987). Efficient analytic approximation of American option values. *Journal of Finance*, 42 (June), 301–320.

Black F (1975). *The Pricing of Complex Options and Corporate Liabilities.* Graduate School of Business, University of Chicago, Chicago, IL.

Merton R (1973). Theory of rational option pricing. *Bell Journal of Economics and Management Science*, 4, 141–183.

Part VI

Mathematical Foundations of Option Pricing Models in a Continuous-Time Setting: Basic Concepts and Extensions

Chapter 21

The Dynamics of Asset Prices and the Role of Information: Analysis and Applications in Asset and Risk Management

Chapter Outline

This chapter is organized as follows:

1. Section 21.1 introduces continuous time stochastic processes for the dynamics of asset prices. In particular, the Wiener process, the generalized Wiener process, and the Ito process are presented and applied to stock prices.
2. In Section 21.2, Ito's lemma is constructed and several of its applications are provided.
3. In Section 21.3, we introduce the concepts of arbitrage, hedging, and replication in connection with the application of Ito's lemma. This allows the derivation of the partial differential equation governing the prices of derivative assets.
4. In Section 21.4, forward and backward equations are presented and some applications are given. In particular, we give the density of the first passage time and the density for the maximum or minimum of diffusion processes.
5. In Section 21.5, a general arbitrage principle is provided.
6. In Section 21.6, we introduce some concepts used in discrete hedging.

Introduction

This chapter explain how assets are priced with complete and incomplete information. Incomplete information reflects illiquidity, and lack of transparency. This can lead to a loss of confidence, as was the case of the financial crisis in 2008. The reader who is unfamiliar with mathematics can skip this part of the book. Most financial models describing the dynamics of price changes, interest rate changes, exchange rate variations, bond price changes, and derivative asset dynamics among other things, present a term known as a Wiener process. This process is a particular type of a general class of stochastic processes known as Markov stochastic processes. A stochastic process can be defined either in a simple way, as throughout this chapter, or in a more mathematical sense, as in supplementary material. Our presentation is at the same time intuitive and rigorous in order to allow the understanding of the necessary tools in continuous time finance. These tools are not as complicated as an uninformed reader might think. Using the definition of a stochastic process enables us to define the standard Brownian motion and the Ito process. The Ito process allows the construction of stochastic integrals and the definition of Ito's theorem or what is commonly known as Ito's lemma. This lemma can be obtained using Taylor's series expansions or a more rigorous mathematical approach. In both cases, some applications of this lemma to the dynamics of asset and derivative asset prices and returns are provided. The introduction of the concepts of arbitrage, replication, and the hedging argument, which are the basic concepts in finance, allows the derivation of a partial differential equation for the pricing of derivative assets. This equation first appeared in Black and Scholes (1973) and Merton (1973). These authors introduced the arbitrage theory of contingent claim pricing and, using Ito's theorem, showed that a continuously revised hedge between a contingent claim and its underlying asset is perfect. Since then, Ito's theorem, the Black and Scholes hedge portfolio, and the concepts of arbitrage and replicating portfolios have been used by many researchers in continuous and discrete time finance. The basic equivalent results in the theory of option pricing in a discrete time setting were obtained by Cox *et al.* (1979) and Rendleman and Barter (1979). They showed that option values calculated with discrete time models converge to option values obtained by continuous time models. In other words, theoretical work on convergence shows that some discrete time processes converge to continuous time processes. For example, in the context of binomial models, an option can be perfectly hedged using the underlying asset, and Ito's theorem can be implemented when constructing the hedging portfolio for infinitesimal time intervals.

Some important questions regarding the use of Ito's lemma and the perfect hedge can be studied. The main question is whether a continuously revised hedge is perfect over each revision interval or only when cumulating the hedging error to zero over a large number of revision intervals. In all such cases, these basic arguments lead to a partial differential equation, which must be satisfied by the prices of derivative assets. This can be derived using one of the two definitions of Ito's lemma: the definition given in the mathematical literature or simply the one obtained by an extension of the Taylor series.

21.1. Continuous Time Processes for Asset Price Dynamics

The dynamics of asset prices are often represented as a function of a Wiener process or what is also known as Brownian motion.

21.1.1. *Asset price dynamics and Wiener process*

The Wiener process has some interesting properties and can be introduced with respect to a change in a variable W over a small interval of time t.

21.1.1.1. *Wiener process or Brownian motion*

Let W denote a variable following a Wiener process and ΔW a change in its value over a small interval of time Δt. The relation between ΔW and Δt is given by the following equation:

$$\Delta W = \xi\sqrt{\Delta t} \tag{21.1}$$

where ξ is a random sample from a normal distribution having a zero mean and a unit standard deviation. If one takes two reasonably short intervals of time, then the values of ΔW are independent. Using these properties, it is clear that ΔW has also a normal distribution with a zero mean, a standard deviation equal to $\sqrt{\Delta t}$, and a variance of Δt.

Now, if one considers the change in W over a longer time period $[0, T]$, composed of N periods of length Δt, i.e., $T = N\Delta t$, then the change in W, from $W(0)$ to $W(T)$, or $W(T) - W(0)$, over this period of time is equal to the sum of changes over shorter periods. Hence, one can write:

$$W(t) - W(0) = \sum_{i=1}^{N} \xi_i \sqrt{\Delta t} \tag{21.2}$$

Using the independence property, it follows from this last equation that the change $W(T) - W(0)$, is normally distributed with a mean of zero, a variance of $N\Delta t = T$, and a standard deviation equal to $\sqrt{T}$. This is the basic Wiener process with a zero mean or drift rate and a unit variance rate. A mean or a drift rate of zero means that the future change is equal to the current change. A variance rate of one means that the change at time T is $1 \times T$.

Example. Consider a variable W following a Wiener process, starting at $W(0) = 20$ (in years). This variable will attain in one year, a value which is normally distributed with a mean of 20 and a standard deviation of 1. In two years, its value follows a similar type of distribution with mean 20 and a standard deviation of $\sqrt{2}$. In n years, its value follows the same distribution with mean 20 and a variance of n. What happens if the interval Δt gets very small, i.e., tends to zero. When Δt gets close to zero, the analogous to Eq. (21.1) is:

$$dW = \xi\sqrt{dt}. \tag{21.3}$$

21.1.1.2. *The martingale property and the Brownian motion*

The notion of martingale is useful in financial models, particularly, when analyzing the concept of arbitrage. A martingale can be defined as follows. Consider a probability space (Ω, F, P) and a filtration $(F_t)_{t\geq 0}$. An adapted family $(M_t)_{t\geq 0}$ of integrable random variables having a finite mean is a martingale when for all $s \leq t$, then we have:

$$E(M_t \mid F_s) = M_s \tag{21.4}$$

where $E(.)$ stands for the mathematical conditional expectation operator. Supplementary material gives the main properties of the conditional expectation operator. The notion of martingale asserts that the best approximation of M_t, given all the available information F_s, is M_s. In terms of financial markets, this means that the best way to predict futures prices is to use the current prices. Hence, using current information is equivalent to using all the historical information, since only the most recent information matters. Using this definition, it must be clear that when $(M_t)_{t\geq 0}$ is a martingale, then $E(M_t) = E(M_0)$. The following result is advanced without proof. If $(M_t)_{t\geq 0}$ is an $(F_t)_t$ – Brownian standard motion, then $(W_t)_t$ is an $(F_t)_t$ – martingale, $W_t^2 - t$ is an $(F_t)_t$ – martingale, and $e^{\left(\sigma W_t - \frac{1}{2}\sigma^2 t\right)}$ is an $(F_t)_t$ – martingale.

The first and second properties characterize the standard Brownian motion. The third property is useful when studying the dynamics of financial asset prices. In fact, as will be shown later, the price of a stock is often written as:

$$S_t = S_0 e^{\left(\sigma W_t - \frac{1}{2}\sigma^2 t\right)}. \tag{21.5}$$

21.1.2. *Asset price dynamics and the generalized Wiener process*

For a variable X, a generalized Wiener process can be expressed as:

$$dX = adt + bdW \tag{21.6}$$

where a and b are constants.

This process shows the dynamics of the variable X in terms of time and dW. The first term, adt, called the deterministic term, means that the expected drift rate of X is 'a' per unit time. The second term, bdW, called the stochastic component, shows the variability or the noise added to the dynamics of X. This noise is given by b times the Wiener process. When the stochastic component is zero, $dX = adt$, or $\frac{dX}{dt} = a$. This is equivalent to $X = X_0 + at$. Hence, the value of X at any time is given by its initial value X_0 plus its drift multiplied by the length of the time period. Now, it is possible to write the equivalent of Eq. (21.6) using Eq. (21.1) for a longer Δt:

$$\Delta X = a\Delta t + b\xi\sqrt{dt}. \tag{21.7}$$

Hence, as before, since ΔX has a normal distribution, its mean is $a\Delta t$, its standard deviation is $b\sqrt{\Delta t}$, and its variance is $b^2\Delta t$.

21.1.3. *Asset price dynamics and the Ito process*

An Ito process for a variable X can be written as follows:

$$dX = a(X,t)dt + b(X,t)dW. \tag{21.8}$$

The dependence of both the expected drift rate and the variance rate on X and time t, is the main difference from the generalized Wiener process. This process has been extensively used in the finance literature, especially for modeling stock price dynamics.

21.1.3.1. *Ito process*

We now give the mathematical definition of an Ito process. Consider a probability space $(\Omega, F_{tt\geq 0}, P)$ with a filtration and $(M_t)_{t\geq T}$ an $(F)_t$-Brownian motion.

An Ito process is a process $(M_t)_{0\leq t\leq T}$ having its values in $\mathcal{R}$ for which for all $t \leq T$:

$$X_t = X_0 + \int_0^t K_s ds + \int_0^t H_s dW_s \tag{21.9}$$

where K_t and H_t are stochastic processes adapted to F_t for which the integral corresponding to the second-order moment is finite. It will be shown later that the second integral in the above expression is a martingale.

21.1.3.2. *The dynamics of stock prices*

The dynamics of the stock price S are represented by the following Ito process with a drift rate, μS, and a variance rate $\sigma^2 S^2$:

$$dS = \mu S dt + \sigma S dW. \tag{21.10}$$

This process for stock prices, also known as the geometric Brownian motion can be written in a discrete time setting as:

$$\frac{\Delta S}{S} = \mu \Delta t + \sigma \xi \sqrt{\Delta t} \tag{21.11}$$

where ξ is a random sample from a normal distribution with a zero mean and a unit standard deviation. When the variance rate of return of the stock price is zero, the expected drift in S over Δt is:

$$dS = \mu S dt \quad \text{or} \quad \frac{dS}{S} = \mu dt \tag{21.12}$$

so that $S = S_0 e^{\mu t}$. When the variance rate is not zero and $\sigma^2 S^2 \Delta t$ is the variance of the actual change in S during Δt, the dynamics of the stock price are given by the expected instantaneous increase in S plus its instantaneous variance times the noise dW. This discrete time version says that the proportional return on the stock S, over a short period of time, is given by an expected return $\mu\Delta t$ and a stochastic return $\sigma\xi\Delta dt$. Hence, $\frac{\Delta S}{S}$ is normally distributed with a mean $\mu\Delta t$ and a standard deviation $\sigma\sqrt{\Delta t}$, or:

$$\frac{\Delta S}{S} \sim N(\mu\Delta t, \sigma\sqrt{\Delta t}) \tag{21.13}$$

21.1.3.3. *Some numerical examples*

Example. Consider the *XYZ* stock price characterized by an expected return of 14% per annum and a standard deviation or volatility of 35% per annum. The initial stock price is 100€. Using Eq. (21.13), the dynamics of this stock price are given by:

$$\frac{dS}{S} = 0.14dt + 0.35dW \tag{21.14}$$

or for a small interval,

$$\Delta t : \frac{dS}{S} = 0.14\Delta t + 0.35\xi\sqrt{\Delta t}.$$

If the time interval Δt is 2 weeks (or 0.03846 year), then the price increase is given by

$$\Delta S = 100[0.14(0.03846) + 0.35\xi\sqrt{0.03846}]$$

or

$$\Delta S = 100(0.005384 + 0.068639\xi).$$

The price increase is a random sample from a normal distribution with a mean of 0.538 and a volatility of 6.86.

Example. Consider the YZ stock price, having an expected return of 20% per annum and a standard deviation or volatility of 25% per annum. Over a time interval of 3 days, or 0.008219178 per year, $\frac{\Delta S}{S}$ is normal with,

$$\frac{\Delta S}{S} \sim N(0.00164, 0.0226)$$

21.1.4. *The log-normal property*

Using the previous example, since the change in the underlying asset price between time t and time t_i, is normally distributed, with a mean $\left(\mu - \frac{1}{2}\sigma^2\right)(t_i - t)$ and a variance $\sigma^2(t_i - t)$, we have

$$\ln(S_{ti}) - \ln(S_t) \sim N\left[\left(\mu - \frac{1}{2}\sigma^2\right)(t_i - t), \sigma\sqrt{(t_i - t)}\right] \quad (21.15)$$

or

$$\ln(S_{ti}) \sim N\left[\left(\mu - \frac{1}{2}\sigma^2\right)(t_i - t) + \ln(S_t), \sigma\sqrt{(t_i - t)}\right].$$

Hence, S_{ti} has a log-normal distribution.

Example. If $S = 100$, the expected return is 15% per annum and the volatility is 30% per annum, the distribution of $\ln(S_{ti})$ in six months is:

$$\ln(S_{ti}) \sim N\left[\ln(100) + [0.15 - 0.5(0.09)](0.5), 0.3\sqrt{\frac{6}{12}}\right]$$

or

$$\ln(S_{ti}) \sim N[4.6576, 0.212].$$

21.1.5. *Distribution of the rate of return*

Let α to be a continuously compounded rate of return. What is the distribution of α?

At a future date t_i, the stock price can be written as:

$$S_{ti} = S_t e^{\alpha(t_i - t)}$$

and $\alpha = \frac{1}{t_i - t}\ln\left(\frac{S_{ti}}{S_t}\right)$. Using the log-normal property, i.e.,

$$\ln\left(\frac{S_{ti}}{S_t}\right) \sim N\left[\left(\mu - \frac{1}{2}\sigma^2\right)(t_i - t), \sigma\sqrt{(t_i - t)}\right]$$

then

$$\alpha \sim N\left[\left(\mu - \frac{1}{2}\sigma^2\right), \frac{\sigma}{\sqrt{(t_i - t)}}\right]. \tag{21.16}$$

Example. What is the distribution of the actual rate of return over two years for a stock having an expected return of 15% per annum and a volatility of 30%?

The distribution is normal with a mean of 10.5%; $(15\% - \frac{0.09}{2})$, and a standard deviation of $\frac{0.3}{\sqrt{2}}$ i.e., 21.21%.

21.2. Ito's Lemma and Its Applications

Financial models are rarely described by a function that depends on a single variable. In general, a function which is itself a function of more than one variable is used. Ito's lemma, which is the fundamental instrument in stochastic calculus, allows such functions to be differentiated. First, we derive Ito's lemma with reference to simple results using Taylor series approximations. We then give a more rigorous definition of Ito's theorem. The formula for Taylor series is given in supplementary material.

21.2.1. *Intuitive form*

Let f be a continuous and differentiable function of a variable x.

If Δx is a small change in x, then using Taylor series, the resulting change in f is given by:

$$\Delta f \sim \left(\frac{df}{dx}\right)\Delta x + \frac{1}{2}\left(\frac{d^2 f}{dx^2}\right)\Delta x^2 + \frac{1}{6}\left(\frac{d^3 f}{dx^3}\right)\Delta x^3 + \cdots \tag{21.17}$$

If f depends on two variables x and y, then Taylor series expansion of Δf is:

$$\Delta f \sim \left(\frac{\partial f}{\partial x}\right)\Delta x + \left(\frac{\partial f}{\partial y}\right)\Delta y + \frac{1}{2}\left(\frac{\partial^2 f}{\partial x^2}\right)\Delta x^2 + \frac{1}{2}\left(\frac{\partial^2 f}{\partial y^2}\right)\Delta y^2 + \left(\frac{\partial^2 f}{\partial y \partial y}\right)\Delta x \Delta y + \cdots \tag{21.18}$$

In the limit case, when Δx and Δy are close to zero, Eq. (21.18) becomes:

$$\Delta f \sim \left(\frac{\partial f}{\partial x}\right) dx + \left(\frac{\partial f}{\partial y}\right) dy. \tag{21.19}$$

Now, if f depends on two variables x and t in lieu of x and y, the analogous to Eq. (21.18) is,

$$\Delta f \sim \left(\frac{\partial f}{\partial x}\right)\Delta x + \left(\frac{\partial f}{\partial t}\right)\Delta t + \frac{1}{2}\left(\frac{\partial^2 f}{\partial x^2}\right)\Delta x^2 + \frac{1}{2}\left(\frac{\partial^2 f}{\partial t^2}\right)\Delta t^2 + \left(\frac{\partial^2 f}{\partial x \partial t}\right)\Delta x \Delta t + \cdots \tag{21.20}$$

Consider a derivative security, $f(x,t)$, whose value depends on time and on the asset price x. Assuming that x follows the general Ito process,

$$dx = a(x,t)dt + b(x,t)dW$$

or

$$\Delta x = a(x,t)\Delta t + b\xi\sqrt{\Delta t}.$$

In the limit, when Δx and Δt are close to zero, we cannot ignore, as before the term in Δx^2 since it is equal to $\Delta x^2 = b^2\xi^2\Delta t +$ terms in higher order in Δt. In this case, the term in Δt cannot be neglected. Since the term ξ is normally distributed with a zero mean, $E(\xi) = 0$ and a unit variance, $E(\xi^2) - E(\xi)^2 = 1$, then $E(\xi^2) = 1$ and $E(\xi)^2\Delta t$ is Δt. The variance of $\xi^2\Delta t$ is of order Δt^2 and consequently, as Δt

approaches zero, $\xi^2\Delta t$ becomes certain and equals its expected value, Δt. In the limit, Eq. (21.20) becomes:

$$df = \left(\frac{\partial f}{\partial x}\right)\Delta x + \left(\frac{\partial f}{\partial t}\right)\Delta t + \frac{1}{2}\left(\frac{\partial^2 f}{\partial x^2}\right)b^2 dt. \tag{21.21}$$

This is exactly Ito's lemma.

Substituting $a(x,t)dt + b(x,t)dW$ for dx, Eq. (21.21) gives:

$$df = \left[\left(\frac{\partial f}{\partial x}\right)a + \left(\frac{\partial f}{\partial t}\right) + \frac{1}{2}\left(\frac{\partial^2 f}{\partial x^2}\right)b^2\right]dt + \left(\frac{\partial f}{\partial x}\right)bdW. \tag{21.22}$$

Example. Let us denote by $X(t)$ a standard Brownian motion. Using $X^4(t)$, show that the following integral is equal to:

$$\int_0^t X^3(\tau)dX(\tau) = \frac{1}{4}X^4(t) - \frac{3}{2}\int_0^t X^2(\tau)d\tau.$$

Solution. We apply Ito's lemma for a function $F(X(t))$:

$$dF = \left(\frac{dF}{dX}\right)dX + \left(\frac{dF}{dt}\right)dt + \left(\frac{1}{2}\frac{d^2F}{dX^2}\right)dt.$$

Let, $F(X(t)) = X^4(t)$ and note that,

$$\int_0^t dF = [F(t)]_0^t.$$

In this case, we have:

$$\int_0^t dF(X(t)) = X^4(t) - X^4(0) = X^4(t) \quad \text{as } X^4(0) = 0.$$

Applying Ito's lemma, we obtain: $dF = 4X^3dX + 6X^2dt$ since $\frac{dF}{dt} = 0$. This gives:

$$\int_0^t dF = \int_0^t 4X^3(\tau)dX(\tau) + 6X^2(\tau)d(\tau) = X^4(t)$$

which can also be written as:

$$\int_0^t 4X^3(\tau)dX(\tau) + \int_0^t 6X^2(\tau)d(\tau)$$
$$= \int_0^t \left(X^3(\tau)dX(\tau) + \frac{6}{4}X^2(\tau)d(\tau)\right) = \frac{1}{4}X^4(t)$$

and we have,

$$\int_0^t X^3(\tau)dX(\tau) = \frac{1}{4}X^4(t) - \frac{3}{2}\int_0^t X^2(\tau)d\tau.$$

Example. Using Ito's lemma, show the following result:

$$\int_0^t \tau^3 X(\tau)dX(\tau) = t^3X^2(t) - \frac{3}{2}\int_0^t \tau^2 X^2(\tau)d\tau - \frac{1}{8}\tau^4$$

or, Ito's lemma will be applied for a function $F(X(t), t) = t^3X^2(t)$:

$$dF = \frac{dF}{dX}dX + \left(\frac{dF}{dt} + \frac{1}{2}\frac{d^2F}{dX^2}\right)dt.$$

In this case:

$$dF = 2t^3X(t)dX + (3t^2X^2(t) + t^3)dt$$

or

$$\int_0^t 2\tau^3X(\tau)dX(\tau) + \int_0^t 3\tau^2X^2(\tau) + \int_0^t \tau^3 d\tau$$
$$= \int_0^t dF = t^3X^2(t) - 0^3X^2(0)$$

since $\int_0^3 X^2(0) = 0$. Hence, we have:

$$\int_0^t \tau^3X(\tau)dX(\tau) + \frac{3}{2}\int_0^t \tau^2X^2(\tau) + \frac{1}{2}\int_0^t \tau^3 d\tau = t^3X^2(t)$$

or, re-arranging the formula, we obtain the following result:

$$\int_0^t \tau^3X(\tau)dX(\tau) = \frac{1}{2}t^3X^2(t) - \frac{3}{2}\int_0^t \tau^2X^2(\tau)d\tau - \frac{1}{2}\int_0^t \tau^3 d\tau$$

or

$$\frac{1}{2}\int_0^t \tau^3 d\tau = \frac{1}{8}\tau^4$$

then:

$$\int_0^t \tau^3X(\tau)dX(\tau) = \frac{1}{2}t^3X^2(t) - \frac{3}{2}\int_0^t \tau^2X^2(\tau)d\tau - \frac{1}{8}\tau^4.$$

Example. Use Ito's lemma to show that:

$$\int_0^t X^5(\tau)dX(\tau) = \frac{1}{5}X^5(t) - 2\int_0^t X^3(\tau)d\tau.$$

Solution. When $F = X^5(t)$, then $\int_0^t dF = X^5(t) - X^5(0) = X^5(t)$ since $X(0) = 0$.

Applying Ito's lemma to the function F gives:

$$dF = 5X^4 dX + 10X^3 dt.$$

Hence:

$$\int_0^t 5X^4(\tau)dX(\tau) + \int_0^t 10X^3(\tau)d\tau = X^5(t)$$

and

$$\int_0^t X^4(\tau)dX(\tau) + 2\int_0^t X^3(\tau)d\tau = \frac{1}{5}X^5(t)$$

or

$$\int_0^t X^4(\tau)dX(\tau) = \frac{1}{5}X^5(t) - 2\int_0^t X^3(\tau)d\tau.$$

21.2.2. *Applications to stock prices*

Example. Apply Ito's lemma to a function $f(S,t)$ when the dynamics of stock prices are described by the following stochastic equation:

$$dS = \mu S dt + \sigma S dW.$$

Equation (21.22) gives:

$$df = \left[\left(\frac{\partial f}{\partial x}\right)\mu S + \left(\frac{\partial f}{\partial t}\right) + \frac{1}{2}\left(\frac{\partial^2 f}{\partial S^2}\right)\sigma^2 S^2\right]dt + \left(\frac{\partial f}{\partial t}\right)\sigma S dW. \tag{21.23}$$

Example. Apply Ito's lemma to derive the process of $f = \ln(S)$.
First calculate the derivatives,

$$\left(\frac{\partial f}{\partial S}\right) = \frac{1}{S}; \quad \left(\frac{\partial^2 f}{\partial S^2}\right) = -\frac{1}{S^2}; \quad \left(\frac{\partial f}{\partial t}\right) = 0.$$

Then from Ito's lemma, one obtains

$$df = \left[\left(\frac{\partial f}{\partial x}\right)\mu S + \left(\frac{\partial f}{\partial t}\right) + \frac{1}{2}\left(\frac{\partial^2 f}{\partial S^2}\right)\sigma^2 S^2\right] dt + \left(\frac{\partial f}{\partial S}\right)\sigma S dW$$

or

$$df = \left[\mu - \frac{1}{2}\sigma^2\right] dt + \sigma dW.$$

This last equation shows that, f follows a generalized Wiener process with a constant drift of $\left(\mu - \frac{1}{2}\sigma^2\right)$ and a variance rate of σ^2.

21.2.3. *Mathematical form*

The following theorem gives Ito's formula.

Theorem. *If* $(Xt)_{0\leq t\leq T}$ *is an Ito process*, i.e.,

$$X_t = X_0 + \int_0^t K_s ds + \int_0^t H_s dW_s \tag{21.24}$$

and f is a continuous function with second-order continuous derivatives, then:

$$f(X_t) = f(X_0) + \int_0^t f'(X_s) dX_s + \frac{1}{2}\int_0^t f''(X_s) d\langle X, X\rangle_s \tag{21.25}$$

where by definition,

$$d\langle X, X\rangle_t = \int_0^t H_s^2 ds.$$

The first integral is given by:

$$\int_0^t f'(X_s) dX_s = \int_0^t f'(X_s) K_s ds + \int_0^t f'(X_s) H_s dW_s.$$

The second integral is given by:

$$\int_0^t f''(X_s)d\langle X, X\rangle_s = \int_0^t f''(X_s)H_s^2 ds.$$

Hence, Ito's formula is:

$$f(X_t) = f(X_0) + \int_0^t f'(X_s)K_s ds + \int_0^t f'(X_s)H_s dW_s + \frac{1}{2}f''(X_s)H_s^2 ds. \quad (21.26)$$

More generally, if $f(x, t)$ has first-order continuous partial derivatives in t and continuous second-order derivatives in x, then:

$$f(t, X_t) = f(0, X_0) + \int_0^t f_s'(s, X_s)ds + \int_0^t f_x'(s, X_s)dX_s + \frac{1}{2}\int_0^t f_{xx}''(s, X_s)d\langle X, X\rangle_s. \quad (21.27)$$

Note that if we put $K_s = 0$ and $H_s = 1$, in the Ito process, i.e.,

$$X_t = X_0 + \int_0^t K_s ds + \int_0^t H_s dW_s \quad (21.28)$$

then it reduces to $X_t = W_t$, which is simply the Brownian motion, since $W_0 = 0$.

Example. In this example, Ito's formula is applied to the dynamics of the squared Brownian motion, W_t^2. When $f(x) = x^2$ and $X_t = W_t$, (the case where $K_s = 0$ and $H_s = 1$), we have:

$$W_t^2 = W_0^2 + \int_0^t 2W_s dW_s + \frac{1}{2}\int_0^t 2d\langle X, X\rangle_s.$$

Since $f'(x) = (x^2)' = 2x$, $f''(x) = (x^2)'' = 2$ and $d\langle X, X\rangle_s = ds$, then:

$$W_t^2 = \int_0^t 2W_s dW_s + \frac{1}{2}\int_0^t 2ds = 2\int_0^t W_s dW_s + t.$$

Since $W_0 = 0$ and $\int_0^t ds = t$, then $W_t^2 - t = 2\int_0^t W_s dW_s$.

Since the expected value of $\int_0^t W_s^2 ds$ is finite, then $(W_s^2 - t)$ is a martingale.

Example. This application of Ito's lemma concerns the calculation of an explicit solution to the process describing the dynamics of stock prices. Let us look for the solutions to $(S_t)_{t\geq 0}$ for the following equation:

$$S_t = S_0 + \int_0^t S_s[\mu S dS + \sigma dW_s] \tag{21.29}$$

which is often written in the form $dS_t = S_t(\mu dt + \sigma dW_t)$.

Let $Y_t = \ln(S_t)$, where S_t is solution to the preceding equation. Since S_t follows an Ito process with $K_s = \mu S_s$ and $H_s = \sigma S_s$, application of Ito's formula to $f(S) = \ln(S)$ gives:

$$\ln(S_t) = \ln(S_0) + \int_0^t \frac{dS_s}{S_s} + \frac{1}{2}\int_0^t \frac{-1}{S_s^2}\sigma^2 S_s^2 ds. \tag{21.30}$$

Since $f(S) = \ln(S), f'(S) = \frac{1}{S}, f''(S) = \frac{-1}{S^2}$, and the term corresponding to the equivalence of $d\langle X, X\rangle_s$ is the instantaneous variance of dS_s, $\mathrm{Var}(dS_s) = \sigma^2 S_s^2 ds$. Substituting Eq. (21.29) in Eq. (21.30) and simplifying gives:

$$Y_t = Y_0 + \int_0^t \left[\mu - \frac{1}{2}\sigma^2\right] ds + \int_0^t \sigma dW_s. \tag{21.31}$$

This result is straightforward since $\int_0^t ds = t, \int_0^t dW_s = W_t - W_0$ with $W_0 = 0$. So, we have $Y_t = \ln(S_t) = \ln(S_0) + \left(\mu - \frac{1}{2}\sigma^2\right)t + \sigma W_t$.

Applying the exponential to Y_t gives the solution to Eq. (21.29)

$$S_t = S_0 e^{\left(\mu - \frac{1}{2}\sigma^2\right)t + \sigma dW_t}.$$

This is the explicit formula for the underlying asset price when its dynamics are given by the stochastic differential equation (21.29). The following theorem which is stated without proof, shows that the solution to Eq. (21.29) is unique.

Theorem. *When $(W_t)_{t\geq 0}$ is a Brownian motion, there is a unique Ito process $(St)_{0\leq t\leq T}$ for which, for every $t \leq T$:*

$$S_t = S_0 + \int_0^t S_s[\mu S dS + \sigma dW_s] \tag{21.32}$$

This process is given by $S_t = S_0 e^{\left(\mu - \frac{1}{2}\sigma^2\right)t + \sigma dW_t}$. This process is used in the derivation of the Black and Scholes formula and is often referred to as the Black–Scholes process.

Example. The Black and Scholes (1973) model for the valuation of a European options uses two assets: a risky asset with a price S_t at time t and a risk-less asset B_t at time t. The dynamics of the risk-less asset or bond are given by the following ordinary differential equation:

$$dB_t = rB_t dt \tag{21.33}$$

where r stands for the risk-less interest rate. The bond's value at time 0, $B_0 = 1$ in a way such that $B_t = e^{rt}$. The dynamics of the risky asset or stock are given by the following stochastic differential equation:

$$dS_t = \mu S_t dt + \sigma S_t dW_t \tag{21.34}$$

where μ and σ are constants and W_t is a standard Brownian motion.

As we have shown, the solution to Eq. (21.34) is:

$$S_t = S_0 e^{\left(\mu - \frac{1}{2}\sigma^2\right)t + \sigma dW_t}$$

where, S_0 is the initial asset price at time 0.

21.2.4. *The generalized Ito's formula*

Ito's formula can be generalized to the case where the function depends on several Ito processes, which are expressed in terms of standard independent Brownian motions. This is the multidimensional Ito's formula or the vector form of Ito's lemma. The formula is useful in deriving interest rate models and models of derivative asset pricing with several state variables.

Generalization of Ito's lemma: The first form: The generalization of Ito's lemma is useful for a function that depends on n stochastic variables x_i, where i varies from 1 to n. Consider the following dynamics for the variables x_i,

$$dx_i = a_i dt + b_i dz_i \tag{21.35}$$

Using Taylor series expansion of f gives:

$$\Delta f = \sum_i \frac{\partial f}{\partial x_i}\Delta x_i + \frac{\partial f}{\partial t}\Delta t + \frac{1}{2}\sum_i\sum_j \frac{\partial^2 f}{\partial x_i \partial x_j}\Delta x_i \Delta x_j + \frac{\partial^2 f}{\partial x_i \partial t}\Delta x_i \Delta t + \cdots \tag{21.36}$$

Equation (21.35) can be discretized as follows $\Delta x_i = a_i \Delta t + b_i \epsilon_i \Delta\sqrt{z_i}$ where the term ϵ_i corresponds to a random sample from a standardized normal distribution. The terms ϵ_i and ϵ_j reflecting the Wiener processes present a correlation coefficient $\rho_{i,j}$. It is possible to show that when the time interval tends to zero, in the limit, the term $\Delta x_i^2 = b_i^2 dt$ and the product $\Delta x_i \Delta x_j = b_i b_j \rho_{i,j} dt$. Hence, in the limit, when the time interval becomes close to zero, Eq. (21.36) can be written as:

$$df = \sum_i \frac{\partial f}{\partial x_i} dx_i + \frac{\partial f}{\partial t} dt + \frac{1}{2}\sum_i\sum_j \frac{\partial^2 f}{\partial x_i \partial x_j} b_i b_j \rho_{i,j} dt.$$

This gives the generalized version of Ito's lemma. Using Eq. (21.35) gives:

$$df = \left(\sum_i \frac{\partial f}{\partial x_i} a_i + \frac{\partial f}{\partial t} + \frac{1}{2}\sum_i\sum_j \frac{\partial^2 f}{\partial x_i \partial x_j} b_i b_j \rho_{ij}\right) + \sum \frac{\partial f}{\partial x_i} b_i dz_i \tag{21.37}$$

Generalization of Ito's lemma: The second form: Consider $W_t = (W_t^1, \ldots, W_t^p)$ where $(W_t^i)_{t\geq 0}$ are independent standard Brownian motions and W_t is a p-dimensional Brownian motion. The mathematical expression of Ito's formula is introduced with respect to n Ito processes $(X_t^1, X_t^2, \ldots, X_t^n)$

$$X_t^i = X_0^i + \int_0^t K_s^i ds + \sum_{i=1}^{p} \int_0^t H_s^{ij} dX_s^i.$$

When the function $f(.)$ has second-order partial derivatives in x and first-order partial derivatives in t, which are continuous in (x, t), then the generalized Ito's lemma is:

$$\begin{aligned} f(t, X_t^1, \ldots, X_t^n) &= f(0, X_0^1, \ldots, X_0^n) + \int_0^t \left(\frac{\partial f}{\partial s}\right)(s, X_s^1, \ldots, X_s^n) ds \\ &\quad + \sum_{i=1}^{n} \int_0^t \left(\frac{\partial f}{\partial x_i}\right)(s, X_s^1, \ldots, X_s^n) dX_s^i \\ &\quad + \frac{1}{2} \sum_{i,j=1}^{n} \int_0^t \left(\frac{\partial^2 f}{\partial x_i \partial x_j}\right)(s, X_s^1, \ldots, X_s^n) d\langle X^i, Xj\rangle_s \end{aligned} \tag{21.38}$$

with

$$dX_s^i = K_s^i ds + \sum_{j=1}^{p} H_s^{i,j} dW_s^j, d\langle X^i, X^j\rangle_s = \sum_{m=1}^{p} H_s^{i,m} H_s^{j,m} ds$$

In the financial literature, the notation is more compact than that used in the mathematical literature. The term $d\langle X^i, Xj\rangle_s$ corresponds to the changes in the instantaneous covariance terms $\text{Cov}(dX_s^i, dX_s^j)$.

21.2.5. *Other applications of Ito's formula*

Example. Use Ito's lemma to show that:

$$\int_0^t X^{n-1}(\tau) dX(\tau) = \frac{1}{n} X^n(t) - \frac{n-1}{2} \int_0^t X^{n-2}(\tau) d\tau$$

Solution. When $F = X^n(t)$, $n \in N^*$ then

$$\int_0^t dF = X^n(t) - X^n(0) = X^n(t)$$

since $X(0) = 0$.

Using Ito's lemma gives:

$$dF = nX^{n-1}dX + \frac{1}{2}n(n-1)X^{n-2}dt.$$

Hence:

$$\int_0^t dF = \int_0^t nX^{n-1}(\tau)dX(\tau) + \frac{1}{2}n(n-1)X^{n-2}(\tau)d\tau = X^n(t)$$

$$\Longleftrightarrow$$

$$\int_0^t X^{n-1}(\tau)dX(\tau) + \frac{1}{2}(n-1)X^{n-2}(\tau)d\tau = \frac{1}{n}X^n(t)$$

$$\Longleftrightarrow$$

$$\int_0^t X^{n-1}(\tau)dX(\tau) = \frac{1}{n}X^n(t) - \int_0^t \frac{n-1}{2}X^{n-2}(\tau)d\tau.$$

Example. Use Ito's lemma to show that:

$$\int_0^t \tau^m X^{n-1}(\tau)dX(\tau) = \frac{1}{n}t^m X^n(t) - \frac{n-1}{2}\int_0^t t^m X^{n-2}(\tau)d\tau$$
$$-\frac{m}{n}\int_0^t t^{m-1}X^n(\tau)d\tau.$$

Solution. When $F = X^n(t)$, where $n,\, m \in N^*$ then

$$\int_0^t dF = t^m X^n(t) - t^m X^n(0) = tmX^n(t)$$

since $X(0) = 0$.

Using Ito's lemma gives:

$$dF = nt^m X^{n-1}dX + \frac{1}{2}n(n-1)X^{n-2}dt + mt^{m-1}X^n(t)dt.$$

Hence, we have:

$$\int_0^t dF = n\int_0^t \tau^m X^{n-1}(\tau)dX(\tau) + \frac{1}{2}n(n-1)\int_0^t \tau^m X^{n-2}(\tau)d\tau$$
$$+m\int_0^t \tau^{m-1}X^n(\tau)d\tau = t^m X^n(t)$$

$$\Longleftrightarrow$$

$$\int_0^t \tau^m X^{n-1}(\tau)dX(\tau) + \frac{1}{2}(n-1)\tau^m X^{n-2}(\tau)d\tau$$
$$+\frac{m}{n}\int_0^t \tau^{m-1}X^n(\tau)d\tau = \frac{1}{n}t^m X^n(t)$$

$$\Longleftrightarrow$$

$$\int_0^t \tau^m X^{n-1}(\tau)dX(\tau) = \frac{1}{n}t^m X^n(t) - \int_0^t \frac{n-1}{2}\tau^m X^{n-2}(\tau)d\tau$$
$$-\frac{m}{n}\int_0^t \tau^{m-1}X^n(\tau)d\tau$$

Example. We consider a function $f(t)$ which is continuous and bounded on the interval $[0,t]$. Using the integration by parts, we want to show that:

$$\int_0^t f(\tau)dX(\tau) = f(t)X(t) - \int_0^t X(t)df(\tau)$$

Solution. Consider the following function $F = f(t)X(t)$. In this case, we have

$$\int_0^t dF = f(t)X(t) - f(0)X(0) = f(t)X(t)$$

since $X(0) = 0$ and by Ito's lemma:

$$dF = fdX + Xdf.$$

Therefore,

$$\int_0^t f(\tau)dX(\tau) + \int_0^t X(\tau)df(\tau) = f(t)X(t)$$

which can be written as:

$$\int_0^t f(\tau)dX(\tau) = f(t)X(t) - \int_0^t X(\tau)df(\tau).$$

21.3. Taylor Series, Ito's Theorem and the Replication Argument

Let us denote by $c(S, t)$ the option value at time t as a function of the underlying asset price S and time t. Assume that the underlying asset price follows a geometric Brownian motion:

$$\frac{dS}{S} = \mu dt + \sigma dW(t) \tag{21.39}$$

where μ and σ^2 correspond, respectively to the instantaneous mean and the variance of the rate of return of the stock.

21.3.1. *The relationship between Taylor series and Ito's differential*

Using Taylor series differential, it is possible to express the price change of the option over a small interval of time $[t, t + dt]$ as:

$$dc = \left(\frac{\partial c}{\partial S}\right) dS + \left(\frac{\partial c}{\partial t}\right) dt + \frac{1}{2}\left(\frac{\partial^2 c}{\partial^2 S}\right)(dS)^2 \tag{21.40}$$

where the last term appears because dS^2 is of order dt. The last term in Eq. (21.40) appears because the term $(dS)^2$ is of order dt.

Omberg (1991) makes a decomposition of the last term in Eq. (21.40) into its expected value and an error term. This allows one to establish a link between Taylor's series (dc) and Ito's differential dc_I as:

$$dc = \left(\frac{\partial c}{\partial S}\right) dS + \left(\frac{\partial c}{\partial t}\right) dt + \frac{1}{2}\left(\frac{\partial^2 c}{\partial^2 S}\right)\sigma^2 S^2 dW^2 + de(t)$$

which can be written as the sum of two components corresponding to the Ito's differential dc_I and an error term $de(t)$:

$$dc = dc_I + de(t) \tag{21.41}$$

where

$$dc_I = \left(\frac{\partial c}{\partial S}\right) dS + \left(\frac{\partial c}{\partial t}\right) dt + \frac{1}{2}\left(\frac{\partial^2 c}{\partial^2 S}\right)\sigma^2 S^2 dt$$

and

$$de(t) = \frac{1}{2}\left(\frac{\partial^2 c}{\partial^2 S}\right)\sigma^2 S^2 \left[dW^2 - dt\right].$$

21.3.2. *Ito's differential and the replication portfolio*

A replication argument is often used in financial theory. It means simply that in complete markets, the payoff of an asset can be created or duplicated using some other assets. A combination of these assets provides a similar payoff as that of the original asset.

The standard case: In general, the payoff of any derivative asset can be created by an investment of a certain amount in the underlying risky asset and another amount in risk-free discount bonds. Also, the payoff of a derivative asset can be created using the discount bond, some options, and the underlying asset. The portfolio which duplicates the payoff of the asset is called the replicating portfolio. When using Ito's lemma, the error term $de(t)$ is often neglected and, the equation for the option is approximated only by the term dc_I. The quantity dc_I is replicated by Q_S units of the underlying asset and an amount of cash Q_c with $Q_S = \left(\frac{\partial c}{\partial S}\right)$ and $Q_c = \frac{1}{r}\left[\left(\frac{\partial c}{\partial S}\right) + \frac{1}{2}\left(\frac{\partial^2 c}{\partial^2 S}\right)\sigma^2 S^2\right]$ where r stands for the risk-free rate of return. Hence, the dynamics of the replicating portfolio are given by:

$$d\Pi_R = \left(\frac{\partial c}{\partial S}\right) dS + rQ_c dt \tag{21.42}$$

where Π_R refers to the replicating portfolio.

An extension to account for information costs: Consider, for example, a financial institution using a given market. If the costs of portfolio selection and models conception, etc., are computed, then it can require at least a return of say, for example $\lambda = 3\%$, before acting in this market. This cost is in some sense the minimal cost before acting in a certain market. It represents somehow, the minimal return required before implementing a given strategy. For the analysis of information costs and valuation, we can refer to Bellalah (1999, 2001), Bellalah *et al.* (2001a, 2001b), Bellalah and Prigent (2001), Bellalah and Selmi (2001), and soon. If you consider the above replicating strategy, then the returns from the replicating portfolio must be at least

$$d\Pi_R = \left(\frac{\partial c}{\partial S}\right) dS + (r + \lambda)Q_c dt$$

with

$$Q_c = \frac{1}{r+\lambda}\left[\left(\frac{\partial c}{\partial S}\right) + \frac{1}{2}\left(\frac{\partial^2 c}{\partial^2 S}\right)\sigma^2 S^2\right] \tag{21.43}$$

where Π_R refers to the replicating portfolio. This shows that the required return must cover at least the costs necessary for constructing the replicating portfolio plus the risk-free rate. In fact, when constructing a portfolio, some money is spent and a return for this must be required. Hence, there must be a minimal cost and a minimal return required for investing in information at the aggregate market level. For this reason, the required return must be at least λ plus the risk-less rate.

21.3.3. *Ito's differential and the arbitrage portfolio*

If one uses arbitrage arguments, then the option value must be equal to the value of its replicating portfolio.

The standard analysis: Using arbitrage arguments, we must have

$$c = Q_s S + Q_c$$

or

$$c = \left(\frac{\partial c}{\partial S}\right) S + \frac{1}{r}\left[\left(\frac{\partial c}{\partial t}\right) + \frac{1}{2}\left(\frac{\partial^2 c}{\partial^2 S}\right)\sigma^2 S^2\right] \tag{21.44}$$

and

$$\frac{1}{2}\frac{\partial^2 c}{\partial^2 S}\sigma^2 S^2 + rc - r\frac{\partial c}{\partial S}S + \left(\frac{\partial c}{\partial t}\right) = 0.$$

This equation is often referred to, in financial economics, as the Black–Scholes–Merton partial differential equation. Note that the value of the replicating portfolio is $\Pi_R = \left(\frac{\partial c}{\partial S}\right) S + Q_c$.

It is possible to implement a hedged position by buying the derivative asset and selling delta units of the underlying asset:

$$\Pi_H = c - \left(\frac{\partial c}{\partial S}\right) S = Q_c \tag{21.45}$$

where the subscript H refers to the hedged portfolio.

A hedged position or portfolio is a portfolio whose return at equilibrium must be equal in theory to the short-term risk-free rate of interest. This is the main contribution of Black–Scholes (1973) to the pricing of derivative assets. Merton (1973) uses the same argument as Black–Scholes (1973) by implementing the concept of self-financing portfolio. This portfolio is also constructed by buying the option and selling the replicating portfolio or vice versa. The condition on the self-financing portfolio is:

$$\Pi_A = c - \left(\frac{\partial c}{\partial S}\right) S - Q_c = 0$$

where S refers to the self-financing portfolio. The omitted error term in the above analysis, $de(t)$, can reflect a replication error, a hedging error or an arbitrage error. It can have different interpretations. The term $de(t)$ is neglected or omitted when the revision of the portfolio is done to allow for the replicating portfolio to be self-financing. When this term is positive, this may refer to an additional cash that must be put in the portfolio. When it is negative, a withdrawal of cash from the portfolio is possible.

An extension to account for information costs: In the same way, the previous analysis can be extended to account for information costs. In this context, we must have:

$$c = Q_S S + Q_c$$

or

$$c = \left(\frac{\partial c}{\partial S}\right) S + \frac{1}{(r+\lambda)}\left[\left(\frac{\partial c}{\partial t}\right) + \frac{1}{2}\left(\frac{\partial^2 c}{\partial^2 S}\right)\sigma^2 S^2\right] \tag{21.46}$$

and

$$\frac{1}{2}\left(\frac{\partial^2 c}{\partial^2 S}\sigma^2 S^2\right) + (r+\lambda)c - (r+\lambda)\left(\frac{\partial c}{\partial S}\right) S + \left(\frac{\partial c}{\partial t}\right) = 0.$$

This equation corresponds to an extended version of the well-known Black–Scholes–Merton partial differential equation accounting for the effect of information costs. For the sake of simplicity, we assume that information costs are equal in both markets: the option market and the underlying asset market. Or in practice, institutions and investors support these costs on both markets. Therefore, a more suitable analysis must account for two costs: cost λ_c on the option market and a cost λ_S on the underlying asset market. In this case, we obtain the following more general equation as in Bellalah and Jacquillat (1995) and Bellalah (1999):

$$\frac{1}{2}\sigma^2 S^2 \frac{\partial^2 c}{\partial^2 S} + (r + \lambda_c)c - (r + \lambda_S)\frac{\partial c}{\partial S}S + \frac{\partial c}{\partial t} = 0. \tag{21.47}$$

21.3.4. *Why are error terms neglected?*

Now, we give an answer to the following question:

If each portfolio revision is self-financing and the hedging error $de(t)$ tends to zero as the interval of time becomes extremely small, is there a mathematical or an economic "rationale" in ignoring the error term?

In the Black and Scholes (1973) theory, the term $de(t)$ is ignored because it is not correlated with the underlying asset price in the context of the capital asset pricing model (CAPM). In this context, it is regarded as a diversifiable risk. This justification is referred to as the "equilibrium option pricing theory". However, if one uses the Black and Scholes theory with respect to the implementation of Ito's lemma, then ignoring the error term, refers to a pure-arbitrage result. Omberg (1991) proposed two explanations for pure arbitrage results with respect to the two following assumptions H_1 and H_2.

According to H_1, the error term is of order $o(dt)$, which is a higher order than dt:

$$H_1: de(t) = o(dt). \tag{21.48}$$

According to H_2, the error term is of order Odt:

$$H_2: de(t) = O(dt) \tag{21.49}$$

and

$$\int_0^\tau de(t) = 0 \quad \text{for } \tau > 0.$$

In H_1, the error is neglected because in the limit, the hedging error disappears more quickly than the risk-free return. This is because the risk-free return is of order dt. In this context, the replicating portfolio is perfect because the smallness of the interval justifies the disparition of the hedging error.

In H_2, the price dynamics are represented by the Taylor's series differential rather than Ito's differential. In this case, cumulation of hedging errors over several time intervals is necessary.

Merton (1973) considered that the error term is $O(dt)$ and neglected it in the context of the law of large numbers.

Omberg (1991) showed that the hedging error is zero over each revision interval in two cases. The first case corresponds to the limit of the binomial discrete option pricing model of Cox *et al.* (1979). The second case concerns a stochastic revision strategy, which succeeds with a certain probability of one-over-one revision interval. However, it remains unproved that the strategy succeeds over a high number of revision intervals.

For other cases, the hedging error over one revision interval is of the same order as the risk-free return and cannot be eliminated.

21.4. Forward and Backward Equations

When the asset price dynamics are described by the following Markov diffusion process:

$$dS_t = \mu(S,t)dt + \sigma(S,t)dW_t$$

the probability density function for S at time t conditional on $S_{t0} = S_0$, denoted by $f(S,t;S_0,t_0)$, satisfies the partial differential equations of motions, which are the backward and the forward Kolmogorov equations. The backward Kolmogorov equation is given by:

$$\frac{1}{2}\sigma^2(S_0,t_0)\left(\frac{\partial^2 f}{\partial S^2}\right) + \mu(S_0,t_0)\left(\frac{\partial f}{\partial S_0}\right) + \left(\frac{\partial f}{\partial t_0}\right) = 0. \qquad (21.50)$$

The forward Kolmogorov or Fokker–Planck equation is given by:

$$\frac{1}{2}\left(\frac{\partial^2 f}{\partial S^2}\right)[\sigma^2(S_0,t_0)f] - \left(\frac{\partial f}{\partial S_0}\right)[\mu(S,t)f] + \left(\frac{\partial f}{\partial t}\right) = 0. \quad (21.51)$$

These equations can be solved under the condition $f(S,t_0;S_0,t_0) = \delta_{S_0}(S)$, i.e., at the initial time, S is equal to S_0 and δ_{S_0} is the Dirac measure at S_0. It is defined by $\delta_{S_0}(S)([a,b]) = 1$, if S_0 is $\in [a,b]$ and zero else where.

Since we are interested only in time-homogeneous processes for which $\sigma = \sigma(S)$ and $\mu = \mu(S)$, two types of constraints are sometimes imposed to obtain an absorbing barrier and a reflecting barrier when the drift is finite. An absorbing barrier means simply that once the process attains a certain value, this value will be conserved for all subsequent instants. A reflecting barrier means that when the process hits a certain level, he/she will return from the direction from which it comes.

When we constrain $f(S_1^+, t)$ to take the value zero, then S_1 is an absorbing barrier from above (+). The intuition of this result is that when $S = S_1$ at t_1, then S will conserve this value for all the subsequent instants t after t_1. When we constrain the term,

$$\frac{1}{2}\left(\frac{\partial^2 f(S,t)\sigma^2(S)}{\partial S^2}\right) - [\mu(S)f(S,t)] \tag{21.52}$$

to zero at $S = S_1$, then S_1 is a reflecting barrier.

It is convenient to note that when $\sigma(S_1) = 0$, then the value at which σ is zero represents a natural barrier. When $\mu(S_1)$ is zero, we have a natural absorbing barrier and when $\mu(S,t)$ is strictly positive (or negative), we have a natural reflecting barrier from above (or below).

Example. When $\mu(S) = \mu$ and $\sigma(S) = \sigma$, then S is a Brownian motion with drift. It is possible to verify that the solution to Eqs. (21.50) and (21.51) is:

$$f(S,t;x_0,t_0) = N\left[\frac{S - x_0 - \mu(T - t_0)}{\sigma\sqrt{T - t_0}}\right] \tag{21.53}$$

where $N[.]$ stands for the density of the standard normal distribution.

21.5. The Main Concepts in Bond Markets and the General Arbitrage Principle

This section presents the main concepts in bond markets and the general arbitrage principle.

21.5.1. *The main concepts in bond pricing*

21.5.1.1. *The yield to maturity (YTM)*

Consider a zero-coupon bond $B(t,T)$ at time t maturing in T years. The present value of one-dollar received at time T is $B(t,T) = e^{-y(T-t)}$. Hence, the YTM is given by $y = -\frac{\log B}{T-t}$. The price of a coupon-paying bond corresponds to the present value of all its cash flows $N+1$: N coupons C_i and principal payment P as follows:

$$V = Pe^{-y(T-t)} + \sum_{i=1}^{N} C_i e^{-y(t_i-t)}. \tag{21.54}$$

When the market bond price is set equal to this equality, this gives the YTM or internal rate of return.

21.5.1.2. *Duration*

If we derive the expression of the bond price with respect to the YTM, this gives the slope of the price/yield curve,

$$\frac{dV}{dy} = -(T-t)Pe^{-y(T-t)} - \sum_{i=1}^{N}(t_i - t)C_i e^{-y(t_i-t)}.$$

Macaulay duration is given by:

$$\frac{-1}{V}\frac{dV}{dy}. \tag{21.55}$$

If the discrete compounded rate is used, this quantity refers to the modified duration. Duration is often computed for small movements in the yield in order to examine the change in the price of the bond.

21.5.1.3. *Convexity*

We denote by δy, the change in the yield y. Using a Taylor's series expansion of V gives:

$$\frac{dV}{V} = \frac{1}{V}\frac{dV}{dy}\delta y + \frac{1}{2V}\frac{d^2V}{dy^2}[\delta y]^2 + \cdots \tag{21.56}$$

Convexity is often computed for large movements in the yield in order to examine the change in the price of the bond with respect to yield.

The dollar convexity is defined with respect to the bond price as:

$$\frac{d^2V}{dy^2} = (T-t)^2 Pe^{-y(T-t)} - \sum_{i=1}^{N}(t_i - t)^2 C_i e^{-y(t_i-t)}. \tag{21.57}$$

Convexity corresponds simply to $\frac{1}{V}\frac{d^2V}{dy^2}$.

21.5.2. *Time-dependent interest rates and information uncertainty*

When the spot interest rate is only a known function of time, then $B = B(t)$. Consider the change in the value of a zero-coupon bond paying 1 at $t = T$ over a time step dt from t to $(t + dt)$. The change in the zero-coupon bond price can be written as $\frac{dB}{dt}$. In this case, this return must be equal to the return from a bank deposit $r(t)$ or $\frac{dB}{dt} = r(t)B$.

However, if this equality is set by arbitrage considerations, then investors must suffer sunk costs to get informed about these opportunities. In fact, it is well known in practice to find only one interest rate for each maturity. This is more difficult to assert in an international context. There will be also some risks related to the re-investments of the coupons and investors must also pay about future investment opportunities. Merton (1987) showed that information costs are specific to each market and are paid when investors want to get informed about investment opportunities. In this case, they require that the return on the bond must be equal to the risk-less rate plus an "additional return" corresponding to information costs. Hence, we have

$$\frac{dB}{dt} = (r(t) + \lambda_B)B.$$

In the standard literature, the additional return $\lambda_B = 0$ and we have:

$$\frac{dB}{dt} = r(t)B.$$

The price of the zero coupon satisfying this equation in the presence of an "additional return" λ_B is $B(t;T) = e^{-\int_t^T (r(\tau)+\lambda_B)d\tau}$.

In the standard literature, the additional return $\lambda_B = 0$ and we have:

$$B(t;T) = e^{-\int_t^T (r\tau)d\tau}.$$

For a coupon-paying bond, when coupons $C(t)dt$ are paid in the time interval $[t, t+dt]$, then the holdings change by an amount $\left[\frac{dB}{dt} + C(t)\right] dt$.

Again, if investors pay sunk costs to get informed about the bond and the coupons, then we have:

$$\left[\frac{dB}{dt} + C(t)\right] dt = (r(t) + \lambda_B)B. \tag{21.58}$$

We obtain the standard case when $\lambda_B = 0$. The solution to this differential equation is given by:

$$\begin{aligned} B(t) &= e^{-\int_t^T (r(\tau)+\lambda_B)d\tau}\left(1 + \int_t^T C(t')e^{\int_{t'}^T (r(\tau)+\lambda_B)d\tau}dt'\right) \\ V(t_c^-) &= V(t_c^+) + C_c. \end{aligned} \tag{21.59}$$

In the standard case, the solution becomes:

$$B(t) = e^{-\int_t^T r(\tau)d\tau}\left(1 + \int_t^T C(t')e^{\int_{t'}^T r\tau d\tau}dt'\right) \tag{21.60}$$

21.5.3. *The general arbitrage principle*

Rogers (1997) considered the general principles of financial modeling in the light of his 1997 approach to interest rate modeling. The general arbitrage principle shows that an asset with price Y_T at time T, is represented at time $t < T$ by:

$$Y_t = E_t\left[\exp\left(-\int_t^T r_s ds\right) Y_T\right] \tag{21.61}$$

where $(r_t)_{t\geq 0}$ is the spot-rate process and E_t is the conditional expectation in a risk-neutral measure P.

The price of a zero-coupon bond at time t with maturity T is:

$$P(t,T) = E_t\left[\exp\left(-\int_t^T r_s ds\right)\right].$$

Rogers (1997) showed that it is a good solution to keep the same model all the time and to express the new assets in terms of this same model. To have another look on interest rate modeling, Rogers (1997) assumed a reference probability $\tilde{P}$ with respect to which the risk-neutral probability has a density:

$$\rho_t = \left.\frac{dP}{d\tilde{P}}\right|_{F_t}$$

on the collection F_t of events. In this context, the bond prices can be written as:

$$\begin{aligned} P(t,T) &= E_t\left[\exp\left(-\int_t^T r_s ds\right)\right] \\ &= \tilde{E}_t\left[\rho_T \exp\left(-\int_t^T r_s ds\right)\right] \Big/ \rho_t = \tilde{E}_t\left[\zeta_T\right]\zeta_t \end{aligned}$$

where ζ_t is a state-price density process defined by:

$$\zeta_t = \exp\left(-\int_0^t r_s ds\right)\rho_t.$$

The final expression for the bond price corresponds to a different approach in the modeling of interest rates called by Rogers (1997), as the "potential approach".

21.6. Discrete Hedging and Option Pricing

The Black–Scholes model is based on the assumption of continuous hedging. This is impossible in practice since hedging is done in a discrete way. In general, re-hedging is done regularly at times separated by a constant interval referred to as the length of the hedging period, δt. This period can vary from a few minutes to some weeks depending on the market activity. It is very short for a market maker and longer for a trader.

21.6.1. *Discrete hedging*

It is possible to use Taylor's series expansions to find a better hedge than the Black–Scholes. This hedge results from the use of a certain number of the underlying assets that minimizes the variance of the hedged portfolio. This allows also to find an option-adjusted value.

Following the analysis in Willmott (1998), consider the discrete model for the underlying asset,

$$S = e^x \tag{21.62}$$

with

$$\delta x = \left(\mu - \frac{\sigma^2}{2}\right)\delta t + \sigma\varphi\delta t^{\frac{1}{2}} \tag{21.63}$$

where φ is a random variable drawn from a standardized normal distribution and $\varphi\delta t^{\frac{1}{2}}$ corresponds to the Wiener process in the continuous time version.

Now, consider the construction of a hedged portfolio by a long position in the derivative security and a short position in Δ units of the underlying asset S,

$$\Pi = V - \Delta S. \tag{21.64}$$

If we determine the right hedge, it is relatively a simple matter to price the option.

Using Taylor's series expansion for the portfolio gives:

$$\begin{aligned}\delta\Pi = \delta t^{\frac{1}{2}} A_1(\varphi, \Delta) + \delta t A_2(\varphi, \Delta) + \delta t^{\frac{3}{2}} A_3(\varphi, \Delta) \\ + \delta t^2 A_4(\varphi, \Delta) + \cdots\end{aligned} \tag{21.65}$$

where A_1 is given by:

$$A_1(\varphi, \Delta) = \sigma\varphi S\left(\frac{\partial V}{\partial S} - \Delta\right),$$

and A_2 is,

$$A_2(\varphi, \Delta) = \frac{\partial V}{\partial t} + S\left(\frac{\partial V}{\partial S} - \Delta\right)\left(\mu + \frac{1}{2}\sigma^2(\varphi^2 - 1)\right) + \frac{1}{2}\sigma^2\varphi^2 S^2\frac{\partial^2 V}{\partial S^2}$$

In this context, the Δ must be chosen in such a way so as to minimize the variance of the change in the portfolio's value. The option is valued by setting the expected return on the portfolio equal to the risk-less rate plus information costs. Using Eq. (21.65), the variance of the change in the portfolio value can be computed as:

$$\mathrm{Var}[\delta\Pi] = E[\delta\Pi^2] - (E[\delta\Pi])^2 \tag{21.66}$$

The value of Δ minimizing the variance is found using:

$$\frac{\partial}{\partial\Delta}\mathrm{Var}[\delta\Pi] = 0$$

Hence, the optimal Δ is:

$$\Delta = \frac{\partial V}{\partial S} + \delta t(\ldots) \tag{21.67}$$

The first term is the Black–Scholes hedge ratio in a context of continuous trading. The second term indicates a reduction in risk.

The leading-order random term in the portfolio is given by $\frac{1}{2}\sigma^2\varphi^2 S^2\frac{\partial^2 V}{\partial S^2}$, which can also be written as $\frac{1}{2}\sigma^2 S^2\frac{\partial^2 V}{\partial S^2} + \frac{1}{2}(\varphi^2 - 1)\sigma^2 S^2\frac{\partial^2 V}{\partial S^2}$.

The second term in this equation corresponding to the hedging error is random. The hedging errors at each re-hedge can add up giving the total hedging error. The latter has a zero mean and a standard deviation of $O(\delta t^{\frac{1}{2}})$.

21.6.2. *Pricing the option*

The determination of the right hedge ratio allows the computation of the option price. Since the expected return on the discretely hedged portfolio must be equal to the risk-less rate plus the information costs, we have:

$$\begin{aligned} E[\delta\Pi] = {} & \left((r+\lambda_V)\delta t + \frac{1}{2}(r+\lambda_V)^2\delta t^2 + \cdots\right)V \\ & - \left((r+\lambda_S)\delta t + \frac{1}{2}(r+\lambda_S)^2\delta t^2 + \cdots\right)\Delta S. \end{aligned} \tag{21.68}$$

If we substitute Eqs. (21.64) and (21.65) in Eq. (21.68), one obtains:

$$\frac{\partial V}{\partial t} + \frac{1}{2}\sigma^2 S^2\frac{\partial^2 V}{\partial S^2} + (r+\lambda_S)S\frac{\partial V}{\partial S} - (r+\lambda_V)V + \delta t(\ldots) = 0. \tag{21.69}$$

When information costs are zero, the first term reduces to the Black–Scholes equation. The second term is a correction to allow for the imperfect hedge. Solving Eqs. (21.67) and (21.69) iteratively as in Willmott (1998), the option price must satisfy.

$$\frac{\partial V}{\partial t} + \frac{1}{2}\sigma^2 S^2 \frac{\partial^2 V}{\partial S^2} + (r + \lambda_S) S \frac{\partial V}{\partial S} - (r + \lambda_V) V$$
$$+ \frac{1}{2}\delta t(\mu - r)(r - \mu - \sigma^2) S^2 \frac{\partial^2 V}{\partial S^2} = 0 \qquad (21.70)$$

and the "better" delta is given by:

$$\Delta = \frac{\partial V}{\partial S} + \delta t \left(\mu - r + \lambda_S + \frac{1}{2}\sigma^2 \right) S \frac{\partial^2 V}{\partial S^2}.$$

This equation shows the growth rate of the asset and information costs on the option and its underlying asset. The second derivative terms in Eq. (21.70) correspond to a constant times the squared value of S. Hence, the corrected option price needs the adjustment of the volatility and using the value σ^* with:

$$\sigma^* = \sigma \left(1 + \frac{\delta t}{2\sigma^2}(\mu - r)(r - \mu - \sigma^2) \right).$$

21.6.3. *The real distribution of returns and the hedging error*

Several studies have shown that the empirical distribution of the underlying assets have a higher peak and fatter tails than the normal distribution. Hence, how this distribution affects the hedging arguments and the hedging errors?

Consider the following return for the underlying asset at time $\delta t \frac{\delta S}{S} = \psi$, where the distribution of the random variable ψ is determined empirically. Now, following the analysis in Willmott (1998), we study the change in the value of the hedged portfolio under the assumption that the option component obeys the Black–Scholes equation with an implied volatility of σ_i. The random return in excess of the risk-free rate for the hedged portfolio is:

$$\delta\Pi - r\Pi\delta t = S\left(\Delta - \frac{\partial V}{\partial S}\right)(r\delta t - \psi) + \frac{1}{2}S^2\frac{\partial^2 V}{\partial S^2}(\psi^2 - \sigma_i^2\delta t) + \cdots \quad (21.71)$$

If a delta hedge is implemented as in Black–Scholes, this gives:

$$\delta\Pi - r\Pi\delta t = \frac{1}{2}S^2\frac{\partial^2 V}{\partial S^2}(\psi^2 - \sigma_i^2\delta t).$$

In an economy with information costs, a factor reflecting these costs must be added to the interest rate r.

Summary

This chapter contains the basic and general material for the dynamics of financial assets and derivative asset prices in a continuous time framework. The presentation is made as simple as possible. The aim is to allow non-familiar readers with these concepts to follow without difficulties the basic methods in continuous time finance. Each concept is proposed in two forms: an intuitive version and a more rigorous mathematical version. The Wiener and Ito processes are used to model the dynamics of asset prices. Ito's lemma is proposed to differentiate a function of one and several stochastic variables. It is illustrated through several examples in different contexts. The Kolmogorov forward and backward equations are presented as well as the first passage time and the maximum (minimum) of a diffusion process. These tools allow the pricing of standard options and more complex derivative assets. The principal of arbitrage simply states that financial assets having identical characteristics must trade at the same price. If this principle is not respected, then selling the high-priced asset and buying the low-priced asset allows a risk-free profit. This principle is used to determine the fair price of a security or a derivative asset. The analysis by Omberg (1991) reveals that the hedging error is zero over each revision interval in the following two cases. The first case represents the limit of the classical binomial discrete option pricing model. The second case corresponds to a stochastic revision strategy, which succeeds with a certain probability of one-over-one revision interval. For other cases, the hedging error over one revision interval is of the same order as the risk-free return and cannot be eliminated. This chapter is necessary for the understanding of the basic techniques behind the theory of rational option pricing in a continuous time framework. However, it is not necessary for the use and applications of all the formulas presented in this book.

References

Bellalah M (1999). The valuation of futures and commodity options with information costs. *Journal of Futures Markets*, 19 (September), 645–664.

Bellalah M (2001). Market imperfections; information costs and the valuation of derivatives: Some general results. *International Journal of Finance*, 13(3), 1895–1927.

Bellalah M and B Jacquillat (1995). Option valuation with information costs: Theory and tests. *The Financial Review*, 30(3) (August), 617–635.

Bellalah M and J-L Prigent (2001). Pricing standard and exotic options in the presence of a finite mixture of Gaussian distributions. *International Journal of Finance*, 13(3), 1975–2000.

Bellalah M and F Selmi (2001). On the quadratic criteria for hedging under transaction costs. *International Journal of Finance*, 13(3), 2001–2020.

Bellalah M, JL Prigent and C Villa (2001a). Skew without skewness: Asymmetric smiles; information costs and stochastic volatilities. *International Journal of Finance*, 13(2), 1826–1837.

Bellalah M, Ma Bellalah and R Portait (2001b). The cost of capital in international finance. *International Journal of Finance*, 13(3), 1958–1973.

Black F and M Scholes (1973). The pricing of options and corporate liabilities. *Journal of Political Economy*, 81, 637–659. Risk premiums (1973). *Journal of Political Economy*, 1387–1404.

Cox J, S Ross and M Rubinstein (1979). Option pricing: A simplified approach. *Journal of Financial Economics*, 7, 229–263.

Merton R (1973). Theory of rational option pricing. *Bell Journal of Economics and Management Science*, 4, 141–183.

Merton RC (1987). A simple model of capital market equilibrium with incomplete information. *Journal of Finance*, 42(3), 483–510.

Omberg E (1991). On the theory of perfect hedging. *Advances in Futures and Options Research*, 5, 1–29.

Rendleman RJ and BJ Barter (1979). The pricing of options on debts securities. *Journal of Financial and Quantitative Analysis*, 15 (March) 11–24.

Rogers C (1997). One for all. *Risk*, 10(3) (March) 56–59.

Willmott P (1998). *Derivatives.* John Wiley and Sons, New York.

Chapter 22

Risk Management: Applications to the Pricing of Assets and Derivatives in Complete Markets

Chapter Outline

This chapter is organized as follows:

1. In Section 22.1, we give some definitions and characterize complete markets.
2. In Section 22.2, equity options are priced with respect to the partial differential equation method and the martingale approach. Both methods are applied to the valuation of equity options.
3. In Section 22.3, bond options and interest rate options are studied and valued. Several models are proposed for the dynamics of interest rates.
4. In Section 22.4, the main techniques are proposed for the pricing of assets in complete markets using the change of numeraire and time.
5. In Section 22.5, the main results in Section 22.4 are extended to account for the effects of information uncertainty.

Introduction

Modern finance allows to quantify risk and its remuneration. The pioneering papers of Arrow (1953) and Merton (1973) assumed that markets are complete. Prices of contingent claims are presented in the form of solutions to partial differential equations (PDE). Prices are also represented as conditional expectation of functionals of stochastic processes. These representations provide solutions to the main pricing problems in modern finance. The pricing of derivative assets is usually based upon two methods which use the same basic arguments. The first method involves the resolution of a PDE under the appropriate boundary conditions corresponding to the derivative asset's payoffs. This is often referred to as the Black–Scholes method. The second method uses the martingale method, initiated by Harrison and Kreps (1979) and Harrison and Pliska (1981), where the current price of any financial asset is given by its discounted future payoffs under the appropriate probability measure. The probability is often referred to as the risk-neutral probability. Both methods are illustrated in detail for the pricing of European call options. Black and Scholes (1973) and Merton (1973) provide the PDE for derivatives and its solutions. The probabilistic method known also as the martingale method, initiated by Cox and Ross (1976), Harrison and Kreps (1979), and Harrison and Pliska (1981) allows to compute the prices of derivatives under a risk-neutral probability, under which the discounted price of any financial claim is a martingale. It must be clear that both methods lead to the same results. Application of the Feynman–Kac formula allows a switch from price as a solution of a PDE to a probability representation. Unfortunately, for most problems in financial economics, and in particular for the pricing of American options, there is often no closed form solutions and option prices must be approximated. Therefore, financial economists often resort to numerical techniques.

22.1. Characterization of Complete Markets

In financial markets, there are two classes of financial assets: securities and derivative assets. Securities correspond fundamentally to common stocks and bonds.

Derivative assets are contingent claims characterized by their intermediate and final payoffs. There are several definitions of a complete market. The idea of complete markets is proposed first by Arrow

(1953) and Debreu (1954). They defined a complete market with respect to state securities or state contingent claims.

A state security or an Arrow–Debreu security is a security which pays off one dollar if and only if a given state of the nature occurs. A state of nature or a possible state in the economy is said to be an insurable state when it is possible to construct a portfolio of assets which has a non-zero return in that state. In this economy, the price of each traded asset at the beginning of the period is p_s. For an economy where every state is insurable, a price vector can be completely determined with unique state prices. This implies the absence of arbitrage opportunities.

A contingent claim is attainable, if there is a strategy that gives at the derivative asset's maturity date the same value as the contingent claim terminal payoff. Hence, a complete market can be defined as a market in which all the contingent claims are attainable, i.e., all the contingent claims can be reached or obtained when implementing a replication or a duplication strategy.

A complete market can be defined with respect to the concept of a viable financial market. A viable financial market is a market where there is no profitable risk-less arbitrage. The absence of risk-less arbitrage or arbitrage opportunities means that a strategy which is implemented at the initial time with a zero-cost must have a nil final or terminal value. It is important to note that there is a relationship between the notion of arbitrage and the martingale property of security prices. The martingale property for security prices means simply that the best estimation of the future price is the last information. Hence, when historical data of security prices are used to predict the future price, only the most recent information matters, i.e., the last price. This concept defines also that of an efficient market. In mathematical terms, a financial market is viable if and only if there is a probability P^* which is equivalent to a probability P, under which the discounted asset prices have the martingale property. This is done under the theorems of the change in probability and in particular, the Girsanov theorem. (See Supplementary material for more detail).

A viable financial market is complete, if and only if there is a probability P^* equivalent to the probability P under which the martingale property is satisfied by security prices. It can be shown that this probability P^* is unique.

If one considers a contingent claim specified by its final payoff h, which is of the form $h = (S_T - K)^+$ for a European call and $h = (K - S_T)^+$ for a European put, then an attainable strategy Φ simulates or duplicates the option price when its payoff at the maturity date T is equal to h, or $V_T(\Phi) = h$. The sequence of the random derivative asset prices between the initial time 0 and the option's maturity date T is a martingale under the unique probability P^*. Hence, we have: $V_0(\Phi) = E^*[V_T(\Phi)]$ and $V_0(\Phi) = E^*[h \mid S_T]$. This gives the general result in complete markets:

$$V_t(\Phi) = S_t E^*[h \mid S_T \mid F_t] \quad \text{for } t : 0, \ldots, T.$$

If at the initial time a derivative asset is sold at its expected price, $E^*[h \mid S_T]$, then an investor following a replication strategy can obtain the exact payoff h at time T. He is said to follow a full hedging strategy.

22.2. Pricing Derivative Assets: The Case of Stock Options

Since each financial asset is specified by its intermediate and terminal payoffs, option pricing consists in finding the fair price at the initial time when the derivative asset is bought or sold. There is a unique approach for the pricing of derivative assets.

22.2.1. *The problem*

The value of each option is given by its expected terminal and intermediate payoffs discounted to the present. However, there are two methods for the pricing of options. The first was initiated by Black and Scholes (1973) and Merton (1973). The second is the martingale approach due to Harrison and Kreps (1979) and Harrison and Pliska (1981). The first method, known as the Black–Scholes method, is based on the resolution of the following PDE:

$$\frac{1}{2}\sigma^2 S^2 \frac{\partial^2 c}{\partial^2 S} + rS\frac{\partial c}{\partial S} + \left(\frac{\partial c}{\partial t}\right) - rc = 0$$

under the appropriate boundary conditions. The second is based on the use of martingale techniques. In either the first or the second approach, the boundary conditions are the same. These conditions refer to the appropriate payoff conditions corresponding to the value of European and American contingent claims. For a European call, the final payoff is given by $c(S, T) = \max[0, S_T - K]$ where K is the option strike price. For a European put, the final payoff is given by $p(S, T) = \max[0, K - S_T]$ where K is the option strike price. For an American call, the additional following condition must be satisfied by the PDE $C(S, t) \geq \max[0, S_t - K]$ where K is the option strike price. The difference from the condition for a European call is that the American call holder can exercise his option at each instant. This condition indicates that at each instant, the American call value must be at least equal to or greater than the intrinsic value, which corresponds to the value of a European call at maturity. For an American put, the additional following condition must be satisfied since the put holder can exercise his option at each instant $P(S, t) \geq \max[0, K - S_T]$ where K is the option strike price. This condition shows that at each instant, the American put value must be at least equal to the intrinsic value. In the presence of dividend distributions, some other conditions must be imposed. All these conditions apply in the absence of dividends. When there are distributions to the underlying asset, there is in general no explicit solutions to these problems and numerical methods are often used. First, we illustrate the PDE method for the valuation of European call options. Second, we illustrate the use of the martingale approach for the pricing of European calls. The reader can verify that the price of the call is the same under both methods. Third, since it is difficult to get closed form solutions for American options with and without distributions to the underlying asset, financial economists often use numerical methods. Therefore, we develop the principles of these techniques in the last section of this chapter.

22.2.2. *The PDE method*

22.2.2.1. *The standard analysis*

Consider the search for the solution of the following PDE:

$$\frac{1}{2}\left(\frac{\partial^2 c}{\partial^2 S}\right)\sigma^2 S^2 + rS\left(\frac{\partial c}{\partial S}\right) + \left(\frac{\partial c}{\partial t}\right) - rc = 0$$

for a European call with the payoff $c(S, T) = \max[0, S_T - K]$ where K is the option strike price. Using the appropriate change of variables, it can be shown that the call price is:

$$c = SN(d_1) - Ke^{-r(T-t)}N(d_2)$$

$$d_1 = \frac{\ln\left(\frac{S}{K}\right) + \left(r + \frac{1}{2}\sigma^2\right)(T-t)}{\sigma\sqrt{T-t}}, \quad d_2 = \frac{\ln\left(\frac{S}{K}\right) + \left(r - \frac{1}{2}\sigma^2\right)(T-t)}{\sigma\sqrt{T-t}}$$

where

$$N(d) = \frac{1}{\sqrt{2\Pi}} \int_{-\infty}^{d} e^{\left(-\frac{x^2}{2}\right)} dx$$

A detailed resolution of this system is given in supplementary material. The payoff of a European put option is $p(S, T) = \max[0, K - S_T]$. Using the appropriate change of variables, it can be shown that the put price is:

$$p = -SN(-d_1) + Ke^{-r(T-t)}N(-d_2)$$

$$d_1 = \frac{\ln\left(\frac{S}{K}\right) + \left(r + \frac{1}{2}\sigma^2\right)(T-t)}{\sigma\sqrt{T-t}}, \quad d_2 = \frac{\ln\left(\frac{S}{K}\right) + \left(r - \frac{1}{2}\sigma^2\right)(T-t)}{\sigma\sqrt{T-t}}.$$

22.2.2.2. *The analysis in the presence of information costs*

Consider the search for the solution of the following PDE:

$$\frac{1}{2}\left(\frac{\partial^2 c}{\partial^2 S}\right)\sigma^2 S^2 + (r + \lambda_S)S\left(\frac{\partial c}{\partial S}\right) + \left(\frac{\partial c}{\partial t}\right) - (r + \lambda_c)c = 0$$

for a European call with the payoff $c(S, T) = \max[0, S_T - K]$ where K is the option strike price.

Using the appropriate change of variables, it can be shown that the call price under information uncertainty is given by:

$$c = Se^{-(\lambda_S - \lambda_c)(T-t)}N(d_1) - Ke^{-(r+\lambda_c)(T-t)}N(d_2)$$

$$d_1 = \frac{\ln\left(\frac{S}{K}\right) + \left(r + \lambda_S + \frac{1}{2}\sigma^2\right)(T-t)}{\sigma\sqrt{T-t}},$$

$$d_2 = \frac{\ln\left(\frac{S}{K}\right) + \left(r + \lambda_S - \frac{1}{2}\sigma^2\right)(T-t)}{\sigma\sqrt{T-t}}$$

where:

$$N(d) = \frac{1}{\sqrt{2\Pi}} \int_{-\infty}^{d} \exp\left(-\frac{x^2}{2}\right) dx$$

The payoff of a European put option is $p(S,T) = \max[0, K - S_T]$. Using the appropriate change of variables, it can be shown that the put price is given by:

$$p = Se^{-(\lambda_S - \lambda_c)(T-t)} N(-d_1) + Ke^{-(r+\lambda_c)(T-t)} N(-d_2)$$

This model appears in Bellalah (2001).

22.2.3. *The martingale method*

The Black and Scholes (1973) pricing of options requires first the knowledge of the probability under which the asset price S_t is a martingale.

22.2.3.1. *The standard analysis*

In the context of the Black–Scholes model, there is an equivalent probability to P under which the discounted expected stock price, $S_t^* = e^{-rt} S_t$ is a martingale. In fact, if one uses the stochastic differential equation for the stock price, we have:

$$dS_t^* = -re^{-rt} S_t dt + e^{-rt} dS_t$$

or

$$dS_t^* = S_t^* [(\mu - r)dt + \sigma dW_t].$$

If we put the change in variables $W_t^* = W_t + \left[\frac{\mu - r}{\sigma}\right] t$ then $dS_t^* = S_t^* \sigma dW_t^*$. Using the Girsanov theorem,

$$\Theta_t = \frac{(\mu - r)}{\sigma},$$

there is a probability P^* equivalent to P under which $(W_t^*)_{0 \leq t \leq T}$ is a standard Brownian motion. Hence, under P^*, we deduce from

Eq. (22.12) that S_t^* is a martingale and

$$S_t^* = S_0^* e^{\sigma W_t^* - \frac{1}{2}\sigma^2 t}$$

The option price in the Black and Scholes (1973) economy can be computed using its discounted expected terminal value under the appropriate probability P^* as:

$$c_t = E^*[e^{-r(T-t)} h \mid F_t]$$

with $h(S_T - K)^+ = f(S_T)$. The option price at time t can be expressed as a function of time and the underlying asset price. In fact,

$$c_t = E^*[e^{-r(T-t)} h \mid F_t]$$

or

$$c_t = E^*\left[e^{-r(T-t)} f\left[S_t e^{-r(T-t)} e^{\sigma(W_T^* - W_t^*) - \frac{1}{2}\sigma^2(T-t)}\right] | F_t\right].$$

Since for all t, $S_t = S_0 e^{\sigma W_t^* - \frac{1}{2}\sigma^2 t}$, and at the option's maturity date $S_T = S_0 e^{\sigma W_T^* - \frac{1}{2}\sigma^2 T}$ the ratio of the stock price between two dates is:

$$\frac{S_T}{S_t} = e^{\left[\sigma(W_T^* - W_t^*) - \frac{1}{2}\sigma^2(T-t)\right]}$$

Since the random stock price S_t is F_t measurable and $(W_T^* - W_t^*)$ is independent of F_t under P^*, it can be shown that $c_t = H(t, S_t)$ with:

$$H(t,S) = E^*\left[e^{-r(T-t)} f\left[S e^{r(T-t)} e^{\sigma(W_T^* - W_t^*) - \frac{\sigma^2}{2}(T-t)}\right]\right] \qquad (22.1)$$

Under the probability P^*, the quantity $(W_T^* - W_t^*)$ follows a Gaussian law, $N(0, \sqrt{(T-t)})$. When $(W_T^* - W_t^*) = Y\sqrt{T-t}$ and Y follows a $N(0,1)$, then

$$H(t,S) = e^{-r(T-t)} \int_{-\infty}^{\infty} f\left[S e^{(r - \frac{\sigma^2}{2})(T-t) + \sigma y \sqrt{T-t}}\right] \frac{1}{\sqrt{2\Pi}} e^{\frac{-y^2}{2}} dy$$

When Y follows $N(0,1)$, under P^*, then

$$E_{p^*}[h(Y)] = \frac{h(y)}{\sqrt{2\Pi}} e^{\frac{-y^2}{2}} dy,$$

since

$$H(t,S) = e^{-r(T-t)} E_{p^*}\left[G(\sqrt{T-t})Y\right]$$

where

$$G(\sqrt{T-t})Y = f\left[Se^{\sigma(\sqrt{T-t})Y+(r-\frac{\sigma^2}{2})(T-t)}\right]$$

and Y follows $N(0,1)$ with density $\frac{1}{\sqrt{2\Pi}} e^{-\frac{1}{2}y^2}$ under P^*.

If one replaces the call's pay off function, then using Eq. (22.1) gives:

$$H(t,S) = E^*\left[\left(e^{-r(T-t)} Se^{(r-\frac{\sigma^2}{2})(T-t)+\sigma(W_T^*-W_t^*)} - K\right)^+\right]$$

or

$$H(t,S) = E^*\left[\left(Se^{(\sigma Y\sqrt{\tau}-\frac{\sigma^2}{2}\tau)} - Ke^{-r\tau}\right)^+\right] \tag{22.2}$$

where $\tau = T - t$.

Equation (22.2) is equivalent to Eq. (22.1) where $f(z)$ is replaced by $(z_T - K)^+$. Now, using the notation,

$$d_1 = \frac{\ln\left(\frac{S}{K}\right) + \left(r + \frac{1}{2}\sigma^2\right)\tau}{\sigma\sqrt{\tau}}, \quad d_2 = d_1 - \sigma\sqrt{\tau}$$

we consider again the equation

$$H(t,S) = E\left[\left(Se^{(r-\frac{\sigma^2}{2})(T-t)+\sigma(W_T^*-W_t^*)} - K\right)^+\right]$$

Using the following lemma

$$E[(Z-K)^+] = E[[(Z-K)]I_{Z\geq K}]$$

with

$$I_{Z\geq K} = \begin{cases} 1, & \text{if } Z \geq K \\ 0 & \text{else} \end{cases}$$

the condition $(Z \geq K)$ is equivalent to:

$$Se^{(\sigma Y\sqrt{\tau}-\frac{1}{2}\sigma^2\tau)} \geq K$$

or

$$\sigma Y\sqrt{\tau} - \frac{1}{2}\sigma^2\tau \geq \ln\left(\frac{K}{S}\right).$$

Hence

$$Y \geq \frac{\ln\left(\frac{K}{S}\right) - \left[r - \frac{1}{2}\sigma^2\tau\right]}{\sigma\sqrt{\tau}}$$

or

$$Y \geq -d_2 \quad \text{or} \quad Y + d_2 \geq 0.$$

Using this remark, $H(t, S)$ can be written as:

$$H(t,S) = E\left[Se^{\left(\sigma Y\sqrt{\tau}-\frac{\sigma^2}{2}\tau\right)} - Ke^{-r\tau}\right]I_{Y+d_2\geq 0}$$

or

$$H(t,S) = \int_{-d_2}^{\infty}\left[Se^{(\sigma Y\sqrt{\tau}-\frac{\sigma^2}{2}\tau)} - Ke^{-rt}\right]\frac{1}{\sqrt{2\Pi}}e^{(-\frac{1}{2}y^2)}dy$$

which is equivalent to:

$$H(t,S) = \int_{-\infty}^{d_2}\left[Se^{(-\sigma Y\sqrt{\tau}-\frac{\sigma^2}{2}\tau)} - Ke^{-rt}\right]\frac{1}{\sqrt{2\Pi}}e^{(-\frac{1}{2}y^2)}dy$$

This integral can be written as the difference between two integrals

$$H(t,S) = \int_{-\infty}^{d_2} Se^{(-\sigma Y\sqrt{\tau}-\frac{\sigma^2}{2}\tau)}\frac{1}{\sqrt{2\Pi}}e^{(-\frac{1}{2}y^2)}dy - \int_{-\infty}^{d_2} Ke^{-r\tau}\frac{1}{\sqrt{2\Pi}}e^{(-\frac{1}{2}y^2)}dy$$

The second integral is equal to $-Ke^{-r\tau}N(d_2)$. Using the change in variable $z = y + \sigma\sqrt{\tau}$ or $y = z - \sigma\sqrt{\tau}$, the first integral can be written as:

$$\int_{-\infty}^{d_2+\sigma\sqrt{\tau}} Se^{\left(-\sigma(z-\sigma\sqrt{\tau})\sqrt{\tau}-\frac{\sigma^2}{2}\tau\right)} \frac{1}{\sqrt{2\Pi}} e^{\left(-\frac{1}{2}(z-\sigma\sqrt{\tau})^2\right)} dz$$

Simple computation of this integral gives exactly $SN(d_1)$. The sum of both integrals corresponds to the Black–Scholes formula:

$$H(t,S) = SN(d_1) - Ke^{-r\tau}N(d_2) \tag{22.3}$$

with

$$d_1 = \frac{\ln\left(\frac{S}{K}\right) + \left(r + \frac{1}{2}\sigma^2\right)(T-t)}{\sigma\sqrt{T-t}}, \quad d_2 = \frac{\ln\left(\frac{S}{K}\right) + \left(r - \frac{1}{2}\sigma^2\right)(T-t)}{\sigma\sqrt{T-t}}.$$

22.2.3.2. *The analysis in the presence of information costs*

It is possible to use the martingale method for the pricing of derivative claims in a Black–Scholes context in the presence of information uncertainty. For the analysis of information costs and valuation, we can refer to Bellalah (2001), Bellalah *et al.* (2001a), Bellalah and Prigent (2001) and Bellalah and Selmi (2001) etc. In this context, we can show that there is an equivalent probability to P under which the discounted expected value of the underlying asset given by $S_t^* = e^{-(r+\lambda_S)t}S_t$ is a martingale. In this expression, the term λ_i refers to information costs.

Consider the stochastic differential equation for the underlying asset:

$$dS_t^* = -(r+\lambda_S)e^{-(r+\lambda_S)t}S_t dt + e^{-(r+\lambda_S)t}dS_t$$

or the following dynamics:

$$dS_t^* = S_t^*[(\mu - r - \lambda_S)dt + \sigma dW_t]$$

If the following change in variables is used

$$W_t^* = W_t + \left[\frac{(\mu - r - \lambda_S)}{\sigma}\right]t$$

then

$$dS_t^* = S_t^* \sigma dW_t^*.$$

Using the Girsanov theorem,

$$\Theta_t = \frac{(\mu - r - \lambda_S)}{\sigma},$$

there is a probability P^* equivalent to P under which W_t^* is a standard Brownian motion. Hence, under P^*, we deduce from this last equation that S_t^* is a martingale and:

$$S_t^* = S_0^* \exp\left[\sigma W_t^* - \frac{1}{2}\sigma^2 t\right].$$

The option price in the Black–Scholes economy can be computed using its discounted expected terminal value under the appropriate probability P^* as

$$c_t = E^*[e^{-(r+\lambda_c)(T-t)} h/F_t] \quad \text{with} \quad h(S_T - K)^+ = f(S_T)$$

The option price at time t for a maturity date is given by:

$$c_t = E^*\left[e^{-(r+\lambda_c)(T-t)} f\left[S_t e^{-(r+\lambda_S)(T-t)}\right.\right.$$
$$\left.\left.\times \exp\left\{\sigma(W_T^* - W_t^*) - \frac{1}{2}\sigma^2(T-t)\right\}\right]\Big/ F_t\right]$$

Since for all t, we have: $S_t = S_0 e^{\left[\sigma W_t^* - \frac{1}{2}\sigma^2 t\right]}$ and the value of the underlying asset at the option's maturity date is $S_T = S_0 \exp\left[\sigma W_T^* - \frac{1}{2}\sigma^2 T\right]$, the ratio of the stock price between two dates is given by:

$$\frac{S_T}{S_t} = \exp\left[\sigma(W_T^* - W_t^*) - \frac{1}{2}\sigma^2(T-t)\right]$$

It can be shown that the option value is given by $c_t = H(t, S_t)$ with:

$$H(t,S) = E^*\left[e^{-(r+\lambda_c)(T-t)} f\left[S e^{(r+\lambda_S)(T-t)} e^{\sigma(W_T^* - W_t^*) - \frac{\sigma^2}{2}(T-t)}\right]\right] \tag{22.4}$$

Under the probability P^*, the quantity $W_T^* - W_t^*$ follows a Gaussian law, $N(0, \sqrt{t})$. When the difference $W_T^* - W_t^* = Y\sqrt{T-t}$ and Y follows an $N(0,1)$, then

$$H(t,S) = e^{-(r+\lambda_c)(T-t)} \int_{-\infty}^{\infty} f\left[S e^{(r+\lambda_S - \frac{\sigma^2}{2})(T-t) + \sigma y\sqrt{T-t}}\right]$$
$$\times \frac{1}{\sqrt{2\Pi}} e^{\frac{-y^2}{2}} dy$$

When Y follows $N(0,1)$, under P^*, then

$$E_{p^*}[h(Y)] = \frac{h(Y)}{\sqrt{2\Pi}} e^{\frac{-y^2}{2}} dy,$$

since

$$H(t,S) = e^{-(r+\lambda_c)(T-t)} E_{p^*}[G(\sqrt{T-t})Y]$$

where

$$G(\sqrt{T-t})Y = f\left[S\exp\left(\sigma(\sqrt{T-t})Y + \left((r+\lambda_S) - \frac{\sigma^2}{2}\right)(T-t)\right)\right]$$

and Y follows $N(0,1)$ with density $\frac{1}{\sqrt{2\Pi}}e^{-\frac{1}{2}y^2}$ under P^*.

22.3. Pricing Derivative Assets: The Case of Bond Options and Interest Rate Options

The value of a zero-coupon bond at maturity is $B(T,T) = 1$.

22.3.1. *Arbitrage-free family of bond prices*

The concept of arbitrage is central to the valuation of financial assets. Musiela (1997) gives the following definition for the arbitrage family of bond prices.

Definition: Consider a process r defined on a filtered probability space (Ω, F, P). An arbitrage-free family of bond prices relative to the interest rate r when $B(T,T) = 1$ for every T in $[0,T^*]$, and when there is a probability P^* on $(\Omega, \mathcal{F})$ equivalent to P such that the relative bond price

$$Z^*(t,T) = B(t,T)/B_t, \quad \forall\, t \in [0,T]$$

is a martingale under P^*. The probability P^* is a martingale measure for the family $B(t,T)$. Hence, for any P^* of an arbitrage-free family of bond prices, we have:

$$B(t,T) = E_{P^*}\left(e^{-\int_t^T r_u du} \,|\, \mathcal{F}_t\right), \quad \forall\, t \in [0,T] \tag{22.5}$$

The reader can refer to supplementary material for more details.

22.3.2. *Time-homogeneous models*

22.3.2.1. *The Vasicek (1977) model*

The diffusion process proposed in the Vasicek (1977) model is a mean-reverting version of the Ornstein–Uhlenbeck process. In this model, the short-term interest rate follows the following dynamics:

$$dr_t = (a - br_t)dt + \sigma dW_t^*$$

where a, b, and σ are positive constants. This Gaussian model allows for the possibility of negative interest rates.

Consider a security paying a continuous dividend at a rate (h, r_t, t) whose payoff is a function of the interest rate r, $F_T = f(r_T)$ at time T.

The price process F_t of this security has the representation $F_t = v(r_t, t)$ where v is solution to the following PDE:

$$\frac{\partial v}{\partial t}(r,t) + \frac{1}{2}\sigma^2\frac{\partial^2 v}{\partial r^2}(r,t) + (a - br)\frac{\partial v}{\partial r}(r,t) - rv(r,t) + h(r,t) = 0, \tag{22.6}$$

The terminal boundary condition is:

$$v(r,T) = f(r) \tag{22.7}$$

When $h = 0$ and $f(r) = 1$, the price of a zero-coupon bond is:

$$B(t,T) = v(r_t, t, T) = e^{m(t,T) - n(t,T)r_t}, \tag{22.8}$$

where

$$n(t,T) = \frac{1}{b}(1 - e^{-b(T-t)})$$

and

$$m(t,T) = \frac{\sigma^2}{2}\int_t^T n^2(u,T)du - a\int_t^T n(u,T)du$$

It is possible to verify this result using Eq. (22.8) with $m(T,T) = n(T,T) = 0$. Using the PDE and separating the terms in r gives the following system:

$$\begin{aligned} n_t(t,T) &= bn(t,T) - 1, \quad n(T,T) = 0, \\ m_t(t,T) &= an(t,T) - \frac{1}{2}\sigma^2 n^2(t,T), \quad m(T,T) = 0 \end{aligned} \tag{22.9}$$

which leads to the above expressions. We can check that we have:

$$dB(t,T) = B(t,T)(r_t dt + \sigma n(t,T) dW_t^*)$$

where the bond price volatility equals $b(t,T) = \sigma n(t,T)$.

Using the expression (22.9) for the bond price, the bond's yield is:

$$Y(t,T) = \frac{n(t,T)r_t - m(t,T)}{T-t}$$

Since this yield is an affine function and therefore the categories of similar models are known as affine models of the term structure.

Jamshidian gives a closed-form solution for a European call on a bond (with and without coupons) with a H-maturity in the context of this model using:

$$C_t = B(t,T)E_Q\left((\xi\eta - K)^+ \,|\, \mathcal{F}_t\right) \tag{22.10}$$

where $\eta = \frac{B(t,H)}{B(t,T)}$;
K: the strike price;
Q: a probability measure equivalent to P^* and
ξ: a random variable with a variance:

$$v_H^2(t,T) = \int_t^T |b(t,T) - b(t,H)|^2 du$$

or

$$v_H^2(t,T) = \frac{\sigma^2}{2b^3}(1 - e^{-2b(T-t)})(1 - e^{-b(H-t)})^2$$

The formula for the call on a bond is given by:

$$C_t = B(t,H)N(d_1(t,T)) - KB(t,T)N(d_2(t,T))$$

with

$$d_{1,2}(t,T) = \frac{\ln\left(B(t,H)/B(t,T)\right) - \ln K \pm \frac{1}{2}v_H^2(t,T)}{v_H(t,T)}$$

for every t less than T and H. This formula does not show the coefficient a and accounts for the bond volatility.

22.3.2.2. *The Cox, Ingersoll and Ross (CIR) (1985) model*

In their general equilibrium approach, CIR (1985) use the familiar square root process for the dynamics of interest rates:

$$dr_t = (a - br_t)dt + \sigma\sqrt{r_t}dW_t^*$$

where a, b, and σ are positive constants. This process does not allow for negative interest rates because of the square root in the diffusion process. The price process of a standard European option $F_t = v(r_t, t)$ must satisfy the following partial differential equation:

$$\frac{\partial v}{\partial t}(r,t) + \frac{1}{2}\sigma^2 r\frac{\partial^2 v}{\partial r^2}(r,t) + (a - br)\frac{\partial v}{\partial r}(r,t) - rv(r,t) + h(r,t) = 0,$$

under the boundary condition:

$$v(r,T) = f(r,T).$$

CIR (1985) provide the following closed-form solutions for the price of a zero-coupon bond.

$$m(t,T) = \frac{2a}{\sigma^2}\ln\left\{\frac{\Gamma e^{br/2}}{\Gamma\cosh\Gamma r + \frac{1}{2}b\sinh\Gamma r}\right\}$$

and

$$n(t,T) = \frac{\sinh\Gamma r}{\Gamma\cosh\Gamma r + \frac{1}{2}b\sinh\Gamma r},$$

with

$$\tau = T - t, \quad 2\Gamma = \sqrt{(b^2 + 2\sigma^2)}.$$

They give also solutions in closed forms for options on zero-coupon and coupon-bearing bonds. Longstaff (1990) proposes closed-form formulas for European options on yields in the context of the CIR (1985) model. The yield on a zero-coupon bond is a linear function of the short-term rate in the CIR model since:

$$Y(t, t+\tau) = \tilde{Y}(r_t, \tau) = \tilde{m}(\tau) + \tilde{n}(\tau) r_t$$

The yield at time t for a zero-coupon bond with a maturity τ for a current level $r_t = r$ is $\tilde{Y}(t, \tau)$. The payoff of a yield European call is given by: $C_T^Y = (\tilde{Y}(r_T, \tau) - K)^+$, where K is the fixed level of the yield.

22.3.2.3. *The Longstaff model*

Longstaff uses the following dynamics for the short-term rate:

$$dr_t = a(b - c\sqrt{r_t})dt + \sigma\sqrt{r_t}dW_t^* \tag{22.11}$$

referred to as a double square root process. In this model, the price of a zero-coupon bond is given by:

$$B(t, T) = v(r_t, t, T) = e^{m(t,T) - n(t,T) r_t - p(t,T)\sqrt{r_t}}$$

where m, n, and p are known functions. In this model, the yield of the bond is a non-linear function of the short-term rate.

22.3.3. *Time-inhomogeneous models*

It is important to note that the Vasicek (1977) and the CIR (1985) models are special cases of the following process:

$$dr_t = a(b - cr_t)dt + \sigma r_t^{\beta} dW_t^*$$

where β is a constant between zero and one.

Hull and White use the following dynamics for the short-term interest rate:

$$dr_t = (a(t) - b(t) r_t)dt + \sigma(t) r_t^{\beta} dW_t^*$$

where β is a positive constant, W^* a Brownian motion and a, b, and σ are locally bounded functions. This model appears as a generalization of the Vasicek (1977) and the CIR (1985) model. When $\beta = 0$, this gives a generalized Vasicek model:

$$dr_t = (a(t) - b(t)r_t)dt + \sigma(t)dW_t^*.$$

When $\beta = 0.5$, this gives a generalized CIR model:

$$dr_t = (a(t) - b(t)r_t)dt + \sigma(t)\sqrt{r_t}dW_t^*$$

22.4. Asset Pricing in Complete Markets: Changing Numeraire and Time

This section introduces two mathematical instruments: the change of numeraire and the change of time. These tools are very effective in solving derivative asset pricing problems.

22.4.1. *Assumptions and the valuation context*

Consider an economy in which transactions take place instantaneously without transactions costs and taxes. The interest rate follows a Gaussian process. The short-term risk-less interest rate $r(t)$ under the risk-neutral probability Q is governed by the following stochastic differential equation

$$dr(t) = a(t)[b(t) - r(t)]dt + \sigma(t)dW_1(t)$$

where the different parameters $a(t), b(t)$ and $\sigma(t)$ are deterministic functions.

Under the risk-neutral probability Q, the dynamics of return on zero-coupon bonds in the absence of default are given by:

$$\frac{dP(t,T)}{P(t,T)} = r(t)dt - \sigma_p(t,T)dW_1(t)$$

where $P(t,T)$ is the price of a zero-coupon bond at time t for a maturity date T.

The volatility in the process describing the dynamics of zero-coupon bond prices is given by:

$$\sigma_p(t,T) = \sigma(t)\int_t^T \exp\left(-\int_t^u a(s)ds\right)du$$

Consider the value at time t of a portfolio which corresponds to an investment of one dollar at time $t = 0$ at the rate $r(t)$:

$$B(t) = e^{\int_0^t r(u)du}$$

This portfolio corresponds to a capitalization factor. Consider the following dynamics for a risky asset S_t:

$$\frac{dS_t}{S_t} = r(t)dt + \sigma_S\left[\rho dW_1(t) + \sqrt{1-\rho^2}dW_2(t)\right]$$

under the risk-neutral probability Q. The coefficient $\rho \in [-1, 1]$ introduces a correlation between the risky asset and the interest rate. The absence of arbitrage opportunities gives the price of any contingent claim under the risk-neutral probability Q as

$$V_0 = E_Q\left[\frac{h(T)}{B(T)}\right],$$

where E_Q corresponds to the conditional expectation under the probability Q.

22.4.2. *Valuation of derivatives in a standard Black–Scholes–Merton economy*

Consider the dynamics of the option's underlying stock

$$\frac{dS_t}{S_t} = rdt + \sigma_S dW_2(t)$$

Using arbitrage arguments, Black and Scholes derived the following PDE:

$$\frac{\partial C}{\partial t} + \frac{1}{2}\sigma_S^2 S^2 \frac{\partial^2 C}{\partial S^2} + rS\frac{\partial C}{\partial S} - rC = 0 \tag{22.12}$$

Consider a replicating portfolio V consisting of a long position in the option and a short position in $\frac{\partial C}{\partial S}$ units of the underlying asset. The portfolio results from investing $\left(\frac{\partial C}{\partial S}\right)$ in the risky asset and an amount $\left(C - S\frac{\partial C}{\partial S}\right)$ in the risk-free asset. Its dynamics are given by:

$$dV = \left(C - S\frac{\partial C}{\partial S}\right)rdt + \frac{\partial C}{\partial S}dS \tag{22.13}$$

Using Ito's lemma gives:

$$dV = \left(\frac{\partial C}{\partial t} + \frac{1}{2}\sigma_S^2 S^2 \frac{\partial^2 C}{\partial S^2}\right) dt + \frac{\partial C}{\partial S} dS \tag{22.14}$$

The solution for a European call is:

$$C(S_0, T, \sigma_S, r) = S_0 N(d_1) - K e^{-rt} N(d_2)$$

$$d_1 = \frac{\ln\left(\frac{S_0}{K}\right) + \left(r + \frac{\sigma_S^2}{2}\right) T}{\sigma_S \sqrt{T}} = d_2 + \sigma_S \sqrt{T}$$

Now, consider the following change of variables in Eq. (22.12)

$$f_t = S_t e^{r(T-t)}, \quad C_f = C e^{r(T-t)}$$

The two changes of variables correspond to a change of numeraire giving respectively the value of a forward contract as a function of its underlying asset and the cost of carry and the value of a forward call as a function of a spot option.

Consider also the following time change in Eq. (22.12) $\tau = \sigma_S^2 t$ and $\tau^* = \sigma_S^2 T$.

The change of underlying asset f in Eq. (22.12) allows to write this equation as:

$$\frac{\partial C}{\partial t} + \frac{1}{2}\sigma_S^2 f^2 \frac{\partial^2 C}{\partial f^2} - rC = 0 \tag{22.15}$$

Equation (22.15) corresponds to the Black (1976) equation providing the value of an option on a forward contract f. A simple comparison between Eqs. (22.15) and (22.12) reveals that the term $rS\frac{\partial C}{\partial S}$ has disappeared. This is because the forward positions cost nothing to initiate and to adjust. Therefore, the dynamics of the replicating portfolio can be written as:

$$dV = rCdt + \frac{\partial C}{\partial f} df$$

Using Ito's lemma

$$dV = \left(\frac{\partial C}{\partial t} + \frac{1}{2}\sigma_A^2 f^2 \frac{\partial^2 C}{\partial f^2}\right) dt + \frac{\partial C}{\partial f} df$$

gives the dynamics of C in Eq. (22.15).

When $C_f = Ce^{r(T-t)}$, this change of variables gives:

$$\frac{\partial C_f}{\partial t} + \frac{1}{2}\sigma_A^2 f^2 \frac{\partial^2 C_f}{\partial f^2} = 0$$

In the same way, no initial investment is required for the call on a forward contract, since it represents a forward option. In this case, the dynamics of the replicating portfolio are given by $dV_f = \frac{\partial C_f}{\partial f} df$ and Ito's lemma gives:

$$dV_f = \left(\frac{\partial C_f}{\partial t} + \frac{1}{2}\sigma_S^2 f^2 \frac{\partial^2 C_f}{\partial f^2}\right) dt + \frac{\partial C_f}{\partial f} df$$

It is possible to use a change of variables for τ and τ^* to simplify the equation to the following form:

$$\frac{\partial C_f}{\partial \tau} + \frac{1}{2} f^2 \frac{\partial^2 C_f}{\partial f^2} = 0 \tag{22.16}$$

Equation (22.16) is useful for the valuation of a forward option on a forward contract maturing in τ^* for which the volatility is equal to one. In this case, the solution to Eq. (22.16) for a forward call on a forward contract is given by:

$$C_f(f_0, \tau^*) = C(f_0, \tau^*, 1, 0) = f_0 N(d_1) - KN(d_2)$$

since

$$\frac{\ln\left(\frac{f_0}{K}\right) + \frac{\tau^*}{2}}{\sqrt{\tau^*}} = \frac{\ln\left(\frac{S_0}{K}\right) + \left(r + \frac{\sigma_S^2}{2}\right) T}{\sigma_S \sqrt{T}}$$

A simple comparison of Eqs. (22.16) and (22.12) reveals that the option is priced as if the interest rate were zero. Besides, the volatility is replaced by 1 and the maturity T by τ^*. This result comes from the changes in numeraires but, in practice, the interest rate enters the cost of carry and the time change comprises the volatility of the forward contract.

22.4.3. *Changing numeraire and time: The martingale approach and the PDE approach*

The change of numeraire and the change of time appear in several papers including Merton (1973), Jamshidian, El Karoui and Geman (1993) etc. In a martingale approach, the change of numeraire and time is useful from a computational point of view. We introduce these concepts and make the analogy with partial differential equations approach.

22.4.3.1. *Change of numeraire*

A numeraire corresponds in general to a process $X(t)$ for which there exists a probability measure Q^X which is defined by its Radon–Nikodym derivative with respect to Q as:

$$\frac{dQ^X}{dQ} = \frac{X(T)}{X(0)}\frac{B(0)}{B(T)}$$

in such a way that the relative price of the asset compared with the numeraire X is a Q^X martingale. In the above expression $B(t)$ corresponds to the capitalization factor and Q is the risk-neutral probability.

In fact, as we know, in the martingale approach, the price of any derivative asset with a payoff $h(T)$ can be computed using the absence of arbitrage opportunities argument. This allows the computation of the price of any contingent claim under the risk-neutral probability Q as $V_0 = E_Q\left[\frac{h(T)}{B(T)}\right]$, where E_Q corresponds to the conditional expectation under the probability Q.

This conditional expectation can also be written as:

$$E_Q\left[\frac{h(T)}{B(T)}\right] = X(0)E_{Q^X}\left[\frac{h(T)}{X(T)}\right]$$

As an example, consider the price of a risk-less zero-coupon bond $P(t,T)$ as a numeraire in an economy with stochastic interest rates. Using this numeraire, it is possible to define for its process a new probability Q^P by giving its Radon–Nikodym derivative with respect to Q as:

$$\frac{dQ^P}{dQ} = \frac{P(T,T)}{P(0,T)} \frac{B(0)}{B(T)}$$

which is also equal to $\frac{dQ^P}{dQ} = \frac{1}{P(0,T)} \frac{1}{B(T)}$ since by definition, the prices $P(T,T)$ and $B(0)$ are equal to 1. Using the two previous equations, it is evident that:

$$E_Q\left[\frac{h(T)}{B(T)}\right] = P(0,T)E_{Q^X}[h(T)]$$

The effect of this change of numeraire can be appreciated using the Black–Scholes context for the pricing of a European call on an asset S in the presence of a stochastic interest rate. We use the following dynamics for the underlying asset:

$$\frac{dS_t}{S_t} = rdt + \sigma_S dW_2(t)$$

and for the short-term interest rate:

$$dr(t) = a(t)[b(t) - r(t)]dt + \sigma(t)dW_1(t)$$

In the presence of stochastic interest rates, the option price can be computed as:

$$C_S = E_Q\left[\left(\frac{S_T - K}{B(T)}\right) I_{S_T \geq K}\right]$$

The indicator function I_E for E is the real-valued random variable defined by $I_E(\omega) = 1$ for all $\omega \in E$ and zero otherwise.

Equivalently, under the probability Q^P, the value of the call can be written as:

$$C_S = P(0,T)E_{Q^P}\left[\left(\frac{S_T}{P(T,T)} - \frac{K}{P(T,T)}\right) I_{\frac{S_T}{P(T,T)} \geq K}\right] \qquad (22.17)$$

where the zero-coupon bond value is by definition equal to one at maturity.

Equation (22.17) allows us to avoid the stochastic character of interest rates. A comparison can be done with respect to the PDE approach. In the presence of stochastic interest rates, the call price is a function of the underlying asset S, the interest rate r and time t. It is also possible to consider the option price as a function of the prices of the underlying asset, the price of zero-coupon bonds, P and time. In this case, it is possible to show that the European call price must satisfy the following partial differential equation:

$$\frac{\partial C_S}{\partial t} + \frac{1}{2}\sigma_S^2 S^2 \frac{\partial^2 C_S}{\partial S^2} + \frac{1}{2}\sigma_p^2 P^2 \frac{\partial^2 C_S}{\partial P^2} - \rho\sigma_S\sigma_P SP \frac{\partial^2 C_S}{\partial S \partial P} + rS\frac{\partial C_S}{\partial S} + rP\frac{\partial C_S}{\partial P} - rC_S = 0 \tag{22.18}$$

This equation must be solved under the terminal condition $C_S = \max[S - K, 0]$. Since the call price C_A is first-degree homogeneous in the underlying asset and the discount bond, or

$$C_S = S\frac{\partial C_S}{\partial S} + P\frac{\partial C_S}{\partial P}$$

Equation (22.18) can be written, after simplification as:

$$\frac{\partial C_S}{\partial t} + \frac{1}{2}\sigma_S^2 S^2 \frac{\partial^2 C_S}{\partial S^2} + \frac{1}{2}\sigma_p^2 P^2 \frac{\partial^2 C_S}{\partial P^2} - \rho\sigma_S\sigma_P SP \frac{\partial^2 C_S}{\partial S \partial P} = 0 \tag{22.19}$$

Now, a change of variables can be made using the bond price $P(t,T)$ as a new numeraire. We denote by F_t the price of a forward contract on the underlying asset S for delivery at time T, $F_t = \frac{S_t}{P(t,T)}$ and by C_F the price of a European call on the forward contract $C_F = \frac{C_S}{P}$.

Using this new change of variables, Eq. (22.19) can be written as:

$$\frac{\partial C_F}{\partial t} + \frac{1}{2}\sigma_F(t,T)^2 F^2 \frac{\partial^2 C_F}{\partial F^2} = 0 \tag{22.20}$$

where the instantaneous variance of the forward contract in this stochastic interest rate economy is

$$\sigma_F(t,T)^2 = \sigma_S^2 + \sigma_P(t,T)^2 + 2\rho\sigma_S\sigma_P(t,T)$$

When the interest rate is constant, the correlation coefficient is zero, and the bond's price volatility is also zero. In this case, the volatility of the forward contract is equivalent to that of the underlying spot asset or $\sigma_F(t,T) = \sigma_S$. The option payoff corresponds to that of a European option on a forward contract $C_F = \max[F-K, 0]$. As it is shown, the change of numeraire P under the martingale approach amounts to a change of variables in the partial differential equation method. The main difference between this economy and the Black–Scholes economy appears in the presence of stochastic interest rates. The intuition of the change in numeraire appears in Merton's (1973) paper for the pricing of a stock option in the presence of stochastic interest rates. Merton (1973) uses a change of variables $\frac{S_t}{KP(t,T)}$. The new probability Q^P corresponds to a "forward-neutral" probability. It is possible to simplify the analysis by considering the underlying asset itself as a numeraire. In this case, a new probability measure Q^S can be defined such that:

$$\frac{dQ^S}{dQ^P} = \frac{S_T}{S_0}\frac{P(0,T)}{P(T,T)}$$

where, as before, the value of $P(T,T)$ is equal to one by definition. When this change of probability is used in the right-hand side of Eq. (22.17), the European call price is given by:

$$C_S = S_0 E^{Q^S}\left[I_{\frac{P(T,T)}{S_T}\leq K}\right] - KP(0,T)E^{Q^P}\left[I_{\frac{S_T}{P(T,T)}\geq K}\right]$$

22.4.3.2. *The change of time*

The main idea behind the change of numeraire in the partial differential equation approach is to operate an appropriate change of variables that facilitates the search of a solution to the price of a derivative contract in the standard Merton (1973) approach. The main idea behind the change of numeraire in the martingale approach is to express under an appropriate probability measure, the relative price of a security as a martingale. Consider a continuous

P-martingale defined by the following stochastic differential equation:

$$dM_t = x_1(t)dW_1(t) + x_2(t)dW_2(t)$$

where the coefficients x_1 and x_2 are deterministic functions.

In this context, it is possible to show the existence of a unique one-dimensional standard Brownian motion Y such that:

$$M_t = \sum_{i=1}^{2} \int_0^t x_i(u)dW_i(u) = Y_{\langle M \rangle_t} \tag{22.21}$$

where

$$\langle M \rangle_t = \sum_{i=1}^{2} \int_0^t x_i^2(u)du.$$

Consider again the pricing of a European call in the presence of stochastic interest rates. Using two changes of numeraire, the call price is:

$$C_S = S_0 E^{Q^S}\left[I_{\frac{P(T,T)}{S_T} \le K}\right] - KP(0,T)E^{Q^P}\left[I_{\frac{S_T}{P(T,T)} \ge K}\right] \tag{22.22}$$

The quantities $\frac{S_t}{P(t,T)}$ and $\frac{P(t,T)}{S}$ are respectively Q^P and Q^S martingales and satisfy

$$\begin{aligned}\left\langle \ln \frac{S_t}{P(t,T)} \right\rangle_t &= \left\langle \ln \frac{P(t,T)}{S_t} \right\rangle_t \\ &= \int_0^t [\sigma_S^2 + \sigma_p(u,T)^2 + 2\rho\sigma_p(u,T)\sigma_S]du\end{aligned}$$

Now, it is possible to introduce the time change τ defined as

$$\tau(t) = \int_0^t [\sigma_S^2 + \sigma_p(u,T)^2 + 2\rho\sigma_p(u,T)\sigma_S]du = \int_0^t \sigma_F(u,T)^2 du$$

with

$$\tau^* = \tau(T) = \int_0^t [\sigma_S^2 + \sigma_p(u,T)^2 + 2\rho\sigma_p(u,T)\sigma_A]du.$$

We can use Eq. (22.21) to show the existence of two standard one-dimensional Brownian motions Y^P and Y^S under the appropriate probabilities Q^P and Q^S such that

$$\frac{S_t}{P(t,T)} = \frac{S_0}{P(0,T)} e^{Y^p_{\tau(t)} - \frac{1}{2}\tau(t)}, \quad \frac{P(t,T)}{A_t} = \frac{P(0,T)}{A_0} e Y^A_{\tau(t)} - \frac{1}{2}\tau(t).$$

Using these two last expressions and Eq. (22.22), the European call price is:

$$C_S = S_0 E_{Q^A}\left[I_{Y^S_{\tau^*} \leq \ln \frac{S_0}{KP(0,T)} + \frac{\tau}{2}}\right] - KP(0,T)E_{Q^S}\left[I_{Y^P_{\tau^*} \geq \ln \frac{S_0}{KP(0,T)} + \frac{\tau^*}{2}}\right]$$

The computation of this equation is straightforward. Hence, the European option price is:

$$C_S = S_0 N\left(\frac{\ln\left(\frac{S_0}{KP(0,T)}\right) + \frac{\tau^*}{2}}{\sqrt{\tau^*}}\right) - KP(0,T)N\left(\frac{\ln\left(\frac{S_0}{KP(0,T)}\right) - \frac{\tau^*}{2}}{\sqrt{\tau^*}}\right) \tag{22.23}$$

We can compare this martingale approach with the PDE approach. Consider the following change of variable in Eq. (22.20)

$$\tau(t) = \int_0^t \sigma_F(u,T)^2$$

In this case, the forward option price C_F as a function of F and τ satisfies the equation:

$$\frac{\partial C_F}{\partial \tau} + \frac{1}{2}F^2\frac{\partial^2 C_F}{\partial F^2} = 0$$

under the appropriate terminal condition $C_F = \max[F - K, 0]$. The equation gives the price of a European option of a forward contract with a strike price K, a maturity date τ^* and a unit volatility for the underlying asset. The solution as given by the martingale approach

(22.23) can also be stated as the solution to the standard Black–Scholes–Merton (1973) equation:

$$C_S = P(0,T)C_F(F_0) = P(0,T)C\left(\frac{S_0}{P(0,T)}, \tau^*, 1, 0\right)$$

where C is the extended Black–Scholes equation defined by:

$$C(S_0, T, \sigma_S, r) = S_0N(d_1) - Ke^{-rt}N(d_2)$$

$$d_1 = \frac{\ln\left(\frac{S_0}{K}\right) + \left(r + \frac{\sigma_S^2}{2}\right)T}{\sigma_S\sqrt{T}} = d_2 + \sigma_S\sqrt{T}.$$

The above analysis shows that the change of numeraire absorbs the stochastic character in the pricing of stock options when interest rates are random. This allows to transform the economy into a new economy in which the forward volatility is unity.

22.5. Valuation in an Extended Black and Scholes Economy in the Presence of Information Costs

Consider the dynamics of the option's underlying stock

$$\frac{dS_t}{S_t} = (r + \lambda_S)dt + \sigma_S dW_2(t)$$

where λ_S corresponds to the shadow cost of incomplete information on asset S. We have shown by arbitrage arguments that the extended Black–Scholes equation in the presence of information costs is given by:

$$\frac{\partial C}{\partial t} + \frac{1}{2}\sigma_S^2 S^2 \frac{\partial^2 C}{\partial S^2} + (r + \lambda_S)S\frac{\partial C}{\partial S} - (r + \lambda_c)C = 0 \tag{22.24}$$

The dynamics of this portfolio are given by:

$$dV = C(r + \lambda_c)dt - \left(S\frac{\partial C}{\partial S}\right)(r + \lambda_c)dt + \frac{\partial C}{\partial S}dS \tag{22.25}$$

Using Ito's lemma gives:

$$dV = \left(\frac{\partial C}{\partial t} + \frac{1}{2}\sigma_S^2 S^2 \frac{\partial^2 C}{\partial S^2}\right) dt + \frac{\partial C}{\partial S} dS \tag{22.26}$$

The difference between Eqs. (22.26) and (22.25) is the partial differential Eq. (22.24). The solution for a European call is:

$$C(S_0, T, \sigma_S, r) = S_0 e^{-(\lambda_S - \lambda_c)t} N(d_1) - K e^{-(r+\lambda_c)t} N(d_2)$$

$$d_1 = \frac{\ln\left(\frac{S_0}{K}\right) + \left(r + \lambda_S + \frac{\sigma_S^2}{2}\right) T}{\sigma_S \sqrt{T}} = d_2 + \sigma_S \sqrt{T}$$

Now, consider the following change of variables:

$$f_t = S_t e^{(r+\lambda_S)(T-t)}, \quad C_f = C e^{(r+\lambda_c)(T-t)}$$

Consider also the time change in Eq. (22.24)

$$\tau = \sigma_S^2 t, \quad \tau^* = \sigma_S^2 T$$

The change of underlying asset f in Eq. (22.24) gives:

$$\frac{\partial C}{\partial t} + \frac{1}{2}\sigma_S^2 f^2 \frac{\partial^2 C}{\partial f^2} - (r + \lambda_c) C = 0 \tag{22.27}$$

This last equation corresponds to the extended Black (1976) equation in the presence of information costs. It gives the value of an option on a forward contract f. The dynamics of the replicating portfolio can be written as:

$$dV = C(r + \lambda_c) dt + \frac{\partial C}{\partial f} df$$

Using Ito's lemma

$$dV = \left(\frac{\partial C}{\partial t} + \frac{1}{2}\sigma_A^2 f^2 \frac{\partial^2 C}{\partial f^2}\right) + \frac{\partial C}{\partial f} df$$

gives the dynamics of C. When $C_f = C e^{(r+\lambda_c)(T-t)}$, this change of variables accounts for the following expression:

$$\frac{\partial C_f}{\partial t} + \frac{1}{2}\sigma_A^2 f^2 \frac{\partial^2 C_f}{\partial f^2} = 0 \tag{22.28}$$

The dynamics of the replicating portfolio are given by $dV_f = \frac{\partial C_f}{\partial f} df$ and Ito's lemma gives:

$$dV_f = \left(\frac{\partial C_f}{\partial t} + \frac{1}{2}\sigma_S^2 f^2 \frac{\partial^2 C_f}{\partial f^2} \right) dt + \frac{\partial C_f}{\partial f} df$$

It is possible to use a change of variables for τ and τ^* to simplify Eq. (22.28) to the following form:

$$\frac{\partial C_f}{\partial \tau} + \frac{1}{2} f^2 \frac{\partial^2 C_f}{\partial f^2} = 0 \tag{22.29}$$

This last equation is useful for the valuation of a forward option on a forward contract maturing in τ^* for which the volatility is equal to one. In this case, the solution for a forward call on a forward contract is given by:

$$C_f(f_0, \tau^*) = C(f_0, \tau^*, 1, 0) = f_0 N(d_1) - KN(d_2)$$

since

$$\frac{\ln\left(\frac{f_0}{K}\right) + \frac{\tau^*}{2}}{\sqrt{\tau^*}} = \frac{\ln\left(\frac{S_0}{K}\right) + \left(r + \lambda_S + \frac{\sigma_S^2}{2}\right) T}{\sigma_S \sqrt{T}}$$

A simple comparison of Eqs. (22.29) and (22.24) reveals that the option is priced as if the interest rate were zero and there are no information costs in the economy. Besides the volatility is replaced by 1 and the maturity T by τ^*.

22.5.1. *Changing numeraire and time*

We know that:

$$E_Q\left[\frac{h(T)}{B(T)}\right] = P(0,T) E_{Q^X}[h(T)]$$

The effect of this change of numeraire can be appreciated using the Black–Scholes context for the pricing of a European call option on an asset S in the presence of a stochastic interest rate. Let us use the following dynamics for the underlying asset

$$\frac{dS_t}{S_t} = (r + \lambda_S)dt + \sigma_S dW_2(t)$$

It is possible to show that the European call price in the presence of information costs must satisfy the following partial differential equation:

$$\frac{\partial C_S}{\partial t} + \frac{1}{2}\sigma_S^2 S^2 \frac{\partial^2 C_S}{\partial S^2} + \frac{1}{2}\sigma_p^2 P^2 \frac{\partial^2 C_S}{\partial P^2} - \rho\sigma_S\sigma_P SP \frac{\partial^2 C_S}{\partial S \partial P} + (r+\lambda_S)S\frac{\partial C_S}{\partial S} + (r+\lambda_P)P\frac{\partial C_S}{\partial P} - (r+\lambda_c)C_S = 0 \tag{22.30}$$

This equation must be solved under the following terminal condition

$$C_S = \max[S - K, 0]$$

Equation (22.30) can be written, after simplification as Eqs. (22.19) and (22.20). When the change of probability is used as before, the European call price is given by:

$$C_S = S_0 E^{Q^S}\left[I_{\frac{P(T,T)}{S_T} \le K}\right] - KP(0,T)\ E^{Q^P}\left[I_{\frac{S_T}{P(T,T)} \ge K}\right]$$

22.5.2. *The change of time*

Consider a continuous P-martingale and the Eqs. (22.21) to (22.23). Using the same procedure, the solution for a call as given by the martingale approach can also be stated as the solution to the standard Black–Scholes–Merton (1973)

$$C_S = P(0,T)C_F(F_0) = P(0,T)C\left(\frac{S_0}{P(0,T)}, \tau^*, 1, 0\right)$$

where C is the extended Black–Scholes equation

$$C(S_0, T, \sigma_S, r) = S_0 e^{-(\lambda_S - \lambda_c)t} N(d_1) - Ke^{-(r+\lambda_c)t} N(d_2)$$

$$d_1 = \frac{\ln\left(\frac{S_0}{K}\right) + (r + \lambda_S + \frac{\sigma_S^2}{2})T}{\sigma_S\sqrt{T}} = d_2 + \sigma_S\sqrt{T}$$

The above analysis shows that the change of numeraire absorbs the stochastic character in the pricing of stock options when interest rates are random. This allows to transform the economy into a new economy in which the forward volatility is unity.

Summary

This chapter contains the basic material for the pricing of derivative assets in a continuous-time framework. The presentation is made as simple as possible in order to enable uninformed readers to understand the main derivations.

First, we present in detail the search for an analytic formula for European call option within the partial differential equation method.

Second, we illustrate in detail the martingale method for the derivation of a European call formula.

Third, we develop the foundations of some interest rate models. Fourth, we present two mathematical tools, the change of numeraire and time change, in order to facilitate the pricing of options. These two transformations have an economic significance and can simplify considerably some valuation problems. While this chapter is necessary for the understanding of the basic techniques of option pricing theory, it is not necessary for the use and applications of all the formulas presented in this book.

References

Arrow, KJ (1953). Le rôle des valeurs boursières pour la rèpartition la meilleur des risques. *International Colloquium on Econometrics*, 1952, CNRS, Paris.

Bellalah, M (2001). Market imperfections; information costs and the valuation of derivatives: some general results. *International Journal of Finance*, 13(3), 1895–1927.

Bellalah, M and JL Prigent (2001). Pricing standard and exotic options in the presence of a finite mixture of Gaussian Distributions. *International Journal of Finance*, 13(3), 1975–2000.

Bellalah, M and F Selmi (2001). On the quadratic criteria for hedging under transaction costs. *International Journal of Finance*, 13(3), 2001–2020.

Bellalah, M, Ma Bellalah and R Portait (2001). The cost of capital in international finance. *International Journal of Finance*, 13(3), 1958–1973.

Bellalah, M, JL Prigent and C Villa (2001a). Skew without Skewness: Asymmetric smiles; information costs and stochastic volatilities. *International Journal of Finance*, 13(2), 1826–1837.

Bellalah M (2018a). On information costs, short sales and the pricing of extendible options, steps and Parisian options. *Annals of Operations Research*, 262(2), (March), 361–387.

Bellalah M (2018b). Pricing derivatives in the presence of shadow costs of incomplete information and short sales. *Annals of Operations Research*, 262(2), (March).

Black, F (1976). The pricing of commodity contracts. *Journal of Financial Economics*, 79(3), 167–179.

Black, F and M Scholes (1973). The pricing of options and corporate liabilities. *Journal of Political Economy*, 81, 637–659.

Cox, JC and SA Ross (1976). The valuation of options for alternative stochastic processes. *Journal of Financial Economics*, 3, 145–66.

Cox, J, J Ingersoll and S Ross (1985). A theory of the term structure of interest rates. *Econometrica* 53, 385–407.

Debreu, G (1954). Representation of a preference ordering by a numerical function. In Thrall R, C Coombs and R Davis (eds.) *Decision Processes*, Wiley, New York, pp. 159–165.

El Karouin N and H Geman (1993). A probabilistic approach to the valuation of general floating rate notes with an application to interest swaps. Unpublished working paper.

Harrison, JM and D Kreps (1979). Martingales and arbitrage in multiperiod securities markets. *Journal of Economic Theory*, 20, 381–408.

Harrison, JM and S Pliska (1981). Martingales and stochastic integrals in the theory of continuous trading. *Stochastic Processes and their Applications*, 11, 215–260.

Longstaff, FA (1990). Time varying term premiums and traditional hypothesis about the term structure. *Journal of Finance*, 45, 1307–1314.

Merton, R (1973). Theory of rational option pricing. *Bell Journal of Economics and Management Science*, 4, 141–183.

Musiela, M (1997). *Martingale Methods in Financial Modelling: Theory and Applications*. Springer: Berlin.

Vasicek, O (1977). A equilibrium characterization of the term structure. *Journal of Financial Economics*, 5, 177–188.

Chapter 23

Simple Extensions and Generalizations of the Black–Scholes Type Models in the Presence of Information Costs

Chapter Outline

This chapter is organized as follows:

1. Section 23.1 provides a simple derivation of the differential equation for a derivative security on a spot asset in the presence of a continuous dividend yield and information costs.
2. Section 23.2 presents the valuation of securities dependent on several variables in the presence of incomplete information.
3. Section 23.3 provides the general differential equation for the pricing of derivatives.
4. Section 23.4 gives the extension of the risk-neutral argument in the presence of information costs.
5. Section 23.5 provides an extension of the analysis to commodity futures prices in the presence of information costs.

Introduction

This chapter develops a general context for the analysis and valuation of options and futures contracts in the presence of one or several state variables and information uncertainty. We provide a simple derivation of the differential equation for a derivative security on a spot asset in the presence of a continuous dividend yield and information costs. Then, we extend this analysis to account for several state variables. This allows the derivation of the valuation equation for securities dependent on several variables in the presence of incomplete information. When a variable does not indicate the price of a traded security, its market price of risk corresponds to the market price of risk of a traded security, whose price is a function only on the value of the variable and time. The value of the market price of risk of the variable is the same at each instant of time. We also show, how to extend the risk-neutral argument in the presence of information costs and how to apply this analysis for the valuation of commodity futures within incomplete information.

23.1. Differential Equation for a Derivative Security on a Spot Asset in the Presence of a Continuous Dividend Yield and Information Costs

We denote by f the price of a derivative security on a stock with a continuous dividend yield q. The dynamics of the underlying asset are given by:

$$dS = \mu S dt + \sigma S dz$$

where the drift term μ and the volatility σ are constants. Using Ito's lemma for the function $f(S,t)$ gives:

$$dV = \left(\frac{\partial V}{dS} \quad \mu S + \frac{dV}{dt} + \frac{1}{2}\frac{\partial^2 V}{\partial S^2}\sigma^2 S^2\right) dt + \frac{\partial V}{\partial S}\sigma S dz.$$

It is possible to construct a portfolio Π by holding a position in the derivative security and a certain number of units of the underlying asset:

$$\Pi = -V + \frac{\partial V}{dS} S.$$

Over a short time interval, the change in the portfolio value can be written as:

$$\Delta\Pi = \left(-\frac{\partial V}{\partial t} - \frac{1}{2}\frac{\partial^2 V}{\partial S^2}\sigma^2 S^2\right)\Delta t.$$

Over the same time interval, dividends are given by $qS\frac{\partial V}{\partial S}\Delta t$.

We denote by ΔW, the change in the wealth of the portfolio holder. In this case, we have:

$$\Delta W = \left(-\frac{\partial V}{\partial t} - \frac{1}{2}\frac{\partial^2 f}{\partial S^2}\sigma^2 S^2 + qS\frac{\partial V}{dS}\right)\Delta t.$$

Since this change is independent of the Wiener process, the portfolio is instantaneously risk less and must earn the risk-free rate plus information costs or:

$$\left(-\frac{\partial V}{\partial t} - \frac{1}{2}\frac{\partial^2 f}{\partial S^2}\sigma^2 S^2 + qS\frac{\partial V}{\partial S}\right)\Delta t = -(r+\lambda_V)V\Delta t+(r+\lambda_S)S\frac{\partial V}{\partial S}\Delta t$$

where λ_i refers to these costs. This gives:

$$\frac{\partial V}{\partial t} + (r + \lambda_S - q)S\frac{\partial V}{\partial S} + \frac{1}{2}\frac{\partial^2 V}{\partial S^2}\sigma^2 S^2 = (r + \lambda_V)V. \tag{23.1}$$

Equation (23.1) must be satisfied by the derivative security in the presence of information costs and a continuous dividend yield.

23.2. The Valuation of Securities Dependent on Several Variables in the Presence of Incomplete Information: A General Method

When a variable does not indicate the price of a traded security, the pricing of derivatives must account for the market price of risk. The market price of risk γ for a traded security is given by:

$$\gamma = \frac{\mu - r - \lambda}{\sigma} \tag{23.2}$$

where μ indicates the expected return from the security.

This equation can also be written as:

$$\mu - r - \lambda = \gamma\sigma. \tag{23.3}$$

The excess return over the risk-free rate in the presence of shadow costs on a security corresponds to its market price of risk multiplied by its volatility.

When $\gamma > 0$, the expected return on an asset is higher than the risk-free rate plus information costs.

When $\gamma = 0$, the expected return on an asset is exactly the risk free rate plus information costs.

When $\gamma < 0$, the expected return on an asset is less than the risk free rate plus information costs.

When a variable does not indicate the price of a traded security, its market price of risk corresponds to the market price of risk of a traded security whose price is a function only on the value of the variable and time. The value of the market price of risk of the variable is the same at each instant of time. In fact, we can show as shown by Hull (for details, refer to Bellalah *et al.*, 1998) that two traded securities depending on the same asset must have the same price of risk, i.e., that Eq. (23.2) must be verified. Consider the following dynamics for a variable θ, which is not a tradable asset:

$$\frac{d\theta}{\theta} = \mu(\theta, t)dt + s(\theta, t)dz.$$

We denote this by V_1 and V_2, respectively the prices of two derivative securities as a function of θ and t. The dynamics of these derivatives can be written as:

$$\frac{dV_1}{V_1} = \mu_1 dt + \sigma_1 dz \tag{23.4}$$

$$\frac{dV_2}{V_2} = \mu_1 dt + \sigma_2 dz. \tag{23.5}$$

These two processes can be written in discrete time as:

$$\Delta V_1 = \mu_1 V_1 \Delta t + \sigma_1 V_1 \Delta z \tag{23.6}$$

$$\Delta V_2 = \mu_2 V_2 \Delta t + \sigma_2 V_2 \Delta z. \tag{23.7}$$

It is possible to construct a portfolio Π which is risk free using $\sigma_2 V_2$ of the first derivative security and $-\sigma_1 V_1$ of the second derivative security.

$$\Pi = \sigma_2 V_2 V_1 - \sigma_1 V_1 V_2.$$

The change in the value of this portfolio can be written as:

$$\Delta\Pi = \sigma_2 V_2 \Delta V_1 - \sigma_1 V_1 \Delta V_2.$$

Using Eqs. (23.6) and (23.7), the change in the portfolio value can be written as:

$$\Delta\Pi = \mu_1 \sigma_2 V_1 V_2 - \mu_2 \sigma_1 V_1 V_2 \Delta t.$$

Since the portfolio Π is instantaneously risk less, it must earn the risk free rate plus information costs on both markets. Hence, we must have:

$$\mu_1 \sigma_2 - \mu_2 \sigma_1 = (r + \lambda_1)\sigma_2 - (r + \lambda_2)\sigma_1$$

or

$$\frac{\mu_1 - (r + \lambda_1)}{\sigma_1} = \frac{\mu_2 - (r + \lambda_2)}{\sigma_2}. \tag{23.8}$$

The term $\frac{\mu-(r+\lambda)}{\sigma}$ must be the same for all securities that depend on time and the variable θ. It is also possible to show that V_1 and V_2 must depend positively on θ. Since, the volatility of V_1 is σ_1, it is possible to use Ito's lemma for σ_1 to obtain:

$$\sigma_1 V_1 = s\theta \frac{\partial V_1}{\partial \theta}.$$

Hence, when V_1 is positively related to the variable θ, the σ_1 is positive and corresponds to the volatility of V_1. But, when f_1 is negatively related to the variable θ, σ_1 is negative and Eq. (23.4) can be written as:

$$\frac{dV_1}{V_1} = \mu_1 dt + (-\sigma_1)(-dz).$$

This indicates that the volatility is $-\sigma_1$ rather than σ_1. The result in Eq. (23.3) can be generalized to n state variables.

Consider n variables, which are assumed to follow Ito diffusion processes, where for each state variable i between 1 and n, we have:

$$\theta_i = m_i\theta_i dt + s_i\theta_i dz_i$$

where dz_i are Wiener processes. The terms m_i and s_i correspond to the expected growth rate and the volatility of the θ_i with $(i = 1, \dots, n)$. The price process for a derivative security that depends on the variables θ_i can be written as:

$$\frac{dV}{V} = \mu dt + \sum_{i=1}^{n} \sigma_i dz_i \tag{23.9}$$

where μ corresponds to the expected return from the security and σ_i is its volatility. The volatility of V is σ_i when all the underlying variables except θ_i are kept fixed. This result is obtained directly using an extension of the generalized version of Ito's lemma in its discrete form. We show in supplementary material that:

$$\mu - r - \lambda_V = \sum_{i=1}^{n} \gamma_i\sigma_i \tag{23.10}$$

where γ_i indicates the market price of risk for the variable θ_i.

Equation (23.10) shows that the expected excess return on the security (option) in the presence of shadow costs depends on γ_i and σ_i.

When $\gamma_i\sigma_i > 0$, a higher return is required by investors to get compensated for the risk arising from the variable θ_i.

When $\gamma_i\sigma_i < 0$, a lower return is required by investors to get compensated for the risk arising from θ_i.

23.3. The General Differential Equation for the Pricing of Derivatives

We denote by

- θ_i: value of ith state variable;
- m_i: expected growth in ith state variable;
- γ_i: market price of risk of ith state variable;
- s_i: volatility of ith state variable;

- r: instantaneous risk-free rate and
- λ_i: shadow cost of incomplete information of ith state variable,

where i takes the values from 1 to n.

Garman (1976) and Cox *et al.* (1985) have shown that the price of any contingent claim must satisfy the following partial differential equation:

$$\frac{\partial V}{\partial t} + \sum_i \theta_i \frac{\partial V}{\partial \theta_i}(m_i - \gamma_i s_i) + \frac{1}{2}\sum_{i,k} \rho_{i,k} s_i s_k \theta_i \theta_k \frac{\partial^2 f}{\partial \theta_i \partial \theta_k} = rf$$

where $\rho_{i,k}$ stands for the correlation coefficient between the variables θ_i and θ_k.

We show in supplementary material, how to obtain a similar equation in the presence of incomplete information. In this context, the equation becomes:

$$\frac{\partial V}{\partial t} + \sum_i \theta_i \frac{\partial V}{\partial \theta_i}(m_i - \gamma_i s_i) + \frac{1}{2}\sum_{i,k} \rho_{i,k} s_i s_k \theta_i \theta_k \frac{\partial^2 V}{\partial \theta_i \partial \theta_k} = (r + \lambda)V. \tag{23.11}$$

In the presence of a single state variable, θ, Eq. (23.11) becomes:

$$\frac{\partial V}{\partial t} + \theta \frac{\partial V}{\partial \theta}(m - \gamma s) + \frac{1}{2} s^2 \theta^2 \frac{\partial^2 V}{\partial^2 \theta} = (r + \lambda)V. \tag{23.12}$$

For a non-dividend paying security, the expected return and volatility must satisfy: $m - r - \lambda = \gamma s$ and $m - \gamma s = r + \lambda$.

In this case, Eq. (23.12) becomes the extended Black–Scholes equation in the presence of information costs.

For a dividend-paying security at a rate q, we have:

$$q + m - r - \lambda = \gamma s \quad \text{or} \quad m - \gamma s = r + \lambda - q.$$

In this case, Eq. (23.12) becomes (23.1)

$$\frac{\partial V}{\partial t} + (r + \lambda_s - q) S \frac{\partial V}{\partial S} + \frac{1}{2} s^2 S^2 \frac{\partial^2 V}{\partial^2 S} = (r + \lambda_V)V.$$

23.4. Extension of the Risk-Neutral Argument in the Presence of Information Costs

We know that the market price of risk is given by

$$\gamma = \frac{\mu - r - \lambda}{\sigma} \quad \text{or} \quad \mu - r - \lambda = \gamma\sigma.$$

Supplementary material shows how to price a derivative as if the world were risk neutral. This is possible when the expected growth rate of each state variable is $(m_i - \gamma_i s_i)$ rather than m_i.

For the case of a non-dividend paying traded asset, using Eq. (23.5), we have

$$m_i - r - \lambda_i = \gamma_i s_i \quad \text{or} \quad m_i - \gamma_i si = r + \lambda_i.$$

This result shows that a change in the expected growth rate of the state variable from θ_i to $(m_i - \gamma_i si)$ is equivalent to using an expected return from the security equal to the risk-less rate plus shadow costs of incomplete information.

For the case of a dividend-paying traded asset, we have

$$q_i + m_i - r - \lambda_i = \gamma_i s_i \quad \text{or} \quad m_i - \gamma_i s_i = r + \lambda_i - q_i.$$

This result shows that a change in the expected growth rate of the state variable from θ_i to $(m_i - \gamma_i si)$ is equivalent to using an expected return (including continuous dividends at a rate q) from the security equal to the risk-less rate plus shadow costs of incomplete information. This analysis allows the pricing of any derivative security as the value of its expected payoff discounted to the present at the risk-free rate plus the information cost on this security or:

$$f = e^{-(r+\lambda_V)(T-t)} \hat{E}[f_T] \tag{23.13}$$

where V_T corresponds to the security's payoff at maturity T and $\hat{E}$ is to the expectation operator in a risk-neutral economy. This refers to an economy where the drift rate in θ_i corresponds to $(m_i - \gamma_i si)$. When the interest rate r is stochastic, it is considered as the other underlying state variables.

In this case, the drift rate in r becomes $\gamma_r s_r$ where γ_r refers to the market price of risk related to r. The term s_r indicates its volatility.

In this case, the pricing of a derivative is given by the discounting of its terminal payoff at the average value of r as:

$$V = \hat{E}[e^{-(\bar{r}+\lambda_V)(T-t)}V_T] \tag{23.14}$$

where $\bar{r}$ corresponds to the average risk-free rate between current time t and maturity T.

23.5. Extension to Commodity Futures Prices within Incomplete Information

Consider the pricing of a long position in a commodity forward contract with delivery price K and maturity T.

23.5.1. *Differential equation for a derivative security dependent on a futures price in the presence of information costs*

Assume that the relationship between the futures price F and the spot price S is given by $F = Se^{\alpha(T-t)}$, where α depends only on time. In this case, if the volatility of the underlying asset is constant, then the volatility of F is constant and equal to that of S. The dynamics of the spot asset are given by $dS = \mu S dt + \sigma S dz$, where μ is the instantaneous expected return, σ is the instantaneous volatility, and dz is an increment of a Wiener process. Using Ito's lemma, the volatility of the futures price σ_F is given by:

$$\sigma_F F = \sigma S \frac{\partial F}{\partial S} = \sigma S e^{\alpha(T-t)} = \sigma F.$$

Hence, the volatility of the futures price is equal to the volatility of the spot price and $\sigma_F = \sigma$. Now, consider the following dynamics for the futures price:

$$dF = \mu_F F dt + \sigma F dz.$$

Since the derivative asset price $f(F, t)$ is a function of the futures price F and time t, using Ito's lemma gives:

$$f = \left(\frac{\partial f}{\partial F}\mu_F F + \frac{\partial f}{\partial t} + \frac{1}{2}\frac{\partial^2 f}{\partial F^2}\sigma^2 F^2\right) dt + \frac{\partial f}{\partial F}\sigma F dz.$$

Consider the value of a portfolio comprising the derivative security and a position in a certain number of the underlying futures contracts. The total change in wealth for the portfolio holder over a short time interval can be written as:

$$\Delta W = \frac{\partial f}{\partial F}\Delta F - \Delta f.$$

The discrete versions of the previous equations for dF and df can be written as:

$$\Delta F = \mu_F F \Delta t + \sigma F \Delta z$$

and

$$\Delta f = \left(-\frac{\partial f}{\partial F}\mu_F F + \frac{\partial f}{\partial t} + \frac{1}{2}\frac{\partial^2 f}{\partial F^2}\sigma^2 F^2\right)\Delta t + \sigma F \frac{\partial f}{\partial F}\Delta z$$

where $\Delta z = \epsilon\sqrt{\Delta t}$.

Hence, we have:

$$\Delta W = \left(-\frac{\partial f}{\partial t} - \frac{1}{2}\frac{\partial^2 f}{\partial F^2}\sigma^2 F^2\right)\Delta t.$$

Since this change in value is risk free, it must earn the risk free rate plus information costs or:

$$\left[-\frac{\partial f}{\partial t} - \frac{1}{2}\frac{\partial^2 f}{\partial F^2}\sigma^2 F^2\right]\Delta t = -(r + \lambda_f) f \Delta t$$

and this gives

$$\frac{\partial f}{\partial t} + \frac{1}{2}\frac{\partial^2 f}{\partial F^2}\sigma^2 F^2 = (r + \lambda_f) f.$$

This equation must be satisfied by a derivative security dependent on a futures price in the presence of information uncertainty.

23.5.2. *Commodity futures prices*

We denote by S the spot price of the commodity, F, the futures price, μ the growth rate of the commodity price, σ its volatility, and Γ its market price of risk. Using the extension of the risk-neutral valuation principle, the price is given by

$$V = e^{-(r+\lambda_V)(T-t)}\hat{E}[S_T - K] \quad \text{or} \quad f = e^{-(r+\lambda_f)(T-t)}(\hat{E}[S_T] - K) \tag{23.15}$$

where $\hat{E}(.)$ refers to the expected value in a risk-neutral economy.

The forward or futures price F corresponds to the value of K that makes the value of the contract f equal to zero in Eq. (23.15). So, we have:

$$F = \hat{E}[S_T]. \tag{23.16}$$

Equation (23.16) shows that the futures price corresponds to the expected spot price in a risk-neutral world. If $(\gamma\sigma)$ is constant and the drift μ is a function of time then:

$$\hat{E}[S_T] = E[S_T]e^{-\gamma\sigma(T-t)}$$

where E corresponds to the real expectations or the expectations in the real world. Using Eq. (23.16), we have:

$$F = E[S_T]e^{-\gamma\sigma(T-t)}. \tag{23.17}$$

If $\gamma = 0$, the futures price is an unbiased estimate of the expected spot price. However, if $\gamma > 0$, the futures price corresponds to a downward-biased estimate of the expected spot price. If $\gamma < 0$, the futures price is a downward-biased estimate of the expected spot price.

23.5.3. *Convenience yields*

When the drift or the expected growth in the commodity price is constant, we have $E(S_T) = Se^{\mu(T-t)}$, Using Eq. (23.17), we have $F = Se^{(\mu-\gamma\sigma)(T-t)}$.

This last equation is consistent with the cost of carry model, when the convenience yield y satisfies the relationship:

$$\mu - \gamma\sigma = r + \lambda + g - y. \tag{23.18}$$

This equation shows that the commodity can be assimilated to a traded security paying a continuous dividend yield equal to the convenience yield y minus the storage costs u. Hence, the convenience yield must satisfy the relationship:

$$y = g + r + \lambda - \mu + \gamma\sigma.$$

When the convenience yield is zero, we have

$$\mu - \gamma\sigma = r + \lambda + g.$$

This result shows that some commodities can be assimilated to traded securities paying negative dividend yields, which are equal to storage costs. The main derivations in this chapter appear in Bellalah (1999).

Summary

This chapter develops a general context for the pricing of derivative assets.

First, we derive the differential equation for a derivative security on a spot asset in the presence of a continuous dividend yield and information costs.

Second, we provide the valuation of securities dependent on several variables in the presence of incomplete information.

Third, we propose the general differential equation in the same context.

Fourth, we show how to extend the risk-neutral argument in the presence of information costs.

Fifth, we extend the analysis to the valuation of commodity futures contracts within incomplete information.

References

Bellalah M (1999). The valuation of futures and commodity options with information costs. *Journal of Futures Markets*, 19 (September), 645–664.

Briys E, M Bellalah, *et al.* (1998). *Options, Futures and Exotic Derivatives.* En collaboration avec E. Briys *et al.* John Wiley & Sons, London.

Cox JC, JE Ingersoll and SA Ross (1985). A theory of the term structure of interest rates. *Econometrica*, 53, 385–407.

Garman M (1976). A general theory of asset valuation under diffusion state processes. *Working Paper*, No. 50, University of California, Berkeley.

Chapter 24

Extension of Asset and Risk Management in the Presence of American Options: Dividends, Early Exercise, and Information Uncertainty

Chapter Outline

This chapter is organized as follows:

1. Section 24.1 is an introduction to the general context for the pricing of American options with and without distributions to the underlying asset.
2. Section 24.2 studies the valuation of American spot and futures options in the context of a constant proportional rate.
3. Section 24.3 deals with the valuation of American spot and futures options in the context of a constant proportional rate within incomplete information.
4. Section 24.4 studies the valuation of American options when there are discrete distributions to the underlying asset.
5. Section 24.5 deals with the valuation of American options when there are discrete distributions to the underlying asset within incomplete information.
6. Section 24.6 is devoted to the valuation of compound options within incomplete information.

Introduction

There are several extensions of the basic Black and Scholes (1973) model. We have already seen the first extension by Black (1976) who takes into account the specificities of futures contracts. The second extension was made by Garman and Kohlhagen (1983) who derive analytical valuation formulas for European options on currencies. In the same year, Grabbe (1983) implemented a similar approach to that used in Black (1976) to provide the value of options on foreign currencies. Merton (1973) indirectly and Barone-Adesi and Whaley (1987), hereafter Barone-Adesi and Whaley (1987) provided the values of European commodity options and commodity futures options. All these models apply only to European options. Since, all the proposed analytical models deal with the pricing of the European options in the absence of discrete distributions to the underlying assets, the extensions of the analytical models to the valuation of American options are proposed in this chapter.

The two important extensions and contributions to the literature on the valuation of American options are those of Merton (1973) and Geske (1979). The pricing of American options is first analyzed by Merton (1973) who showed the difficulties in obtaining closed-form solutions when there are discrete distributions to the underlying asset. However, he provided closed-form solutions for American options when the time to maturity is infinite. Geske (1979) provided analytical formulas for the valuation of options on options or compound options. He used a valuation by duplication technique for the pricing of American options. A compound option can be defined as an option on the firm's equity. For a levered equity firm (a firm with debt in its capital structure), equity can be seen as a call on the value of the assets. This was first noted by Black and Scholes (1973); B–S, who considered the option on equity as an option on the value of the firm's asset. Geske's approach is interesting since it allows the valuation of American options and includes the question of dividend.

American option pricing models have been proposed by several authors. However, given the difficulties in obtaining closed-form solutions, it became quite a natural way to resort to analytical approximation models, binomial methods, and numerical techniques. When there are continuous distributions to the underlying asset, the literature on the valuation of American options provides some analytical approximation formulas. Barone-Adesi and Whaley (1987) presented simple analytic approximations for the pricing of American options on commodity futures contracts. These formulas are accurate and computationally more efficient than compound-option pricing models, binomial models, and finite difference methods. The approach relies on a quadratic approximation method similar to that used by McMillan (1986) for the valuation of the American put option on a non-dividend-paying stock. However, the formulas apply only for a constant proportional rate.

When there are discrete distributions to the underlying asset, the valuation of American options is more complex. In this context, models were proposed by several authors including Roll (1977), Geske (1979), and Whaley (1981, 1986) for call options. Put formulas were proposed by Johnson (1983), Geske and Johnson (1984), Geske and Shastri (1985), Blomeyer (1986), and Barone-Adesi and Whaley (1987), among others. Most of these models, if not all, are based on the concept of compound options. The compound option or an option on an option has been studied in a context of complete information by several authors. The concept of an option on an option is important in the study of several opportunities with a sequential nature where some of them are available only if earlier opportunities are undertaken. Black and Scholes (1973), Black and Cox (1976), Galai and Masulis (1976), and Geske (1979) show that several corporate liabilities may be considered as options. In a context of complete information, they studied the pricing of a firm's common stock and bonds by considering the stock as an option on the firm's value. They showed that corporate investment opportunities may be analyzed as options and compound options. However, their analysis does not account for information uncertainty. We use arbitrage arguments to derive the formula in a Black and Scholes (1973) economy. Such a formula might be applied to the valuation of equity in the capital structure of the firm. The information uncertainty about the firm and its cash flows reflects the agency costs and the asymmetric information problems. By assuming the stock as an option on the value of the firm, the value of the call as a compound option can be derived as a function of the firm's value by accounting for information costs and the effects of leverage. We present two alternative derivations for the value of the firm's stock as a compound option in the presence of information costs. For the analysis of information costs and valuation, we can refer to Bellalah (2001), Bellalah *et al.* (2001a, 2001b), Bellalah and Prigent (2001), Bellalah and Selmi (2001), etc.

24.1. The Valuation of American Options: The General Problem

Two problems arise in the valuation of American options. The first is associated with the possibility of early exercise. The second is linked to the distributions to the underlying asset. The nonexistence of a put call parity theorem for American options implies a distinct treatment for call and put options. The problem is different according to the pattern of distributions to the underlying asset. In fact, if the dividend stream is continuous, it may not induce the optimal early exercise of American options. However, when the dividends are discrete, this may induce early exercise of American options.

24.1.1. *Early exercise of American calls*

We deal with the main reasons behind rational exercise of American options.

24.1.1.1. *Exercise without distributions*

When there are no distributions to the underlying asset, there is no incentive to exercise an American call option before its maturity date. Hence, the value of an American call is equal to that of a European call. This result is due to Theorems 1 and 2 of Merton (1973) where it is shown that in the absence of dividend payments, an American call will never be exercised prior to expiration. In this context, the value of an American call is equivalent to that of a European call when the interest rates are constant. The intuition of this result is simple. In the absence of dividends, the option is worth more "alive" than "dead" because of its time value. Killing the option would mean pocketing its intrinsic value while losing its speculative. The investor is better off in selling the option rather than killing it.

24.1.1.2. *Early exercise with continuous distributions*

When dividends are paid continuously at a constant rate of d dollars per unit time, and when the interest rate is constant, a sufficient condition for no premature exercise is that:

$$K > \frac{d}{r} \tag{24.1}$$

This condition shows that the call strike price must be greater than the ratio of the continuous dividend rate to the short-term risk-less rate.

24.1.1.3. *Early exercise with discrete distributions*

When the amounts of dividends per share d_j are paid at different dates τ_j, for $j = 1$ to n, are known and the interest rate is constant, then a sufficient condition for no premature exercise is:

$$K > \sum_{j=1}^{p} \left[\frac{P(\tau_j)}{1 - P(\tau_n)} \right] d(\tau_j) \tag{24.2}$$

where $P(\tau)$ is the price of a discount bond paying one-Dollar in τ years.

This condition shows that the net present value of future dividends must be less than the present value of earnings from investing the strike price for τ periods. The intuition of this result is simple. In fact, if the losses from dividends are less than the gains from investing the required funds to exercise the option and hold the stock, the option is exercised. When the dividend per share is $D(S,t)$, the B–S differential equation is slightly modified. In fact, the instantaneous rate of return is no longer $\mu S dt$ but rather $\frac{\mu - D(S,t)}{S} dt$. This gives the following partial differential equation, which was formulated first by Merton (1973):

$$\frac{1}{2}\sigma^2 S^2 \left(\frac{\partial^2 C}{\partial^2 S} \right) + [rS - D] \left(\frac{\partial C}{\partial S} \right) + \left(\frac{\partial C}{\partial t} \right) - rC = 0 \tag{24.3}$$

where $C(S, \tau, K)$ is the American call value. This partial differential equation must satisfy the following boundary conditions:

$$C(0, \tau, K) = 0 \tag{24.4}$$

$$C(S, 0, K) = \max[0, S - K] \tag{24.5}$$

$$C(S, \tau, K) \geq \max[0, S - K] \tag{24.6}$$

Equation (24.4) shows that the option is worthless when the underlying asset is zero for any time to maturity τ. Equation (24.5) indicates that the option price is equal to the greater of zero and its intrinsic value at the option maturity date. Equation (24.6) is an arbitrage condition. It indicates the American option value at any time during the option's life. It shows also that at each instant τ, there is a positive probability of early exercise. This implies that there exists a certain level $I(\tau)$ of the underlying asset price such that for each $S > I(\tau)$, the option is worth more "dead" than in "life". Since the value of an immediate exercise is $(S - K)$, the structure of the problem implies the additional condition $C(I(\tau), \tau, K) = I(\tau) - K = h$, where $C(I(\tau), \tau, K)$ satisfies the partial differential equation for $0 \leq S \leq I(\tau)$. Since $I(\tau)$ is an unknown function of time, the structure of the problem is complex. Indeed the boundary conditions are semi-infinite and time dependent. The value of $I(\tau)$ must be determined as part of the solution. As defined by Samuelson (1972) and Merton (1973), this is rather a difficult problem since the unknown function $I(\tau)$ must be determined from the behavior of the call's holder, who maximizes the option value at each instant, by adding a condition of regularity.

To make this point explicit, consider a function $f(S, \tau; K, I(\tau))$, which is a solution to this problem for a given $I(\tau)$, or:

$$C(S, \tau, K) = \max_{(I)} f(S, \tau; K, I).$$

The optimal $I(\tau)$ is independent of the current underlying asset price, and the following condition, which is "high contact" at the boundary must be accounted for $\frac{\partial C(I(\tau), \tau, K)}{\partial S} = 1$. This means that the option's partial derivative with respect to the underlying asset price is equal to one. Intuitively, this condition corresponds to the point of tangency between the call function and its intrinsic value, since only in-the-money options are exercised. The proof of this condition is relatively a simple matter. In fact, for the function $f(x, I)$, (differentiable and concave with respect to its second argument), the total derivative with respect to I along the boundary $x = I$ is given by:

$$\frac{df}{dI} = \frac{dh}{dI} = f_1(I, I) + f_2(I, I).$$

When the function has a maximum for a level $I = I^*$, $f_2(x, I^*) = 0$.

Since, $\frac{df}{dI} = \frac{dh}{dI} = f_1(I^*, I^*)$ and $h = I - K$, so $f_1(I^*, I^*) = \frac{dh}{dI} = 1$. This is the proof that the derivative must be equal to one. The solution to this problem gives the value of the American call when there are dividends. Samuelson (1972) and Merton (1973) analyzed this "free boundary" problem and did not provide solutions for a finite-life option. However, a solution for an infinite-life option (a perpetual warrant) was provided by Merton (Eq. (46), p. 172).

24.1.2. *Early exercise of American puts*

The valuation of American calls is simpler than the valuation of American puts with and without discrete cash distributions to the underlying asset. While European and American calls have the same value when there are no distributions to the underlying asset, this result does not hold for European and American puts. While there is no incentive to exercise an American call option before its maturity date in the absence of dividends, there is always a probability of premature exercise of an American put. This is due to the first arbitrage condition, according to which the value of an American put must be greater than its intrinsic value at each instant, and second, to the fact that the value of a European put with an infinite time to maturity or a perpetual put is zero.

24.1.2.1. *Exercise without distributions*

Since there is no put-call parity relationship for American options, American puts must be treated separately. The problem with the rational pricing of European or American put options is somewhat different from that of European or American calls. This results from the work of Merton (1973) who showed that an American put option can be exercised early even in the absence of distributions to the underlying asset. The American put must satisfy the Black and

Scholes (1973) or Merton's (1973) partial differential equation:

$$\frac{1}{2}\sigma^2 S^2\left(\frac{\partial^2 P}{\partial^2 S}\right)+rS\left(\frac{\partial P}{\partial S}\right)+\left(\frac{\partial P}{\partial t}\right)-rP=0$$

under the following boundary conditions:

$$P(\infty,\tau,K)=0 \tag{24.7}$$

$$P(S,0,K)=\max[0,K-S] \tag{24.8}$$

$$P(S,\tau,K)\geq \max[0,K-S] \tag{24.9}$$

Equation (24.7) shows that the put is worthless when the underlying asset price tends to infinity. This result is rather intuitive. In fact, the put intrinsic value is given by the difference between a constant (the strike price) and the infinite underlying asset price. Equation (24.8) is standard and gives the put value at the option's maturity date. Equation (24.9) shows that it is sometimes optimal to exercise the put before its maturity date. This happens when the underlying asset price tends to zero. In this situation, it is interesting to exercise the put as soon as possible to benefit from the investment of the strike price until the option's maturity date. From the analyses of McKean (1969), Samuelson (1972), and Merton (1973), there is no-closed form solution for a finite-life put when the above boundary conditions are applied to the partial differential equation. However, for an infinite time to maturity, a closed-form solution is given by Merton (1973), (Eq. (52), p. 174). The structure of this problem implies the existence of a certain level of the underlying asset $I(t)$, referred to as the critical asset price level, for which the exercise depends on the maximization behavior of the put's holder. The determination of this critical level implies adding the following condition on the put's derivative with respect to the underlying asset $\frac{\partial P(I^*,\infty,K)}{\partial t}=-1$. This condition is the Samuelson's "high contact" or boundary condition. The analysis of this problem (the free boundary problem) by Merton (1973) allows the derivation of the put's value when the time to maturity is infinite.

24.1.2.2. *Early exercise with continuous distributions*

When there are continuous distributions to the underlying asset, the pricing of American puts is rather difficult. However, an interesting approach was proposed by Barone-Adesi and Whaley (1987) for the valuation of American options. This approach is referred to as the quadratic approximation method.

24.1.2.3. *Early exercise with discrete distributions*

When there are no dividends, the American put option may be exercised early. In fact, since interest income can be earned on the exercisable proceeds of the option when exercised, this is sufficient to justify early exercise. When the American option holder delays exercise, this means that he forgoes the interest income on the exercisable proceeds.

When there are dividends, the American put option holder must compare the effect of dividends on the put value and the interest income. If the holder does not exercise his put, he forgoes the interest income. If he exercises before the ex-dividend date, he will not profit from the increase in the exercisable proceeds when the underlying stock goes ex-dividend. There is a trade-off between the interest income and the dividend. Hence, between dividend dates, the option holder is always in a dilemma. Some interesting approximations of American values are given in the literature. These approximations include, Johnson (1983), Geske and Johnson (1984), Geske and Shastri (1985), Blomeyer (1986), and Barone-Adesi and Whaley among others. However, most of them work less well than binomial models and finite difference methods.

24.1.3. *The American put option and its critical stock price*

We provide an expression for the critical stock price for the American put. The put price is expressed in an integral form which involves first passage probabilities. Using the fact that:

- the put ceases to depend on time when the critical stock price is reached and
- the result that an American put corresponds to the value of a European put plus the early exercise premium, Bunch and Johnson (2000) provide a formula for the critical price.

24.1.3.1. *The first-passage approach and the perpetual put option case*

The American put price P is exercised when the stock price S hits the critical stock price S_c. When the stock price and its critical value have no discontinuities, we can write:

$$P = \max_{S_c} \int_0^T e^{-rt}(K - S_c) f dt, \quad (S \succ S_c) \tag{24.10}$$

where T is the maturity date and K is the strike price. The first factor in the integral corresponds to a discount factor. The second factor corresponds to the payoff among exercise. The third factor f is the first-passage probability, i.e., the probability that the stock price declines from its value S to the critical value S_c for the first time t. The maximization concerns all possible functions $S_c(\tau)$ where $\tau = T - t$. For values of the underlying asset less than the critical price, the put value is simply its intrinsic value. For an infinite time to maturity, the critical asset price is constant and can be determined using the first-order condition. The first-passage probability is provided by Feller (1971).

First, define:

$$Z = \frac{1}{\sigma}\left[\log\left(\frac{S}{S_t}\right) + \left(r - \frac{1}{2}\sigma^2\right)t\right]$$

where σ corresponds to the volatility of the underlying asset.

Second, define:

$$a = \frac{1}{\sigma}\left[\log\left(\frac{S}{S_c}\right) + \left(r - \frac{1}{2}\sigma^2\right)t\right]$$

This term can be seen as a standardized measure of how the put is from early exercise. When $\gamma = \frac{2r}{\sigma^2} = 1$, so that a is constant, Eq. (24.10) requires an expression for the first-passage time of a standardized Brownian motion. Feller (1971) shows that the following density function must be used:

$$f(x)d(x) = \frac{1}{\sqrt{2\pi x^3}} e^{-1/(2x)} dx.$$

The American put value can be computed using the appropriate density obtained via the transformation $x = \frac{t}{a^2}$ so that

$$f(t)d(t) = \frac{a}{\sqrt{2\pi t^3}} e^{-a^2/(2t)} dt$$

in Eq. (24.10). It is possible to choose the constant in this last equation to normalize $f(t)$, so the integral of $f(t)$ from zero to infinity is one. Since the critical price is constant in this case, we have:

$$P = \frac{K - S_c}{\sqrt{2\pi}} \int_0^\infty \frac{ae^{-rt} e^{-a^2/(2t)}}{t^{3/2}} dt.$$

When $\gamma = 1$, a is constant: $a = \frac{1}{\sigma} \log(S/S_c)$.

Using the Laplace transform Table of Abramowitz and Stegun (1972, p. 1026), the result is

$$\int_0^\infty \frac{k}{\sqrt{2\pi t^3}} e^{-k^2/(4t)} e^{-st} dt = e^{-k\sqrt{s}}.$$

When $s = r$ and $k^2 = a^2$, we have:

$$P = (K - S_c) \exp\left[-(\sqrt{2r}/\sigma) \log\left(\frac{S}{S_c}\right)\right]$$

which is equivalent to:

$$P = (K - S_c) \left(\frac{S}{S_c}\right) \tag{24.11}$$

A similar result is obtained by Merton (1973). In fact, the Black and Scholes (1973) partial differential equation,

$$\frac{\partial P}{\partial t} = rP - rS\frac{\partial P}{\partial S} - \frac{1}{2}\sigma^2 S^2 \frac{\partial^2 P}{\partial S^2} \tag{24.12}$$

simplifies to an ordinary equation for an infinite maturity.

When $\gamma = 1$, by substituting Eq. (24.11) into:

$$rP - rS\frac{\partial P}{\partial S} - \frac{1}{2}\sigma^2 S^2 \frac{\partial^2 P}{\partial S^2} \tag{24.13}$$

we can show that Eq. (24.11) satisfies Eq. (24.13). Equation (24.11) can be written as:

$$P = K\left(\frac{S_c}{S}\right) - S\left(\frac{S_c}{S}\right)^2. \tag{24.14}$$

Since in Eq. (24.11) $\frac{\partial P}{\partial S} = -(K - S_c)S_c/S^2$, we have $\frac{\partial P}{\partial S} = -(S_c/S)^2$.

Equation (24.14) shows that the American put price corresponds to the exercise price times the expected discount factor plus the stock price times the hedge ratio. This is similar to a European put given in Black and Scholes (1973) as:

$$p = Ke^{-rT}N(-d_2) - SN(-d_1). \tag{24.15}$$

It is possible to obtain expressions when γ is different from one. Bunch and Johnson (2000) show that:

$$P = (K - S_c)\left(\frac{S_c}{S}\right)^{\gamma} \tag{24.16}$$

Equations (24.11) and (24.16) do not contain normal density functions. This is the exact result and the exact density is

$$f(t) = \frac{\log \frac{S}{S_c} e^{-a^2/(2t)}}{\sqrt{2\pi}\sigma t^{3/2}}.$$

Now, we consider the more difficult case of finite-lived puts.

24.1.3.2. *The critical stock price function for a finite time to maturity*

When the time to maturity is finite, the critical stock price is no longer constant. The first-passage probabilities may be estimated using the tangent approximation:

$$f = \frac{\log \frac{S}{S_c} + \frac{\dot{S}}{S_c} t}{\sqrt{2\pi}\sigma t^{3/2}} e^{-a^2/(2t)}$$

where the dot indicates the time derivative. The variables S_c and a are general functions of t. Bunch and Johnson (2000) derive an expression for the critical stock price using the tangent approximation:

$$S_c/X = \frac{\gamma}{1+\gamma} + \frac{e^{-\beta_2\tau-\alpha_1\sqrt{\tau}}}{1+\gamma}$$

where

$$\beta_2 = \frac{\sigma a}{2t} + \frac{a^2}{2t^2} - r - \frac{3}{2t} - \frac{ar}{\sigma t}$$

and α_1 is a positive constant.

When $S = S_c$, we have $\frac{\partial P}{\partial \tau} = 0$.

It is possible to use the equation providing a relationship between the American put, P and the European put p as:

$$P = p + \int_0^T rKe^{-rt}N(-d_2(S, S_c, t))dt$$

where,

$$d_2(S, S_c, t) = \frac{\log\left(\frac{S}{S_c}\right) + (r - \frac{1}{2}\sigma^2)t}{\sigma\sqrt{t}}.$$

The second term corresponds to the early exercise premium. Bunch and Johnson (2000) shows that:

$$\frac{S_c}{K} = e^{-(r+(1/2)\sigma^2)\tau-g\sigma\sqrt{\tau}} \tag{24.17}$$

where,

$$g = \pm\sqrt{2\log\frac{\sigma^2}{\frac{2r}{\sqrt{\alpha}}x\log xe^{-\alpha(r+(1/2)\sigma^2)^2\tau/(2\sigma^2)}}} \quad \text{where, } x = \frac{K}{S_c}. \tag{24.18}$$

The function g has typically a value about 1.5. Equation (24.17) has the appropriate asymptote for very large τ when,

$$g = \frac{1}{\sqrt{\tau}}\left[\log\frac{1+\gamma}{\gamma} - \left(r + \frac{1}{2}\sigma^2\right)\tau\right]. \tag{24.19}$$

It is important to know, when $g = 0$ and the corresponding time τ_0 by setting $g = 0$ in Eq. (24.19):

$$\tau_0 \approx \frac{\log \frac{1+\gamma}{\gamma}}{r + \frac{1}{2}\sigma^2}. \tag{24.20}$$

The exact expression can be obtained when $g = 0$ in Eq. (24.18) to:

$$\tau_0 = \frac{2 \log \frac{2\sqrt{\alpha}}{\gamma(1+\gamma)\sigma^2 \tau_0}}{\sigma^2(1+\gamma)\left[1 - \frac{\alpha}{4}(1+\gamma)\right]}$$

This equation can be solved iteratively. Bunch and Johnson (2000) shows that

$$\alpha = 1 - \frac{A}{1 + \frac{(1+\gamma)^2}{4}\gamma^2 \tau}, \quad \text{where } A = \frac{1}{2}\left(\frac{\gamma}{1+\gamma}\right)^2.$$

The approximation for g corresponding to a small τ is:

$$g = \sqrt{\log \frac{\sigma^2}{4er^2\tau/\alpha}} \tag{24.21}$$

The analysis in Bunch and Johnson (2000) shows that for typical puts, the values of g are between one and two. Equation (24.21) shows that when $r = 0$, there is no reason to early exercise, so S_c should be zero. In fact, when the interest rate is zero in Eq. (24.21), g tends to infinity and the critical stock price is worthless.

24.2. Valuation of American Commodity Options and Futures Options with Continuous Distributions

Most options written on commodities and commodity futures are of the American type. Hence, an early exercise premium is embedded in American call and put prices. Analytical solutions for the American option pricing problems with several dividends have not yet been found.

The quadratic approximation method used by Barone–Adesi and Whaley (1987), is computationally efficient. It provides an accurate, inexpensive method for the valuation of American call and put options traded on commodities and commodity futures.

24.2.1. *Valuation of American commodity options*

The following analysis applies to commodity options for which the cost of carrying the underlying commodity is a constant proportional rate, to commodity futures options and to stock options. The model used here is an extension of the Merton (1973) and Barone-Adesi and Whaley's (1987) model to American options. The pricing of American options involves the valuation of the early exercise premium attached to the possibility of early exercise. It is possible to show that, under certain conditions, American options should be exercised early. In fact, when the cost of carrying the underlying commodity, b, is less than the risk-less interest rate of interest r, and the option becomes deep-in-the money, the values of $N(d_1)$ and $N(d_2)$ approach 1. The European call value tends toward the quantity $Se^{(b-r)T} - Ke^{-rT}$.

Since an American option may be exercised for its intrinsic value, $(S - K)$, this value may be higher than $Se^{(b-r)T} - Ke^{-rT}$.

When $b = r$, there is no possibility of early exercise for an American call option. This argument does not hold for American put options since for puts, as shown by Merton (1973), there is always some probability of early exercise.

Since the cost of carrying any futures position is nil, i.e., $b = 0$, then all formulas proposed here can be used to price commodity futures options by substituting the futures price F for the commodity price S and setting $b = 0$. Also, when the option's underlying asset is a non-dividend paying stock, $b = r$, and the formulas can be applied to stock options.

European and American option values must satisfy the following partial differential equation,

$$\frac{1}{2}\sigma^2 S^2 \frac{\partial^2 C(S,t)}{\partial^2 S} + bS\frac{\partial C(S,t)}{\partial S} + \frac{\partial C(S,t)}{\partial t} - rC(S,t) = 0. \quad (24.22)$$

This equation applies to American options, European options, and the early exercise premium. This premium is given by the difference in value between the American and European option values, i.e., $\epsilon_c = C(S,T) - c(S,T)$ and $\epsilon_p = P(S,T) - p(S,T)$. Using this notation, Eq. (24.22) can be re-written for the early exercise premium as:

$$\frac{1}{2}\sigma^2 S^2 \frac{\partial^2 \epsilon(S,t)}{\partial^2 S} + bS\frac{\partial \epsilon(S,t)}{\partial S} + \frac{\partial \epsilon(S,t)}{\partial t} - r\epsilon(S,t) = 0. \quad (24.23)$$

Let $M = \frac{2r}{\sigma^2}, N = \frac{2b}{\sigma^2}, \tau = T - t$. Multiplying Eq. (24.23) by $(\frac{2}{\sigma^2})$ gives:

$$S^2 \frac{\partial^2 \epsilon(S,t)}{\partial^2 S} + NS \frac{\partial \epsilon(S,t)}{\partial S} - \frac{M}{r} \frac{\partial \epsilon(S,t)}{\partial \tau} - M\epsilon(S,t) = 0. \quad (24.24)$$

Now, define the early exercise premium as $\epsilon(S,k) = k(\tau) f(S,k)$. Hence,

$$\left(\frac{\partial^2 \epsilon(S,t)}{\partial^2 S}\right) = k\left(\frac{\partial^2 f}{\partial^2 S}\right) \quad \text{and} \quad \left(\frac{\partial \epsilon(S,t)}{\partial \tau}\right) = k_\tau f + k k_\tau \left(\frac{\partial f}{\partial k}\right).$$

When substituting into Eq. (24.24), we obtain:

$$S^2\left(\frac{\partial^2 f}{\partial^2 S}\right) + NS\left(\frac{\partial f}{\partial S}\right) - Mf\left[1 + \left(\frac{k_\tau}{rk}\right)\left(1 + \frac{k}{f}\left(\frac{\partial f}{\partial k}\right)\right)\right] = 0.$$

If you choose $k(\tau) = 1 - e^{-r\tau}$, this equation becomes,

$$S^2\left(\frac{\partial^2 f}{\partial^2 S}\right) + NS\left(\frac{\partial f}{\partial S}\right) - \frac{Mf}{k} - M(1-k)\left(\frac{\partial f}{\partial k}\right) = 0. \quad (24.25)$$

Now, the quadratic approximation is applied to Eq. (24.25) in order to eliminate the term $M(1-k)(\frac{\partial f}{\partial k})$. In fact, as τ approaches $0, (\infty), (\frac{\partial f}{\partial k})$ approaches 0 (k approaches 1). Hence, Eq. (24.25) becomes a second-order differential equation

$$S^2\left(\frac{\partial^2 f}{\partial^2 S}\right) + NS\left(\frac{\partial f}{\partial S}\right) - \frac{Mf}{k} = 0.$$

The above equation presents two linearly independent solutions of the form $f(S) = a_1 S^{q_1} + a_2 S^{q_2}$.

Solving this equation, the American call option value presented by Barone-Adesi and Whaley (1987) is:

$$C(S,T) = c(S,T) + A_2\left(\frac{S}{S^*}\right)^{q_2} \quad \text{when } S < S^*$$

$$C(S,T) = S - K \quad \text{when } S \geq S^*$$

with

$$A_2 = \frac{S^*}{q_2}\left[1 - e^{(b-r)T} N(d_1(S^*))\right]$$

$$q_2 = \frac{1}{2}\left[-(N-1) + \sqrt{(N-1)^2 + 4\frac{M}{k}}\right]$$

$$N = \frac{2r}{\sigma^2}, \quad M = \frac{2b}{\sigma^2}, \quad k = 1 - e^{-rT}.$$

In this formula, S^* stands for the critical commodity price, which can be determined iteratively using the following system:

$$S^* - K = c(S^*, T) + \frac{S^*[1 - e^{(b-r)T} N(d_1(S^*)]}{q_2}.$$

The value of S^* corresponds to the value of S above which the call's value is equal to its exercisable proceeds, $(S - K)$. This value can be determined by a Newton–Raphson procedure or using the efficient algorithm presented by Barone-Adesi and Whaley (1987). When b is less than r, the American call value is given by the above formula. Otherwise, when b is greater or equal to r, $C(S,T) = c(S,T)$ since the call will never be exercised early.

In the same context, the American commodity option value $P(S,T)$ is given by:

$$P(S,T) = p(S,T) + A_1\left(\frac{S}{S^*}\right)^{q_1} \quad \text{when } S > S^*$$

$$P(S,T) = K - S \quad \text{when } S \leq S^*$$

with,

$$A_1 = \frac{-S^*}{q_1}\left[1 - e^{(b-r)T} N(-d_1(S^*))\right]$$

$$q_1 = \frac{1}{2}\left[-(N-1) - \sqrt{(N-1)^2 + 4\frac{M}{k}}\right],$$

$$N = \frac{2r}{\sigma^2}, \quad M = \frac{2b}{\sigma^2}, \quad k = 1 - e^{-rT}.$$

The critical underlying commodity price is given by an iterative procedure from the following equation

$$K - S^* = p(S^*, T) - \frac{S^*[1 - e^{(b-r)T} N(-d_1(S^*))]}{q_1}.$$

24.2.2. *Examples and applications*

Tables 24.1 and 24.2 provide the values of European and American call options and the critical underlying asset price level for different parameters.

Tables 24.3 and 24.4 provide the values of European and American put options and the critical underlying asset price level for different parameters.

Table 24.1. European and American call option prices. $K = 100$, $r = 0.08$, $T = 0.25$, $b = 0.04$, and $\sigma = 0.2$.

S	c	C	S^*
90	0.84	0.849	214.952
100	4.439	4.431	214.952
110	11.451	11.662	214.952
120	20.891	20.898	214.952

Table 24.2. European and American call option prices. $K = 100$, $r = 0.08$, $T = 0.25$, $b = 0.08$, and $\sigma = 0.2$.

S	c	C	S^*
90	0.698	0.705	120.323
100	3.909	3.934	120.323
110	10.737	10.823	120.323
120	19.748	20.009	120.323

Table 24.3. European and American put option prices. $S = 100$, $r = 0.08$, $T = 0.25$, $b = -0.04$, and $\sigma = 0.2$.

S	p	P	S^*
90	9.765	10.180	87.438
100	3.455	3.544	87.438
110	0.777	0.798	87.438
120	0.112	0.118	87.438

Table 24.4. European and American put option prices. $K = 100$, $r = 0.08$, $T = 0.25$, $b = 0.08$, and $\sigma = 0.2$.

S	p	P	S^*
90	10.500	10.565	83.501
100	3.909	3.921	83.501
110	0.935	0.938	83.501
120	0.144	0.145	83.501

24.2.3. *Valuation of American futures options*

From the analysis by Barone-Adesi and Whaley (1987), American futures call option formula when there are no carrying costs is:

$$C(F,T) = c(F,T) + A_2(F/F^*)^{q_2} \quad \text{when } F < F^*$$
$$C(F,T) = F - K \quad \text{when } F \geq F^*$$

with

$$A_2 = \frac{F^*}{q_2}\left[1 - e^{-rT}N(d_1(F^*))\right]$$

$$q_2 = \frac{1}{2}\left(1 + \sqrt{4\frac{M}{k}}\right), \quad M = \frac{2r}{\sigma^2}, \quad k = 1 - e^{-rT}.$$

When there are carrying costs, the formula becomes:

$$C(F,T) = c(F,T) + A_2(F/F^*)^{q_2} \quad \text{when } F < F^*$$
$$C(F,T) = F - K \quad \text{when } F \geq F^*$$

with,

$$A_2 = \frac{F^*}{q_2}\left[1 - e^{(b-r)T}N(d_1(F^*))\right]$$
$$q_2 = \frac{1}{2}\left(-(N-1) + \sqrt{(N-1)^2 + 4\frac{M}{k}}\right)$$
$$N = \frac{2r}{\sigma^2}, \quad M = \frac{2b}{\sigma^2}, \quad k = 1 - e^{-rT}.$$

The price of an American call futures option $C(F,T)$, is equal to the price of a European futures option $c(F,T)$, plus a term corresponding to the probability of early exercise $A_2(F/F^*)^{q_2}$. The critical futures price, F^*, is calculated using the following equation:

$$F^* - K = c(F^*,T) + \frac{F^*\left[1 - e^{(b-r)T}N(d_1(F^*))\right]}{q_2}.$$

When the futures price is below F^*, the American option price is given by the European price plus the early exercise premium. When the futures price is above F^*, the American option price is given by the intrinsic value, $(F - K)$.

In the absence of carrying costs, the formula for the American futures put is:

$$P(F,T) = p(F,T) + A_1(F/F^*)^{q_1} \quad \text{when } F > F^*$$
$$P(F,T) = K - F \quad \text{when } F \leq F^*$$

with,

$$A_1 = \frac{-F^{**}}{q_1}\left[1 - e^{rT}N(-d_1(F^*))\right]$$
$$q_1 = \frac{1}{2}\left(1 - \sqrt{4\frac{M}{k}}\right), \quad M = \frac{2r}{\sigma^2}, \quad k = 1 - e^{-rT}.$$

When there are carrying costs, the formula for the American put is:

$$P(F,T) = p(F,T) + A_1(F/F^*)^{q_1} \quad \text{when } F > F^*$$
$$P(F,T) = K - F \quad \text{when } F \leq F^*$$

with,

$$A_1 = \frac{-F^*}{q_1}\left[1 - e^{(b-r)T}N(-d_1(F^*))\right]$$
$$q_1 = \frac{1}{2}\left(-(N-1) - \sqrt{(N-1)^2 + 4\frac{M}{k}}\right),$$
$$N = \frac{2r}{\sigma^2}, \quad M = \frac{2b}{\sigma^2}, \quad k = 1 - e^{-rT}.$$

The critical futures price corresponding to an optimal early exercise is calculated using the following equation:

$$K - F^* = p(F^*,T) - \frac{F^*\left[1 - e^{(b-r)T}N(-d_1(F^*))\right]}{q_1}.$$

When the futures price is above the critical price, the American futures option price is given by the sum of the European price and the early exercise premium $A_1(F/F^*)^{q_1}$. When the futures price is above the critical futures price, the American futures option value is equal to its intrinsic value, $(K - F)$.

24.2.4. *Examples and applications*

Tables 24.5 and 24.6 provide the values of European and American call and put futures options for different parameters.

Table 24.5. European and American futures call prices. $K = 100$, $r = 0.08$, $T = 0.25$, $b = 0$, and $\sigma = 0.2$.

S	$N(d_1)$	$N(d_2)$	c	C
90	0.1624	0.1417	0.4360	0.4402
100	0.5199	0.4801	3.900	3.9251
110	0.8428	0.8173	10.7600	10.8380
120	0.9710	0.9635	19.7750	20.0250

Table 24.6. European and American futures put prices. $K = 100$, $r = 0.08$, $T = 0.25$, $b = 0$, and $\sigma = 0.2$.

S	$N(-d_1)$	$N(-d_2)$	p	P
90	0.8522	0.8375	10.2300	10.6500
100	0.5199	0.4801	3.9087	4.0199
110	0.1826	0.1571	0.9607	0.9807
120	0.0364	0.0289	0.1714	0.1795

The difference between European and American call option prices correspond to the early exercise premium attached to American options.

24.3. Valuation of American Commodity and Futures Options with Continuous Distributions within Information Uncertainty

This section is devoted to the valuation of American commodity options within information uncertainty.

24.3.1. *Commodity option valuation with information costs*

Following Black (1976), we assume that the fractional change in the futures price is distributed log-normally, with a known constant variance rate, σ. We also assume, that all the parameters of the CAPM of Merton (1987), CAPMI, are constant through time. In this context, it is possible to create a risk-less hedge by taking a long position in the option and a short position in the futures contract with the same transaction date. Black (1976) assumed that a continuously rebalanced self-financing portfolio of the underlying futures contracts and the risk-less asset can be constructed to duplicate the payoff of the futures option. The absence of costless arbitrage opportunities implies the following relationship between the futures or the forward price and its underlying asset: $F = Se^{(b+\lambda_S)T}$ where F is the current forward price, T is the option's maturity date, b is the constant proportional cost of carrying the commodity, and λ_S is the information cost on the spot asset. When a hedged position is constructed and "continuously" re-balanced, using limiting arguments as in Omberg (1991), yields:

$$\frac{1}{2}\sigma^2 S^2 C_{SS} + (b + \lambda_S) S C_S - (r + \lambda_C) C + C_t = 0.$$

When λ_S and λ_C are set equal to zero, this equation collapses to that in Barone-Adesi and Whaley (1987).

Let T be the maturity date of the call and K be its strike price. This equation must be solved under the call boundary condition at maturity. The value of a European commodity call by Bellalah (1999) is:

$$C(S, T) = Se^{((b-r-(\lambda_C-\lambda_S))T)} N(d_1) - Ke^{-(r+\lambda_C)T} N(d_2)$$

with

$$d_1 = \left[\ln\left(\frac{S}{K}\right) + \left(b + \frac{1}{2}\sigma^2 + \lambda_S\right) T\right] \Big/ \sigma\sqrt{T}, \quad d_2 = d_1 - \sigma\sqrt{T}$$

and where $N(\cdot)$ is the cumulative normal density function.

When λ_S and λ_C are equal to zero and $b = r$, this formula is the same as that in Black and Scholes.[1] If besides, the cost of carrying

[1]In fact, to obtain this equation, the CAPMI can be written as:

$$\bar{R}_S - r - \lambda_S = \beta_S \left[\bar{R}_m - r - \lambda_m\right],$$

or

$$\bar{R}_S - r - \lambda_S = a\beta_S \quad \text{with } a = \left[\bar{R}_m - r - \lambda_m\right].$$

This equation can be written for the expected return on the spot asset and the option as:

$$E\left(\frac{\Delta S}{S}\right) = (r + \lambda_S)\Delta t + a\beta_S \Delta t$$

$$E\left(\frac{\Delta C}{C}\right) = (r + \lambda_C)\Delta t + a\beta_C \Delta t$$

Multiplying this last equation by C and substituting for β_C gives:

$$E(\Delta C) = (r + \lambda_C) C \Delta t + aS\beta_S C_S \Delta t.$$

Taking the expected value b and replacing $E(\Delta S)$ gives:

$$E(\Delta C) = (r + \lambda_S) S C_S \Delta t + aS\beta_S C_S \Delta t + C_t \Delta t + \frac{1}{2} C_{SS} S^2 \sigma^2 \Delta t.$$

the commodity is zero, this equation is equivalent to that in Black. Using the futures price $F = Se^{(b+\lambda_S)T}$ instead of the spot price, the equation becomes for a European futures call as:

$$C(F,T) = e^{-(r+\lambda_C)T}(FN(d_1) - KN(d_2))$$

with

$$d_1 = \left[\ln\left(\frac{F}{K}\right) + \frac{1}{2}\sigma^2 T\right] \Big/ \sigma\sqrt{T}, \quad d_2 = d_1 - \sigma\sqrt{T}.$$

The solution for a European futures put option in the same context is:

$$P(F,T) = e^{-(r+\lambda_C)T}(-FN(-d_1) + KN(-d_2))$$

The term $FN(d_1) - KN(d_2)$ shows that the expected value of the futures call at expiration, is the expected difference between the futures price and the strike price conditional upon the option being in-the-money times the probability that it will be in-the-money. The term $e^{-(r+\lambda_C)T}$ is the appropriate discount factor within a framework of incomplete information by which the expected expiration value is brought to the present. The following equation (with information costs) is the analogous of that as given by Black (1976)[2]:

$$\frac{1}{2}C_{SS}S^2\sigma^2 - (r + \lambda_C)C + C_t = 0.$$

This valuation equation applies to forward contracts, European, and American options. The American commodity option value $C_A(S,T)$

Making the equality between this equation, and

$$E(\Delta C) = (r + \lambda_C)C\Delta t + aS\beta_S C_S \Delta t,$$

and simplifying gives:

$$\frac{1}{2}C_{SS}S^2\sigma^2 + (r + \lambda_S)SC_S - (r + \lambda_C)C + C_t = 0.$$

If $\lambda_S = \lambda_C = 0$, this equation is the Black and Scholes equation.

[2]It is possible to use the previous footnote to see this result. In fact, since the value of a futures contract is zero, the equity in the position is just the value of the option. In this context, the system:

$$E(\Delta C) = (r + \lambda_S)SC_S\Delta t + aS\beta_S C_S\Delta t + C_t\Delta t + \frac{1}{2}C_{SS}S^2\sigma^2\Delta t$$

$$E(\Delta C) = (r + \lambda_C)C\Delta t + aS\beta_S C_S\Delta t,$$

is given by:

$$C_A(S,T) = C(S,T) + A_2 \left(\frac{S}{S^*}\right)^{q_2} \quad \text{when } S < S^*$$

$$C_A(S,T) = S - K \quad \text{when } S \geq S^*$$

with

$$A_2 = \frac{S^*}{q2}(1 - e^{(b+\lambda_S - r - \lambda_C)T} N(d_1(S^*)))$$

$$q_2 = \frac{1}{2}\left(-(N-1) + \sqrt{(N-1)^2 + 4\frac{M}{k}}\right)$$

$$N = \frac{2(r+\lambda_C)}{\sigma^2}, \quad M = \frac{2(b+\lambda_S)}{\sigma^2}, \quad k = 1 - e^{-(r+\lambda_C)T}.$$

The critical underlying commodity price is given by an iterative procedure from the following equation:

$$S^* - K = C\left((S^*,T) + \frac{S^*\left(1 - e^{(b+\lambda_S - r - \lambda_C)T} N(d_1(S^*))\right)}{q_2}\right).$$

The American commodity option value $P_A(S,T)$ is:

$$P_A(S,T) = P(S,T) + A_1 \left(\frac{S}{S^*}\right)^{q1} \quad \text{when } S > S^{**}$$

$$P_A(S,T) = K - S \quad \text{when } S \leq S^{**}$$

---

becomes:

$$E(\Delta C) = C_t \Delta t + \frac{1}{2} C_{SS} S^2 \sigma^2 \Delta t$$

$$E(\Delta C) = (r + \lambda_C) C \Delta t,$$

which gives:

$$\frac{1}{2} C_{SS} S^2 \sigma^2 - (r + \lambda_C) C + C_t = 0.$$

If $\lambda_C = 0$, this equation is the Black equation with information costs.

with:

$$A_1 = \frac{-S^{**}}{q1}(1 - e^{(b+\lambda_S-r-\lambda_C)T}N(-d_1(S^{**})))$$

$$q_1 = \frac{1}{2}\left(-(N-1) - \sqrt{(N-1)^2 + 4\frac{M}{k}}\right), \quad N = \frac{2(r+\lambda_C)}{\sigma^2},$$

$$M = \frac{2(b+\lambda_S)}{\sigma^2}, \quad k = 1 - e^{-(r+\lambda_C)T}.$$

The critical underlying commodity price is given by an iterative procedure from the following equation[3]:

$$K - S^* = P(S^*, T) - \frac{S^*(1 - e^{(b+\lambda_S-r-\lambda_C)T}N(-d_1(S^*)))}{q1}.$$

A similar algorithm as the one developed by Barone-Adesi and Whaley (1987) can be used to determine the critical underlying price.

24.3.2. *Simulation results*

Table 24.7 presents a sensitivity analysis of the theoretical European futures call and put values as given by Black's model and the model derived in the previous section. The calculations are based on two alternative assumptions regarding information costs, 1% and 5%. When $F = K = 100$, $T = 0.25$, $\sigma = 0.2$, $r = 0.08$, and $b = 0$, results show that an increase in information costs from 1% to 5% reduces call values respectively from 3.8990 to 3.8602. The simulations show that model prices are less than Black's prices for out-of-the-money and in-the-money calls and are nearly equal to Black's prices for at-the-money calls. This result shows that our model explains at least the relative mispricing of out and at-the-money calls, which is an advantage with respect to Black's model. It is important to note that the differences in option values increase with the interaction between information costs and the other option valuation parameters.

When the information costs vary from 1% to 5%, a decrease is observed in put values. The simulations performed indicate that model prices are nearly equivalent to Black's prices for at and

[3]The above solutions are written as in Barone–Adesi and Whaley (1987). They can be re-written as a function of the futures price as given by Whaley (1986) using the cost-of carry model: the relationship between the futures price and the spot price.

Table 24.7. Simulations of Futures call (put) option values using Black's model, C_{Black}, (P_{Black}) and the proposed model, C_M, (P_M) for the following parameters. $K = 100$, $T = 0.25$, $\sigma = 0.2$, $r = 0.08$, and $b = 0$.

Panel A, F	C_{Black}	$C_{M,\lambda_C=0.01}$	$C_{M,\lambda_C=0.05}$	P_{Black}	$P_{M,\lambda_C=0.01}$	$P_{M,\lambda_C=0.05}$
80	0	0	0	19.6611	19.6203	19.4549
90	0.6963	0.6353	0.6310	10.4365	10.3128	10.3112
100	3.9087	3.8990	3.8602	3.9087	3.8990	3.8602
110	10.7427	10.7358	10.6290	0.9487	0.9483	0.9482
120	19.7554	19.7260	19.5297	0.1414	0.1370	0.1363
Panel B	$T = 0.25$	$\sigma = 0.2$	$r = 0.12$			
80	0	0	0	19.4461	19.4249	19.2912
90	0.6820	0.6810	0.6767	10.4356	10.4112	10.3106
100	3.8698	3.8602	3.8217	3.8698	3.8602	3.8217
110	10.6356	10.6290	10.5237	0.9412	0.9408	0.9393
120	19.5487	19.5297	19.3354	0.1497	0.1493	0.1476
Panel C	$T = 0.5$	$\sigma = 0.2$	$r = 0.08$			
80	0	0	0	18.1417	18.0566	17.6991
90	1.6913	1.6833	1.6520	11.3091	11.2433	11.1226
100	5.4161	5.3890	5.2823	5.4161	5.3870	5.2823
110	11.7325	11.6939	11.4235	2.1246	2.1139	2.0916
120	19.9157	19.8562	19.4630	0.6999	0.6961	0.6916
Panel D	$T = 0.5$	$\sigma = 0.4$	$r = 0.08$			
80	2.6940	2.6806	2.6275	21.9098	21.8005	21.3688
90	6.1331	6.1025	5.9817	15.7410	15.6625	15.3524
100	10.8051	10.7512	10.5383	10.8151	10.7512	10.5383
110	16.7917	16.7080	16.6123	7.1838	7.1480	7.0165
120	19.9557	19.8562	19.4630	4.6800	4.6567	4.5645

out-of-the money puts. However, model prices are less than those reported in Black's model for in-the-money puts. Since our model eliminates the overvaluation bias of these puts, this is an advantage with respect to Black's model. The calculations performed are based on three alternative assumptions regarding information costs for European and American call options when the futures price varies from 90 to 120. Table 24.8 shows that our model prices are most of the time less or equal to Barone-Adesi and Whaley's model prices for call options. Table 24.9 provides the theoretical values for European and American futures put options.

Table 24.8. Comparisons of European and American Futures call option values using the proposed models, C_{European}, C_{American}, C_{BAW} for the following parameters. $K = 100$, $T = 0.25$, $\sigma = 0.2$, $r = 0.08$, $b = 0$, and $\lambda_C = 0.01$.

Panel, A, F	C_{European}	C_{American}	F_{Critical}	C_{BAW}
90	0.6950	0.7407	121.770	0.70
100	3.8000	3.9380	121.758	3.93
110	10.7427	10.8158	121.778	10.81
120	19.7500	20.0270	121.770	20.02
Panel B	$T = 0.25$	$\sigma = 0.2$	$r = 0.08$	$\lambda_C = 0.02$
90	0.6340	0.6419	121.629	0.70
100	3.8800	3.9201	121.612	3.93
110	10.7000	10.8186	121.629	10.81
120	19.6700	20.0230	121.624	20.02
Panel C	$T = 0.25$	$\sigma = 0.2$	$r = 0.08$	$\lambda_C = 0.05$
90	0.6310	0.6478	121.3529	0.70
100	3.8602	3.910	121.3110	3.93
110	10.6290	10.8056	121.3244	10.81
120	19.5297	20.0183	121.3240	20.02
Panel D	$T = 0.5$	$\sigma = 0.2$	$r = 0.08$	$\lambda_C = 0.01$
90	1.5830	1.61087	128.240	1.72
100	5.3800	5.46840	128.290	5.48
110	11.6930	11.9060	128.136	11.90
120	19.8560	20.3413	121.139	20.34
Panel E	$T = 0.5$	$\sigma = 0.2$	$r = 0.08$	$\lambda_C = 0.02$
90	1.5750	1.61220	127.920	1.72
100	5.3600	5.4639	127.929	5.48
110	11.6300	11.8896	127.935	11.90
120	19.7500	20.3423	127.922	20.34
Panel F	$T = 0.5$	$\sigma = 0.2$	$r = 0.08$	$\lambda_C = 0.05$
90	1.6520	1.6265	127.5502	1.72
100	5.2823	5.4647	127.5533	5.48
110	11.4235	11.8724	127.5430	11.90
120	19.4630	20.3218	127.5470	20.34

Table 24.9. Comparisons of European and American Futures put option values using the proposed models, P_{European}, P_{American}, P_{BAW} for the following parameters. $K = 100$, $T = 0.25$, $\sigma = 0.2$, $r = 0.08$, $b = 0$, and $\lambda_C = 0.01$.

Panel, A, F	P_{European}	P_{American}	F_{Critical}	P_{BAW}
90	10.3128	10.6440	86.780	10.58
100	3.8990	4.0130	86.132	3.93
110	0.9584	0.9850	86.770	0.94
120	0.1710	0.1800	86.710	0.15
Panel B	$T = 0.25$	$\sigma = 0.2$	$r = 0.08$	$\lambda_C = 0.02$
90	10.1870	10.6310	86.821	10.58
100	3.8890	4.00600	86.190	3.93
110	0.9450	0.98420	86.817	0.94
120	0.1370	0.17950	86.756	0.15
Panel C	$T = 0.25$	$\sigma = 0.2$	$r = 0.08$	$\lambda_C = 0.05$
90	10.3112	10.6050	86.9420	10.58
100	3.8602	3.99600	86.3589	3.93
110	0.9482	0.98000	86.940	0.94
120	0.1363	0.17900	86.889	0.15
Panel D	$T = 0.5$	$\sigma = 0.2$	$r = 0.08$	$\lambda_C = 0.01$
90	11.2433	11.7240	82.251	11.48
100	5.3890	5.5846	82.144	5.48
110	2.1139	2.21400	82.190	2.15
120	0.6961	0.7757	82.228	0.70
Panel E	$T = 0.5$	$\sigma = 0.2$	$r = 0.08$	$\lambda_C = 0.02$
90	11.0870	11.69200	82.3570	11.48
100	5.3620	5.5656	82.2556	5.48
110	2.1232	2.20680	82.299	2.15
120	0.7325	0.77000	82.336	0.70
Panel F	$T = 0.5$	$\sigma = 0.2$	$r = 0.08$	$\lambda_C = 0.05$
90	11.1226	11.6400	82.6640	11.48
100	5.2823	5.5209	82.5700	5.48
110	2.0916	2.1843	82.614	2.15
120	0.6916	0.77100	82.640	0.70

24.4. Valuation of American Options with Discrete Cash Distributions

Most of the traded stock and index options around the world may be exercised before their expiration dates and are therefore of the American type.

24.4.1. *Early exercise of American options*

Early exercise of these options is often induced by the payment of dividends on the underlying asset. For stock options, it may be optimal to exercise a call on the last cum-dividend day to receive the dividend. In this case, the adapted versions of the Black–Scholes model proposed by Roll (1977), Geske (1979), and Whaley (1981) can be used.

For an index option, when the dividends are distributed fairly evenly over time, B–S type models may be used. However, when the dividends tend to be clustered, early exercise may be triggered at many points in time and B–S type models can not be applied. Another potential dividend-induced reason of early exercise is due to asset carrying costs. When these costs are different from the risk-less interest rate, early exercise is also possible. Hence, for many reasons, the B–S model does not price adequately American commodity and futures options, since by definition, the model is "reserved" to European options on non-dividend paying stocks.

Harvey and Whaley (1992) showed that ad-hoc valuation procedures sometimes produce large pricing errors because of the discrete and seasonal pattern of dividends on some indexes like the S&P 100 index portfolio. The most commonly used methods are the B–S model adjusted for dividends because of its ease of computation and the American-style option pricing approximations with a constant proportional dividend yield. These include the quadratic approximation of Barone-Adesi and Whaley (1987) and the Cox *et al.* (1979) binomial method under the assumption of a constant proportional dividend yield rate. The appropriate approach for the valuation of American options when there are discrete dividends is based on the compound option approach. Several models are proposed in this context. Given the contribution of the compound option approach to the pricing of American options, this approach is presented in detail.

24.4.2. *Valuation of American options with dividends*

The valuation of American stock options is equivalent to the valuation of a portfolio which contains a commodity option on a stock with some distributions. These distributions are reflected in the assumed proportional rate of carrying the stock, y, and the amount of cash dividend paid once a year. For the sake of simplicity, let us use the context in Roll (1977), Geske (1979), and Whaley (1981) and assume that:

- Investors can borrow and lend without restrictions at the short-term instantaneous risk-less rate r during the option's life T.
- The stock pays a cash income at some dates t_i, ($t_i < T$).
- The stock pays a dividend D and the ex-dividend instant is t, ($t < T$).
- The stock price net of the discounted dividend, S, is given by:

$$S_\tau = P_\tau - De^{-r(t-\tau)} \quad \text{for } \tau < t$$

$$S_\tau = P_\tau \quad \text{for } \tau \geq t$$

where P is the stock price cum-dividend. The price dynamics of the stock S are given by the stochastic differential equation:

$$dS/S = \mu dt + \sigma dz$$

where μ and σ stand respectively for the instantaneous expected rate of return and the standard deviation of the stock price return and dz is a standard Wiener process. We can show that there exists some finite ex-dividend stock price S_t above (under) which the early exercise of an American call (put) may be optimal. We call this value of S_t, S_t^*, which is easily calculated by an iterative procedure. Once this critical value is determined, the valuation by duplication technique can be implemented.

Consider the following portfolio of options:

(a) The purchase of a European call having a strike price K and a maturity date T;
(b) The purchase of a European call with a strike price S_t^* and a maturity date $(t - \epsilon)$ and
(c) The sale of a European call option on the option defined in (a) with a strike price $(S_t^* + D - K)$ and a maturity date $(t - \epsilon)$.

The contingent payoff of this portfolio of options is identical to that of an American call. In a perfect capital market, the absence of costless arbitrage opportunities ensures that the American call value is identical to that of this portfolio. The American call value must be equal to the algebraic sum of the three options in the portfolio. The option described in (a), C_a, can be valued using the commodity option formula. Its value is given by:

$$c_a = Se^{(y-r)T}N_1(a_1) - Ke^{-rT}N_1(a_2)$$

$$a_1 = \left[\ln\left(\frac{S}{K}\right) + \left(y + \frac{1}{2}\sigma^2\right)T\right] \Big/ \sigma\sqrt{T}, \quad a_2 = a_1 - \sigma\sqrt{T}$$

where $N_1(\cdot)$ stands for the cumulative normal distribution.

The option described in (b/), C_b can be priced using an extension of Merton's (1973) formula for which the strike price is S_t^*. Its value is given by:

$$C_b = Se^{(y-r)t}N(b_1) - S_t^* e^{-rt}N(b_2)$$

$$b_1 = \left[\ln(S/S_t^*) + \left(y + \frac{1}{2}\sigma^2\right)t\right] \Big/ \sigma\sqrt{t}, \quad b_2 = b_1 - \sigma\sqrt{t}$$

where S_t^* is the solution to the following equation,

$$c(S_t^*, T - t, K) = S_t^* + D - K.$$

The option described in (c/) can be priced using the compound option formula proposed in Geske (1979). Its value is given by:

$$c_c = Se^{(y-r)T}N_2\left(a_1, b_1, \sqrt{\frac{t}{T}}\right) - Ke^{-rT}N_2$$

$$\times \left(a_2, b_2, \sqrt{\frac{t_i}{T}}\right) - (S_t^* + D - K)e^{-rt}N_1(b_2)$$

where,

$$a_1 = \left[\ln(S/K) + \left(y + \frac{1}{2}\sigma^2\right)T\right] \Big/ \sigma\sqrt{T}, \quad a_2 = a_1 - \sigma\sqrt{T}$$

$$b_1 = \left[\ln(S/S_t^*) + \left(y + \frac{1}{2}\sigma^2\right)t\right] \Big/ \sigma\sqrt{t}, \quad b_2 = b_1 - \sigma\sqrt{t}.$$

Where $N_2(\ldots)$ is the bivariate cumulative normal density function with upper integral limits a and b and a correlation coefficient ρ. Since the value of the American call is equivalent to the algebraic sum of the three options in the portfolio, we have: $C = c_a + c_b - c_c$.

Using the properties of the bivariate cumulative normal density function, little algebra allows the derivation of the following formula for the American call on a stock,

$$C = S\left[e^{(y-r)t}N_1(b_1) + e^{(y-r)T}N_2\left(a_1, -b_1, -\sqrt{\frac{t}{T}}\right)\right]$$
$$- K\left[e^{-rt}N_1(b_2) + e^{-rT}N_2\left(a_2, -b_2, -\sqrt{\frac{t}{T}}\right)\right] + De^{-rt}N_1(b_2)$$

24.4.2.1. *Simulations*

The formula obtained by Whaley (1981) is used to generate call option prices. Using the following parameters:

Strike price, $K = 100$, Ex-dividend date, $t = 6$ months, Time to maturity, $T = 1$ year, Interest rate for 6 months, $r = 0.04$, Volatility of the stock, (6 months), $\sigma = 0.2$, and Dividend, $D = 5$. Option prices are reported in Table 24.10.

The different applications presented for European options can be used with American options. Besides, the compound option approach

Table 24.10. American call prices in the presence of dividends.

S	S_{cr}	S_{cr}	$C(S,T,K)$
82	77.196	123.5818	3.8050
85	80.196	123.5818	4.8175
87	82.196	123.5818	5.5758
90	85.196	123.5818	6.8389
92	87.196	123.5818	7.7645
95	90.196	123.5818	9.2759
97	92.196	123.5818	10.3636
100	95.196	123.5818	12.1113
102	97.196	123.5818	13.3506
105	100.196	123.5818	15.3155
107	102.196	123.5818	16.6922
110	105.196	123.5818	18.8509
112	107.196	123.5818	20.3486
115	110.196	123.5818	22.6759
117	112.196	123.5818	24.2774
120	115.196	123.5818	26.7476
122	117.196	123.5818	28.4363
125	120.196	123.5818	31.0255

apply to the valuation of wildcard options, some exotic and complex options. These applications will be studied in this book.

24.5. Valuation of American Options with Discrete Cash Distributions within Information Uncertainty

24.5.1. *The model*

We use a similar context as that in Roll (1977), Geske (1979), and Whaley (1981) and assume besides that the stock price net of the discounted dividend, S, is:

$$S_\tau = P_\tau - De^{-(r+\lambda_S)(t-\tau)} \quad \text{for } \tau < t$$
$$S_\tau = P_\tau \quad \text{for } \tau \geq t$$

where P is the stock price cum-dividend and λ_S is the information cost regarding the underlying asset price.

If we account for information costs as given by Bellalah (1999), then the cost of carry model is $F = Se^{(y+\lambda_S)T}$ where F is the current forward price. The option C_a is given by:

$$c_a = Se^{(y-r-(\lambda_C-\lambda_S))T} N_1(a_1) - Ke^{-(r+\lambda_C)T} N_1(a_2)$$
$$a_1 = \left[\ln\left(\frac{S}{K}\right) + \left(y + \lambda_S + \frac{1}{2}\sigma^2\right) T\right] \Big/ \sigma\sqrt{T}$$
$$a_2 = a_1 - \sigma\sqrt{T}$$

where λ_C stands for information cost on the option market.

The option described in (b/), C_b can be priced using Bellalah's (1999) formula:

$$C_b = Se^{(y-r-(\lambda_C-\lambda_S))t} N(b_1) - S_t^* e^{-(r+\lambda_C)t} N(b_2)$$
$$b_1 = \left[\ln\left(\frac{S}{S_t^*}\right) + \left(y + \frac{1}{2}\sigma^2 + \lambda_S\right) t\right] \Big/ \sigma\sqrt{t},$$
$$b_2 = b_1 - \sigma\sqrt{t}$$

where S_t^* is the solution to the following equation:

$$c(S_t^*, T - t, E) = S_t^* + D - K.$$

The option described in (c/) can be priced using:

$$c_c = Se^{(y-r-(\lambda_C-\lambda_S))T} N_2\left(a_1, b_1, \sqrt{\frac{t}{T}}\right)$$
$$- Ke^{-(r+\lambda_C)T} N_2\left(a_2, b_2, \sqrt{\frac{t_i}{T}}\right) - (S_t^* + D - K)e^{-(r+\lambda_C)t} N_1(b_2)$$

with:

$$a_1 = \left[\ln\left(\frac{S}{K}\right) + \left(y + \frac{1}{2}\sigma^2 + \lambda_S\right) T\right] \Big/ \sigma\sqrt{T}, \quad a_2 = a_1 - \sigma\sqrt{T}$$
$$b_1 = \left[\ln\left(\frac{S}{S_t^*}\right) + \left(y + \frac{1}{2}\sigma^2 + \lambda_S\right) t\right] \Big/ \sigma\sqrt{t}, \quad b_2 = b_1 - \sigma\sqrt{t}$$

where $N_2(\ldots)$ is the bivariate cumulative normal density function with upper integral limits a and b and a correlation coefficient ρ.

The American call is given by:

$$C = S\left[e^{(y-r-(\lambda_C-\lambda_S))t} N_1(b_1)\right.$$
$$\left. + e^{(y-r-(\lambda_C-\lambda_S))T} N_2\left(a_1, -b_1, -\sqrt{\frac{t}{T}}\right)\right]$$
$$- K\left[e^{-(r+\lambda_C)t} N_1(b_2) + e^{-(r+\lambda_C)T} N_2\left(a_2, -b_2, -\sqrt{\frac{t}{T}}\right)\right]$$
$$+ De^{-(r+\lambda_C)t} N_1(b_2).$$

24.5.2. *Simulation results*

Table 24.11 gives the computation of the American call value referred to as call, the option c_a, the option c_b, the option c_c, the CRR price, the algebric sum of the three options $(c_a + c_b - c_c)$, the critical underlying asset price, and the difference between our call formula and the benchmark. Table 24.12 uses the same data except for information costs. Information costs are set equal to $\lambda_S = 0.01$ and $\lambda_C = 0.001$. Table 24.13 uses the same parameters except for the information

Table 24.11. Simulations of option values for the continuous-time model and the discrete time model using the following parameters. $S = 175$, $r = 0.1$, $D = 1.5$, $T = 30$, $t = 24$, $\sigma = 0.32$, $\lambda_c = 0$, and $\lambda_s = 0$.

Strike	Call	ca	cb	cc	CRR	$ca + cb - cc$	S^*	Call-CRR
100	76.03	74.42	74.25	72.65	75.81	76.03	100.02	0.22
105	71.06	69.46	69.11	67.51	70.85	71.06	105	0.21
110	66.09	64.51	63.96	62.37	65.89	66.09	110	0.20
115	61.13	59.55	59.07	57.49	60.93	61.13	115	0.19
120	56.16	54.59	53.65	52.07	55.97	56.16	120	0.19
125	51.19	49.63	48.48	46.92	51.01	51.19	125	0.18
130	46.22	44.67	43.32	41.76	46.05	46.23	130	0.17
135	41.26	39.72	38.49	36.94	41.09	41.26	135	0.16
140	36.30	34.79	32.99	31.47	36.16	36.30	140	0.14
145	31.37	29.90	27.87	26.39	31.25	31.37	145	0.11
150	26.50	25.11	22.85	21.46	26.42	26.50	150	0.07
155	21.78	20.52	18.05	16.80	21.77	21.78	154.99	0.01
160	17.31	16.23	13.64	12.56	17.37	17.31	159.99	−0.05
165	13.25	12.38	9.78	8.92	13.39	13.25	164.99	−0.13
170	9.72	9.07	6.63	5.98	9.91	9.72	169.99	−0.19
175	6.82	6.37	4.22	3.77	7.03	6.82	174.99	−0.20
180	4.56	4.27	2.52	2.23	4.77	4.56	179.99	−0.21
185	2.91	2.74	1.41	1.24	3.10	2.91	184.99	−0.18
190	1.77	1.68	0.74	0.64	1.92	1.77	189.99	−0.14
195	1.03	0.98	0.36	0.31	1.13	1.03	194.99	−0.10
200	0.57	0.55	0.16	0.14	0.64	0.57	200	−0.06
240	0	0	0	0	0	0	240	−0

costs which are set equal to $\lambda_S = 0.1$ and $\lambda_C = 0.05$. The results reveal that the difference between our model prices and the CRR prices are very small. Information costs offer a simple way to calibrate model prices to market data as shown in Bellalah and Jacquillat (1995) and Bellalah (1999, 2001, 2018a, 2018b). If we invert the information costs as in Table 24.14, we see that the mispricing bias in inverted. Table 24.14 gives the results for the different parameter values, except for information costs, which are set respectively equal to $\lambda_S = 0.05$ and $\lambda_C = 0.1$.

Table 24.12. Simulations of option values for the continuous-time model and the discrete time model using the following parameters. $S = 175$, $r = 0.1$, $D = 1.5$, $T = 30$, $t = 24$, $\sigma = 0.32$, $\lambda_c = 0.001$, and $\lambda_s = 0.01$.

Strike	Call	*ca*	*cb*	*cc*	CRR	$ca + cb - cc$	S^*	Call-CRR
100	76.14	74.56	74.34	72.76	75.94	76.14	100.02	0.19
120	56.427	54.73	53.73	52.19	56.11	56.27	120	0.16
140	36.41	34.93	33.06	31.57	36.30	36.41	140.01	0.11
145	31.48	30.04	27.94	26.49	31.39	31.48	145	0.09
150	26.61	25.25	22.92	21.55	26.56	26.61	150	0.05
155	21.89	20.65	18.11	16.87	21.90	21.89	154.99	−0.01
160	17.42	16.35	13.67	12.61	17.49	17.42	159.99	−0.07
165	13.34	12.49	9.83	8.97	13.50	13.34	164.99	−0.15
170	9.80	9.16	6.66	6.02	10.01	9.80	169.99	−0.34
175	6.89	6.44	4.24	3.80	7.10	6.89	174.99	−0.21
180	4.62	4.33	2.53	2.25	4.84	4.62	179.99	−0.22
185	2.95	2.78	1.42	1.25	3.14	2.95	184.99	−0.19
190	1.80	1.71	0.74	0.65	1.95	1.80	189.99	−0.14
195	1.05	1	0.36	0.32	1.16	1.05	194.99	−0.10
200	0.58	0.56	0.17	0.14	0.65	0.58	200	−0.06
240	0	0	0	0	0	0	240	−0

Table 24.13. Simulations of option values for the continuous-time model and the discrete time model using the following parameters. $S = 175$, $r = 0.1$, $D = 1.5$, $T = 30$, $t = 24$, $\sigma = 0.32$, $\lambda_c = 0.05$, and $\lambda_s = 0.1$.

Strike	Call	*ca*	*cb*	*cc*	CRR	$ca + cb - cc$	S^*	Call-CRR
100	76.92	75.55	74.95	73.58	76.92	76.92	100.02	−0
120	57.12	55.79	54.31	52.98	57.17	57.12	120	−0.05
140	37.32	36.06	33.59	32.33	37.43	37.32	140.01	−0.10
145	32.40	31.18	28.45	27.23	32.53	32.40	145	−0.13
150	27.54	26.38	23.40	22.25	27.70	27.54	150	−0.16
155	22.80	21.75	18.55	17.51	23.01	22.80	154.99	−0.21
160	18.29	17.39	14.08	13.18	18.56	18.29	159.99	−0.26
165	14.15	13.43	10.15	9.42	14.47	14.15	164.99	−0.32
170	10.52	9.97	6.90	6.36	10.86	10.52	169.99	−0.34
175	7.49	7.11	4.41	4.04	7.81	7.49	174.99	−0.32
180	5.09	4.85	2.65	2.41	5.40	5.09	179.99	−0.30
185	3.31	3.16	1.49	1.34	3.56	3.31	184.99	−0.25
190	2.05	1.97	0.78	0.70	2.25	2.05	189.99	−0.19
195	1.22	1.18	0.38	0.34	1.35	1.22	194.99	−0.13
200	0.69	0.67	0.18	0.16	0.78	0.69	200	−0.08
240	0	0	0	0	0	0	240	−0

Table 24.14. Simulations of option values for the continuous-time model and the discrete time model using the following parameters. $S = 175$, $r = 0.1$, $D = 1.5$, $T = 30$, $t = 24$, $\sigma = 0.32$, $\lambda_c = 0.1$, and $\lambda_s = 0.05$.

Strike	Call	ca	cb	cc	CRR	$ca + cb - cc$	S^*	Call-CRR
100	76.10	74.52	74.25	72.67	75.90	76.10	100.02	0.20
120	56.36	54.85	53.73	52.22	56.22	56.36	120	0.13
140	36.63	35.21	33.15	31.72	36.57	36.63	140.01	0.06
145	31.73	30.35	28.03	26.66	31.70	31.73	145	0.03
150	26.89	25.59	23.04	21.74	26.90	26.89	150	−0.01
155	22.18	21	18.24	17.07	22.25	22.18	154.99	−0.07
160	17.71	16.70	13.82	12.81	17.85	17.71	159.99	−0.13
165	13.63	12.82	9.93	9.12	13.84	13.63	164.99	−0.21
170	10.07	9.46	6.75	6.15	10.32	10.07	169.99	−0.25
175	7.11	6.69	4.31	3.89	7.37	7.11	174.99	−0.25
180	4.80	4.53	2.58	2.31	5.05	4.80	179.99	−0.24
185	3.09	2.93	1.45	1.29	3.30	3.09	184.99	−0.21
190	1.90	1.81	0.76	0.67	2.07	1.90	189.99	−0.16
195	1.12	1.07	0.37	0.33	1.23	1.12	194.99	−0.11
200	0.63	0.60	0.17	0.15	0.70	0.63	200	−0.07
240	0	0	0	0	0	0	240	−0

24.6. The Valuation Equations for Standard and Compound Options with Information Costs

We denote by $S(V, t)$ the value of the option as a function of the underlying asset and time.

24.6.1. *The pricing of assets under incomplete information*

Using the same assumptions as in the seminal paper of Black and Scholes and the additional assumption of information uncertainty on the option $S(V, t)$ and its underlying asset, V, it is possible to construct a hedged position which contains one share of stock long and $\frac{1}{S_V}$ options short. The term S_V is the first derivative of the option with respect to its underlying asset. Since the return in the hedged position is certain, the return must be equal to $(r + \lambda_V)\Delta t$ for the underlying asset and $(r + \lambda_S)\Delta t$ for the option where λ_V and λ_S refer respectively to the information costs on the underlying asset and the option. The differential equation for the value of the option:

$$\frac{1}{2}\sigma^2 V^2 S_{VV} + (r + \lambda_V)VS_V - (r + \lambda_S)S + S_t = 0. \qquad (24.26)$$

Let T be the maturity date of the call and M be its strike price. Equation (24.26) subject to the following boundary condition at maturity:

$$S(V,T) = V_T - M \quad \text{if } V_T \geq M$$
$$S(V,T) = 0 \quad \text{if } V_T < M$$

is solved using standard methods for the price of a European call, which is found to be equal to:

$$S(V,T) = Ve^{-(\lambda_S - \lambda_V)T} N_1(d_1) - Me^{-(r+\lambda_S)T} N_1(d_2) \qquad (24.27)$$

with:

$$d_1 = \left[\ln\left(\frac{V}{M}\right) + \left(r + \frac{1}{2}\sigma^2 + \lambda_V\right)T\right] \Big/ \sigma\sqrt{T} d_2 = d_1 - \sigma\sqrt{T}$$

and where $N_1(\cdot)$ is the univariate cumulative normal density function.

24.6.2. *The valuation of equity as a compound option*

Following Geske (1979), consider a levered firm for which the debt corresponds to pure discount bonds maturing in T years with a face value M. Under the standard assumptions of liquidating the firm in T years, payingoff the bondholders and giving the residual value (if any) to stockholders, the bondholders have given the stockholders the option to buy back the assets at the debt maturity date. In this context, a call on the firm's stock is a compound option, $C(S,t) = f(g(V,t),t)$ where t stands for the current time. The return on the firm's assets follows the stochastic differential equation:

$$dV/V = \alpha_v dt + \sigma_v dz_v$$

where α_v and σ_v refer to the instantaneous rate of return and the standard deviation of the return of the firm per unit time, and dz_v is a Brownian motion. Using the definition of the call $C(V,t)$, its return can be described by: $dC/C = \alpha_c dt + \sigma_c dz_c$ where α_c and σ_c refer to the instantaneous rate of return and the standard deviation of the return on the call per unit time, and dz_C is a Brownian motion. Using Ito's lemma as before, the dynamics of the call can be expressed as:

$$dC = \frac{1}{2}C_{vv}\sigma_v^2 V^2 dt + C_v dV + C_t dt.$$

It is possible to create a risk-less hedge with two securities, between the firm and a call to get the partial differential equation:

$$\frac{1}{2}\sigma_v^2 V^2 C_{vv} + (r + \lambda_v)VC_v - (r + \lambda_C)C + C_t = 0 \qquad (24.28)$$

where λ_v in an information cost relative to the firm's value. At the option's maturity date, $t = T_0$, the value of the call option on the firm's stock must satisfy the following condition: $C_{T_0} = \max[S_{T_0} - K, 0]$ where K stands for the strike price. Since the stock is viewed as an option on the value of the firm, re-call the value of S_{T_0}:

$$S(V_{T_0}, T_0) = V_{T_0}e^{-(\lambda_S - \lambda_V)(T - T_0)}N_1(d_1) - Me^{-(r+\lambda_S)(T-T_0)}N_1(d_2)$$

with:

$$d_1 = \left[\ln\left(\frac{V}{M}\right) + \left(r + \frac{1}{2}\sigma^2 + \lambda_V\right)(T - T_0)\right] \Big/ \sigma\sqrt{(T - T_0)}$$

$$d_2 = d_1 - \sigma\sqrt{(T - T_0)}.$$

It is convenient to note that Eq. (24.28) is more difficult to solve than Eq. (24.26) because its boundary condition is a function of the solution to Eq. (24.26). At date T_0, the value of the firm making the holder of the call on the stock indifferent with regard to the exercise decision is solution to $S_{T_0} - K = 0$ where S_{T_0} is given by the last formula. Following the methodology in Geske (1979), the compound call option value with information costs is:

$$C_0 = V_0 e^{-(\lambda_c - \lambda_v)T_0} e^{-(\lambda_s - \lambda_v)(T - T_0)} N_2\left(h + \sigma_v\sqrt{T_0}, k + \sigma_v\sqrt{T}, \sqrt{\frac{T_0}{T}}\right)$$

$$- Me^{-(r+\lambda_s)T} e^{-(\lambda_c - \lambda_s)(T_0)} N_2\left(h, k, \sqrt{\frac{T_0}{T}}\right).$$

$$- Ke^{-(r+\lambda_c)T_0} N_1(h).$$

With:

$$h = \left[\ln\left(\frac{V_0}{\bar{V}}\right) + \left(r + \lambda_v - \frac{1}{2}\sigma_v^2\right)T_0\right] \Big/ \sigma_v\sqrt{T_0}$$

$$k = \left[\ln\left(\frac{V_0}{M}\right) + \left(r + \lambda_v - \frac{1}{2}\sigma_v^2\right)T\right] \Big/ \sigma_v\sqrt{T}$$

The value $\bar{V}$ is determined by the following equation:

$$\begin{aligned} S_{T_0} - K = {} & \bar{V}e^{-(\lambda_s - \lambda_v)(T - T_0)}N_1(k(\bar{V}) + \sigma_v\sqrt{T - T_0}) \\ & - Me^{-(r+\lambda_s)(T-T_0)}N_1(k(\bar{V})) - K = \end{aligned}$$

where:

$$k(\bar{V}) = \left[\ln\left(\frac{\bar{V}}{M}\right) + \left(r + \lambda_v - \frac{1}{2}\sigma_v^2\right)T\right] \Big/ \sigma_v\sqrt{T}$$

and $N_2\left(x, y, \sqrt{\frac{T_0}{T}}\right)$ is the bivariate cumulative normal distribution with upper integral limits x and y and $\sqrt{\frac{T_0}{T}}$ is the correlation coefficient.

A first special case is obtained when information costs regarding the call are equal to information costs for the stocks, i.e., $\lambda_c = \lambda_s$. In this case, the investors suffer sunk costs to get informed about the equity and the assets of the firm. The costs regarding the equity and the firm's cash flows reflect the agency costs and the asymmetric information costs. The formula is:

$$\begin{aligned} C_0 = {} & V_0e^{-(\lambda_c - \lambda_v)T}N_2\left(h + \sigma_v\sqrt{T_0}, k + \sigma_v\sqrt{T}, \sqrt{\frac{T_0}{T}}\right) \\ & - Me^{-(r+\lambda_c)T}N_2\left(h, k, \sqrt{\frac{T_0}{T}}\right) - Ke^{-(r+\lambda_c)T_0}N_1(h). \end{aligned}$$

The value $\bar{V}$ is determined by the following equation:

$$\begin{aligned} S_{T_0} - K = {} & \bar{V}e^{-(\lambda_c - \lambda_v)(T - T_0)}N_1(k + \sigma_v\sqrt{T - T_0}) \\ & - Me^{-(r+\lambda_c)(T-T_0)}N_1(k) - K = 0. \end{aligned}$$

A second special case of the compound option formula is obtained when the incurred information costs are equal to a same value λ for the stock, the firm's value and the call. In this context, the compound option formula becomes:

$$C_0 = V_0 N_2\left(h + \sigma_v\sqrt{T_0}, k + \sigma_v\sqrt{T}, \sqrt{\frac{T_0}{T}}\right)$$
$$- Me^{-(r+\lambda)T} N_2\left(h, k, \sqrt{\frac{T_0}{T}}\right) - Ke^{-(r+\lambda)T_0} N_1(h)$$

where the value $\bar{V}$ is determined from the following equation:

$$S_{T_0} - K = \bar{V} N_1\left(k + \sigma_v\sqrt{T - T_0}\right)$$
$$- Me^{-(r+\lambda)(T-T_0)} N_1(k) - K = 0.$$

If the information cost is zero, this compound option pricing formula becomes the one as given by Geske (1979). The following tables present the simulation results of the above models. Table 24.15 gives the call equity values using the Black and Scholes model and our model. The following parameters are used for the simulations: $M = 100$, $r = 0.08$, $T = 0.25$, and $\sigma_v = 0.4$. The following information costs are used to generate option values: $(\lambda_s = \lambda_v = 0)$ which correspond to the Black and Scholes case, and $(\lambda_s = 0.1\%, \lambda_v = 1\%)$, $(\lambda_s = 0\%, \lambda_v = 1\%)$, and $(\lambda_s = 0.1\%, \lambda_v = 3\%)$. The results show

Table 24.15. Simulation and comparison of the Black and Scholes model and our model for the values of European equity options. $M = 100$, $r = 0.08$, $T = 0.25$, and $\sigma_v = 0.4$.

V	$\lambda_s = \lambda_v = 0$	$\lambda_s = 0.1\%$, $\lambda_v = 1\%$	$\lambda_s = 0\%$, $\lambda_v = 1\%$	$\lambda_s = 0.1\%$, $\lambda_v = 3\%$
70	0	0	0	0
80	0.9800	0.9829	0.9775	0.9780
90	4.1206	4.1189	4.1103	4.0984
100	8.9163	8.9085	8.8941	8.8641
110	15.6302	15.6119	15.5912	15.5340
120	23.8003	23.7660	23.7409	23.6489

Table 24.16. Simulation and comparisons of European equity values as compound options in the presence of information costs using Geske's model and our model. $K = 20$, $M = 100$, $r = 0.08$, $T = 0.25$, $T_0 = 0.125$, and $\sigma_v = 0.4$.

V_0	$\lambda_c = 0\%$ $\lambda_s = 0\%$ $\lambda_v = 0\%$	$\lambda_c = 2\%$ $\lambda_s = 2\%$ $\lambda_v = 2\%$	$\lambda_c = 1\%$ $\lambda_s = 1\%$ $\lambda_v = 2\%$	$\lambda_c = 1\%$ $\lambda_s = 2\%$ $\lambda_v = 2\%$
110	6.82	7.13	7.16	7.14
120	15.17	15.65	15.70	15.67
130	26.52	27.16	27.25	27.20

that in all cases our option values are less than those reported for the Black and Scholes model. The difference between the two models depends on the magnitude of information costs. Since the Black and Scholes model overvalues call option prices, our model reduces the amount of this mispricing bias.

Table 24.16 gives the simulation results for the compound option formula with information costs and the Geske's compound call formula for the following parameters: $K = 20$, $M = 100$, $r = 0.08$, $T = 0.25$, $T_0 = 0.125$, and $\sigma_v = 0.4$. The parameters used for information costs in Table 24.2 are:

Case a: $(\lambda_c = \lambda_s = \lambda_v = 0\%)$;
Case b: $(\lambda_c = \lambda_s = \lambda_v = 2\%)$;
Case c: $(\lambda_c = \lambda_s = 1\%,\ \lambda_v = 2\%)$ and
Case d: $(\lambda_c = 1\%, \lambda_s = \lambda_v = 2\%)$.

In case (a), we have exactly the same values as those generated by the formula given by Geske (1979). This case is a benchmark for the comparisons of our results. The table shows that the compound option price is an increasing function of the firm's assets V. This result is independent of the values attributed to information costs. Note also that the compound option price is an increasing function of the information costs regarding the firm's assets, λ_v. When λ_v is fixed, this allows the study of the effects of the other information costs on the option value. In this case, the option price seems to be a decreasing function of the two information costs λ_c and λ_s.

When comparing cases (b) and (c) on one hand and the cases (c) and (d) on the other hand, we observe this decreasing feature.

Summary

The option pricing literature has evolved since the work of Black–Scholes (1973) and Merton (1973). Even if models now exist for the valuation of European and American call and put options on a variety of underlying assets and commodities including common stocks, bonds, agricultural futures contracts, and financial futures, there is still no-known analytical solutions for options written on commodities that have known discrete cash payments during the option's life. Bunch and Johnson (2000) use the first-passage probability approach to derive exact expressions for the critical stock price function and for the American put price. The analysis considers the infinite or perpetual put and the finite case. The derivation is based on the fact that exercise occurs when the interest rate effect is exactly offset by the volatility effect. A similar result can be obtained, if we account for the effects of shadow costs of incomplete information since these costs are added to the interest rate. The method in Bunch and Johnson (2000) can be extended to currency options, options on futures, to exotic options, etc. This chapter presents in detail the basic concepts and techniques underlying rational pricing of American options. This is done in the context of analytical European models along the lines of Black–Scholes (1973), Merton (1973), Black (1976), Barone-Adesi and Whaley (1987). Our attention is focused on the question of dividend and the privilege feature of early exercise and information uncertainty.

When there are no distributions to the underlying asset, there is no incentive to exercise an American call option before its maturity date. Hence, the value of an American call is equal to that of a European call. The valuation of American calls is simpler than the valuation of American puts with and without discrete cash distributions to the underlying asset. While European and American calls have the same value when there are no distributions to the underlying asset, this result does not hold for European and American puts. The nonexistence of a put-call parity theorem for American options imply a specific treatment for put options. The pricing of American puts is rather a difficult task, even in the absence of distributions to the underlying asset. However, some interesting results are presented in the absence of dividends and when there is a continuous dividend rate. Most options written on commodities and commodity futures are of the American type. Hence, an early exercise premium is embedded in American call and put prices. Analytical solutions for the American option pricing problems with several dividends have not yet been found. The quadratic approximation method used by Barone-Adesi and Whaley (1987) is computationally efficient. It provides an accurate, inexpensive method for the valuation of American call and put options traded on commodities and commodity futures. In the case of discrete distributions to the underlying asset, the formulas proposed in the literature are not so efficient as those proposed for American calls. The valuation of American stock options is equivalent to the valuation of a portfolio which contains a commodity option on a stock with some distributions. The general problem of valuing American options is analyzed in three different contexts: when there are no distributions to the underlying asset, when there is a constant proportional distribution rate, and in the presence of discrete cash distributions. The analysis covers American options on spot assets and American futures options. The main results reported in the literature regarding the pricing of American calls are reviewed. Some models are presented in detail and simulations are run.

Information costs play a central role in the analysis and the valuation of financial assets, firms and their cash flows. We present an arbitrage argument to derive an option pricing formula within a context of information uncertainty. The formula collapses to that in Black and Scholes in the absence of these costs. By analogy between the option theory and the assets in the capital structure of the firm, the formula can be used to value equity in a levered firm. The compound option formulas derived in this chapter shed light on the effects of leverage and information uncertainty in the valuation of corporate assets. Since several corporate liabilities can be valued with the compound option approach, our results are useful in the pricing of the capital structure of the firm.

References

Abramowitz M and IA Stegun (1972). *Handbook of Mathematical Functions with Formulas, Graphs, and Mathematical Tables.* U.S. Government Printing Office, Washington, D.C.

Barone-Adesi G and RE Whaley (1987). Efficient analytic approximation of American option values. *Journal of Finance*, 42 (June), 301–320.

Bellalah M. (1999). The valuation of futures and commodity options with information costs. *Journal of Futures Markets*, 19 (September), 645–664.

Bellalah M (2001). Market imperfections; information costs and the valuation of derivatives: Some general results. *International Journal of Finance*, 13(3), 1895–1927.

Bellalah M and B Jacquillat (1995). Option valuation with information costs: Theory and tests. *The Financial Review*, 30(3) (August), 617–635.

Bellalah M and JL Prigent (2001). Pricing standard and exotic options in the presence of a finite mixture of Gaussian distributions. *International Journal of Finance*, 13(3), 1975–2000.

Bellalah M and F Selmi (2001). On the quadratic criteria for hedging under transaction costs. *International Journal of Finance*, 13(3), 2001–2020.

Bellalah M, JL Prigent and C Villa (2001a). Skew without skewness: Asymmetric smiles; information costs and stochastic volatilities. *International Journal of Finance*, 13(2), 1826–1837.

Bellalah M, Ma Bellalah and R Portait (2001b). The cost of capital in international finance. *International Journal of Finance*, 13(3), 1958–1973.

Bellalah M. (2018a). On information costs, short sales and the pricing of extendible options, steps and Parisian options. *Annals of Operations Research*, 262(2) (March) 361–387.

Bellalah M. (2018b). Pricing derivatives in the presence of shadow costs of incomplete information and short sales, *Annals of Operations Research*, 262(2) (March).

Black F (1976). The pricing of commodity contracts. *Journal of Financial Economics*, 3, 167–179.

Black F and M Scholes (1973). The pricing of options and corporate liabilities. *Journal of Political Economy*, 81, 637–659.

Black F and J Cox (1976). Valuing corporate securities: Some effects of bond indenture conditions. *Journal of Finance*, 31 (May), 351–367.

Blomeyer EC (1986). An analytic approximation for the American put price for options on stocks with dividends. *Journal of Financial and Quantitative Analysis*, 21 (June), 229–233.

Bunch DS and H Johnson (2000). The American put option and its critical stock price. *Journal of Finance*, 55(5), 2333–2357.

Cox J, S Ross and M Rubinstein (1979). Option pricing: A simplified approach. *Journal of Financial Economics*, 7, 229–263.

Feller W (1971). *An Introduction to Probability Theory and Its Applications.* John Wiley, New York.

Galai D and R Masulis (1976). The option pricing model and the risk factor of stock. *Journal of Financial Economics*, 3, 53–81.

Garman M and S Kohlhagen (1983). Foreign currency option values. *Journal of International Money and Finance*, 2, 231–237.

Geske R (1979). The valuation of compound options. *Journal of Financial Economic*, 7, 375–380.

Geske R and HE Johnson (1984). The American put option valued analytically. *Journal of Finance*, 39 (December), 1511–1524.

Geske R and K Shastri (1985). Valuation by approximation: A comparison of alternative option valuation techniques. *Journal of Financial and Quantitative Analysis*, 20 (March), 45–71.

Grabbe JO (1983). The pricing of call and put options on foreign exchange. *Journal of International Money and Finance*, 2, 239–253.

Harvey C and R Whaley (1992). Dividends and the S-P 100 index option valuation. *Journal of Futures Markets*, 12(2), 123–137.

Johnson HE (1983). An analytic approximation to the American put price. *Journal of Financial and Quantitative Analysis*, 18 (March), 141–148.

McKean Jr HP (1969). *Stochastic Integrals.* Academic Press, New York.

McMillan L (1986). Analytic approximation for the American put option. *Advances in Futures and Options Research*, 1, 119–139.

Merton R (1973). Theory of rational option pricing. *Bell Journal of Economics and Management Science*, 4, 141–183.

Merton R (1987). An equilibrium market model with incomplete information. *Journal of Finance*, 42, 483–511.

Omberg E (1991). On the theory of perfect hedging. *Advances in Futures and Options Research*, 5, 1–29.

Roll R (1977). An analytical valuation formula for unprotected American call options with known dividends. *Journal of Financial Economics*, 5, 251–258.

Samuelson P (1972). *The Collected Scientific Papers of Paul Samuelson*. In Merton RC (ed.). MIT Press, Cambridge, MA.

Whaley R (1981). On the valuation of American call options on stocks with known dividends. *Journal of Financial Economics*, 9, 207–211.

Whaley RE (1986). Valuation of American futures options: Theory and empirical tests. *Journal of Finance*, 41 (March), 127–150.

Supplementary Material

The supplementary material includes questions, exercises and appendices.

Online access is automatically assigned if you purchase the ebook online via www.worldscientific.com. If you have purchased the print copy of this book or the ebook via other sales channels, please follow the instructions below to download the files:

1. Register for an account or log in at: www.worldscientific.com/.
2. Go to: https://www.worldscientific.com/r/q0551-supp or scan the QR code below.
3. Download the files from: https://www.worldscientific.com/worldscibooks/10.1142/q0551#t=suppl.

For subsequent access, simply log in with the same login details in order to access.

For enquiries, please email: sales@wspc.com.sg.

Index

A

B

C

D

E

F

G

H

I

J

K

L

M

N

O

P

Q

R

S

T

V

W

Y

www.ingramcontent.com/pod-product-compliance
Lightning Source LLC
LaVergne TN
LVHW070906300926
849162LV00010B/1837